MORE SERVLETS AND JAVASERVER™ PAGES

MARTY HALL

PH PTR Prentice Hall PTR,
Upper Saddle River, NJ 07458
www.phptr.com

Sun Microsystems Press
A Prentice Hall Title

Library of Congress Cataloging-in-Publication Data

Hall, Marty
    More Servlets and JavaServer Pages / Marty Hall.
        p. cm.
    Includes index.
    ISBN 0-13-067614-4
        1. Java (Computer programming language) 2. Servlets. 3. Active server pages. I. Title.

QA76.73.J38 H3455 2001
005.2'762--dc21

2001056014

The publisher offers discounts on this book when ordered in bulk quantities.
For more information, contact Corporate Sales Department, Prentice Hall PTR ,
One Lake Street, Upper Saddle River, NJ 07458. Phone: 800-382-3419; FAX: 201- 236-7141.
E-mail: corpsales@prenhall.com.

Production Editor and Compositor: *Vanessa Moore*
Copy Editor: *Mary Lou Nohr*
Project Coordinator: *Anne R. Garcia*
Acquisitions Editor: *Gregory G. Doench*
Editorial Assistant: *Brandt Kenna*
Cover Design Director: *Jerry Votta*
Cover Designer: *Design Source*
Art Director: *Gail Cocker-Bogusz*
Manufacturing Manager: *Alexis R. Heydt-Long*
Marketing Manager: *Debby vanDijk*

Sun Microsystems Press Publisher: *Michael Llwyd Alread*

10   9   8   7   6   5   4   3   2   1

ISBN 0-13-067614-4

Sun Microsystems Press
A Prentice Hall Title

Contents

PART I
THE BASICS   2

CHAPTER 1
SERVER SETUP AND CONFIGURATION   4

CHAPTER 2
A FAST INTRODUCTION TO
BASIC SERVLET PROGRAMMING   34

CHAPTER 3
A FAST INTRODUCTION TO BASIC JSP PROGRAMMING 120

PART II
WEB APPLICATIONS   240

CHAPTER 4
USING AND DEPLOYING WEB APPLICATIONS   242

CHAPTER 5
CONTROLLING WEB APPLICATION
BEHAVIOR WITH WEB.XML   276

CHAPTER 6
A SAMPLE WEB APPLICATION: AN ONLINE BOAT SHOP   324

PART III
WEB APPLICATION SECURITY   350

CHAPTER 7
DECLARATIVE SECURITY   352

CHAPTER 8
PROGRAMMATIC SECURITY   408

PART IV
MAJOR NEW SERVLET AND JSP CAPABILITIES   432

CHAPTER 9
SERVLET AND JSP FILTERS   434

CHAPTER 10
THE APPLICATION EVENTS FRAMEWORK   488

PART V
NEW TAG LIBRARY CAPABILITIES   560

CHAPTER 11
NEW TAG LIBRARY FEATURES IN JSP 1.2   562

CHAPTER 12
THE JSP STANDARD TAG LIBRARY 618

APPENDIX
SERVER ORGANIZATION AND STRUCTURE   696

Acknowledgments

Many people helped me with this book. Without their assistance, I would still be on the third chapter. Larry Brown (U.S. Navy), John Guthrie (American Institutes for Research), Randal Hanford (Boeing, University of Washington), Bill Higgins (IBM), and Rich Slywczak (NASA) provided valuable technical feedback on many different chapters. Others providing useful suggestions or corrections include Nathan Abramson (ATG), Wayne Bethea (Johns Hopkins University Applied Physics Lab—JHU/APL), Lien Duong (JHU/APL), Bob Evans (JHU/APL), Lis Immer (JHU/APL), Makato Ishii (Casa Real), Tyler Jewell (BEA), Jim Mayfield (JHU/APL), Matt McGinty (New Atlanta), Paul McNamee (JHU/APL), Karl Moss (Macromedia), and Jim Stafford (Capita). I hope I learned from their advice. Mary Lou "Eagle Eyes" Nohr spotted my errant commas, awkward sentences, typographical errors, and grammatical inconsistencies. She improved the result immensely. Vanessa Moore designed the book layout and produced the final version; she did a great job despite my many last-minute changes. Greg Doench of Prentice Hall believed in the concept from the beginning and encouraged me to write the book. Mike Alread persuaded Sun Microsystems Press to believe in it also. Thanks to all.

Most of all, thanks to B.J., Lindsay, and Nathan for their patience and encouragement. God has blessed me with a great family.

About the Author

Marty Hall is president of coreservlets.com, a small company that provides training courses and consulting services related to server-side Java technology. He also teaches Java and Web programming in the Johns Hopkins University part-time graduate program in Computer Science, where he directs the Distributed Computing and Web Technology concentration areas. Marty is the author of *Core Web Programming* and *Core Servlets and JavaServer Pages*, both from Sun Microsystems Press and Prentice Hall. You can reach Marty at hall@coreservlets.com; you can find out about his on-site training courses at *http://courses.coreservlets.com*.

Introduction

Suppose your company wants to sell products online. You have a database that gives the price and inventory status of each item. But, your database doesn't speak HTTP, the protocol that Web browsers use. Nor does it output HTML, the format Web browsers need. What can you do? Once users know what they want to buy, how do you gather that information? You want to customize your site based on visitors' preferences and interests—how? You want to let users see their previous purchases, but you don't want to reveal that information to other visitors. How do you enforce these security restrictions? When your Web site becomes popular, you might want to compress pages to reduce bandwidth. How can you do this without causing your site to fail for the 30% of visitors whose browsers don't support compression? In all these cases, you need a program to act as the intermediary between the browser and some server-side resource. This book is about using the Java platform for this type of program.

"Wait a second," you say. "Didn't you *already* write a book about that?" Well, yes. In May of 2000, Sun Microsystems Press and Prentice Hall released my second book, *Core Servlets and JavaServer Pages*. It was successful beyond everyone's wildest expectations, selling approximately 100,000 copies in the first year, getting translated into Bulgarian, Chinese, Czech, French, German, Hebrew, Japanese, Korean, Polish, Russian, and Spanish, and being chosen by Amazon.com as one of the top five computer programming books of 2001. Even better, I was swamped with requests for what I *really* like doing: teaching short courses for developers in industry. Despite having to decline most of the requests, I was still able to teach servlet and JSP short courses in Australia, Canada, Japan, the Philippines, and at a variety of U.S. venues. What fun!

Since then, use of servlets and JSP has continued to grow at a phenomenal rate. The Java 2 Platform has become the technology of choice for developing e-commerce applications, dynamic Web sites, and Web-enabled applications and service. Servlets and JSP continue to be the foundation of this platform—they provide the link between Web clients and server-side applications. Virtually all major Web servers for Windows, Unix (including Linux), MacOS, VMS, and mainframe operating systems now support servlet and JSP technology either natively or by means of a plugin. With only a small amount of configuration, you can run servlets and JSP in Microsoft IIS, iPlanet/Netscape Enterprise Server, the Apache Web Server, IBM WebSphere, BEA WebLogic, and dozens of other servers. Performance of both commercial and open-source servlet and JSP engines has improved significantly.

However, the field continues to evolve rapidly. For example:

- The official servlet and JSP reference implementation is no longer developed by Sun. Instead, it is Apache Tomcat, an open-source product developed by a team from many different organizations.
- Use of Web applications to bundle groups of servlets and JSP pages has grown significantly.
- Portable mechanisms for enforcing Web application security have started to displace the server-specific mechanisms that were formerly used.
- Version 2.3 of the servlet specification was released (August 2001). New features in this specification include servlet and JSP filters, application life-cycle event handlers, and a number of smaller additions and changes to existing APIs and to the deployment descriptor (*web.xml*).
- Version 1.2 of the JSP specification was released (also August 2001). This version lets you bundle event listeners with tag libraries, lets you designate XML-based programs to check the syntax of pages that use custom tags, and supplies interfaces that let your custom tags loop more efficiently and handle errors more easily. JSP 1.2 also makes a number of smaller changes and additions to existing APIs and to the TLD file format.
- XML has become firmly entrenched as a data-interchange language. Servlet and JSP pages use it for configuration files. Tag library validators can use it to verify custom tag syntax. JSP pages can be represented entirely in XML.
- Throughout 2000 and 2001, the JSR-052 expert group put together a standard tag library for JSP. In November of 2001 they released early access version 1.2 of this library, called JSTL (JSP Standard Tag Library). This library provides standard tags for simple looping, iterating over a variety of data structures, evaluating content conditionally, and accessing objects without using explicit scripting code.

Whew. Lots of changes. The new features are very useful, but is there a single place where you can learn about all of them? Here! That's why I wrote this book: to show developers how to make use of all of these new features. If you aren't familiar with basic servlet and JSP development, don't worry. I provide a thorough review at the beginning of the book.

Who Should Read This Book

This book is aimed at two main groups.

The first group is composed of people who are familiar with basic servlet and JSP development and want to learn how to make use of all the new capabilities I just described.

However, if you are new to this technology, there is no need to go away and learn older servlet and JSP versions and then come back to this book. Assuming you are familiar with the basics of the Java programming language itself, you fit into the second main group for whom this book is designed. For you, I start the book with a detailed review of the foundations of servlet and JSP programming, set in the context of the servlet 2.3 and JSP 1.2 specifications. Furthermore, when space prevents coverage of some of the finer points of basic development, I cite the specific sections of *Core Servlets and JavaServer Pages* that provide details and put those sections online at *http://www.moreservlets.com*. In fact, I put the *entire* text of *Core Servlets and JavaServer Pages* on the Web site (in PDF).

Although this book is well suited for both experienced servlet and JSP programmers and newcomers to the technology, it assumes that you are familiar with basic Java programming. You don't have to be an expert Java developer, but if you know nothing about the Java programming language, this is not the place to start. After all, servlet and JSP technology is an *application* of the Java programming language. If you don't know the language, you can't apply it. So, if you know nothing about basic Java development, start with a good introductory book like *Thinking in Java*, *Core Java*, or *Core Web Programming*. Come back here after you are comfortable with at least the basics.

Book Distinctives

This book has four important characteristics that set it apart from many other similar-sounding books:

- **Integrated coverage of servlets and JSP.** The two technologies are closely related; you should learn and use them together.

- **Real code.** Complete, working, documented programs are essential to learning; I provide lots of them.
- **Step-by-step instructions.** Complex tasks are broken down into simple steps that are illustrated with real examples.
- **Server configuration and usage details.** I supply lots of concrete examples to get you going quickly.

Integrated Coverage of Servlets and JSP

One of the key philosophies behind *Core Servlets and JavaServer Pages* was that servlets and JSP should be learned (and used!) together, not separately. After all, they aren't two entirely distinct technologies: JSP is just a different way of writing servlets. If you don't know servlet programming, you can't use servlets when they are a better choice than JSP, you can't use the MVC architecture to integrate servlets and JSP, you can't understand complex JSP constructs, and you can't understand how JSP scripting elements work (since they are really just servlet code). If you don't understand JSP development, you can't use JSP when it is a better option than servlet technology, you can't use the MVC architecture, and you are stuck using `print` statements even for pages that consist almost entirely of static HTML.

In this book, an integrated approach is more important than ever. Web applications let you bundle both servlets and JSP pages into a single file or directory. The custom URLs, initialization parameters, preload settings, and session timeouts of the deployment descriptor apply equally to servlets and JSP pages. Declarative security applies equally to both technologies. The new filtering capability applies to both. Event listeners apply to both. The jx portion of the JSP standard tag library (JSTL) is mostly predicated on the assumption that the JSP page is presenting data that was established by a servlet. Servlets and JSP go together!

Real Code

Sure, small code snippets are useful for introducing concepts. The book has lots of them. But, for you to *really* understand how to use various techniques, you also need to see the techniques in the context of complete working programs. Not huge programs: just ones that have no missing pieces and thus really run. I provide plenty of such programs, all of them documented and available for unrestricted use at *www.moreservlets.com*.

Step-by-Step Instructions

When I was a graduate student (long before Java existed), I had an Algorithms professor who explained in class that he was a believer in step-by-step instructions. I was puzzled: wasn't everyone? Not at all. Sure, most instructors explained simple tasks that way, but this professor took even highly theoretical concepts and said "first you do *this*, then you do *that*," and so on. The other instructors didn't explain things this way; neither did my textbooks. But, it helped me enormously.

If such an approach works even for theoretical subjects, how much more should it work with applied tasks like those described in this book?

Server Configuration and Usage Details

When I first tried to learn server-side programming, I grabbed a couple of books, the official specifications, and some online papers. Almost without fail, they said something like "since this technology is portable, we won't cover specifics of any one server." Aargh. I couldn't even get started. After hunting around, I downloaded a server. I wrote some code. How did I compile it? Where did I put it? How did I invoke it?

Servlet and JSP *code* is portable. The *APIs* are standardized. But, server structure and organization are not standardized. The directory in which you place your code is different on ServletExec than it is on JRun. You set up SSL differently with Tomcat than you do with other servers. These details are important.

Now, I'm not saying that this is a book that is specific to any particular server. I'm just saying that when a topic requires server-specific knowledge, it is important to say so. Furthermore, specific examples are helpful. So, when I describe a topic that requires server-specific information like the directory in which to place a Web application, I first explain the general pattern that servers tend to follow. Then, I give very specific details for three of the most popular servers that are available without cost for desktop development: Apache Tomcat, Macromedia/Allaire JRun, and New Atlanta ServletExec.

How This Book Is Organized

This book consists of five parts:

- **Part I: The Basics.** Server setup and configuration. Basic servlet programming. Basic JSP programming.
- **Part II: Web Applications.** Using and deploying Web applications. Controlling behavior with *web.xml*. A larger example.
- **Part III: Web Application Security.** Declarative security. Programmatic security. SSL.
- **Part IV: Major New Servlet and JSP Capabilities.** Servlet and JSP filters. Application life-cycle event listeners.
- **Part V: New Tag Library Capabilities.** New tag library features in JSP 1.2. The JSP Standard Tag Library (JSTL).

Part I: The Basics

- Server setup and configuration.
- Downloading the JDK.
- Obtaining a development server.
- Configuring and testing the server.
- Deploying and accessing HTML and JSP pages.
- Setting up your development environment.
- Deploying and accessing servlets.
- Simplifying servlet and JSP deployment.
- Basic servlet programming.
- The advantages of servlets over competing technologies.
- The basic servlet structure and life cycle.
- Servlet initialization parameters.
- Access to form data.
- HTTP 1.1 request headers, response headers, and status codes.
- The servlet equivalent of the standard CGI variables.
- Cookies in servlets.
- Session tracking.
- Basic JSP programming.
- Understanding the benefits of JSP.
- Invoking Java code with JSP expressions, scriptlets, and declarations.
- Structuring the servlet that results from a JSP page.
- Including files and applets in JSP documents.
- Using JavaBeans with JSP.
- Creating custom JSP tag libraries.
- Combining servlets and JSP: the Model View Controller (Model 2) architecture.

Part II: Web Applications

- Using and deploying Web applications.
- Registering Web applications with the server.
- Organizing Web applications.
- Deploying applications in WAR files.
- Recording Web application dependencies on shared libraries.
- Dealing with relative URLs.
- Sharing data among Web applications.
- Controlling Web application behavior with *web.xml*.
- Customizing URLs.
- Turning off default URLs.
- Initializing servlets and JSP pages.
- Preloading servlets and JSP pages.

- Declaring filters for servlets and JSP pages.
- Designating welcome pages and error pages.
- Restricting access to Web resources.
- Controlling session timeouts.
- Documenting Web applications.
- Specifying MIME types.
- Locating tag library descriptors.
- Declaring event listeners.
- Accessing J2EE Resources.
- Defining and using a larger Web application.
- The interaction among components in a Web application.
- Using sessions for per-user data.
- Using the servlet context for multiuser data.
- Managing information that is accessed by multiple servlets and JSP pages.
- Eliminating dependencies on the Web application name.

Part III: Web Application Security

- Declarative security.
- Understanding the major aspects of Web application security.
- Authenticating users with HTML forms.
- Using BASIC HTTP authentication.
- Defining passwords in Tomcat, JRun, and ServletExec.
- Designating protected resources with the `security-constraint` element.
- Using `login-config` to specify the authentication method.
- Mandating the use of SSL.
- Configuring Tomcat to use SSL.
- Programmatic security.
- Combining container-managed and programmatic security.
- Using the `isUserInRole` method.
- Using the `getRemoteUser` method.
- Using the `getUserPrincipal` method.
- Programmatically controlling all aspects of security.
- Using SSL with programmatic security.

Part IV: Major New Servlet and JSP Capabilities

- Servlet and JSP filters.
- Designing basic filters.
- Reading request data.
- Accessing the servlet context.

- Initializing filters.
- Blocking the servlet or JSP response.
- Modifying the servlet or JSP response.
- Using filters for debugging and logging.
- Using filters to monitor site access.
- Using filters to replace strings.
- Using filters to compress the response.
- Application life-cycle event listeners.
- Understanding the general event-handling strategy.
- Monitoring servlet context initialization and shutdown.
- Setting application-wide values.
- Detecting changes in attributes of the servlet context.
- Recognizing creation and destruction of HTTP sessions.
- Analyzing overall session usage.
- Watching for changes in session attributes.
- Tracking purchases at an e-commerce site.
- Using multiple cooperating listeners.
- Packaging listeners in JSP tag libraries.

Part V: New Tag Library Capabilities

- New tag library features in JSP 1.2.
- Converting TLD files to the new format.
- Bundling life-cycle event listeners with tag libraries.
- Checking custom tag syntax with `TagLibraryValidator`.
- Using the Simple API for XML (SAX) in validators.
- Handling errors with the `TryCatchFinally` interface.
- Changing names of method return values.
- Looping without creating `BodyContent`.
- Declaring scripting variables in the TLD file.
- The JSP Standard Tag Library (JSTL).
- Downloading and installing the standard JSP tag library.
- Reading attributes without using Java syntax.
- Accessing bean properties without using Java syntax.
- Looping an explicit number of times.
- Iterating over various data structures.
- Checking iteration status.
- Iterating with string-based tokens.
- Evaluating expressions conditionally.
- Using the JSTL expression language to set attributes, return values, and declare scripting variables.

Conventions

Throughout the book, concrete programming constructs or program output are presented in a monospaced font. For example, when abstractly discussing server-side programs that use HTTP, I might refer to "HTTP servlets" or just "servlets," but when I say HttpServlet I am talking about a specific Java class.

User input is indicated in boldface, and command-line prompts are either generic (Prompt>) or indicate the operating system to which they apply (DOS>). For instance, the following indicates that "Some Output" is the result when "java SomeProgram" is executed on any platform.

```
Prompt> java SomeProgram
Some Output
```

URLs, filenames, and directory names are presented with italics. So, for example, I would say "the StringTokenizer class" (monospaced because I'm talking about the class name) and "Listing such and such shows *SomeFile.java*" (italic because I'm talking about the filename). Paths use forward slashes as in URLs unless they are specific to the Windows operating system. So, for instance, I would use a forward slash when saying "look in *install_dir/bin*" (OS neutral) but use backslashes when saying "*C:\Windows\Temp*" (Windows specific).

Important standard techniques are indicated by specially marked entries, as in the following example.

Core Approach

Pay particular attention to items in "Core Approach" sections. They indicate techniques that should always or almost always be used.

Notes and warnings are called out in a similar manner.

About the Web Site

The book has a companion Web site at *http://www.moreservlets.com/*. This free site includes:

- Documented source code for all examples shown in the book; this code can be downloaded for unrestricted use.

- The complete text of *Core Servlets and JavaServer Pages* in PDF format.
- Up-to-date download sites for servlet and JSP software.
- Links to all URLs mentioned in the text of the book.
- Information on book discounts.
- Reports on servlet and JSP short courses.
- Book additions, updates, and news.

MORE SERVLETS AND JAVASERVER™ PAGES

THE BASICS

Part I

SERVER SETUP AND CONFIGURATION

Topics in This Chapter

- Downloading the JDK
- Obtaining a development server
- Configuring and testing the server
- Deploying and accessing HTML and JSP pages
- Setting up your development environment
- Deploying and accessing servlets
- Simplifying servlet and JSP deployment

Chapter 1

Before you can start learning specific servlet and JSP techniques, you need to have the right software and know how to use it. This introductory chapter explains how to obtain, configure, test, and use free versions of all the software needed to run servlets and JavaServer Pages.

1.1 Download the Java Development Kit (JDK)

You probably already have the JDK installed, but if not, installing it should be your first step. Version 2.3 of the servlet API and version 1.2 of the JSP API require the Java 2 platform (standard or enterprise edition). If you aren't using J2EE features like EJB or JNDI, I recommend that you use the standard edition, JDK 1.3 or 1.4.

For Solaris, Windows, and Linux, obtain JDK 1.3 at *http://java.sun.com/j2se/1.3/* and JDK 1.4 at *http://java.sun.com/j2se/1.4/*. For other platforms, check first whether a Java 2 implementation comes preinstalled as it does with MacOS X. If not, see Sun's list of third-party Java implementations at *http://java.sun.com/cgi-bin/java-ports.cgi*.

1.2   Download a Server for Your Desktop

Your second step is to download a server that implements the Java Servlet 2.3 and JSP 1.2 specifications for use on your desktop. In fact, I typically keep *two* servers installed on my desktop (Apache's free Tomcat server and one commercial server) and test my applications on both to keep myself from accidentally using nonportable constructs.

Regardless of the server that you will use for final deployment, you will want at least one server *on your desktop* for development. Even if the deployment server is in the office next to you connected by a lightning-fast network connection, you still don't want to use it for your development. Even a test server on your intranet that is inaccessible to customers is much less convenient for development purposes than a server right on your desktop. Running a development server on your desktop simplifies development in a number of ways, as compared to deploying to a remote server each and every time you want to test something.

1. **It is faster to test.** With a server on your desktop, there is no need to use FTP or another upload program. The harder it is for you to test changes, the less frequently you will test. Infrequent testing will let errors persist that will slow you down in the long run.

2. **It is easier to debug.** When running on your desktop, many servers display the standard output in a normal window. This is in contrast to deployment servers where the standard output is almost always either completely hidden or only available on the screen of the system administrator. So, with a desktop server, plain old `System.out.println` statements become useful tracing and debugging utilities.

3. **It is simple to restart.** During development, you will find that you need to restart the server frequently. For example, the server typically reads the *web.xml* file (see Chapter 4, "Using and Deploying Web Applications") only at startup. So, you normally have to restart the server each time you modify *web.xml*. Although some servers (e.g., ServletExec) have an interactive method of reloading *web.xml*, tasks such as clearing session data, resetting the `ServletContext`, or replacing modified class files used indirectly by servlets or JSP pages (e.g., beans or utility classes) may still necessitate restarting the server. Some older servers also need to be restarted because they implement servlet reloading unreliably. (Normally, servers instantiate the class that corresponds to a servlet only once and keep the instance in memory between requests. With *servlet reloading*, a server automatically replaces servlets that are in memory but whose class file has changed

on the disk). Besides, some deployment servers recommend completely disabling servlet reloading in order to increase performance.
So, it is much more productive to develop in an environment where
you can restart the server with a click of the mouse without asking for
permission from other developers who might be using the server.

4. **It is more reliable to benchmark.** Although it is difficult to collect
    accurate timing results for short-running programs even in the best of
    circumstances, running benchmarks on systems that have heavy and
    varying system loads is notoriously unreliable.

5. **It is under your control.** As a developer, you may not be the admin-
    istrator of the system on which the test or deployment server runs. You
    might have to ask some system administrator every time you want the
    server restarted. Or, the remote system may be down for a system
    upgrade at the most critical juncture of your development cycle. Not
    fun.

Now, if you can run on your desktop the same server you use for deployment, all
the better. But one of the beauties of servlets and JSP is that you don't *have* to; you
can develop with one server and deploy with another. Following are some of the most
popular free options for desktop development servers. In all cases, the free version
runs as a standalone Web server; in most cases, you have to pay for the deployment
version that can be integrated with a regular Web server like Microsoft IIS,
iPlanet/Netscape, or the Apache Web Server. However, the performance difference
between using one of the servers as a servlet and JSP engine within a regular Web
server and using it as a complete standalone Web server is not significant enough to
matter during development. See *http://java.sun.com/products/servlet/industry.html*
for a more complete list of servers.

- **Apache Tomcat.**
  Tomcat 4 is the official reference implementation of the servlet 2.3 and
  JSP 1.2 specifications. Tomcat 3 is the official reference implementation
  for servlets 2.2 and JSP 1.1. Both versions can be used as a standalone
  server during development or can be plugged into a standard Web
  server for use during deployment. Like all Apache products, Tomcat is
  entirely free and has complete source code available. Of all the servers,
  it also tends to be the one that is most compliant with the latest servlet
  and JSP specifications. However, the commercial servers tend to be
  better documented, easier to configure, and a bit faster. To download
  Tomcat, see *http://jakarta.apache.org/tomcat/*.

- **Allaire/Macromedia JRun.**
  JRun is a servlet and JSP engine that can be used in standalone mode
  for development or plugged into most common commercial Web
  servers for deployment. It is free for development purposes, but you

have to purchase a license before deploying with it. It is a popular choice among developers that are looking for easier administration than Tomcat. For details, see *http://www.allaire.com/products/JRun/*.

- **New Atlanta's ServletExec.** ServletExec is another popular servlet and JSP engine that can be used in standalone mode for development or, for deployment, plugged into the Microsoft IIS, Apache, and iPlanet/Netscape Web servers. Version 4.0 supports servlets 2.3 and JSP 1.2. You can download and use it for free, but some of the high-performance capabilities and administration utilities are disabled until you purchase a license. The ServletExec Debugger is the configuration you would use as a standalone desktop development server. For details, see *http://www.servletexec.com/*.

- **Caucho's Resin.**
  Resin is a fast servlet and JSP engine with extensive XML support. It is free for development and noncommercial deployment purposes. For details, see *http://www.caucho.com/*.

- **LiteWebServer from Gefion Software.**
  LWS is a small standalone Web server that supports servlets and JSP. It is free for both development and deployment purposes, but a license will entitle you to increased support and the complete server source code. See *http://www.gefionsoftware.com/LiteWebServer/* for details.

1.3　Change the Port and Configure Other Server Settings

Most of the free servers listed in Section 1.2 use a nonstandard default port in order to avoid conflicts with other Web servers that may be using the standard port (80). However, if you are using the servers in standalone mode and have no other server running permanently on port 80, you will find it more convenient to use port 80. That way, you don't have to use the port number in every URL you type in your browser. There are one or two other settings that you might want to modify as well.

Changing the port or other configuration settings is a server-specific process, so you need to read your server's documentation for definitive instructions. However, I'll give a quick summary of the process for three of the most popular free servers here: Tomcat, JRun, and ServletExec.

Apache Tomcat

Tomcat Port Number

With Tomcat 4, modifying the port number involves editing *install_dir/conf/server.xml*, changing the `port` attribute of the `Connector` element from 8080 to 80, and restarting the server. Remember that this section applies to the use of Tomcat in standalone mode on your desktop system where no other server is already running permanently on port 80. On Unix/Linux, you must have system administrator privileges to start services on port 80 or other port numbers below 1024. You probably have such privileges on your desktop machine; you do not necessarily have them on deployment servers.

The original element will look something like the following:

```
<Connector
  className="org.apache.catalina.connector.http.HttpConnector"
  port="8080" ...
  ... />
```

It should change to something like the following:

```
<Connector
  className="org.apache.catalina.connector.http.HttpConnector"
  port="80" ...
  ... />
```

The easiest way to find the correct entry is to search for 8080 in *server.xml*; there should only be one noncomment occurrence. Be sure to make a backup of *server.xml* before you edit it, just in case you make a mistake that prevents the server from running. Also, remember that XML is case sensitive, so for instance, you cannot replace port with `Port` or `Connector` with `connector`.

With Tomcat 3, you modify the same file (*install_dir/conf/server.xml*), but you need to use slightly different `Connector` elements for different minor releases of Tomcat. With version 3.2, you replace 8080 with 80 in the following `Parameter` element.

```
<Connector ...>
  <Parameter name="port" value="8080"/>
</Connector>
```

Again, restart the server after making the change.

Other Tomcat Settings

Besides the port, three additional Tomcat settings are important: the JAVA_HOME variable, the DOS memory settings, and the CATALINA_HOME or TOMCAT_HOME variable.

The most critical Tomcat setting is the JAVA_HOME environment variable—failing to set it properly prevents Tomcat from handling JSP pages. This variable should list the base JDK installation directory, not the *bin* subdirectory. For example, if you are on Windows 98/Me and installed the JDK in *C:\JDK1.3*, you might put the following line in your *autoexec.bat* file.

```
set JAVA_HOME=C:\JDK1.3
```

On Windows NT/2000, you would go to the Start menu and select Settings, then Control Panel, then System, then Environment. Then, you would enter the JAVA_HOME value.

On Unix/Linux, if the JDK is installed in */usr/j2sdk1_3_1* and you use the C shell, you would put the following into your *.cshrc* file.

```
setenv JAVA_HOME /usr/j2sdk1_3_1
```

Rather than setting the JAVA_HOME environment variable globally in the operating system, some developers prefer to edit the startup script to set it there. If you prefer this strategy, edit *install_dir/bin/catalina.bat* (Tomcat 4; Windows) or *install_dir/bin/tomcat.bat* (Tomcat 3; Windows) and change the following:

```
if not "%JAVA_HOME%" == "" goto gotJavaHome
echo You must set JAVA_HOME to point at ...
goto cleanup
:gotJavaHome
```

to:

```
if not "%JAVA_HOME%" == "" goto gotJavaHome
set JAVA_HOME=C:\JDK1.3
:gotJavaHome
```

Be sure to make a backup copy of *catalina.bat* or *tomcat.bat* before making the changes. Unix/Linux users would make similar changes in *catalina.sh* or *tomcat.sh*.

If you use Windows, you may also have to change the DOS memory settings for the startup and shutdown scripts. If you get an "Out of Environment Space" error message when you start the server, you will need to right-click on *install_dir/bin/startup.bat*, select Properties, select Memory, and change the Initial Environment entry from Auto to 2816. Repeat the process for *install_dir/bin/shutdown.bat*.

In some cases, it is also helpful to set the CATALINA_HOME (Tomcat 4) or TOMCAT_HOME (Tomcat 3) environment variables. This variable identifies the Tomcat installation directory to the server. However, if you are careful to avoid copying the server startup scripts and you use only shortcuts (called "symbolic links" on Unix/Linux) instead, you are not required to set this variable. See Section 1.6 for more information on using these shortcuts.

Please note that this section describes the use of Tomcat as a standalone server for servlet and JSP *development*. It requires a totally different configuration to deploy Tomcat as a servlet and JSP container integrated within a regular Web server. For information on the use of Tomcat for deployment, please see *http://jakarta.apache.org/tomcat/tomcat-4.0-doc/*.

Allaire/Macromedia JRun

When using JRun in standalone mode (vs. integrated with a standard Web server), there are several options that you probably want to change from their default values. All can be set from the graphical JRun Management Console and/or through the JRun installation wizard.

JRun Port Number

To change the JRun port, first start the JRun Admin Server by clicking on the appropriate icon (on Windows, go to the Start menu, then Programs, then JRun 3.x). Then, click on the JRun Management Console (JMC) button or enter the URL *http://localhost:8000/* in a browser. Log in, using a username of `admin` and the password that you specified when you installed JRun, choose JRun Default Server, then select JRun Web Server. Figure 1–1 shows the result. Next, select Web Server Port, enter 80, and press Update. See Figure 1–2. Finally, select JRun Default Server again and press the Restart Server button.

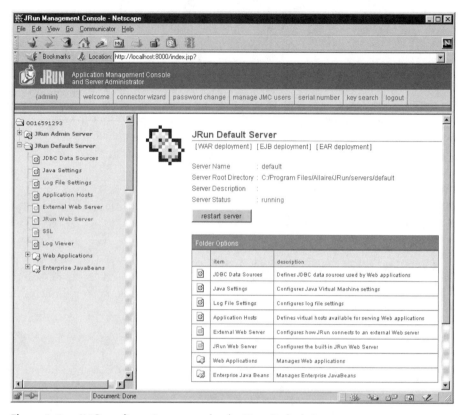

Figure 1–1   JMC configuration screen for the JRun Default Server.

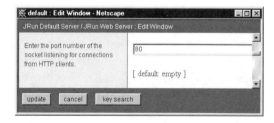

Figure 1–2   JRun Default Server port configuration window.

Other JRun Settings

When you install JRun, the installation wizard will ask you three questions that are particularly relevant to using JRun in standalone mode for development purposes. First, it will ask for a serial number. You can leave that blank; it is only required for deployment servers. Second, it will ask if you want to start JRun as a service. You should *deselect* this option; starting JRun automatically is useful for deployment but inconvenient for development because the server icon does not appear in the taskbar, thus making it harder to restart the server. The wizard clearly states that using JRun as a service should be reserved for deployment, but since the service option is selected by default, you can easily miss it. Finally, you will be asked if you want to configure an external Web server. Decline this option; you need no separate Web server when using JRun in standalone mode.

New Atlanta ServletExec

The following settings apply to use of the ServletExec Debugger 4.0, the version of ServletExec that you would use for standalone desktop development (vs. integrated with a regular Web server for deployment).

ServletExec Port Number

To change the port number from 8080 to 80, edit *install_dir/StartSED40.bat* and add "-port 80" to the end of the line that starts the server, as below.

```
%JAVA_HOME%\bin\java ... ServletExecDebuggerMain -port 80
```

Remember that this section applies to the use of ServletExec in standalone mode on your desktop system where no other server is already running permanently on port 80. On Unix/Linux, you must have system administrator privileges to start services on port 80 or other port numbers below 1024. You probably have such privileges on your desktop machine; you do not necessarily have them on deployment servers.

Other ServletExec Settings

ServletExec shares two settings with Tomcat. The one required setting is the JAVA_HOME environment variable. As with Tomcat, this variable refers to the base installation directory of the JDK (not the *bin* subdirectory). For example, if the JDK is installed in *C:\JDK1.3*, you should modify the JAVA_HOME entry in *install_dir/StartSED40.bat* to look like the following.

```
set JAVA_HOME=C:\JDK1.3
```

Also as with Tomcat, if you use Windows, you may have to change the DOS memory settings for the startup script. If you get an "Out of Environment Space" error message when you start the server, you will need to right-click on *install_dir/bin/StartSED40.bat*, select Properties, select Memory, and change the Initial Environment entry from Auto to 2816.

1.4   Test the Server

Before trying your own servlets or JSP pages, you should make sure that the server is installed and configured properly. For Tomcat, click on *install_dir/bin/startup.bat* (Windows) or execute *install_dir/bin/startup.sh* (Unix/Linux). For JRun, go to the Start menu and select Programs, JRun 3.1, and JRun Default Server. For Servlet-Exec, click on *install_dir/bin/StartSED40.bat*. In all three cases, enter the URL *http://localhost/* in your browser and make sure you get a regular Web page, not an error message saying that the page cannot be displayed or that the server cannot be found. Figures 1–3 through 1–5 show typical results. If you chose not to change the port number to 80 (see Section 1.3, "Change the Port and Configure Other Server Settings"), you will need to use a URL like *http://localhost:8080/* that includes the port number.

Figure 1–3   Initial home page for Tomcat 4.0.

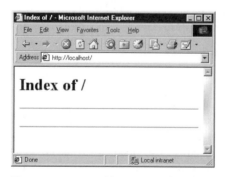

Figure 1–4   Initial home page for JRun 3.1.

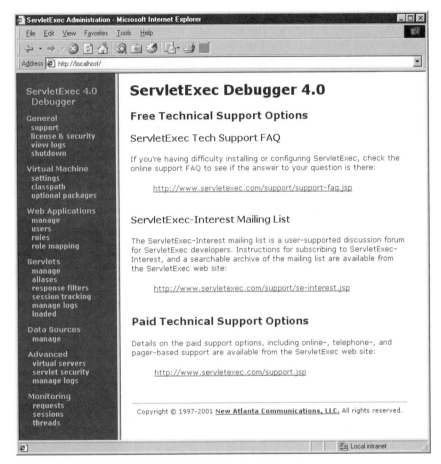

Figure 1–5   Initial home page for ServletExec 4.0.

1.5   Try Some Simple HTML and JSP Pages

After you have verified that the server is running, you should make sure that you can install and access simple HTML and JSP pages. This test, if successful, shows two important things. First, successfully accessing an HTML page shows that you understand which directories should hold HTML and JSP files. Second, successfully accessing a new JSP page shows that the Java compiler (not just the Java virtual machine) is configured properly.

Eventually, you will almost certainly want to create and use your own Web applications (see Chapter 4, "Using and Deploying Web Applications"), but for initial testing I recommend that you use the default Web application. Although Web applications follow a common directory structure, the exact location of the default Web application is server specific. Check your server's documentation for definitive instructions, but I summarize the locations for Tomcat, JRun, and ServletExec in the following list. Where I list *SomeDirectory* you can use any directory name you like. (But you are never allowed to use *WEB-INF* or *META-INF* as directory names. For the default Web application, you also have to avoid a directory name that matches the URL prefix of any other Web application.)

- **Tomcat Directory**
  install_dir/webapps/ROOT
  (or *install_dir/webapps/ROOT/SomeDirectory*)

- **JRun Directory**
  install_dir/servers/default/default-app
  (or *install_dir/servers/default/default-app/SomeDirectory*)

- **ServletExec Directory**
  install_dir/public_html[1]
  (or *install_dir/public_html/SomeDirectory*)

- **Corresponding URLs**
  http://host/Hello.html
  (or *http://host/SomeDirectory/Hello.html*)
  http://host/Hello.jsp
  (or *http://host/SomeDirectory/Hello.jsp*)

For your first tests, I suggest you simply take *Hello.html* (Listing 1.1, Figure 1–6) and *Hello.jsp* (Listing 1.2, Figure 1–7) and drop them into the appropriate locations. The code for these files, as well as *all* the code from the book, is available online at *http://www.moreservlets.com*. That Web site also contains updates, additions, information on short courses, and the full text of *Core Servlets and JavaServer Pages* (in PDF). If neither the HTML file nor the JSP file works (e.g., you get File Not Found—404—errors), you likely are using the wrong directory for the files. If the HTML file works but the JSP file fails, you probably have incorrectly specified the base JDK directory (e.g., with the JAVA_HOME variable).

---

1. Note that the *public_html* directory is created automatically by ServletExec the first time you run the server. So, you will be unable to find *public_html* if you have not yet tested the server as described in Section 1.4 (Test the Server).

Listing 1.1 *Hello.html*

```
<!DOCTYPE HTML PUBLIC "-//W3C//DTD HTML 4.0 Transitional//EN">
<HTML>
<HEAD><TITLE>HTML Test</TITLE></HEAD>
<BODY BGCOLOR="#FDF5E6">
<H1>HTML Test</H1>
Hello.
</BODY>
</HTML>
```

Listing 1.2 *Hello.jsp*

```
<!DOCTYPE HTML PUBLIC "-//W3C//DTD HTML 4.0 Transitional//EN">
<HTML>
<HEAD><TITLE>JSP Test</TITLE></HEAD>
<BODY BGCOLOR="#FDF5E6">
<H1>JSP Test</H1>
Time: <%= new java.util.Date() %>
</BODY>
</HTML>
```

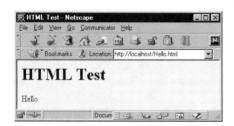

Figure 1–6 Result of *Hello.html*.

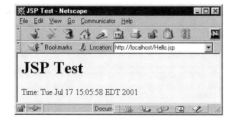

Figure 1–7 Result of *Hello.jsp*.

1.6   Set Up Your Development Environment

The server startup script automatically sets the server's CLASSPATH to include the standard servlet and JSP classes and the *WEB-INF/classes* directory (containing compiled servlets) of each Web application. But *you* need similar settings, or you will be unable to compile servlets in the first place. This section summarizes the configuration needed for servlet development.

Create a Development Directory

The first thing you should do is create a directory in which to place the servlets and JSP pages that you develop. This directory can be in your home directory (e.g., *~/ServletDevel* on Unix) or in a convenient general location (e.g., *C:\ServletDevel* on Windows). It should *not*, however, be in the server's installation directory.

Eventually, you will organize this development directory into different Web applications (each with a common structure—see Chapter 4). For initial testing of your environment, however, you can just put servlets either directly in the development directory (for packageless servlets) or in a subdirectory that matches the servlet package name. Many developers simply put all their code in the server's deployment directory (see Section 1.9). I strongly discourage this practice and instead recommend one of the approaches described in Section 1.8 (Establish a Simplified Deployment Method). Although developing in the deployment directory seems simpler at the beginning since it requires no copying of files, it significantly complicates matters in the long run. Mixing locations makes it hard to separate an operational version from a version you are testing, makes it difficult to test on multiple servers, and makes organization much more complicated. Besides, your desktop is almost certainly not the final deployment server, so you'll eventually have to develop a good system for deploying anyhow.

Core Warning

Don't use the server's deployment directory as your development location. Instead, keep a separate development directory.

Make Shortcuts to Start and Stop the Server

Since I find myself frequently restarting the server, I find it convenient to place shortcuts to the server startup and shutdown icons inside my main development directory. You will likely find it convenient to do the same.

For example, for Tomcat on Windows, go to *install_dir/bin*, right-click on *startup.bat*, and select Copy. Then go to your development directory, right-click in the window, and select Paste Shortcut (not just Paste). Repeat the process for *install_dir/bin/shutdown.bat*. On Unix, you would use `ln -s` to make a symbolic link to *startup.sh*, *tomcat.sh* (needed even though you don't directly invoke this file), and *shutdown.sh*.

For JRun on Windows, go to the Start menu, select Programs, select JRun 3.x, right-click on the JRun Default Server icon, and select Copy. Then go to your development directory, right-click in the window, and select Paste Shortcut. Repeat the process for the JRun Admin Server and JRun Management Console.

For the ServletExec Debugger (i.e., standalone development server), go to *install_dir*, right-click on *StartSED40.bat*, and select Copy. Then go to your development directory, right-click in the window, and select Paste Shortcut (not just Paste). There is no separate shutdown file; to stop ServletExec, just go to *http://localhost/* (see Figure 1–5) and click on the Shutdown link in the General category on the left-hand side.

Set Your CLASSPATH

Since servlets and JSP are not part of the Java 2 platform, standard edition, you have to identify the servlet classes to the compiler. The *server* already knows about the servlet classes, but the *compiler* (i.e., `javac`) you use for development probably doesn't. So, if you don't set your CLASSPATH, attempts to compile servlets, tag libraries, or other classes that use the servlet API will fail with error messages about unknown classes. The exact location of the servlet JAR file varies from server to server. In most cases, you can hunt around for a file called *servlet.jar*. Or, read your server's documentation to discover the location. Once you find the JAR file, add the location to your development CLASSPATH. Here are the locations for some common development servers:

- **Tomcat 4 Location.**
  install_dir/common/lib/servlet.jar
- **Tomcat 3 Location.**
  install_dir/lib/servlet.jar
- **JRun Location.**
  install_dir/lib/ext/servlet.jar

- **ServletExec Location.**
  install_dir/ServletExecDebugger.jar

Now, in addition to the servlet JAR file, you also need to put your development directory in the `CLASSPATH`. Although this is not necessary for simple packageless servlets, once you gain experience you will almost certainly use packages. Compiling a file that is in a package and that uses another class in the same package requires the `CLASSPATH` to include the directory that is at the top of the package hierarchy. In this case, that's the development directory I just discussed in the first subsection. Forgetting this setting is perhaps *the* most common mistake made by beginning servlet programmers.

Core Approach

Remember to add your development directory to your `CLASSPATH`. Otherwise, you will get "Unresolved symbol" error messages when you attempt to compile servlets that are in packages and that make use of other classes in the same package.

Finally, you should include "." (the current directory) in the `CLASSPATH`. Otherwise, you will only be able to compile packageless classes that are in the top-level development directory.

Here are a few representative methods of setting the `CLASSPATH`. They assume that your development directory is *C:\devel* (Windows) or */usr/devel* (Unix/Linux) and that you are using Tomcat 4. Replace *install_dir* with the actual base installation location of the server. Be sure to use the appropriate case for the filenames. Note that these examples represent only one approach for setting the `CLASSPATH`. Many Java integrated development environments have a global or project-specific setting that accomplishes the same result. But these settings are totally IDE-specific and won't be discussed here.

- **Windows 98/Me.** Put the following in your *autoexec.bat*. (Note that this all goes on one line with no spaces—it is broken here for readability.)

  ```
  set CLASSPATH=.;
              C:\devel;
              install_dir\common\lib\servlet.jar
  ```

- **Windows NT/2000.** Go to the Start menu and select Settings, then Control Panel, then System, then Environment. Then, enter the `CLASSPATH` value from the previous bullet.

- **Unix/Linux (C shell).** Put the following in your *.cshrc*. (Again, in the real file it goes on a single line without spaces.)
  ```
  setenv CLASSPATH .:
                   /usr/devel:
                   install_dir/common/lib/servlet.jar
  ```

Bookmark or Install the Servlet and JSP API Documentation

Just as no serious programmer should develop general-purpose Java applications without access to the JDK 1.3 or 1.4 API documentation (in Javadoc format), no serious programmer should develop servlets or JSP pages without access to the API for classes in the `javax.servlet` packages. Here is a summary of where to find the API:

- *http://java.sun.com/products/jsp/download.html*
  This site lets you download the Javadoc files for either the servlet 2.3 and JSP 1.2 API or for the servlet 2.2 and JSP 1.1 API. You will probably find this API so useful that it will be worth having a local copy instead of browsing it online. However, some servers bundle this documentation, so check before downloading.

- *http://java.sun.com/products/servlet/2.3/javadoc/*
  This site lets you browse the servlet 2.3 API online.

- *http://java.sun.com/products/servlet/2.2/javadoc/*
  This site lets you browse the servlet 2.2 and JSP 1.1 API online.

- *http://java.sun.com/j2ee/j2sdkee/techdocs/api/*
  This address lets you browse the complete API for the Java 2 Platform, Enterprise Edition (J2EE), which includes the servlet 2.2 and JSP 1.1 packages.

1.7 Compile and Test Some Simple Servlets

OK, so your environment is all set. At least you *think* it is. It would be nice to confirm that hypothesis. Following are three tests that help verify this.

Test 1: A Servlet That Does Not Use Packages

The first servlet to try is a basic one: no packages, no utility (helper) classes, just simple HTML output. Rather than writing your own test servlet, you can just grab *HelloServlet.java* (Listing 1.3) from the book's source code archive at *http://www.moreservlets.com*. If you get compilation errors, go back and check your CLASSPATH settings (Section 1.6)—you most likely erred in listing the location of the JAR file that contains the servlet classes (e.g., *servlet.jar*). Once you compile *Hello-Servlet.java*, put *HelloServlet.class* in the appropriate location (usually the *WEB-INF/classes* directory of your server's default Web application). Check your server's documentation for this location, or see the following list for a summary of the locations used by Tomcat, JRun, and ServletExec. Then, access the servlet with the URL *http://localhost/servlet/HelloServlet* (or *http://localhost:8080/servlet/HelloServlet* if you chose not to change the port number as described in Section 1.3). You should get something similar to Figure 1–8. If this URL fails but the test of the server itself (Section 1.4) succeeded, you probably put the class file in the wrong directory.

- **Tomcat Directory.**
  install_dir/webapps/ROOT/WEB-INF/classes

- **JRun Directory.**
  install_dir/servers/default/default-app/WEB-INF/classes

- **ServletExec Directory.**
  install_dir/Servlets

- **Corresponding URL.**
  http://host/servlet/HelloServlet

Listing 1.3	*HelloServlet.java*

```
import java.io.*;
import javax.servlet.*;
import javax.servlet.http.*;

/** Simple servlet used to test server. */

public class HelloServlet extends HttpServlet {
  public void doGet(HttpServletRequest request,
                    HttpServletResponse response)
      throws ServletException, IOException {
    response.setContentType("text/html");
    PrintWriter out = response.getWriter();
```

Listing 1.3	*HelloServlet.java (continued)*

```
    String docType =
      "<!DOCTYPE HTML PUBLIC \"-//W3C//DTD HTML 4.0 " +
      "Transitional//EN\">\n";
    out.println(docType +
                "<HTML>\n" +
                "<HEAD><TITLE>Hello</TITLE></HEAD>\n" +
                "<BODY BGCOLOR=\"#FDF5E6\">\n" +
                "<H1>Hello</H1>\n" +
                "</BODY></HTML>");
  }
}
```

Figure 1–8   Result of `HelloServlet`.

Test 2: A Servlet That Uses Packages

The second servlet to try is one that uses packages but no utility classes. Again, rather than writing your own test, you can grab *HelloServlet2.java* (Listing 1.4) from the book's source code archive at *http://www.moreservlets.com*. Since this servlet is in the `moreservlets` package, it should go in the *moreservlets* directory, both during development and when deployed to the server. If you get compilation errors, go back and check your `CLASSPATH` settings (Section 1.6)—you most likely forgot to include "." (the current directory). Once you compile *Hello-Servlet2.java*, put *HelloServlet2.class* in the *moreservlets* subdirectory of whatever directory the server uses for servlets that are not in custom Web applications (usually the *WEB-INF/classes* directory of the default Web application). Check your server's documentation for this location, or see the following list for a summary of the locations for Tomcat, JRun, and ServletExec. For now, you can simply copy the class file from the development directory to the deployment directory, but Section 1.8 (Establish a Simplified Deployment Method) will provide some options for simplifying the process.

    Once you have placed the servlet in the proper directory, access it with the URL *http://localhost/servlet/moreservlets.HelloServlet2*. You should get something similar to Figure 1–9. If this test fails, you probably either typed the URL wrong (e.g., used a slash instead of a dot after the package name) or put *HelloServlet2.class* in the wrong location (e.g., directly in the server's *WEB-INF/classes* directory instead of in the *moreservlets* subdirectory).

- **Tomcat Directory.**
  install_dir/webapps/ROOT/WEB-INF/classes/moreservlets
- **JRun Directory.**
  install_dir/servers/default/default-app/WEB-INF/classes/moreservlets
- **ServletExec Directory.**
  install_dir/Servlets/moreservlets
- **Corresponding URL.**
  http://host/servlet/moreservlets.HelloServlet2

Listing 1.4	*moreservlets/HelloServlet2.java*

```java
package moreservlets;

import java.io.*;
import javax.servlet.*;
import javax.servlet.http.*;

/** Simple servlet used to test the use of packages. */

public class HelloServlet2 extends HttpServlet {
  public void doGet(HttpServletRequest request,
                    HttpServletResponse response)
      throws ServletException, IOException {
    response.setContentType("text/html");
    PrintWriter out = response.getWriter();
    String docType =
      "<!DOCTYPE HTML PUBLIC \"-//W3C//DTD HTML 4.0 " +
      "Transitional//EN\">\n";
    out.println(docType +
                "<HTML>\n" +
                "<HEAD><TITLE>Hello (2)</TITLE></HEAD>\n" +
                "<BODY BGCOLOR=\"#FDF5E6\">\n" +
                "<H1>Hello (2)</H1>\n" +
                "</BODY></HTML>");
  }
}
```

Figure 1–9   Result of `HelloServlet2`.

Test 3: A Servlet That Uses Packages and Utilities

The final servlet you should test to verify the configuration of your server and development environment is one that uses both packages and utility classes. Listing 1.5 presents *HelloServlet3.java*, a servlet that uses the `ServletUtilities` class (Listing 1.6) to simplify the generation of the `DOCTYPE` (specifies the HTML version—useful when using HTML validators) and `HEAD` (specifies the title) portions of the HTML page. Those two parts of the page are useful (technically required, in fact), but are tedious to generate with servlet `println` statements. Again, the source code can be found at *http://www.moreservlets.com*.

Since both the servlet and the utility class are in the `moreservlets` package, they should go in the *moreservlets* directory. If you get compilation errors, go back and check your `CLASSPATH` settings (Section 1.6)—you most likely forgot to include the top-level development directory. I've said it before, but I'll say it again: your `CLASSPATH` must include the top-level directory of your package hierarchy before you can compile a packaged class that makes use of another class from the same package. This requirement is not particular to servlets; it is the way packages work on the Java platform in general. Nevertheless, many servlet developers are unaware of this fact, and it is one of the (perhaps *the*) most common errors beginning developers encounter.

Core Warning

Your `CLASSPATH` must include your top-level development directory. Otherwise, you cannot compile servlets that are in packages and that also use classes from the same package.

Once you compile *HelloServlet3.java* (which will automatically cause *Servlet-Utilities.java* to be compiled), put *HelloServlet3.class* and *ServletUtilities.class* in the *moreservlets* subdirectory of whatever directory the server uses for servlets that are not in custom Web applications (usually the *WEB-INF/classes* directory of the default Web application). Check your server's documentation for this location, or see the following list for a summary of the locations used by Tomcat, JRun, and ServletExec. Then, access the servlet with the URL *http://localhost/servlet/moreservlets.HelloServlet3*. You should get something similar to Figure 1–10.

- **Tomcat Directory.**
  install_dir/webapps/ROOT/WEB-INF/classes/moreservlets

- **JRun Directory.**
  install_dir/servers/default/default-app/WEB-INF/classes/moreservlets

- **ServletExec Directory.**
  install_dir/Servlets/moreservlets

- **Corresponding URL.**
  http://host/servlet/moreservlets.HelloServlet3

Listing 1.5 | *moreservlets/HelloServlet3.java*

```java
package moreservlets;

import java.io.*;
import javax.servlet.*;
import javax.servlet.http.*;

/** Simple servlet used to test the use of packages
 *  and utilities from the same package.
 */

public class HelloServlet3 extends HttpServlet {
  public void doGet(HttpServletRequest request,
                    HttpServletResponse response)
      throws ServletException, IOException {
    response.setContentType("text/html");
    PrintWriter out = response.getWriter();
    String title = "Hello (3)";
    out.println(ServletUtilities.headWithTitle(title) +
                "<BODY BGCOLOR=\"#FDF5E6\">\n" +
                "<H1>" + title + "</H1>\n" +
                "</BODY></HTML>");
  }
}
```

Listing 1.6   *moreservlets/ServletUtilities.java*

```
package moreservlets;

import javax.servlet.*;
import javax.servlet.http.*;

/** Some simple time savers. Note that most are static methods. */

public class ServletUtilities {
  public static final String DOCTYPE =
    "<!DOCTYPE HTML PUBLIC \"-//W3C//DTD HTML 4.0 " +
    "Transitional//EN\">";

  public static String headWithTitle(String title) {
    return(DOCTYPE + "\n" +
           "<HTML>\n" +
           "<HEAD><TITLE>" + title + "</TITLE></HEAD>\n");
  }

  ...
}
```

Figure 1–10   Result of `HelloServlet3`.

1.8   Establish a Simplified Deployment Method

OK, so you have a development directory. You can compile servlets with or without packages. You know which directory the servlet classes belong in. You know the URL that should be used to access them (at least the default URL; in Section 5.3, "Assigning Names and Custom URLs," you'll see how to customize that address). But how do you move the class files from the development directory to the deployment directory? Copying each one by hand every time is tedious and error prone. Once you start using Web applications (see Chapter 4), copying individual files becomes even more cumbersome.

There are several options to simplify the process. Here are a few of the most popular ones. If you are just beginning with servlets and JSP, you probably want to start with the first option and use it until you become comfortable with the development process. Note that I do *not* list the option of putting your code directly in the server's deployment directory. Although this is one of the most common choices among beginners, it scales so poorly to advanced tasks that I recommend you steer clear of it from the start.

1. Copy to a shortcut or symbolic link.
2. Use the -d option of javac.
3. Let your IDE take care of deployment.
4. Use ant or a similar tool.

Details on these four options are given in the following subsections.

Copy to a Shortcut or Symbolic Link

On Windows, go to the server's default Web application, right-click on the *classes* directory, and select Copy. Then go to your development directory, right-click, and select Paste Shortcut (not just Paste). Now, whenever you compile a packageless servlet, just drag the class files onto the shortcut. When you develop in packages, use the right mouse to drag the entire directory (e.g., the *moreservlets* directory) onto the shortcut, release the mouse, and select Copy. On Unix/Linux, you can use symbolic links (created with ln -s) in a manner similar to that for Windows shortcuts.

An advantage of this approach is that it is simple. So, it is good for beginners who want to concentrate on learning servlets and JSP, not deployment tools. Another advantage is that a variation applies once you start using your own Web applications (see Chapter 4). Just make a shortcut to the main Web application directory (one level up from the top of the default Web application), and copy the entire Web application each time by using the right mouse to drag the directory that contains your Web application onto this shortcut and selecting Copy.

One disadvantage of this approach is that it requires repeated copying if you use multiple servers. For example, I keep at least two different servers on my development system and regularly test my code with both servers. A second disadvantage is that this approach copies both the Java source code files and the class files to the server, whereas only the class files are needed. This may not matter much on your desktop server, but when you get to the "real" deployment server, you won't want to include the source code files.

Use the -d Option of javac

By default, the Java compiler (javac) places class files in the same directory as the source code files that they came from. However, javac has an option (-d) that lets you designate a different location for the class files. You need only specify the top-level directory for class files—javac will automatically put packaged classes in subdirectories that match the package names. So, for example, with Tomcat I could compile the HelloServlet2 servlet (Listing 1.4, Section 1.7) as follows (line break added only for clarity; omit it in real life).

```
javac -d install_dir/webapps/ROOT/WEB-INF/classes
        HelloServlet2.java
```

You could even make a Windows batch file or Unix shell script or alias that makes a command like servletc expand to javac -d install_dir/.../classes. See *http://java.sun.com/j2se/1.3/docs/tooldocs/win32/javac.html* for more details on -d and other javac options.

An advantage of this approach is that it requires no manual copying of class files. Furthermore, the exact same command can be used for classes in different packages since javac automatically puts the class files in a subdirectory matching the package.

The main disadvantage is that this approach applies only to Java class files; it won't work for deploying HTML and JSP pages, much less entire Web applications.

Let Your IDE Take Care of Deployment

Most servlet- and JSP-savvy development environments (e.g., IBM WebSphere Studio, Macromedia JRun Studio, Borland JBuilder) have options that let you tell the IDE where to deploy class files for your project. Then, when you tell the IDE to build the project, the class files are automatically deployed to the proper location (package-specific subdirectories and all).

An advantage of this approach, at least in some IDEs, is that it can deploy HTML and JSP pages and even entire Web applications, not just Java class files. A disadvantage is that it is an IDE-specific technique and thus is not portable across systems.

Use ant or a Similar Tool

Developed by the Apache foundation, ant is a tool similar to the Unix make utility. However, ant is written in the Java programming language (and thus is portable) and is touted to be both simpler to use and more powerful than make. Many servlet and JSP developers use ant for compiling and deploying. The use of ant is especially popular among Tomcat users and with those developing Web applications (see Chapter 4).

For general information on using `ant`, see *http://jakarta.apache.org/ant/manual/*. See *http://jakarta.apache.org/tomcat/tomcat-4.0-doc/appdev/processes.html* for specific guidance on using `ant` with Tomcat.

The main advantage of this approach is flexibility: `ant` is powerful enough to handle everything from compiling the Java source code to copying files to producing WAR files (Section 4.3). The disadvantage of `ant` is the overhead of learning to use it; there is more of a learning curve with `ant` than with the other techniques in this section.

1.9   Deployment Directories for Default Web Application: Summary

The following subsections summarize the way to deploy and access HTML files, JSP pages, servlets, and utility classes in Tomcat, JRun, and ServletExec. The summary assumes that you are deploying files in the default Web application, have changed the port number to 80 (see Section 1.3), and are accessing servlets through the default URL (i.e., *http://host/servlet/ServletName*). Later chapters explain how to deploy user-defined Web applications and how to customize the URLs. But you'll probably want to start with the defaults just to confirm that everything is working properly. The Appendix (Server Organization and Structure) gives a unified summary of the directories used by Tomcat, JRun, and ServletExec for both the default Web application and custom Web applications.

If you are using a server on your desktop, you can use *localhost* for the *host* portion of each of the URLs in this section.

Tomcat

HTML and JSP Pages

- **Main Location.**
  install_dir/webapps/ROOT
- **Corresponding URLs.**
  http://host/SomeFile.html
  http://host/SomeFile.jsp
- **More Specific Location (Arbitrary Subdirectory).**
  install_dir/webapps/ROOT/SomeDirectory
- **Corresponding URLs.**
  http://host/SomeDirectory/SomeFile.html
  http://host/SomeDirectory/SomeFile.jsp

Individual Servlet and Utility Class Files

- **Main Location (Classes without Package).**
  install_dir/webapps/ROOT/WEB-INF/classes
- **Corresponding URL (Servlets).**
  http://host/servlet/ServletName
- **More Specific Location (Classes in Packages).**
  install_dir/webapps/ROOT/WEB-INF/classes/packageName
- **Corresponding URL (Servlets in Packages).**
  http://host/servlet/packageName.ServletName

Servlet and Utility Class Files Bundled in JAR Files

- **Location.**
  install_dir/webapps/ROOT/WEB-INF/lib
- **Corresponding URLs (Servlets).**
  http://host/servlet/ServletName
  http://host/servlet/packageName.ServletName

JRun

HTML and JSP Pages

- **Main Location.**
  install_dir/servers/default/default-app
- **Corresponding URLs.**
  http://host/SomeFile.html
  http://host/SomeFile.jsp
- **More Specific Location (Arbitrary Subdirectory).**
  install_dir/servers/default/default-app/SomeDirectory
- **Corresponding URLs.**
  http://host/SomeDirectory/SomeFile.html
  http://host/SomeDirectory/SomeFile.jsp

Individual Servlet and Utility Class Files

- **Main Location (Classes without Package).**
  install_dir/servers/default/default-app/WEB-INF/classes
- **Corresponding URL (Servlets).**
  http://host/servlet/ServletName

- **More Specific Location (Classes in Packages).**
  install_dir/servers/default/default-app/WEB-INF/classes/packageName
- **Corresponding URL (Servlets in Packages).**
  http://host/servlet/packageName.ServletName

Servlet and Utility Class Files Bundled in JAR Files

- **Location.**
  install_dir/servers/default/default-app/WEB-INF/lib
- **Corresponding URLs (Servlets).**
  http://host/servlet/ServletName
  http://host/servlet/packageName.ServletName

ServletExec

HTML and JSP Pages

- **Main Location.**
  install_dir/public_html
- **Corresponding URLs.**
  http://host/SomeFile.html
  http://host/SomeFile.jsp
- **More Specific Location (Arbitrary Subdirectory).**
  install_dir/public_html/SomeDirectory
- **Corresponding URLs.**
  http://host/SomeDirectory/SomeFile.html
  http://host/SomeDirectory/SomeFile.jsp

Individual Servlet and Utility Class Files

- **Main Location (Classes without Package).**
  install_dir/Servlets
- **Corresponding URL (Servlets).**
  http://host/servlet/ServletName
- **More Specific Location (Classes in Packages).**
  install_dir/Servlets/packageName
- **Corresponding URL (Servlets in Packages).**
  http://host/servlet/packageName.ServletName

Servlet and Utility Class Files Bundled in JAR Files

- **Location.**
  install_dir/Servlets
- **Corresponding URLs (Servlets).**
  http://host/servlet/ServletName
  http://host/servlet/packageName.ServletName

A FAST
INTRODUCTION TO
BASIC SERVLET
PROGRAMMING

Topics in This Chapter

- The advantages of servlets over competing technologies
- The basic servlet structure and life cycle
- Servlet initialization parameters
- Access to form data
- HTTP 1.1 request headers, response headers, and status codes
- The servlet equivalent of the standard CGI variables
- Cookies in servlets
- Session tracking

Chapter

2

Servlets are Java technology's answer to Common Gateway Interface (CGI) programming. They are programs that run on a Web server, acting as a middle layer between a request coming from a Web browser or other HTTP client and databases or applications on the HTTP server. Their job is to perform the following tasks, as illustrated in Figure 2–1.

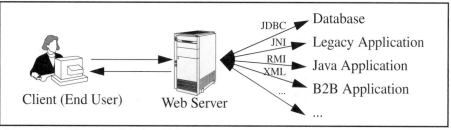

Figure 2–1   The role of Web middleware.

1. **Read the explicit data sent by the client.**
    The end user normally enters this data in an HTML form on a Web page. However, the data could also come from an applet or a custom HTTP client program.

2. **Read the implicit HTTP request data sent by the browser.**
    Figure 2–1 shows a single arrow going from the client to the Web server (the layer where servlets and JSP execute), but there are really *two* varieties of data: the explicit data the end user enters in a form

and the behind-the-scenes HTTP information. Both varieties are critical to effective development. The HTTP information includes cookies, media types and compression schemes the browser understands, and so forth.

3. **Generate the results.**
   This process may require talking to a database, executing an RMI or CORBA call, invoking a legacy application, or computing the response directly. Your real data may be in a relational database. Fine. But your database probably doesn't speak HTTP or return results in HTML, so the Web browser can't talk directly to the database. The same argument applies to most other applications. You need the Web middle layer to extract the incoming data from the HTTP stream, talk to the application, and embed the results inside a document.

4. **Send the explicit data (i.e., the document) to the client.**
   This document can be sent in a variety of formats, including text (HTML), binary (GIF images), or even a compressed format like gzip that is layered on top of some other underlying format.

5. **Send the implicit HTTP response data.**
   Figure 2–1 shows a single arrow going from the Web middle layer (the servlet or JSP page) to the client. But, there are really *two* varieties of data sent: the document itself and the behind-the-scenes HTTP information. Both varieties are critical to effective development. Sending HTTP response data involves telling the browser or other client what type of document is being returned (e.g., HTML), setting cookies and caching parameters, and other such tasks.

Many client requests can be satisfied by prebuilt documents, and the server would handle these requests without invoking servlets. In many cases, however, a static result is not sufficient, and a page needs to be generated for each request. There are a number of reasons why Web pages need to be built on-the-fly like this:

- **The Web page is based on data sent by the client.**
  For instance, the results page from search engines and order-confirmation pages at online stores are specific to particular user requests. Just remember that the user submits two kinds of data: explicit (i.e., HTML form data) and implicit (i.e., HTTP request headers). Either kind of input can be used to build the output page. In particular, it is quite common to build a user-specific page based on a cookie value.

- **The Web page is derived from data that changes frequently.**
  For example, a weather report or news headlines site might build the pages dynamically, perhaps returning a previously built page if that page is still up to date.

- **The Web page uses information from corporate databases or other server-side sources.**
  For example, an e-commerce site could use a servlet to build a Web page that lists the current price and availability of each sale item.

In principle, servlets are not restricted to Web or application servers that handle HTTP requests but can be used for other types of servers as well. For example, servlets could be embedded in FTP or mail servers to extend their functionality. In practice, however, this use of servlets has not caught on, and I'll only be discussing HTTP servlets.

2.1   The Advantages of Servlets Over "Traditional" CGI

Java servlets are more efficient, easier to use, more powerful, more portable, safer, and cheaper than traditional CGI and many alternative CGI-like technologies.

Efficient

With traditional CGI, a new process is started for each HTTP request. If the CGI program itself is relatively short, the overhead of starting the process can dominate the execution time. With servlets, the Java virtual machine stays running and handles each request with a lightweight Java thread, not a heavyweight operating system process. Similarly, in traditional CGI, if there are N requests to the same CGI program, the code for the CGI program is loaded into memory N times. With servlets, however, there would be N threads, but only a single copy of the servlet class would be loaded. This approach reduces server memory requirements and saves time by instantiating fewer objects. Finally, when a CGI program finishes handling a request, the program terminates. This approach makes it difficult to cache computations, keep database connections open, and perform other optimizations that rely on persistent data. Servlets, however, remain in memory even after they complete a response, so it is straightforward to store arbitrarily complex data between client requests.

Convenient

Servlets have an extensive infrastructure for automatically parsing and decoding HTML form data, reading and setting HTTP headers, handling cookies, tracking sessions, and many other such high-level utilities. Besides, you already know the Java programming language. Why learn Perl too? You're already convinced that Java technology makes for more reliable and reusable code than does Visual Basic, VBScript, or C++. Why go back to those languages for server-side programming?

Powerful

Servlets support several capabilities that are difficult or impossible to accomplish with regular CGI. Servlets can talk directly to the Web server, whereas regular CGI programs cannot, at least not without using a server-specific API. Communicating with the Web server makes it easier to translate relative URLs into concrete path names, for instance. Multiple servlets can also share data, making it easy to implement database connection pooling and similar resource-sharing optimizations. Servlets can also maintain information from request to request, simplifying techniques like session tracking and caching of previous computations.

Portable

Servlets are written in the Java programming language and follow a standard API. Servlets are supported directly or by a plug-in on virtually *every* major Web server. Consequently, servlets written for, say, iPlanet Enterprise Server can run virtually unchanged on Apache, Microsoft Internet Information Server (IIS), IBM WebSphere, or StarNine WebStar. They are part of the Java 2 Platform, Enterprise Edition (J2EE; see *http://java.sun.com/j2ee/*), so industry support for servlets is becoming even more pervasive.

Secure

One of the main sources of vulnerabilities in traditional CGI stems from the fact that the programs are often executed by general-purpose operating system shells. So, the CGI programmer must be careful to filter out characters such as backquotes and semicolons that are treated specially by the shell. Implementing this precaution is harder than one might think, and weaknesses stemming from this problem are constantly being uncovered in widely used CGI libraries.

A second source of problems is the fact that some CGI programs are processed by languages that do not automatically check array or string bounds. For example, in C and C++ it is perfectly legal to allocate a 100-element array and then write into the 999th "element," which is really some random part of program memory. So, programmers who forget to perform this check open up their system to deliberate or accidental buffer overflow attacks.

Servlets suffer from neither of these problems. Even if a servlet executes a system call (e.g., with `Runtime.exec` or JNI) to invoke a program on the local operating system, it does not use a shell to do so. And, of course, array bounds checking and other memory protection features are a central part of the Java programming language.

Inexpensive

There are a number of free or very inexpensive Web servers that are good for development use or deployment of low- or medium-volume Web sites. Thus, with servlets and JSP you can start with a free or inexpensive server and migrate to more expensive servers with high-performance capabilities or advanced administration utilities only after your project meets initial success. This is in contrast to many of the other CGI alternatives, which require a significant initial investment for the purchase of a proprietary package.

2.2 Basic Servlet Structure

Listing 2.1 outlines a basic servlet that handles GET requests. GET requests, for those unfamiliar with HTTP, are the usual type of browser requests for Web pages. A browser generates this request when the user enters a URL on the address line, follows a link from a Web page, or submits an HTML form that either does not specify a METHOD or specifies METHOD="GET". Servlets can also easily handle POST requests, which are generated when someone submits an HTML form that specifies METHOD="POST". For details on using HTML forms, see Chapter 16 of *Core Servlets and JavaServer Pages* (available in PDF at *http://www.moreservlets.com*).

Listing 2.1 *ServletTemplate.java*

```java
import java.io.*;
import javax.servlet.*;
import javax.servlet.http.*;

public class ServletTemplate extends HttpServlet {
  public void doGet(HttpServletRequest request,
                    HttpServletResponse response)
      throws ServletException, IOException {

    // Use "request" to read incoming HTTP headers
    // (e.g., cookies) and query data from HTML forms.

    // Use "response" to specify the HTTP response status
    // code and headers (e.g. the content type, cookies).

    PrintWriter out = response.getWriter();
    // Use "out" to send content to browser.
  }
}
```

To be a servlet, a class should extend `HttpServlet` and override `doGet` or `doPost`, depending on whether the data is being sent by `GET` or by `POST`. If you want a servlet to take the same action for both `GET` and `POST` requests, simply have `doGet` call `doPost`, or vice versa.

Both `doGet` and `doPost` take two arguments: an `HttpServletRequest` and an `HttpServletResponse`. The `HttpServletRequest` has methods by which you can find out about incoming information such as form (query) data, HTTP request headers, and the client's hostname. The `HttpServletResponse` lets you specify outgoing information such as HTTP status codes (200, 404, etc.) and response headers (`Content-Type`, `Set-Cookie`, etc.). Most importantly, it lets you obtain a `PrintWriter` with which you send the document content back to the client. For simple servlets, most of the effort is spent in `println` statements that generate the desired page. Form data, HTTP request headers, HTTP responses, and cookies are all discussed in the following sections.

Since `doGet` and `doPost` throw two exceptions, you are required to include them in the declaration. Finally, you must import classes in `java.io` (for `PrintWriter`, etc.), `javax.servlet` (for `HttpServlet`, etc.), and `javax.servlet.http` (for `HttpServletRequest` and `HttpServletResponse`).

A Servlet That Generates Plain Text

Listing 2.2 shows a simple servlet that outputs plain text, with the output shown in Figure 2–2. Before we move on, it is worth spending some time reviewing the process of installing, compiling, and running this simple servlet. See Chapter 1 (Server Setup and Configuration) for a much more detailed description of the process.

First, be sure that your server is set up properly as described in Section 1.4 (Test the Server) and that your CLASSPATH refers to the necessary three entries (the JAR file containing the `javax.servlet` classes, your development directory, and "."), as described in Section 1.6 (Set Up Your Development Environment).

Second, type "`javac HelloWorld.java`" or tell your development environment to compile the servlet (e.g., by clicking Build in your IDE or selecting Compile from the emacs JDE menu). This will compile your servlet to create *HelloWorld.class*.

Third, move *HelloWorld.class* to the directory that your server uses to store servlets (usually *install_dir/.../WEB-INF/classes*—see Section 1.7). Alternatively, you can use one of the techniques of Section 1.8 (Establish a Simplified Deployment Method) to automatically place the class files in the appropriate location.

Finally, invoke your servlet. This last step involves using either the default URL of *http://host/servlet/ServletName* or a custom URL defined in the *web.xml* file as described in Section 5.3 (Assigning Names and Custom URLs). Figure 2–2 shows the servlet being accessed by means of the default URL, with the server running on the local machine.

Listing 2.2 *HelloWorld.java*

```java
import java.io.*;
import javax.servlet.*;
import javax.servlet.http.*;

public class HelloWorld extends HttpServlet {
  public void doGet(HttpServletRequest request,
                    HttpServletResponse response)
      throws ServletException, IOException {
    PrintWriter out = response.getWriter();
    out.println("Hello World");
  }
}
```

Figure 2–2 Result of `HelloWorld` servlet.

A Servlet That Generates HTML

Most servlets generate HTML, not plain text as in the previous example. To build HTML, you need two additional steps:

1. Tell the browser that you're sending back HTML.
2. Modify the `println` statements to build a legal Web page.

You accomplish the first step by setting the HTTP `Content-Type` response header. In general, headers are set by the `setHeader` method of `HttpServlet-Response`, but setting the content type is such a common task that there is also a special `setContentType` method just for this purpose. The way to designate HTML is with a type of `text/html`, so the code would look like this:

```java
response.setContentType("text/html");
```

Although HTML is the most common type of document that servlets create, it is not unusual for servlets to create other document types. For example, it is quite common to use servlets to generate GIF images (content type image/gif) and Excel spreadsheets (content type application/vnd.ms-excel).

Don't be concerned if you are not yet familiar with HTTP response headers; they are discussed in Section 2.8. Note that you need to set response headers *before* actually returning any of the content with the PrintWriter. That's because an HTTP response consists of the status line, one or more headers, a blank line, and the actual document, *in that order*. The headers can appear in any order, and servlets buffer the headers and send them all at once, so it is legal to set the status code (part of the first line returned) even after setting headers. But servlets do not necessarily buffer the document itself, since users might want to see partial results for long pages. Servlet engines are permitted to partially buffer the output, but the size of the buffer is left unspecified. You can use the getBufferSize method of HttpServletResponse to determine the size, or you can use setBufferSize to specify it. You can set headers until the buffer fills up and is actually sent to the client. If you aren't sure whether the buffer has been sent, you can use the isCommitted method to check. Even so, the simplest approach is to simply put the setContentType line before any of the lines that use the PrintWriter.

Core Approach

*Always set the content type **before** transmitting the actual document.*

The second step in writing a servlet that builds an HTML document is to have your println statements output HTML, not plain text. Listing 2.3 shows *Hello-Servlet.java*, the sample servlet used in Section 1.7 to verify that the server is functioning properly. As Figure 2–3 illustrates, the browser formats the result as HTML, not as plain text.

Listing 2.3   *HelloServlet.java*

```
import java.io.*;
import javax.servlet.*;
import javax.servlet.http.*;

public class HelloServlet extends HttpServlet {
  public void doGet(HttpServletRequest request,
                    HttpServletResponse response)
      throws ServletException, IOException {
```

Listing 2.3	*HelloServlet.java (continued)*

```
response.setContentType("text/html");
PrintWriter out = response.getWriter();
String docType =
  "<!DOCTYPE HTML PUBLIC \"-//W3C//DTD HTML 4.0 " +
  "Transitional//EN\">\n";
out.println(docType +
            "<HTML>\n" +
            "<HEAD><TITLE>Hello</TITLE></HEAD>\n" +
            "<BODY BGCOLOR=\"#FDF5E6\">\n" +
            "<H1>Hello</H1>\n" +
            "</BODY></HTML>");
  }
}
```

Figure 2–3   Result of `HelloServlet`.

Servlet Packaging

In a production environment, multiple programmers can be developing servlets for the same server. So, placing all the servlets in the same directory results in a massive, hard-to-manage collection of classes and risks name conflicts when two developers accidentally choose the same servlet name. Packages are the natural solution to this problem. As we'll see in Chapter 4, even the use of Web applications does not obviate the need for packages.

When you use packages, you need to perform the following two additional steps.

1. **Move the files to a subdirectory that matches the intended package name.** For example, I'll use the `moreservlets` package for most of the rest of the servlets in this book. So, the class files need to go in a subdirectory called *moreservlets*.

2. **Insert a package statement in the class file.** For example, to place a class in a package called `somePackage`, the class should be in the *somePackage* directory and the *first* non-comment line of the file should read

```
package somePackage;
```

For example, Listing 2.4 presents a variation of `HelloServlet` that is in the `moreservlets` package and thus the *moreservlets* directory. As discussed in Section 1.7 (Compile and Test Some Simple Servlets), the class file should be placed in *install_dir/webapps/ROOT/WEB-INF/classes/moreservlets* for Tomcat, in *install_dir/servers/default/default-app/WEB-INF/classes/moreservlets* for JRun, and in *install_dir/Servlets/moreservlets* for ServletExec.

Figure 2–4 shows the servlet accessed by means of the default URL.

Listing 2.4   *HelloServlet2.java*

```java
package moreservlets;

import java.io.*;
import javax.servlet.*;
import javax.servlet.http.*;

/** Simple servlet used to test the use of packages. */

public class HelloServlet2 extends HttpServlet {
  public void doGet(HttpServletRequest request,
                    HttpServletResponse response)
      throws ServletException, IOException {
    response.setContentType("text/html");
    PrintWriter out = response.getWriter();
    String docType =
      "<!DOCTYPE HTML PUBLIC \"-//W3C//DTD HTML 4.0 " +
      "Transitional//EN\">\n";
    out.println(docType +
                "<HTML>\n" +
                "<HEAD><TITLE>Hello (2)</TITLE></HEAD>\n" +
                "<BODY BGCOLOR=\"#FDF5E6\">\n" +
                "<H1>Hello (2)</H1>\n" +
                "</BODY></HTML>");
  }
}
```

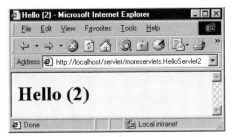

Figure 2–4   Result of `HelloServlet2`.

Simple HTML-Building Utilities

As you probably already know, an HTML document is structured as follows:

```
<!DOCTYPE ...>
<HTML>
<HEAD><TITLE>...</TITLE>...</HEAD>
<BODY ...>...</BODY>
</HTML>
```

When using servlets to build the HTML, you might be tempted to omit part of this structure, especially the DOCTYPE line, noting that virtually all major browsers ignore it even though the HTML 3.2 and 4.0 specifications require it. I strongly discourage this practice. The advantage of the DOCTYPE line is that it tells HTML validators which version of HTML you are using so they know which specification to check your document against. These validators are valuable debugging services, helping you catch HTML syntax errors that your browser guesses well on but that other browsers will have trouble displaying.

The two most popular online validators are the ones from the World Wide Web Consortium (*http://validator.w3.org/*) and from the Web Design Group (*http://www.htmlhelp.com/tools/validator/*). They let you submit a URL, then they retrieve the page, check the syntax against the formal HTML specification, and report any errors to you. Since, to a visitor, a servlet that generates HTML looks exactly like a regular Web page, it can be validated in the normal manner unless it requires POST data to return its result. Since GET data is attached to the URL, you can even send the validators a URL that includes GET data. If the servlet is available only inside your corporate firewall, simply run it, save the HTML to disk, and choose the validator's File Upload option.

Core Approach

Use an HTML validator to check the syntax of pages that your servlets generate.

Admittedly, it is a bit cumbersome to generate HTML with `println` statements, especially long tedious lines like the `DOCTYPE` declaration. Some people address this problem by writing detailed HTML-generation utilities, then use the utilities throughout their servlets. I'm skeptical of the usefulness of such an extensive library. First and foremost, the inconvenience of generating HTML programmatically is one of the main problems addressed by JavaServer Pages. Second, HTML generation routines can be cumbersome and tend not to support the full range of HTML attributes (`CLASS` and `ID` for style sheets, JavaScript event handlers, table cell background colors, and so forth).

Despite the questionable value of a full-blown HTML generation library, if you find you're repeating the same constructs many times, you might as well create a simple utility file that simplifies those constructs. For standard servlets, two parts of the Web page (`DOCTYPE` and `HEAD`) are unlikely to change and thus could benefit from being incorporated into a simple utility file. These are shown in Listing 2.5, with Listing 2.6 showing a variation of `HelloServlet` that makes use of this utility. I'll add a few more utilities throughout the chapter.

Listing 2.5   *moreservlets/ServletUtilities.java*

```
package moreservlets;

import javax.servlet.*;
import javax.servlet.http.*;

/** Some simple time savers. Note that most are static methods. */

public class ServletUtilities {
  public static final String DOCTYPE =
    "<!DOCTYPE HTML PUBLIC \"-//W3C//DTD HTML 4.0 " +
    "Transitional//EN\">";

  public static String headWithTitle(String title) {
    return(DOCTYPE + "\n" +
           "<HTML>\n" +
           "<HEAD><TITLE>" + title + "</TITLE></HEAD>\n");
  }

  ...
}
```

Listing 2.6	*moreservlets/HelloServlet3.java*

```java
package moreservlets;

import java.io.*;
import javax.servlet.*;
import javax.servlet.http.*;

/** Simple servlet used to test the use of packages
 *  and utilities from the same package.
 */

public class HelloServlet3 extends HttpServlet {
  public void doGet(HttpServletRequest request,
                    HttpServletResponse response)
      throws ServletException, IOException {
    response.setContentType("text/html");
    PrintWriter out = response.getWriter();
    String title = "Hello (3)";
    out.println(ServletUtilities.headWithTitle(title) +
                "<BODY BGCOLOR=\"#FDF5E6\">\n" +
                "<H1>" + title + "</H1>\n" +
                "</BODY></HTML>");
  }
}
```

After you compile *HelloServlet3.java* (which results in *ServletUtilities.java* being compiled automatically), you need to move the two class files to the *moreservlets* subdirectory of the server's default deployment location. If you get an "Unresolved symbol" error when compiling *HelloServlet3.java*, go back and review the CLASS-PATH settings described in Section 1.6 (Set Up Your Development Environment). If you don't know where to put the class files, review Sections 1.7 and 1.9. Figure 2–5 shows the result when the servlet is invoked with the default URL.

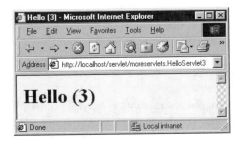

Figure 2–5   Result of `HelloServlet3`.

2.3 The Servlet Life Cycle

In Section 2.1 (The Advantages of Servlets Over "Traditional" CGI), I referred to the fact that only a single instance of a servlet gets created, with each user request resulting in a new thread that is handed off to doGet or doPost as appropriate. I'll now be more specific about how servlets are created and destroyed, and how and when the various methods are invoked. I give a quick summary here, then elaborate in the following subsections.

When the servlet is first created, its init method is invoked, so init is where you put one-time setup code. After this, each user request results in a thread that calls the service method of the previously created instance. Multiple concurrent requests normally result in multiple threads calling service simultaneously, although your servlet can implement a special interface (SingleThreadModel) that stipulates that only a single thread is permitted to run at any one time. The service method then calls doGet, doPost, or another doXxx method, depending on the type of HTTP request it received. Finally, when the server decides to unload a servlet, it first calls the servlet's destroy method.

The init Method

The init method is called when the servlet is first created; it is *not* called again for each user request. So, it is used for one-time initializations, just as with the init method of applets. The servlet is normally created when a user first invokes a URL corresponding to the servlet, but you can also specify that the servlet be loaded when the server is first started (see Section 5.5, "Initializing and Preloading Servlets and JSP Pages").

The init method definition looks like this:

```
public void init() throws ServletException {
  // Initialization code...
}
```

One of the most common tasks that init performs is reading server-specific initialization parameters. For example, the servlet might need to know about database settings, password files, server-specific performance parameters, hit count files, or serialized cookie data from previous requests. Initialization parameters are particularly valuable because they let the servlet *deployer* (e.g., the server administrator), not just the servlet *author*, customize the servlet.

To read initialization parameters, you first obtain a ServletConfig object by means of getServletConfig, then call getInitParameter on the result. Here is an example:

```
public void init() throws ServletException {
  ServletConfig config = getServletConfig();
  String param1 = config.getInitParameter("parameter1");
}
```

Notice two things about this code. First, the `init` method uses `getServlet-Config` to obtain a reference to the `ServletConfig` object. Second, `Servlet-Config` has a `getInitParameter` method with which you can look up initialization parameters associated with the servlet. Just as with the `getParameter` method used in the `init` method of applets, both the input (the parameter name) and the output (the parameter value) are strings.

You *read* initialization parameters by calling the `getInitParameter` method of `ServletConfig`. But how do you *set* them? That's the job of the *web.xml* file, called the *deployment descriptor*. This file belongs in the *WEB-INF* directory of the Web application you are using, and it controls many aspects of servlet and JSP behavior. Many servers provide graphical interfaces that let you specify initialization parameters and control various aspects of servlet and JSP behavior. Although those interfaces are server specific, behind the scenes they use the *web.xml* file, and this file is completely portable. Use of *web.xml* is discussed in detail in Chapter 4 (Using and Deploying Web Applications) and Chapter 5 (Controlling Web Application Behavior with web.xml), but for a quick preview, *web.xml* contains an XML header, a `DOCTYPE` declaration, and a `web-app` element. For the purpose of initialization parameters, the `web-app` element should contain a `servlet` element with three subelements: `servlet-name`, `servlet-class`, and `init-param`. The `serv-let-name` element is the name that you want to use to access the servlet. The `servlet-class` element gives the fully qualified (i.e., including packages) class name of the servlet, and `init-param` gives names and values to initialization parameters.

For example, Listing 2.7 shows a *web.xml* file that gives a value to the initialization parameter called `parameter1` of the `OriginalServlet` class that is in the some-Package package. However, the initialization parameter is available only when the servlet is accessed with the registered servlet name (or a custom URL as described in Section 5.3). So, the `param1` variable in the previous code snippet would have the value `"First Parameter Value"` when the servlet is accessed by means of *http://host/servlet/SomeName*, but would have the value `null` when the servlet is accessed by means of *http://host/servlet/somePackage.OriginalServlet*.

Core Warning

Initialization parameters are not available to servlets that are accessed by means of their default URL. A registered name or custom URL must be used.

For more information on the *web.xml* file, including new parameters available with servlets version 2.3, see Chapter 5 (Controlling Web Application Behavior with web.xml). For specific details on initialization parameters and a complete working example, see Section 5.5 (Initializing and Preloading Servlets and JSP Pages).

Listing 2.7   *web.xml* (Excerpt illustrating initialization parameters)

```
<?xml version="1.0" encoding="ISO-8859-1"?>
<!DOCTYPE web-app PUBLIC
    "-//Sun Microsystems, Inc.//DTD Web Application 2.2//EN"
    "http://java.sun.com/j2ee/dtds/web-app_2_2.dtd">

<web-app>
  <servlet>
    <servlet-name>SomeName</servlet-name>
    <servlet-class>somePackage.OriginalServlet</servlet-class>
    <init-param>
      <param-name>parameter1</param-name>
      <param-value>First Parameter Value</param-value>
    </init-param>
  </servlet>
  <!-- ... -->
</web-app>
```

The service Method

Each time the server receives a request for a servlet, the server spawns a new thread (perhaps by reusing an idle `Thread` from a thread pool) and calls `service`. The service method checks the HTTP request type (GET, POST, PUT, DELETE, etc.) and calls `doGet`, `doPost`, `doPut`, `doDelete`, etc., as appropriate. A GET request results from a normal request for a URL or from an HTML form that has no METHOD specified. A POST request results from an HTML form that specifically lists POST as the METHOD. Other HTTP requests are generated only by custom clients. If you aren't familiar with HTML forms, see Chapter 16 of *Core Servlets and JavaServer Pages* (available in PDF at *http://www.moreservlets.com*).

Now, if you have a servlet that needs to handle both POST and GET requests identically, you may be tempted to override `service` directly rather than implementing both `doGet` and `doPost`. This is not a good idea. Instead, just have `doPost` call `doGet` (or vice versa), as below.

```
public void doGet(HttpServletRequest request,
                  HttpServletResponse response)
   throws ServletException, IOException {
  // Servlet code
}

public void doPost(HttpServletRequest request,
                   HttpServletResponse response)
   throws ServletException, IOException {
  doGet(request, response);
}
```

Although this approach takes a couple of extra lines of code, it has several advantages over directly overriding `service`. First, you can later add support for other HTTP request methods by adding `doPut`, `doTrace`, etc., perhaps in a subclass. Overriding `service` directly precludes this possibility. Second, you can add support for modification dates by adding a `getLastModified` method. Since `getLastModified` is invoked by the default `service` method, overriding `service` eliminates this option. Finally, you get automatic support for HEAD, OPTION, and TRACE requests.

Core Approach

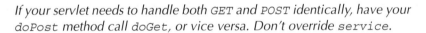

If your servlet needs to handle both GET and POST identically, have your doPost method call doGet, or vice versa. Don't override service.

The doGet, doPost, and doXxx Methods

These methods contain the real meat of your servlet. Ninety-nine percent of the time, you only care about GET or POST requests, so you override `doGet` and/or `doPost`. However, if you want to, you can also override `doDelete` for DELETE requests, `doPut` for PUT, `doOptions` for OPTIONS, and `doTrace` for TRACE. Recall, however, that you have automatic support for OPTIONS and TRACE.

In versions 2.1 and 2.2 of the servlet API, there is no `doHead` method. That's because the system automatically uses the status line and header settings of `doGet` to answer HEAD requests. In version 2.3, however, `doHead` was added so that you can generate responses to HEAD requests (i.e., requests from custom clients that want just the HTTP headers, not the actual document) more quickly—without building the actual document output.

The SingleThreadModel Interface

Normally, the system makes a single instance of your servlet and then creates a new thread for each user request, with multiple concurrent threads running if a new request comes in while a previous request is still executing. This means that your doGet and doPost methods must be careful to synchronize access to fields and other shared data, since multiple threads may access the data simultaneously. If you want to prevent this multithreaded access, you can have your servlet implement the SingleThreadModel interface, as below.

```
public class YourServlet extends HttpServlet
    implements SingleThreadModel {
  . . .
}
```

If you implement this interface, the system guarantees that there is never more than one request thread accessing a single instance of your servlet. In most cases, it does so by queuing all the requests and passing them one at a time to a single servlet instance. However, the server is permitted to create a pool of multiple instances, each of which handles one request at a time. Either way, this means that you don't have to worry about simultaneous access to regular fields (instance variables) of the servlet. You *do*, however, still have to synchronize access to class variables (static fields) or shared data stored outside the servlet.

Synchronous access to your servlets can significantly hurt performance (latency) if your servlet is accessed frequently. When a servlet waits for I/O, the server remains idle instead of handling pending requests. So, think twice before using the Single-ThreadModel approach.

Core Warning

Avoid implementing SingleThreadModel for high-traffic servlets. Use explicit synchronized blocks instead.

The destroy Method

The server may decide to remove a previously loaded servlet instance, perhaps because it is explicitly asked to do so by the server administrator, or perhaps because the servlet is idle for a long time. Before it does, however, it calls the servlet's destroy method. This method gives your servlet a chance to close database connections, halt background threads, write cookie lists or hit counts to disk, and perform other such cleanup activities. Be aware, however, that it is possible for the Web server to crash. So, don't count on destroy as the *only* mechanism for saving state to disk. Activities like hit counting or accumulating lists of cookie values that indicate special access should also proactively write their state to disk periodically.

2.4   The Client Request: Form Data

One of the main motivations for building Web pages dynamically is to base the result upon query data submitted by the user. This section briefly shows you how to access that data. More details are provided in Chapter 3 of *Core Servlets and JavaServer Pages* (available in PDF at *http://www.moreservlets.com*).

If you've ever used a search engine, visited an online bookstore, tracked stocks on the Web, or asked a Web-based site for quotes on plane tickets, you've probably seen funny-looking URLs like *http://host/path?user=Marty+Hall&origin=bwi&dest=nrt*. The part after the question mark (i.e., *user=Marty+Hall&origin=bwi&dest=nrt*) is known as *form data* (or *query data*) and is the most common way to get information from a Web page to a server-side program. Form data can be attached to the end of the URL after a question mark (as above) for GET requests or sent to the server on a separate line for POST requests. If you're not familiar with HTML forms, see Chapter 16 of *Core Servlets and JavaServer Pages* (in PDF at *http://www.moreservlets.com*) for details on how to build forms that collect and transmit data of this sort.

Reading Form Data from CGI Programs

Extracting the needed information from form data is traditionally one of the most tedious parts of CGI programming. First, you have to read the data one way for GET requests (in traditional CGI, this is usually through the QUERY_STRING environment variable) and a different way for POST requests (by reading the standard input in traditional CGI). Second, you have to chop the pairs at the ampersands, then separate the parameter names (left of the equal signs) from the parameter values (right of the equal signs). Third, you have to URL-decode the values. Alphanumeric characters are sent unchanged, but spaces are converted to plus signs and other characters are converted to %XX where XX is the ASCII (or ISO Latin-1) value of the character, in hex.

Reading Form Data from Servlets

One of the nice features of servlets is that all the form parsing is handled automatically. You simply call the getParameter method of HttpServletRequest, supplying the case-sensitive parameter name as an argument. You use getParameter exactly the same way when the data is sent by GET as you do when it is sent by POST.

The servlet knows which request method was used and automatically does the right thing behind the scenes. The return value is a `String` corresponding to the URL-decoded value of the first occurrence of that parameter name. An empty `String` is returned if the parameter exists but has no value, and `null` is returned if there is no such parameter in the request.

Technically, it is legal for a single HTML form to use the same parameter name twice, and in fact this situation really occurs when you use `SELECT` elements that allow multiple selections (see Section 16.6 of *Core Servlets and JavaServer Pages*). If the parameter could potentially have more than one value, you should call `get-ParameterValues` (which returns an array of strings) instead of `getParameter` (which returns a single string). The return value of `getParameterValues` is `null` for nonexistent parameter names and is a one-element array when the parameter has only a single value.

Parameter names are case sensitive, so, for example, `request.get-Parameter("Param1")` and `request.getParameter("param1")` are *not* interchangeable.

Core Note

The values supplied to `getParameter` and `getParameterValues` are case sensitive.

Finally, although most real servlets look for a specific set of parameter names, for debugging purposes it is sometimes useful to get a full list. Use `getParameter-Names` to get this list in the form of an `Enumeration`, each entry of which can be cast to a `String` and used in a `getParameter` or `getParameterValues` call. Just note that the `HttpServletRequest` API does not specify the order in which the names appear within that `Enumeration`.

Example: Reading Three Explicit Parameters

Listing 2.8 presents a simple servlet called `ThreeParams` that reads form data parameters named `param1`, `param2`, and `param3` and places their values in a bulleted list. Listing 2.9 shows an HTML form that collects user input and sends it to this servlet. By use of an `ACTION` URL that begins with a slash (e.g., */servlet/more-servlets.ThreeParams*), the form can be installed anywhere in the server's Web document hierarchy; there need not be any particular association between the directory containing the form and the servlet installation directory. When you use Web applications, HTML files (and images and JSP pages) go in the directory above the one containing the *WEB-INF* directory; see Section 4.2 (Structure of a Web Application) for details. The directory for HTML files that are not part of an explicit Web application varies from server to server. As described in Section 1.5 (Try Some Simple HTML and JSP Pages) HTML and JSP pages go in *install_dir/webapps/ROOT* for Tomcat, in *install_dir/servers/default/default-app* for JRun, and in *install_dir/public_html* for ServletExec. For other servers, see the appropriate server documentation.

Also note that the `ThreeParams` servlet reads the query data after it starts generating the page. Although you are required to specify *response* settings before beginning to generate the content, there is no requirement that you read the *request* parameters at any particular time.

Listing 2.8   *ThreeParams.java*

```java
package moreservlets;

import java.io.*;
import javax.servlet.*;
import javax.servlet.http.*;

/** Simple servlet that reads three parameters from the
 *  form data.
 */

public class ThreeParams extends HttpServlet {
  public void doGet(HttpServletRequest request,
                    HttpServletResponse response)
      throws ServletException, IOException {
    response.setContentType("text/html");
    PrintWriter out = response.getWriter();
    String title = "Reading Three Request Parameters";
    out.println(ServletUtilities.headWithTitle(title) +
                "<BODY BGCOLOR=\"#FDF5E6\">\n" +
                "<H1 ALIGN=\"CENTER\">" + title + "</H1>\n" +
                "<UL>\n" +
                "  <LI><B>param1</B>: "
              + request.getParameter("param1") + "\n" +
                "  <LI><B>param2</B>: "
              + request.getParameter("param2") + "\n" +
                "  <LI><B>param3</B>: "
              + request.getParameter("param3") + "\n" +
                "</UL>\n" +
                "</BODY></HTML>");
  }
}
```

Listing 2.9	*ThreeParamsForm.html*

```
<!DOCTYPE HTML PUBLIC "-//W3C//DTD HTML 4.0 Transitional//EN">
<HTML>
<HEAD>
  <TITLE>Collecting Three Parameters</TITLE>
</HEAD>
<BODY BGCOLOR="#FDF5E6">
<H1 ALIGN="CENTER">Collecting Three Parameters</H1>

<FORM ACTION="/servlet/moreservlets.ThreeParams">
  First Parameter:   <INPUT TYPE="TEXT" NAME="param1"><BR>
  Second Parameter:  <INPUT TYPE="TEXT" NAME="param2"><BR>
  Third Parameter:   <INPUT TYPE="TEXT" NAME="param3"><BR>
  <CENTER><INPUT TYPE="SUBMIT"></CENTER>
</FORM>

</BODY>
</HTML>
```

Figure 2–6 shows the HTML form after the user enters the home directories of three famous Internet personalities (OK, *two* famous Internet personalities). Figure 2–7 shows the result of the form submission. Note that, although the form contained ~, a non-alphanumeric character that was transmitted by use of its hex-encoded Latin-1 value (%7E), the servlet had to do nothing special to get the value as it was typed into the HTML form. This conversion (called URL decoding) is done automatically. Servlet authors simply specify the parameter name as it appears in the HTML source code and get back the parameter value as it was entered by the end user: a big improvement over CGI and many alternatives to servlets and JSP.

If you're accustomed to the traditional CGI approach where you read POST data through the standard input, you should note that it is possible to do the same thing with servlets by calling getReader or getInputStream on the HttpServlet-Request and then using that stream to obtain the raw input. This is a bad idea for regular parameters; getParameter is simpler and yields results that are parsed and URL-decoded. However, reading the raw input might be of use for uploaded files or POST data being sent by custom clients. Note, however, that if you read the POST data in this manner, it might no longer be found by getParameter.

Core Warning

Do not use getParameter when you also call getInputStream and read the raw servlet input.

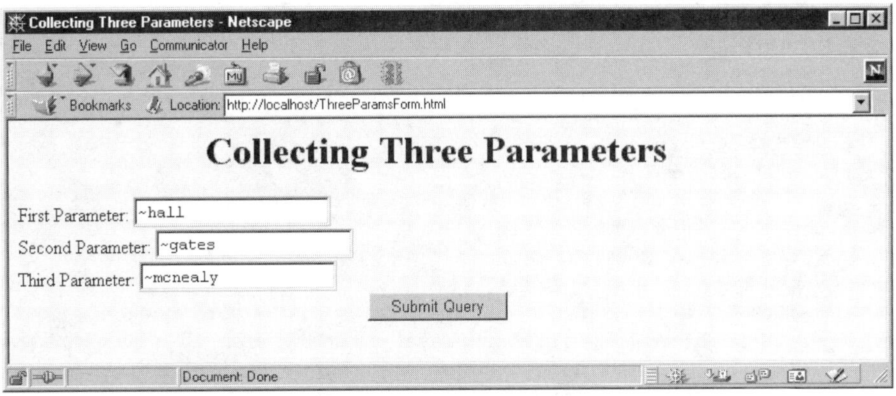

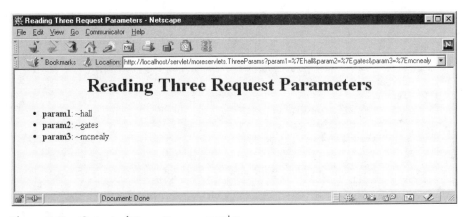

Figure 2–6   HTML front end resulting from *ThreeParamsForm.html.*

Figure 2–7   Output of `ThreeParams` servlet.

Filtering Query Data

In the previous example, we read the `param1`, `param2`, and `param3` request parameters and inserted them verbatim into the page being generated. This is not necessarily safe, since the request parameters might contain HTML characters such as "<" that could disrupt the rest of the page processing, causing some of the subsequent tags to be interpreted incorrectly. For an example, see Section 3.6 of *Core Servlets and JavaServer Pages* (available in PDF at *http://www.moreservlets.com*). A safer approach is to filter out the HTML-specific characters before inserting the values into the page. Listing 2.10 shows a static `filter` method that accomplishes this task.

Listing 2.10 *ServletUtilities.java*

```java
package moreservlets;

import javax.servlet.*;
import javax.servlet.http.*;

public class ServletUtilities {
  // Other parts shown elsewhere.

  // Given a string, this method replaces all occurrences of
  //   '<' with '&lt;', all occurrences of '>' with
  //   '&gt;', and (to handle cases that occur inside attribute
  //   values), all occurrences of double quotes with
  //   '&quot;' and all occurrences of '&' with '&amp;'.
  //   Without such filtering, an arbitrary string
  //   could not safely be inserted in a Web page.

  public static String filter(String input) {
    StringBuffer filtered = new StringBuffer(input.length());
    char c;
    for(int i=0; i<input.length(); i++) {
      c = input.charAt(i);
      if (c == '<') {
        filtered.append("&lt;");
      } else if (c == '>') {
        filtered.append("&gt;");
      } else if (c == '"') {
        filtered.append("&quot;");
      } else if (c == '&') {
        filtered.append("&amp;");
      } else {
        filtered.append(c);
      }
    }
    return(filtered.toString());
  }
}
```

2.5 The Client Request: HTTP Request Headers

One of the keys to creating effective servlets is understanding how to manipulate the HyperText Transfer Protocol (HTTP). Getting a thorough grasp of this protocol is not an esoteric, theoretical concept, but rather a practical issue that can have an immediate impact on the performance and usability of your servlets. This section discusses the HTTP information that is sent from the browser to the server in the form of request headers. It explains a few of the most important HTTP 1.1 request headers, summarizing how and why they would be used in a servlet. For more details and examples, see Chapter 4 of *Core Servlets and JavaServer Pages* (available in PDF at *http://www.moreservlets.com*).

Note that HTTP request headers are distinct from the form (query) data discussed in the previous section. Form data results directly from user input and is sent as part of the URL for GET requests and on a separate line for POST requests. Request headers, on the other hand, are indirectly set by the browser and are sent immediately following the initial GET or POST request line. For instance, the following example shows an HTTP request that might result from a user submitting a book-search request to a servlet at *http://www.somebookstore.com/servlet/Search*. The request includes the headers Accept, Accept-Encoding, Connection, Cookie, Host, Referer, and User-Agent, all of which might be important to the operation of the servlet, but none of which can be derived from the form data or deduced automatically: the servlet needs to explicitly read the request headers to make use of this information.

```
GET /servlet/Search?keywords=servlets+jsp HTTP/1.1
Accept: image/gif, image/jpg, */*
Accept-Encoding: gzip
Connection: Keep-Alive
Cookie: userID=id456578
Host: www.somebookstore.com
Referer: http://www.somebookstore.com/findbooks.html
User-Agent: Mozilla/4.7 [en] (Win98; U)
```

Reading Request Headers from Servlets

Reading headers is straightforward; just call the getHeader method of HttpServletRequest, which returns a String if the specified header was supplied on this request, null otherwise. Header names are not case sensitive. So, for example, request.getHeader("Connection") is interchangeable with request.getHeader("connection").

Although getHeader is the general-purpose way to read incoming headers, a few headers are so commonly used that they have special access methods in HttpServletRequest. Following is a summary.

- **getCookies**
  The getCookies method returns the contents of the Cookie header, parsed and stored in an array of Cookie objects. This method is discussed in more detail in Section 2.9 (Cookies).

- **getAuthType and getRemoteUser**
  The getAuthType and getRemoteUser methods break the
  Authorization header into its component pieces.

- **getContentLength**
  The getContentLength method returns the value of the
  Content-Length header (as an int).

- **getContentType**
  The getContentType method returns the value of the
  Content-Type header (as a String).

- **getDateHeader and getIntHeader**
  The getDateHeader and getIntHeader methods read the
  specified headers and then convert them to Date and int values,
  respectively.

- **getHeaderNames**
  Rather than looking up one particular header, you can use the
  getHeaderNames method to get an Enumeration of all header
  names received on this particular request. This capability is
  illustrated in Listing 2.11.

- **getHeaders**
  In most cases, each header name appears only once in the request.
  Occasionally, however, a header can appear multiple times, with each
  occurrence listing a separate value. Accept-Language is one such
  example. You can use getHeaders to obtain an Enumeration of the
  values of all occurrences of the header.

Finally, in addition to looking up the request headers, you can get information on
the main request line itself, also by means of methods in HttpServletRequest.
Here is a summary of the three main methods.

- **getMethod**
  The getMethod method returns the main request method (normally
  GET or POST, but methods like HEAD, PUT, and DELETE are possible).

- **getRequestURI**
  The getRequestURI method returns the part of the URL that comes
  after the host and port but before the form data. For example, for a URL
  of *http://randomhost.com/servlet/search.BookSearch*, getRequestURI
  would return "/servlet/search.BookSearch".

- **getProtocol**
  The getProtocol method returns the third part of the request line,
  which is generally HTTP/1.0 or HTTP/1.1. Servlets should usually
  check getProtocol before specifying *response* headers (Section 2.8)
  that are specific to HTTP 1.1.

Example: Making a Table of All Request Headers

Listing 2.11 shows a servlet that simply creates a table of all the headers it receives, along with their associated values. It also prints out the three components of the main request line (method, URI, and protocol). Figures 2–8 and 2–9 show typical results with Netscape and Internet Explorer.

Listing 2.11 *ShowRequestHeaders.java*

```java
package moreservlets;

import java.io.*;
import javax.servlet.*;
import javax.servlet.http.*;
import java.util.*;

/** Shows all the request headers sent on this request. */

public class ShowRequestHeaders extends HttpServlet {
  public void doGet(HttpServletRequest request,
                    HttpServletResponse response)
      throws ServletException, IOException {
    response.setContentType("text/html");
    PrintWriter out = response.getWriter();
    String title = "Servlet Example: Showing Request Headers";
    out.println(ServletUtilities.headWithTitle(title) +
                "<BODY BGCOLOR=\"#FDF5E6\">\n" +
                "<H1 ALIGN=\"CENTER\">" + title + "</H1>\n" +
                "<B>Request Method: </B>" +
                request.getMethod() + "<BR>\n" +
                "<B>Request URI: </B>" +
                request.getRequestURI() + "<BR>\n" +
                "<B>Request Protocol: </B>" +
                request.getProtocol() + "<BR><BR>\n" +
                "<TABLE BORDER=1 ALIGN=\"CENTER\">\n" +
                "<TR BGCOLOR=\"#FFAD00\">\n" +
                "<TH>Header Name<TH>Header Value");
    Enumeration headerNames = request.getHeaderNames();
    while(headerNames.hasMoreElements()) {
      String headerName = (String)headerNames.nextElement();
      out.println("<TR><TD>" + headerName);
      out.println("    <TD>" + request.getHeader(headerName));
    }
    out.println("</TABLE>\n</BODY></HTML>");
  }
```

Listing 2.11 *ShowRequestHeaders.java (continued)*

```
/** Let the same servlet handle both GET and POST. */

public void doPost(HttpServletRequest request,
                   HttpServletResponse response)
   throws ServletException, IOException {
  doGet(request, response);
 }
}
```

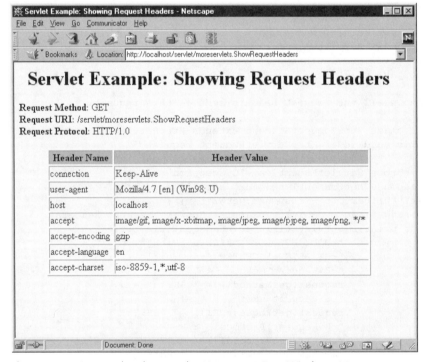

Figure 2–8   Request headers sent by Netscape 4.7 on Windows 98.

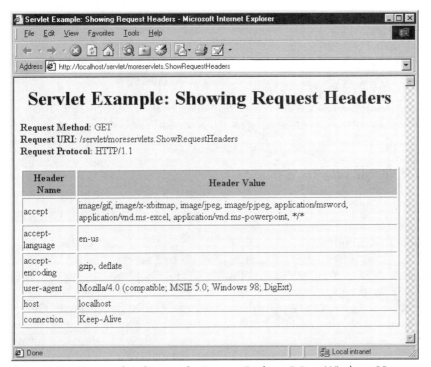

Figure 2–9   Request headers sent by Internet Explorer 5.0 on Windows 98.

Understanding HTTP 1.1 Request Headers

Access to the request headers permits servlets to perform a number of optimizations and to provide a number of features not otherwise possible. This subsection summarizes the headers most often used by servlets; more details are given in *Core Servlets and JavaServer Pages*, Chapter 4 (in PDF at *http://www.moreservlets.com*). Note that HTTP 1.1 supports a superset of the headers permitted in HTTP 1.0. For additional details on these and other headers, see the HTTP 1.1 specification, given in RFC 2616. The official RFCs are archived in a number of places; your best bet is to start at *http://www.rfc-editor.org/* to get a current list of the archive sites.

Accept

This header specifies the MIME types that the browser or other clients can handle. A servlet that can return a resource in more than one format can examine the Accept header to decide which format to use. For example, images in PNG format have some compression advantages over those in GIF, but only a few browsers support PNG. If you had images in both formats, a servlet could call `request.getHeader("Accept")`, check for `image/png`, and if it finds a match, use *xxx.png* filenames in all the `IMG` elements it generates. Otherwise, it would just use *xxx.gif*.

See Table 2.1 in Section 2.8 (The Server Response: HTTP Response Headers) for the names and meanings of the common MIME types

Note that Internet Explorer 5 has a bug whereby the `Accept` header is not sent properly when you reload a page. It is sent properly on the original request, however.

Accept-Charset

This header indicates the character sets (e.g., ISO-8859-1) the browser can use.

Accept-Encoding

This header designates the types of encodings that the client knows how to handle. If the server receives this header, it is free to encode the page by using one of the formats specified (usually to reduce transmission time), sending the `Content-Encoding` response header to indicate that it has done so. This encoding type is completely distinct from the MIME type of the actual document (as specified in the `Content-Type` response header), since this encoding is reversed *before* the browser decides what to do with the content. On the other hand, using an encoding the browser doesn't understand results in totally incomprehensible pages. Consequently, it is critical that you explicitly check the `Accept-Encoding` header before using any type of content encoding. Values of `gzip` or `compress` are the two most common possibilities.

Compressing pages before returning them is a valuable service because the decoding time is likely to be small compared to the savings in transmission time. See Section 9.5 where gzip compression is used to reduce download times by a factor of 10.

Accept-Language

This header specifies the client's preferred languages in case the servlet can produce results in more than one language. The value of the header should be one of the standard language codes such as `en`, `en-us`, `da`, etc. See RFC 1766 for details (start at *http://www.rfc-editor.org/* to get a current list of the RFC archive sites).

Authorization

This header is used by clients to identify themselves when accessing password-protected Web pages. For details, see Chapters 7 and 8.

Connection

This header indicates whether the client can handle persistent HTTP connections. Persistent connections permit the client or other browser to retrieve multiple files (e.g., an HTML file and several associated images) with a single socket connection, saving the overhead of negotiating several independent connections. With an HTTP 1.1 request, persistent connections are the default, and the client must specify a value of `close` for this header to use old-style connections. In HTTP 1.0, a value of `Keep-Alive` means that persistent connections should be used.

Each HTTP request results in a new invocation of a servlet (i.e., a thread calling the servlet's `service` and `doXxx` methods), regardless of whether the request is a separate connection. That is, the server invokes the servlet only after the server has already read the HTTP request. This means that servlets need help from the server to handle persistent connections. Consequently, the servlet's job is just to make it *possible* for the server to use persistent connections, which the servlet does by setting the `Content-Length` response header.

Content-Length

This header is applicable only to POST requests and gives the size of the POST data in bytes. Rather than calling `request.getIntHeader("Content-Length")`, you can simply use `request.getContentLength()`. However, since servlets take care of reading the form data for you (see Section 2.4), you rarely use this header explicitly.

Cookie

This header is used to return cookies to servers that previously sent them to the browser. Never read this header directly; use `request.getCookies` instead. For details, see Section 2.9 (Cookies). Technically, `Cookie` is not part of HTTP 1.1. It was originally a Netscape extension but is now widely supported, including in both Netscape Navigator/Communicator and Microsoft Internet Explorer.

Host

In HTTP 1.1, browsers and other clients are *required* to specify this header, which indicates the host and port as given in the original URL. Due to request forwarding and machines that have multiple hostnames, it is quite possible that the server could not otherwise determine this information. This header is not new in HTTP 1.1, but in HTTP 1.0 it was optional, not required.

If-Modified-Since

This header indicates that the client wants the page only if it has been changed after the specified date. The server sends a 304 (Not Modified) header if no newer result is available. This option is useful because it lets browsers cache documents and reload them over the network only when they've changed. However, servlets don't need to deal directly with this header. Instead, they should just implement the getLastModified method to have the system handle modification dates automatically. See Section 2.8 of *Core Servlets and JavaServer Pages* (available in PDF at *http://www.moreservlets.com*) for an example of the use of getLastModified.

If-Unmodified-Since

This header is the reverse of If-Modified-Since; it specifies that the operation should succeed only if the document is older than the specified date. Typically, If-Modified-Since is used for GET requests ("give me the document only if it is newer than my cached version"), whereas If-Unmodified-Since is used for PUT requests ("update this document only if nobody else has changed it since I generated it"). This header is new in HTTP 1.1.

Referer

This header indicates the URL of the referring Web page. For example, if you are at Web page 1 and click on a link to Web page 2, the URL of Web page 1 is included in the Referer header when the browser requests Web page 2. All major browsers set this header, so it is a useful way of tracking where requests come from. This capability is helpful for tracking advertisers who refer people to your site, for slightly changing content depending on the referring site, or simply for keeping track of where your traffic comes from. In the last case, most people simply rely on Web server log files, since the Referer is typically recorded there. Although the Referer header is useful, don't rely too heavily on it since it can easily be spoofed by a custom client. Finally, note that, due to a spelling mistake by one of the original HTTP authors, this header is Referer, not the expected Referrer.

User-Agent

This header identifies the browser or other client making the request and can be used to return different content to different types of browsers. Be wary of this usage when dealing only with Web browsers; relying on a hard-coded list of browser versions and associated features can make for unreliable and hard-to-modify servlet code. Whenever possible, use something specific in the HTTP headers instead. For example, instead of trying to remember which browsers support gzip on which platforms, simply check the Accept-Encoding header.

However, the User-Agent header is quite useful for distinguishing among different *categories* of client. For example, Japanese developers might see if the User-Agent is an Imode cell phone (in which case you would redirect to a chtml page), a Skynet cell phone (in which case you would redirect to a wml page), or a Web browser (in which case you would generate regular HTML).

Most Internet Explorer versions list a "Mozilla" (Netscape) version first in their User-Agent line, with the real browser version listed parenthetically. This is done for compatibility with JavaScript, where the User-Agent header is sometimes used to determine which JavaScript features are supported. Also note that this header can be easily spoofed, a fact that calls into question the reliability of sites that use this header to "show" market penetration of various browser versions.

2.6   The Servlet Equivalent of the Standard CGI Variables

If you come to servlets with a background in traditional Common Gateway Interface (CGI) programming, you are probably used to the idea of "CGI variables." These are a somewhat eclectic collection of information about the current request. Some are based on the HTTP request line and headers (e.g., form data), others are derived from the socket itself (e.g., the name and IP address of the requesting host), and still others are taken from server installation parameters (e.g., the mapping of URLs to actual paths).

Although it probably makes more sense to think of different sources of data (request data, server information, etc.) as distinct, experienced CGI programmers may find it useful to see the servlet equivalent of each of the CGI variables. If you don't have a background in traditional CGI, first, count your blessings; servlets are easier to use, more flexible, and more efficient than standard CGI. Second, just skim this section, noting the parts not directly related to the incoming HTTP request. In particular, observe that you can use getServletContext().getRealPath to map a URI (here, URI refers to the part of the URL that comes after the host and port) to an actual path and that you can use request.getRemoteHost() and request.getRemoteAddress() to get the name and IP address of the client.

AUTH_TYPE

If an Authorization header was supplied, this variable gives the scheme specified (basic or digest). Access it with request.getAuthType().

CONTENT_LENGTH

For POST requests only, this variable stores the number of bytes of data sent, as given by the Content-Length request header. Technically, since the CONTENT_LENGTH CGI variable is a string, the servlet equivalent is String.valueOf(request.getContentLength()) or request.get-Header("Content-Length"). You'll probably want to just call request.getContentLength(), which returns an int.

CONTENT_TYPE

CONTENT_TYPE designates the MIME type of attached data, if specified.

See Table 2.1 in Section 2.8 (The Server Response: HTTP Response Headers) for the names and meanings of the common MIME types. Access CONTENT_TYPE with request.getContentType().

DOCUMENT_ROOT

The DOCUMENT_ROOT variable specifies the real directory corresponding to the URL *http://host/*. Access it with getServletContext().getReal-Path("/"). In older servlet specifications, you accessed this variable with request.getRealPath("/"); however, the older access method is no longer supported. Also, you can use getServletContext().getRealPath to map an arbitrary URI (i.e., URL suffix that comes after the hostname and port) to an actual path on the local machine.

HTTP_XXX_YYY

Variables of the form HTTP_HEADER_NAME were how CGI programs obtained access to arbitrary HTTP request headers. The Cookie header became HTTP_COOKIE, User-Agent became HTTP_USER_AGENT, Referer became HTTP_REFERER, and so forth. Servlets should just use request.getHeader or one of the shortcut methods described in Section 2.5 (The Client Request: HTTP Request Headers).

PATH_INFO

This variable supplies any path information attached to the URL after the address of the servlet but before the query data. For example, with *http://host/servlet/moreservlets.SomeServlet/foo/bar?baz=quux*, the path information is */foo/bar*. Since servlets, unlike standard CGI programs, can talk directly to the server, they don't need to treat path information specially. Path information could be sent as part of the regular form data and then translated by getServletContext().getRealPath. Access the value of PATH_INFO by using request.getPathInfo().

PATH_TRANSLATED

PATH_TRANSLATED gives the path information mapped to a real path on the server. Again, with servlets there is no need to have a special case for path information, since a servlet can call getServletContext().getReal-Path() to translate partial URLs into real paths. This translation is not possible with standard CGI because the CGI program runs entirely separately from the server. Access this variable by means of request.getPath-Translated().

QUERY_STRING

For GET requests, this variable gives the attached data as a single string with values still URL-encoded. You rarely want the raw data in servlets; instead, use request.getParameter to access individual parameters, as described in Section 2.5 (The Client Request: HTTP Request Headers). However, if you do want the raw data, you can get it with request.getQueryString().

REMOTE_ADDR

This variable designates the IP address of the client that made the request, as a String (e.g., "198.137.241.30"). Access it by calling request.get-RemoteAddr().

REMOTE_HOST

REMOTE_HOST indicates the fully qualified domain name (e.g., *whitehouse.gov*) of the client that made the request. The IP address is returned if the domain name cannot be determined. You can access this variable with request.getRemoteHost().

REMOTE_USER

If an Authorization header was supplied and decoded by the server itself, the REMOTE_USER variable gives the user part, which is useful for session tracking in protected sites. Access it with request.getRemoteUser().

REQUEST_METHOD

This variable stipulates the HTTP request type, which is usually GET or POST but is occasionally HEAD, PUT, DELETE, OPTIONS, or TRACE. Servlets rarely need to look up REQUEST_METHOD explicitly, since each of the request types is typically handled by a different servlet method (doGet, doPost, etc.). An exception is HEAD, which is handled automatically by the service method returning whatever headers and status codes the doGet method would use. Access this variable by means of request.getMethod().

SCRIPT_NAME

This variable specifies the path to the server-side program (i.e., the servlet in our case), relative to the server's root directory. It can be accessed through `request.getServletPath()`.

SERVER_NAME

`SERVER_NAME` gives the host name of the server machine. It can be accessed by means of `request.getServerName()`.

SERVER_PORT

This variable stores the port the server is listening on. Technically, the servlet equivalent is `String.valueOf(request.getServerPort())`, which returns a `String`. You'll usually just want `request.getServerPort()`, which returns an `int`.

SERVER_PROTOCOL

The `SERVER_PROTOCOL` variable indicates the protocol name and version used in the request line (e.g., `HTTP/1.0` or `HTTP/1.1`). Access it by calling `request.getProtocol()`.

SERVER_SOFTWARE

This variable gives identifying information about the Web server. Access it with `getServletContext().getServerInfo()`.

2.7   The Server Response: HTTP Status Codes

When a Web server responds to a request from a browser or other Web client, the response typically consists of a status line, some response headers, a blank line, and the document. Here is a minimal example:

```
HTTP/1.1 200 OK
Content-Type: text/plain

Hello World
```

The status line consists of the HTTP version (`HTTP/1.1` in the example above), a status code (an integer; `200` in the example), and a very short message corresponding to the status code (`OK` in the example). In most cases, all of the headers are optional except for `Content-Type`, which specifies the MIME type of the document that follows. Although most responses contain a document, some don't. For example, responses to HEAD requests should never include a document, and a variety of status codes essentially indicate failure and either don't include a document or include only a short error-message document.

Servlets can perform a variety of important tasks by manipulating the status line and the response headers. For example, they can forward the user to other sites; indicate that the attached document is an image, Adobe Acrobat file, or HTML file; tell the user that a password is required to access the document; and so forth. This section briefly summarizes the most important status codes and what can be accomplished with them; see Chapter 6 of *Core Servlets and JavaServer Pages* (in PDF at *http://www.moreservlets.com*) for more details. The following section discusses the response headers.

Specifying Status Codes

As just described, the HTTP response status line consists of an HTTP version, a status code, and an associated message. Since the message is directly associated with the status code and the HTTP version is determined by the server, all a servlet needs to do is to set the status code. A code of 200 is set automatically, so servlets don't usually need to specify a status code at all. When they do set a code, they do so with the setStatus method of HttpServletResponse. If your response includes a special status code *and* a document, be sure to call setStatus *before* actually returning any of the content with the PrintWriter. That's because an HTTP response consists of the status line, one or more headers, a blank line, and the actual document, *in that order*. As discussed in Section 2.2 (Basic Servlet Structure), servlets do not necessarily buffer the document (version 2.1 servlets never do so), so you have to either set the status code before first using the PrintWriter or carefully check that the buffer hasn't been flushed and content actually sent to the browser.

Core Approach

*Set status codes **before** sending any document content to the client.*

The setStatus method takes an int (the status code) as an argument, but instead of using explicit numbers, for clarity and reliability use the constants defined in HttpServletResponse. The name of each constant is derived from the standard HTTP 1.1 message for each constant, all upper case with a prefix of SC (for *Status Code*) and spaces changed to underscores. Thus, since the message for 404 is Not Found, the equivalent constant in HttpServletResponse is SC_NOT_FOUND. There are two exceptions, however. The constant for code 302 is derived from the HTTP 1.0 message (Moved Temporarily), not the HTTP 1.1 message (Found), and the constant for code 307 (Temporary Redirect) is missing altogether.

Although the general method of setting status codes is simply to call `response.setStatus(int)`, there are two common cases where a shortcut method in `HttpServletResponse` is provided. Just be aware that both of these methods throw `IOException`, whereas `setStatus` does not.

- **`public void sendError(int code, String message)`**
  The `sendError` method sends a status code (usually 404) along with a short message that is automatically formatted inside an HTML document and sent to the client.
- **`public void sendRedirect(String url)`**
  The `sendRedirect` method generates a 302 response along with a `Location` header giving the URL of the new document. With servlets version 2.1, this must be an absolute URL. In version 2.2 and 2.3, either an absolute or a relative URL is permitted; the system automatically translates relative URLs into absolute ones before putting them in the `Location` header.

Setting a status code does not necessarily mean that you don't need to return a document. For example, although most servers automatically generate a small File Not Found message for 404 responses, a servlet might want to customize this response. Again, remember that if you do send output, you have to call `setStatus` or `sendError` *first*.

HTTP 1.1 Status Codes

In this subsection I describe the most important status codes available for use in servlets talking to HTTP 1.1 clients, along with the standard message associated with each code. A good understanding of these codes can dramatically increase the capabilities of your servlets, so you should at least skim the descriptions to see what options are at your disposal. You can come back for details when you are ready to make use of some of the capabilities.

The complete HTTP 1.1 specification is given in RFC 2616. In general, you can access RFCs online by going to *http://www.rfc-editor.org/* and following the links to the latest RFC archive sites, but since this one came from the World Wide Web Consortium, you can just go to *http://www.w3.org/Protocols/*. Codes that are new in HTTP 1.1 are noted, since some browsers support only HTTP 1.0. You should only send the new codes to clients that support HTTP 1.1, as verified by checking `request.getRequestProtocol`.

The rest of this section describes the specific status codes available in HTTP 1.1. These codes fall into five general categories:

- **100–199**
  Codes in the 100s are informational, indicating that the client should respond with some other action.

- **200–299**
  Values in the 200s signify that the request was successful.
- **300–399**
  Values in the 300s are used for files that have moved and usually include a `Location` header indicating the new address.
- **400–499**
  Values in the 400s indicate an error by the client.
- **500–599**
  Codes in the 500s signify an error by the server.

The constants in `HttpServletResponse` that represent the various codes are derived from the standard messages associated with the codes. In servlets, you usually refer to status codes only by means of these constants. For example, you would use `response.setStatus(response.SC_NO_CONTENT)` rather than `response.setStatus(204)`, since the latter is unclear to readers and is prone to typographical errors. However, you should note that servers are allowed to vary the messages slightly, and clients pay attention only to the numeric value. So, for example, you might see a server return a status line of `HTTP/1.1 200 Document Follows` instead of `HTTP/1.1 200 OK`.

100 (Continue)

If the server receives an `Expect` request header with a value of `100-continue`, it means that the client is asking if it can send an attached document in a follow-up request. In such a case, the server should either respond with status 100 (`SC_CONTINUE`) to tell the client to go ahead or use 417 (`Expectation Failed`) to tell the browser it won't accept the document. This status code is new in HTTP 1.1.

200 (OK)

A value of 200 (`SC_OK`) means that everything is fine. The document follows for `GET` and `POST` requests. This status is the default for servlets; if you don't use `setStatus`, you'll get 200.

202 (Accepted)

A value of 202 (`SC_ACCEPTED`) tells the client that the request is being acted upon, but processing is not yet complete.

204 (No Content)

A status code of 204 (`SC_NO_CONTENT`) stipulates that the browser should continue to display the previous document because no new document is available. This behavior is useful if the user periodically reloads a page by pressing the Reload button, and you can determine that the previous page is already up-to-date.

205 (Reset Content)

A value of 205 (SC_RESET_CONTENT) means that there is no new document, but the browser should reset the document view. This status code instructs browsers to clear form fields. It is new in HTTP 1.1.

301 (Moved Permanently)

The 301 (SC_MOVED_PERMANENTLY) status indicates that the requested document is elsewhere; the new URL for the document is given in the Location response header. Browsers should automatically follow the link to the new URL.

302 (Found)

This value is similar to 301, except that in principle the URL given by the Location header should be interpreted as a temporary replacement, not a permanent one. In practice, most browsers treat 301 and 302 identically. Note: In HTTP 1.0, the message was Moved Temporarily instead of Found, and the constant in HttpServletResponse is SC_MOVED_TEMPORARILY, not the expected SC_FOUND.

Core Note

The constant representing 302 is SC_MOVED_TEMPORARILY, not SC_FOUND.

Status code 302 is useful because browsers automatically follow the reference to the new URL given in the Location response header. It is so useful, in fact, that there is a special method for it, sendRedirect. Using response.sendRedirect(url) has a couple of advantages over using response.setStatus(response.SC_MOVED_TEMPORARILY) and response.setHeader("Location", url). First, it is shorter and easier. Second, with sendRedirect, the servlet automatically builds a page containing the link to show to older browsers that don't automatically follow redirects. Finally, with version 2.2 and 2.3 of servlets, sendRedirect can handle relative URLs, automatically translating them into absolute ones.

Technically, browsers are only supposed to automatically follow the redirection if the original request was GET. For details, see the discussion of the 307 status code.

303 (See Other)

The 303 (`SC_SEE_OTHER`) status is similar to 301 and 302, except that if the original request was POST, the new document (given in the `Location` header) should be retrieved with GET. This code is new in HTTP 1.1.

304 (Not Modified)

When a client has a cached document, it can perform a conditional request by supplying an `If-Modified-Since` header to indicate that it wants the document only if it has been changed since the specified date. A value of 304 (`SC_NOT_MODIFIED`) means that the cached version is up-to-date and the client should use it. Otherwise, the server should return the requested document with the normal (200) status code. Servlets normally should not set this status code directly. Instead, they should implement the `getLastModified` method and let the default `service` method handle conditional requests based upon this modification date. For an example, see Section 2.8 of *Core Servlets and JavaServer Pages*.

307 (Temporary Redirect)

The rules for how a browser should handle a 307 status are identical to those for 302. The 307 value was added to HTTP 1.1 since many browsers erroneously follow the redirection on a 302 response even if the original message is a POST. Browsers are supposed to follow the redirection of a POST request only when they receive a 303 response status. This new status is intended to be unambiguously clear: follow redirected GET *and* POST requests in the case of 303 responses; follow redirected GET but *not* POST requests in the case of 307 responses. Note: For some reason there is no constant in `HttpServlet-Response` corresponding to this status code, so you have to use 307 explicitly. This status code is new in HTTP 1.1.

400 (Bad Request)

A 400 (`SC_BAD_REQUEST`) status indicates bad syntax in the client request.

401 (Unauthorized)

A value of 401 (`SC_UNAUTHORIZED`) signifies that the client tried to access a password-protected page without proper identifying information in the `Authorization` header. The response must include a `WWW-Authenticate` header.

403 (Forbidden)

A status code of 403 (`SC_FORBIDDEN`) means that the server refuses to supply the resource, regardless of authorization. This status is often the result of bad file or directory permissions on the server.

404 (Not Found)

The infamous 404 (`SC_NOT_FOUND`) status tells the client that no resource could be found at that address. This value is the standard "no such page" response. It is such a common and useful response that there is a special method for it in the `HttpServletResponse` class: `send-Error("message")`. The advantage of `sendError` over `setStatus` is that, with `sendError`, the server automatically generates an error page showing the error message. 404 errors need not merely say "Sorry, the page cannot be found." Instead, they can give information on why the page couldn't be found or supply search boxes or alternative places to look. The sites at *www.microsoft.com* and *www.ibm.com* have particularly good examples of useful error pages. In fact, there is an entire site dedicated to the good, the bad, the ugly, and the bizarre in 404 error messages: *http://www.plinko.net/404/*. I find *http://www.plinko.net/404/category.asp?Category=Funny* particularly amusing.

Unfortunately, however, the default behavior of Internet Explorer 5 is to ignore the error page you send back and to display its own, even though doing so contradicts the HTTP specification. To turn off this setting, you can go to the Tools menu, select Internet Options, choose the Advanced tab, and make sure "Show friendly HTTP error messages" box is not checked. Unfortunately, however, few users are aware of this setting, so this "feature" prevents most users of Internet Explorer version 5 from seeing any informative messages you return. Other major browsers and version 4 of Internet Explorer properly display server-generated error pages.

Core Warning

By default, Internet Explorer version 5 improperly ignores server-generated error pages.

To make matters worse, some versions of Tomcat 3 fail to properly handle strings that are passed to `sendError`. So, if you are using Tomcat 3, you may need to generate 404 error messages by hand. Fortunately, it is relatively uncommon for individual servlets to build their own 404 error pages. A more common approach is to set up error pages for each Web application; see Section 5.8 (Designating Pages to Handle Errors) for details. Tomcat correctly handles these pages.

Core Warning

Some versions of Tomcat 3.x fail to properly display strings that are supplied to sendError.

405 (Method Not Allowed)

A 405 (SC_METHOD_NOT_ALLOWED) value indicates that the request method (GET, POST, HEAD, PUT, DELETE, etc.) was not allowed for this particular resource. This status code is new in HTTP 1.1.

415 (Unsupported Media Type)

A value of 415 (SC_UNSUPPORTED_MEDIA_TYPE) means that the request had an attached document of a type the server doesn't know how to handle. This status code is new in HTTP 1.1.

417 (Expectation Failed)

If the server receives an Expect request header with a value of 100-continue, it means that the client is asking if it can send an attached document in a follow-up request. In such a case, the server should either respond with this status (417) to tell the browser it won't accept the document or use 100 (SC_CONTINUE) to tell the client to go ahead. This status code is new in HTTP 1.1.

500 (Internal Server Error)

500 (SC_INTERNAL_SERVER_ERROR) is the generic "server is confused" status code. It often results from CGI programs or (heaven forbid!) servlets that crash or return improperly formatted headers.

501 (Not Implemented)

The 501 (SC_NOT_IMPLEMENTED) status notifies the client that the server doesn't support the functionality to fulfill the request. It is used, for example, when the client issues a command like PUT that the server doesn't support.

503 (Service Unavailable)

A status code of 503 (SC_SERVICE_UNAVAILABLE) signifies that the server cannot respond because of maintenance or overloading. For example, a servlet might return this header if some thread or database connection pool is currently full. The server can supply a Retry-After header to tell the client when to try again.

505 (HTTP Version Not Supported)

The 505 (SC_HTTP_VERSION_NOT_SUPPORTED) code means that the server doesn't support the version of HTTP named in the request line. This status code is new in HTTP 1.1.

A Front End to Various Search Engines

Listing 2.12 presents an example that makes use of the two most common status codes other than 200 (OK): 302 (Found) and 404 (Not Found). The 302 code is set by the shorthand sendRedirect method of HttpServletResponse, and 404 is specified by sendError.

In this application, an HTML form (see Figure 2–10 and the source code in Listing 2.14) first displays a page that lets the user specify a search string, the number of results to show per page, and the search engine to use. When the form is submitted, the servlet extracts those three parameters, constructs a URL with the parameters embedded in a way appropriate to the search engine selected (see the SearchSpec class of Listing 2.13), and redirects the user to that URL (see Figure 2–11). If the user fails to choose a search engine or specify search terms, an error page informs the client of this fact (but see warnings under the 404 status code in the previous subsection).

Listing 2.12 *SearchEngines.java*

```
package moreservlets;

import java.io.*;
import javax.servlet.*;
import javax.servlet.http.*;
import java.net.*;

/** Servlet that takes a search string, number of results per
 *  page, and a search engine name, sending the query to
 *  that search engine. Illustrates manipulating
 *  the response status line. It sends a 302 response
 *  (via sendRedirect) if it gets a known search engine,
 *  and sends a 404 response (via sendError) otherwise.
 */

public class SearchEngines extends HttpServlet {
  public void doGet(HttpServletRequest request,
                    HttpServletResponse response)
      throws ServletException, IOException {
    String searchString = request.getParameter("searchString");
```

Listing 2.12 *SearchEngines.java (continued)*

```java
    if ((searchString == null) ||
        (searchString.length() == 0)) {
      reportProblem(response, "Missing search string.");
      return;
    }
    // The URLEncoder changes spaces to "+" signs and other
    // non-alphanumeric characters to "%XY", where XY is the
    // hex value of the ASCII (or ISO Latin-1) character.
    // Browsers always URL-encode form values, so the
    // getParameter method decodes automatically. But since
    // we're just passing this on to another server, we need to
    // re-encode it.
    searchString = URLEncoder.encode(searchString);
    String numResults = request.getParameter("numResults");
    if ((numResults == null) ||
        (numResults.equals("0")) ||
        (numResults.length() == 0)) {
      numResults = "10";
    }
    String searchEngine =
      request.getParameter("searchEngine");
    if (searchEngine == null) {
      reportProblem(response, "Missing search engine name.");
      return;
    }
    SearchSpec[] commonSpecs = SearchSpec.getCommonSpecs();
    for(int i=0; i<commonSpecs.length; i++) {
      SearchSpec searchSpec = commonSpecs[i];
      if (searchSpec.getName().equals(searchEngine)) {
        String url =
          searchSpec.makeURL(searchString, numResults);
        response.sendRedirect(url);
        return;
      }
    }
    reportProblem(response, "Unrecognized search engine.");
  }

  private void reportProblem(HttpServletResponse response,
                             String message)
      throws IOException {
    response.sendError(response.SC_NOT_FOUND,
                       "<H2>" + message + "</H2>");
  }
```

Listing 2.12 *SearchEngines.java (continued)*

```
public void doPost(HttpServletRequest request,
                   HttpServletResponse response)
    throws ServletException, IOException {
  doGet(request, response);
  }
}
```

Listing 2.13 *SearchSpec.java*

```
package moreservlets;

/** Small class that encapsulates how to construct a
 *  search string for a particular search engine.
 */

public class SearchSpec {
  private String name, baseURL, numResultsSuffix;

  private static SearchSpec[] commonSpecs =
    { new SearchSpec
      ("google",
       "http://www.google.com/search?q=",
       "&num="),
      new SearchSpec
      ("altavista",
       "http://www.altavista.com/sites/search/web?q=",
       "&nbq="),
      new SearchSpec
      ("lycos",
       "http://lycospro.lycos.com/cgi-bin/" +
       "pursuit?query=",
       "&maxhits="),
      new SearchSpec
      ("hotbot",
       "http://www.hotbot.com/?MT=",
       "&DC=")
    };

  public SearchSpec(String name,
                    String baseURL,
                    String numResultsSuffix) {
```

Listing 2.13 *SearchSpec.java (continued)*

```
    this.name = name;
    this.baseURL = baseURL;
    this.numResultsSuffix = numResultsSuffix;
  }

  public String makeURL(String searchString,
                        String numResults) {
    return(baseURL + searchString +
           numResultsSuffix + numResults);
  }

  public String getName() {
    return(name);
  }

  public static SearchSpec[] getCommonSpecs() {
    return(commonSpecs);
  }
}
```

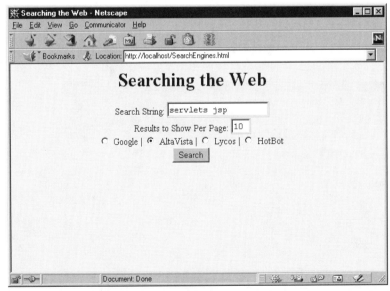

Figure 2–10 Front end to the `SearchEngines` servlet. See Listing 2.14 for the HTML source code.

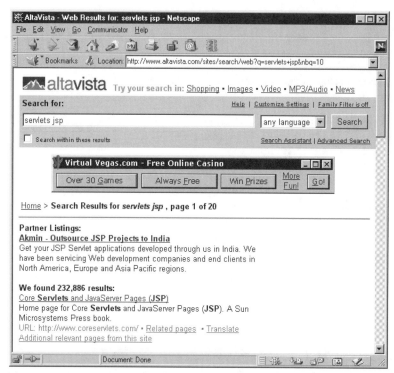

Figure 2–11 Result of the `SearchEngines` servlet when the form of Figure 2–10 is submitted.

Figure 2–12 Result of the `SearchEngines` servlet when a form that has no search string is submitted. This result is for JRun 3.1; results can vary slightly among servers and will omit the "Missing search string" message in most Tomcat versions.

Listing 2.14 *SearchEngines.html*

```
<!DOCTYPE HTML PUBLIC "-//W3C//DTD HTML 4.0 Transitional//EN">
<HTML>
<HEAD>
  <TITLE>Searching the Web</TITLE>
</HEAD>
<BODY BGCOLOR="#FDF5E6">
<H1 ALIGN="CENTER">Searching the Web</H1>

<FORM ACTION="/servlet/moreservlets.SearchEngines">
  <CENTER>
    Search String:
    <INPUT TYPE="TEXT" NAME="searchString"><BR>
    Results to Show Per Page:
    <INPUT TYPE="TEXT" NAME="numResults"
                       VALUE=10 SIZE=3><BR>
    <INPUT TYPE="RADIO" NAME="searchEngine"
                       VALUE="google">
    Google |
    <INPUT TYPE="RADIO" NAME="searchEngine"
                       VALUE="altavista">
    AltaVista |
    <INPUT TYPE="RADIO" NAME="searchEngine"
                       VALUE="lycos">
    Lycos |
    <INPUT TYPE="RADIO" NAME="searchEngine"
                       VALUE="hotbot">
    HotBot
    <BR>
    <INPUT TYPE="SUBMIT" VALUE="Search">
  </CENTER>
</FORM>

</BODY>
</HTML>
```

2.8   The Server Response: HTTP Response Headers

As discussed in the previous section, a response from a Web server normally consists of a status line, one or more response headers (one of which must be Content-Type), a blank line, and the document. To get the most out of your servlets, you need to know how to use the status line and response headers effectively, not just how to generate the document.

Setting the HTTP response headers often goes hand in hand with setting the status codes in the status line, as discussed in the previous section. For example, all the "document moved" status codes (300 through 307) have an accompanying `Location` header, and a 401 (`Unauthorized`) code always includes an accompanying `WWW-Authenticate` header. However, specifying headers can also play a useful role even when no unusual status code is set. Response headers can be used to specify cookies, to supply the page modification date (for client-side caching), to instruct the browser to reload the page after a designated interval, to give the file size so that persistent HTTP connections can be used, to designate the type of document being generated, and to perform many other tasks. This section gives a brief summary of the handling of response headers. See Chapter 7 of *Core Servlets and JavaServer Pages* (available in PDF at *http://www.moreservlets.com*) for more details and examples.

Setting Response Headers from Servlets

The most general way to specify headers is to use the `setHeader` method of `HttpServletResponse`. This method takes two strings: the header name and the header value. As with setting status codes, you must specify headers *before* returning the actual document.

In addition to the general-purpose `setHeader` method, `HttpServlet-Response` also has two specialized methods to set headers that contain dates and integers:

- **setDateHeader(String header, long milliseconds)**
  This method saves you the trouble of translating a Java date in milliseconds since 1970 (as returned by `System.currentTimeMillis`, `Date.getTime`, or `Calendar.getTimeInMillis`) into a GMT time string.
- **setIntHeader(String header, int headerValue)**
  This method spares you the minor inconvenience of converting an int to a `String` before inserting it into a header.

HTTP allows multiple occurrences of the same header name, and you sometimes want to add a new header rather than replace any existing header with the same name. For example, it is quite common to have multiple `Accept` and `Set-Cookie` headers that specify different supported MIME types and different cookies, respectively. With servlets version 2.1, `setHeader`, `setDateHeader`, and `setInt-Header` always *add* new headers, so there is no way to "unset" headers that were set earlier (e.g., by an inherited method). With servlets versions 2.2 and 2.3, `set-Header`, `setDateHeader`, and `setIntHeader` *replace* any existing headers of the same name, whereas `addHeader`, `addDateHeader`, and `addIntHeader` add a header regardless of whether a header of that name already exists. If it matters to you whether a specific header has already been set, use `containsHeader` to check.

Finally, `HttpServletResponse` also supplies a number of convenience methods for specifying common headers. These methods are summarized as follows.

- **`setContentType`**
  This method sets the `Content-Type` header and is used by the majority of servlets.
- **`setContentLength`**
  This method sets the `Content-Length` header, which is useful if the browser supports persistent (keep-alive) HTTP connections.
- **`addCookie`**
  This method inserts a cookie into the `Set-Cookie` header. There is no corresponding `setCookie` method, since it is normal to have multiple `Set-Cookie` lines. See Section 2.9 (Cookies) for a discussion of cookies.
- **`sendRedirect`**
  As discussed in the previous section, the `sendRedirect` method sets the `Location` header as well as setting the status code to 302. See Listing 2.12 for an example.

Understanding HTTP 1.1 Response Headers

Following is a summary of the most useful HTTP 1.1 response headers. A good understanding of these headers can increase the effectiveness of your servlets, so you should at least skim the descriptions to see what options are at your disposal. You can come back for details when you are ready to use the capabilities.

These headers are a superset of those permitted in HTTP 1.0. The official HTTP 1.1 specification is given in RFC 2616. The RFCs are online in various places; your best bet is to start at *http://www.rfc-editor.org/* to get a current list of the archive sites. Header names are not case sensitive but are traditionally written with the first letter of each word capitalized.

Be cautious in writing servlets whose behavior depends on response headers that are only available in HTTP 1.1, especially if your servlet needs to run on the WWW "at large" rather than on an intranet—many older browsers support only HTTP 1.0. It is best to explicitly check the HTTP version with `request.getRequest-Protocol` before using new headers.

Allow

The `Allow` header specifies the request methods (`GET`, `POST`, etc.) that the server supports. It is required for 405 (`Method Not Allowed`) responses.

The default `service` method of servlets automatically generates this header for `OPTIONS` requests.

Cache-Control

This useful header tells the browser or other client the circumstances in which the response document can safely be cached. It has the following possible values:

- **public.** Document is cacheable, even if normal rules (e.g., for password-protected pages) indicate that it shouldn't be.
- **private.** Document is for a single user and can only be stored in private (nonshared) caches.
- **no-cache.** Document should never be cached (i.e., used to satisfy a later request). The server can also specify "no-cache="header1,header2,...,headerN"" to indicate the headers that should be omitted if a cached response is later used. Browsers normally do not cache documents that were retrieved by requests that include form data. However, if a servlet generates different content for different requests even when the requests contain no form data, it is critical to tell the browser not to cache the response. Since older browsers use the `Pragma` header for this purpose, the typical servlet approach is to set *both* headers, as in the following example.

```
response.setHeader("Cache-Control", "no-cache");
response.setHeader("Pragma", "no-cache");
```

- **no-store.** Document should never be cached and should not even be stored in a temporary location on disk. This header is intended to prevent inadvertent copies of sensitive information.
- **must-revalidate.** Client must revalidate document with original server (not just intermediate proxies) each time it is used.
- **proxy-revalidate.** This is the same as `must-revalidate`, except that it applies only to shared caches.
- **max-age=xxx.** Document should be considered stale after *xxx* seconds. This is a convenient alternative to the `Expires` header but only works with HTTP 1.1 clients. If both `max-age` and `Expires` are present in the response, the `max-age` value takes precedence.
- **s-max-age=xxx.** Shared caches should consider the document stale after *xxx* seconds.

The `Cache-Control` header is new in HTTP 1.1.

Connection

A value of `close` for this response header instructs the browser not to use persistent HTTP connections. Technically, persistent connections are the default when the client supports HTTP 1.1 and does *not* specify a `Connection: close` request header (or when an HTTP 1.0 client specifies `Connection: keep-alive`). However, since persistent connections require a `Content-Length` response header, there is no reason for a servlet to explicitly use the `Connection` header. Just omit the `Content-Length` header if you aren't using persistent connections.

Content-Encoding

This header indicates the way in which the page was encoded during transmission. The browser should reverse the encoding before deciding what to do with the document. Compressing the document with gzip can result in huge savings in transmission time; for an example, see Section 9.5.

Content-Language

The `Content-Language` header signifies the language in which the document is written. The value of the header should be one of the standard language codes such as en, en-us, da, etc. See RFC 1766 for details on language codes (you can access RFCs online at one of the archive sites listed at *http://www.rfc-editor.org/*).

Content-Length

This header indicates the number of bytes in the response. This information is needed only if the browser is using a persistent (keep-alive) HTTP connection. See the `Connection` header for determining when the browser supports persistent connections. If you want your servlet to take advantage of persistent connections when the browser supports it, your servlet should write the document into a `ByteArrayOutputStream`, look up its size when done, put that into the `Content-Length` field with `response.setContentLength`, then send the content by `byteArrayStream.writeTo(response.getOutputStream())`. See *Core Servlets and JavaServer Pages* Section 7.4 for an example.

Content-Type

The `Content-Type` header gives the MIME (Multipurpose Internet Mail Extension) type of the response document. Setting this header is so common that there is a special method in `HttpServletResponse` for it: `setContentType`. MIME types are of the form *maintype/subtype* for officially registered types and of the form *maintype/x-subtype* for unregistered types. Most servlets specify `text/html`; they can, however, specify other types instead.

In addition to a basic MIME type, the `Content-Type` header can also designate a specific character encoding. If this is not specified, the default is `ISO-8859_1` (Latin). For example, the following instructs the browser to interpret the document as HTML in the `Shift_JIS` (standard Japanese) character set.

```
response.setContentType("text/html; charset=Shift_JIS");
```

Table 2.1 lists some the most common MIME types used by servlets. RFC 1521 and RFC 1522 list more of the common MIME types (again, see *http://www.rfc-editor.org/* for a list of RFC archive sites). However, new MIME types are registered all the time, so a dynamic list is a better place to look. The officially registered types are listed at *http://www.isi.edu/in-notes/iana/assignments/media-types/media-types*. For common unregistered types, *http://www.ltsw.se/knbase/internet/mime.htp* is a good source.

Table 2.1   Common MIME Types

Type	Meaning
application/msword	Microsoft Word document
application/octet-stream	Unrecognized or binary data
application/pdf	Acrobat (*.pdf*) file
application/postscript	PostScript file
application/vnd.lotus-notes	Lotus Notes file
application/vnd.ms-excel	Excel spreadsheet
application/vnd.ms-powerpoint	PowerPoint presentation
application/x-gzip	Gzip archive
application/x-java-archive	JAR file
application/x-java-serialized-object	Serialized Java object
application/x-java-vm	Java bytecode (*.class*) file
application/zip	Zip archive
audio/basic	Sound file in *.au* or *.snd* format

Table 2.1	Common MIME Types *(continued)*

Type	*Meaning*
audio/midi	MIDI sound file
audio/x-aiff	AIFF sound file
audio/x-wav	Microsoft Windows sound file
image/gif	GIF image
image/jpeg	JPEG image
image/png	PNG image
image/tiff	TIFF image
image/x-xbitmap	X Windows bitmap image
text/css	HTML cascading style sheet
text/html	HTML document
text/plain	Plain text
text/xml	XML
video/mpeg	MPEG video clip
video/quicktime	QuickTime video clip

Expires

This header stipulates the time at which the content should be considered out-of-date and thus no longer be cached. A servlet might use this for a document that changes relatively frequently, to prevent the browser from displaying a stale cached value. Furthermore, since some older browsers support `Pragma` unreliably (and `Cache-Control` not at all), an `Expires` header with a date in the past is often used to prevent browser caching.

For example, the following would instruct the browser not to cache the document for more than 10 minutes.

```
long currentTime = System.currentTimeMillis();
long tenMinutes = 10*60*1000; // In milliseconds
response.setDateHeader("Expires", currentTime + tenMinutes);
```

Also see the `max-age` value of the `Cache-Control` header.

Last-Modified

This very useful header indicates when the document was last changed.
The client can then cache the document and supply a date by an
`If-Modified-Since` request header in later requests. This request is
treated as a conditional `GET`, with the document being returned only
if the `Last-Modified` date is later than the one specified for
`If-Modified-Since`. Otherwise, a 304 (`Not Modified`) status line is
returned, and the client uses the cached document. If you set this header
explicitly, use the `setDateHeader` method to save yourself the bother of for-
matting GMT date strings. However, in most cases you simply implement the
`getLastModified` method (see *Core Servlets and JavaServer Pages* Section
2.8) and let the standard `service` method handle `If-Modified-Since`
requests.

Location

This header, which should be included with all responses that have a status
code in the 300s, notifies the browser of the document address. The browser
automatically reconnects to this location and retrieves the new document. This
header is usually set indirectly, along with a 302 status code, by the
`sendRedirect` method of `HttpServletResponse`. An example is given in
the previous section (Listing 2.12).

Pragma

Supplying this header with a value of `no-cache` instructs HTTP 1.0 clients
not to cache the document. However, support for this header was inconsistent
with HTTP 1.0 browsers, so `Expires` with a date in the past is often used
instead. In HTTP 1.1, `Cache-Control: no-cache` is a more reliable
replacement.

Refresh

This header indicates how soon (in seconds) the browser should ask for an
updated page. For example, to tell the browser to ask for a new copy in 30
seconds, you would specify a value of 30 with

```
response.setIntHeader("Refresh", 30)
```

Note that `Refresh` does not stipulate continual updates; it just specifies
when the *next* update should be. So, you have to continue to supply `Refresh`
in all subsequent responses. This header is extremely useful because it lets
servlets return partial results quickly while still letting the client see the complete results at a later time. For an example, see Section 7.3 of *Core Servlets
and JavaServer Pages* (in PDF at *http://www.moreservlets.com*).

Instead of having the browser just reload the current page, you can specify the page to load. You do this by supplying a semicolon and a URL after the refresh time. For example, to tell the browser to go to *http://host/path* after 5 seconds, you would do the following.

```
response.setHeader("Refresh", "5; URL=http://host/path/")
```

This setting is useful for "splash screens," where an introductory image or message is displayed briefly before the real page is loaded.

Note that this header is commonly set indirectly by putting

```
<META HTTP-EQUIV="Refresh"
      CONTENT="5; URL=http://host/path/">
```

in the HEAD section of the HTML page, rather than as an explicit header from the server. That usage came about because automatic reloading or forwarding is something often desired by authors of static HTML pages. For servlets, however, setting the header directly is easier and clearer.

This header is not officially part of HTTP 1.1 but is an extension supported by both Netscape and Internet Explorer.

Retry-After

This header can be used in conjunction with a 503 (Service Unavailable) response to tell the client how soon it can repeat its request.

Set-Cookie

The Set-Cookie header specifies a cookie associated with the page. Each cookie requires a separate Set-Cookie header. Servlets should not use response.setHeader("Set-Cookie", ...) but instead should use the special-purpose addCookie method of HttpServletResponse. For details, see Section 2.9 (Cookies). Technically, Set-Cookie is not part of HTTP 1.1. It was originally a Netscape extension but is now widely supported, including in both Netscape and Internet Explorer.

WWW-Authenticate

This header is always included with a 401 (Unauthorized) status code. It tells the browser what authorization type (BASIC or DIGEST) and realm the client should supply in its Authorization header. See Chapters 7 and 8 for a discussion of the various security mechanisms available to servlets.

2.9   Cookies

Cookies are small bits of textual information that a Web server sends to a browser and that the browser later returns unchanged when visiting the same Web site or domain. By letting the server read information it sent the client previously, the site can provide visitors with a number of conveniences such as presenting the site the way the visitor previously customized it or letting identifiable visitors in without their having to reenter a password.

This section discusses how to explicitly set and read cookies from within servlets, and the next section shows how to use the servlet session tracking API (which can use cookies behind the scenes) to keep track of users as they move around to different pages within your site.

Benefits of Cookies

There are four typical ways in which cookies can add value to your site.

Identifying a User During an E-commerce Session

Many online stores use a "shopping cart" metaphor in which the user selects an item, adds it to his shopping cart, then continues shopping. Since the HTTP connection is usually closed after each page is sent, when the user selects a new item to add to the cart, how does the store know that it is the same user who put the previous item in the cart? Persistent (keep-alive) HTTP connections do not solve this problem, since persistent connections generally apply only to requests made very close together in time, as when a browser asks for the images associated with a Web page. Besides, many servers and browsers lack support for persistent connections. Cookies, however, *can* solve this problem. In fact, this capability is so useful that servlets have an API specifically for session tracking, and servlet authors don't need to manipulate cookies directly to take advantage of it. Session tracking is discussed in Section 2.10.

Avoiding Username and Password

Many large sites require you to register to use their services, but it is inconvenient to remember and enter the username and password each time you visit. Cookies are a good alternative for low-security sites. When a user registers, a cookie containing a unique user ID is sent to him. When the client reconnects at a later date, the user ID is returned automatically, the server looks it up, determines it belongs to a registered user, and permits access without an explicit username and password. The site might also store the user's address, credit card number, and so forth in a database and use the user ID from the cookie as a key to retrieve the data. This approach prevents the user from having to reenter the data each time.

Customizing a Site

Many "portal" sites let you customize the look of the main page. They might let you pick which weather report you want to see, what stock and sports results you care about, how search results should be displayed, and so forth. Since it would be inconvenient for you to have to set up your page each time you visit their site, they use cookies to remember what you wanted. For simple settings, the site could accomplish this customization by storing the page settings directly in the cookies. For more complex customization, however, the site just sends the client a unique identifier and keeps a server-side database that associates identifiers with page settings.

Focusing Advertising

Most advertiser-funded Web sites charge their advertisers much more for displaying "directed" ads than "random" ads. Advertisers are generally willing to pay much more to have their ads shown to people that are known to have some interest in the general product category. For example, if you go to a search engine and do a search on "Java Servlets," the search site can charge an advertiser much more for showing you an ad for a servlet development environment than for an ad for an online travel agent specializing in Indonesia. On the other hand, if the search had been for "Java Hotels," the situation would be reversed. Without cookies, the sites have to show a random ad when you first arrive and haven't yet performed a search, as well as when you search on something that doesn't match any ad categories. With cookies, they can identify your interests by remembering your previous searches.

Some Problems with Cookies

Providing convenience to the user and added value to the site owner is the purpose behind cookies. And despite much misinformation, cookies are not a serious security threat. Cookies are never interpreted or executed in any way and thus cannot be used to insert viruses or attack your system. Furthermore, since browsers generally only accept 20 cookies per site and 300 cookies total, and since browsers can limit each cookie to 4 kilobytes, cookies cannot be used to fill up someone's disk or launch other denial-of-service attacks.

However, even though cookies don't present a serious *security* threat, they can present a significant threat to *privacy*. First, some people don't like the fact that search engines can remember that they're the user who usually does searches on certain topics. For example, they might search for job openings or sensitive health data and don't want some banner ad tipping off their coworkers next time they do a search. Even worse, two sites can share data on a user by each loading small images off the same third-party site, where that third party uses cookies and shares the data with both original sites. The doubleclick.net service is the prime example of this technique. (Netscape, however, provides a nice feature that lets you refuse cookies from sites other than that to which you connected, but without disabling cookies altogether.) This trick of associating cookies with images can even be exploited through e-mail if you use an HTML-enabled e-mail reader that "supports" cookies and is associated with a browser. Thus, people could send you e-mail that loads images, attach cookies to those images, then identify you (e-mail address and all) if you subsequently visit their Web site. Boo.

A second privacy problem occurs when sites rely on cookies for overly sensitive data. For example, some of the big online bookstores use cookies to remember users and let you order without reentering much of your personal information. This is not a particular problem since they don't actually display the full credit card number and only let you send books to an address that was specified when you *did* enter the credit card in full or use the username and password. As a result, someone using your computer (or stealing your cookie file) could do no more harm than sending a big book order to your address, where the order could be refused. However, other companies might not be so careful, and an attacker who gained access to someone's computer or cookie file could get online access to valuable personal information. Even worse, incompetent sites might embed credit card or other sensitive information directly in the cookies themselves, rather than using innocuous identifiers that are only linked to real users on the server. This is dangerous, since most users don't view leaving their computer unattended in their office as being tantamount to leaving their credit card sitting on their desk.

The point of this discussion is twofold. First, due to real and perceived privacy problems, some users turn off cookies. So, even when you use cookies to give added value to a site, your site shouldn't *depend* on them. Second, as the author of servlets that use cookies, you should be careful not to use cookies for particularly sensitive information, since this would open users up to risks if somebody accessed their computer or cookie files.

The Servlet Cookie API

To send cookies to the client, a servlet should create one or more cookies with designated names and values with new Cookie(name, value), set any optional attributes with cookie.setXxx (readable later by cookie.getXxx), and insert the cookies into the response headers with response.addCookie(cookie). To read incoming cookies, a servlet should call request.getCookies, which returns an array of Cookie objects corresponding to the cookies the browser has associated with your site (null if there are no cookies in the request). In most cases, the servlet loops down this array until it finds the one whose name (getName) matches the name it had in mind, then calls getValue on that Cookie to see the value associated with that name. Each of these topics is discussed in more detail in the following sections.

Creating Cookies

You create a cookie by calling the `Cookie` constructor, which takes two strings: the cookie name and the cookie value. Neither the name nor the value should contain white space or any of the following characters:

```
[ ] ( ) = , " / ? @ : ;
```

If you want the browser to store the cookie on disk instead of just keeping it in memory, use `setMaxAge` to specify how long (in seconds) the cookie should be valid.

Placing Cookies in the Response Headers

The cookie is inserted into a `Set-Cookie` HTTP response header by means of the `addCookie` method of `HttpServletResponse`. The method is called `addCookie`, not `setCookie`, because any previously specified `Set-Cookie` headers are left alone and a new header is set. Here's an example:

```
Cookie userCookie = new Cookie("user", "uid1234");
userCookie.setMaxAge(60*60*24*365); // Store cookie for 1 year
response.addCookie(userCookie);
```

Reading Cookies from the Client

To send cookies *to* the client, you create a `Cookie`, then use `addCookie` to send a `Set-Cookie` HTTP response header. To read the cookies that come back *from* the client, you call `getCookies` on the `HttpServletRequest`. This call returns an array of `Cookie` objects corresponding to the values that came in on the `Cookie` HTTP request header. If the request contains no cookies, `getCookies` should return `null`. However, Tomcat 3.x returns a zero-length array instead.

Core Warning

In Tomcat 3.x, calls to `request.getCookies` *return a zero-length array instead of* `null` *when there are no cookies in the request. Tomcat 4 and most commercial servers properly return* `null`.

Once you have this array, you typically loop down it, calling `getName` on each `Cookie` until you find one matching the name you have in mind. You then call `getValue` on the matching `Cookie` and finish with some processing specific to the resultant value. This is such a common process that, at the end of this section, I present two utilities that simplify retrieving a cookie or cookie value that matches a designated cookie name.

Using Cookie Attributes

Before adding the cookie to the outgoing headers, you can set various characteristics of the cookie by using one of the following *setXxx* methods, where *Xxx* is the name of the attribute you want to specify. Each *setXxx* method has a corresponding *getXxx* method to retrieve the attribute value. Except for name and value, the cookie attributes apply only to *outgoing* cookies from the server to the client; they aren't set on cookies that come *from* the browser to the server. So, don't expect these attributes to be available in the cookies you get by means of `request.get-Cookies`.

public String getComment()
public void setComment(String comment)

These methods look up or specify a comment associated with the cookie. With version 0 cookies (see the upcoming entry on `getVersion` and `setVersion`), the comment is used purely for informational purposes on the server; it is not sent to the client.

public String getDomain()
public void setDomain(String domainPattern)

These methods get or set the domain to which the cookie applies. Normally, the browser returns cookies only to the same hostname that sent them. You can use `setDomain` method to instruct the browser to return them to other hosts within the same domain. To prevent servers from setting cookies that apply to hosts outside their domain, the specified domain must meet the following two requirements: It must start with a dot (e.g., *.prenhall.com*); it must contain two dots for noncountry domains like *.com*, *.edu*, and *.gov*; and it must contain three dots for country domains like *.co.uk* and *.edu.es*. For instance, cookies sent from a servlet at *bali.vacations.com* would not normally get returned by the browser to pages at *mexico.vacations.com*. If the site wanted this to happen, the servlets could specify `cookie.set-Domain(".vacations.com")`.

public int getMaxAge()
public void setMaxAge(int lifetime)

These methods tell how much time (in seconds) should elapse before the cookie expires. A negative value, which is the default, indicates that the cookie will last only for the current session (i.e., until the user quits the browser) and will not be stored on disk. See the `LongLivedCookie` class (Listing 2.18), which defines a subclass of `Cookie` with a maximum age automatically set one year in the future. Specifying a value of 0 instructs the browser to delete the cookie.

public String getName()
public void setName(String cookieName)

This pair of methods gets or sets the name of the cookie. The name and the value are the two pieces you virtually *always* care about. However, since the name is supplied to the Cookie constructor, you rarely need to call setName. On the other hand, getName is used on almost every cookie received on the server. Since the getCookies method of HttpServletRequest returns an array of Cookie objects, a common practice is to loop down the array, calling getName until you have a particular name, then to check the value with getValue. For an encapsulation of this process, see the getCookieValue method shown in Listing 2.17.

public String getPath()
public void setPath(String path)

These methods get or set the path to which the cookie applies. If you don't specify a path, the browser returns the cookie only to URLs in or below the directory containing the page that sent the cookie. For example, if the server sent the cookie from *http://ecommerce.site.com/toys/ specials.html*, the browser would send the cookie back when connecting to *http:// ecommerce.site.com/toys/bikes/beginners.html*, but not to *http://ecommerce.site.com/cds/classical.html*. The setPath method can specify something more general. For example, someCookie.set-Path("/") specifies that *all* pages on the server should receive the cookie. The path specified must include the current page; that is, you may specify a more general path than the default, but not a more specific one. So, for example, a servlet at *http://host/store/cust-service/request* could specify a path of */store/* (since */store/* includes */store/cust-service/*) but not a path of */store/cust-service/returns/* (since this directory does not include */store/cust-service/*).

public boolean getSecure()
public void setSecure(boolean secureFlag)

This pair of methods gets or sets the boolean value indicating whether the cookie should only be sent over encrypted (i.e., SSL) connections. The default is false; the cookie should apply to all connections.

public String getValue()
public void setValue(String cookieValue)

The getValue method looks up the value associated with the cookie; the setValue method specifies it. Again, the name and the value are the two parts of a cookie that you almost *always* care about, although in a few cases, a name is used as a boolean flag and its value is ignored (i.e., the existence of a cookie with the designated name is all that matters).

public int getVersion()
public void setVersion(int version)

These methods get and set the cookie protocol version the cookie complies with. Version 0, the default, follows the original Netscape specification (*http://www.netscape.com/newsref/std/cookie_spec.html*). Version 1, not yet widely supported, adheres to RFC 2109 (retrieve RFCs from the archive sites listed at *http://www.rfc-editor.org/*).

Examples of Setting and Reading Cookies

Listing 2.15 and Figure 2–13 show the SetCookies servlet, a servlet that sets six cookies. Three have the default expiration date, meaning that they should apply only until the user next restarts the browser. The other three use setMaxAge to stipulate that they should apply for the next hour, regardless of whether the user restarts the browser or reboots the computer to initiate a new browsing session.

Listing 2.16 shows a servlet that creates a table of all the cookies sent to it in the request. Figure 2–14 shows this servlet immediately after the SetCookies servlet is visited. Figure 2–15 shows it within an hour of when SetCookies is visited but when the browser has been closed and restarted. Figure 2–16 shows it within an hour of when SetCookies is visited but when the browser has been closed and restarted.

Listing 2.15	*SetCookies.java*

```
package moreservlets;

import java.io.*;
import javax.servlet.*;
import javax.servlet.http.*;

/** Sets six cookies: three that apply only to the current
 *  session (regardless of how long that session lasts)
 *  and three that persist for an hour (regardless of
 *  whether the browser is restarted).
 */
```

Listing 2.15	*SetCookies.java (continued)*

```java
public class SetCookies extends HttpServlet {
  public void doGet(HttpServletRequest request,
                    HttpServletResponse response)
      throws ServletException, IOException {
    for(int i=0; i<3; i++) {
      // Default maxAge is -1, indicating cookie
      // applies only to current browsing session.
      Cookie cookie = new Cookie("Session-Cookie-" + i,
                                 "Cookie-Value-S" + i);
      response.addCookie(cookie);
      cookie = new Cookie("Persistent-Cookie-" + i,
                          "Cookie-Value-P" + i);
      // Cookie is valid for an hour, regardless of whether
      // user quits browser, reboots computer, or whatever.
      cookie.setMaxAge(3600);
      response.addCookie(cookie);
    }
    response.setContentType("text/html");
    PrintWriter out = response.getWriter();
    String title = "Setting Cookies";
    out.println
      (ServletUtilities.headWithTitle(title) +
       "<BODY BGCOLOR=\"#FDF5E6\">\n" +
       "<H1 ALIGN=\"CENTER\">" + title + "</H1>\n" +
       "There are six cookies associated with this page.\n" +
       "To see them, visit the\n" +
       "<A HREF=\"/servlet/moreservlets.ShowCookies\">\n" +
       "<CODE>ShowCookies</CODE> servlet</A>.\n" +
       "<P>\n" +
       "Three of the cookies are associated only with the\n" +
       "current session, while three are persistent.\n" +
       "Quit the browser, restart, and return to the\n" +
       "<CODE>ShowCookies</CODE> servlet to verify that\n" +
       "the three long-lived ones persist across sessions.\n" +
       "</BODY></HTML>");
  }
}
```

Figure 2–13 Result of SetCookies servlet.

Listing 2.16 *ShowCookies.java*

```
package moreservlets;

import java.io.*;
import javax.servlet.*;
import javax.servlet.http.*;

/** Creates a table of the cookies associated with
 *  the current page.
 */

public class ShowCookies extends HttpServlet {
  public void doGet(HttpServletRequest request,
                    HttpServletResponse response)
      throws ServletException, IOException {
    response.setContentType("text/html");
    PrintWriter out = response.getWriter();
    String title = "Active Cookies";
```

Listing 2.16   *ShowCookies.java (continued)*

```java
    out.println(ServletUtilities.headWithTitle(title) +
                "<BODY BGCOLOR=\"#FDF5E6\">\n" +
                "<H1 ALIGN=\"CENTER\">" + title + "</H1>\n" +
                "<TABLE BORDER=1 ALIGN=\"CENTER\">\n" +
                "<TR BGCOLOR=\"#FFAD00\">\n" +
                "  <TH>Cookie Name\n" +
                "  <TH>Cookie Value");
    Cookie[] cookies = request.getCookies();
    if (cookies == null) {
      out.println("<TR><TH COLSPAN=2>No cookies");
    } else {
      Cookie cookie;
      for(int i=0; i<cookies.length; i++) {
        cookie = cookies[i];
        out.println("<TR>\n" +
                    "  <TD>" + cookie.getName() + "\n" +
                    "  <TD>" + cookie.getValue());
      }
    }
    out.println("</TABLE></BODY></HTML>");
  }
}
```

Figure 2–14   Result of visiting the ShowCookies servlet within an hour of visiting SetCookies (same browser session).

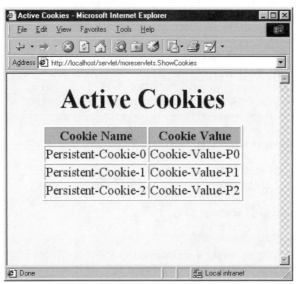

Figure 2–15   Result of visiting the ShowCookies servlet within an hour of visiting SetCookies (different browser session).

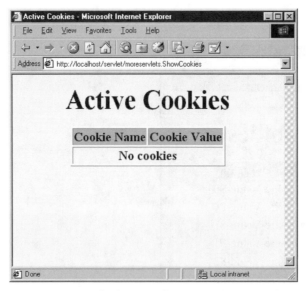

Figure 2–16   Result of visiting the ShowCookies servlet more than an hour after visiting SetCookies (different browser session).

Basic Cookie Utilities

This section presents some simple but useful utilities for dealing with cookies.

Finding Cookies with Specified Names

Listing 2.17 shows a section of *ServletUtilities.java* that simplifies the retrieval of a cookie or cookie value, given a cookie name. The getCookieValue method loops through the array of available Cookie objects, returning the value of any Cookie whose name matches the input. If there is no match, the designated default value is returned. So, for example, our typical approach for dealing with cookies is as follows:

```
Cookie[] cookies = request.getCookies();
String color =
  ServletUtilities.getCookieValue(cookies, "color", "black");
String font =
  ServletUtilities.getCookieValue(cookies, "font", "Arial");
```

The getCookie method also loops through the array comparing names but returns the actual Cookie object instead of just the value. That method is for cases when you want to do something with the Cookie other than just read its value.

Listing 2.17 *ServletUtilities.java*

```
package moreservlets;

import javax.servlet.*;
import javax.servlet.http.*;

public class ServletUtilities {
  // Other parts of ServletUtilities shown elsewhere.


  /** Given an array of Cookies, a name, and a default value,
   *  this method tries to find the value of the cookie with
   *  the given name. If there is no cookie matching the name
   *  in the array, then the default value is returned instead.
   */
```

Listing 2.17   *ServletUtilities.java (continued)*

```java
public static String getCookieValue(Cookie[] cookies,
                                    String cookieName,
                                    String defaultValue) {
  if (cookies != null) {
    for(int i=0; i<cookies.length; i++) {
      Cookie cookie = cookies[i];
      if (cookieName.equals(cookie.getName()))
        return(cookie.getValue());
    }
  }
  return(defaultValue);
}

/** Given an array of cookies and a name, this method tries
 *  to find and return the cookie from the array that has
 *  the given name. If there is no cookie matching the name
 *  in the array, null is returned.
 */

public static Cookie getCookie(Cookie[] cookies,
                               String cookieName) {
  if (cookies != null) {
    for(int i=0; i<cookies.length; i++) {
      Cookie cookie = cookies[i];
      if (cookieName.equals(cookie.getName()))
        return(cookie);
    }
  }
  return(null);
}
}
```

Creating Long-Lived Cookies

Listing 2.18 shows a small class that you can use instead of Cookie if you want your cookie to automatically persist for a year when the client quits the browser. For an example of the use of this class, see the customized search engine interface of Section 8.6 of *Core Servlets and JavaServer Pages* (available in PDF at *http://www.more-servlets.com*).

Listing 2.18 *LongLivedCookie.java*

```
package moreservlets;

import javax.servlet.http.*;

/** Cookie that persists 1 year. Default Cookie doesn't
 *  persist past current session.
 */

public class LongLivedCookie extends Cookie {
  public static final int SECONDS_PER_YEAR = 60*60*24*365;

  public LongLivedCookie(String name, String value) {
    super(name, value);
    setMaxAge(SECONDS_PER_YEAR);
  }
}
```

2.10 Session Tracking

This section briefly introduces the servlet session-tracking API, which keeps track of visitors as they move around at your site. For additional details and examples, see Chapter 9 of *Core Servlets and JavaServer Pages* (in PDF at *http://www.moreservlets.com*).

The Need for Session Tracking

HTTP is a "stateless" protocol: each time a client retrieves a Web page, it opens a separate connection to the Web server. The server does not automatically maintain contextual information about a client. Even with servers that support persistent (keep-alive) HTTP connections and keep a socket open for multiple client requests that occur close together in time, there is no built-in support for maintaining contextual information. This lack of context causes a number of difficulties. For example, when clients at an online store add an item to their shopping carts, how does the server know what's already in the carts? Similarly, when clients decide to proceed to checkout, how can the server determine which previously created shopping carts are theirs?

There are three typical solutions to this problem: cookies, URL rewriting, and hidden form fields. The following subsections quickly summarize what would be required if you had to implement session tracking yourself (without using the built-in session tracking API) each of the three ways.

Cookies

You can use HTTP cookies to store information about a shopping session, and each subsequent connection can look up the current session and then extract information about that session from some location on the server machine. For example, a servlet could do something like the following:

```
String sessionID = makeUniqueString();
Hashtable sessionInfo = new Hashtable();
Hashtable globalTable = findTableStoringSessions();
globalTable.put(sessionID, sessionInfo);
Cookie sessionCookie = new Cookie("JSESSIONID", sessionID);
sessionCookie.setPath("/");
response.addCookie(sessionCookie);
```

Then, in later requests the server could use the `globalTable` hash table to associate a session ID from the `JSESSIONID` cookie with the `sessionInfo` hash table of data associated with that particular session. This is an excellent solution and is the most widely used approach for session handling. Still, it is nice that servlets have a higher-level API that handles all this plus the following tedious tasks:

- Extracting the cookie that stores the session identifier from the other cookies (there may be many cookies, after all).
- Setting an appropriate expiration time for the cookie.
- Associating the hash tables with each request.
- Generating the unique session identifiers.

URL Rewriting

With this approach, the client appends some extra data on the end of each URL that identifies the session, and the server associates that identifier with data it has stored about that session. For example, with *http://host/path/file.html;jsessionid=1234*, the session information is attached as *jsessionid=1234*. This is also an excellent solution and even has the advantage that it works when browsers don't support cookies or when the user has disabled them. However, it has most of the same problems as cookies, namely, that the server-side program has a lot of straightforward but tedious processing to do. In addition, you have to be very careful that every URL that references your site and is returned to the user (even by indirect means like `Location` fields in server redirects) has the extra information appended. And, if the user leaves the session and comes back via a bookmark or link, the session information can be lost.

Hidden Form Fields

HTML forms can have an entry that looks like the following:

```
<INPUT TYPE="HIDDEN" NAME="session" VALUE="...">
```

This entry means that, when the form is submitted, the specified name and value are included in the GET or POST data. This hidden field can be used to store information about the session but has the major disadvantage that it only works if every page is dynamically generated by a form submission. Thus, hidden form fields cannot support general session tracking, only tracking within a specific series of operations.

Session Tracking in Servlets

Servlets provide an outstanding technical solution: the HttpSession API. This high-level interface is built on top of cookies or URL rewriting. All servers are required to support session tracking with cookies, and many have a setting that lets you globally switch to URL rewriting. In fact, some servers use cookies if the browser supports them but automatically revert to URL rewriting when cookies are unsupported or explicitly disabled.

Either way, the servlet author doesn't need to bother with many of the details, doesn't have to explicitly manipulate cookies or information appended to the URL, and is automatically given a convenient place to store arbitrary objects that are associated with each session.

The Session-Tracking API

Using sessions in servlets is straightforward and involves looking up the session object associated with the current request, creating a new session object when necessary, looking up information associated with a session, storing information in a session, and discarding completed or abandoned sessions. Finally, if you return any URLs to the clients that reference your site and URL rewriting is being used, you need to attach the session information to the URLs.

Looking Up the HttpSession Object Associated with the Current Request

You look up the HttpSession object by calling the getSession method of HttpServletRequest. Behind the scenes, the system extracts a user ID from a cookie or attached URL data, then uses that as a key into a table of previously created HttpSession objects. But this is all done transparently to the programmer: you just call getSession. If getSession returns null, this means that the user is not already participating in a session, so you can create a new session. Creating a new session in this case is so commonly done that there is an option to automatically create a new session if one doesn't already exist. Just pass `true` to `getSession`. Thus, your first step usually looks like this:

```
HttpSession session = request.getSession(true);
```

If you care whether the session existed previously or is newly created, you can use `isNew` to check.

Looking Up Information Associated with a Session

`HttpSession` objects live on the server; they're just automatically associated with the client by a behind-the-scenes mechanism like cookies or URL rewriting. These session objects have a built-in data structure that lets you store any number of keys and associated values. In version 2.1 and earlier of the servlet API, you use `session.getValue("attribute")` to look up a previously stored value. The return type is `Object`, so you have to do a typecast to whatever more specific type of data was associated with that attribute name in the session. The return value is `null` if there is no such attribute, so you need to check for `null` before calling methods on objects associated with sessions.

In versions 2.2 and 2.3 of the servlet API, `getValue` is deprecated in favor of `getAttribute` because of the better naming match with `setAttribute` (in version 2.1, the match for `getValue` is `putValue`, not `setValue`).

Here's a representative example, assuming `ShoppingCart` is some class you've defined to store information on items being purchased.

```
HttpSession session = request.getSession(true);
ShoppingCart cart =
  (ShoppingCart)session.getAttribute("shoppingCart");
if (cart == null) { // No cart already in session
  cart = new ShoppingCart();
  session.setAttribute("shoppingCart", cart);
}
doSomethingWith(cart);
```

In most cases, you have a specific attribute name in mind and want to find the value (if any) already associated with that name. However, you can also discover all the attribute names in a given session by calling `getValueNames`, which returns an array of strings. This method was your only option for finding attribute names in version 2.1, but in servlet engines supporting versions 2.2 and 2.3 of the servlet specification, you can use `getAttributeNames`. That method is more consistent in that it returns an `Enumeration`, just like the `getHeaderNames` and `getParameterNames` methods of `HttpServletRequest`.

Although the data that was explicitly associated with a session is the part you care most about, some other pieces of information are sometimes useful as well. Here is a summary of the methods available in the `HttpSession` class.

public Object getAttribute(String name)
public Object getValue(String name) [deprecated]

These methods extract a previously stored value from a session object. They return `null` if no value is associated with the given name. Use `getValue` only if you need to support servers that run version 2.1 of the servlet API. Versions 2.2 and 2.3 support both methods, but `getAttribute` is preferred and `getValue` is deprecated.

public void setAttribute(String name, Object value)
public void putValue(String name, Object value) [deprecated]

These methods associate a value with a name. Use `putValue` only if you need to support servers that run version 2.1 of the servlet API. If the object supplied to `setAttribute` or `putValue` implements the `HttpSession-BindingListener` interface, the object's `valueBound` method is called after it is stored in the session. Similarly, if the previous value implements `HttpSessionBindingListener`, its `valueUnbound` method is called.

public void removeAttribute(String name)
public void removeValue(String name) [deprecated]

These methods remove any values associated with the designated name. If the value being removed implements `HttpSessionBindingListener`, its `valueUnbound` method is called. Use `removeValue` only if you need to support servers that run version 2.1 of the servlet API. In versions 2.2 and 2.3, `removeAttribute` is preferred, but `removeValue` is still supported (albeit deprecated) for backward compatibility.

public Enumeration getAttributeNames()
public String[] getValueNames() [deprecated]

These methods return the names of all attributes in the session. Use `get-ValueNames` only if you need to support servers that run version 2.1 of the servlet API.

public String getId()

This method returns the unique identifier generated for each session. It is useful for debugging or logging.

public boolean isNew()

This method returns `true` if the client (browser) has never seen the session, usually because it was just created rather than being referenced by an incoming client request. It returns `false` for preexisting sessions.

public long getCreationTime()

This method returns the time in milliseconds since midnight, January 1, 1970 (GMT) at which the session was first built. To get a value useful for printing, pass the value to the `Date` constructor or the `setTimeInMillis` method of `GregorianCalendar`.

public long getLastAccessedTime()

This method returns the time in milliseconds since midnight, January 1, 1970 (GMT) at which the session was last sent from the client.

public int getMaxInactiveInterval()
public void setMaxInactiveInterval(int seconds)

These methods get or set the amount of time, in seconds, that a session should go without access before being automatically invalidated. A negative value indicates that the session should never time out. Note that the timeout is maintained on the server and is *not* the same as the cookie expiration date, which is sent to the client. See Section 5.10 (Controlling Session Timeouts) for instructions on changing the default session timeout interval.

public void invalidate()

This method invalidates the session and unbinds all objects associated with it. Use this method with caution; remember that sessions are associated with users (i.e., clients), not with individual servlets or JSP pages. So, if you invalidate a session, you might be destroying data that another servlet or JSP page is using.

Associating Information with a Session

As discussed in the previous section, you *read* information associated with a session by using `getAttribute`. To *specify* information, use `setAttribute`. To let your values perform side effects when they are stored in a session, simply have the object you are associating with the session implement the `HttpSessionBinding-Listener` interface. That way, every time `setAttribute` (or `putValue`) is called on one of those objects, its `valueBound` method is called immediately afterward.

Be aware that `setAttribute` replaces any previous values; if you want to remove a value without supplying a replacement, use `removeAttribute`. This method triggers the `valueUnbound` method of any values that implement `HttpSessionBindingListener`.

Following is an example of adding information to a session. You can add information in two ways: by adding a new session attribute (as with the first bold line in the example) or by augmenting an object that is already in the session (as in the last line of the example).

```
HttpSession session = request.getSession(true);
ShoppingCart cart =
  (ShoppingCart)session.getAttribute("shoppingCart");
if (cart == null) { // No cart already in session
  cart = new ShoppingCart();
  session.setAttribute("shoppingCart", cart);
}
addSomethingTo(cart);
```

Terminating Sessions

Sessions automatically become inactive when the amount of time between client accesses exceeds the interval specified by `getMaxInactiveInterval`. When this happens, any objects bound to the `HttpSession` object automatically get unbound. Then, your attached objects are automatically notified if they implement the `HttpSessionBindingListener` interface.

Rather than waiting for sessions to time out, you can explicitly deactivate a session with the session's `invalidate` method.

Encoding URLs Sent to the Client

If you are using URL rewriting for session tracking and you send a URL that references your site to the client, you need to explicitly add the session data. There are two possible places where you might use URLs that refer to your own site.

The first is where the URLs are embedded in the Web page that the servlet generates. These URLs should be passed through the `encodeURL` method of `HttpServletResponse`. The method determines if URL rewriting is currently in use and appends the session information only if necessary. The URL is returned unchanged otherwise.

Here's an example:

```
String originalURL = someRelativeOrAbsoluteURL;
String encodedURL = response.encodeURL(originalURL);
out.println("<A HREF=\"" + encodedURL + "\">...</A>");
```

The second place you might use a URL that refers to your own site is in a send-Redirect call (i.e., placed into the Location response header). In this second situation, different rules determine whether session information needs to be attached, so you cannot use encodeURL. Fortunately, HttpServletResponse supplies an encodeRedirectURL method to handle that case. Here's an example:

```
String originalURL = someURL;
String encodedURL = response.encodeRedirectURL(originalURL);
response.sendRedirect(encodedURL);
```

Since you often don't know if your servlet will later become part of a series of pages that use session tracking, it is good practice to plan ahead and encode URLs that reference your own site.

A Servlet Showing Per-Client Access Counts

Listing 2.19 presents a simple servlet that shows basic information about the client's session. When the client connects, the servlet uses request.getSession(true) either to retrieve the existing session or, if there was no session, to create a new one. The servlet then looks for an attribute of type Integer called accessCount. If it cannot find such an attribute, it uses 0 as the number of previous accesses. This value is then incremented and associated with the session by setAttribute. Finally, the servlet prints a small HTML table showing information about the session. Figures 2–17 and 2–18 show the servlet on the initial visit and after the page was reloaded several times.

Listing 2.19	*ShowSession.java*

```java
package moreservlets;

import java.io.*;
import javax.servlet.*;
import javax.servlet.http.*;
import java.net.*;
import java.util.*;

/** Simple example of session tracking. */

public class ShowSession extends HttpServlet {
  public void doGet(HttpServletRequest request,
                    HttpServletResponse response)
      throws ServletException, IOException {
    response.setContentType("text/html");
    PrintWriter out = response.getWriter();
```

Listing 2.19 *ShowSession.java (continued)*

```java
String title = "Session Tracking Example";
HttpSession session = request.getSession(true);
String heading;
Integer accessCount =
  (Integer)session.getAttribute("accessCount");
if (accessCount == null) {
  accessCount = new Integer(0);
  heading = "Welcome, Newcomer";
} else {
  heading = "Welcome Back";
  accessCount = new Integer(accessCount.intValue() + 1);
}
session.setAttribute("accessCount", accessCount);
out.println(ServletUtilities.headWithTitle(title) +
            "<BODY BGCOLOR=\"#FDF5E6\">\n" +
            "<H1 ALIGN=\"CENTER\">" + heading + "</H1>\n" +
            "<H2>Information on Your Session:</H2>\n" +
            "<TABLE BORDER=1 ALIGN=\"CENTER\">\n" +
            "<TR BGCOLOR=\"#FFAD00\">\n" +
            "  <TH>Info Type<TH>Value\n" +
            "<TR>\n" +
            "  <TD>ID\n" +
            "  <TD>" + session.getId() + "\n" +
            "<TR>\n" +
            "  <TD>Creation Time\n" +
            "  <TD>" +
            new Date(session.getCreationTime()) + "\n" +
            "<TR>\n" +
            "  <TD>Time of Last Access\n" +
            "  <TD>" +
            new Date(session.getLastAccessedTime()) + "\n" +
            "<TR>\n" +
            "  <TD>Number of Previous Accesses\n" +
            "  <TD>" + accessCount + "\n" +
            "</TABLE>\n" +
            "</BODY></HTML>");

}

/** Handle GET and POST requests identically. */

public void doPost(HttpServletRequest request,
                   HttpServletResponse response)
    throws ServletException, IOException {
  doGet(request, response);
}
}
```

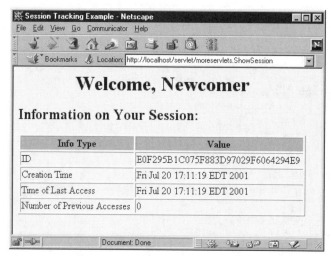

Figure 2–17 First visit by client to ShowSession servlet.

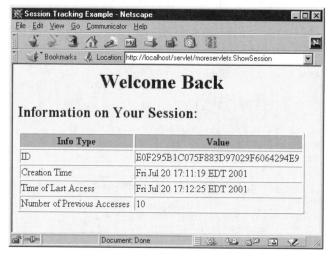

Figure 2–18 Eleventh visit to ShowSession servlet. Access count is independent of number of visits by other clients.

A Simplified Shopping Cart Application

Core Servlets and JavaServer Pages (available in PDF at *http://www.moreservlets.com*) presents a full-fledged shopping cart example. Most of the code in that example is for automatically building the Web pages that display the items and for the shopping cart itself. Although these application-specific pieces can be somewhat complicated, the basic session tracking is quite simple. This section illustrates the fundamental approach to session tracking, but without a full-featured shopping cart.

Listing 2.20 shows an application that uses a simple ArrayList (the Java 2 platform's replacement for Vector) to keep track of all the items each user has previously purchased. In addition to finding or creating the session and inserting the newly purchased item (the value of the newItem request parameter) into it, this example outputs a bulleted list of whatever items are in the "cart" (i.e., the ArrayList). Notice that the code that outputs this list is synchronized on the ArrayList. This precaution is worth taking, but you should be aware that the circumstances that make synchronization necessary are exceedingly rare. Since each user has a separate session, the only way a race condition could occur is if the same user submits two purchases very close together in time. Although unlikely, this *is* possible, so synchronization is worthwhile.

Listing 2.20   *ShowItems.java*

```java
package moreservlets;

import java.io.*;
import javax.servlet.*;
import javax.servlet.http.*;
import java.util.ArrayList;
import moreservlets.*;

/** Servlet that displays a list of items being ordered.
 *  Accumulates them in an ArrayList with no attempt at
 *  detecting repeated items. Used to demonstrate basic
 *  session tracking.
 */

public class ShowItems extends HttpServlet {
  public void doGet(HttpServletRequest request,
                    HttpServletResponse response)
      throws ServletException, IOException {
    HttpSession session = request.getSession(true);
    ArrayList previousItems =
      (ArrayList)session.getAttribute("previousItems");
    if (previousItems == null) {
      previousItems = new ArrayList();
      session.setAttribute("previousItems", previousItems);
    }
    String newItem = request.getParameter("newItem");
    response.setContentType("text/html");
    PrintWriter out = response.getWriter();
    String title = "Items Purchased";
```

Listing 2.20 *ShowItems.java (continued)*

```
    out.println(ServletUtilities.headWithTitle(title) +
                "<BODY BGCOLOR=\"#FDF5E6\">\n" +
                "<H1>" + title + "</H1>");
    synchronized(previousItems) {
      if (newItem != null) {
        previousItems.add(newItem);
      }
      if (previousItems.size() == 0) {
        out.println("<I>No items</I>");
      } else {
        out.println("<UL>");
        for(int i=0; i<previousItems.size(); i++) {
          out.println("<LI>" + (String)previousItems.get(i));
        }
        out.println("</UL>");
      }
    }
    out.println("</BODY></HTML>");
  }
}
```

Listing 2.21 shows an HTML form that collects values of the `newItem` parameter and submits them to the servlet. Figure 2–19 shows the result of the form; Figures 2–20 and 2–21 show the results of the servlet before visiting the order form and after visiting the order form several times, respectively.

Listing 2.21 *OrderForm.html*

```
<!DOCTYPE HTML PUBLIC "-//W3C//DTD HTML 4.0 Transitional//EN">
<HTML>
<HEAD>
  <TITLE>Order Form</TITLE>
</HEAD>
<BODY BGCOLOR="#FDF5E6">
<H1 ALIGN="CENTER">Order Form</H1>
<FORM ACTION="/servlet/moreservlets.ShowItems">
  New Item to Order:
  <INPUT TYPE="TEXT" NAME="newItem" VALUE="yacht"><BR>
  <CENTER>
    <INPUT TYPE="SUBMIT" VALUE="Order and Show All Purchases">
  </CENTER>
</FORM>
</BODY>
</HTML>
```

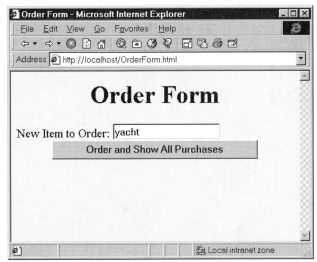

Figure 2–19   Front end to the item display servlet.

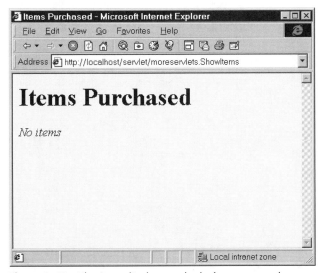

Figure 2–20   The item display servlet before any purchases are made.

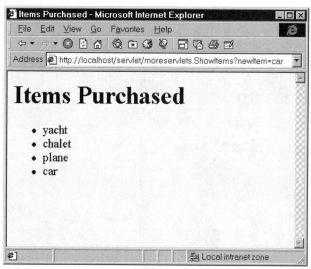

Figure 2–21   The item display servlet after a few small purchases are made.

A FAST
INTRODUCTION TO
BASIC JSP
PROGRAMMING

Topics in This Chapter

- Understanding the benefits of JSP

- Invoking Java code with JSP expressions, scriptlets, and declarations

- Structuring the servlet that results from a JSP page

- Including files and applets in JSP documents

- Using JavaBeans with JSP

- Creating custom JSP tag libraries

- Combining servlets and JSP: the Model View Controller (Model 2) architecture

Chapter 3

JavaServer Pages (JSP) technology enables you to mix regular, static HTML with dynamically generated content. You simply write the regular HTML in the normal manner, using familiar Web-page-building tools. You then enclose the code for the dynamic parts in special tags, most of which start with <% and end with %>. For example, here is a section of a JSP page that results in "Thanks for ordering *Core Web Programming*" for a URL of *http://host/OrderConfirmation.jsp?title= Core+Web+Programming*:

```
Thanks for ordering <I><%= request.getParameter("title") %></I>
```

Separating the static HTML from the dynamic content provides a number of benefits over servlets alone, and the approach used in JavaServer Pages offers several advantages over competing technologies such as ASP, PHP, or ColdFusion. Section 3.2 gives some details on these advantages, but they basically boil down to two facts: JSP is widely supported and thus doesn't lock you into a particular operating system or Web server; and JSP gives you full access to the Java programming language and Java servlet technology for the dynamic part, rather than requiring you to use an unfamiliar and weaker special-purpose language.

3.1   JSP Overview

The process of making JavaServer Pages accessible on the Web is much simpler than that for servlets. Assuming you have a Web server that supports JSP, you give your file a *.jsp* extension and simply place it in any of the designated JSP locations (which, on many servers, is any place you could put a normal Web page): no compiling, no packages, and no user CLASSPATH settings. However, although your *personal* environment doesn't need any special settings, the *server* still has to be set up with access to the servlet and JSP class files and the Java compiler. For details, see Chapter 1 (Server Setup and Configuration).

Although what you write often looks more like a regular HTML file than like a servlet, behind the scenes the JSP page is automatically converted to a normal servlet, with the static HTML simply being printed to the output stream associated with the servlet. This translation is normally done the first time the page is requested. To ensure that the first real user doesn't experience a momentary delay when the JSP page is translated into a servlet and compiled, developers can simply request the page themselves after first installing it. Alternatively, if you deliver your applications on the same server you develop them on, you can deliver the precompiled servlet class files in their server-specific directories (see example locations on page 128). You can even omit the JSP source code in such a case.

One warning about the automatic translation process is in order. If you make an error in the dynamic portion of your JSP page, the system may not be able to properly translate it into a servlet. If your page has such a fatal translation-time error, the server will present an HTML error page describing the problem to the client. Internet Explorer 5, however, typically replaces server-generated error messages with a canned page that it considers friendlier. You will need to turn off this "feature" when debugging JSP pages. To do so with Internet Explorer 5, go to the Tools menu, select Internet Options, choose the Advanced tab, and make sure the "Show friendly HTTP error messages" box is not checked.

Core Approach

When debugging JSP pages, be sure to turn off Internet Explorer's "friendly" HTTP error messages.

Aside from the regular HTML, there are three main types of JSP constructs that you embed in a page: *scripting elements*, *directives*, and *actions*. Scripting elements let you specify Java code that will become part of the resultant servlet, directives let you control the overall structure of the servlet, and actions let you specify existing components that should be used and otherwise control the behavior of the JSP engine. To simplify the scripting elements, you have access to a number of pre-defined variables, such as `request` in the code snippet just shown.

This book covers versions 1.1 and 1.2 of the JavaServer Pages specification. Basic JSP constructs are backward-compatible with JSP 1.0, but custom tags, Web applications, and use of the deployment descriptor (*web.xml*) are specific to JSP 1.1 and later. Furthermore, JSP 1.1 did not mandate the use of Java 2; JSP 1.2 does. Consequently, if you use constructs specific to Java 2 (e.g., collections), your JSP 1.2 code will not run on JSP 1.1-compatible servers that are running on top of JDK 1.1. Finally, note that all JSP 1.x versions are completely incompatible with the long-obsolete JSP 0.92. If JSP 0.92 was your only exposure to JSP, you have a pleasant surprise in store; JSP technology has been totally revamped (and improved) since then.

3.2 Advantages of JSP

JSP has a number of advantages over many of its alternatives. Here are a few of them.

Versus Active Server Pages (ASP) or ColdFusion

ASP is a competing technology from Microsoft. The advantages of JSP are twofold.

First, the dynamic part is written in Java, not VBScript or another ASP-specific language, so JSP is more powerful and better suited to complex applications that require reusable components.

Second, JSP is portable to other operating systems and Web servers; you aren't locked into Windows and IIS. Even if ASP.NET (not yet available as of fall 2001) succeeds in addressing the problem of developing server-side code with VBScript, you cannot expect to use ASP on multiple servers and operating systems.

You could make the same argument when comparing JSP to the current version of ColdFusion; with JSP you can use Java for the "real code" and are not tied to a particular server product. Note, however, that the next release of ColdFusion (version 5.0) will be within the context of a J2EE server, allowing developers to easily mix Cold-Fusion and servlet/JSP code.

Versus PHP

PHP (a recursive acronym for "PHP: Hypertext Preprocessor") is a free, open-source, HTML-embedded scripting language that is somewhat similar to both ASP and JSP. One advantage of JSP is that the dynamic part is written in Java, which already has an extensive API for networking, database access, distributed objects, and the like, whereas PHP requires learning an entirely new, less widely used language. A second advantage is that JSP is much more widely supported by tool and server vendors than is PHP.

Versus Pure Servlets

JSP doesn't provide any capabilities that couldn't, in principle, be accomplished with a servlet. In fact, JSP documents are automatically translated into servlets behind the scenes. But it is more convenient to write (and to modify!) regular HTML than to have a zillion `println` statements that generate the HTML. Plus, by separating the presentation from the content, you can put different people on different tasks: your Web page design experts can build the HTML by using familiar tools and either leave places for your servlet programmers to insert the dynamic content or invoke the dynamic content indirectly by means of XML tags.

Does this mean that you can just learn JSP and forget about servlets? By no means! JSP developers need to know servlets for four reasons:

1. JSP pages get translated into servlets. You can't understand how JSP works without understanding servlets.

2. JSP consists of static HTML, special-purpose JSP tags, and Java code. What kind of Java code? Servlet code! You can't write that code if you don't understand servlet programming.

3. Some tasks are better accomplished by servlets than by JSP. JSP is good at generating pages that consist of large sections of fairly well structured HTML or other character data. Servlets are better for generating binary data, building pages with highly variable structure, and performing tasks (such as redirection) that involve little or no output.

4. Some tasks are better accomplished by a *combination* of servlets and JSP than by *either* servlets or JSP alone. See Section 3.8 (Integrating Servlets and JSP: The MVC Architecture) for details.

Versus JavaScript

JavaScript, which is completely distinct from the Java programming language, is normally used to generate HTML dynamically on the *client*, building parts of the Web page as the browser loads the document. This is a useful capability and does not normally overlap with the capabilities of JSP (which runs only on the *server*). JSP pages still include `SCRIPT` tags for JavaScript, just as normal HTML pages do. In fact, JSP can even be used to dynamically generate the JavaScript that will be sent to the client.

It is also possible to use JavaScript on the server, most notably on Netscape, IIS, and BroadVision servers. However, Java is more powerful, flexible, reliable, and portable.

3.3   Invoking Code with JSP Scripting Elements

There are a number of different ways to generate dynamic content from JSP, as illustrated in Figure 3–1. Each of these approaches has a legitimate place; the size and complexity of the project is the most important factor in deciding which approach is appropriate. However, be aware that people err on the side of placing too much code directly in the page much more often than they err on the opposite end of the spectrum. Although putting small amounts of Java code directly in JSP pages works fine for simple applications, using long and complicated blocks of Java code in JSP pages yields a result that is hard to maintain, hard to debug, and hard to divide among different members of the development team. Nevertheless, many pages are quite simple, and the first two approaches of Figure 3–1 (placing explicit Java code directly in the page) work quite well. This section discusses those approaches.

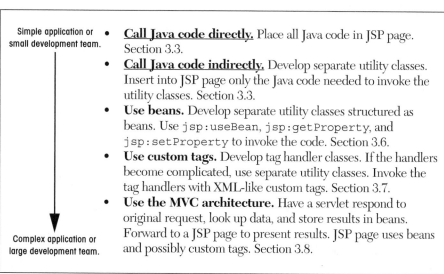

Simple application or small development team.

- **Call Java code directly.** Place all Java code in JSP page. Section 3.3.
- **Call Java code indirectly.** Develop separate utility classes. Insert into JSP page only the Java code needed to invoke the utility classes. Section 3.3.
- **Use beans.** Develop separate utility classes structured as beans. Use `jsp:useBean`, `jsp:getProperty`, and `jsp:setProperty` to invoke the code. Section 3.6.
- **Use custom tags.** Develop tag handler classes. If the handlers become complicated, use separate utility classes. Invoke the tag handlers with XML-like custom tags. Section 3.7.
- **Use the MVC architecture.** Have a servlet respond to original request, look up data, and store results in beans. Forward to a JSP page to present results. JSP page uses beans and possibly custom tags. Section 3.8.

Complex application or large development team.

Figure 3–1   Strategies for invoking dynamic code from JSP.

JSP scripting elements let you insert code into the servlet that will be generated from the JSP page. There are three forms:

1. *Expressions* of the form `<%= Expression %>`, which are evaluated and inserted into the servlet's output.
2. *Scriptlets* of the form `<% Code %>`, which are inserted into the servlet's `_jspService` method (called by `service`).
3. *Declarations* of the form `<%! Code %>`, which are inserted into the body of the servlet class, outside of any existing methods.

Each of these scripting elements is described in more detail in the following sections.

In many cases, a large percentage of your JSP page just consists of static HTML, known as *template text*. In almost all respects, this HTML looks just like normal HTML, follows all the same syntax rules, and is simply "passed through" to the client by the servlet created to handle the page. Not only does the HTML look normal, it can be created by whatever tools you already are using for building Web pages. For example, I used Macromedia's HomeSite for most of the JSP pages in this book.

There are two minor exceptions to the "template text is passed straight through" rule. First, if you want to have `<%` in the output, you need to put `<\%` in the template text. Second, if you want a comment to appear in the JSP page but not in the resultant document, use

```
<%-- JSP Comment --%>
```

HTML comments of the form

```
<!-- HTML Comment -->
```

are passed through to the resultant HTML normally.

Expressions

A JSP expression is used to insert values directly into the output. It has the following form:

```
<%= Java Expression %>
```

The expression is evaluated, converted to a string, and inserted in the page. That is, this evaluation is performed at run time (when the page is requested) and thus has full access to information about the request. For example, the following shows the date/time that the page was requested.

```
Current time: <%= new java.util.Date() %>
```

Predefined Variables

To simplify these expressions, you can use a number of predefined variables (or "implicit objects"). There is nothing magic about these variables; the system simply tells you what names it will use for the local variables in _jspService. These implicit objects are discussed in more detail later in this section, but for the purpose of expressions, the most important ones are:

- **request**, the HttpServletRequest
- **response**, the HttpServletResponse
- **session**, the HttpSession associated with the request (unless disabled with the session attribute of the page directive—see Section 3.4)
- **out**, the Writer (a buffered version called JspWriter) used to send output to the client

Here is an example:

```
Your hostname: <%= request.getRemoteHost() %>
```

JSP/Servlet Correspondence

Now, I just stated that a JSP expression is evaluated and inserted into the page output. Although this is true, it is sometimes helpful to understand in a bit more detail what is going on.

It is actually pretty simple: JSP expressions basically become print (or write) statements in the servlet that results from the JSP page. Whereas regular HTML becomes print statements with double quotes around the text, JSP expressions become print statements with no double quotes. Instead of being placed in the doGet method, these print statements are placed in a new method called _jspService that is called by service for both GET and POST requests. For instance, Listing 3.1 shows a small JSP sample that includes some static HTML and a JSP expression. Listing 3.2 shows a _jspService method that might result. Of course, different vendors will produce code in slightly different ways, and optimizations such as reading the HTML from a static byte array are quite common.

Also, I oversimplified the definition of the out variable; out in a JSP page is a JspWriter, so you have to modify the slightly simpler PrintWriter that directly results from a call to getWriter. So, don't expect the code your server generates to look *exactly* like this.

Listing 3.1	Sample JSP Expression: Random Number

```
<H1>A Random Number</H1>
<%= Math.random() %>
```

Listing 3.2	Representative Resulting Servlet Code: Random Number

```
public void _jspService(HttpServletRequest request,
                        HttpServletResponse response)
    throws ServletException, IOException {
  response.setContentType("text/html");
  HttpSession session = request.getSession(true);
  JspWriter out = response.getWriter(); // Oversimplified a bit
  out.println("<H1>A Random Number</H1>");
  out.println(Math.random());
    ...
}
```

If you want to see the exact code that your server generates, you'll have to dig around a bit to find it. In fact, some servers delete the source code files once they are successfully compiled. But here is a summary of the locations used by three common, free development servers.

Tomcat 4.0 Autogenerated Servlet Source Code
install_dir/work/localhost/_
(The final directory is an underscore.)

JRun 3.1 Autogenerated Servlet Source Code
install_dir/servers/default/default-app/WEB-INF/jsp
(More generally, in the *WEB-INF/jsp* directory of the Web application to which the JSP page belongs.)

ServletExec 4.0 Autogenerated Servlet Source Code
install_dir/Servlets/pagecompile
(More generally, in *install_dir/ServletExec Data/virtual-server-name/ web-app-name/pagecompile*.)

XML Syntax for Expressions

On some servers, XML authors can use the following alternative syntax for JSP expressions:

```
<jsp:expression>Java Expression</jsp:expression>
```

However, in JSP 1.1 and earlier, servers are not required to support this alternative syntax, and in practice few do. In JSP 1.2, servers are required to support this syntax as long as authors don't mix the XML version (`<jsp:expression>` ... `</jsp:expression>`) and the standard JSP version that follows ASP syntax

(`<%= ... %>`) in the same page. Note that XML elements, unlike HTML ones, are case sensitive, so be sure to use `jsp:expression` in lower case.

Installing JSP Pages

Servlets require you to set your CLASSPATH, use packages to avoid name conflicts, install the class files in servlet-specific locations, and use special-purpose URLs. Not so with JSP pages. JSP pages can be placed in the same directories as normal HTML pages, images, and style sheets; they can also be accessed through URLs of the same form as those for HTML pages, images, and style sheets. Here are a few examples of default installation locations (i.e., locations that apply when you aren't using custom Web applications) and associated URLs. Where I list *SomeDirectory*, you can use any directory name you like. (But you are never allowed to use *WEB-INF* or *META-INF* as directory names. For the default Web application, you also have to avoid a directory name that matches the URL prefix of any other Web application. For information on defining your own Web application, see Chapter 4, "Using and Deploying Web Applications.")

- **Tomcat Directory**
  install_dir/webapps/ROOT
  (or *install_dir/webapps/ROOT/SomeDirectory*)
- **JRun Directory**
  install_dir/servers/default/default-app
  (or *install_dir/servers/default/default-app/SomeDirectory*)
- **ServletExec Directory**
  install_dir/public_html
  (or *install_dir/public_html/SomeDirectory*)
- **Corresponding URLs**
  http://host/Hello.html
  (or *http://host/SomeDirectory/Hello.html*)
  http://host/Hello.jsp
  (or *http://host/SomeDirectory/Hello.jsp*)

Note that, although JSP pages *themselves* need no special installation directories, any Java classes called *from* JSP pages still need to go in the standard locations used by servlet classes (e.g., *.../WEB-INF/classes*; see Sections 1.7 and 1.9).

Example: JSP Expressions

Listing 3.3 gives an example JSP page called *Expressions.jsp*. I placed the file in a subdirectory called *jsp-intro*, copied the entire directory from my development directory to the deployment location just discussed, and used a base URL of *http://host/jsp-intro/Expressions.jsp*. Figures 3–2 and 3–3 show some typical results.

Notice that I included META tags and a style sheet link in the HEAD section of the JSP page. It is good practice to include these elements, but there are two reasons why they are often omitted from pages generated by normal servlets.

First, with servlets, it is tedious to generate the required println statements. With JSP, however, the format is simpler and you can make use of the code reuse options in your usual HTML building tools.

Second, servlets cannot use the simplest form of relative URLs (ones that refer to files in the same directory as the current page) since the servlet directories are not mapped to URLs in the same manner as are URLs for normal Web pages. JSP pages, on the other hand, are installed in the normal Web page hierarchy on the server, and relative URLs are resolved properly as long as the JSP page is accessed directly by the client, rather than indirectly by means of a RequestDispatcher. Even then, there are some techniques you can use to simplify the use of relative URLs. For details, see Section 4.5 (Handling Relative URLs in Web Applications).

Thus, in most cases style sheets and JSP pages can be kept together in the same directory. The source code for the style sheet, like all code shown or referenced in the book, can be found at *http://www.moreservlets.com*.

Listing 3.3   *Expressions.jsp*

```
<!DOCTYPE HTML PUBLIC "-//W3C//DTD HTML 4.0 Transitional//EN">
<HTML>
<HEAD>
<TITLE>JSP Expressions</TITLE>
<META NAME="keywords"
      CONTENT="JSP,expressions,JavaServer Pages,servlets">
<META NAME="description"
      CONTENT="A quick example of JSP expressions.">
<LINK REL=STYLESHEET
      HREF="JSP-Styles.css"
      TYPE="text/css">
</HEAD>

<BODY>
<H2>JSP Expressions</H2>
<UL>
  <LI>Current time: <%= new java.util.Date() %>
  <LI>Server: <%= application.getServerInfo() %>
  <LI>Session ID: <%= session.getId() %>
  <LI>The <CODE>testParam</CODE> form parameter:
      <%= request.getParameter("testParam") %>
</UL>
</BODY>
</HTML>
```

Figure 3–2   Result of *Expressions.jsp* using JRun 3.1 and omitting the `testParam` request parameter.

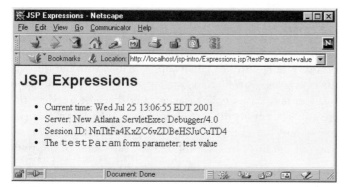

Figure 3–3   Result of *Expressions.jsp* using ServletExec 4.0 and specifying `test+value` as the value of the `testParam` request parameter.

Scriptlets

If you want to do something more complex than output a simple expression, JSP scriptlets let you insert arbitrary code into the servlet's `_jspService` method (which is called by `service`). Scriptlets have the following form:

```
<% Java Code %>
```

Scriptlets have access to the same automatically defined variables as do expressions (`request`, `response`, `session`, `out`, etc.). So, for example, if you want to explicitly send output to the resultant page, you could use the `out` variable, as in the following example.

```
<%
String queryData = request.getQueryString();
out.println("Attached GET data: " + queryData);
%>
```

In this particular instance, you could have accomplished the same effect more easily by using the following JSP expression:

```
Attached GET data: <%= request.getQueryString() %>
```

In general, however, scriptlets can perform a number of tasks that cannot be accomplished with expressions alone. These tasks include setting response headers and status codes, invoking side effects such as writing to the server log or updating a database, or executing code that contains loops, conditionals, or other complex constructs. For instance, the following snippet specifies that the current page is sent to the client as plain text, not as HTML (which is the default).

```
<% response.setContentType("text/plain"); %>
```

It is important to note that you can set response headers or status codes at various places within a JSP page, even though this capability appears to violate the rule that this type of response data needs to be specified before any document content is sent to the client. Setting headers and status codes is permitted because servlets that result from JSP pages use a special variety of `Writer` (of type `JspWriter`) that partially buffers the document. This buffering behavior can be changed, however; see Section 3.4 for a discussion of the `buffer` and `autoflush` attributes of the `page` directive.

JSP/Servlet Correspondence

It is easy to understand how JSP scriptlets correspond to servlet code: the scriptlet code is just directly inserted into the `_jspService` method: no strings, no `print` statements, no changes whatsoever. For instance, Listing 3.4 shows a small JSP sample that includes some static HTML, a JSP expression, and a JSP scriptlet. Listing 3.5 shows a `_jspService` method that might result. Again, different vendors will produce this code in slightly different ways, and I oversimplified the `out` variable (which is a `JspWriter`, not the slightly simpler `PrintWriter` that results from a call to `getWriter`). So, don't expect the code your server generates to look *exactly* like this.

Listing 3.4	Sample JSP Expression/Scriptlet

```
<H2>foo</H2>
<%= bar() %>
<% baz(); %>
```

Listing 3.5 Representative Resulting Servlet Code: Expression/Scriptlet

```
public void _jspService(HttpServletRequest request,
                        HttpServletResponse response)
    throws ServletException, IOException {
  response.setContentType("text/html");
  HttpSession session = request.getSession(true);
  JspWriter out = response.getWriter();
  out.println("<H2>foo</H2>");
  out.println(bar());
  baz();
  ...
}
```

Scriptlet Example

As an example of code that is too complex for a JSP expression alone, Listing 3.6 presents a JSP page that uses the `bgColor` request parameter to set the background color of the page. *JSP-Styles.css* is omitted so that the style sheet does not override the background color. Figures 3–4, 3–5, and 3–6 show the default result, the result for a background of `C0C0C0`, and the result for `papayawhip` (one of the oddball X11 color names still supported for historical reasons), respectively.

Listing 3.6 *BGColor.jsp*

```
<!DOCTYPE HTML PUBLIC "-//W3C//DTD HTML 4.0 Transitional//EN">
<HTML>
<HEAD>
  <TITLE>Color Testing</TITLE>
</HEAD>
<%
String bgColor = request.getParameter("bgColor");
if (bgColor == null) { bgColor = "WHITE"; }
%>
<BODY BGCOLOR="<%= bgColor %>">
<H2 ALIGN="CENTER">Testing a Background of "<%= bgColor %>"</H2>
</BODY>
</HTML>
```

Figure 3–4   Default result of *BGColor.jsp*.

Figure 3–5   Result of *BGColor.jsp* when accessed with a `bgColor` parameter having the RGB value `C0C0C0`.

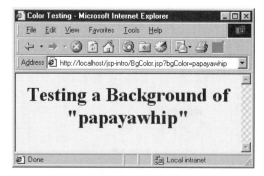

Figure 3–6   Result of *BGColor.jsp* when accessed with a `bgColor` parameter having the X11 color name `papayawhip`.

Using Scriptlets to Make Parts of the JSP Page Conditional

Another use of scriptlets is to conditionally output HTML or other content that is *not* within any JSP tags. The key to this approach is the fact that code inside a scriptlet gets inserted into the resultant servlet's `_jspService` method (called by `service`) *exactly* as written and that any static HTML (template text) before or after a scriptlet gets converted to `print` statements. This means that scriptlets need not contain complete Java statements and that blocks left open can affect the static HTML or JSP outside of the scriptlets. For example, consider the following JSP fragment containing mixed template text and scriptlets.

```
<% if (Math.random() < 0.5) { %>
Have a <B>nice</B> day!
<% } else { %>
Have a <B>lousy</B> day!
<% } %>
```

You probably find that a bit confusing. I certainly did the first few times. Neither the "have a nice day" nor the "have a lousy day" lines are contained within a JSP tag, so it seems odd that only one of the two becomes part of the output for any given request. But, when you think about how this example will be converted to servlet code by the JSP engine, you get the following easily understandable result.

```
if (Math.random() < 0.5) {
  out.println("Have a <B>nice</B> day!");
} else {
  out.println("Have a <B>lousy</B> day!");
}
```

XML and Other Special Scriptlet Syntax

There are two special constructs you should take note of. First, if you want to use the characters `%>` inside a scriptlet, enter `%\>` instead. Second, the XML equivalent of `<% Java Code %>` is

```
<jsp:scriptlet>Java Code</jsp:scriptlet>
```

In JSP 1.1 and earlier, servers are not required to support this alternative syntax, and in practice few do. In JSP 1.2, servers are required to support this syntax as long as authors don't mix the XML version (`<jsp:scriptlet> ... </jsp:scriptlet>`) and the ASP-like version (`<% ... %>`) in the same page. Remember that XML elements are case sensitive; be sure to use `jsp:scriptlet` in lower case.

Declarations

A JSP declaration lets you define methods or fields that get inserted into the main body of the servlet class (*outside* of the _jspService method that is called by service to process the request). A declaration has the following form:

```
<%! Java Code %>
```

Since declarations do not generate any output, they are normally used in conjunction with JSP expressions or scriptlets. The declarations define methods or fields that are later used by expressions or scriptlets. One caution is warranted however: do not use JSP declarations to override the standard servlet life-cycle methods (service, doGet, init, etc.). The servlet into which the JSP page gets translated already makes use of these methods. There is no need for declarations to gain access to service, doGet, or doPost, since calls to service are automatically dispatched to _jspService, which is where code resulting from expressions and scriptlets is put. However, for initialization and cleanup, you can use jspInit and jspDestroy—the standard init and destroy methods are guaranteed to call these two methods when in servlets that come from JSP.

Core Approach

For initialization and cleanup in JSP pages, use JSP declarations to override jspInit and/or jspDestroy.

Aside from overriding standard methods like jspInit and jspDestroy, the utility of JSP declarations for defining methods is somewhat questionable. Moving the methods to separate classes (possibly as static methods) makes them easier to write (since you are using a Java environment, not an HTML-like one), easier to test (no need to run a server), easier to debug (no tricks are needed to see the standard output), and easier to reuse (many different JSP pages can use the same utility class). However, using JSP declarations to define fields, as we will see shortly, gives you something not easily reproducible with separate utility classes: a place to store data that is persistent between requests.

Core Approach

Consider separate helper classes instead of methods defined by means of JSP declarations.

JSP/Servlet Correspondence

JSP declarations result in code that is placed inside the servlet class definition but outside the _jspService method. Since fields and methods can be declared in any order, it does not matter if the code from declarations goes at the top or bottom of the servlet. For instance, Listing 3.7 shows a small JSP snippet that includes some static HTML, a JSP declaration, and a JSP expression. Listing 3.8 shows a servlet that might result. Note that the specific name of the resultant servlet is not defined by the JSP specification, and in fact different servers have different conventions. Besides, as already stated, different vendors will produce this code in slightly different ways, and I oversimplified the out variable (which is a JspWriter, not the slightly simpler PrintWriter that results from a call to getWriter). So, don't expect the code your server generates to look *exactly* like this.

Listing 3.7   Sample JSP Declaration

```
<H1>Some Heading</H1>
<%!
  private String randomHeading() {
    return("<H2>" + Math.random() + "</H2>");
  }
%>
<%= randomHeading() %>
```

Listing 3.8   Representative Resulting Servlet Code: Declaration

```
public class xxxx implements HttpJspPage {
  private String randomHeading() {
    return("<H2>" + Math.random() + "</H2>");
  }

  public void _jspService(HttpServletRequest request,
                          HttpServletResponse response)
      throws ServletException, IOException {
    response.setContentType("text/html");
    HttpSession session = request.getSession(true);
    JspWriter out = response.getWriter();
    out.println("<H1>Some Heading</H1>");
    out.println(randomHeading());
    ...
  }

  ...
}
```

Declaration Example

In this example, a JSP fragment prints the number of times the current page has been requested since the server was booted (or the servlet class was changed and reloaded). A hit counter in one line of code!

```
<%! private int accessCount = 0; %>
Accesses to page since server reboot:
<%= ++accessCount %>
```

Recall that multiple client requests to the same servlet result only in multiple threads calling the `service` method of a single servlet instance. They do *not* result in the creation of multiple servlet instances except possibly when the servlet implements `SingleThreadModel` (see Section 2.3, "The Servlet Life Cycle"). Thus, instance variables (fields) of a normal servlet are shared by multiple requests, and `accessCount` does not have to be declared `static`. Now, advanced readers might wonder if the snippet just shown is thread safe; does the code guarantee that each visitor gets a unique count? The answer is no; in unusual situations multiple users could see the same value. For access counts, as long as the count is correct in the long run, it does not matter if two different users occasionally see the same count. But, for values such as session identifiers, it is critical to have unique values. For an example similar to the previous snippet but that guarantees thread safety, see the discussion of the `isThreadSafe` attribute of the `page` directive in Section 3.4.

Listing 3.9 shows the full JSP page; Figure 3–7 shows a representative result. Now, before you rush out and use this approach to track access to all your pages, a couple of cautions are in order. First of all, you couldn't use this for a real hit counter, since the count starts over whenever you restart the server. So, a real hit counter would need to use `jspInit` and `jspDestroy` to read the previous count at startup and store the old count when the server is shut down. Even then, it would be possible for the server to crash unexpectedly (e.g., when a rolling blackout strikes Silicon Valley). So, you would have to periodically write the hit count to disk. Finally, some advanced servers support distributed applications whereby a cluster of servers appears to the client as a single server. If your servlets or JSP pages might need to support distribution in this way, plan ahead and avoid the use of fields for persistent data. Use a database instead.

Listing 3.9 *AccessCounts.jsp*

```
<!DOCTYPE HTML PUBLIC "-//W3C//DTD HTML 4.0 Transitional//EN">
<HTML>
<HEAD>
<TITLE>JSP Declarations</TITLE>
<META NAME="keywords"
      CONTENT="JSP,declarations,JavaServer,Pages,servlets">
<META NAME="description"
      CONTENT="A quick example of JSP declarations.">
<LINK REL=STYLESHEET
      HREF="JSP-Styles.css"
      TYPE="text/css">
</HEAD>
<BODY>
<H1>JSP Declarations</H1>
<%! private int accessCount = 0; %>
<H2>Accesses to page since server reboot:
<%= ++accessCount %></H2>
</BODY>
</HTML>
```

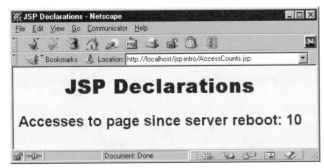

Figure 3–7   Visiting *AccessCounts.jsp* after it has been requested nine previous times by the same or different clients.

XML and Special Declaration Syntax

As with scriptlets, if you want to output %>, enter %\> instead. Finally, note that the XML equivalent of <%! *Java Code* %> is

```
<jsp:declaration>Java Code</jsp:declaration>
```

In JSP 1.1 and earlier, servers are not required to support this alternative syntax, and in practice few do. In JSP 1.2, servers are required to support this syntax as long as authors don't mix the XML version (`<jsp:declaration> ... </jsp:declaration>`) and the standard ASP-like version (`<%! ... %>`) in the same page. Remember that XML elements are case sensitive; be sure to use `jsp:declaration` in lower case.

Predefined Variables

To simplify code in JSP expressions and scriptlets, you are supplied with eight automatically defined local variables in `_jspService`, sometimes called *implicit objects*. Since JSP declarations result in code that appears outside of the `_jspService` method, these variables are not accessible in declarations. The available variables are `request`, `response`, `out`, `session`, `application`, `config`, `pageContext`, and `page`. Details for each are given below.

- **request**
  This variable is the `HttpServletRequest` associated with the request; it gives you access to the request parameters, the request type (e.g., `GET` or `POST`), and the incoming HTTP headers (e.g., cookies).

- **response**
  This variable is the `HttpServletResponse` associated with the response to the client. Since the output stream (see `out`) is normally buffered, it is usually legal to set HTTP status codes and response headers in the body of JSP pages, even though the setting of headers or status codes is not permitted in servlets once any output has been sent to the client. If you turn buffering off, however (see the `buffer` attribute in Section 3.4), you must set status codes and headers before supplying any output.

- **out**
  This variable is the `Writer` used to send output to the client. However, to make it easy to set response headers at various places in the JSP page, `out` is not the standard `PrintWriter` but rather a buffered version of `Writer` called `JspWriter`. You can adjust the buffer size through use of the `buffer` attribute of the `page` directive. The `out` variable is used almost exclusively in scriptlets, since JSP expressions are automatically placed in the output stream and thus rarely need to refer to `out` explicitly.

- **session**
  This variable is the `HttpSession` object associated with the request. Recall that sessions are created automatically in JSP, so this variable is bound even if there is no incoming session reference. The one exception is when you use the `session` attribute of the `page` directive (Section 3.4) to disable session tracking. In that case,

attempts to reference the `session` variable cause errors at the time the JSP page is translated into a servlet.

- **application**
  This variable is the `ServletContext` as obtained by `getServletContext`. Servlets and JSP pages can store persistent data in the `ServletContext` object rather than in instance variables. `ServletContext` has `setAttribute` and `getAttribute` methods that let you store arbitrary data associated with specified keys. The difference between storing data in instance variables and storing it in the `ServletContext` is that the `ServletContext` is shared by all servlets in the Web application, whereas instance variables are available only to the same servlet that stored the data.

- **config**
  This variable is the `ServletConfig` object for this page. The `jspInit` method would use it to read initialization parameters.

- **pageContext**
  JSP introduced a class called `PageContext` to give a single point of access to many of the page attributes. The `pageContext` variable stores the value of the `PageContext` object associated with the current page. If a method or constructor needs access to multiple page-related objects, passing `pageContext` is easier than passing many separate references to `out`, `request`, `response`, and so forth.

- **page**
  This variable is simply a synonym for `this` and is not very useful. It was created as a placeholder for the time when the scripting language could be something other than Java.

3.4 Structuring Autogenerated Servlets: The JSP page Directive

A JSP *directive* affects the overall structure of the servlet that results from the JSP page. The following templates show the two possible forms for directives. Single quotes can be substituted for the double quotes around the attribute values, but the quotation marks cannot be omitted altogether. To obtain quote marks within an attribute value, precede them with a backslash, using \' for ' and \" for ".

```
<%@ directive attribute="value" %>

<%@ directive attribute1="value1"
              attribute2="value2"
              ...
              attributeN="valueN" %>
```

In JSP, there are three types of directives: page, include, and taglib. The page directive lets you control the structure of the servlet by importing classes, customizing the servlet superclass, setting the content type, and the like. A page directive can be placed anywhere within the document; its use is the topic of this section. The second directive, include, lets you insert a file into the servlet class at the time the JSP file is translated into a servlet. An include directive should be placed in the document at the point at which you want the file to be inserted; it is discussed in Section 3.5. JSP 1.1 introduced a third directive, taglib, which is used to define custom markup tags; it is discussed in Section 3.7.

The page directive lets you define one or more of the following case-sensitive attributes: import, contentType, isThreadSafe, session, buffer, autoflush, extends, info, errorPage, isErrorPage, language, and pageEncoding. These attributes are explained in the following subsections.

The import Attribute

The import attribute of the page directive lets you specify the packages that should be imported by the servlet into which the JSP page gets translated. As illustrated in Figure 3–8, using separate utility classes makes your dynamic code easier to maintain, debug, and reuse, and your utility classes are sure to use packages.

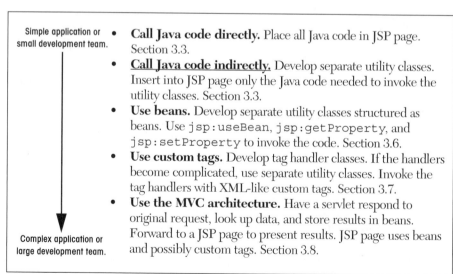

Figure 3–8   Strategies for invoking dynamic code from JSP.

In fact, *all* of your utility classes should be placed in packages. For one thing, packages are a good strategy on any large project because they help protect against name conflicts. With JSP, however, packages are absolutely required. That's because, in the absence of packages, classes you reference are assumed to be in the same package as the current class. For example, suppose that a JSP page contains the following scriptlet.

```
<% Test t = new Test(); %>
```

Now, if `Test` is in an imported package, there is no ambiguity. But, if `Test` is not in a package, or the package to which `Test` belongs is not explicitly imported, then the system will assume that `Test` is in the same package as the autogenerated servlet. The problem is that the autogenerated servlet's package is not known! It is quite common for servers to create servlets whose package is determined by the directory in which the JSP page is placed. Other servers use different approaches. So, you simply cannot rely on packageless classes to work properly. The same argument applies to beans (Section 3.6), since beans are just classes that follow some simple naming and structure conventions.

Core Approach

Always put your utility classes and beans in packages.

By default, the servlet imports `java.lang.*`, `javax.servlet.*`, `javax.servlet.jsp.*`, `javax.servlet.http.*`, and possibly some number of server-specific entries. Never write JSP code that relies on any server-specific classes being imported automatically.

Use of the `import` attribute takes one of the following two forms.

```
<%@ page import="package.class" %>
<%@ page import="package.class1,...,package.classN" %>
```

For example, the following directive signifies that all classes in the `java.util` package should be available to use without explicit package identifiers.

```
<%@ page import="java.util.*" %>
```

The `import` attribute is the only `page` attribute that is allowed to appear multiple times within the same document. Although `page` directives can appear anywhere within the document, it is traditional to place `import` statements either near the top of the document or just before the first place that the referenced package is used.

Note that, although the JSP pages go in the normal HTML directories of the server, the classes you write that are used by JSP pages must be placed in the special servlet directories (e.g., *.../WEB-INF/classes*; see Sections 1.7 and 1.9).

For example, Listing 3.10 presents a page that uses three classes not in the standard JSP import list: `java.util.Date`, `moreservlets.ServletUtilities` (see Listing 2.17), and `moreservlets.LongLivedCookie` (see Listing 2.18). To simplify references to these classes, the JSP page uses

```
<%@ page import="java.util.*,moreservlets.*" %>
```

Figures 3–9 and 3–10 show some typical results.

Listing 3.10 *ImportAttribute.jsp*

```
<!DOCTYPE HTML PUBLIC "-//W3C//DTD HTML 4.0 Transitional//EN">
<HTML>
<HEAD>
<TITLE>The import Attribute</TITLE>
<LINK REL=STYLESHEET
      HREF="JSP-Styles.css"
      TYPE="text/css">
</HEAD>
<BODY>
<H2>The import Attribute</H2>
<%-- JSP page directive --%>
<%@ page import="java.util.*,moreservlets.*" %>
<%-- JSP Declaration --%>
<%!
private String randomID() {
  int num = (int)(Math.random()*10000000.0);
  return("id" + num);
}
private final String NO_VALUE = "<I>No Value</I>";
%>
<%-- JSP Scriptlet --%>
<%
Cookie[] cookies = request.getCookies();
String oldID =
  ServletUtilities.getCookieValue(cookies, "userID", NO_VALUE);
if (oldID.equals(NO_VALUE)) {
  String newID = randomID();
  Cookie cookie = new LongLivedCookie("userID", newID);
  response.addCookie(cookie);
}
%>
<%-- JSP Expressions --%>
This page was accessed on <%= new Date() %> with a userID
cookie of <%= oldID %>.
</BODY>
</HTML>
```

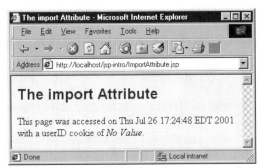

Figure 3–9   *ImportAttribute.jsp* when first accessed.

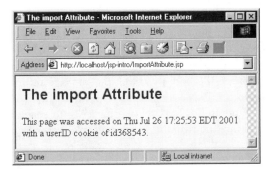

Figure 3–10   *ImportAttribute.jsp* when accessed in a subsequent request.

The contentType Attribute

The `contentType` attribute sets the `Content-Type` response header, indicating the MIME type of the document being sent to the client. For more information on MIME types, see Table 2.1 (Common MIME Types) in Section 2.8 (The Server Response: HTTP Response Headers).

Use of the `contentType` attribute takes one of the following two forms.

```
<%@ page contentType="MIME-Type" %>
<%@ page contentType="MIME-Type; charset=Character-Set" %>
```

For example, the directive

```
<%@ page contentType="application/vnd.ms-excel" %>
```

has the same effect as the scriptlet

```
<% response.setContentType("application/vnd.ms-excel"); %>
```

The main difference between the two forms is that `response.setContent-Type` can be invoked conditionally whereas the `page` directive cannot be. Setting the content type conditionally is occasionally useful when the same content can be displayed in different forms—for an example, see the Section "Generating Excel Spreadsheets" starting on page 254 of *Core Servlets and JavaServer Pages* (available in PDF at *http://www.moreservlets.com*).

Unlike regular servlets, where the default MIME type is `text/plain`, the default for JSP pages is `text/html` (with a default character set of `ISO-8859-1`). Thus, JSP pages that output HTML in a Latin character set need not use `content-Type` at all. But, pages in JSP 1.1 and earlier that output other character sets need to use `contentType` even when they generate HTML. For example, Japanese JSP pages might use the following.

```
<%@ page contentType="text/html; charset=Shift_JIS" %>
```

In JSP 1.2, however, the `pageEncoding` attribute (see details later in this section) can be used to directly specify the character set.

Listing 3.11 shows a JSP page that generates tab-separated Excel output. Note that the `page` directive and comment are at the bottom so that the carriage returns at the ends of the lines don't show up in the Excel document (remember: JSP does not ignore white space—JSP usually generates HTML where most white space is ignored by the browser). Figure 3–11 shows the result in Internet Explorer on a system that has Microsoft Office installed.

Listing 3.11   *Excel.jsp*

```
First   Last     Email Address
Marty   Hall     hall@moreservlets.com
Larry   Brown    brown@corewebprogramming.com
Steve   Balmer   balmer@sun.com
Scott   McNealy  mcnealy@microsoft.com
<%@ page contentType="application/vnd.ms-excel" %>
<%-- There are tabs, not spaces, between columns. --%>
```

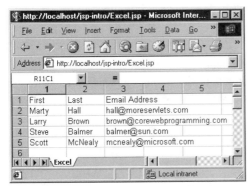

Figure 3–11   Excel document (*Excel.jsp*) in Internet Explorer.

The isThreadSafe Attribute

The isThreadSafe attribute controls whether the servlet that results from the JSP page will implement the SingleThreadModel interface (Section 2.3). Use of the isThreadSafe attribute takes one of the following two forms.

```
<%@ page isThreadSafe="true" %> <%-- Default --%>
<%@ page isThreadSafe="false" %>
```

With normal servlets, simultaneous user requests result in multiple threads concurrently accessing the service method of the same servlet instance. This behavior assumes that the servlet is *thread safe*; that is, that the servlet synchronizes access to data in its fields so that inconsistent values will not result from an unexpected ordering of thread execution. In some cases (such as page access counts), you may not care if two visitors occasionally get the same value, but in other cases (such as user IDs), identical values can spell disaster. For example, the following snippet is not thread safe since a thread could be preempted after reading idNum but before updating it, yielding two users with the same user ID.

```
<%! private static int idNum = 0; %>
<%
String userID = "userID" + idNum;
out.println("Your ID is " + userID + ".");
idNum = idNum + 1;
%>
```

The code should have used a `synchronized` block. This construct is written

```
synchronized(someObject) { ... }
```

and means that once a thread enters the block of code, no other thread can enter the same block (or any other block marked with the same object reference) until the first thread exits. So, the previous snippet should have been written in the following manner.

```
<%! private static int idNum = 0; %>
<%
synchronized(this) {
  String userID = "userID" + idNum;
  out.println("Your ID is " + userID + ".");
  idNum = idNum + 1;
}
%>
```

That's the normal servlet behavior: multiple simultaneous requests are dispatched to multiple threads that concurrently access the same servlet instance. However, if a servlet implements the `SingleThreadModel` interface, the system guarantees that there will not be simultaneous access to the same servlet instance. The system can satisfy this guarantee either by queuing all requests and passing them to the same servlet instance or by creating a pool of instances, each of which handles a single request at a time. The possibility of a pool of instances explains the need for the `static` qualifier in the `idNum` field declaration in the previous examples.

You use `<%@ page isThreadSafe="false" %>` to indicate that your code is *not* thread safe and thus that the resulting servlet should implement `Single-ThreadModel`. The default value is `true`, which means that the system assumes you made your code thread safe and it can consequently use the higher-performance approach of multiple simultaneous threads accessing a single servlet instance.

Explicitly synchronizing your code as in the previous snippet is preferred whenever possible. In particular, explicit synchronization yields higher performance pages that are accessed frequently. However, using `isThreadSafe="false"` is useful when the problematic code is hard to find (perhaps it is in a class for which you have no source code) and for quick testing to see if a problem stems from race conditions at all.

Core Note

With frequently accessed pages, you get better performance by using explicit synchronization than by using the `isThreadSafe` attribute.

The session Attribute

The `session` attribute controls whether the page participates in HTTP sessions. Use of this attribute takes one of the following two forms.

```
<%@ page session="true" %> <%-- Default --%>
<%@ page session="false" %>
```

A value of `true` (the default) indicates that the predefined variable `session` (of type `HttpSession`) should be bound to the existing session if one exists; otherwise, a new session should be created and bound to `session`. A value of `false` means that no sessions will be used automatically and attempts to access the variable `session` will result in errors at the time the JSP page is translated into a servlet. Turning off session tracking may save significant amounts of server memory on high-traffic sites. Just remember that sessions are *user specific*, not *page specific*. Thus, it doesn't do any good to turn off session tracking for one page unless you also turn it off for related pages that are likely to be visited in the same client session.

The buffer Attribute

The `buffer` attribute specifies the size of the buffer used by the `out` variable, which is of type `JspWriter`. Use of this attribute takes one of two forms.

```
<%@ page buffer="sizekb" %>
<%@ page buffer="none" %>
```

Servers can use a larger buffer than you specify, but not a smaller one. For example, `<%@ page buffer="32kb" %>` means the document content should be buffered and not sent to the client until at least 32 kilobytes have been accumulated, the page is completed, or the output is explicitly flushed (e.g., with `response.flushBuffer`). The default buffer size is server specific, but must be at least 8 kilobytes. Be cautious about turning off buffering; doing so requires JSP elements that set headers or status codes to appear at the top of the file, before any HTML content.

The autoflush Attribute

The `autoflush` attribute controls whether the output buffer should be automatically flushed when it is full or whether an exception should be raised when the buffer overflows. Use of this attribute takes one of the following two forms.

```
<%@ page autoflush="true" %> <%-- Default --%>
<%@ page autoflush="false" %>
```

A value of `false` is illegal when `buffer="none"` is also used.

The extends Attribute

The `extends` attribute designates the superclass of the servlet that will be generated for the JSP page and takes the following form.

```
<%@ page extends="package.class" %>
```

This attribute is normally reserved for developers or vendors that implement fundamental changes to the way that pages operate (e.g., to add in personalization features). Ordinary mortals should steer clear of this attribute.

The info Attribute

The `info` attribute defines a string that can be retrieved from the servlet by means of the `getServletInfo` method. Use of `info` takes the following form.

```
<%@ page info="Some Message" %>
```

The errorPage Attribute

The `errorPage` attribute specifies a JSP page that should process any exceptions (i.e., something of type `Throwable`) thrown but not caught in the current page. The designated error page must use `isErrorPage="true"` (see next entry) to indicate that it permits use as an error page. The `errorPage` attribute is used as follows.

```
<%@ page errorPage="Relative URL" %>
```

The exception thrown will be automatically available to the designated error page by means of the `exception` variable. For an example, see Section 11.10 of *Core Servlets and JavaServer Pages* (available in PDF at *http://www.moreservlets.com*).

Note that the `errorPage` attribute is used to designate *page-specific* error pages. To designate error pages that apply to an entire Web application or to various categories of errors within an application, use the `error-page` element in *web.xml*. For details, see Section 5.8 (Designating Pages to Handle Errors).

The isErrorPage Attribute

The `isErrorPage` attribute indicates whether the current page can act as the error page for another JSP page. Use of `isErrorPage` takes one of the following two forms:

```
<%@ page isErrorPage="true" %>
<%@ page isErrorPage="false" %> <%-- Default --%>
```

The language Attribute

At some point, the `language` attribute is intended to specify the underlying programming language being used, as below.

```
<%@ page language="cobol" %>
```

For now, don't bother with this attribute since `java` is both the default and the only legal choice.

The pageEncoding Attribute

The `pageEncoding` attribute, available only in JSP 1.2, defines the character encoding for the page. The default value is ISO-8859-1 unless the `contentType` attribute of the `page` directive is specified, in which case the `charset` entry of `contentType` is the default.

XML Syntax for Directives

All JSP 1.2 servers (containers) and some JSP 1.1 servers permit you to use an alternative XML-compatible syntax for directives as long as you don't mix the XML version and the normal version in the same page. These constructs take the following form:

```
<jsp:directive.directiveType attribute="value" />
```

For example, the XML equivalent of

```
<%@ page import="java.util.*" %>
```

is

```
<jsp:directive.page import="java.util.*" />
```

3.5 Including Files and Applets in JSP Documents

JSP has three main capabilities for including external pieces into a JSP document.

1. **The `include` directive.** The construct lets you insert JSP code into the main page before that main page is translated into a servlet. The included code can contain JSP constructs such as field definitions and

content-type settings *that affect the main page as a whole*. This capability is discussed in the first of the following subsections.

2. **The jsp:include action.** Although reusing chunks of JSP code is a powerful capability, most times you would rather sacrifice a small amount of power for the convenience of being able to change the included documents without updating the main JSP page. The jsp:include action lets you include the output of a page at request time. Note that jsp:include only lets you include the *output* of the secondary page, not the secondary page's actual code as with the include directive. Consequently, the secondary page cannot use any JSP constructs that affect the main page as a whole. Use of jsp:include is discussed in the second subsection.

3. **The jsp:plugin action.** Although this chapter is primarily about server-side Java, client-side Java in the form of Web-embedded applets continues to play a role, especially within corporate intranets. The jsp:plugin element is used to insert applets that use the Java Plug-In into JSP pages. This capability is discussed in the third subsection.

Including Files at Page Translation Time: The include Directive

You use the include directive to include a file in the main JSP document at the time the document is translated into a servlet (which is typically the first time it is accessed). The syntax is as follows:

```
<%@ include file="Relative URL" %>
```

There are two ramifications of the fact that the included file is inserted at page translation time, not at request time as with jsp:include (see the next subsection).

First, the included file is permitted to contain JSP code such as response header settings and field definitions *that affect the main page*. For example, suppose snippet.jsp contained the following code:

```
<%! int accessCount = 0; %>
```

In such a case, you could do the following:

```
<%@ include file="snippet.jsp" %> <%-- Defines accessCount --%>
<%= accessCount++ %>              <%-- Uses accessCount --%>
```

Second, if the included file changes, all the JSP files that use it may need to be updated. Unfortunately, although servers are *allowed* to support a mechanism for detecting when an included file has changed (and then recompiling the servlet), they are not *required* to do so. So, you may have to update the modification dates of each JSP page that uses the included code. Some operating systems have commands that update the modification date without your actually editing the file (e.g., the Unix touch command), but a simple portable alternative is to include a JSP comment in the top-level page. Update the comment whenever the included file changes. For example, you might put the modification date of the included file in the comment, as below.

```
<%-- Navbar.jsp modified 3/1/00 --%>
<%@ include file="Navbar.jsp" %>
```

Core Warning

If you change an included JSP file, you may have to update the modification dates of all JSP files that use it.

XML Syntax for the include Directive

The XML-compatible equivalent of

```
<%@ include file="..." %>
```

is

```
<jsp:directive.include file="..." />
```

Remember that only servlet and JSP containers (servers) that support JSP 1.2 are required to support the XML version.

Including Pages at Request Time: The jsp:include Action

The include directive (see the previous subsection) lets you include actual JSP code into multiple different pages. Including the code itself is sometimes a useful capability, but the include directive requires you to update the modification date of the page whenever the included file changes. This is a significant inconvenience. The jsp:include action includes the *output* of a secondary page at the time the main page is requested. Thus, jsp:include does not require you to update the main file when an included file changes. On the other hand, the main page has already been translated into a servlet by request time, so the included pages cannot contain JSP that affects the main page as a whole. Also, inclusion at page translation time is marginally faster. These are relatively minor considerations, and jsp:include is almost always preferred.

Core Approach

For file inclusion, use `jsp:include` *whenever possible. Reserve the include directive for cases when the included file defines fields or methods that the main page uses or when the included file sets response headers of the main page.*

Although the *output* of the included pages cannot contain JSP, the pages can be the result of resources that use JSP to *create* the output. That is, the URL that refers to the included resource is interpreted in the normal manner by the server and thus can be a servlet or JSP page. The server runs the included page in the usual manner and places the output into the main page. This is precisely the behavior of the `include` method of the `RequestDispatcher` class (Section 3.8), which is what servlets use if they want to do this type of file inclusion.

The `jsp:include` element has two attributes, as shown in the sample below: `page` and `flush`. The `page` attribute is required and designates a relative URL referencing the file to be included. The `flush` attribute specifies whether the output stream of the main page should flushed before the inclusion of the page. In JSP 1.2, `flush` is an optional attribute and the default value is `false`. In JSP 1.1, `flush` is a required attribute and the only legal value is `true`.

```
<jsp:include page="Relative URL" flush="true" />
```

The included file automatically is given the same request parameters as the originally requested page. If you want to augment those parameters, you can use the `jsp:param` element (which has `name` and `value` attributes). For example, consider the following snippet.

```
<jsp:include page="/fragments/StandardHeading.jsp">
  <jsp:param name="bgColor" value="YELLOW" />
</jsp:include>
```

Now, suppose that the main page is invoked by means of *http://host/path/MainPage.jsp?fgColor=RED*. In such a case, the main page receives `"RED"` for calls to `request.getParameter("fgColor")` and `null` for calls to `request.getParameter("bgColor")` (regardless of whether the `bgColor` attribute is accessed before or after the inclusion of the *StandardHeading.jsp* page). The *StandardHeading.jsp* page would receive `"RED"` for calls to `request.getParameter("fgColor")` and `"YELLOW"` for calls to `request.getParameter("bgColor")`. If the main page receives a request parameter that is also specified with the `jsp:param` element, the value from `jsp:param` takes precedence in the included page.

As an example of a typical use of `jsp:include`, consider the simple news summary page shown in Listing 3.12. Page developers can change the news items in the files `Item1.html` through `Item3.html` (Listings 3.13 through 3.15) without having to update the main news page. Figure 3–12 shows the result.

Listing 3.12   *WhatsNew.jsp*

```
<!DOCTYPE HTML PUBLIC "-//W3C//DTD HTML 4.0 Transitional//EN">
<HTML>
<HEAD>
<TITLE>What's New at JspNews.com</TITLE>
<LINK REL=STYLESHEET
      HREF="JSP-Styles.css"
      TYPE="text/css">
</HEAD>
<BODY>
<TABLE BORDER=5 ALIGN="CENTER">
  <TR><TH CLASS="TITLE">
      What's New at JspNews.com</TABLE>
<P>
Here is a summary of our three most recent news stories:
<OL>
  <LI><jsp:include page="news/Item1.html" flush="true" />
  <LI><jsp:include page="news/Item2.html" flush="true" />
  <LI><jsp:include page="news/Item3.html" flush="true" />
</OL>
</BODY>
</HTML>
```

Listing 3.13   *Item1.html*

```
<B>Bill Gates acts humble.</B> In a startling and unexpected
development, Microsoft big wig Bill Gates put on an open act of
humility yesterday.
<A HREF="http://www.microsoft.com/Never.html">More details...</A>
```

Listing 3.14   *Item2.html*

```
<B>Scott McNealy acts serious.</B> In an unexpected twist,
wisecracking Sun head Scott McNealy was sober and subdued at
yesterday's meeting.
<A HREF="http://www.sun.com/Imposter.html">More details...</A>
```

Listing 3.15   *Item3.html*

```
<B>Larry Ellison acts conciliatory.</B> Catching his competitors
off guard yesterday, Oracle prez Larry Ellison referred to his
rivals in friendly and respectful terms.
<A HREF="http://www.oracle.com/Mistake.html">More details...</A>
```

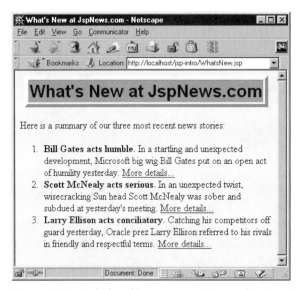

Figure 3–12   Including files at request time makes it easier to update the individual files.

Including Applets for the Java Plug-In

With JSP, you don't need any special syntax to include ordinary applets: just use the normal HTML APPLET tag. However, except for intranets that use Netscape 6 exclusively, these applets must use JDK 1.1 or JDK 1.02 since neither Netscape 4.x nor Internet Explorer 5.x supports the Java 2 platform (i.e., JDK 1.2–1.4). This lack of support imposes several restrictions on applets:

- To use Swing, you must send the Swing files over the network. This process is time consuming and fails in Internet Explorer 3 and Netscape 3.x and 4.01–4.05 (which only support JDK 1.02), since Swing depends on JDK 1.1.

- You cannot use Java 2D.

- You cannot use the Java 2 collections package.

- Your code runs more slowly, since most compilers for the Java 2 platform are significantly improved over their 1.1 predecessors.

To address these problems, Sun developed a browser plug-in for Netscape and Internet Explorer that lets you use the Java 2 platform in a variety of browsers. This plug-in is available at *http://java.sun.com/products/plugin/* and also comes bundled with JDK 1.2.2 and later. Since the plug-in is quite large (several megabytes), it is not reasonable to expect users on the WWW at large to download and install it just to run your applets. On the other hand, it is a reasonable alternative for fast corporate intranets, especially since applets can automatically prompt browsers that lack the plug-in to download it.

Unfortunately, however, the normal `APPLET` tag will not work with the plug-in, since browsers are specifically designed to use only their built-in virtual machine when they see `APPLET`. Instead, you have to use a long and messy `OBJECT` tag for Internet Explorer and an equally long `EMBED` tag for Netscape. Furthermore, since you typically don't know which browser type will be accessing your page, you have to either include both `OBJECT` and `EMBED` (placing the `EMBED` within the `COMMENT` section of `OBJECT`) or identify the browser type at the time of the request and conditionally build the right tag. This process is straightforward but tedious and time consuming.

The `jsp:plugin` element instructs the server to build a tag appropriate for applets that use the plug-in. This element does not add any Java capabilities to the client. How could it? JSP runs entirely on the server; the client knows nothing about JSP. The `jsp:plugin` element merely simplifies the generation of the `OBJECT` or `EMBED` tags.

Servers are permitted some leeway in exactly how they implement `jsp:plugin` but most simply include both `OBJECT` and `EMBED`. To see exactly how your server translates `jsp:plugin`, insert into a page a simple `jsp:plugin` element with `type`, `code`, `width`, and `height` attributes as in the following example. Then, access the page from your browser and view the HTML source. You don't need to create an applet to perform this experiment.

Note that JRun 3.0 SP2 does not support `jsp:plugin`; JRun 3.1 supports it properly.

The jsp:plugin Element

The simplest way to use `jsp:plugin` is to supply four attributes: `type`, `code`, `width`, and `height`. You supply a value of `applet` for the `type` attribute and use the other three attributes in exactly the same way as with the `APPLET` element, with two exceptions: the attribute names are case sensitive, and single or double quotes are always required around the attribute values. So, for example, you could replace

```
<APPLET CODE="MyApplet.class"
        WIDTH=475 HEIGHT=350>
</APPLET>
```

with

```
<jsp:plugin type="applet"
            code="MyApplet.class"
            width="475" height="350">
</jsp:plugin>
```

The jsp:plugin element has a number of other optional attributes. Most parallel the attributes of the APPLET element. Here is a full list.

- **type**
  For applets, this attribute should have a value of applet. However, the Java Plug-In also permits you to embed JavaBeans components in Web pages. Use a value of bean in such a case.
- **code**
  This attribute is used identically to the CODE attribute of APPLET, specifying the top-level applet class file that extends Applet or JApplet.
- **width**
  This attribute is used identically to the WIDTH attribute of APPLET, specifying the width in pixels to be reserved for the applet.
- **height**
  This attribute is used identically to the HEIGHT attribute of APPLET, specifying the height in pixels to be reserved for the applet.
- **codebase**
  This attribute is used identically to the CODEBASE attribute of APPLET, specifying the base directory for the applets. The code attribute is interpreted relative to this directory. As with the APPLET element, if you omit this attribute, the directory of the current page is used as the default. In the case of JSP, this default location is the directory where the original JSP file resided, not the system-specific location of the servlet that results from the JSP file.
- **align**
  This attribute is used identically to the ALIGN attribute of APPLET and IMG, specifying the alignment of the applet within the Web page. Legal values are left, right, top, bottom, and middle.
- **hspace**
  This attribute is used identically to the HSPACE attribute of APPLET, specifying empty space in pixels reserved on the left and right of the applet.
- **vspace**
  This attribute is used identically to the VSPACE attribute of APPLET, specifying empty space in pixels reserved on the top and bottom of the applet.

- **archive**
  This attribute is used identically to the ARCHIVE attribute of APPLET, specifying a JAR file from which classes and images should be loaded.
- **name**
  This attribute is used identically to the NAME attribute of APPLET, specifying a name to use for interapplet communication or for identifying the applet to scripting languages like JavaScript.
- **title**
  This attribute is used identically to the very rarely used TITLE attribute of APPLET (and virtually all other HTML elements in HTML 4.0), specifying a title that could be used for a tool-tip or for indexing.
- **jreversion**
  This attribute identifies the version of the Java Runtime Environment (JRE) that is required. The default is 1.1.
- **iepluginurl**
  This attribute designates a URL from which the plug-in for Internet Explorer can be downloaded. Users who don't already have the plug-in installed will be prompted to download it from this location. The default value will direct the user to the Sun site, but for intranet use you might want to direct the user to a local copy.
- **nspluginurl**
  This attribute designates a URL from which the plug-in for Netscape can be downloaded. The default value will direct the user to the Sun site, but for intranet use you might want to direct the user to a local copy.

The jsp:param and jsp:params Elements

The jsp:param element is used with jsp:plugin in a manner similar to the way that PARAM is used with APPLET, specifying a name and value that are accessed from within the applet by getParameter. There are two main differences, however. First, since jsp:param follows XML syntax, attribute names must be lower case, attribute values must be enclosed in single or double quotes, and the element must end with />, not just >. Second, all jsp:param entries must be enclosed within a jsp:params element.

So, for example, you would replace

```
<APPLET CODE="MyApplet.class"
        WIDTH=475 HEIGHT=350>
  <PARAM NAME="PARAM1" VALUE="VALUE1">
  <PARAM NAME="PARAM2" VALUE="VALUE2">
</APPLET>
```

with

```
<jsp:plugin type="applet"
            code="MyApplet.class"
            width="475" height="350">
  <jsp:params>
    <jsp:param name="PARAM1" value="VALUE1" />
    <jsp:param name="PARAM2" value="VALUE2" />
  </jsp:params>
</jsp:plugin>
```

The jsp:fallback Element

The `jsp:fallback` element provides alternative text to browsers that do not support OBJECT or EMBED. You use this element in almost the same way as you would use alternative text placed within an APPLET element. So, for example, you would replace

```
<APPLET CODE="MyApplet.class"
        WIDTH=475 HEIGHT=350>
  <B>Error: this example requires Java.</B>
</APPLET>
```

with

```
<jsp:plugin type="applet"
            code="MyApplet.class"
            width="475" height="350">
  <jsp:fallback>
    <B>Error: this example requires Java.</B>
  </jsp:fallback>
</jsp:plugin>
```

A jsp:plugin Example

Listing 3.16 shows a JSP page that uses the `jsp:plugin` element to generate an entry for the Java 2 Plug-In. Listings 3.17 through 3.20 show the code for the applet itself (which uses Swing and Java 2D), and Figure 3–13 shows the result.

Listing 3.16 *PluginApplet.jsp*

```
<!DOCTYPE HTML PUBLIC "-//W3C//DTD HTML 4.0 Transitional//EN">
<HTML>
<HEAD>
<TITLE>Using jsp:plugin</TITLE>
<LINK REL=STYLESHEET
      HREF="JSP-Styles.css"
      TYPE="text/css">
</HEAD>
<BODY>
<TABLE BORDER=5 ALIGN="CENTER">
  <TR><TH CLASS="TITLE">
      Using jsp:plugin</TABLE>
<P>
<CENTER>
<jsp:plugin type="applet"
            code="PluginApplet.class"
            width="370" height="420">
</jsp:plugin>
</CENTER>
</BODY>
</HTML>
```

Listing 3.17 *PluginApplet.java*

```
import javax.swing.*;

/** An applet that uses Swing and Java 2D and thus requires
 *  the Java Plug-In.
 */

public class PluginApplet extends JApplet {
  public void init() {
    WindowUtilities.setNativeLookAndFeel();
    setContentPane(new TextPanel());
  }
}
```

Listing 3.18 *TextPanel.java*

```java
import java.awt.*;
import java.awt.event.*;
import javax.swing.*;

/** JPanel that places a panel with text drawn at various angles
 *  in the top part of the window and a JComboBox containing
 *  font choices in the bottom part.
 */

public class TextPanel extends JPanel
                       implements ActionListener {
  private JComboBox fontBox;
  private DrawingPanel drawingPanel;

  public TextPanel() {
    GraphicsEnvironment env =
      GraphicsEnvironment.getLocalGraphicsEnvironment();
    String[] fontNames = env.getAvailableFontFamilyNames();
    fontBox = new JComboBox(fontNames);
    setLayout(new BorderLayout());
    JPanel fontPanel = new JPanel();
    fontPanel.add(new JLabel("Font:"));
    fontPanel.add(fontBox);
    JButton drawButton = new JButton("Draw");
    drawButton.addActionListener(this);
    fontPanel.add(drawButton);
    add(fontPanel, BorderLayout.SOUTH);
    drawingPanel = new DrawingPanel();
    fontBox.setSelectedItem("Serif");
    drawingPanel.setFontName("Serif");
    add(drawingPanel, BorderLayout.CENTER);
  }

  public void actionPerformed(ActionEvent e) {
    drawingPanel.setFontName((String)fontBox.getSelectedItem());
    drawingPanel.repaint();
  }
}
```

Listing 3.19   *DrawingPanel.java*

```java
import java.awt.*;
import java.awt.geom.*;
import javax.swing.*;

/** A window with text drawn at an angle. The font is
 *  set by means of the setFontName method.
 */

class DrawingPanel extends JPanel {
  private Ellipse2D.Double circle =
    new Ellipse2D.Double(10, 10, 350, 350);
  private GradientPaint gradient =
    new GradientPaint(0, 0, Color.red, 180, 180, Color.yellow,
                      true); // true means to repeat pattern
  private Color[] colors = { Color.white, Color.black };

  public void paintComponent(Graphics g) {
    super.paintComponent(g);
    Graphics2D g2d = (Graphics2D)g;
    g2d.setPaint(gradient);
    g2d.fill(circle);
    g2d.translate(185, 185);
    for (int i=0; i<16; i++) {
      g2d.rotate(Math.PI/8.0);
      g2d.setPaint(colors[i%2]);
      g2d.drawString("jsp:plugin", 0, 0);
    }
  }

  public void setFontName(String fontName) {
    setFont(new Font(fontName, Font.BOLD, 35));
  }
}
```

Listing 3.20   *WindowUtilities.java*

```
import javax.swing.*;
import java.awt.*;

/** A few utilities that simplify using windows in Swing. */

public class WindowUtilities {

  /** Tell system to use native look and feel, as in previous
   *  releases. Metal (Java) LAF is the default otherwise.
   */

  public static void setNativeLookAndFeel() {
    try {
      UIManager.setLookAndFeel
        (UIManager.getSystemLookAndFeelClassName());
    } catch(Exception e) {
      System.out.println("Error setting native LAF: " + e);
    }
  }

  ... // See www.moreservlets.com for remaining code.
}
```

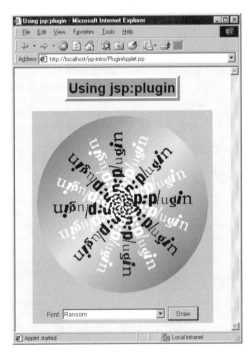

Figure 3–13 Result of *PluginApplet.jsp* in Internet Explorer when the Java 2 Plug-In is installed.

3.6   Using JavaBeans with JSP

This section discusses the third general strategy for inserting dynamic content in JSP pages (see Figure 3–14): by means of JavaBeans components.

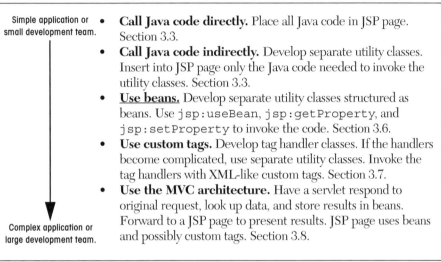

Simple application or small development team.

- **Call Java code directly.** Place all Java code in JSP page. Section 3.3.
- **Call Java code indirectly.** Develop separate utility classes. Insert into JSP page only the Java code needed to invoke the utility classes. Section 3.3.
- **Use beans.** Develop separate utility classes structured as beans. Use `jsp:useBean`, `jsp:getProperty`, and `jsp:setProperty` to invoke the code. Section 3.6.
- **Use custom tags.** Develop tag handler classes. If the handlers become complicated, use separate utility classes. Invoke the tag handlers with XML-like custom tags. Section 3.7.
- **Use the MVC architecture.** Have a servlet respond to original request, look up data, and store results in beans. Forward to a JSP page to present results. JSP page uses beans and possibly custom tags. Section 3.8.

Complex application or large development team.

Figure 3–14   Strategies for invoking dynamic code from JSP.

The JavaBeans API provides a standard format for Java classes. Visual manipulation tools and other programs can automatically discover information about classes that follow this format and can then create and manipulate the classes without the user having to explicitly write any code. Use of JavaBeans components in JSP provides three advantages over scriptlets and JSP expressions.

1. **No Java syntax.** By using beans, page authors can manipulate Java objects, using only XML-compatible syntax: no parentheses, semicolons, or curly braces. This promotes a stronger separation between the content and the presentation and is especially useful in large development teams that have separate Web and Java developers.
2. **Simpler object sharing.** The JSP bean constructs make it much easier to share objects among multiple pages or between requests than if the equivalent explicit Java code were used.
3. **Convenient correspondence between request parameters and object properties.** The JSP bean constructs greatly simplify the process of reading request parameters, converting from strings, and stuffing the results inside objects.

Full coverage of JavaBeans is beyond the scope of this book. If you want details, pick up one of the many books on the subject or see the documentation and tutorials at *http://java.sun.com/products/javabeans/docs/*. For the purposes of this chapter, however, all you need to know about beans are three simple points:

1. **A bean class must have a zero-argument (empty) constructor.** You can satisfy this requirement either by explicitly defining such a constructor or by omitting all constructors, which results in an empty constructor being created automatically. The empty constructor will be called when JSP elements create beans. In fact, as we will see in Section 3.8 (Integrating Servlets and JSP: The MVC Architecture), it is quite common for a servlet to create a bean and a JSP page to merely look up data from the existing bean. In that case, the requirement that the bean have a zero-argument constructor is waived.

2. **A bean class should have no public instance variables (fields).** I hope you already follow this practice and use accessor methods instead of allowing direct access to the instance variables. Use of accessor methods lets you do three things without users of your class changing their code: (a) impose constraints on variable values (e.g., have the `setSpeed` method of your `Car` class disallow negative speeds); (b) change your internal data structures (e.g., change from English units to metric units internally, but still have `getSpeedIn-MPH` and `getSpeedInKPH` methods); (c) perform side effects automatically when values change (e.g., update the user interface when `setPosition` is called).

3. **Persistent values should be accessed through methods called getXxx and setXxx.** For example, if your `Car` class stores the current number of passengers, you might have methods named `getNum-Passengers` (which takes no arguments and returns an `int`) and `setNumPassengers` (which takes an `int` and has a `void` return type). In such a case, the `Car` class is said to have a *property* named `numPassengers` (notice the lowercase n in the property name, but the uppercase N in the method names). If the class has a `getXxx` method but no corresponding `setXxx`, the class is said to have a read-only property named *xxx*.

   The one exception to this naming convention is with boolean properties: they use a method called `isXxx` to look up their values. So, for example, your `Car` class might have methods called `isLeased` (which takes no arguments and returns a `boolean`) and `setLeased` (which takes a `boolean` and has a `void` return type), and would be said to have a `boolean` property named `leased` (again, notice the lowercase leading letter in the property name).

Although you can use JSP scriptlets or expressions to access arbitrary methods of a class, standard JSP actions for accessing beans can only make use of methods that use the get*Xxx*/set*Xxx* or is*Xxx*/set*Xxx* naming convention.

Basic Bean Use

The `jsp:useBean` action lets you load a bean to be used in the JSP page. Beans provide a very useful capability because they let you exploit the reusability of Java classes without sacrificing the convenience that JSP adds over servlets alone.

The simplest syntax for specifying that a bean should be used is the following.

```
<jsp:useBean id="name" class="package.Class" />
```

This statement usually means "instantiate an object of the class specified by `Class`, and bind it to a variable with the name specified by `id`."

So, for example, the JSP action

```
<jsp:useBean id="book1" class="moreservlets.Book" />
```

can normally be thought of as equivalent to the scriptlet

```
<% moreservlets.Book book1 = new moreservlets.Book(); %>
```

The bean class definition should be placed in the server's class path (generally, in the same directories where servlets can be installed), *not* in the directory that contains the JSP file. Thus, on most servers, the proper location for bean classes is the *.../WEB-INF/classes* directory discussed in Sections 1.7 and 1.9. With some servers, however (e.g., ServletExec), you have to explicitly add bean classes to the server's `CLASSPATH` *if* you are using the default servlet directories (i.e., not using user-defined Web applications). With user-defined Web applications (see Chapter 4), *all* servers permit individual bean classes to be placed in the application's *WEB-INF/classes* directory and JAR files containing bean classes to be placed in the *WEB-INF/lib* directory.

Although it is convenient to think of `jsp:useBean` as being equivalent to building an object, `jsp:useBean` has additional options that make it more powerful. As we'll see later, you can specify a `scope` attribute that associates the bean with more than just the current page. If beans can be shared, it is useful to obtain references to existing beans, rather than always building a new object. So, the `jsp:useBean` action specifies that a new object is instantiated only if there is no existing one with the same `id` and `scope`.

Rather than using the `class` attribute, you are permitted to use `beanName` instead. The difference is that `beanName` can refer either to a class or to a file containing a serialized bean object. The value of the `beanName` attribute is passed to the `instantiate` method of `java.beans.Bean`.

In most cases, you want the local variable to have the same type as the object being created. In a few cases, however, you might want the variable to be declared to have a type that is a superclass of the actual bean type or is an interface that the bean implements. Use the `type` attribute to control this declaration, as in the following example.

```
<jsp:useBean id="thread1" class="MyClass" type="Runnable" />
```

This use results in code similar to the following being inserted into the `_jspService` method.

```
Runnable thread1 = new MyClass();
```

Note that since `jsp:useBean` uses XML syntax, the format differs in three ways from HTML syntax: the attribute names are case sensitive, either single or double quotes can be used (but one or the other *must* be used), and the end of the tag is marked with `/>`, not just `>`. The first two syntactic differences apply to all JSP elements that look like `jsp:xxx`. The third difference applies unless the element is a container with a separate start and end tag.

A few character sequences also require special handling in order to appear inside attribute values. To get `'` within an attribute value, use `\'`. Similarly, to get `"`, use `\"`; to get `\`, use `\\`; to get `%>`, use `%\>`; and to get `<%`, use `<\%`.

Accessing Bean Properties

Once you have a bean, you can access its properties with `jsp:getProperty`, which takes a `name` attribute that should match the `id` given in `jsp:useBean` and a `property` attribute that names the property of interest. Alternatively, you could use a JSP expression and explicitly call a method on the object that has the variable name specified with the `id` attribute. For example, assuming that the `Book` class has a `String` property called `title` and that you've created an instance called `book1` by using the `jsp:useBean` example just given, you could insert the value of the `title` property into the JSP page in either of the following two ways.

```
<jsp:getProperty name="book1" property="title" />
<%= book1.getTitle() %>
```

The first approach is preferable in this case, since the syntax is more accessible to Web page designers who are not familiar with the Java programming language. However, direct access to the variable is useful when you are using loops, conditional statements, and methods not represented as properties.

If you are not familiar with the concept of bean properties, the standard interpretation of the statement "this bean has a property of type `T` called `foo`" is "this class has a method called `getFoo` that returns something of type `T`, and it has another method called `setFoo` that takes a `T` as an argument and stores it for later access by `getFoo`."

Setting Bean Properties: Simple Case

To modify bean properties, you normally use jsp:setProperty. This action has several different forms, but with the simplest form you just supply three attributes: name (which should match the id given by jsp:useBean), property (the name of the property to change), and value (the new value). Later in this section I present some alternate forms of jsp:setProperty that let you automatically associate a property with a request parameter. That section also explains how to supply values that are computed at request time (rather than fixed strings) and discusses the type conversion conventions that let you supply string values for parameters that expect numbers, characters, or boolean values.

An alternative to using the jsp:setProperty action is to use a scriptlet that explicitly calls methods on the bean object. For example, given the book1 object shown earlier in this section, you could use either of the following two forms to modify the title property.

```
<jsp:setProperty name="book1"
                 property="title"
                 value="Core Servlets and JavaServer Pages" />
<% book1.setTitle("Core Servlets and JavaServer Pages"); %>
```

Using jsp:setProperty has the advantage that it is more accessible to the non-programmer, but direct access to the object lets you perform more complex operations such as setting the value conditionally or calling methods other than get*Xx* or set*Xx* on the object.

Example: StringBean

Listing 3.21 presents a simple class called StringBean that is in the moreservlets package. Because the class has no public instance variables (fields) and has a zero-argument constructor since it doesn't declare any explicit constructors, it satisfies the basic criteria for being a bean. Since StringBean has a method called get-Message that returns a String and another method called setMessage that takes a String as an argument, in beans terminology the class is said to have a String property called message.

Listing 3.22 shows a JSP file that uses the StringBean class. First, an instance of StringBean is created with the jsp:useBean action as follows.

```
<jsp:useBean id="stringBean" class="moreservlets.StringBean" />
```

After this, the message property can be inserted into the page in either of the following two ways.

```
<jsp:getProperty name="stringBean" property="message" />
<%= stringBean.getMessage() %>
```

The `message` property can be modified in either of the following two ways.

```
<jsp:setProperty name="stringBean"
                 property="message"
                 value="some message" />
<% stringBean.setMessage("some message"); %>
```

Please note that I do not recommend that you really mix the explicit Java syntax and the XML syntax in the same page; this example is just meant to illustrate the equivalent results of the two forms.

Figure 3–15 shows the result.

Listing 3.21 *StringBean.java*

```java
package moreservlets;

/** A simple bean that has a single String property
 *  called message.
 */

public class StringBean {
  private String message = "No message specified";

  public String getMessage() {
    return(message);
  }

  public void setMessage(String message) {
    this.message = message;
  }
}
```

Listing 3.22 *StringBean.jsp*

```html
<!DOCTYPE HTML PUBLIC "-//W3C//DTD HTML 4.0 Transitional//EN">
<HTML>
<HEAD>
<TITLE>Using JavaBeans with JSP</TITLE>
<LINK REL=STYLESHEET
      HREF="JSP-Styles.css"
      TYPE="text/css">
</HEAD>
<BODY>
<TABLE BORDER=5 ALIGN="CENTER">
  <TR><TH CLASS="TITLE">
      Using JavaBeans with JSP</TABLE>
```

Listing 3.22 *StringBean.jsp (continued)*

```
<jsp:useBean id="stringBean" class="moreservlets.StringBean" />
<OL>
<LI>Initial value (getProperty):
    <I><jsp:getProperty name="stringBean"
                        property="message" /></I>
<LI>Initial value (JSP expression):
    <I><%= stringBean.getMessage() %></I>
<LI><jsp:setProperty name="stringBean"
                     property="message"
                     value="Best string bean: Fortex" />
    Value after setting property with setProperty:
    <I><jsp:getProperty name="stringBean"
                        property="message" /></I>
<LI><% stringBean.setMessage("My favorite: Kentucky Wonder"); %>
    Value after setting property with scriptlet:
    <I><%= stringBean.getMessage() %></I>
</OL>
</BODY>
</HTML>
```

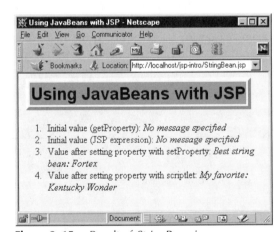

Figure 3–15   Result of *StringBean.jsp.*

Setting Bean Properties

You normally use jsp:setProperty to set bean properties. The simplest form of this action takes three attributes: name (which should match the id given by jsp:useBean), property (the name of the property to change), and value (the new value).

For example, the `SaleEntry` class shown in Listing 3.23 has an `itemID` property (a `String`), a `numItems` property (an `int`), a `discountCode` property (a `double`), and two read-only properties `itemCost` and `totalCost` (each of type `double`). Listing 3.24 shows a JSP file that builds an instance of the `SaleEntry` class by means of:

```
<jsp:useBean id="entry" class="moreservlets.SaleEntry" />
```

The results are shown in Figure 3–16.

Once the bean is instantiated, using an input parameter to set the `itemID` is straightforward, as shown below.

```
<jsp:setProperty
    name="entry"
    property="itemID"
    value='<%= request.getParameter("itemID") %>' />
```

Notice that I used a JSP expression for the `value` parameter. Most JSP attribute values have to be fixed strings, but the `value` attribute of `jsp:setProperty` is permitted to be a request time expression. If the expression uses double quotes internally, recall that single quotes can be used instead of double quotes around attribute values and that `\'` and `\"` can be used to represent single or double quotes within an attribute value. In any case, the point is that it is *possible* to use JSP expressions here, but doing so requires the use of explicit Java code. In some applications, avoiding such explicit code is the main reason for using beans in the first place. Besides, as the next examples will show, the situation becomes much more complicated when the bean property is not of type `String`. The next two subsections will discuss how to solve these problems.

Listing 3.23 *SaleEntry.java*

```java
package moreservlets;

/** Simple bean to illustrate the various forms
 *  of jsp:setProperty.
 */

public class SaleEntry {
  private String itemID = "unknown";
  private double discountCode = 1.0;
  private int numItems = 0;

  public String getItemID() {
    return(itemID);
  }
```

Listing 3.23 *SaleEntry.java (continued)*

```java
  public void setItemID(String itemID) {
    if (itemID != null) {
      this.itemID = itemID;
    } else {
      this.itemID = "unknown";
    }
  }

  public double getDiscountCode() {
    return(discountCode);
  }

  public void setDiscountCode(double discountCode) {
    this.discountCode = discountCode;
  }

  public int getNumItems() {
    return(numItems);
  }

  public void setNumItems(int numItems) {
    this.numItems = numItems;
  }

  // In real life, replace this with database lookup.

  public double getItemCost() {
    double cost;
    if (itemID.equals("a1234")) {
      cost = 12.99*getDiscountCode();
    } else {
      cost = -9999;
    }
    return(roundToPennies(cost));
  }

  private double roundToPennies(double cost) {
    return(Math.floor(cost*100)/100.0);
  }

  public double getTotalCost() {
    return(getItemCost() * getNumItems());
  }
}
```

Listing 3.24 *SaleEntry1.jsp*

```
<!DOCTYPE HTML PUBLIC "-//W3C//DTD HTML 4.0 Transitional//EN">
<HTML>
<HEAD>
<TITLE>Using jsp:setProperty</TITLE>
<LINK REL=STYLESHEET
      HREF="JSP-Styles.css"
      TYPE="text/css">
</HEAD>
<BODY>
<TABLE BORDER=5 ALIGN="CENTER">
  <TR><TH CLASS="TITLE">
      Using jsp:setProperty</TABLE>
<jsp:useBean id="entry" class="moreservlets.SaleEntry" />
<jsp:setProperty
    name="entry"
    property="itemID"
    value='<%= request.getParameter("itemID") %>' />
<%
int numItemsOrdered = 1;
try {
  numItemsOrdered =
    Integer.parseInt(request.getParameter("numItems"));
} catch(NumberFormatException nfe) {}
%>
<jsp:setProperty
    name="entry"
    property="numItems"
    value="<%= numItemsOrdered %>" />
<%
double discountCode = 1.0;
try {
  String discountString =
    request.getParameter("discountCode");
  // In JDK 1.1 use Double.valueOf(discountString).doubleValue()
  discountCode =
    Double.parseDouble(discountString);
} catch(NumberFormatException nfe) {}
%>
<jsp:setProperty
    name="entry"
    property="discountCode"
    value="<%= discountCode %>" />
<BR>
```

Listing 3.24 *SaleEntry1.jsp (continued)*

```
<TABLE ALIGN="CENTER" BORDER=1>
<TR CLASS="COLORED">
  <TH>Item ID<TH>Unit Price<TH>Number Ordered<TH>Total Price
<TR ALIGN="RIGHT">
  <TD><jsp:getProperty name="entry" property="itemID" />
  <TD>$<jsp:getProperty name="entry" property="itemCost" />
  <TD><jsp:getProperty name="entry" property="numItems" />
  <TD>$<jsp:getProperty name="entry" property="totalCost" />
</TABLE>
</BODY>
</HTML>
```

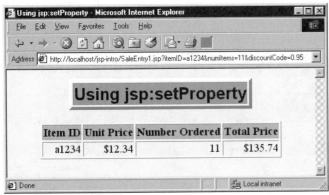

Figure 3–16   Result of *SaleEntry1.jsp*.

Associating Individual Properties with Input Parameters

Setting the `itemID` property is easy since its value is a `String`. Setting the `numItems` and `discountCode` properties is a bit more problematic since their values must be numbers and `getParameter` returns a `String`. Here is the somewhat cumbersome code required to set `numItems`:

```
<%
int numItemsOrdered = 1;
try {
  numItemsOrdered =
    Integer.parseInt(request.getParameter("numItems"));
} catch(NumberFormatException nfe) {}
%>
```

```
<jsp:setProperty
    name="entry"
    property="numItems"
    value="<%= numItemsOrdered %>" />
```

Fortunately, JSP has a nice solution to this problem. It lets you associate a property with a request parameter and automatically perform type conversion from strings to numbers, characters, and boolean values. Instead of using the value attribute, you use param to name an input parameter. The value of the named request parameter is automatically used as the value of the bean property, and simple type conversions are performed automatically. If the specified parameter is missing from the request, no action is taken (the system does not pass null to the associated property). So, for example, setting the numItems property can be simplified to:

```
<jsp:setProperty
    name="entry"
    property="numItems"
    param="numItems" />
```

Listing 3.25 shows the relevant part of the JSP page reworked in this manner.

Listing 3.25 *SaleEntry2.jsp*

```
. . .
<jsp:useBean id="entry" class="moreservlets.SaleEntry" />
<jsp:setProperty
    name="entry"
    property="itemID"
    param="itemID" />
<jsp:setProperty
    name="entry"
    property="numItems"
    param="numItems" />
<jsp:setProperty
    name="entry"
    property="discountCode"
    param="discountCode" />
. . .
```

Converting Types Automatically

When bean properties are associated with input parameters, the system automatically performs simple type conversions for properties that expect primitive types (byte, int, double, etc.) or the corresponding wrapper types (Byte, Integer, Double, etc.).

Associating All Properties with Input Parameters

Associating a property with an input parameter saves you the bother of performing conversions for many of the simple built-in types. JSP lets you take the process one step further by associating *all* properties with identically named input parameters. All you have to do is to supply "*" for the `property` parameter. So, for example, all three of the `jsp:setProperty` statements of Listing 3.25 can be replaced by the following simple line. Listing 3.26 shows the relevant part of the page.

```
<jsp:setProperty name="entry" property="*" />
```

Although this approach is simple, three small warnings are in order. First, as with individually associated properties, no action is taken when an input parameter is missing. In particular, the system does not supply `null` as the property value. Second, automatic type conversion does not guard against illegal values as effectively as does manual type conversion. So, you might consider error pages when using automatic type conversion. Third, since both bean property names and request parameters are case sensitive, the property name and request parameter name must match exactly.

Listing 3.26	*SaleEntry3.jsp*

```
...
<jsp:useBean id="entry" class="msajsp.SaleEntry" />
<jsp:setProperty name="entry" property="*" />
...
```

Sharing Beans

Up to this point, I have treated the objects that were created with `jsp:useBean` as though they were simply bound to local variables in the `_jspService` method (which is called by the `service` method of the servlet that is generated from the page). Although the beans are indeed bound to local variables, that is not the only behavior. They are also stored in one of four different locations, depending on the value of the optional `scope` attribute of `jsp:useBean`. The `scope` attribute has the following possible values:

- **page**
  This is the default value. It indicates that, in addition to being bound to a local variable, the bean object should be placed in the `PageContext` object for the duration of the current request. Storing the object there means that servlet code can access it by calling `getAttribute` on the predefined `pageContext` variable.

- `application`
  This very useful value means that, in addition to being bound to a local variable, the bean will be stored in the shared `ServletContext` available through the predefined `application` variable or by a call to `getServletContext()`. The `ServletContext` is shared by all servlets in the same Web application. Values in the `ServletContext` can be retrieved by the `getAttribute` method. This sharing has a couple of ramifications.

  First, it provides a simple mechanism for multiple servlets and JSP pages to access the same object. See the following subsection (Creating Beans Conditionally) for details and an example.

  Second, it lets a servlet *create* a bean that will be used in JSP pages, not just *access* one that was previously created. This approach lets a servlet handle complex user requests by setting up beans, storing them in the `ServletContext`, then forwarding the request to one of several possible JSP pages to present results appropriate to the request data. For details on this approach, see Section 3.8 (Integrating Servlets and JSP: The MVC Architecture).

- `session`
  This value means that, in addition to being bound to a local variable, the bean will be stored in the `HttpSession` object associated with the current request, where it can be retrieved with `getAttribute`.

- `request`
  This value signifies that, in addition to being bound to a local variable, the bean object should be placed in the `ServletRequest` object for the duration of the current request, where it is available by means of the `getAttribute` method. Storing values in the request object is common when using the MVC (Model 2) architecture. For details, see Section 3.8 (Integrating Servlets and JSP: The MVC Architecture).

Creating Beans Conditionally

To make bean sharing more convenient, you can conditionally evaluate bean-related elements in two situations.

First, a `jsp:useBean` element results in a new bean being instantiated only if no bean with the same `id` and `scope` can be found. If a bean with the same `id` and `scope` *is* found, the preexisting bean is simply bound to the variable referenced by `id`. A typecast is performed if the preexisting bean is of a more specific type than the bean being declared, and a `ClassCastException` results if this typecast is illegal.

Second, instead of

```
<jsp:useBean ... />
```

you can use

```
<jsp:useBean ...>statements</jsp:useBean>
```

The point of using the second form is that the statements between the `jsp:use-`
`Bean` start and end tags are executed *only* if a new bean is created, *not* if an existing
bean is used. This conditional execution is convenient for setting initial bean properties for beans that are shared by multiple pages. Since you don't know which page
will be accessed first, you don't know which page should contain the initialization
code. No problem: they can all contain the code, but only the page first accessed
actually executes it. For example, Listing 3.27 shows a simple bean that can be used
to record cumulative access counts to any of a set of related pages. It also stores the
name of the first page that was accessed. Since there is no way to predict which page
in a set will be accessed first, each page that uses the shared counter has statements
like the following to ensure that only the first page that is accessed sets the
`firstPage` attribute.

```
<jsp:useBean id="counter"
             class="moreservlets.AccessCountBean"
             scope="application">
  <jsp:setProperty name="counter"
                   property="firstPage"
                   value="Current Page Name" />
</jsp:useBean>
```

Listing 3.28 shows the first of three pages that use this approach. The source code
archive at *http://www.moreservlets.com* contains the other two nearly identical
pages. Figure 3–17 shows a typical result.

Listing 3.27   *AccessCountBean.java*

```
package moreservlets;

/** Simple bean to illustrate sharing beans through
 *  use of the scope attribute of jsp:useBean.
 */

public class AccessCountBean {
  private String firstPage;
  private int accessCount = 1;

  public String getFirstPage() {
    return(firstPage);
  }

  public void setFirstPage(String firstPage) {
    this.firstPage = firstPage;
  }
```

Listing 3.27   *AccessCountBean.java (continued)*

```java
  public int getAccessCount() {
    return(accessCount);
  }

  public void setAccessCountIncrement(int increment) {
    accessCount = accessCount + increment;
  }
}
```

Listing 3.28   *SharedCounts1.jsp*

```html
<!DOCTYPE HTML PUBLIC "-//W3C//DTD HTML 4.0 Transitional//EN">
<HTML>
<HEAD>
<TITLE>Shared Access Counts: Page 1</TITLE>
<LINK REL=STYLESHEET
      HREF="JSP-Styles.css"
      TYPE="text/css">
</HEAD>
<BODY>
<TABLE BORDER=5 ALIGN="CENTER">
  <TR><TH CLASS="TITLE">
      Shared Access Counts: Page 1</TABLE>
<P>
<jsp:useBean id="counter"
             class="moreservlets.AccessCountBean"
             scope="application">
  <jsp:setProperty name="counter"
                   property="firstPage"
                   value="SharedCounts1.jsp" />
</jsp:useBean>
Of SharedCounts1.jsp (this page),
<A HREF="SharedCounts2.jsp">SharedCounts2.jsp</A>, and
<A HREF="SharedCounts3.jsp">SharedCounts3.jsp</A>,
<jsp:getProperty name="counter" property="firstPage" />
was the first page accessed.
<P>
Collectively, the three pages have been accessed
<jsp:getProperty name="counter" property="accessCount" />
times.
<jsp:setProperty name="counter" property="accessCountIncrement"
                 value="1" />
</BODY>
</HTML>
```

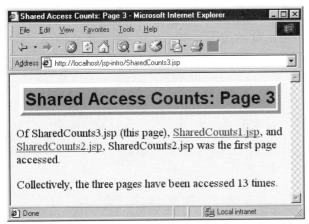

Figure 3–17   Result of a user visiting *SharedCounts3.jsp*. The first page visited by any user was *SharedCounts2.jsp*. *SharedCounts1.jsp*, *SharedCounts2.jsp*, and *SharedCounts3.jsp* were collectively visited a total of twelve times after the server was last started but before the visit shown in this figure.

3.7 Defining Custom JSP Tag Libraries

JSP 1.1 introduced an extremely valuable new capability: the ability to create your own JSP tags. You define how a tag, its attributes, and its body are interpreted, then group your tags into collections called *tag libraries* that can be used in any number of JSP files. The ability to define tag libraries in this way permits Java developers to boil down complex server-side behaviors into simple and easy-to-use elements that content developers can easily incorporate into their JSP pages. This section introduces the basic capabilities of custom tags. New features introduced in JSP 1.2 are covered in Chapter 11 (New Tag Library Features in JSP 1.2).

Custom tags accomplish some of the same goals as beans that are accessed with `jsp:useBean` (see Figure 3–18)—encapsulating complex behaviors into simple and accessible forms. There are several differences, however:

1. Custom tags can manipulate JSP content; beans cannot.
2. Complex operations can be reduced to a significantly simpler form with custom tags than with beans.
3. Custom tags require quite a bit more work to set up than do beans.

4. Custom tags usually define relatively self-contained behavior, whereas beans are often defined in one servlet and then used in a different servlet or JSP page (see the following section on integrating servlets and JSP).

5. Custom tags are available only in JSP 1.1 and later, but beans can be used in all JSP 1.x versions.

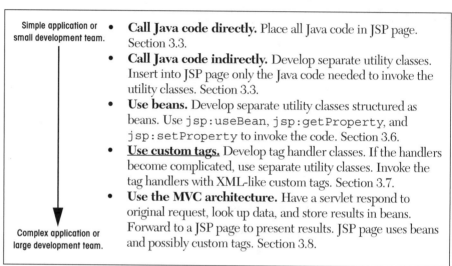

Simple application or small development team.

- **Call Java code directly.** Place all Java code in JSP page. Section 3.3.
- **Call Java code indirectly.** Develop separate utility classes. Insert into JSP page only the Java code needed to invoke the utility classes. Section 3.3.
- **Use beans.** Develop separate utility classes structured as beans. Use `jsp:useBean`, `jsp:getProperty`, and `jsp:setProperty` to invoke the code. Section 3.6.
- **Use custom tags.** Develop tag handler classes. If the handlers become complicated, use separate utility classes. Invoke the tag handlers with XML-like custom tags. Section 3.7.
- **Use the MVC architecture.** Have a servlet respond to original request, look up data, and store results in beans. Forward to a JSP page to present results. JSP page uses beans and possibly custom tags. Section 3.8.

Complex application or large development team.

Figure 3–18 Strategies for invoking dynamic code from JSP.

The Components That Make Up a Tag Library

To use custom JSP tags, you need to define three separate components: the tag handler class that defines the tag's behavior, the tag library descriptor file that maps the XML element names to the tag implementations, and the JSP file that uses the tag library. The rest of this subsection gives an overview of each of these components, and the following subsections give details on how to build these components for various styles of tags. Most people find that the first tag they write is the hardest—the difficulty being in knowing where each component should go, not in writing the components. So, I suggest that you start by just downloading the examples of this subsection and getting the example tag working. After that, you can move on to the following subsections and try some of your own tags.

The Tag Handler Class

When defining a new tag, your first task is to define a Java class that tells the system what to do when it sees the tag. This class must implement the `javax.servlet.jsp.tagext.Tag` interface. You usually accomplish this by extending the `TagSupport` or `BodyTagSupport` class.

Listing 3.29 is an example of a simple tag that just inserts "`Custom tag example (msajsp.tags.ExampleTag)`" into the JSP page wherever the corresponding tag is used. Don't worry about understanding the exact behavior of this class; that will be made clear in the next subsection. For now, just note that the class is in the more-servlets.tags package and is called `ExampleTag`. Consequently, the class file needs to be placed in *tags* subdirectory of the *moreservlets* subdirectory of whatever directory the current Web application is using for Java class files (i.e., *.../WEB-INF/classes*—see Sections 1.7 and 1.9). With Tomcat, for example, the class file would be in *install_dir/webapps/ROOT/WEB-INF/classes/moreservlets/tags/ExampleTag.class*.

Listing 3.29 *ExampleTag.java*

```
package moreservlets.tags;

import javax.servlet.jsp.*;
import javax.servlet.jsp.tagext.*;
import java.io.*;

/** Very simple JSP tag that just inserts a string
 *  ("Custom tag example...") into the output.
 *  The actual name of the tag is not defined here;
 *  that is given by the Tag Library Descriptor (TLD)
 *  file that is referenced by the taglib directive
 *  in the JSP file.
 */

public class ExampleTag extends TagSupport {
  public int doStartTag() {
    try {
      JspWriter out = pageContext.getOut();
      out.print("Custom tag example " +
                "(moreservlets.tags.ExampleTag)");
    } catch(IOException ioe) {
      System.out.println("Error in ExampleTag: " + ioe);
    }
    return(SKIP_BODY);
  }
}
```

The Tag Library Descriptor File

Once you have defined a tag handler, your next task is to identify the class to the server and to associate it with a particular XML tag name. This task is accomplished by means of a tag library descriptor file (in XML format) like the one shown in Listing 3.30. This file contains some fixed information, an arbitrary short name for your library, a short description, and a series of tag descriptions. The nonbold part of the listing is the same in virtually all tag library descriptors and can be copied verbatim from the source code archive at *http://www.moreservlets.com*.

The format of tag descriptions is described in later sections. For now, just note that the `tag` element defines the main name of the tag (really tag suffix, as will be seen shortly) and identifies the class that handles the tag. Since the tag handler class is in the `moreservlets.tags` package, the fully qualified class name of `moreservlets.tags.ExampleTag` is used. Note that this is a class name, not a URL or relative path name. The class can be installed anywhere on the server that beans or other supporting classes can be put. With Tomcat, the base location for classes in the default Web application is *install_dir/webapps/ROOT/WEB-INF/classes*, so *ExampleTag.class* would be in *install_dir/webapps/ROOT/WEB-INF/classes/moreservlets/tags*. Although it is always a good idea to put your servlet classes in packages, a surprising feature of Tomcat is that tag handlers are *required* to be in packages.

Listing 3.30   *msajsp-taglib.tld*

```
<?xml version="1.0" encoding="ISO-8859-1" ?>
<!DOCTYPE taglib
  PUBLIC "-//Sun Microsystems, Inc.//DTD JSP Tag Library 1.1//EN"
  "http://java.sun.com/j2ee/dtds/web-jsptaglibrary_1_1.dtd">

<taglib>
  <tlibversion>1.0</tlibversion>
  <jspversion>1.1</jspversion>
  <shortname>msajsp-tags</shortname>
  <info>
    A tag library from More Servlets and JavaServer Pages,
    http://www.moreservlets.com/.
  </info>
  <tag>
    <name>example</name>
    <tagclass>moreservlets.tags.ExampleTag</tagclass>
    <bodycontent>empty</bodycontent>
    <info>Simplest example: inserts one line of output</info>
  </tag>
  ...
</taglib>
```

The JSP File

Once you have a tag handler implementation and a tag library description, you are ready to write a JSP file that makes use of the tag. Listing 3.31 gives an example. Somewhere before the first use of your tag, you need to use the `taglib` directive. This directive has the following form:

```
<%@ taglib uri="..." prefix="..." %>
```

The required `uri` attribute can be either an absolute or relative URL referring to a tag library descriptor file like the one shown in Listing 3.30. For now, we will use a simple relative URL corresponding to a TLD file that is in the same directory as the JSP page that uses it. When we get to Web applications, however (see Chapter 4), we will see that it makes more sense for larger applications to put the TLD files in a subdirectory inside the *WEB-INF* directory. This configuration makes it easier to reuse the same TLD file from JSP pages in multiple directories, and it prevents end users from retrieving the TLD file. Furthermore, as we will see in Section 5.13 (Locating Tag Library Descriptors), you can use the Web application deployment descriptor (i.e., *web.xml*) to change the meaning of strings supplied to the `uri` attribute of the `taglib` directive. When starting out, however, you will probably find it easiest to put the TLD file in the same directory as the JSP page that uses it and then use a simple filename as the value of the `uri` attribute.

The `prefix` attribute, also required, specifies a prefix that will be used in front of whatever tag name the tag library descriptor defined. For example, if the TLD file defines a tag named `tag1` and the `prefix` attribute has a value of `test`, the actual tag name would be `test:tag1`. This tag could be used in either of the following two ways, depending on whether it is defined to be a container that makes use of the tag body:

```
<test:tag1>Arbitrary JSP</test:tag1>
```

or just

```
<test:tag1 />
```

To illustrate, the descriptor file of Listing 3.30 is called `msajsp-taglib.tld` and resides in the same directory as the JSP file shown in Listing 3.31 (i.e., any of the standard locations for JSP files described in Section 3.3, *not* the directory where Java class files are placed). Thus, the `taglib` directive in the JSP file uses a simple relative URL giving just the filename, as shown below.

```
<%@ taglib uri="msajsp-taglib.tld" prefix="msajsp" %>
```

Furthermore, since the `prefix` attribute is `msajsp` (for *More Servlets and Java-Server Pages*), the rest of the JSP page uses `msajsp:example` to refer to the `example` tag defined in the descriptor file. Figure 3–19 shows the result.

Listing 3.31 *SimpleExample.jsp*

```
<!DOCTYPE HTML PUBLIC "-//W3C//DTD HTML 4.0 Transitional//EN">
<HTML>
<HEAD>
<%@ taglib uri="msajsp-taglib.tld" prefix="msajsp" %>
<TITLE><msajsp:example /></TITLE>
<LINK REL=STYLESHEET
      HREF="JSP-Styles.css"
      TYPE="text/css">
</HEAD>
<BODY>
<H1><msajsp:example /></H1>
<msajsp:example />
</BODY>
</HTML>
```

Figure 3–19   Result of *SimpleExample.jsp*.

Defining a Basic Tag

This subsection gives details on defining simple tags without attributes or tag bodies; the tags are thus of the form `<prefix:tagname />`.

A Basic Tag: Tag Handler Class

Tags that either have no body or that merely include the body verbatim should extend the `TagSupport` class. This is a built-in class in the `javax.servlet.jsp.tagext` package that implements the `Tag` interface and contains much of the standard functionality basic tags need. Because of other classes you will use, your tag should normally import classes in the `javax.servlet.jsp` and `java.io` packages as well. So, most tag implementations contain the following `import` statements after the package declaration:

```
import javax.servlet.jsp.*;
import javax.servlet.jsp.tagext.*;
import java.io.*;
```

I recommend that you grab an example from *http://www.moreservlets.com* and use it as the starting point for your own implementations.

For a tag without attributes or body, all you need to do is override the `doStart-Tag` method, which defines code that gets called *at request time* at the place where the element's start tag is found. To generate output, the method should obtain the `JspWriter` (the specialized `Writer` available in JSP pages through use of the predefined `out` variable) from the automatically defined `pageContext` field by means of `getOut`. In addition to the `getOut` method, the `pageContext` field (of type `PageContext`) has methods for obtaining other data structures associated with the request. The most important ones are `getRequest`, `getResponse`, `getServlet-Context`, and `getSession`.

Since the `print` method of `JspWriter` throws `IOException`, the `print` statements should be inside a `try/catch` block. To report other types of errors to the client, you can declare that your `doStartTag` method throws a `JspException` and then throw one when the error occurs.

If your tag does not have a body, your `doStartTag` should return the `SKIP_BODY` constant. This instructs the system to ignore any content between the tag's start and end tags. As we will see shortly, `SKIP_BODY` is sometimes useful even when there is a tag body (e.g., if you sometimes include it and other times omit it), but the simple tag we're developing here will be used as a stand-alone tag (`<prefix:tagname />`) and thus does not have body content.

Listing 3.32 shows a tag implementation that uses this approach to generate a random 50-digit prime number through use of the `Primes` class (Listing 3.33), which is adapted from Section 7.3 (Persistent Servlet State and Auto-Reloading Pages) of *Core Servlets and JavaServer Pages*. Remember that the full text of *Core Servlets and JavaServer Pages* is available in PDF at *http://www.moreservlets.com*.

Listing 3.32 *SimplePrimeTag.java*

```java
package moreservlets.tags;

import javax.servlet.jsp.*;
import javax.servlet.jsp.tagext.*;
import java.io.*;
import java.math.*;
import moreservlets.*;

/** Generates a prime of approximately 50 digits.
 *  (50 is actually the length of the random number
 *  generated -- the first prime above that number will
 *  be returned.)
 */

public class SimplePrimeTag extends TagSupport {
  protected int len = 50;

  public int doStartTag() {
    try {
      JspWriter out = pageContext.getOut();
      BigInteger prime = Primes.nextPrime(Primes.random(len));
      out.print(prime);
    } catch(IOException ioe) {
      System.out.println("Error generating prime: " + ioe);
    }
    return(SKIP_BODY);
  }
}
```

Listing 3.33 *Primes.java*

```java
package moreservlets;

import java.math.BigInteger;

/** A few utilities to generate a large random BigInteger,
 *  and find the next prime number above a given BigInteger.
 */
```

Listing 3.33   *Primes.java (continued)*

```java
public class Primes {
  // Note that BigInteger.ZERO and BigInteger.ONE are
  // unavailable in JDK 1.1.
  private static final BigInteger ZERO = BigInteger.ZERO;
  private static final BigInteger ONE = BigInteger.ONE;
  private static final BigInteger TWO = new BigInteger("2");

  // Likelihood of false prime is less than 1/2^ERR_VAL
  // Assumedly BigInteger uses the Miller-Rabin test or
  // equivalent, and thus is NOT fooled by Carmichael numbers.
  // See section 33.8 of Cormen et al.'s Introduction to
  // Algorithms for details.
  private static final int ERR_VAL = 100;

  public static BigInteger nextPrime(BigInteger start) {
    if (isEven(start))
      start = start.add(ONE);
    else
      start = start.add(TWO);
    if (start.isProbablePrime(ERR_VAL))
      return(start);
    else
      return(nextPrime(start));
  }

  private static boolean isEven(BigInteger n) {
    return(n.mod(TWO).equals(ZERO));
  }

  private static StringBuffer[] digits =
    { new StringBuffer("0"), new StringBuffer("1"),
      new StringBuffer("2"), new StringBuffer("3"),
      new StringBuffer("4"), new StringBuffer("5"),
      new StringBuffer("6"), new StringBuffer("7"),
      new StringBuffer("8"), new StringBuffer("9") };

  private static StringBuffer randomDigit(boolean isZeroOK) {
    int index;
    if (isZeroOK) {
      index = (int)Math.floor(Math.random() * 10);
    } else {
      index = 1 + (int)Math.floor(Math.random() * 9);
    }
    return(digits[index]);
  }
```

Listing 3.33   *Primes.java (continued)*

```java
/** Create a random big integer where every digit is
 *  selected randomly (except that the first digit
 *  cannot be a zero).
 */

public static BigInteger random(int numDigits) {
  StringBuffer s = new StringBuffer("");
  for(int i=0; i<numDigits; i++) {
    if (i == 0) {
      // First digit must be non-zero.
      s.append(randomDigit(false));
    } else {
      s.append(randomDigit(true));
    }
  }
  return(new BigInteger(s.toString()));
}

/** Simple command-line program to test. Enter number
 *  of digits, and it picks a random number of that
 *  length and then prints the first 50 prime numbers
 *  above that.
 */

public static void main(String[] args) {
  int numDigits;
  try {
    numDigits = Integer.parseInt(args[0]);
  } catch (Exception e) { // No args or illegal arg.
    numDigits = 150;
  }
  BigInteger start = random(numDigits);
  for(int i=0; i<50; i++) {
    start = nextPrime(start);
    System.out.println("Prime " + i + " = " + start);
  }
}
}
```

A Basic Tag: Tag Library Descriptor File

The general format of a descriptor file is almost always the same: it should contain an XML version identifier followed by a DOCTYPE declaration followed by a taglib container element, as shown earlier in Listing 3.30. To get started, just download a sample from the source code archive at *http://www.moreservlets.com*. The important part to understand is what goes *in* the `taglib` element: the `tag` element. For tags without attributes, the `tag` element should contain four elements between `<tag>` and `</tag>`:

1. **name**, whose body defines the base tag name to which the prefix of the `taglib` directive will be attached. In this case, I use

   `<name>simplePrime</name>`

   to assign a base tag name of `simplePrime`.

2. **tagclass**, which gives the fully qualified class name of the tag handler. In this case, I use

   `<tagclass>moreservlets.tags.SimplePrimeTag</tagclass>`

   Note that `tagclass` was renamed `tag-class` in JSP 1.2. So, if you use features specific to JSP 1.2 and use the JSP 1.2 `DOCTYPE`, you should use `tag-class`, not `tagclass`.

3. **bodycontent**, which can be omitted, but if present should have the value `empty` for tags without bodies. Tags with normal bodies that might be interpreted as normal JSP use a value of `JSP` (the default value), and the rare tags whose handlers completely process the body themselves use a value of `tagdependent`. For the `SimplePrime-Tag` discussed here, I use `empty` as below:

   `<bodycontent>empty</bodycontent>`

   Note that `bodycontent` was renamed `body-content` in JSP 1.2. However, as with the other new element names, you are only required to make the change if you use the JSP 1.2 `DOCTYPE`.

4. **info**, which gives a short description. Here, I use

   `<info>Outputs a random 50-digit prime.</info>`

   Note that `info` was renamed `description` in JSP 1.2.

Core Note

In JSP 1.2, `tagclass` was renamed `tag-class`, `bodycontent` was renamed `body-content`, and `info` was renamed `description`. However, the old element names still work in JSP 1.2 servers as long as the TLD file uses the JSP 1.1 `DOCTYPE`.

Listing 3.34 shows the relevant part of the TLD file.

Listing 3.34	*msajsp-taglib.tld* (Excerpt 1)

```xml
<?xml version="1.0" encoding="ISO-8859-1" ?>
<!DOCTYPE ...>
<taglib>
  ...
  <tag>
    <name>simplePrime</name>
    <tagclass>moreservlets.tags.SimplePrimeTag</tagclass>
    <bodycontent>empty</bodycontent>
    <info>Outputs a random 50-digit prime.</info>
  </tag>
  ...
</taglib>
```

A Basic Tag: JSP File

JSP documents that make use of custom tags need to use the `taglib` directive, supplying a `uri` attribute that gives the location of the tag library descriptor file and a `prefix` attribute that specifies a short string that will be attached (along with a colon) to the main tag name. Remember that the `uri` attribute can be an absolute or relative URL. When first learning, it is easiest to use a simple relative URL corresponding to a TLD file that is in the same directory as the JSP page that uses it. When we get to Web applications, however (see Chapter 4), we will see that it makes more sense for larger applications to put the TLD files in a subdirectory inside the *WEB-INF* directory. This configuration makes it easier to reuse the same TLD file from JSP pages in multiple directories, and it prevents end users from retrieving the TLD file.

Furthermore, as we will see in Section 5.13 (Locating Tag Library Descriptors), you can use the Web application deployment descriptor (i.e., *web.xml*) to change the meaning of strings supplied to the `uri` attribute of the `taglib` directive. For now, however, you will probably find it easiest to put the TLD file in the same directory as the JSP page that uses it and then use a simple filename as the value of the `uri` attribute.

Listing 3.35 shows a JSP document that uses

```
<%@ taglib uri="msajsp-taglib.tld" prefix="msajsp" %>
```

to use the TLD file just shown in Listing 3.34 with a prefix of `msajsp`. Since the base tag name is `simplePrime`, the full tag used is

```
<msajsp:simplePrime />
```

Figure 3–20 shows the result.

Listing 3.35 *SimplePrimeExample.jsp*

```
<!DOCTYPE HTML PUBLIC "-//W3C//DTD HTML 4.0 Transitional//EN">
<HTML>
<HEAD>
<TITLE>Some 50-Digit Primes</TITLE>
<LINK REL=STYLESHEET
      HREF="JSP-Styles.css"
      TYPE="text/css">
</HEAD>
<BODY>
<H1>Some 50-Digit Primes</H1>
<%@ taglib uri="msajsp-taglib.tld" prefix="msajsp" %>
<UL>
  <LI><msajsp:simplePrime />
  <LI><msajsp:simplePrime />
  <LI><msajsp:simplePrime />
  <LI><msajsp:simplePrime />
</UL>
</BODY>
</HTML>
```

Figure 3–20   Result of *SimplePrimeExample.jsp*.

Assigning Attributes to Tags

Allowing tags like

```
<prefix:name attribute1="value1" attribute2="value2" ... />
```

adds significant flexibility to your tag library. This subsection explains how to add attribute support to your tags.

Tag Attributes: Tag Handler Class

Providing support for attributes is straightforward. Use of an attribute called attribute1 simply results in a call to a method called setAttribute1 in your class that extends TagSupport (or that otherwise implements the Tag interface). Consequently, adding support for an attribute named attribute1 is merely a matter of implementing the following method:

```
public void setAttribute1(String value1) {
  doSomethingWith(value1);
}
```

Note that an attribute of attributeName (lowercase a) corresponds to a method called setAttributeName (uppercase A).

Static values (i.e., those determined at page translation time) are always supplied to the method as type String. However, you can use rtexprvalue and type elements in the TLD file to permit attributes of other types to be dynamically calculated. See the following subsection for details.

One of the most common things to do in the attribute handler is to simply store the attribute in a field that will later be used by doStartTag or a similar method. For example, the following is a section of a tag implementation that adds support for the message attribute.

```
private String message = "Default Message";

public void setMessage(String message) {
  this.message = message;
}
```

If the tag handler will be accessed from other classes, it is a good idea to provide a getAttributeName method in addition to the setAttributeName method. Only setAttributeName is required, however.

Listing 3.36 shows a subclass of SimplePrimeTag that adds support for the length attribute. When such an attribute is supplied, it results in a call to set-Length, which converts the input String to an int and stores it in the len field already used by the doStartTag method in the parent class.

| Listing 3.36 | *PrimeTag.java* |

```
package moreservlets.tags;

/** Generates an N-digit random prime (default N = 50).
 *  Extends SimplePrimeTag, adding a length attribute
 *  to set the size of the prime. The doStartTag
 *  method of the parent class uses the len field
 *  to determine the length of the prime.
 */

public class PrimeTag extends SimplePrimeTag {
  public void setLength(String length) {
    try {
      len = Integer.parseInt(length);
    } catch(NumberFormatException nfe) {
      len = 50;
    }
  }
}
```

Tag Attributes: Tag Library Descriptor File

Tag attributes must be declared inside the `tag` element by means of an `attribute` element. The `attribute` element has five nested elements that can appear between `<attribute>` and `</attribute>`.

1. **name**, a required element that defines the case-sensitive attribute name. In this case, I use

    `<name>length</name>`

2. **required**, a required element that stipulates whether the attribute must always be supplied (`true`) or is optional (`false`). In this case, to indicate that `length` is optional, I use

    `<required>false</required>`

    If `required` is `false` and the JSP page omits the attribute, no call is made to the `setAttributeName` method. So, be sure to give default values to the fields that the method sets. Omitting a required attribute results in an error at page translation time.

3. **rtexprvalue**, an optional element that indicates whether the attribute value can be a JSP expression like `<%= expression %>` (`true`) or whether it must be a fixed string (`false`). The default value is `false`, so this element is usually omitted except when you want to allow attributes to have values determined at request time.

4. **type**, an optional element that designates the class to which the value should be typecast. Designating a type is only legal when rtexprvalue is true.

5. **example**, an optional element that gives an example of how to use the tag. This element is intended for development environments and has no effect on execution; it is available only in JSP 1.2.

Listing 3.37 shows the relevant tag element within the tag library descriptor file. In addition to supplying an attribute element to describe the length attribute, the tag element also contains the standard name (prime), tagclass (moreservlets.tags.PrimeTag), bodycontent (empty), and info (short description) elements. Note that if you use features specific to JSP 1.2 and the JSP 1.2 DOCTYPE (see Chapter 11, "New Tag Library Features in JSP 1.2"), you should change tagclass, bodycontent, and info to tag-class, body-content, and description, respectively.

Listing 3.37   *msajsp-taglib.tld* (Excerpt 2)

```xml
<?xml version="1.0" encoding="ISO-8859-1" ?>
<!DOCTYPE ...>
<taglib>
  ...
  <tag>
    <name>prime</name>
    <tagclass>moreservlets.tags.PrimeTag</tagclass>
    <bodycontent>empty</bodycontent>
    <info>Outputs a random N-digit prime.</info>
    <attribute>
      <name>length</name>
      <required>false</required>
    </attribute>
  </tag>
  ...
</taglib>
```

Tag Attributes: JSP File

Listing 3.38 shows a JSP document that uses the taglib directive to load the tag library descriptor file and to specify a prefix of msajsp. Since the prime tag is defined to permit a length attribute, Listing 3.38 uses

```
<msajsp:prime length="xxx" />
```

Remember that custom tags follow XML syntax, which requires attribute values to be enclosed in either single or double quotes. Also, since the `length` attribute is not required, it is permissible to just use

```
<msajsp:prime />
```

The tag handler is responsible for using a reasonable default value in such a case. Figure 3–21 shows the result of Listing 3.38.

Listing 3.38   *PrimeExample.jsp*

```
<!DOCTYPE HTML PUBLIC "-//W3C//DTD HTML 4.0 Transitional//EN">
<HTML>
<HEAD>
<TITLE>Some N-Digit Primes</TITLE>
<LINK REL=STYLESHEET
      HREF="JSP-Styles.css"
      TYPE="text/css">
</HEAD>
<BODY>
<H1>Some N-Digit Primes</H1>
<%@ taglib uri="msajsp-taglib.tld" prefix="msajsp" %>
<UL>
  <LI>20-digit: <msajsp:prime length="20" />
  <LI>40-digit: <msajsp:prime length="40" />
  <LI>80-digit: <msajsp:prime length="80" />
  <LI>Default (50-digit): <msajsp:prime />
</UL>
</BODY>
</HTML>
```

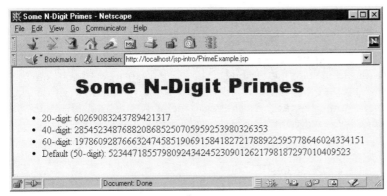

Figure 3–21   Result of *PrimeExample.jsp*.

Including the Tag Body

Up to this point, all of the custom tags you have seen ignore the tag body and thus are used as stand-alone tags of the form

```
<prefix:tagname />
```

In this section, we see how to define tags that use their body content and are thus written in the following manner:

```
<prefix:tagname>body</prefix:tagname>
```

Tag Bodies: Tag Handler Class

In the previous examples, the tag handlers defined a `doStartTag` method that returned `SKIP_BODY`. To instruct the system to make use of the body that occurs between the new element's start and end tags, your `doStartTag` method should return `EVAL_BODY_INCLUDE` instead. The body content can contain JSP scripting elements, directives, and actions, just like the rest of the page. The JSP constructs are translated into servlet code at page translation time, and that code is invoked at request time.

If you make use of a tag body, then you might want to take some action *after* the body as well as before it. Use the `doEndTag` method to specify this action. In almost all cases, you want to continue with the rest of the page after finishing with your tag, so the `doEndTag` method should return `EVAL_PAGE`. If you want to abort the processing of the rest of the page, you can return `SKIP_PAGE` instead.

Listing 3.39 defines a tag for a heading element that is more flexible than the standard HTML `H1` through `H6` elements. This new element allows a precise font size, a list of preferred font names (the first entry that is available on the client system will be used), a foreground color, a background color, a border, and an alignment (`LEFT`, `CENTER`, `RIGHT`). Only the alignment capability is available with the `H1` through `H6` elements. The heading is implemented through use of a one-cell table enclosing a `SPAN` element that has embedded style sheet attributes. The `doStartTag` method generates the `TABLE` and `SPAN` start tags, then returns `EVAL_BODY_INCLUDE` to instruct the system to include the tag body. The `doEndTag` method generates the `</SPAN>` and `</TABLE>` tags, then returns `EVAL_PAGE` to continue with normal page processing. Various `setAttributeName` methods are used to handle the attributes like `bgColor` and `fontSize`.

Listing 3.39   *HeadingTag.java*

```java
package moreservlets.tags;

import javax.servlet.jsp.*;
import javax.servlet.jsp.tagext.*;
import java.io.*;

/** Generates an HTML heading with the specified background
 *  color, foreground color, alignment, font, and font size.
 *  You can also turn on a border around it, which normally
 *  just barely encloses the heading, but which can also
 *  stretch wider. All attributes except the background
 *  color are optional.
 */

public class HeadingTag extends TagSupport {
  private String bgColor; // The one required attribute
  private String color = null;
  private String align="CENTER";
  private String fontSize="36";
  private String fontList="Arial, Helvetica, sans-serif";
  private String border="0";
  private String width=null;

  public void setBgColor(String bgColor) {
    this.bgColor = bgColor;
  }

  public void setColor(String color) {
    this.color = color;
  }

  public void setAlign(String align) {
    this.align = align;
  }

  public void setFontSize(String fontSize) {
    this.fontSize = fontSize;
  }

  public void setFontList(String fontList) {
    this.fontList = fontList;
  }
```

Listing 3.39 *HeadingTag.java (continued)*

```java
public void setBorder(String border) {
  this.border = border;
}

public void setWidth(String width) {
  this.width = width;
}

public int doStartTag() {
  try {
    JspWriter out = pageContext.getOut();
    out.print("<TABLE BORDER=" + border +
              " BGCOLOR=\"" + bgColor + "\"" +
              " ALIGN=\"" + align + "\"");
    if (width != null) {
      out.print(" WIDTH=\"" + width + "\"");
    }
    out.print("><TR><TH>");
    out.print("<SPAN STYLE=\"" +
              "font-size: " + fontSize + "px; " +
              "font-family: " + fontList + "; ");
    if (color != null) {
      out.println("color: " + color + ";");
    }
    out.print("\"> "); // End of <SPAN ...>
  } catch(IOException ioe) {
    System.out.println("Error in HeadingTag: " + ioe);
  }
  return(EVAL_BODY_INCLUDE); // Include tag body
}

public int doEndTag() {
  try {
    JspWriter out = pageContext.getOut();
    out.print("</SPAN></TABLE>");
  } catch(IOException ioe) {
    System.out.println("Error in HeadingTag: " + ioe);
  }
  return(EVAL_PAGE); // Continue with rest of JSP page
}
}
```

Tag Bodies: Tag Library Descriptor File

There is only one new feature in the use of the `tag` element for tags that use body content: the `bodycontent` element should contain the value `JSP` as below.

```
<bodycontent>JSP</bodycontent>
```

Remember, however, that `bodycontent` is optional (`JSP` is the default value) and is mainly intended for IDEs. The `name`, `tagclass`, `info`, and `attribute` elements are used in the same manner as described previously. Listing 3.40 gives the relevant part of the code.

Listing 3.40   *msajsp-taglib.tld* (Excerpt 3)

```xml
<?xml version="1.0" encoding="ISO-8859-1" ?>
<!DOCTYPE ...>
<taglib>
  ...
  <tag>
    <name>heading</name>
    <tagclass>moreservlets.tags.HeadingTag</tagclass>
    <bodycontent>JSP</bodycontent>
    <info>Outputs a 1-cell table used as a heading.</info>
    <attribute>
      <name>bgColor</name>
      <required>true</required>  <!-- bgColor is required -->
    </attribute>
    <attribute>
      <name>color</name>
      <required>false</required>
    </attribute>
    <attribute>
      <name>align</name>
      <required>false</required>
    </attribute>
    <attribute>
      <name>fontSize</name>
      <required>false</required>
    </attribute>
    <attribute>
      <name>fontList</name>
      <required>false</required>
    </attribute>
    <attribute>
      <name>border</name>
      <required>false</required>
    </attribute>
```

Listing 3.40   *msajsp-taglib.tld* (Excerpt 3) *(continued)*

```
  <attribute>
    <name>width</name>
    <required>false</required>
  </attribute>
</tag>

...
</taglib>
```

Tag Bodies: JSP File

Listing 3.41 shows a document that uses the heading tag just defined. Since the bgColor attribute was defined to be required, all uses of the tag include it. Figure 3–22 shows the result.

Listing 3.41   *HeadingExample.jsp*

```
<!DOCTYPE HTML PUBLIC "-//W3C//DTD HTML 4.0 Transitional//EN">
<HTML>
<HEAD>
<TITLE>Some Tag-Generated Headings</TITLE>
</HEAD>
<BODY>
<%@ taglib uri="msajsp-taglib.tld" prefix="msajsp" %>
<msajsp:heading bgColor="#C0C0C0">
Default Heading
</msajsp:heading>
<P>
<msajsp:heading bgColor="BLACK" color="WHITE">
White on Black Heading
</msajsp:heading>
<P>
<msajsp:heading bgColor="#EF8429" fontSize="60" border="5">
Large Bordered Heading
</msajsp:heading>
<P>
<msajsp:heading bgColor="CYAN" width="100%">
Heading with Full-Width Background
</msajsp:heading>
<P>
<msajsp:heading bgColor="CYAN" fontSize="60"
                fontList="Brush Script MT, Times, serif">
Heading with Non-Standard Font
</msajsp:heading>
</BODY>
</HTML>
```

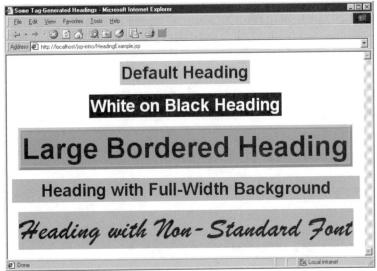

Figure 3–22 The custom `msajsp:heading` element gives you much more succinct control over heading format than do the standard `H1` through `H6` elements in HTML.

Optionally Including the Tag Body

Most tags either *never* make use of body content or *always* do so. In either case, you decide in advance whether the body content is used. However, you are also permitted to make this decision at request time. This subsection shows you how to use request time information to decide whether to include the tag body.

Optional Body Inclusion: Tag Handler Class

Optionally including the tag body is a trivial exercise: just return `EVAL_BODY_INCLUDE` or `SKIP_BODY`, depending on the value of some request time expression. The important thing to know is how to discover that request time information, since `doStartTag` does not have `HttpServletRequest` and `HttpServlet-Response` arguments as do `service`, `_jspService`, `doGet`, and `doPost`. The solution to this dilemma is to use `getRequest` to obtain the `HttpServlet-Request` from the automatically defined `pageContext` field of `TagSupport`. Strictly speaking, the return type of `getRequest` is `ServletRequest`, so you have to do a typecast to `HttpServletRequest` if you want to call a method that is not inherited from `ServletRequest`. However, in this case I just use `getParameter`, so no typecast is required.

Listing 3.42 defines a tag that ignores its body unless a request time `debug` parameter is supplied. Such a tag provides a useful capability whereby you embed debugging information directly in the JSP page during development but activate it only when a problem occurs.

Listing 3.42 *DebugTag.java*

```java
package moreservlets.tags;

import javax.servlet.jsp.*;
import javax.servlet.jsp.tagext.*;
import java.io.*;
import javax.servlet.*;

/** A tag that includes the body content only if
 *  the "debug" request parameter is set.
 */

public class DebugTag extends TagSupport {
  public int doStartTag() {
    ServletRequest request = pageContext.getRequest();
    String debugFlag = request.getParameter("debug");
    if ((debugFlag != null) &&
        (!debugFlag.equalsIgnoreCase("false"))) {
      return(EVAL_BODY_INCLUDE);
    } else {
      return(SKIP_BODY);
    }
  }
}
```

Optional Body Inclusion: Tag Library Descriptor File

If your tag *ever* makes use of its body, you should provide the value `JSP` inside the `bodycontent` element (if you use `bodycontent` at all). Other than that, all the elements within `tag` are used in the same way as described previously. Listing 3.43 shows the entries needed for `DebugTag`.

Listing 3.43 *msajsp-taglib.tld* (Excerpt 4)

```
<?xml version="1.0" encoding="ISO-8859-1" ?>
<!DOCTYPE ...>
<taglib>
  ...
  <tag>
    <name>debug</name>
    <tagclass>moreservlets.tags.DebugTag</tagclass>
    <bodycontent>JSP</bodycontent>
    <info>Includes body only if debug param is set.</info>
  </tag>
  ...
</taglib>
```

Optional Body Inclusion: JSP File

Suppose that you have an application where most of the problems that occur are due to requests occurring close together in time, the host making the request, or session tracking. In such a case, the time, requesting host, and session ID would be useful information to track. Listing 3.43 shows a page that encloses debugging information between `<msajsp:debug>` and `</msajsp:debug>`. Figures 3–23 and 3–24 show the normal result and the result when a request time `debug` parameter is supplied, respectively.

Listing 3.44 *DebugExample.jsp*

```
<!DOCTYPE HTML PUBLIC "-//W3C//DTD HTML 4.0 Transitional//EN">
<HTML>
<HEAD>
<TITLE>Using the Debug Tag</TITLE>
<LINK REL=STYLESHEET
      HREF="JSP-Styles.css"
      TYPE="text/css">
</HEAD>
<BODY>
<H1>Using the Debug Tag</H1>
<%@ taglib uri="msajsp-taglib.tld" prefix="msajsp" %>
Top of regular page. Blah, blah, blah. Yadda, yadda, yadda.
<P>
<msajsp:debug>
<B>Debug:</B>
```

Listing 3.44   *DebugExample.jsp (continued)*

```
<UL>
  <LI>Current time: <%= new java.util.Date() %>
  <LI>Requesting hostname: <%= request.getRemoteHost() %>
  <LI>Session ID: <%= session.getId() %>
</UL>
</msajsp:debug>
<P>
Bottom of regular page. Blah, blah, blah. Yadda, yadda, yadda.
</BODY>
</HTML>
```

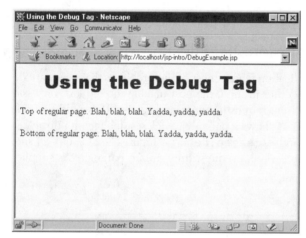

Figure 3–23   The body of the msajsp:debug element is normally ignored.

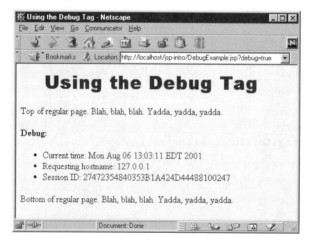

Figure 3–24   The body of the msajsp:debug element is included when a debug request parameter is supplied.

Manipulating the Tag Body

The msajsp:prime element ignored any body content, the msajsp:heading element used body content, and the msajsp:debug element ignored or used it, depending on a request time parameter. The common thread among these elements is that the body content was never modified; it was either ignored or included verbatim (after JSP translation). This section shows you how to process the tag body.

Tag Body Processing: Tag Handler Class

Up to this point, all of the tag handlers have extended the TagSupport class. This is a good standard starting point, since it implements the required Tag interface and performs a number of useful setup operations like storing the PageContext reference in the pageContext field. However, TagSupport is not powerful enough for tag implementations that need to manipulate their body content, and BodyTagSupport should be used instead.

BodyTagSupport extends TagSupport, so the doStartTag and doEndTag methods are used in the same way as before. Two important new methods are defined by BodyTagSupport:

1. **doAfterBody**, a method that you should override to handle the manipulation of the tag body. This method should normally return SKIP_BODY when it is done, indicating that no further body processing should be performed.
2. **getBodyContent**, a method that returns an object of type Body-Content that encapsulates information about the tag body. In tag libraries that are intended only for JSP 1.2, you can use the body-Content field of BodyTagSupport instead of calling getBody-Content. Most libraries, however, are intended to run in either JSP version.

The BodyContent class has three important methods:

1. **getEnclosingWriter**, a method that returns the JspWriter being used by doStartTag and doEndTag.
2. **getReader**, a method that returns a Reader that can read the tag's body.
3. **getString**, a method that returns a String containing the entire tag body.

The ServletUtilities class (see Listing 2.10) contains a static filter method that takes a string and replaces <, >, ", and & with <, >, ", and &, respectively. This method is useful when servlets output strings that might contain characters that would interfere with the HTML structure of the page in which the strings are embedded. Listing 3.45 shows a tag implementation that gives this filtering functionality to a custom JSP tag.

Listing 3.45   *FilterTag.java*

```
package moreservlets.tags;

import javax.servlet.jsp.*;
import javax.servlet.jsp.tagext.*;
import java.io.*;
import moreservlets.*;

/** A tag that replaces <, >, ", and & with their HTML
 *  character entities (&lt;, &gt;, &quot;, and &amp;).
 *  After filtering, arbitrary strings can be placed
 *  in either the page body or in HTML attributes.
 */

public class FilterTag extends BodyTagSupport {
  public int doAfterBody() {
    BodyContent body = getBodyContent();
    String filteredBody =
      ServletUtilities.filter(body.getString());
    try {
      JspWriter out = body.getEnclosingWriter();
      out.print(filteredBody);
    } catch(IOException ioe) {
      System.out.println("Error in FilterTag: " + ioe);
    }
    // SKIP_BODY means we're done. If we wanted to evaluate
    // and handle the body again, we'd return EVAL_BODY_TAG
    // (JSP 1.1/1.2) or EVAL_BODY_AGAIN (JSP 1.2 only)
    return(SKIP_BODY);
  }
}
```

Tag Body Processing: Tag Library Descriptor File

Tags that manipulate their body content should use the `bodycontent` element the same way as tags that simply include it verbatim; they should supply a value of JSP. Other than that, nothing new is required in the descriptor file, as you can see by examining Listing 3.46, which shows the relevant portion of the TLD file.

Listing 3.46 *msajsp-taglib.tld* (Excerpt 5)

```
<?xml version="1.0" encoding="ISO-8859-1" ?>
<!DOCTYPE ...>
<taglib>
  ...
  <tag>
    <name>filter</name>
    <tagclass>moreservlets.tags.FilterTag</tagclass>
    <bodycontent>JSP</bodycontent>
    <info>Replaces HTML-specific characters in body.</info>
  </tag>
  ...
</taglib>
```

Tag Body Processing: JSP File

Listing 3.47 shows a page that uses a table to show some sample HTML and its result. Creating this table would be tedious in regular HTML since the table cell that shows the original HTML would have to change all the < and > characters to < and >. This necessity is particularly onerous during development when the sample HTML is frequently changing. Use of the <msajsp:filter> tag greatly simplifies the process, as Listing 3.47 illustrates. Figure 3–25 shows the result.

Listing 3.47 *FilterExample.jsp*

```
<!DOCTYPE HTML PUBLIC "-//W3C//DTD HTML 4.0 Transitional//EN">
<HTML>
<HEAD>
<TITLE>HTML Logical Character Styles</TITLE>
<LINK REL=STYLESHEET
      HREF="JSP-Styles.css"
      TYPE="text/css">
</HEAD>
<BODY>
<H1>HTML Logical Character Styles</H1>
Physical character styles (B, I, etc.) are rendered consistently
in different browsers. Logical character styles, however,
may be rendered differently by different browsers.
Here's how your browser
(<%= request.getHeader("User-Agent") %>)
renders the HTML 4.0 logical character styles:
<P>
<%@ taglib uri="msajsp-taglib.tld" prefix="msajsp" %>
```

Listing 3.47 *FilterExample.jsp (continued)*

```
<TABLE BORDER=1 ALIGN="CENTER">
<TR CLASS="COLORED"><TH>Example<TH>Result
<TR>
<TD><PRE><msajsp:filter>
<EM>Some emphasized text.</EM><BR>
<STRONG>Some strongly emphasized text.</STRONG><BR>
<CODE>Some code.</CODE><BR>
<SAMP>Some sample text.</SAMP><BR>
<KBD>Some keyboard text.</KBD><BR>
<DFN>A term being defined.</DFN><BR>
<VAR>A variable.</VAR><BR>
<CITE>A citation or reference.</CITE>
</msajsp:filter></PRE>
<TD>
<EM>Some emphasized text.</EM><BR>
<STRONG>Some strongly emphasized text.</STRONG><BR>
<CODE>Some code.</CODE><BR>
<SAMP>Some sample text.</SAMP><BR>
<KBD>Some keyboard text.</KBD><BR>
<DFN>A term being defined.</DFN><BR>
<VAR>A variable.</VAR><BR>
<CITE>A citation or reference.</CITE>
</TABLE>
</BODY>
</HTML>
```

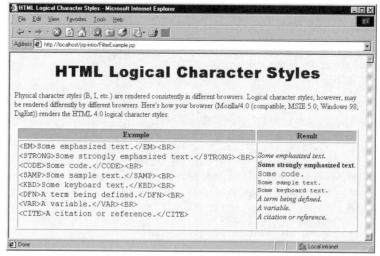

Figure 3–25   The `msajsp:filter` element lets you insert text without worrying about it containing special HTML characters.

Including or Manipulating the Tag Body Multiple Times

Rather than just including or processing the body of the tag a single time, you sometimes want to do so more than once. The ability to support multiple body inclusion lets you define a variety of iteration tags that repeat JSP fragments a variable number of times, repeat them until a certain condition occurs, and so forth. This subsection shows you how to build such tags.

Multiple Body Actions: the Tag Handler Class

Tags that process the body content multiple times should start by extending `BodyTagSupport` and implementing `doStartTag`, `doEndTag`, and, most importantly, `doAfterBody` as before. The difference lies in the return value of `doAfter-Body`. If this method returns `EVAL_BODY_TAG`, then the tag body is evaluated again, resulting in a new call to `doAfterBody`. This process continues until `doAfterBody` returns `SKIP_BODY`. In JSP 1.2, the `EVAL_BODY_TAG` constant is deprecated and replaced with `EVAL_BODY_AGAIN`. The two constants have the same value, but `EVAL_BODY_AGAIN` is a clearer name. So, if your tag library is designed to be used only in JSP 1.2 containers (e.g., it uses some features specific to JSP 1.2 as described in Chapter 11), you should use `EVAL_BODY_AGAIN`. Most tag libraries, however, are designed to run in either JSP version and thus use `EVAL_BODY_TAG`.

Core Note

EVAL_BODY_TAG is renamed EVAL_BODY_AGAIN in JSP 1.2.

Listing 3.48 defines a tag that repeats the body content the number of times specified by the `reps` attribute. Since the body content can contain JSP (which is converted into servlet code at page translation time but is invoked at request time), each repetition does not necessarily result in the same output to the client.

Listing 3.48   *RepeatTag.java*

```java
package moreservlets.tags;

import javax.servlet.jsp.*;
import javax.servlet.jsp.tagext.*;
import java.io.*;

/** A tag that repeats the body the specified
 *  number of times.
 */

public class RepeatTag extends BodyTagSupport {
  private int reps;

  public void setReps(String repeats) {
    try {
      reps = Integer.parseInt(repeats);
    } catch(NumberFormatException nfe) {
      reps = 1;
    }
  }

  public int doAfterBody() {
    if (reps-- >= 1) {
      BodyContent body = getBodyContent();
      try {
        JspWriter out = body.getEnclosingWriter();
        out.println(body.getString());
        body.clearBody(); // Clear for next evaluation
      } catch(IOException ioe) {
        System.out.println("Error in RepeatTag: " + ioe);
      }
      // Replace EVAL_BODY_TAG with EVAL_BODY_AGAIN in JSP 1.2.
      return(EVAL_BODY_TAG);
    } else {
      return(SKIP_BODY);
    }
  }
}
```

Multiple Body Actions: the Tag Library Descriptor File

Listing 3.49 shows the relevant section of the TLD file that gives the name msa-jsp:repeat to the tag just defined. To accommodate request time values in the reps attribute, the file uses an rtexprvalue element (enclosing a value of true) within the attribute element.

Listing 3.49 *msajsp-taglib.tld* (Excerpt 6)

```
<?xml version="1.0" encoding="ISO-8859-1" ?>
<!DOCTYPE ...>
<taglib>
  ...
  <tag>
    <name>repeat</name>
    <tagclass>moreservlets.tags.RepeatTag</tagclass>
    <bodycontent>JSP</bodycontent>
    <info>Repeats body the specified number of times.</info>
    <attribute>
      <name>reps</name>
      <required>true</required>
      <!-- rtexprvalue indicates whether attribute
           can be a JSP expression. -->
      <rtexprvalue>true</rtexprvalue>
    </attribute>
  </tag>
  ...
</taglib>
```

Multiple Body Actions: the JSP File

Listing 3.50 shows a JSP document that creates a numbered list of prime numbers. The number of primes in the list is taken from the request time `repeats` parameter. Figure 3–26 shows one possible result.

Listing 3.50 *RepeatExample.jsp*

```
<!DOCTYPE HTML PUBLIC "-//W3C//DTD HTML 4.0 Transitional//EN">
<HTML>
<HEAD>
<TITLE>Some 40-Digit Primes</TITLE>
<LINK REL=STYLESHEET
      HREF="JSP-Styles.css"
      TYPE="text/css">
</HEAD>
<BODY>
<H1>Some 40-Digit Primes</H1>
Each entry in the following list is the first prime number
higher than a randomly selected 40-digit number.
<%@ taglib uri="msajsp-taglib.tld" prefix="msajsp" %>
<OL>
<!-- Repeats N times. A null reps value means repeat once. -->
```

Listing 3.50 *RepeatExample.jsp (continued)*

```
<msajsp:repeat reps='<%= request.getParameter("repeats") %>'>
  <LI><msajsp:prime length="40" />
</msajsp:repeat>
</OL>
</BODY>
</HTML>
```

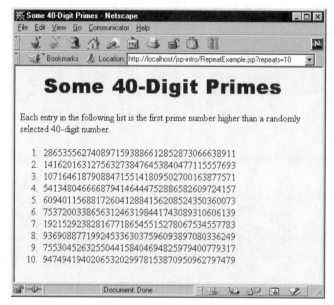

Figure 3–26   Result of *RepeatExample.jsp* when accessed with a `repeats` parameter of 10.

Using Nested Tags

Although Listing 3.50 places the `msajsp:prime` element within the `msajsp:repeat` element, the two elements are independent of each other. The first generates a prime number regardless of where it is used, and the second repeats the enclosed content regardless of whether that content uses an `msajsp:prime` element.

Some tags, however, depend on a particular nesting. For example, in standard HTML, the `TD` and `TH` elements can only appear within `TR`, which in turn can only appear within `TABLE`. The color and alignment settings of `TABLE` are inherited by `TR`, and the values of `TR` affect how `TD` and `TH` behave. So, the nested elements cannot act in isolation even when nested properly. Similarly, the tag library descriptor file makes use of a number of elements like `taglib`, `tag`, `attribute`, and `required` where a strict nesting hierarchy is imposed.

This subsection shows you how to define tags that depend on a particular nesting order and where the behavior of certain tags depends on values supplied by earlier ones.

Nested Tags: the Tag Handler Classes

Class definitions for nested tags can extend *either* `TagSupport` *or* `BodyTag-Support`, depending on whether they need to manipulate their body content (these extend `BodyTagSupport`) or, more commonly, just ignore it or include it verbatim (these extend `TagSupport`).

Although nested tags use the standard tag handler classes, they use two new techniques within those classes. First, nested tags can use `findAncestorWithClass` to find the tag in which they are nested. This method takes a reference to the current class (e.g., `this`) and the `Class` object of the enclosing class (e.g., `Enclosing-Tag.class`) as arguments. If no enclosing class is found, the method in the nested class can throw a `JspTagException` that reports the problem. Second, if one tag wants to store data that a later tag will use, it can place that data in the instance of the enclosing tag. The definition of the enclosing tag should provide methods for storing and accessing this data.

Suppose that we want to define a set of tags that would be used like this:

```
<msajsp:if>
  <msajsp:condition><%= someExpression %></msajsp:condition>
  <msajsp:then>JSP to include if condition is true</msajsp:then>
  <msajsp:else>JSP to include if condition is false</msajsp:else>
</msajsp:if>
```

To accomplish this task, the first step is to define an `IfTag` class to handle the `msajsp:if` tag. This handler should have methods to specify and check whether the condition is `true` or `false` (`setCondition` and `getCondition`). The handler should also have methods to designate and check whether the condition has ever been explicitly set (`setHasCondition` and `getHasCondition`), since we want to disallow `msajsp:if` tags that contain no `msajsp:condition` entry. Listing 3.51 shows the code for `IfTag`.

The second step is to define a tag handler for `msajsp:condition`. This class, called `IfConditionTag`, defines a `doStartTag` method that merely checks whether the tag appears within `IfTag`. It returns `EVAL_BODY_TAG` (`EVAL_BODY_BUFFERED` in tag libraries that are specific to JSP 1.2) if so and throws an exception if not. The handler's `doAfterBody` method looks up the body content (`getBodyContent`), converts it to a `String` (`getString`), and compares that to `"true"`. This approach means that an explicit value of `true` can be substituted for a

JSP expression like `<%= expression %>` if, during initial page development, you want to temporarily designate that the `then` portion should always be used. Using a comparison to `"true"` also means that *any* other value will be considered false. Once this comparison is performed, the result is stored in the enclosing tag by means of the `setCondition` method of `IfTag`. The code for `IfConditionTag` is shown in Listing 3.52.

Listing 3.51 *IfTag.java*

```java
package moreservlets.tags;

import javax.servlet.jsp.*;
import javax.servlet.jsp.tagext.*;
import java.io.*;
import javax.servlet.*;

/** A tag that acts like an if/then/else. */

public class IfTag extends TagSupport {
  private boolean condition;
  private boolean hasCondition = false;

  public void setCondition(boolean condition) {
    this.condition = condition;
    hasCondition = true;
  }

  public boolean getCondition() {
    return(condition);
  }

  public void setHasCondition(boolean flag) {
    this.hasCondition = flag;
  }

  /** Has the condition field been explicitly set? */

  public boolean hasCondition() {
    return(hasCondition);
  }

  public int doStartTag() {
    return(EVAL_BODY_INCLUDE);
  }
}
```

| Listing 3.52 | *IfConditionTag.java* |

```java
package moreservlets.tags;

import javax.servlet.jsp.*;
import javax.servlet.jsp.tagext.*;
import java.io.*;
import javax.servlet.*;

/** The condition part of an if tag. */

public class IfConditionTag extends BodyTagSupport {
  public int doStartTag() throws JspTagException {
    IfTag parent =
      (IfTag)findAncestorWithClass(this, IfTag.class);
    if (parent == null) {
      throw new JspTagException("condition not inside if");
    }
    // If your tag library is intended to be used ONLY
    // in JSP 1.2, replace EVAL_BODY_TAG with
    // EVAL_BODY_BUFFERED.
    return(EVAL_BODY_TAG);
  }

  public int doAfterBody() {
    IfTag parent =
      (IfTag)findAncestorWithClass(this, IfTag.class);
    String bodyString = getBodyContent().getString();
    if (bodyString.trim().equals("true")) {
      parent.setCondition(true);
    } else {
      parent.setCondition(false);
    }
    return(SKIP_BODY);
  }
}
```

The third step is to define a class to handle the msajsp:then tag. The doStart-Tag method of this class verifies that it is inside IfTag and also checks that an explicit condition has been set (i.e., that the IfConditionTag has already appeared within the IfTag). The doAfterBody method checks for the condition in the IfTag class, and, if it is true, looks up the body content and prints it. Listing 3.53 shows the code.

The final step in defining tag handlers is to define a class for msajsp:else. This class is very similar to the one that handles the then part of the tag, except that this handler only prints the tag body from doAfterBody if the condition from the surrounding IfTag is false. The code is shown in Listing 3.54.

Listing 3.53   *IfThenTag.java*

```java
package moreservlets.tags;

import javax.servlet.jsp.*;
import javax.servlet.jsp.tagext.*;
import java.io.*;
import javax.servlet.*;

/** The then part of an if tag. */

public class IfThenTag extends BodyTagSupport {
  public int doStartTag() throws JspTagException {
    IfTag parent =
      (IfTag)findAncestorWithClass(this, IfTag.class);
    if (parent == null) {
      throw new JspTagException("then not inside if");
    } else if (!parent.hasCondition()) {
      String warning =
        "condition tag must come before then tag";
      throw new JspTagException(warning);
    }
    // If your tag library is intended to be used ONLY
    // in JSP 1.2, replace EVAL_BODY_TAG with
    // EVAL_BODY_BUFFERED.
    return(EVAL_BODY_TAG);
  }

  public int doAfterBody() {
    IfTag parent =
      (IfTag)findAncestorWithClass(this, IfTag.class);
    if (parent.getCondition()) {
      try {
        BodyContent body = getBodyContent();
        JspWriter out = body.getEnclosingWriter();
        out.print(body.getString());
      } catch(IOException ioe) {
        System.out.println("Error in IfThenTag: " + ioe);
      }
    }
    return(SKIP_BODY);
  }
}
```

Listing 3.54   *IfElseTag.java*

```java
package moreservlets.tags;

import javax.servlet.jsp.*;
import javax.servlet.jsp.tagext.*;
import java.io.*;
import javax.servlet.*;

/** The else part of an if tag. */

public class IfElseTag extends BodyTagSupport {
  public int doStartTag() throws JspTagException {
    IfTag parent =
      (IfTag)findAncestorWithClass(this, IfTag.class);
    if (parent == null) {
      throw new JspTagException("else not inside if");
    } else if (!parent.hasCondition()) {
      String warning =
        "condition tag must come before else tag";
      throw new JspTagException(warning);
    }
    // If your tag library is intended to be used ONLY
    // in JSP 1.2, replace EVAL_BODY_TAG with
    // EVAL_BODY_BUFFERED.
    return(EVAL_BODY_TAG);
  }

  public int doAfterBody() {
    IfTag parent =
      (IfTag)findAncestorWithClass(this, IfTag.class);
    if (!parent.getCondition()) {
      try {
        BodyContent body = getBodyContent();
        JspWriter out = body.getEnclosingWriter();
        out.print(body.getString());
      } catch(IOException ioe) {
        System.out.println("Error in IfElseTag: " + ioe);
      }
    }
    return(SKIP_BODY);
  }
}
```

Nested Tags: the Tag Library Descriptor File

Even though there is an explicit required nesting structure for the tags just defined, the tags must be declared separately in the TLD file. This means that nesting validation is performed only at request time, not at page translation time. In JSP 1.1, you could instruct the system to do some validation at page translation time by using a `TagExtraInfo` class. This class has a `getVariableInfo` method that you can use to check whether attributes exist and where they are used. Once you have defined a subclass of `TagExtraInfo`, you associate it with your tag in the tag library descriptor file by means of the `teiclass` element (`tei-class` in JSP 1.2), which is used just like `tagclass`. In practice, however, `TagExtraInfo` is a bit cumbersome to use. Fortunately, JSP 1.2 introduced a very useful new class for this purpose: `Tag-LibraryValidator`. See Chapter 11 (New Tag Library Features in JSP 1.2) for information on using this class.

Listing 3.55 *msajsp-taglib.tld* (Excerpt 7)

```xml
<?xml version="1.0" encoding="ISO-8859-1" ?>
<!DOCTYPE ...>
<taglib>
  ...
  <tag>
    <name>if</name>
    <tagclass>moreservlets.tags.IfTag</tagclass>
    <bodycontent>JSP</bodycontent>
    <info>if/condition/then/else tag.</info>
  </tag>
  <tag>
    <name>condition</name>
    <tagclass>moreservlets.tags.IfConditionTag</tagclass>
    <bodycontent>JSP</bodycontent>
    <info>condition part of if/condition/then/else tag.</info>
  </tag>
  <tag>
    <name>then</name>
    <tagclass>moreservlets.tags.IfThenTag</tagclass>
    <bodycontent>JSP</bodycontent>
    <info>then part of if/condition/then/else tag.</info>
  </tag>
  <tag>
    <name>else</name>
    <tagclass>moreservlets.tags.IfElseTag</tagclass>
    <bodycontent>JSP</bodycontent>
    <info>else part of if/condition/then/else tag.</info>
  </tag>
  ...
</taglib>
```

Nested Tags: the JSP File

Listing 3.56 shows a page that uses the `msajsp:if` tag three different ways. In the first instance, a value of `true` is hardcoded for the condition. In the second instance, a parameter from the HTTP request is used for the condition, and in the third case, a random number is generated and compared to a fixed cutoff. Figure 3–27 shows a typical result.

Listing 3.56   *IfExample.jsp*

```
<!DOCTYPE HTML PUBLIC "-//W3C//DTD HTML 4.0 Transitional//EN">
<HTML>
<HEAD>
<TITLE>If Tag Example</TITLE>
<LINK REL=STYLESHEET
      HREF="JSP-Styles.css"
      TYPE="text/css">
</HEAD>
<BODY>
<H1>If Tag Example</H1>
<%@ taglib uri="msajsp-taglib.tld" prefix="msajsp" %>
<msajsp:if>
  <msajsp:condition>true</msajsp:condition>
  <msajsp:then>Condition is true</msajsp:then>
  <msajsp:else>Condition is false</msajsp:else>
</msajsp:if>
<P>
<msajsp:if>
  <msajsp:condition><%= request.isSecure() %></msajsp:condition>
  <msajsp:then>Request is using SSL (https)</msajsp:then>
  <msajsp:else>Request is not using SSL</msajsp:else>
</msajsp:if>
<P>
Some coin tosses:<BR>
<msajsp:repeat reps="10">
  <msajsp:if>
    <msajsp:condition><%= Math.random() < 0.5 %></msajsp:condition>
    <msajsp:then><B>Heads</B><BR></msajsp:then>
    <msajsp:else><B>Tails</B><BR></msajsp:else>
  </msajsp:if>
</msajsp:repeat>
</BODY>
</HTML>
```

Figure 3–27   Result of *IfExample.jsp*.

3.8   Integrating Servlets and JSP: The MVC Architecture

Servlets are great when your application requires a lot of real programming to accomplish its task. Servlets can manipulate HTTP status codes and headers, use cookies, track sessions, save information between requests, compress pages, access databases, generate GIF images on-the-fly, and perform many other tasks flexibly and efficiently. But, generating HTML with servlets can be tedious and can yield a result that is hard to modify.

That's where JSP comes in; it lets you separate much of the presentation from the dynamic content. That way, you can write the HTML in the normal manner, even using HTML-specific tools and putting your Web content developers to work on your JSP documents. JSP expressions, scriptlets, and declarations let you insert simple Java code into the servlet that results from the JSP page, and directives let you control the overall layout of the page. For more complex requirements, you can wrap up Java code inside beans or define your own JSP tags.

Great. We have everything we need, right? Well, no, not quite. The assumption behind a JSP document is that it provides a *single* overall presentation. What if you want to give totally different results depending on the data that you receive? Beans and custom tags (see Figure 3–28), although extremely powerful and flexible, don't overcome the limitation that the JSP page defines a relatively fixed top-level page appearance. The solution is to use *both* servlets and JavaServer Pages. If you have a complicated application that may require several substantially different presentations, a servlet can handle the initial request, partially process the data, set up beans, and then forward the results to one of a number of different JSP pages, depending on the circumstances. This approach is known as the *Model View Controller (MVC)* or *Model 2* architecture. For code that supports a formalization of this approach, see the Apache Struts Framework at *http://jakarta.apache.org/struts/*.

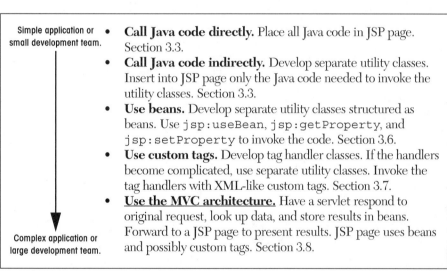

Figure 3–28 Strategies for invoking dynamic code from JSP.

Forwarding Requests

The key to letting servlets forward requests or include external content is to use a `RequestDispatcher`. You obtain a `RequestDispatcher` by calling the `get-RequestDispatcher` method of `ServletContext`, supplying a URL relative to the server root. For example, to obtain a `RequestDispatcher` associated with *http://yourhost/presentations/presentation1.jsp*, you would do the following:

```
String url = "/presentations/presentation1.jsp";
RequestDispatcher dispatcher =
  getServletContext().getRequestDispatcher(url);
```

Once you have a `RequestDispatcher`, you use `forward` to completely transfer control to the associated URL and you use `include` to output the associated URL's content. In both cases, you supply the `HttpServletRequest` and `HttpServlet-Response` as arguments. Both methods throw `ServletException` and `IOException`. For example, Listing 3.57 shows a portion of a servlet that forwards the request to one of three different JSP pages, depending on the value of the `operation` parameter. To avoid repeating the `getRequestDispatcher` call, I use a utility method called `gotoPage` that takes the URL, the `HttpServlet-Request`, and the `HttpServletResponse`; gets a `RequestDispatcher`; and then calls `forward` on it.

Listing 3.57 Request Forwarding Example

```
public void doGet(HttpServletRequest request,
                  HttpServletResponse response)
    throws ServletException, IOException {
  String operation = request.getParameter("operation");
  if (operation == null) {
    operation = "unknown";
  }
  if (operation.equals("operation1")) {
    gotoPage("/operations/presentation1.jsp",
             request, response);
  } else if (operation.equals("operation2")) {
    gotoPage("/operations/presentation2.jsp",
             request, response);
  } else {
    gotoPage("/operations/unknownRequestHandler.jsp",
             request, response);
  }
}

private void gotoPage(String address,
                      HttpServletRequest request,
                      HttpServletResponse response)
    throws ServletException, IOException {
  RequestDispatcher dispatcher =
    getServletContext().getRequestDispatcher(address);
  dispatcher.forward(request, response);
}
```

Using Static Resources

In most cases, you forward requests to a JSP page or another servlet. In some cases, however, you might want to send the request to a static HTML page. In an e-commerce site, for example, requests that indicate that the user does not have a valid account name might be forwarded to an account application page that uses HTML forms to gather the requisite information. With GET requests, forwarding requests to a static HTML page is perfectly legal and requires no special syntax; just supply the address of the HTML page as the argument to getRequest-Dispatcher. However, since forwarded requests use the same request method as the original request, POST requests cannot be forwarded to normal HTML pages. The solution to this problem is to simply rename the HTML page to have a *.jsp* extension. Renaming *somefile.html* to *somefile.jsp* does not change its output for GET requests, but *somefile.html* cannot handle POST requests, whereas *somefile.jsp* gives an identical response for both GET and POST.

Supplying Information to the Destination Pages

A servlet can store data for JSP pages in three main places: in the HttpServlet-Request, in the HttpSession, and in the ServletContext. These storage locations correspond to the three nondefault values of the scope attribute of jsp:useBean: that is, request, session, and application.

1. **Storing data that servlet looked up and that JSP page will use only in this request.** The servlet would create and store data as follows:

   ```
   SomeClass value = new SomeClass(...);
   request.setAttribute("key", value);
   ```

   Then, the servlet would forward to a JSP page that uses the following to retrieve the data:

   ```
   <jsp:useBean id="key" class="SomeClass"
                scope="request" />
   ```

2. **Storing data that servlet looked up and that JSP page will use in this request and in later requests from same client.** The servlet would create and store data as follows:

   ```
   SomeClass value = new SomeClass(...);
   HttpSession session = request.getSession(true);
   session.setAttribute("key", value);
   ```

Then, the servlet would forward to a JSP page that uses the following to retrieve the data:

```
<jsp:useBean id="key" class="SomeClass"
             scope="session" />
```

3. **Storing data that servlet looked up and that JSP page will use in this request and in later requests from any client.** The servlet would create and store data as follows:

```
SomeClass value = new SomeClass(...);
getServletContext().setAttribute("key", value);
```

Then, the servlet would forward to a JSP page that uses the following to retrieve the data:

```
<jsp:useBean id="key" class="SomeClass"
             scope="application" />
```

Interpreting Relative URLs in the Destination Page

Although a servlet can forward the request to an arbitrary location on the same server, the process is quite different from that of using the `sendRedirect` method of `HttpServletResponse`. First, `sendRedirect` requires the client to reconnect to the new resource, whereas the `forward` method of `RequestDispatcher` is handled completely on the server. Second, `sendRedirect` does not automatically preserve all of the request data; `forward` does. Third, `sendRedirect` results in a different final URL, whereas with `forward`, the URL of the original servlet is maintained.

This final point means that if the destination page uses relative URLs for images or style sheets, it needs to make them relative to the server root, not to the destination page's actual location. For example, consider the following style sheet entry:

```
<LINK REL=STYLESHEET
      HREF="my-styles.css"
      TYPE="text/css">
```

If the JSP page containing this entry is accessed by means of a forwarded request, `my-styles.css` will be interpreted relative to the URL of the *originating* servlet, not relative to the JSP page itself, almost certainly resulting in an error. Section 4.5 (Handling Relative URLs in Web Applications) discusses several approaches to this problem. One simple solution, however, is to give the full server path to the style sheet file, as follows.

```
<LINK REL=STYLESHEET
      HREF="/path/my-styles.css"
      TYPE="text/css">
```

The same approach is required for addresses used in `<IMG  SRC=...>` and `<A HREF=...>`.

Using Alternative Means to Get a RequestDispatcher

Servers that support version 2.2 or 2.3 of the servlet specification have two additional ways of obtaining a `RequestDispatcher` besides the `getRequestDispatcher` method of `ServletContext`.

First, since most servers let you register explicit names for servlets or JSP pages, it makes sense to access them by name rather than by path. Use the `getNamed-Dispatcher` method of `ServletContext` for this task.

Second, you might want to access a resource by a path relative to the current servlet's location, rather than relative to the server root. This approach is not common when servlets are accessed in the standard manner (*http://host/servlet/ServletName*), because JSP files would not be accessible by means of *http://host/servlet/...* since that URL is reserved especially for servlets. However, it is common to register servlets under another path (see Section 5.3, "Assigning Names and Custom URLs"), and in such a case you can use the `getRequestDispatcher` method of `HttpServlet-Request` rather than the one from `ServletContext`. For example, if the originating servlet is at *http://host/travel/TopLevel*,

```
getServletContext().getRequestDispatcher("/travel/cruises.jsp")
```

could be replaced by

```
request.getRequestDispatcher("cruises.jsp");
```

Example: An Online Travel Agent

Consider the case of an online travel agent that has a quick-search page, as shown in Figure 3–29 and Listing 3.58. Users need to enter their email address and password to associate the request with their previously established customer account. Each request also includes a trip origin, trip destination, start date, and end date. However, the action that will result will vary substantially in accordance with the action requested. For example, pressing the "Book Flights" button should show a list of available flights on the dates specified, ordered by price (see Figure 3–30). The user's real name, frequent flyer information, and credit card number should be used to generate the page. On the other hand, selecting "Edit Account" should show any previously entered customer information, letting the user modify values or add entries. Likewise, the actions resulting from choosing "Rent Cars" or "Find Hotels" will share much of the same customer data but will have a totally different presentation.

To accomplish the desired behavior, the front end (Listing 3.58) submits the request to the top-level travel servlet shown in Listing 3.59. This servlet looks up the customer information (see *http://www.moreservlets.com* for the actual code used, but this would be replaced by a database lookup in real life), puts it in the `HttpSession` object associating the value (of type `moreservlets.TravelCustomer`) with the name `customer`, and then forwards the request to a different JSP page corresponding to each of the possible actions. The destination page (see Listing 3.60 and the result in Figure 3–30) looks up the customer information by means of

```
<jsp:useBean id="customer"
             class="moreservlets.TravelCustomer"
             scope="session" />
```

and then uses `jsp:getProperty` to insert customer information into various parts of the page.

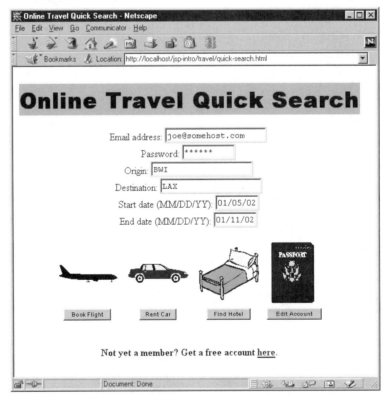

Figure 3–29 Front end to travel servlet (see Listing 3.58).

Listing 3.58	*quick-search.html* (Excerpt)

```html
<!DOCTYPE HTML PUBLIC "-//W3C//DTD HTML 4.0 Transitional//EN">
<HTML>
<HEAD>
  <TITLE>Online Travel Quick Search</TITLE>
  <LINK REL=STYLESHEET
        HREF="travel-styles.css"
        TYPE="text/css">
</HEAD>
<BODY>
<BR>
<H1>Online Travel Quick Search</H1>
<FORM ACTION="/servlet/moreservlets.Travel" METHOD="POST">
<CENTER>
Email address: <INPUT TYPE="TEXT" NAME="emailAddress"><BR>
Password: <INPUT TYPE="PASSWORD" NAME="password" SIZE=10><BR>
...
<TABLE CELLSPACING=1>
<TR>
  <TH> <IMG SRC="airplane.gif" WIDTH=100 HEIGHT=29
                ALIGN="TOP" ALT="Book Flight"> 
  ...
<TR>
  <TH><SMALL>
      <INPUT TYPE="SUBMIT" NAME="flights" VALUE="Book Flight">
      </SMALL>
  ...
</TABLE>
</CENTER>
</FORM>
...
</BODY>
</HTML>
```

Figure 3–30 Result of travel servlet (Listing 3.59) dispatching request to *BookFlights.jsp* (Listing 3.60).

Listing 3.59 *Travel.java*

```java
package moreservlets;

import java.io.*;
import javax.servlet.*;
import javax.servlet.http.*;

/** Top-level travel-processing servlet. This servlet sets up
 *  the customer data as a bean, then forwards the request
 *  to the airline booking page, the rental car reservation
 *  page, the hotel page, the existing account modification
 *  page, or the new account page.
 */

public class Travel extends HttpServlet {
  private TravelCustomer[] travelData;

  public void init() {
    travelData = TravelData.getTravelData();
  }

  /** Since password is being sent, use POST only. However,
   *  the use of POST means that you cannot forward
   *  the request to a static HTML page, since the forwarded
   *  request uses the same request method as the original
   *  one, and static pages cannot handle POST. Solution:
   *  have the "static" page be a JSP file that contains
   *  HTML only. That's what accounts.jsp is. The other
   *  JSP files really need to be dynamically generated,
   *  since they make use of the customer data.
   */

  public void doPost(HttpServletRequest request,
                     HttpServletResponse response)
      throws ServletException, IOException {
    String emailAddress = request.getParameter("emailAddress");
    String password = request.getParameter("password");
    TravelCustomer customer =
      TravelCustomer.findCustomer(emailAddress, travelData);
    if ((customer == null) || (password == null) ||
        (!password.equals(customer.getPassword()))) {
      gotoPage("/jsp-intro/travel/accounts.jsp",
               request, response);
    }
```

Listing 3.59	*Travel.java (continued)*

```java
    // The methods that use the following parameters will
    // check for missing or malformed values.
    customer.setStartDate(request.getParameter("startDate"));
    customer.setEndDate(request.getParameter("endDate"));
    customer.setOrigin(request.getParameter("origin"));
    customer.setDestination(request.getParameter
                                  ("destination"));
    HttpSession session = request.getSession(true);
    session.setAttribute("customer", customer);
    if (request.getParameter("flights") != null) {
      gotoPage("/jsp-intro/travel/BookFlights.jsp",
               request, response);
    } else if (request.getParameter("cars") != null) {
      gotoPage("/jsp-intro/travel/RentCars.jsp",
               request, response);
    } else if (request.getParameter("hotels") != null) {
      gotoPage("/jsp-intro/travel/FindHotels.jsp",
               request, response);
    } else if (request.getParameter("account") != null) {
      gotoPage("/jsp-intro/travel/EditAccounts.jsp",
               request, response);
    } else {
      gotoPage("/jsp-intro/travel/IllegalRequest.jsp",
               request, response);
    }
  }

  private void gotoPage(String address,
                        HttpServletRequest request,
                        HttpServletResponse response)
      throws ServletException, IOException {
    RequestDispatcher dispatcher =
      getServletContext().getRequestDispatcher(address);
    dispatcher.forward(request, response);
  }
}
```

Listing 3.60   *BookFlights.jsp*

```
<!DOCTYPE HTML PUBLIC "-//W3C//DTD HTML 4.0 Transitional//EN">
<HTML>
<HEAD>
  <TITLE>Best Available Flights</TITLE>
  <LINK REL=STYLESHEET
        HREF="/jsp-intro/travel/travel-styles.css"
        TYPE="text/css">
</HEAD>
<BODY>
<H1>Best Available Flights</H1>
<CENTER>
<jsp:useBean id="customer"
             class="moreservlets.TravelCustomer"
             scope="session" />
Finding flights for
<jsp:getProperty name="customer" property="fullName" />
<P>
<jsp:getProperty name="customer" property="flights" />
<P><BR><HR><BR>
<FORM ACTION="/servlet/BookFlight">
<jsp:getProperty name="customer"
                 property="frequentFlyerTable" />
<P>
<B>Credit Card:</B>
<jsp:getProperty name="customer" property="creditCard" />
<P>
<INPUT TYPE="SUBMIT" NAME="holdButton" VALUE="Hold for 24 Hrs">
<P>
<INPUT TYPE="SUBMIT" NAME="bookItButton" VALUE="Book It!">
</FORM>
</CENTER>
</BODY>
</HTML>
```

You should pay careful attention to the `TravelCustomer` class (shown partially in Listing 3.61, with the complete code available at *http://www.moreservlets.com*). In particular, note that the class spends a considerable amount of effort making the customer information accessible as plain strings or even HTML-formatted strings through simple properties. Every task that requires any substantial amount of programming is spun off into the bean, rather than being performed in the JSP page itself. This is typical of servlet/JSP integration—the use of JSP does not *entirely* obviate the need to format data as strings or HTML in Java code. Significant up-front effort to make the data conveniently available to JSP more than pays for itself when multiple JSP pages access the same type of data. Other supporting classes (*Frequent-FlyerInfo.java*, *TravelData.java*, etc.), JSP pages (*RentCars.jsp*, *FindHotels.jsp*, etc.), and the *travel-styles.css* style sheet can be found at *http://www.moreservlets.com*.

Listing 3.61 *TravelCustomer.java*

```java
package moreservlets;

import java.util.*;
import java.text.*;

/** Describes a travel services customer. Implemented
 *  as a bean with some methods that return data in HTML
 *  format, suitable for access from JSP.
 */

public class TravelCustomer {
  private String emailAddress, password, firstName, lastName;
  private String creditCardName, creditCardNumber;
  private String phoneNumber, homeAddress;
  private String startDate, endDate;
  private String origin, destination;
  private FrequentFlyerInfo[] frequentFlyerData;
  private RentalCarInfo[] rentalCarData;
  private HotelInfo[] hotelData;

  public TravelCustomer(String emailAddress,
                        String password,
                        String firstName,
                        String lastName,
                        String creditCardName,
                        String creditCardNumber,
                        String phoneNumber,
                        String homeAddress,
                        FrequentFlyerInfo[] frequentFlyerData,
                        RentalCarInfo[] rentalCarData,
                        HotelInfo[] hotelData) {
    setEmailAddress(emailAddress);
    setPassword(password);
    setFirstName(firstName);
    setLastName(lastName);
    setCreditCardName(creditCardName);
    setCreditCardNumber(creditCardNumber);
    setPhoneNumber(phoneNumber);
    setHomeAddress(homeAddress);
```

Listing 3.61   *TravelCustomer.java (continued)*

```java
      setStartDate(startDate);
      setEndDate(endDate);
      setFrequentFlyerData(frequentFlyerData);
      setRentalCarData(rentalCarData);
      setHotelData(hotelData);
    }

    public String getEmailAddress() {
      return(emailAddress);
    }

    public void setEmailAddress(String emailAddress) {
      this.emailAddress = emailAddress;
    }

    // See http://www.moreservlets.com for missing code.
    public String getFrequentFlyerTable() {
      FrequentFlyerInfo[] frequentFlyerData =
        getFrequentFlyerData();
      if (frequentFlyerData.length == 0) {
        return("<I>No frequent flyer data recorded.</I>");
      } else {
        String table =
          "<TABLE>\n" +
          "  <TR><TH>Airline<TH>Frequent Flyer Number\n";
        for(int i=0; i<frequentFlyerData.length; i++) {
          FrequentFlyerInfo info = frequentFlyerData[i];
          table = table +
                  "<TR ALIGN=\"CENTER\">" +
                  "<TD>" + info.getAirlineName() +
                  "<TD>" + info.getFrequentFlyerNumber() + "\n";
        }
        table = table + "</TABLE>\n";
        return(table);
      }
    }

    // This would be replaced by a database lookup
    // in a real application.

    public String getFlights() {
      String flightOrigin =
        replaceIfMissing(getOrigin(), "Nowhere");
      String flightDestination =
        replaceIfMissing(getDestination(), "Nowhere");
      Date today = new Date();
```

Listing 3.61   *TravelCustomer.java (continued)*

```
DateFormat formatter =
  DateFormat.getDateInstance(DateFormat.MEDIUM);
String dateString = formatter.format(today);
String flightStartDate =
  replaceIfMissing(getStartDate(), dateString);
String flightEndDate =
  replaceIfMissing(getEndDate(), dateString);
String [][] flights =
  { { "Java Airways", "1522", "455.95", "Java, Indonesia",
      "Sun Microsystems", "9:00", "3:15" },
    { "Servlet Express", "2622", "505.95", "New Atlanta",
      "New Atlanta", "9:30", "4:15" },
    { "Geek Airlines", "3.14159", "675.00", "JHU",
      "MIT", "10:02:37", "2:22:19" } };
String flightString = "";
for(int i=0; i<flights.length; i++) {
  String[] flightInfo = flights[i];
  flightString =
    flightString + getFlightDescription(flightInfo[0],
                                        flightInfo[1],
                                        flightInfo[2],
                                        flightInfo[3],
                                        flightInfo[4],
                                        flightInfo[5],
                                        flightInfo[6],
                                        flightOrigin,
                                        flightDestination,
                                        flightStartDate,
                                        flightEndDate);
}
return(flightString);
}

private String getFlightDescription(String airline,
                                    String flightNum,
                                    String price,
                                    String stop1,
                                    String stop2,
                                    String time1,
                                    String time2,
                                    String flightOrigin,
                                    String flightDestination,
                                    String flightStartDate,
                                    String flightEndDate) {
```

Listing 3.61   *TravelCustomer.java (continued)*

```java
    String flight =
      "<P><BR>\n" +
      "<TABLE WIDTH=\"100%\"><TR><TH CLASS=\"COLORED\">\n" +
      "<B>" + airline + " Flight " + flightNum +
      " ($" + price + ")</B></TABLE><BR>\n" +
      "<B>Outgoing:</B> Leaves " + flightOrigin +
      " at " + time1 + " AM on " + flightStartDate +
      ", arriving in " + flightDestination +
      " at " + time2 + " PM (1 stop -- " + stop1 + ").\n" +
      "<BR>\n" +
      "<B>Return:</B> Leaves " + flightDestination +
      " at " + time1 + " AM on " + flightEndDate +
      ", arriving in " + flightOrigin +
      " at " + time2 + " PM (1 stop -- " + stop2 + ").\n";
    return(flight);
  }

  private String replaceIfMissing(String value,
                                  String defaultValue) {
    if ((value != null) && (value.length() > 0)) {
      return(value);
    } else {
      return(defaultValue);
    }
  }

  public static TravelCustomer findCustomer
                             (String emailAddress,
                              TravelCustomer[] customers) {
    if (emailAddress == null) {
      return(null);
    }
    for(int i=0; i<customers.length; i++) {
      String custEmail = customers[i].getEmailAddress();
      if (emailAddress.equalsIgnoreCase(custEmail)) {
        return(customers[i]);
      }
    }
    return(null);
  }
}
```

Forwarding Requests from JSP Pages

The most common request-forwarding scenario is that the request first comes to a servlet and the servlet forwards the request to a JSP page. The reason a servlet usually handles the original request is that checking request parameters and setting up beans requires a lot of programming, and it is more convenient to do this programming in a servlet than in a JSP document. The reason that the destination page is usually a JSP document is that JSP simplifies the process of creating the HTML content.

However, just because this is the *usual* approach doesn't mean that it is the *only* way of doing things. It is certainly possible for the destination page to be a servlet. Similarly, it is quite possible for a JSP page to forward requests elsewhere. For example, a request might go to a JSP page that normally presents results of a certain type and that forwards the request elsewhere only when it receives unexpected values.

Sending requests to servlets instead of JSP pages requires no changes whatsoever in the use of the `RequestDispatcher`. However, there is special syntactic support for forwarding requests from JSP pages. In JSP, the `jsp:forward` action is simpler and easier to use than wrapping up `RequestDispatcher` code in a scriptlet. This action takes the following form:

```
<jsp:forward page="Relative URL" />
```

The page attribute is allowed to contain JSP expressions so that the destination can be computed at request time. For example, the following code sends about half the visitors to *http://host/examples/page1.jsp* and the others to *http://host/examples/page2.jsp*.

```
<% String destination;
   if (Math.random() > 0.5) {
     destination = "/examples/page1.jsp";
   } else {
     destination = "/examples/page2.jsp";
   }
%>
<jsp:forward page="<%= destination %>" />
```

The `jsp:forward` action, like `jsp:include`, can make use of `jsp:param` elements to supply extra request parameters to the destination page. For details, see the discussion of `jsp:include` in Section 3.5.

WEB
APPLICATIONS

Part II

USING AND DEPLOYING WEB APPLICATIONS

Topics in This Chapter

- Registering Web applications with the server
- Organizing Web applications
- Deploying applications in WAR files
- Recording Web application dependencies on shared libraries
- Dealing with relative URLs
- Sharing data among Web applications

Chapter 4

Web applications (or "Web apps") let you bundle a set of servlets, JSP pages, tag libraries, HTML documents, images, style sheets, and other Web content into a single collection that can be used on any server compatible with servlet version 2.2 or later (JSP 1.1 or later). When designed carefully, Web apps can be moved from server to server or placed at different locations on the same server, all without making any changes to any of the servlets, JSP pages, or HTML files in the application.

This capability lets you move complex applications around with a minimum of effort, streamlining application reuse. In addition, since each Web app has its own directory structure, sessions, `ServletContext`, and class loader, using a Web app simplifies even the initial development because it reduces the amount of coordination needed among various parts of your overall system.

4.1 Registering Web Applications

With servlets 2.2 and later (JSP 1.1 and later), Web applications are portable. Regardless of the server, you store files in the same directory structure and access them with URLs in identical formats. For example, Figure 4–1 summarizes the directory structure and URLs that would be used for a simple Web application called `webapp1`. This section will illustrate how to install and execute this simple Web application on different platforms.

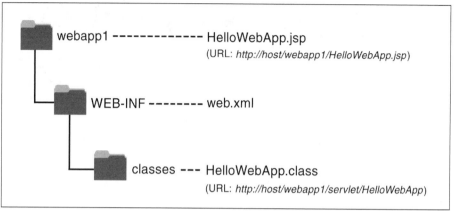

Figure 4–1 Structure of the `webapp1` Web application.

Although Web applications themselves are completely portable, the registration process is server specific. For example, to move the `webapp1` application from server to server, you don't have to modify anything *inside* any of the directories shown in Figure 4–1. However, the location *in which* the top-level directory (*webapp1* in this case) is placed will vary from server to server. Similarly, you use a server-specific process to tell the system that URLs that begin with *http://host/webapp1/* should apply to the Web application. In general, you will need to read your server's documentation to get details on the registration process. I'll present a few brief examples here, then give explicit details for Tomcat, JRun, and ServletExec in the following subsections.

My usual strategy is to build Web applications in my personal development environment and periodically copy them to various deployment directories for testing on different servers. I never place my development directory directly within a server's deployment directory—doing so makes it hard to deploy on multiple servers, hard to develop while a Web application is executing, and hard to organize the files. I recommend you avoid this approach as well; instead, use a separate development directory and deploy by means of one of the strategies outlined in Section 1.8 (Establish a Simplified Deployment Method). The simplest approach is to keep a shortcut (Windows) or symbolic link (Unix/Linux) to the deployment directories of various servers and simply copy the entire development directory whenever you want to deploy. For example, on Windows you can use the right mouse button to drag the development folder onto the shortcut, release the button, and select Copy.

To illustrate the registration process, the iPlanet Server 6.0 provides you with two choices for creating Web applications. First, you can edit iPlanet's *web-apps.xml* file (not *web.xml*!) and insert a `web-app` element with attributes `dir` (the directory containing the Web app files) and `uri` (the URL prefix that designates the Web application). Second, you can create a Web Archive (WAR) file and then use the `wdeploy` command-line program to deploy it. WAR files are simply JAR files that contain a Web application directory and use *.war* instead of *.jar* for file extensions. See Section 4.3 for a discussion of creating and using WAR files.

With the Resin server from Caucho, you use a `web-app` element within *web.xml* and supply `app-dir` (directory) and `id` (URL prefix) attributes. Resin even lets you use regular expressions in the `id`. So, for example, you can automatically give users their own Web apps that are accessed with URLs of the form *http://hostname/~username/*.

With the BEA WebLogic 6 Server, you have two choices. First, you can place a directory (see Section 4.2) containing a Web application into the *config/domain/app-lications* directory, and the server will automatically assign the Web application a URL prefix that matches the directory name. Second, you can create a WAR file (see Section 4.3) and use the Web Applications entry of the Administration Console to deploy it.

Registering a Web Application with Tomcat

With Tomcat 4, creating a Web application consists simply of creating the appropriate directory structure and restarting the server. For extra control over the process, you can modify *install_dir/conf/server.xml* (a Tomcat-specific file) to refer to the Web application. The following steps walk you through what is required to create a Web app that is accessed by means of URLs that start with *http://host/webapp1/*. These examples are taken from Tomcat 4.0, but the process for Tomcat 3 is very similar.

1. **Create a simple directory called *webapp1*.** Since this is your personal development directory, it can be located at any place you find convenient. Once you have a *webapp1* directory, place a simple JSP page called *HelloWebApp.jsp* (Listing 4.1) in it. Put a simple servlet called *HelloWebApp.class* (compiled from Listing 4.2) in the *WEB-INF/classes* subdirectory. Section 4.2 gives details on the directory structure of a Web application, but for now just note that the JSP pages, HTML documents, images, and other regular Web documents go in the top-level directory of the Web app, whereas servlets are placed in the *WEB-INF/classes* subdirectory.

    You can also use subdirectories relative to those locations, although recall that a servlet in a subdirectory must use a package name that matches the directory name.

    Finally, although Tomcat doesn't actually require it, it is a good idea to include a *web.xml* file in the *WEB-INF* directory. The *web.xml* file, called *the deployment descriptor*, is completely portable across servers. We'll see some uses for this deployment descriptor later in this chapter, and Chapter 5 (Controlling Web Application Behavior with web.xml) will discuss it in detail. For now, however, just copy the existing *web.xml* file from *install_dir/webapps/ROOT/WEB-INF* or use the version that is online under Chapter 4 of the source code archive at *http://www.moreservlets.com*. In fact, for purposes of testing Web application deployment, you might want to start by simply downloading the entire *webapp1* directory from *http://www.moreservlets.com*.

2. **Copy that directory to *install_dir/webapps*.** For example, suppose that you are running Tomcat version 4.0, and it is installed in *C:\jakarta-tomcat-4.0*. You would then copy the *webapp1* directory to the *webapps* directory, resulting in *C:\jakarta-tomcat-4.0\webapps\ webapp1\HelloWebApp.jsp, C:\jakarta-tomcat-4.0\webapps\webapp1\ WEB-INF\classes\HelloWebApp.class*, and *C:\jakarta-tomcat-4.0\ webapps\webapp1\WEB-INF\web.xml*. You could also wrap the directory inside a WAR file (Section 4.3) and simply drop the WAR file into *C:\jakarta-tomcat-4.0\webapps*.

3. **Optional: add a `Context` entry to *install_dir/conf/server.xml*.** If you want your Web application to have a URL prefix that exactly matches the directory name and you are satisfied with the default Tomcat settings for Web applications, you can omit this step. But, if you want a bit more control over the Web app registration process, you can supply a `Context` element in *install_dir/conf/server.xml*. If you do edit *server.xml*, be sure to make a backup copy first; a small syntax error in *server.xml* can completely prevent Tomcat from running.

   The `Context` element has several possible attributes that are documented at *http://jakarta.apache.org/tomcat/tomcat-4.0-doc/config/ context.html*. For instance, you can decide whether to use cookies or URL rewriting for session tracking, you can enable or disable servlet reloading (i.e., monitoring of classes for changes and reloading servlets whose class file changes on disk), and you can set debugging levels. However, for basic Web apps, you just need to deal with the two required attributes: `path` (the URL prefix) and `docBase` (the base installation directory of the Web application, relative to *install_dir/webapps*). This entry should look like the following snippet. See Listing 4.3 for more detail.

   ```
   <Context path="/webapp1" docBase="webapp1" />
   ```

   Note that you should not use */examples* as the URL prefix; Tomcat already uses that prefix for a sample Web application.

Core Warning

Do not use /examples *as the URL prefix of a Web application in Tomcat.*

4. **Restart the server.** I keep a shortcut to *install_dir/bin/startup.bat* (*install_dir/bin/startup.sh* on Unix) and *install_dir/bin/shutdown.bat* (*install_dir/bin/shutdown.sh* on Unix) in my development directory. I recommend you do the same. Thus, restarting the server involves simply double-clicking the shutdown link and then double-clicking the startup link.

5. **Access the JSP page and the servlet.** The URL *http://hostname/ webapp1/HelloWebApp.jsp* invokes the JSP page (Figure 4–2), and *http://hostname/webapp1/servlet/HelloWebApp* invokes the servlet (Figure 4–3). During development, you probably use *localhost* for the host name. These URLs assume that you have modified the Tomcat configuration file (*install_dir/conf/server.xml*) to use port 80 as recommended in Chapter 1 (Server Setup and Configuration). If you haven't made this change, use *http://hostname:**8080**/webapp1/HelloWeb-App.jsp* and *http://hostname:**8080**/webapp1/servlet/HelloWebApp*.

Figure 4–2   Invoking a JSP page that is in a Web application.

Figure 4–3   Invoking a servlet that is in a Web application.

Listing 4.1 *HelloWebApp.jsp*

```
<!DOCTYPE HTML PUBLIC "-//W3C//DTD HTML 4.0 Transitional//EN">
<HTML>
<HEAD><TITLE>JSP: Hello Web App</TITLE></HEAD>
<BODY BGCOLOR="#FDF5E6">
<H1>JSP: Hello Web App</H1>
</BODY>
</HTML>
```

Listing 4.2 *HelloWebApp.java*

```java
import java.io.*;
import javax.servlet.*;
import javax.servlet.http.*;

public class HelloWebApp extends HttpServlet {
  public void doGet(HttpServletRequest request,
                    HttpServletResponse response)
      throws ServletException, IOException {
    response.setContentType("text/html");
    PrintWriter out = response.getWriter();
    String docType =
      "<!DOCTYPE HTML PUBLIC \"-//W3C//DTD HTML 4.0 " +
      "Transitional//EN\">\n";
    String title = "Servlet: Hello Web App";
    out.println(docType +
                "<HTML>\n" +
                "<HEAD><TITLE>" + title + "</TITLE></HEAD>\n" +
                "<BODY BGCOLOR=\"#FDF5E6\">\n" +
                "<H1>" + title + "</H1>\n" +
                "</BODY></HTML>");
  }
}
```

Listing 4.3   Partial *server.xml* for Tomcat 4

```
<?xml version="1.0" encoding="ISO-8859-1"?>
<Server>
  <!-- ... -->

  <!-- Having the URL prefix (path) match the actual directory
       (docBase) is a convenience, not a requirement. -->
  <Context path="/webapp1" docBase="webapp1" />
</Server>
```

Registering a Web Application with JRun

Registering a Web app with JRun 3.1 involves nine simple steps. The process is nearly identical to other versions of JRun.

1. **Create the directory.** Use the directory structure illustrated in Figure 4–1: a *webapp1* directory containing *HelloWebApp.jsp*, *WEB-INF/classes/HelloWebApp.class*, and *WEB-INF/web.xml*.

2. **Copy the entire *webapp1* directory to *install_dir/servers/default*.** The *install_dir/servers/default* directory is the standard location for Web applications in JRun. Again, I recommend that you simplify the process of copying the directory by using one of the methods described in Section 1.8 (Establish a Simplified Deployment Method). The easiest approach is to make a shortcut or symbolic link from your development directory to *install_dir/servers/default* and then simply copy the *webapp1* directory onto the shortcut whenever you redeploy. You can also deploy using WAR files (Section 4.3).

3. **Start the JRun Management Console.** You can invoke the Console either by selecting JRun Management Console from the JRun menu (on Microsoft Windows, this is available by means of Start, Programs, JRun) or by opening *http://hostname:8000/*. Either way, the JRun Admin Server has to be running first.

4. **Click on JRun Default Server.** This entry is in the left-hand pane, as shown in Figure 4–4.

5. **Click on Web Applications.** This item is in the bottom of the list that is created when you select the default server from the previous step. Again, see Figure 4–4.

6. **Click on Create an Application.** This entry is in the right-hand pane that is created when you select Web Applications from the previous step. If you deploy using WAR files (see Section 4.3) instead of an unpacked directory, choose Deploy an Application instead.

7. **Specify the directory name and URL prefix.** To tell the system that the files are in the directory *webapp1*, specify `webapp1` for the Application Name entry. To designate a URL prefix of */webapp1*, put `/webapp1` in the Application URL textfield. Note that you do not have to modify the Application Root Dir entry; that is done automatically when you enter the directory name. Press the Create button when done. See Figure 4–5.

8. **Restart the server.** From the JRun Management Console, click on JRun Default Server and then press the Restart Server button. Assuming JRun is not running as a Windows NT or Windows 2000 service, you can also double-click the JRun Default Server icon from the taskbar and then press Restart. See Figure 4–6.

9. **Access the JSP page and the servlet.** The URL *http://hostname/ webapp1/HelloWebApp.jsp* invokes the JSP page (Figure 4–2), and *http://hostname/webapp1/servlet/HelloWebApp* invokes the servlet (Figure 4–3). During development, you probably use *localhost* for the host name. These are exactly the same URLs and results as with Tomcat and ServletExec. This approach assumes that you have modified JRun to use port 80 as recommended in Chapter 1 (Server Setup and Configuration). If you haven't made this change, use *http://hostname:8100/webapp1/HelloWebApp.jsp* and *http://hostname:8100/webapp1/servlet/HelloWebApp*.

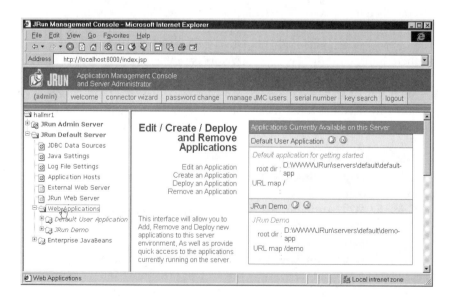

Figure 4–4   JRun Web application setup screen.

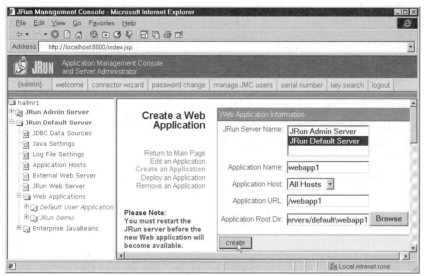

Figure 4–5 JRun Web application creation screen. You only need to fill in the Application Name and Application Root Dir entries.

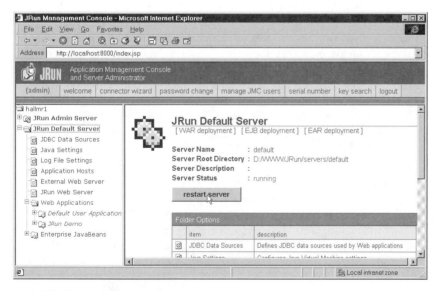

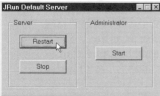

Figure 4–6 You must restart JRun for a newly created Web app to take effect.

Registering a Web Application with ServletExec

The process of registering Web applications is particularly simple with ServletExec 4. To make a Web app with a prefix *webapp1*, just create a directory called *webapp1* with the structure described in the previous two subsections. Drop this directory into *install_dir/webapps/default*, restart the server, and access resources in the Web app with URLs that begin with *http://hostname/webapp1/*. You can also drop WAR files (Section 4.3) in the same directory; the name of the WAR file (minus the *.war* extension) automatically is used as the URL prefix.

For more control over the process or to add a Web application when the server is already running, perform the following steps. Note that, using this approach, you do *not* need to restart the server after registering the Web app.

1. **Create a simple directory called *webapp1*.** Use the structure summarized in Figure 4–1: place a simple JSP page called *HelloWebApp.jsp* (Listing 4.1) in the top-level directory and put a simple servlet called *AppTest.class* (compiled from Listing 4.2) in the *WEB-INF/classes* subdirectory. Section 4.2 gives details on the directory structure of a Web app, but for now just note that the JSP pages, HTML documents, images, and other regular Web documents go in the top-level directory of the Web app, whereas servlets are placed in the *WEB-INF/classes* subdirectory. You can also use subdirectories relative to those locations, although recall that a servlet in a subdirectory must use a package name that matches the directory name. Later in this chapter (and throughout Chapter 5), we'll see uses for the *web.xml* file that goes in the *WEB-INF* directory. For now, however, you can omit this file and let ServletExec create one automatically, or you can copy a simple example from *http://www.moreservlets.com*. In fact, you can simply download the entire *webapp1* directory from the Web site.

2. **Optional: copy that directory to *install_dir/webapps/default*.** ServletExec allows you to store your Web application directory at any place on the system, so it is possible to simply tell ServletExec where the existing *webapp1* directory is located. However, I find it convenient to keep separate development and deployment copies of my Web applications. That way, I can develop continually but only deploy periodically. Since *install_dir/webapps/default* is the standard location for ServletExec Web applications, that's a good location for your deployment directories.

3. **Go to the ServletExec Web app management interface.** Access the ServletExec administration interface by means of the URL *http://hostname* and select Manage under the Web Applications heading. During development, you probably use *localhost* for the

host name. See Figure 4–7. This assumes that you have modified ServletExec to use port 80 as recommended in Chapter 1 (Server Setup and Configuration). If you haven't made this change, use *http://hostname:8080*.

4. **Enter the Web app name, URL prefix, and directory location.** From the previous user interface, select Add Web Application (see Figure 4–7). This results in an interface (Figure 4–8) with text fields for the Web application configuration information. It is traditional, but not required, to use the same name (e.g., *webapp1*) for the Web app name, the URL prefix, and the main directory that contains the Web application.

Figure 4–7 ServletExec interface for managing Web applications.

5. **Add the Web application.** After entering the information from Item 4, select Add Web Application. See Figure 4–8.

6. **Access the JSP page and the servlet.** The URL *http://hostname/ webapp1/HelloWebApp.jsp* invokes the JSP page (Figure 4–2), and *http://hostname/webapp1/servlet/HelloWebApp* invokes the servlet (Figure 4–3). During development, you probably use *localhost* for the host name. These are exactly the same URLs and results as with Tomcat and JRun. This assumes that you have modified ServletExec to use port 80 as recommended in Chapter 1 (Server Setup and Configuration). If you haven't made this change, use *http://hostname:**8080**/webapp1/HelloWebApp.jsp* and *http://hostname:**8080**/webapp1/servlet/HelloWebApp.*

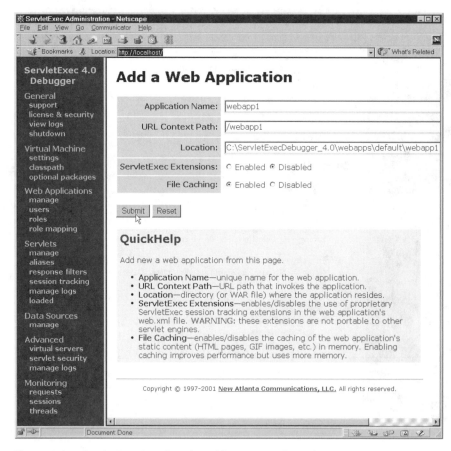

Figure 4–8 ServletExec interface for adding new Web applications.

4.2   Structure of a Web Application

The process of *registering* a Web application is not standardized; it frequently involves server-specific configuration files or user interfaces. However, the Web application *itself* has a completely standardized format and is totally portable across all Web or application servers that support version 2.2 or later of the servlet specification. The top-level directory of a Web application is simply a directory with a name of your choosing. Within that directory, certain types of content go in designated locations. This section provides details on the type of content that is placed in various locations; it also gives a sample Web application layout.

Locations for Various File Types

Quick summary: JSP pages and other normal Web documents go in the top-level directory, unbundled Java classes go in the *WEB-INF/classes* directory, JAR files go in *WEB-INF/lib*, and the *web.xml* file goes in *WEB-INF*. Figure 4–9 shows a representative example. For details or a more explicit sample hierarchy, check out the following subsections.

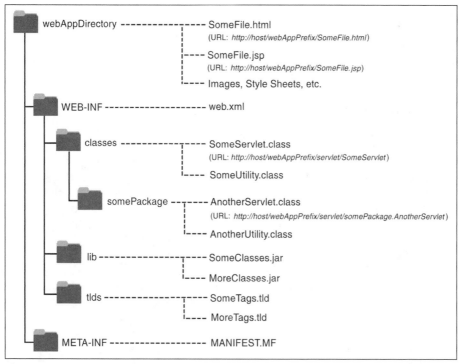

Figure 4–9   A representative Web application.

JSP Pages

JSP pages should be placed in the top-level Web application directory or in a subdirectory with any name other than *WEB-INF* or *META-INF*. Servers are prohibited from serving files from *WEB-INF* or *META-INF* to the user. When you register a Web application (see Section 4.1), you tell the server the URL prefix that designates the Web app and define where the Web app directory is located. It is common, but by no means mandatory, to use the name of the main Web application directory as the URL prefix. Once you register a prefix, JSP pages are then accessed with URLs of the form *http://hostname/webAppPrefix/filename.jsp* (if the pages are in the top-level directory of the Web application) or *http://hostname/webAppPrefix/subdirectory/filename.jsp* (if the pages are in a subdirectory).

It depends on the server whether a default file such as *index.jsp* can be accessed with a URL that specifies only a directory (e.g., *http://hostname/webAppPrefix/*) without the developer first making an entry in the Web app's *WEB-INF/web.xml* file. If you want *index.jsp* to be the default filename, I strongly recommend that you make an explicit `welcome-file-list` entry in your Web app's *web.xml* file. For example, the following *web.xml* entry specifies that if a URL gives a directory name but no filename, the server should try *index.jsp* first and *index.html* second. If neither is found, the result is server specific (e.g., a directory listing).

```
<welcome-file-list>
  <welcome-file>index.jsp</welcome-file>
  <welcome-file>index.html</welcome-file>
</welcome-file-list>
```

For details, see Section 5.7 (Specifying Welcome Pages).

HTML Documents, Images, and Other Regular Web Content

As far as the servlet and JSP engine is concerned, HTML files, GIF and JPEG images, style sheets, and other Web documents follow exactly the same rules as do JSP pages. They are placed in exactly the same locations and accessed with URLs of exactly the same form. In deployment scenarios, however, a servlet or JSP engine such as JRun, ServletExec, Tomcat, or Resin is often plugged into a regular Web server like Microsoft IIS, Apache, or older versions of the Netscape Web server. In such a case, the regular Web server usually serves regular Web pages more quickly than does the servlet and JSP engine. So, if your static Web documents are accessed extremely frequently, you are faced with a portability vs. performance trade-off. Putting the static documents in the Web application hierarchy lets you move the servlets, the JSP pages, *and* the static documents from server to server with a minimum of changes. Putting the static resources in the regular Web server's hierarchy increases performance but requires server-specific changes when you move the Web app to another server. Fortunately, this issue is important only for the highest-traffic pages.

It depends on the server whether a default file such as *index.html* can be accessed with a URL that specifies only a directory (e.g., *http://hostname/webAppPrefix/*) without the developer first making an entry in the Web app's *WEB-INF/web.xml* file. If you want *index.html* to be the default filename, I recommend that you make an explicit `welcome-file-list` entry in *web.xml*. For details, see Section 5.7 (Specifying Welcome Pages).

Servlets, Beans, and Helper Classes (Unbundled)

Servlets and other *.class* files are placed either in *WEB-INF/classes* or in a subdirectory of *WEB-INF/classes* that matches their package name. During development, don't forget that your `CLASSPATH` should include the *classes* directory. The *server* already knows about this location, but your *development* environment does not. In order to compile servlets that are in packages, the compiler needs to know the location of the top-level directory of your package hierarchy. See Section 1.6 (Set Up Your Development Environment) for details.

The default way to access servlets is with URLs of the form *http://hostname/webAppPrefix/servlet/ServletName* or *http://hostname/webAppPrefix/servlet/package-Name.ServletName*. To designate a different URL, you use the `servlet-mapping` element in the *web.xml* deployment descriptor file that is located within the *WEB-INF* directory of the Web application. See Section 5.3 (Assigning Names and Custom URLs) for details.

Servlets, Beans, and Helper Classes (Bundled in JAR Files)

If the servlets or other *.class* files are bundled inside JAR files, then the JAR files should be placed in *WEB-INF/lib*. If the classes are in packages, then within the JAR file they should be in a directory that matches their package name.

Deployment Descriptor

The deployment descriptor file, *web.xml*, should be placed in the *WEB-INF* subdirectory of the main Web application directory. For details on using *web.xml*, see Chapter 5 (Controlling Web Application Behavior with web.xml). Note that a few servers (e.g., Tomcat) have a global *web.xml* file that applies to all Web applications. That file is entirely server specific; the only standard *web.xml* file is the per-application one that is placed within the *WEB-INF* directory of the Web app.

Tag Library Descriptor Files

TLD files can be placed almost anywhere within the Web application. However, I recommend that you put them in a *tlds* directory within *WEB-INF*. Grouping them in a common directory (e.g., *tlds*) simplifies their management. Placing that directory within *WEB-INF* prevents end users from retrieving them. JSP pages, however, can access TLD files that are in *WEB-INF*. They just use a `taglib` element as follows

```
<%@ taglib uri="/WEB-INF/tlds/myTaglibFile.tld" ...%>
```

Since it is the server, not the client, that accesses the TLD file in this case, the prohibition that content inside of *WEB-INF* is not Web accessible does not apply.

WAR Manifest File

When you create a WAR file (see Section 4.3), a *MANIFEST.MF* file is placed in the *META-INF* subdirectory. Normally, the `jar` utility automatically creates *MANIFEST.MF* and places it in the *META-INF* directory, and you ignore it if you unpack the WAR file. Occasionally, however, you modify *MANIFEST.MF* explicitly (see Section 4.4), so it is useful to know where it is stored.

Sample Hierarchy

Suppose you have a Web application that is in a directory named *widgetStore* and is registered (see Section 4.1) with the URL prefix */widgetStore*. Following is one possible structure for the Web app.

widgetStore/orders.jsp
widgetStore/specials.html

These files would be accessed with the URLs *http://hostname/widgetStore/orders.jsp* and *http://hostname/widgetStore/specials.html*, respectively.

widgetStore/info/company-profile.jsp
widgetStore/info/contacts.html

These files would be accessed with the URLs *http://hostname/widgetStore/info/company-profile.jsp* and *http://hostname/widgetStore/info/contacts.html*, respectively.

widgetStore/founder.jpg

Since the *orders.jsp* and *specials.html* files are in the same directory as this file, they would use a simple relative URL to refer to the image, as below.

```
<IMG SRC="founder.jpg" ...>
```

Since *company-profile.jsp* and *contacts.html* are in a lower-level directory, they would use a relative URL that contains "..", as below.

```
<IMG SRC="../founder.jpg" ...>
```

But what if you want to support the flexibility of moving a JSP page to a different directory without changing the URL that refers to the image? Or what if a servlet wants to refer to this image? This is slightly more complicated; see Section 4.5 (Handling Relative URLs in Web Applications) for a discussion of the problem and its solutions.

widgetStore/images/button1.gif

Since the *orders.jsp* and *specials.html* files are in the parent directory of this file, they would refer to the image by using a relative URL that contains the directory name, as below.

```
<IMG SRC="images/button1.gif" ...>
```

Since *company-profile.jsp* and *contacts.html* are in a sibling directory, they would use a relative URL that contains ".." and the directory name, as below.

```
<IMG SRC="../images/founder.gif" ...>
```

Again, if you want to be able to move the JSP page without changing the image URL or if you want to refer to the image from a servlet, things are a bit complicated. See Section 4.5 (Handling Relative URLs in Web Applications) for a discussion of the problem and its solutions.

widgetStore/WEB-INF/tlds/widget-taglib.tld

This tag library descriptor file would be referenced from a JSP page by use of a `taglib` element as follows.

```
<%@ taglib uri="/WEB-INF/tlds/widget-taglib.tld" ...%>
```

Note that the JSP page that uses this TLD file can be located anywhere within the *widgetStore* Web app directory. Note, too, that there is no potential problem regarding relative URLs as there is with images (as mentioned in the previous two subsections). Also note that it is legal (recommended, in fact) to place the *tlds* directory within the *WEB-INF* directory, even though the *WEB-INF* directory is not accessible to Web clients. It is legal because the server, not the client, retrieves the TLD file.

widgetStore/WEB-INF/web.xml

This is the deployment descriptor. It is not accessible by Web clients; it is used only by the server itself. See Chapter 5 (Controlling Web Application Behavior with web.xml) for details on its use.

widgetStore/WEB-INF/classes/CheckoutServlet.class

This packageless servlet would be accessed either with the URL *http://hostname/widgetStore/servlet/CheckoutServlet* or with a custom URL that starts with *http://hostname/widgetStore/*. The *web.xml* file would define the custom URL; see Section 5.3 (Assigning Names and Custom URLs) for details.

widgetStore/WEB-INF/classes/cart/ShowCart.class

This servlet from the `cart` package would be accessed either with the URL *http://hostname/widgetStore/servlet/cart.ShowCart* or with a custom URL that starts with *http://hostname/widgetStore/*. Again, the *web.xml* file would define the custom URL. Remember that dots, not slashes, separate package names from class names in URLs that refer to servlets. So be sure to use *http://hostname/widgetStore/servlet/cart.ShowCart*, not *http://hostname/widgetStore/servlet/cart/ShowCart*.

widgetStore/WEB-INF/lib/Utils.jar

The *Utils.jar* file could contain utility classes used by the servlets and by various JSP pages. If the classes are in packages, they should be in subdirectories within the JAR file, and the servlets or JSP pages that use them must utilize `import` statements.

4.3 Deploying Web Applications in WAR Files

WAR (Web ARchive) files provide a convenient way of bundling Web apps in a single file. Having a single large file instead of many small files makes it easier to transfer the Web application from server to server.

A WAR file is really just a JAR file with a *.war* extension, and you use the normal `jar` command to create it. For example, to bundle the entire `widgetStore` Web app into a WAR file named *widgetStore.war*, you would just change directory to the *widgetStore* directory and execute the following command.

```
jar cvf widgetStore.war *
```

For simple WAR files, that's it! However, in version 2.3 of the servlet API, you can create WAR files that designate that they need shared but nonstandard libraries installed on the server. This topic is covered in Section 4.4.

Of course, you can use other `jar` options (e.g., to digitally sign classes) with WAR files just as you can with regular JAR files. For details, see *http://java.sun.com/j2se/*

1.3/docs/tooldocs/win32/jar.html (Windows) or *http://java.sun.com/j2se/1.3/docs/tool-docs/solaris/jar.html* (Unix/Linux).

Finally, remember that you have to follow slightly different procedures to register Web apps that are contained in WAR files than you do to deploy unbundled Web applications. For details, see Section 4.1 (Registering Web Applications).

4.4 Recording Dependencies on Server Libraries

With servlet and JSP engines (or "containers") supporting the servlet 2.2 and JSP 1.1 API, there is no portable way to designate that a Web app depends on some shared library that is not part of the servlet or JSP API itself. You have to either copy the library's JAR file into the *WEB-INF/lib* directory of each and every Web application, or you have to make server-specific changes that lack mechanisms for verification.

With servlet version 2.3 (JSP version 1.2), you can use the *META-INF/MANI-FEST.MF* file to express dependencies on shared libraries. Compliant containers are required to detect when these dependencies are unfulfilled and provide a warning. Note that although support for these dependencies is a new capability in servlet version 2.3, the actual method of expressing the dependencies is the standard one for the Java 2 Platform Standard Edition, as described at *http://java.sun.com/j2se/1.3/docs/guide/extensions/versioning.html*. Furthermore, although the method for *expressing* dependencies is now standardized, the way to actually *implement* shared libraries is nonstandard. For example, with Tomcat 4, individual class files placed in *install_dir/classes* and JAR files placed in *install_dir/lib* are made available to all Web applications. Other servers might use an entirely different approach or might completely disallow code sharing across Web applications.

Creating a Manifest File

The *MANIFEST.MF* file is created automatically by the `jar` utility. Unless you are using shared libraries, you normally ignore this file altogether. Even if you do want to customize the manifest file so that you can use shared libraries more portably, you rarely edit it directly. Instead, you typically create a text file with a subset of manifest file entries and then use the m option to tell `jar` to add the contents of the text file to the autogenerated manifest file. For example, suppose that you have a file called *myAppdependencies.txt* that is in the top-level directory of your Web application. You can create a WAR file called *myApp.war* by changing directory to the top-level Web application directory and then issuing the following `jar` command.

```
jar cvmf myAppDependencies.txt myApp.war *
```

There are two small problems with this approach, however. First, *myApp-Dependencies.txt* is actually part of the WAR file. This inclusion is unnecessary and may confuse the deployer who sees an unneeded file mixed in with *index.jsp* and other top-level Web files. Second, the WAR file itself (*myApp.war*) is created in the top-level directory of the Web application. It is slightly more convenient to place the WAR file one directory level up from there, so that configuration and archive files are kept distinct from the Web application contents. Both of these minor problems can be solved by use of the C option to `jar`, which instructs `jar` to change directories before adding files to the archive. You place *myAppDependencies.txt* one level *up* from the main Web application directory (*myApp* in the following example), change directory to the location containing *myAppDependencies.txt*, and issue the following jar command:

```
jar cvmf myAppDependencies.txt myApp.war -C myApp *
```

This way, the dependency file and the WAR file itself are located in the directory that contains the top-level Web application directory (*myApp*), not in *myApp* itself. Note that it is not legal to go to the parent directory of *myApp* and then use a directory name when specifying the files, as below.

```
jar cvmf myAppDependencies.txt myApp.war myApp/* // Wrong!
```

The reason this fails is that the name *myApp* incorrectly becomes part of all of the WAR entries except for *MANIFEST.MF*.

Contents of the Manifest File

OK, ok. So you know how to use `jar` to create manifest files. But what do you put *in* the manifest file that lets you specify dependencies on shared libraries? There are four main entries that you need, each of which consists of a single plain-text line of the form "`Entry: value`".

- **Extension-List.** This entry designates one or more names of your choosing, separated by spaces. The names will be used in the rest of the manifest file to identify the library of interest. For example, suppose that several of your Web applications use JavaMail to send email. Rather than repeating the JavaMail JAR file in each and every Web application, you might use a server-specific mechanism to make it available to all Web applications. Then, your dependency file would contain a line like the following.

  ```
  Extension-List: javaMail
  ```

- *name*-**Extension-Name.** This entry designates the standard name for the library of interest. You cannot choose an arbitrary name here; you must supply the name exactly as it is given in the `Extension-Name` entry of the JAR file that contains the actual library of interest. For most standard extensions, the package name is used as the extension name. Note that the leading name must match whatever you specified for `Extension-List`. So, if the standard JavaMail JAR file uses an `Extension-Name` of `javax.mail`, the first two entries in your dependency file would look like the following.

```
Extension-List: javaMail
javaMail-Extension-Name: javax.mail
```

- *name*-**Specification-Version.** This entry gives the minimum required specification version of the library of interest. When the server finds an installed library, it compares the listed `Specification-Version` to the minimum specified here. For example, if your Web apps require JavaMail version 1.2 or later, your dependency file might start as follows.

```
Extension-List: javaMail
javaMail-Extension-Name: javax.mail
javaMail-Specification-Version: 1.2
```

- *name*-**Implementation-URL.** This entry lets you specify the location where the server can find the JAR file. Note, however, that it is unclear how many servers (if any) will automatically download the JAR file when necessary, rather than simply generating an error message. Combining all four entries results in a dependency file like the following.

```
Extension-List: javaMail
javaMail-Extension-Name: javax.mail
javaMail-Specification-Version: 1.2
javaMail-Implementation-URL: http://somehost.com/javaMail.jar
```

Although these are the four most important entries, there are a number of other possible entries. For details, see *http://java.sun.com/j2se/1.3/docs/guide/extensions/versioning.html*. For information on JavaMail, see *http://java.sun.com/products/javamail/*.

4.5   Handling Relative URLs in Web Applications

Suppose you have an image that you want displayed in a JSP page. If the image is used only by that particular JSP page, you can place the image and the JSP page in the same directory; the JSP page can then use a simple relative URL to name the image, as below:

```
<IMG SRC="MyImage.gif" WIDTH="..." HEIGHT="..." ALT="...">
```

If there are lots of different images, it is usually convenient to group them in a subdirectory. But each URL remains simple:

```
<IMG SRC="images/MyImage.gif" ...>
```

So far, so good. But what if the same image is used by JSP or HTML pages that are scattered throughout your application? Copying the image lots of places would be wasteful and would make updating the image difficult. And even that wouldn't solve all your problems. For example, what if you have a servlet that uses an image? After all, you can't just use

```
out.println("<IMG SRC=\"MyImage.gif\" ...>"); // Fails!
```

because the browser would treat the image location as relative to the servlet's URL. But the default URL of a servlet is *http://host/webAppPrefix/servlet/ServletName*. Thus, the browser would resolve the relative URL *MyImage.gif* to *http://host/web-AppPrefix/servlet/MyImage.gif*. That, of course, will fail since *servlet* is not really the name of a directory; it is just an artifact of the default URL mapping. You have precisely the same problem when using the MVC architecture (see Section 3.8) where a `RequestDispatcher` forwards the request from a servlet to a JSP page. The browser only knows about the URL of the original servlet and thus treats image URLs as relative to that location.

If you aren't using Web applications, you can solve all these problems the same way: by using a URL that is relative to the server's root directory, not relative to the location of the file that uses the image. For example, you could put the images in a directory called *images* that is in the root directory. Then, a JSP page could use

```
<IMG SRC="/images/MyImage.gif" ...>
```

and a servlet could do

```
out.println("<IMG SRC=\"/images/MyImage.gif\" ...>");
```

Unfortunately, however, this trick fails when you use Web applications. If a JSP page uses an image URL of

```
<IMG SRC="/images/MyImage.gif" ...>
```

the browser will request the image from the main server root, not from the base location of the Web application.

Exactly the same problem occurs with style sheets, applet class files, and even simple hypertext links that use URLs that begin with slashes. Note, however, that this problem does not occur in situations where the server resolves the URLs, only in cases where the browser does so. So, for example, it is perfectly safe for a JSP page that is in a Web app to do

```
<%@ taglib uri="/tlds/SomeFile.tld" ... %>
```

The server will correctly treat that URL as referring to the *tlds* directory within the Web application. Similarly, there is no problem using URLs that begin with / in locations passed to the `getRequestDispatcher` method of `ServletContext`; the server resolves them with respect to the Web application's root directory, not the overall server root.

Core Approach

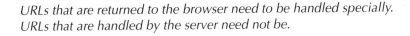

URLs that are returned to the browser need to be handled specially.
URLs that are handled by the server need not be.

There are three possible solutions to this dilemma. The first is the most commonly used but the least flexible. I recommend option (2) or (3).

1. **Use the Web application name in the URL.** For example, you could create a subdirectory called *images* within your Web application, and a JSP page could refer to an image with the following URL.
   `<IMG SRC="/webAppPrefix/images/MyImage.gif" ...>`
   This would work both for regular JSP pages and JSP pages that are invoked by means of a `RequestDispatcher`. Servlets could use the same basic strategy. However, this approach has one serious drawback: if you change the URL prefix of the Web application, you have to change a large number of JSP pages and servlets. This restriction is unacceptable in many situations; you want to be able to change the Web application's URL prefix without changing any of the files *within* the Web app.

2. **Assign URLs that are at the top level of the Web application.**
   For example, suppose you had a servlet named `WithdrawServlet` that was in the `banking` package of a Web application named `financial`. The default URL to invoke that servlet would be *http://host/financial/servlet/banking.WithdrawServlet*. Thus, the servlet would suffer from the problems just discussed when using images, style sheets, and so forth. But, there is no requirement that you use the default URL. In fact, many people feel that you should avoid default URLs in deployment scenarios. Instead, you can use the *web.xml* file to assign a URL that does not contain the *servlet* "subdirectory" (see Section 5.3, "Assigning Names and Custom URLs"). For example, Listing 4.4 shows a *web.xml* file that could be used to change the URL from *http://host/financial/servlet/banking.WithdrawServlet* to *http://host/financial/Withdraw*. Now, since the URL does not contain a "subdirectory" named *servlet*, the servlet can use simple relative URLs that contain only the filename or the subdirectory and the file, but without using a /. For instance, if the Web application contained an image called *Cash.jpg*, you could place it in the Web app's *images* directory and the servlet could use

   ```
   out.println("<IMG SRC=\"images/Cash.jpg\" ...>");
   ```

Listing 4.4 *web.xml* that assigns top-level URL

```
<?xml version="1.0" encoding="ISO-8859-1"?>
<!DOCTYPE web-app PUBLIC
    "-//Sun Microsystems, Inc.//DTD Web Application 2.2//EN"
    "http://java.sun.com/j2ee/dtds/web-app_2_2.dtd">
<web-app>
  <servlet>
    <servlet-name>WithdrawServlet</servlet-name>
    <servlet-class>banking.WithdrawServlet</servlet-class>
  </servlet>
  <servlet-mapping>
    <servlet-name>WithdrawServlet</servlet-name>
    <url-pattern>Withdraw</url-pattern>
  </servlet-mapping>
</web-app>
```

3. **Use `getContextPath`.** The most general solution is to explicitly add the Web application name to the front of each URL that begins with /. However, instead of hardcoding the name, you can use the `getContextPath` method of `HttpServletRequest` to determine

the name at execution time. For example, a JSP page could do the following.

```
<% String prefix = request.getContextPath();
   String url = prefix + "/images/MyImage.jpg"; %>
<IMG SRC="<%= url %>" ...>
```

If you have a number of URLs of this nature, you can make use of the BASE element to standardize the location to which relative URLs are resolved. For example:

```
<HEAD>
<BASE HREF="<%= request.getContextPath() %>">
<TITLE>...</TITLE>
</HEAD>
```

The use of getContextPath is so generally applicable that it is worth capturing some of this functionality in a reusable utility. Listing 4.5 presents one such utility that not only modifies regular URLs, but also handles URLs that are to be used for session tracking that is based on URL rewriting.

Listing 4.5 *AppUtils.java*

```java
package moreservlets;

import javax.servlet.http.*;

/** A small set of utilities to simplify the use of URLs in
 *  Web applications.
 */

public class AppUtils {

  /** For use in URLs referenced by JSP pages or servlets, where
   *  you want to avoid hardcoding the Web app name. Replace
   *         <PRE><XMP>
   *  <IMG SRC="/images/foo.gif" ...>
   *  with the following two lines:
   *  <% String imageURL = webAppURL("/images/foo.gif",
   *                                 request); %>
   *  <IMG SRC="<%= imageURL %>"...>
   *
   *         </XMP></PRE>
   */
```

Listing 4.5 *AppUtils.java (continued)*

```java
public static String webAppURL(String origURL,
                               HttpServletRequest request) {
  return(request.getContextPath() + origURL);
}

/** For use when you want to support session tracking with
 *  URL encoding and you are putting a URL
 *  beginning with a slash into a page from a Web app.
 */

public static String encodeURL(String origURL,
                               HttpServletRequest request,
                               HttpServletResponse response) {
  return(response.encodeURL(webAppURL(origURL, request)));
}

/** For use when you want to support session tracking with
 *  URL encoding and you are using sendRedirect to send a URL
 *  beginning with a slash to the client.
 */

public static String encodeRedirectURL
                         (String origURL,
                          HttpServletRequest request,
                          HttpServletResponse response) {
  return(response.encodeRedirectURL
                     (webAppURL(origURL, request)));
}
}
```

4.6 Sharing Data Among Web Applications

One of the major purposes of Web applications is to keep data separate. Each Web application maintains its own table of sessions and its own servlet context. Each Web application also uses its own class loader; this behavior eliminates problems with name conflicts but means that static methods and fields can't be used to share data among applications. However, it *is* still possible to share data with cookies or by using ServletContext objects that are associated with specific URLs. These two approaches are summarized below.

- **Cookies.** Cookies are maintained by the browser, not by the server. Consequently, cookies can be shared across multiple Web applications as long as they are set to apply to any path on the server. By default, the browser sends cookies only to URLs that have the same prefix as the one from which it first received the cookies. For example, if the server sends a cookie from the page associated with *http://host/path1/ SomeFile.jsp*, the browser sends the cookie back to *http://host/path1/ SomeOtherFile.jsp* and *http://host/path1/path2/Anything*, but not to *http://host/path3/Anything*. Since Web applications always have unique URL prefixes, this behavior means that default-style cookies will never be shared between two different Web applications.

  However, as described in Section 2.9 (Cookies), you can use the setPath method of the Cookie class to change this behavior. Supplying a value of "/", as shown below, instructs the browser to send the cookie to *all* URLs at the host from which the original cookie was received.

  ```
  Cookie c = new Cookie("name", "value");
  c.setMaxAge(...);
  c.setPath("/");
  response.addCookie(c);
  ```

- **ServletContext objects associated with a specific URL.** In a servlet, you obtain the Web application's servlet context by calling the getServletContext method of the servlet itself (inherited from GenericServlet). In a JSP page, you use the predefined application variable. Either way, you get the servlet context associated with the servlet or JSP page that is making the request. However, you can also call the getContext method of ServletContext to obtain a servlet context—not necessarily your own—associated with a particular URL. This approach is illustrated below.

  ```
  ServletContext myContext = getServletContext();
  String url = "/someWebAppPrefix";
  ServletContext otherContext = myContext.getContext(url);
  Object someData = otherContext.getAttribute("someKey");
  ```

Neither of these two data-sharing approaches is perfect.

The drawback to cookies is that only limited data can be stored in them. Each cookie value is a string, and the length of each value is limited to 4 kilobytes. So, robust data sharing requires a database: you use the cookie value as a key into the database and store the real data in the database.

One drawback to sharing servlet contexts is that you have to know the URL prefix that the other Web application is using. You normally want the freedom to change a Web application's prefix without changing any associated code. Use of the get-Context method restricts this flexibility. A second drawback is that, for security reasons, servers are permitted to prohibit access to the ServletContext of certain Web applications. Calls to getContext return null in such a case. For example, in Tomcat you can use a value of false for the crossContext attribute of the Context or DefaultContext element (specified in *install_dir/conf/server.xml*) to indicate that a Web application should run in a security-conscious environment and prohibit access to its ServletContext.

These two data-sharing approaches are illustrated by the SetSharedInfo and ShowSharedInfo servlets shown in Listings 4.6 and 4.7. The SetSharedInfo servlet creates custom entries in the session object and the servlet context. It also sets two cookies: one with the default path, indicating that the cookie should apply only to URLs with the same URL prefix as the original request, and one with a path of "/", indicating that the cookie should apply to all URLs on the host. Finally, the Set-SharedInfo servlet redirects the client to the ShowSharedInfo servlet, which displays the names of all session attributes, all attributes in the current servlet context, all attributes in the servlet context that applies to URLs with the prefix */shareTest1*, and all cookies.

Listing 4.6   *SetSharedInfo.java*

```
package moreservlets;

import java.io.*;
import javax.servlet.*;
import javax.servlet.http.*;

/** Puts some data into the session, the servlet context, and
 *  two cookies. Then redirects the user to the servlet
 *  that displays info on sessions, the servlet context,
 *  and cookies.
 */

public class SetSharedInfo extends HttpServlet {
  public void doGet(HttpServletRequest request,
                    HttpServletResponse response)
      throws ServletException, IOException {
    HttpSession session = request.getSession(true);
    session.setAttribute("sessionTest", "Session Entry One");
    ServletContext context = getServletContext();
    context.setAttribute("servletContextTest",
                    "Servlet Context Entry One");
```

Listing 4.6   *SetSharedInfo.java (continued)*

```
   Cookie c1 = new Cookie("cookieTest1", "Cookie One");
   c1.setMaxAge(3600);      // One hour
   response.addCookie(c1); // Default path
   Cookie c2 = new Cookie("cookieTest2", "Cookie Two");
   c2.setMaxAge(3600);      // One hour
   c2.setPath("/");          // Explicit path: all URLs
   response.addCookie(c2);
   String url = request.getContextPath() +
              "/servlet/moreservlets.ShowSharedInfo";
   // In case session tracking is based on URL rewriting.
   url = response.encodeRedirectURL(url);
   response.sendRedirect(url);
  }
}
```

Listing 4.7   *ShowSharedInfo.java*

```
package moreservlets;

import java.io.*;
import javax.servlet.*;
import javax.servlet.http.*;
import java.util.*;

/** Summarizes information on sessions, the servlet
 *  context and cookies. Illustrates that sessions
 *  and the servlet context are separate for each Web app
 *  but that cookies are shared as long as their path is
 *  set appropriately.
 */

public class ShowSharedInfo extends HttpServlet {
  public void doGet(HttpServletRequest request,
                    HttpServletResponse response)
      throws ServletException, IOException {
    response.setContentType("text/html");
    PrintWriter out = response.getWriter();
    String title = "Shared Info";
    out.println(ServletUtilities.headWithTitle(title) +
              "<BODY BGCOLOR=\"#FDF5E6\">\n" +
              "<H1 ALIGN=\"CENTER\">" + title + "</H1>\n" +
              "<UL>\n" +
              "  <LI>Session:");
```

Listing 4.7   *ShowSharedInfo.java (continued)*

```java
    HttpSession session = request.getSession(true);
    Enumeration attributes = session.getAttributeNames();
    out.println(getAttributeList(attributes));
    out.println("  <LI>Current Servlet Context:");
    ServletContext application = getServletContext();
    attributes = application.getAttributeNames();
    out.println(getAttributeList(attributes));
    out.println("  <LI>Servlet Context of /shareTest1:");
    application = application.getContext("/shareTest1");
    attributes = application.getAttributeNames();
    out.println(getAttributeList(attributes));
    out.println("  <LI>Cookies:<UL>");
    Cookie[] cookies = request.getCookies();
    if ((cookies == null) || (cookies.length == 0)) {
      out.println("    <LI>No cookies found.");
    } else {
      Cookie cookie;
      for(int i=0; i<cookies.length; i++) {
        cookie = cookies[i];
        out.println("    <LI>" + cookie.getName());
      }
    }
    out.println("    </UL>\n" +
                "</UL>\n" +
                "</BODY></HTML>");
  }

  private String getAttributeList(Enumeration attributes) {
    StringBuffer list = new StringBuffer("  <UL>\n");
    if (!attributes.hasMoreElements()) {
      list.append("    <LI>No attributes found.");
    } else {
      while(attributes.hasMoreElements()) {
        list.append("    <LI>");
        list.append(attributes.nextElement());
        list.append("\n");
      }
    }
    list.append("  </UL>");
    return(list.toString());
  }
}
```

Figure 4–10 shows the result after the user visits the `SetSharedInfo` and `ShowSharedInfo` servlets from within the Web application that is assigned *shareTest1* as a URL prefix. The `ShowSharedInfo` servlet sees:

- The custom session attribute.
- The custom (explicitly created by the `SetSharedInfo` servlet) and standard (automatically created by the server) attributes that are contained in the default servlet context.
- The custom and standard attributes that are contained in the servlet context that is found by means of `getContext("/shareTest1")`, which in this case is the same as the default servlet context.
- The two explicitly created cookies and the system-created cookie used behind the scenes by the session tracking API.

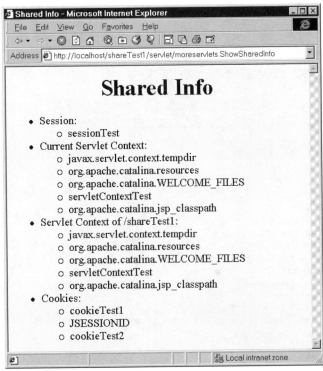

Figure 4–10 Result of visiting the `SetSharedInfo` and `ShowSharedInfo` servlets from within the same Web application.

Figure 4–11 shows the result when the user later visits an identical copy of the ShowSharedInfo servlet that is installed in a Web application that has */shareTest2* as the URL prefix. The servlet sees:

- The standard attributes that are contained in the default servlet context.
- The custom and standard attributes that are contained in the servlet context that is found by means of getContext("/shareTest1"), which in this case is different from the default servlet context.
- Two cookies: the explicitly created one that has its path set to "/" and the system-created one used behind the scenes for session tracking (which also uses a custom path of "/").

The servlet does *not* see:

- Any attributes in its session object.
- Any custom attributes contained in the default servlet context.
- The explicitly created cookie that uses the default path.

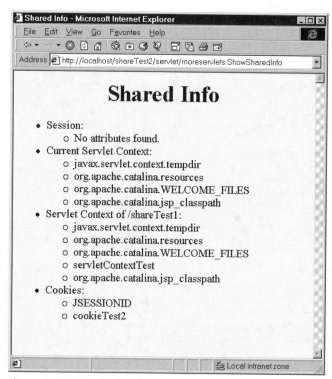

Figure 4–11   Result of visiting the SetSharedInfo servlet in one Web application and the ShowSharedInfo servlet in a different Web application.

CONTROLLING
WEB APPLICATION
BEHAVIOR WITH
WEB.XML

Topics in This Chapter

- Customizing URLs
- Turning off default URLs
- Initializing servlets and JSP pages
- Preloading servlets and JSP pages
- Declaring filters for servlets and JSP pages
- Designating welcome pages and error pages
- Restricting access to Web resources
- Controlling session timeouts
- Documenting Web applications
- Specifying MIME types
- Locating tag library descriptors
- Declaring event listeners
- Accessing J2EE resources

Chapter 5

This chapter describes the makeup of the deployment descriptor file that is placed in *WEB-INF/web.xml* within each Web application. I'll summarize all the legal elements here; for the formal specification see *http://java.sun.com/dtd/web-app_2_3.dtd* (for version 2.3 of the servlet API) or *http://java.sun.com/j2ee/dtds/web-app_2_2.dtd* (for version 2.2).

Most of the servlet and JSP examples in this chapter assume that they are part of a Web application named `deployDemo`. For details on how to set up and register Web applications, please see Chapter 4 (Using and Deploying Web Applications).

5.1 Defining the Header and Root Elements

The deployment descriptor, like all XML files, must begin with an XML header. This header declares the version of XML that is in effect and gives the character encoding for the file.

A `DOCTYPE` declaration must appear immediately after the header. This declaration tells the server the version of the servlet specification (e.g., 2.2 or 2.3) that applies and specifies the Document Type Definition (DTD) that governs the syntax of the rest of the file.

The top-level (root) element for all deployment descriptors is `web-app`. Remember that XML elements, unlike HTML elements, are case sensitive. Consequently, `Web-App` and `WEB-APP` are not legal; you must use `web-app` in lower case.

Core Warning

XML elements are case sensitive.

Thus, the *web.xml* file should be structured as follows for Web apps that will run in servlet 2.2 containers (servers) or that will run in 2.3 containers but not make use of the new *web.xml* capabilities (e.g., filter or listener declarations) introduced in version 2.3.

```
<?xml version="1.0" encoding="ISO-8859-1"?>
<!DOCTYPE web-app PUBLIC
    "-//Sun Microsystems, Inc.//DTD Web Application 2.2//EN"
    "http://java.sun.com/j2ee/dtds/web-app_2_2.dtd">
<web-app>
  <!-- Other elements go here. All are optional. -->
</web-app>
```

Rather than typing in this template by hand, you can (and should) download an example from *http://www.moreservlets.com* or copy and edit the version that comes in the default Web application of whatever server you use. However, note that the *web.xml* file that is distributed with Allaire JRun 3 (e.g., in *install_dir/servers/default/ default-app/WEB-INF* for JRun 3.0 or the *samples* directory for JRun 3.1) incorrectly omits the XML header and DOCTYPE line. As a result, although JRun accepts properly formatted *web.xml* files from other servers, other servers might not accept the *web.xml* file from JRun 3. So, if you use JRun 3, be sure to insert the header and DOCTYPE lines.

Core Warning

The web.xml file that is distributed with JRun 3 is illegal; it is missing the XML header and DOCTYPE declaration.

If you want to use servlet/JSP filters, application life-cycle listeners, or other features specific to servlets 2.3, you must use the servlet 2.3 DTD, as shown in the *web.xml* file below. Of course, you must also use a server that supports this version of the specification—version 4 of Tomcat, JRun, or ServletExec, for example. Just be aware that your Web application will not run in servers that support only version 2.2 of the servlet API (e.g., version 3 of Tomcat, JRun, or ServletExec).

```
<?xml version="1.0" encoding="ISO-8859-1"?>
<!DOCTYPE web-app PUBLIC
    "-//Sun Microsystems, Inc.//DTD Web Application 2.3//EN"
    "http://java.sun.com/dtd/web-app_2_3.dtd">
```

```
<web-app>
  <!-- Other elements go here. All are optional. -->
</web-app>
```

5.2   The Order of Elements within the Deployment Descriptor

Not only are XML elements case sensitive, they are also sensitive to the order in which they appear within other elements. For example, the XML header must be the first entry in the file, the DOCTYPE declaration must be second, and the web-app element must be third. Within the web-app element, the order of the elements also matters. Servers are not required to enforce this ordering, but they are permitted to, and some do so in practice, completely refusing to run Web applications that contain elements that are out of order. This means that *web.xml* files that use nonstandard element ordering are not portable.

Core Approach

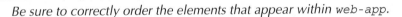

Be sure to correctly order the elements that appear within web-app.

The following list gives the required ordering of all legal elements that can appear directly within the web-app element. For example, the list shows that any servlet elements must appear before any servlet-mapping elements. If there are any mime-mapping elements, they must go after all servlet and servlet-mapping elements but before welcome-file-list. Remember that all these elements are optional. So, you can omit any element but you cannot place it in a nonstandard location.

- **icon**. The icon element designates the location of either one or two image files that an IDE or GUI tool can use to represent the Web application. For details, see Section 5.11 (Documenting Web Applications).
- **display-name**. The display-name element provides a name that GUI tools might use to label this particular Web application. See Section 5.11.
- **description**. The description element gives explanatory text about the Web application. See Section 5.11.

- **distributable**. The `distributable` element tells the system that it is safe to distribute the Web application across multiple servers. See Section 5.15.

- **context-param**. The `context-param` element declares application-wide initialization parameters. For details, see Section 5.5 (Initializing and Preloading Servlets and JSP Pages).

- **filter**. The filter element associates a name with a class that implements the `javax.servlet.Filter` interface. For details, see Section 5.6 (Declaring Filters).

- **filter-mapping**. Once you have named a filter, you associate it with one or more servlets or JSP pages by means of the `filter-mapping` element. See Section 5.6.

- **listener**. Version 2.3 of the servlet API added support for event listeners that are notified when the session or servlet context is created, modified, or destroyed. The `listener` element designates the event listener class. See Section 5.14 for details.

- **servlet**. Before you assign initialization parameters or custom URLs to servlets or JSP pages, you must first name the servlet or JSP page. You use the `servlet` element for that purpose. For details, see Section 5.3.

- **servlet-mapping**. Servers typically provide a default URL for servlets: *http://host/webAppPrefix/servlet/ServletName*. However, you often change this URL so that the servlet can access initialization parameters (Section 5.5) or more easily handle relative URLs (Section 4.5). When you do change the default URL, you use the `servlet-mapping` element to do so. See Section 5.3.

- **session-config**. If a session has not been accessed for a certain period of time, the server can throw it away to save memory. You can explicitly set the timeout for individual session objects by using the `setMaxInactiveInterval` method of `HttpSession`, or you can use the `session-config` element to designate a default timeout. For details, see Section 5.10.

- **mime-mapping**. If your Web application has unusual files that you want to guarantee are assigned certain MIME types, the `mime-mapping` element can provide this guarantee. For more information, see Section 5.12.

- **welcome-file-list**. The `welcome-file-list` element instructs the server what file to use when the server receives URLs that refer to a directory name but not a filename. See Section 5.7 for details.

- **error-page**. The `error-page` element lets you designate the pages that will be displayed when certain HTTP status codes are returned or when certain types of exceptions are thrown. For details, see Section 5.8.
- **taglib**. The `taglib` element assigns aliases to Tag Library Descriptor files. This capability lets you change the location of the TLD files without editing the JSP pages that use those files. See Section 5.13 for more information.
- **resource-env-ref**. The `resource-env-ref` element declares an administered object associated with a resource. See Section 5.15.
- **resource-ref**. The `resource-ref` element declares an external resource used with a resource factory. See Section 5.15.
- **security-constraint**. The `security-constraint` element lets you designate URLs that should be protected. It goes hand-in-hand with the `login-config` element. See Section 5.9 for details.
- **login-config**. You use the `login-config` element to specify how the server should authorize users who attempt to access protected pages. It goes hand-in-hand with the `security-constraint` element. See Section 5.9 for details.
- **security-role**. The `security-role` element gives a list of security roles that will appear in the `role-name` subelements of the `security-role-ref` element inside the `servlet` element. Declaring the roles separately could make it easier for advanced IDEs to manipulate security information. See Section 5.9 for details.
- **env-entry**. The `env-entry` element declares the Web application's environment entry. See Section 5.15.
- **ejb-ref**. The `ejb-ref` element declares a reference to the home of an enterprise bean. See Section 5.15.
- **ejb-local-ref**. The `ejb-local-ref` element declares a reference to the local home of an enterprise bean. See Section 5.15.

5.3 Assigning Names and Custom URLs

One of the most common tasks that you perform in *web.xml* is giving names and custom URLs to your servlets or JSP pages. You use the `servlet` element to assign names; you use the `servlet-mapping` element to associate custom URLs with the name just assigned.

Assigning Names

In order to provide initialization parameters, define a custom URL, or assign a security role to a servlet or JSP page, you must first give the servlet or page a name. You assign a name by means of the `servlet` element. The most common format includes `servlet-name` and `servlet-class` subelements (inside the `web-app` element), as follows.

```
<servlet>
  <servlet-name>Test</servlet-name>
  <servlet-class>moreservlets.TestServlet</servlet-class>
</servlet>
```

This means that the servlet at *WEB-INF/classes/moreservlets/TestServlet* is now known by the registered name `Test`. Giving a servlet a name has two major implications. First, initialization parameters, custom URL patterns, and other customizations refer to the servlet by the registered name, not by the class name. Second, the name can be used in the URL instead of the class name. Thus, with the definition just given, the URL *http://host/webAppPrefix/servlet/**Test*** can be used in lieu of *http://host/webAppPrefix/servlet/**moreservlets.TestServlet***.

Remember: not only are XML elements case sensitive, but the order in which you define them also matters. For example, all `servlet` elements within the `web-app` element must come before any of the `servlet-mapping` elements that are introduced in the next subsection, but before the filter or documentation-related elements (if any) that are discussed in Sections 5.6 and 5.11. Similarly, the `servlet-name` subelement of `servlet` must come before `servlet-class`. Section 5.2 (The Order of Elements within the Deployment Descriptor) describes the required ordering in detail.

Core Approach

Be sure to properly order the elements within the `web-app` element of web.xml. In particular, the `servlet` element must come before `servlet-mapping`.

For example, Listing 5.1 shows a simple servlet called `TestServlet` that resides in the `moreservlets` package. Since the servlet is part of a Web application rooted in a directory named *deployDemo*, *TestServlet.class* is placed in *deployDemo/WEB-INF/classes/moreservlets*. Listing 5.2 shows a portion of the *web.xml* file that would be placed in *deployDemo/WEB-INF/*. This *web.xml* file uses the `servlet-name` and `servlet-class` elements to associate the name `Test` with *TestServlet.class*.

Figures 5–1 and 5–2 show the results when `TestServlet` is invoked by means of the default URL and the registered name, respectively.

Listing 5.1   *TestServlet.java*

```java
package moreservlets;

import java.io.*;
import javax.servlet.*;
import javax.servlet.http.*;

/** Simple servlet used to illustrate servlet naming
 *   and custom URLs.
 */

public class TestServlet extends HttpServlet {
  public void doGet(HttpServletRequest request,
                    HttpServletResponse response)
      throws ServletException, IOException {
    response.setContentType("text/html");
    PrintWriter out = response.getWriter();
    String uri = request.getRequestURI();
    out.println(ServletUtilities.headWithTitle("Test Servlet") +
                "<BODY BGCOLOR=\"#FDF5E6\">\n" +
                "<H2>URI: " + uri + "</H2>\n" +
                "</BODY></HTML>");
  }
}
```

Listing 5.2   *web.xml* (Excerpt showing servlet name)

```xml
<?xml version="1.0" encoding="ISO-8859-1"?>
<!DOCTYPE web-app PUBLIC
    "-//Sun Microsystems, Inc.//DTD Web Application 2.3//EN"
    "http://java.sun.com/dtd/web-app_2_3.dtd">

<web-app>
  <!-- ... -->
  <servlet>
    <servlet-name>Test</servlet-name>
    <servlet-class>moreservlets.TestServlet</servlet-class>
  </servlet>
  <!-- ... -->
</web-app>
```

Figure 5–1   TestServlet when invoked with the default URL.

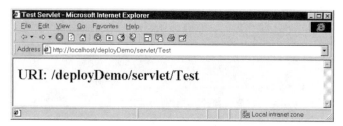

Figure 5–2   TestServlet when invoked with the registered name.

Defining Custom URLs

Most servers have a default URL for servlets: *http://host/webAppPrefix/servlet/ packageName.ServletName*. Although it is convenient to use this URL during development, you often want a different URL for deployment. For instance, you might want a URL that appears in the top level of the Web application (e.g., *http://host/ webAppPrefix/AnyName*), without the *servlet* entry in the URL. A URL at the top level simplifies the use of relative URLs, as described in Section 4.5 (Handling Relative URLs in Web Applications). Besides, top-level URLs are shorter and simply *look* better to many developers than the long and cumbersome default URLs.

In fact, sometimes you are *required* to use a custom URL. For example, you might turn off the default URL mapping so as to better enforce security restrictions or to prevent users from accidentally accessing servlets that have no init parameters. This idea is discussed further in Section 5.4 (Disabling the Invoker Servlet). If you disable the default URL, how do you access the servlet? Only by using a custom URL.

To assign a custom URL, you use the `servlet-mapping` element along with its `servlet-name` and `url-pattern` subelements. The `servlet-name` element provides an arbitrary name with which to refer to the servlet; `url-pattern` describes a URL relative to the Web application root. The value of the `url-pattern` element must begin with a slash (`/`).

Here is a simple *web.xml* excerpt that lets you use the URL *http://host/webApp-Prefix/UrlTest* instead of either *http://host/webAppPrefix/servlet/Test* or *http://host/webAppPrefix/servlet/moreservlets.TestServlet*. Figure 5–3 shows a typical result. Remember that you still need the XML header, the DOCTYPE declaration, and the enclosing web-app element as described in Section 5.1 (Defining the Header and Root Elements). Furthermore, recall that the order in which XML elements appears is not arbitrary. In particular, you are required to put all the servlet elements before any of the servlet-mapping elements. For a complete breakdown of the required ordering of elements within web-app, see Section 5.2 (The Order of Elements within the Deployment Descriptor).

```
<servlet>
  <servlet-name>Test</servlet-name>
  <servlet-class>moreservlets.TestServlet</servlet-class>
</servlet>
<!-- ... -->
<servlet-mapping>
  <servlet-name>Test</servlet-name>
  <url-pattern>/UrlTest</url-pattern>
</servlet-mapping>
```

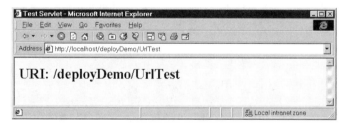

Figure 5–3   TestServlet invoked with a URL pattern.

The URL pattern can also include wildcards. For example, the following snippet instructs the server to send to all requests beginning with the Web app's URL prefix (see Section 4.1, "Registering Web Applications") and ending with *.asp* to the servlet named BashMS.

```
<servlet>
  <servlet-name>BashMS</servlet-name>
  <servlet-class>msUtils.ASPTranslator</servlet-class>
</servlet>
<!-- ... -->
<servlet-mapping>
  <servlet-name>BashMS</servlet-name>
  <url-pattern>/*.asp</url-pattern>
</servlet-mapping>
```

Naming JSP Pages

Since JSP pages get translated into servlets, it is natural to expect that you can name JSP pages just as you can name servlets. After all, JSP pages might benefit from initialization parameters, security settings, or custom URLs, just as regular servlets do. Although it is true that JSP pages are really servlets behind the scenes, there is one key difference: you don't know the actual class name of JSP pages (since the system picks the name). So, to name JSP pages, you substitute the `jsp-file` element for the `servlet-class` element, as follows.

```
<servlet>
  <servlet-name>PageName</servlet-name>
  <jsp-file>/TestPage.jsp</jsp-file>
</servlet>
```

You name JSP pages for exactly the same reason that you name servlets: to provide a name to use with customization settings (e.g., initialization parameters and security settings) and so that you can change the URL that invokes the JSP page (e.g., so that multiple URLs get handled by the same page or to remove the *.jsp* extension from the URL). However, when setting initialization parameters, remember that JSP pages read initialization parameters by using the `jspInit` method, not the `init` method. See Section 5.5 (Initializing and Preloading Servlets and JSP Pages) for details.

For example, Listing 5.3 is a simple JSP page named *TestPage.jsp* that just prints out the local part of the URL used to invoke it. *TestPage.jsp* is placed in the top level of the *deployDemo* directory. Listing 5.4 shows a portion of the *web.xml* file (i.e., *deployDemo/WEB-INF/web.xml*) used to assign a registered name of `PageName` and then to associate that registered name with URLs of the form *http://host/webApp-Prefix/UrlTest2/anything*. Figures 5–4 through 5–6 show the results for the URLs *http://localhost/deployDemo/TestPage.jsp* (the real name), *http://localhost/deploy-Demo/servlet/PageName* (the registered servlet name), and *http://localhost/deploy-Demo/UrlTest2/foo/bar/baz.html* (a URL matching `url-pattern`), respectively.

Listing 5.3   *TestPage.jsp*

```
<!DOCTYPE HTML PUBLIC "-//W3C//DTD HTML 4.0 Transitional//EN">
<HTML>
<HEAD><TITLE>JSP Test Page</TITLE></HEAD>
<BODY BGCOLOR="#FDF5E6">
<H2>URI:  <%= request.getRequestURI() %></H2>
</BODY></HTML>
```

Listing 5.4	*web.xml* (Excerpt illustrating the naming of JSP pages)

```xml
<?xml version="1.0" encoding="ISO-8859-1"?>
<!DOCTYPE web-app PUBLIC
    "-//Sun Microsystems, Inc.//DTD Web Application 2.3//EN"
    "http://java.sun.com/dtd/web-app_2_3.dtd">

<web-app>
  <!-- ... -->
  <servlet>
    <servlet-name>PageName</servlet-name>
    <jsp-file>/TestPage.jsp</jsp-file>
  </servlet>
  <!-- ... -->
  <servlet-mapping>
    <servlet-name>PageName</servlet-name>
    <url-pattern>/UrlTest2/*</url-pattern>
  </servlet-mapping>
  <!-- ... -->
</web-app>
```

Figure 5–4   *TestPage.jsp* invoked with the normal URL.

Figure 5–5   *TestPage.jsp* invoked with the registered servlet name.

Figure 5–6   *TestPage.jsp* invoked with a URL that matches the designated
`url-pattern`.

5.4   Disabling the Invoker Servlet

One reason for setting up a custom URL for a servlet or JSP page is so that you can
register initialization parameters to be read from the `init` (servlets) or `jspInit`
(JSP pages) methods. However, as discussed in Section 5.5 (Initializing and Preloading Servlets and JSP Pages), the initialization parameters are available only when the
servlet or JSP page is accessed by means of a custom URL pattern or a registered
name, not when it is accessed with the default URL of *http://host/webAppPrefix/
servlet/ServletName*. Consequently, you might want to turn off the default URL so
that nobody accidentally calls the uninitialized servlet. This process is sometimes
known as disabling *the invoker servlet*, since most servers have a standard servlet that
is registered with the default servlet URLs and simply invokes the real servlet that
the URL refers to.

There are two main approaches for disabling the default URL:

- Remapping the */servlet/* pattern in each Web application.
- Globally turning off the invoker servlet.

It is important to note that, although remapping the */servlet/* pattern in each Web
application is more work than disabling the invoker servlet in one fell swoop, remapping can be done in a completely portable manner. In contrast, the process for globally disabling the invoker servlet is completely machine specific, and in fact some
servers (e.g., ServletExec) have no such option. The first following subsection discusses the per-Web-application strategy of remapping the */servlet/* URL pattern. The
next two subsections provide details on globally disabling the invoker servlet in Tomcat and JRun.

Remapping the /servlet/ URL Pattern

It is quite straightforward to disable processing of URLs that begin with *http://host/
webAppPrefix/servlet/* in a particular Web application. All you need to do is create an

error message servlet and use the `url-pattern` element discussed in the previous section to direct all matching requests to that servlet. Simply use

```
<url-pattern>/servlet/*</url-pattern>
```

as the pattern within the `servlet-mapping` element.

For example, Listing 5.5 shows a portion of the deployment descriptor that associates the `SorryServlet` servlet (Listing 5.6) with all URLs that begin with *http://host/webAppPrefix/servlet/*. Figures 5–7 and 5–8 illustrate attempts to access the `TestServlet` servlet (Listing 5.1 in Section 5.3) before (Figure 5–7) and after (Figure 5–8) the *web.xml* entries of Listing 5.5 are made.

All compliant servers yield the results of Figures 5–7 and 5–8. However, ServletExec 4.0 has a bug whereby mappings of the `/servlet/*` pattern are ignored (other mappings work fine). Furthermore, since ServletExec has no global method of disabling the invoker servlet, in version 4.0 you are left with no alternative but to leave the invoker servlet enabled. The problem is resolved in ServletExec version 4.1.

Core Warning

You cannot disable the invoker servlet in ServletExec 4.0.

Listing 5.5   *web.xml* (Excerpt showing how to disable default URLs)

```xml
<?xml version="1.0" encoding="ISO-8859-1"?>
<!DOCTYPE web-app PUBLIC
    "-//Sun Microsystems, Inc.//DTD Web Application 2.3//EN"
    "http://java.sun.com/dtd/web-app_2_3.dtd">

<web-app>
  <!-- ... -->
  <servlet>
    <servlet-name>Sorry</servlet-name>
    <servlet-class>moreservlets.SorryServlet</servlet-class>
  </servlet>
  <!-- ... -->
  <servlet-mapping>
    <servlet-name>Sorry</servlet-name>
    <url-pattern>/servlet/*</url-pattern>
  </servlet-mapping>
  <!-- ... -->
</web-app>
```

| Listing 5.6 | *SorryServlet.java* |

```java
package moreservlets;

import java.io.*;
import javax.servlet.*;
import javax.servlet.http.*;

/** Simple servlet used to give error messages to
 *  users who try to access default servlet URLs
 *  (i.e., http://host/webAppPrefix/servlet/ServletName)
 *  in Web applications that have disabled this
 *  behavior.
 */

public class SorryServlet extends HttpServlet {
  public void doGet(HttpServletRequest request,
                    HttpServletResponse response)
     throws ServletException, IOException {
    response.setContentType("text/html");
    PrintWriter out = response.getWriter();
    String title = "Invoker Servlet Disabled.";
    out.println(ServletUtilities.headWithTitle(title) +
                "<BODY BGCOLOR=\"#FDF5E6\">\n" +
                "<H2>" + title + "</H2>\n" +
                "Sorry, access to servlets by means of\n" +
                "URLs that begin with\n" +
                "http://host/webAppPrefix/servlet/\n" +
                "has been disabled.\n" +
                "</BODY></HTML>");
  }

  public void doPost(HttpServletRequest request,
                     HttpServletResponse response)
     throws ServletException, IOException {
    doGet(request, response);
  }
}
```

Figure 5–7   Successful attempt to invoke the `TestServlet` servlet by means of the default URL. The invoker servlet is enabled.

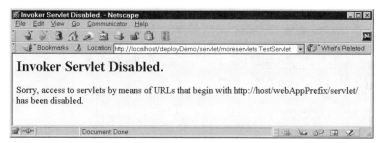

Figure 5–8   Unsuccessful attempt to invoke the `TestServlet` servlet by means of the default URL. The invoker servlet is disabled.

Globally Disabling the Invoker: Tomcat

The method you use to turn off the default URL in Tomcat 4 is quite different from the approach used in Tomcat 3. The following two subsections summarize the two approaches.

Disabling the Invoker: Tomcat 4

Tomcat 4 turns off the invoker servlet in the same way that I turned it off in the previous section: by means of a `url-mapping` element in *web.xml*. The difference is that Tomcat uses a server-specific global *web.xml* file that is stored in *install_dir/conf*, whereas I used the standard *web.xml* file that is stored in the *WEB-INF* directory of each Web application.

Thus, to turn off the invoker servlet in Tomcat 4, you simply comment out the `/servlet/*` URL mapping entry in *install_dir/conf/web.xml*, as shown below.

```
<!--
<servlet-mapping>
  <servlet-name>invoker</servlet-name>
```

```
    <url-pattern>/servlet/*</url-pattern>
</servlet-mapping>
-->
```

Again, note that this entry is in the Tomcat-specific *web.xml* file that is stored in *install_dir/conf*, not the standard *web.xml* file that is stored in the *WEB-INF* directory of each Web application.

Figures 5–9 and 5–10 show the results when the `TestServlet` (Listing 5.1 from the previous section) is invoked with the default URL and with the registered servlet name in a version of Tomcat that has the invoker servlet disabled. Both URLs are of the form *http://host/webAppPrefix/servlet/something*, and both fail. Figure 5–11 shows the result when the explicit URL pattern is used; this request succeeds.

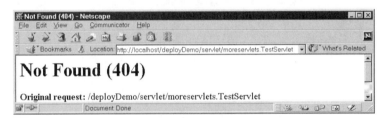

Figure 5–9   `TestServlet` when invoked with the default URL in a server that has globally disabled the invoker servlet.

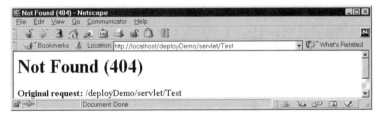

Figure 5–10   `TestServlet` when invoked with a registered name in a server that has globally disabled the invoker servlet.

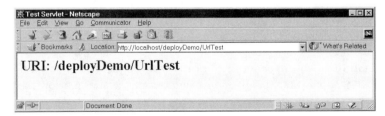

Figure 5–11   `TestServlet` when invoked with a custom URL in a server that has globally disabled the invoker servlet.

Disabling the Invoker: Tomcat 3

In version 3 of Apache Tomcat, you globally disable the default servlet URL by commenting out the `InvokerInterceptor` entry in *install_dir/conf/server.xml*. For example, following is a section of a *server.xml* file that prohibits use of the default servlet URL.

```
<!--
<RequestInterceptor
  className="org.apache.tomcat.request.InvokerInterceptor"
  debug="0" prefix="/servlet/" />
-->
```

With this entry commented out, Tomcat 3 gives the same results as shown in Figures 5–9 through 5–11.

Globally Disabling the Invoker: JRun

In JRun 3.1, you disable the invoker servlet by editing *install_dir/lib/global.properties* and inserting a # at the beginning of the line that defines the invoker, thus commenting out the line. This is illustrated below.

```
# webapp.servlet-mapping./servlet=invoker
```

With these settings, JRun gives about the same results as shown in Figures 5–9 through 5–11; the only minor difference is that it gives 500 (Internal Server Error) messages for the first two cases instead of the 404 (Not Found) messages that Tomcat gives.

5.5 Initializing and Preloading Servlets and JSP Pages

This section discusses methods for controlling the startup behavior of servlets and JSP pages. In particular, it explains how you can assign initialization parameters and how you can change the point in the server life cycle at which servlets and JSP pages are loaded.

Assigning Servlet Initialization Parameters

You provide servlets with initialization parameters by means of the `init-param` element, which has `param-name` and `param-value` subelements. For instance, in the following example, if the `InitServlet` servlet is accessed by means of its registered name (`InitTest`), it could call `getServletConfig().getInit-Parameter("param1")` from its init method to get "`Value 1`" and `getServletConfig().getInitParameter("param2")` to get "`2`".

```
<servlet>
  <servlet-name>InitTest</servlet-name>
  <servlet-class>myPackage.InitServlet</servlet-class>
  <init-param>
    <param-name>param1</param-name>
    <param-value>Value 1</param-value>
  </init-param>
  <init-param>
    <param-name>param2</param-name>
    <param-value>2</param-value>
  </init-param>
</servlet>
```

There are a few common gotchas that are worth keeping in mind when dealing with initialization parameters:

- **Return values.** The return value of `getInitParameter` is always a `String`. So, for instance, in the previous example you might use `Integer.parseInt` on `param2` to obtain an `int`.
- **Initialization in JSP.** JSP pages use `jspInit`, not `init`. JSP pages also require use of the `jsp-file` element in place of `servlet-class`, as described in Section 5.3 (Assigning Names and Custom URLs). Initializing JSP pages is discussed in the next subsection.
- **Default URLs.** Initialization parameters are only available when servlets are accessed by means of their registered names or through custom URL patterns associated with their registered names. So, in this example, the `param1` and `param2` init parameters would be available when you used the URL *http://host/webAppPrefix/servlet/InitTest*, but not when you used the URL *http://host/webAppPrefix/servlet/myPackage.InitServlet*.

Core Warning

Initialization parameters are not available in servlets that are accessed by their default URL.

For example, Listing 5.7 shows a simple servlet called `InitServlet` that uses the `init` method to set the `firstName` and `emailAddress` fields. Listing 5.8 shows the *web.xml* file that assigns the name `InitTest` to the servlet. Figures 5–12 and 5–13 show the results when the servlet is accessed with the registered name (correct) and the original name (incorrect), respectively.

Listing 5.7 *InitServlet.java*

```java
package moreservlets;

import java.io.*;
import javax.servlet.*;
import javax.servlet.http.*;

/** Simple servlet used to illustrate servlet
 *  initialization parameters.
 */

public class InitServlet extends HttpServlet {
  private String firstName, emailAddress;

  public void init() {
    ServletConfig config = getServletConfig();
    firstName = config.getInitParameter("firstName");
    emailAddress = config.getInitParameter("emailAddress");
  }

  public void doGet(HttpServletRequest request,
                    HttpServletResponse response)
      throws ServletException, IOException {
    response.setContentType("text/html");
    PrintWriter out = response.getWriter();
    String uri = request.getRequestURI();
    out.println(ServletUtilities.headWithTitle("Init Servlet") +
                "<BODY BGCOLOR=\"#FDF5E6\">\n" +
                "<H2>Init Parameters:</H2>\n" +
                "<UL>\n" +
                "<LI>First name: " + firstName + "\n" +
                "<LI>Email address: " + emailAddress + "\n" +
                "</UL>\n" +
                "</BODY></HTML>");
  }
}
```

Listing 5.8	*web.xml* (Excerpt illustrating initialization parameters)

```xml
<?xml version="1.0" encoding="ISO-8859-1"?>
<!DOCTYPE web-app PUBLIC
    "-//Sun Microsystems, Inc.//DTD Web Application 2.3//EN"
    "http://java.sun.com/dtd/web-app_2_3.dtd">

<web-app>
  <!-- ... -->
  <servlet>
    <servlet-name>InitTest</servlet-name>
    <servlet-class>moreservlets.InitServlet</servlet-class>
    <init-param>
      <param-name>firstName</param-name>
      <param-value>Larry</param-value>
    </init-param>
    <init-param>
      <param-name>emailAddress</param-name>
      <param-value>ellison@microsoft.com</param-value>
    </init-param>
  </servlet>
  <!-- ... -->
</web-app>
```

Figure 5–12   The `InitServlet` when correctly accessed with its registered name.

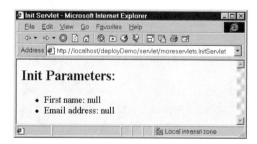

Figure 5–13   The `InitServlet` when incorrectly accessed with the default URL.

Assigning JSP Initialization Parameters

Providing initialization parameters to JSP pages differs in three ways from providing them to servlets.

1. **You use `jsp-file` instead of `servlet-class`.** So, the `servlet` element of the *WEB-INF/web.xml* file would look something like this:

   ```
   <servlet>
     <servlet-name>PageName</servlet-name>
     <jsp-file>/RealPage.jsp</jsp-file>
     <init-param>
       <param-name>...</param-name>
       <param-value>...</param-value>
     </init-param>
     ...
   </servlet>
   ```

2. **You almost always assign an explicit URL pattern.** With servlets, it is moderately common to use the default URL that starts with *http://host/webAppPrefix/**servlet**/*; you just have to remember to use the registered name instead of the original name. This is technically legal with JSP pages also. For example, with the example just shown in item 1, you could use a URL of *http://host/webAppPrefix/servlet/Page-Name* to access the version of *RealPage.jsp* that has access to initialization parameters. But, many users dislike URLs that appear to refer to regular servlets when used for JSP pages. Furthermore, if the JSP page is in a directory for which the server provides a directory listing (e.g., a directory with neither an *index.html* nor an *index.jsp* file), the user might get a link to the JSP page, click on it, and thus accidentally invoke the uninitialized page. So, a good strategy is to use `url-pattern` (Section 5.3) to associate the *original* URL of the JSP page with the registered servlet name. That way, clients can use the normal name for the JSP page but still invoke the customized version. For example, given the `servlet` definition from item 1, you might use the following `servlet-mapping` definition:

   ```
   <servlet-mapping>
     <servlet-name>PageName</servlet-name>
     <url-pattern>/RealPage.jsp</url-pattern>
   </servlet-mapping>
   ```

3. **The JSP page uses `jspInit`, not `init`.** The servlet that is automatically built from a JSP page may already be using the `init` method. Consequently, it is illegal to use a JSP declaration to provide an `init` method. You must name the method `jspInit` instead.

To illustrate the process of initializing JSP pages, Listing 5.9 shows a JSP page called *InitPage.jsp* that contains a `jspInit` method and is placed at the top level of the `deployDemo` Web page hierarchy. Normally, a URL of *http://localhost/deploy-Demo/InitPage.jsp* would invoke a version of the page that has no access to initialization parameters and would thus show `null` for the `firstName` and `emailAddress` variables. However, the *web.xml* file (Listing 5.10) assigns a registered name and then associates that registered name with the URL pattern */InitPage.jsp*. As Figure 5–14 shows, the result is that the normal URL for the JSP page now invokes the version of the page that has access to the initialization parameters.

Listing 5.9   *InitPage.jsp*

```
<!DOCTYPE HTML PUBLIC "-//W3C//DTD HTML 4.0 Transitional//EN">
<HTML>
<HEAD><TITLE>JSP Init Test</TITLE></HEAD>

<BODY BGCOLOR="#FDF5E6">

<H2>Init Parameters:</H2>
<UL>
  <LI>First name: <%= firstName %>
  <LI>Email address: <%= emailAddress %>
</UL>

</BODY></HTML>

<%!
private String firstName, emailAddress;

public void jspInit() {
  ServletConfig config = getServletConfig();
  firstName = config.getInitParameter("firstName");
  emailAddress = config.getInitParameter("emailAddress");
}
%>
```

Listing 5.10 *web.xml* (Excerpt showing init params for JSP pages)

```xml
<?xml version="1.0" encoding="ISO-8859-1"?>
<!DOCTYPE web-app PUBLIC
    "-//Sun Microsystems, Inc.//DTD Web Application 2.3//EN"
    "http://java.sun.com/dtd/web-app_2_3.dtd">

<web-app>
  <!-- ... -->
  <servlet>
    <servlet-name>InitPage</servlet-name>
    <jsp-file>/InitPage.jsp</jsp-file>
    <init-param>
      <param-name>firstName</param-name>
      <param-value>Bill</param-value>
    </init-param>
    <init-param>
      <param-name>emailAddress</param-name>
      <param-value>gates@oracle.com</param-value>
    </init-param>
  </servlet>
  <!-- ... -->
  <servlet-mapping>
    <servlet-name>InitPage</servlet-name>
    <url-pattern>/InitPage.jsp</url-pattern>
  </servlet-mapping>
  <!-- ... -->
</web-app>
```

Figure 5–14 Mapping a JSP page's original URL to the registered servlet name prevents users from accidentally accessing the uninitialized version.

Supplying Application-Wide Initialization Parameters

Normally, you assign initialization parameters to individual servlets or JSP pages. The designated servlet or JSP page reads the parameters by means of the `getInit-Parameter` method of `ServletConfig`. However, in some situations you want to supply system-wide initialization parameters that can be read by *any* servlet or JSP page by means of the `getInitParameter` method of `ServletContext`.

You use the `context-param` element to declare these system-wide initialization values. The `context-param` element should contain `param-name`, `param-value`, and, optionally, `description` subelements, as below.

```
<context-param>
  <param-name>support-email</param-name>
  <param-value>blackhole@mycompany.com</param-value>
</context-param>
```

Recall that, to ensure portability, the elements within *web.xml* must be declared in the proper order. Complete details are given in Section 5.2 (The Order of Elements within the Deployment Descriptor). Here, however, just note that the `context-param` element must appear after any documentation-related elements (`icon`, `display-name`, and `description`—see Section 5.11) and before any `filter` (Section 5.6), `filter-mapping` (Section 5.6), `listener` (Section 5.14), or `servlet` (Section 5.3) elements.

Loading Servlets When the Server Starts

Suppose that a servlet or JSP page has an `init` (servlet) or `jspInit` (JSP) method that takes a long time to execute. For example, suppose that the `init` or `jspInit` method looks up constants from a database or `ResourceBundle`. In such a case, the default behavior of loading the servlet at the time of the first client request results in a significant delay for that first client. So, you can use the `load-on-startup` subelement of `servlet` to stipulate that the server load the servlet when the server first starts. Here is an example.

```
<servlet>
  <servlet-name>...</servlet-name>
  <servlet-class>...</servlet-class> <!-- Or jsp-file -->
  <load-on-startup />
</servlet>
```

Rather than using an empty `load-on-startup` element, you can supply an integer for the element body. The idea is that the server should load lower-numbered servlets or JSP pages before higher-numbered ones. For example, the following `servlet` entries (placed within the `web-app` element in the *web.xml* file that goes in the *WEB-INF* directory of your Web application) would instruct the server to first load and initialize `SearchServlet`, then load and initialize the servlet resulting from the *index.jsp* file that is in the Web app's *results* directory.

```
<servlet>
  <servlet-name>Search</servlet-name>
  <servlet-class>myPackage.SearchServlet</servlet-class>
  <load-on-startup>1</load-on-startup>
</servlet>
<servlet>
  <servlet-name>Results</servlet-name>
  <jsp-file>/results/index.jsp</jsp-file>
  <load-on-startup>2</load-on-startup>
</servlet>
```

5.6 Declaring Filters

Servlet version 2.3 introduced the concept of filters. Although filters are supported by all servers that support version 2.3 of the servlet API, you must use the version 2.3 DTD in *web.xml* in order to use the filter-related elements. For details on the DTD, see Section 5.1 (Defining the Header and Root Elements).

Core Note

Filters and the filter-related elements in web.xml *are available only in servers that support the Java servlet API version 2.3. Even with compliant servers, you must use the version 2.3 DTD.*

Filters are discussed in detail in Chapter 9, but the basic idea is that filters can intercept and modify the request coming into or the response going out of a servlet or JSP page. Before a servlet or JSP page is executed, the `doFilter` method of the first associated filter is executed. When that filter calls `doFilter` on its `Filter-Chain` object, the next filter in the chain is executed. If there is no other filter, the servlet or JSP page itself is executed. Filters have full access to the incoming `ServletRequest` object, so they can check the client's hostname, look for incoming cookies, and so forth. To access the output of the servlet or JSP page, a filter can wrap the response object inside a stand-in object that, for example, accumulates the output into a buffer. After the call to the `doFilter` method of the `FilterChain` object, the filter can examine the buffer, modify it if necessary, and then pass it on to the client.

For example, Listing 5.11 defines a simple filter that intercepts requests and prints a report on the standard output (available with most servers when you run them on your desktop during development) whenever the associated servlet or JSP page is accessed.

Listing 5.11	*ReportFilter.java*

```
package moreservlets;

import java.io.*;
import javax.servlet.*;
import javax.servlet.http.*;
import java.util.*;

/** Simple filter that prints a report on the standard output
 *  whenever the associated servlet or JSP page is accessed.
 */

public class ReportFilter implements Filter {
  public void doFilter(ServletRequest request,
                       ServletResponse response,
                       FilterChain chain)
      throws ServletException, IOException {
    HttpServletRequest req = (HttpServletRequest)request;
    System.out.println(req.getRemoteHost() +
                       " tried to access " +
                       req.getRequestURL() +
                       " on " + new Date() + ".");
    chain.doFilter(request,response);
  }

  public void init(FilterConfig config)
      throws ServletException {
  }

  public void destroy() {}
}
```

Once you have created a filter, you declare it in the *web.xml* file by using the filter element along with the filter-name (arbitrary name), filter-class (fully qualified class name), and, optionally, init-params subelements. Remember that the order in which elements appear within the web-app element of *web.xml* is not arbitrary; servers are allowed (but not required) to enforce the expected ordering, and in practice some servers do so. Complete ordering requirements are given in

Section 5.2 (The Order of Elements within the Deployment Descriptor), but note here that all `filter` elements must come before any `filter-mapping` elements, which in turn must come before any `servlet` or `servlet-mapping` elements.

Core Warning

Be sure to put all your `filter` and `filter-mapping` elements before any `servlet` and `servlet-mapping` elements in web.xml.

For instance, given the `ReportFilter` class just shown, you could make the following `filter` declaration in *web.xml*. It associates the name `Reporter` with the actual class `ReportFilter` (which is in the `moreservlets` package).

```
<filter>
  <filter-name>Reporter</filter-name>
  <filter-class>moreservlets.ReportFilter</filter-class>
</filter>
```

Once you have named a filter, you associate it with one or more servlets or JSP pages by means of the `filter-mapping` element. You have two choices in this regard.

First, you can use `filter-name` and `servlet-name` subelements to associate the filter with a specific servlet name (which must be declared with a `servlet` element later in the same *web.xml* file). For example, the following snippet instructs the system to run the filter named `Reporter` whenever the servlet or JSP page named `SomeServletName` is accessed by means of a custom URL.

```
<filter-mapping>
  <filter-name>Reporter</filter-name>
  <servlet-name>SomeServletName</servlet-name>
</filter-mapping>
```

Second, you can use the `filter-name` and `url-pattern` subelements to associate the filter with groups of servlets, JSP pages, or static content. For example, the following snippet instructs the system to run the filter named `Reporter` when *any* URL in the Web application is accessed.

```
<filter-mapping>
  <filter-name>Reporter</filter-name>
  <url-pattern>/*</url-pattern>
</filter-mapping>
```

For example, Listing 5.12 shows a portion of a *web.xml* file that associates the `ReportFilter` filter with the servlet named `PageName`. The name `PageName`, in turn, is associated with a JSP file named *TestPage.jsp* and URLs that begin with the pattern *http://host/webAppPrefix/UrlTest2/*. The source code for *TestPage.jsp* and a discussion of the naming of JSP pages were given earlier in Section 5.3 (Assigning Names and Custom URLs). In fact, the `servlet` and `servlet-name` entries in Listing 5.12 are taken unchanged from that section. Given these *web.xml* entries, you see debugging reports in the standard output of the following sort (line breaks added for readability).

```
audit.irs.gov tried to access
http://mycompany.com/deployDemo/UrlTest2/business/tax-plan.html
on Tue Dec 25 13:12:29 EDT 2001.
```

Listing 5.12 *web.xml* (Excerpt showing filter usage)

```
<?xml version="1.0" encoding="ISO-8859-1"?>
<!DOCTYPE web-app PUBLIC
    "-//Sun Microsystems, Inc.//DTD Web Application 2.3//EN"
    "http://java.sun.com/dtd/web-app_2_3.dtd">

<web-app>
  <filter>
    <filter-name>Reporter</filter-name>
    <filter-class>moreservlets.ReportFilter</filter-class>
  </filter>
  <!-- ... -->
  <filter-mapping>
    <filter-name>Reporter</filter-name>
    <servlet-name>PageName</servlet-name>
  </filter-mapping>
  <!-- ... -->
  <servlet>
    <servlet-name>PageName</servlet-name>
    <jsp-file>/TestPage.jsp</jsp-file>
  </servlet>
  <!-- ... -->
  <servlet-mapping>
    <servlet-name>PageName</servlet-name>
    <url-pattern>/UrlTest2/*</url-pattern>
  </servlet-mapping>
  <!-- ... -->
</web-app>
```

5.7   Specifying Welcome Pages

Suppose a user supplies a URL like *http://host/webAppPrefix/directoryName/* that contains a directory name but no filename. What happens? Does the user get a directory listing? An error? The contents of a standard file? If so, which one—*index.html*, *index.jsp*, *default.html*, *default.htm*, or what?

The `welcome-file-list` element, along with its subsidiary `welcome-file` element, resolves this ambiguity. For example, the following *web.xml* entry specifies that if a URL gives a directory name but no filename, the server should try *index.jsp* first and *index.html* second. If neither is found, the result is server specific (e.g., a directory listing).

```
<welcome-file-list>
  <welcome-file>index.jsp</welcome-file>
  <welcome-file>index.html</welcome-file>
</welcome-file-list>
```

Although many servers follow this behavior by default, they are not required to do so. As a result, it is good practice to explicitly use `welcome-file-list` to ensure portability.

Core Approach

Make `welcome-file-list` a standard entry in your web.xml *files.*

5.8   Designating Pages to Handle Errors

Now, I realize that *you* never make any mistakes when developing servlets and JSP pages and that all of your pages are so clear that no rational person could be confused by them. Still, however, the world is full of irrational people, and users could supply illegal parameters, use incorrect URLs, or fail to provide values for required form fields. Besides, *other* developers might not be as careful as you are, and they should have some tools to overcome their deficiencies.

The `error-page` element is used to handle problems. It has two possible subelements: `error-code` and `exception-type`. The first of these, `error-code`, designates what URL to use when a designated HTTP error code occurs. (If you aren't familiar with HTTP error codes, they are discussed in Chapter 6 of *Core Servlets and*

JavaServer Pages, which is available in PDF in its entirety at *http://www.more-servlets.com.*) The second of these subelements, `exception-type`, designates what URL to use when a designated Java exception is thrown but not caught. Both `error-code` and `exception-type` use the `location` element to designate the URL. This URL must begin with /. The page at the place designated by `location` can access information about the error by looking up two special-purpose attributes of the `HttpServletRequest` object: `javax.servlet.error.status_code` and `javax.servlet.error.message`.

Recall that it is important to declare the `web-app` subelements in the proper order within *web.xml*. Section 5.2 (The Order of Elements within the Deployment Descriptor) gives complete details on the required ordering. For now, however, just remember that `error-page` comes near the end of the *web.xml* file, after `servlet`, `servlet-name`, and `welcome-file-list`.

The error-code Element

To better understand the value of the `error-code` element, consider what happens at most sites when you type the filename incorrectly. You typically get a 404 error message that tells you that the file can't be found but provides little useful information. On the other hand, try typing unknown filenames at *www.microsoft.com*, *www.ibm.com*, or especially *www.bea.com*. There, you get useful messages that provide alternative places to look for the page of interest. Providing such useful error pages is a valuable addition to your Web application. In fact, *http://www.plinko.net/404/* has an entire site devoted to the topic of 404 error pages. This site includes examples of the best, worst, and funniest 404 pages from around the world.

Listing 5.13 shows a JSP page that could be returned to clients that provide unknown filenames. Listing 5.14 shows the *web.xml* file that designates Listing 5.13 as the page that gets displayed when a 404 error code is returned. Figure 5–15 shows a typical result. Note that the URL displayed in the browser remains the one supplied by the client; the error page is a behind-the-scenes implementation technique.

Finally, remember that the default configuration of Internet Explorer version 5, in clear violation of the HTTP spec, ignores server-generated error messages and displays its own standard error message instead. Fix this by going to the Tools menu, selecting Internet Options, clicking on Advanced, then deselecting Show Friendly HTTP Error Messages.

Core Warning

In the default configuration, Internet Explorer improperly ignores server-generated error messages.

Listing 5.13 *NotFound.jsp*

```
<!DOCTYPE HTML PUBLIC "-//W3C//DTD HTML 4.0 Transitional//EN">
<HTML>
<HEAD><TITLE>404: Not Found</TITLE></HEAD>
<BODY BGCOLOR="#FDF5E6">
<H2>Error!</H2>
I'm sorry, but I cannot find a page that matches
<%= request.getRequestURI() %> on the system. Maybe you should
try one of the following:
<UL>
  <LI>Go to the server's <A HREF="/">home page</A>.
  <LI>Search for relevant pages.<BR>
      <FORM ACTION="http://www.google.com/search">
      <CENTER>
      Keywords: <INPUT TYPE="TEXT" NAME="q"><BR>
      <INPUT TYPE="SUBMIT" VALUE="Search">
      </CENTER>
      </FORM>
  <LI>Admire a random multiple of 404:
      <%= 404*((int)(1000*Math.random())) %>.
  <LI>Try a <A HREF="http://www.plinko.net/404/rndindex.asp"
            TARGET="_blank">
      random 404 error message</A>. From the amazing and
      amusing plinko.net <A HREF="http://www.plinko.net/404/">
      404 archive</A>.
</UL>
</BODY></HTML>
```

Listing 5.14 *web.xml* (Excerpt designating error pages for HTTP error codes)

```
<?xml version="1.0" encoding="ISO-8859-1"?>
<!DOCTYPE web-app PUBLIC
    "-//Sun Microsystems, Inc.//DTD Web Application 2.3//EN"
    "http://java.sun.com/dtd/web-app_2_3.dtd">

<web-app>
  <error-page>
    <error-code>404</error-code>
    <location>/NotFound.jsp</location>
  </error-page>
  <!-- ... -->
</web-app>
```

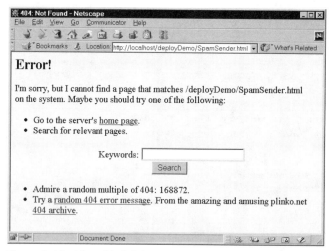

Figure 5–15   Use of helpful 404 messages can enhance the usability of your site.

The exception-type Element

The `error-code` element handles the case when a request results in a particular HTTP status code. But what about the equally common case when the servlet or JSP page returns 200 but generates a runtime exception? That's the situation handled by the `exception-type` element. You only need to supply two things: a fully qualified exception class and a location, as below:

```
<error-page>
  <exception-type>packageName.className</exception-type>
  <location>/SomeURL</location>
</error-page>
```

Then, if any servlet or JSP page in the Web application generates an uncaught exception of the specified type, the designated URL is used. The exception type can be a standard one like `javax.ServletException` or `java.lang.OutOf-MemoryError`, or it can be an exception specific to your application.

For instance, Listing 5.15 shows an exception class named `DumbDeveloper-Exception` that might be used to flag particularly knuckle-headed mistakes by clueless programmers (not that you have any of those types on *your* development team). The class also contains a static method called `dangerousComputation` that sometimes generates this type of exception. Listing 5.16 shows a JSP page that calls `dangerousComputation` on random integer values. When the exception is thrown, *DDE.jsp* (Listing 5.17) is displayed to the client, as designated by the `exception-type` entry shown in the *web.xml* version of Listing 5.18. Figures 5–16 and 5–17 show lucky and unlucky results, respectively.

Listing 5.15 *DumbDeveloperException.java*

```java
package moreservlets;

/** Exception used to flag particularly onerous
    programmer blunders. Used to illustrate the
    exception-type web.xml element.
 */

public class DumbDeveloperException extends Exception {
  public DumbDeveloperException() {
    super("Duh. What was I *thinking*?");
  }

  public static int dangerousComputation(int n)
      throws DumbDeveloperException {
    if (n < 5) {
      return(n + 10);
    } else {
      throw(new DumbDeveloperException());
    }
  }
}
```

Listing 5.16 *RiskyPage.jsp*

```jsp
<!DOCTYPE HTML PUBLIC "-//W3C//DTD HTML 4.0 Transitional//EN">
<HTML>
<HEAD><TITLE>Risky JSP Page</TITLE></HEAD>
<BODY BGCOLOR="#FDF5E6">
<H2>Risky Calculations</H2>
<%@ page import="moreservlets.*" %>
<% int n = ((int)(10 * Math.random())); %>
<UL>
  <LI>n: <%= n %>
  <LI>dangerousComputation(n):
      <%= DumbDeveloperException.dangerousComputation(n) %>
</UL>
</BODY></HTML>
```

Listing 5.17 *DDE.jsp*

```
<!DOCTYPE HTML PUBLIC "-//W3C//DTD HTML 4.0 Transitional//EN">
<HTML>
<HEAD><TITLE>Dumb</TITLE></HEAD>
<BODY BGCOLOR="#FDF5E6">
<H2>Dumb Developer</H2>
We're brain dead. Consider using our competitors.
</BODY></HTML>
```

Listing 5.18 *web.xml* (Excerpt designating error pages for exceptions)

```
<?xml version="1.0" encoding="ISO-8859-1"?>
<!DOCTYPE web-app PUBLIC
    "-//Sun Microsystems, Inc.//DTD Web Application 2.3//EN"
    "http://java.sun.com/dtd/web-app_2_3.dtd">

<web-app>
  <!-- ... -->
  <servlet>...</servlet>
  <!-- ... -->
  <error-page>
    <exception-type>
      moreservlets.DumbDeveloperException
    </exception-type>
    <location>/DDE.jsp</location>
  </error-page>
  <!-- ... -->
</web-app>
```

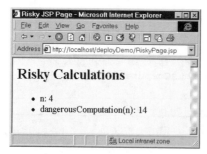

Figure 5–16 Fortuitous results of *RiskyPage.jsp*.

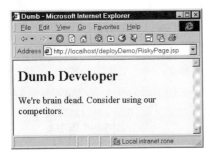

Figure 5–17   Unlucky results of *RiskyPage.jsp*.

5.9   Providing Security

Use of the server's built-in capabilities to manage security is discussed in Chapter 7 (Declarative Security). This section summarizes the *web.xml* elements that relate to this topic.

Designating the Authorization Method

You use the `login-config` element to specify how the server should authorize users who attempt to access protected pages. It contains three possible subelements: `auth-method`, `realm-name`, and `form-login-config`. The `login-config` element should appear near the end of the *web.xml* deployment descriptor, immediately after the `security-constraint` element discussed in the next subsection. For complete details on the ordering of elements within *web.xml*, see Section 5.2. For details and examples on the use of the `login-config` element, see Chapter 7 (Declarative Security).

auth-method

This subelement of `login-config` lists the specific authentication mechanism that the server should use. Legal values are `BASIC`, `DIGEST`, `FORM`, and `CLIENT-CERT`. Servers are only required to support `BASIC` and `FORM`.

`BASIC` specifies that standard HTTP authentication should be used, in which the server checks for an `Authorization` header, returning a 401 status code and a `WWW-Authenticate` header if the header is missing. This causes the client to pop up a dialog box that is used to populate the `Authorization` header. Details of this process are discussed in Section 7.3 (BASIC Authentication). Note that this mechanism provides little or no security against attackers who are snooping on the Internet connection (e.g., by running a packet sniffer on the client's subnet) since the username and password are sent with the easily reversible base64 encoding. All compliant servers are required to support BASIC authentication.

DIGEST indicates that the client should transmit the username and password using the encrypted Digest Authentication form. This provides more security against network intercepts than does BASIC authentication, but the encryption can be reversed more easily than the method used in SSL (HTTPS). The point is somewhat moot, however, since few browsers currently support Digest Authentication, and consequently servlet containers are not required to support it.

FORM specifies that the server should check for a reserved session cookie and should redirect users who do not have it to a designated login page. That page should contain a normal HTML form to gather the username and password. After logging in, users are tracked by means of the reserved session-level cookie. Although in and of itself, FORM authentication is no more secure against network snooping than is BASIC authentication, additional protection such as SSL or network-level security (e.g., IPSEC or VPN) can be layered on top if necessary. All compliant servers are required to support FORM authentication.

CLIENT-CERT stipulates that the server must use HTTPS (HTTP over SSL) and authenticate users by means of their Public Key Certificate. This provides strong security against network intercept, but only J2EE-compliant servers are required to support it.

realm-name

This element applies only when the auth-method is BASIC. It designates the name of the security realm that is used by the browser in the title of the dialog box and as part of the Authorization header.

form-login-config

This element applies only when the auth-method is FORM. It designates two pages: the page that contains the HTML form that collects the username and password (by means of the form-login-page subelement), and the page that should be used to indicate failed authentication (by means of the form-error-page subelement). As discussed in Chapter 7, the HTML form given by the form-login-page must have an ACTION attribute of j_security_check, a username textfield named j_username, and a password field named j_password.

For example, Listing 5.19 instructs the server to use form-based authentication. A page named *login.jsp* in the top-level directory of the Web app should collect the username and password, and failed login attempts should be reported by a page named *login-error.jsp* in the same directory.

Listing 5.19 *web.xml* (Excerpt showing `login-config`)

```
<?xml version="1.0" encoding="ISO-8859-1"?>
<!DOCTYPE web-app PUBLIC
    "-//Sun Microsystems, Inc.//DTD Web Application 2.3//EN"
    "http://java.sun.com/dtd/web-app_2_3.dtd">

<web-app>
  <!-- ... -->
  <security-constraint>...</security-constraint>
  <login-config>
    <auth-method>FORM</auth-method>
    <form-login-config>
      <form-login-page>/login.jsp</form-login-page>
      <form-error-page>/login-error.jsp</form-error-page>
    </form-login-config>
  </login-config>
  <!-- ... -->
</web-app>
```

Restricting Access to Web Resources

So, you can tell the server which authentication method to use. "Big deal," you say, "that's not much use unless I can designate the URLs that ought to be protected." Right. Designating these URLs and describing the protection they should have is the purpose of the `security-constraint` element. This element should come immediately *before* login-config in *web.xml*. It contains four possible subelements: web-resource-collection, auth-constraint, user-data-constraint, and display-name. Each of these is described in the following subsections.

web-resource-collection

This element identifies the resources that should be protected. All security-constraint elements must contain at least one web-resource-collection entry. This element consists of a web-resource-name element that gives an arbitrary identifying name, a url-pattern element that identifies the URLs that should be protected, an optional http-method element that designates the HTTP commands to which the protection applies

(GET, POST, etc.; the default is all methods), and an optional `description`
element that provides documentation. For example, the following `web-
resource-collection` entry (within a `security-constraint` element)
designates that all documents in the *proprietary* directory of the Web application should be protected.

```
<security-constraint>
  <web-resource-collection>
    <web-resource-name>Proprietary</web-resource-name>
    <url-pattern>/proprietary/*</url-pattern>
  </web-resource-collection>
  <!-- ... -->
</security-constraint>
```

It is important to note that the `url-pattern` applies only to clients that
access the resources directly. In particular, it does *not* apply to pages that are
accessed through the MVC architecture with a `RequestDispatcher` or by
the similar means of `jsp:forward`. This asymmetry is good if used properly.
For example, with the MVC architecture a servlet looks up data, places it in
beans, and forwards the request to a JSP page that extracts the data from the
beans and displays it (see Section 3.8). You want to ensure that the JSP page is
never accessed directly but instead is accessed only through the servlet that sets
up the beans the page will use. The `url-pattern` and `auth-constraint`
(see next subsection) elements can provide this guarantee by declaring that *no*
user is permitted direct access to the JSP page. But, this asymmetric behavior
can catch developers off guard and allow them to accidentally provide unrestricted access to resources that should be protected.

Core Warning

*These protections apply only to direct client access. The security model
does not apply to pages accessed by means of a `RequestDispatcher`
or `jsp:forward`.*

auth-constraint

Whereas the `web-resource-collection` element designates which URLs
should be protected, the `auth-constraint` element designates which users
should have access to protected resources. It should contain one or more
`role-name` elements identifying the class of users that have access and,
optionally, a `description` element describing the role. For instance, the following part of the `security-constraint` element in *web.xml* states that

only users who are designated as either Administrators or Big Kahunas (or both) should have access to the designated resource.

```
<security-constraint>
  <web-resource-collection>...</web-resource-collection>
  <auth-constraint>
    <role-name>administrator</role-name>
    <role-name>kahuna</role-name>
  </auth-constraint>
</security-constraint>
```

It is important to realize that this is the point at which the portable portion of the process ends. How a server determines which users are in which roles and how it stores user passwords is completely system dependent. See Section 7.1 (Form-Based Authentication) for information on the approaches used by Tomcat, JRun, and ServletExec.

For example, Tomcat uses *install_dir/conf/tomcat-users.xml* to associate usernames with role names and passwords, as in the example below that designates users joe (with password bigshot) and jane (with password enaj) as belonging to the administrator and/or kahuna roles.

```
<tomcat-users>
  <user name="joe"
        password="bigshot" roles="administrator,kahuna" />
  <user name="jane"
        password="enaj" roles="kahuna" />
  <!-- ... -->
</tomcat-users>
```

Core Warning

Container-managed security requires a significant server-specific component. In particular, you must use nonportable methods to associate passwords with usernames and to map usernames to role names.

user-data-constraint
This optional element indicates which transport-level protections should be used when the associated resource is accessed. It must contain a transport-guarantee subelement (with legal values NONE, INTEGRAL, or CONFIDENTIAL) and may optionally contain a description element. A value of NONE (the default) for transport-guarantee puts no restrictions on the commu-

nication protocol used. A value of INTEGRAL means that the communication must be of a variety that prevents data from being changed in transit without detection. A value of CONFIDENTIAL means that the data must be transmitted in a way that prevents anyone who intercepts it from reading it. Although in principle (and in future HTTP versions) there may be a distinction between INTEGRAL and CONFIDENTIAL, in current practice they both simply mandate the use of SSL. For example, the following instructs the server to only permit HTTPS connections to the associated resource:

```
<security-constraint>
  <!-- ... -->
  <user-data-constraint>
    <transport-guarantee>CONFIDENTIAL</transport-guarantee>
  </user-data-constraint>
</security-constraint>
```

display-name

This rarely used subelement of security-constraint gives a name to the security constraint entry that might be used by a GUI tool.

Assigning Role Names

Up to this point, the discussion has focused on security that was completely managed by the container (server). Servlets and JSP pages, however, can also manage their own security. For details, see Chapter 8 (Programmatic Security).

For example, the container might let users from either the bigwig or big-cheese role access a page showing executive perks but permit only the bigwig users to modify the page's parameters. One common way to accomplish this more fine-grained control is to call the isUserInRole method of HttpServlet-Request and modify access accordingly (for an example, see Section 8.2).

The security-role-ref subelement of servlet provides an alias for a security role name that appears in the server-specific password file. For instance, suppose a servlet was written to call request.isUserInRole("boss") but is then used in a server whose password file calls the role manager instead of boss. The following would permit the servlet to use either name.

```
<servlet>
  <!-- ... -->
  <security-role-ref>
    <role-name>boss</role-name>      <!-- New alias -->
    <role-link>manager</role-link> <!-- Real name -->
  </security-role-ref>
</servlet>
```

You can also use a `security-role` element within `web-app` to provide a global list of all security roles that will appear in the `role-name` elements. Declaring the roles separately could make it easier for advanced IDEs to manipulate security information.

5.10 Controlling Session Timeouts

If a session has not been accessed for a certain period of time, the server can throw it away to save memory. You can explicitly set the timeout for individual session objects by using the `setMaxInactiveInterval` method of `HttpSession`. If you do not use this method, the default timeout is server specific. However, the `session-config` and `session-timeout` elements can be used to give an explicit timeout that will apply on all servers. The units are minutes, so the following example sets the default session timeout to three hours (180 minutes).

```
<session-config>
  <session-timeout>180</session-timeout>
</session-config>
```

5.11 Documenting Web Applications

More and more development environments are starting to provide explicit support for servlets and JSP. Examples include Borland JBuilder Enterprise Edition, Macromedia UltraDev, Allaire JRun Studio, and IBM VisualAge for Java.

A number of the *web.xml* elements are designed not for the server, but for the visual development environment. These include `icon`, `display-name`, and `description`.

Recall that it is important to declare the `web-app` subelements in the proper order within *web.xml*. Section 5.2 (The Order of Elements within the Deployment Descriptor) gives complete details on the required ordering. For now, however, just remember that `icon`, `display-name`, and `description` are the first three legal elements within the `web-app` element of *web.xml*.

icon

The `icon` element designates the location of either one or two image files that the GUI tool can use to represent the Web application. A 16 × 16 GIF or JPEG image can be specified with the `small-icon` element, and a 32 × 32 image can be specified with `large-icon`. Here is an example:

```
<icon>
  <small-icon>/images/small-book.gif</small-icon>
  <large-icon>/images/tome.jpg</large-icon>
</icon>
```

display-name

The `display-name` element provides a name that the GUI tools might use to label this particular Web application. Here is an example.

```
<display-name>Rare Books</display-name>
```

description

The `description` element provides explanatory text, as below.

```
<description>
This Web application represents the store developed for
rare-books.com, an online bookstore specializing in rare
and limited-edition books.
</description>
```

5.12 Associating Files with MIME Types

Servers typically have a way for Webmasters to associate file extensions with media types. So, for example, a file named *mom.jpg* would automatically be given a MIME type of `image/jpeg`. However, suppose that your Web application has unusual files that you want to guarantee are assigned a certain MIME type when sent to clients. The `mime-mapping` element, with `extension` and `mime-type` subelements, can provide this guarantee. For example, the following code instructs the server to assign a MIME type of `application/x-fubar` to all files that end in *.foo*.

```
<mime-mapping>
  <extension>foo</extension>
  <mime-type>application/x-fubar</mime-type>
</mime-mapping>
```

Or, perhaps your Web application wants to override standard mappings. For instance, the following would tell the server to designate *.ps* files as plain text (`text/plain`) rather than as PostScript (`application/postscript`) when sending them to clients.

```
<mime-mapping>
  <extension>ps</extension>
  <mime-type>text/plain</mime-type>
</mime-mapping>
```

For more information on MIME types, see Table 2.1 on page 88.

5.13 Locating Tag Library Descriptors

The JSP `taglib` element has a required `uri` attribute that gives the location of a Tag Library Descriptor (TLD) file relative to the Web application root. The actual name of the TLD file might change when a new version of the tag library is released, but you might want to avoid changing all the existing JSP pages. Furthermore, you might want to use a short `uri` to keep the `taglib` elements concise. That's where the deployment descriptor's `taglib` element comes in. It contains two subelements: `taglib-uri` and `taglib-location`. The `taglib-uri` element should exactly match whatever is used for the `uri` attribute of the JSP `taglib` element. The `taglib-location` element gives the real location of the TLD file. For example, suppose that you place the file *chart-tags-1.3beta.tld* in *yourWebApp/WEB-INF/tlds*. Now, suppose that *web.xml* contains the following within the `web-app` element.

```
<taglib>
  <taglib-uri>/charts.tld</taglib-uri>
  <taglib-location>
    /WEB-INF/tlds/chart-tags-1.3beta.tld
  </taglib-location>
</taglib>
```

Given this specification, JSP pages can now make use of the tag library by means of the following simplified form.

```
<% taglib uri="/charts.tld" prefix="somePrefix" %>
```

5.14 Designating Application Event Listeners

Application event listeners are classes that are notified when the servlet context or a session object is created or modified. They are new in version 2.3 of the servlet specification and are discussed in detail in Chapter 10 (The Application Events Framework). Here, though, I just want to briefly illustrate the use of the *web.xml* elements that are used to register a listener with the Web application.

Registering a listener involves simply placing a `listener` element inside the `web-app` element of *web.xml*. Inside the `listener` element, a `listener-class` element lists the fully qualified class name of the listener, as below.

```
<listener>
  <listener-class>package.ListenerClass</listener-class>
</listener>
```

Although the structure of the `listener` element is simple, don't forget that you have to properly order the subelements inside the `web-app` element. The `listener` element goes immediately before all the `servlet` elements and immediately after any `filter-mapping` elements. Furthermore, since application life-cycle listeners are new in version 2.3 of the servlet specification, you have to use the 2.3 version of the *web.xml* DTD, not the 2.2 version.

For example, Listing 5.20 shows a simple listener called `ContextReporter` that prints a message on the standard output whenever the Web application's `ServletContext` is created (e.g., the Web application is loaded) or destroyed (e.g., the server is shut down). Listing 5.21 shows the portion of the *web.xml* file that is required for registration of the listener.

Listing 5.20 *ContextReporter.java*

```java
package moreservlets;

import javax.servlet.*;
import java.util.*;

/** Simple listener that prints a report on the standard output
 *  when the ServletContext is created or destroyed.
 */

public class ContextReporter implements ServletContextListener {
  public void contextInitialized(ServletContextEvent event) {
    System.out.println("Context created on " +
                       new Date() + ".");
  }

  public void contextDestroyed(ServletContextEvent event) {
    System.out.println("Context destroyed on " +
                       new Date() + ".");
  }
}
```

Listing 5.21	*web.xml* (Excerpt declaring a listener)

```
<?xml version="1.0" encoding="ISO-8859-1"?>
<!DOCTYPE web-app PUBLIC
    "-//Sun Microsystems, Inc.//DTD Web Application 2.3//EN"
    "http://java.sun.com/dtd/web-app_2_3.dtd">

<web-app>
  <!-- ... -->
  <filter-mapping>...</filter-mapping>
  <listener>
    <listener-class>moreservlets.ContextReporter</listener-class>
  </listener>
  <servlet>...</servlet>
  <!-- ... -->
</web-app>
```

5.15 J2EE Elements

This section describes the *web.xml* elements that are used for Web applications that are part of a J2EE environment. I'll provide a brief summary here; for details, see Chapter 5 of the Java 2 Platform Enterprise Edition version 1.3 specification at *http://java.sun.com/j2ee/j2ee-1_3-fr-spec.pdf.*

distributable

The `distributable` element indicates that the Web application is programmed in such a way that servers that support clustering can safely distribute the Web application across multiple servers. For example, a distributable application must use only `Serializable` objects as attributes of its `HttpSession` objects and must avoid the use of instance variables (fields) for implementing persistence. The `distributable` element appears directly after the `description` element (Section 5.11) and contains no subelements or data—it is simply a flag (as below).

```
<distributable />
```

resource-env-ref

The `resource-env-ref` element declares an administered object associated with a resource. It consists of an optional `description` element, a `resource-env-ref-name` element (a JNDI name relative to the `java:comp/env` context), and a `resource-env-type` element (the fully qualified class designating the type of the resource), as below.

```
<resource-env-ref>
  <resource-env-ref-name>
    jms/StockQueue
  </resource-env-ref-name>
  <resource-env-ref-type>
    javax.jms.Queue
  </resource-env-ref-type>
</resource-env-ref>
```

resource-ref

The `resource-ref` element declares an external resource used with a resource factory. It consists of an optional `description` element, a `res-ref-name` element (the resource manager connection-factory reference name), a `res-type` element (the fully qualified class name of the factory type), a `res-auth` element (the type of authentication used—`Application` or `Container`), and an optional `res-sharing-scope` element (a specification of the shareability of connections obtained from the resource—`Shareable` or `Unshareable`). Here is an example.

```
<resource-ref>
  <res-ref-name>jdbc/EmployeeAppDB</res-ref-name>
  <res-type>javax.sql.DataSource</res-type>
  <res-auth>Container</res-auth>
  <res-sharing-scope>Shareable</res-sharing-scope>
</resource-ref>
```

env-entry

The `env-entry` element declares the Web application's environment entry. It consists of an optional `description` element, an `env-entry-name` element (a JNDI name relative to the `java:comp/env` context), an `env-entry-value` element (the entry value), and an `env-entry-type` element (the fully qualified class name of a type in the `java.lang` package—`java.lang.Boolean`, `java.lang.String`, etc.). Here is an example.

```
<env-entry>
  <env-entry-name>minAmount</env-entry-name>
  <env-entry-value>100.00</env-entry-value>
  <env-entry-type>java.lang.Double</env-entry-type>
</env-entry>
```

ejb-ref

The `ejb-ref` element declares a reference to the home of an enterprise bean. It consists of an optional `description` element, an `ejb-ref-name` element (the name of the EJB reference relative to `java:comp/env`), an `ejb-ref-type` element (the type of the bean—`Entity` or `Session`), a home element (the fully qualified name of the bean's home interface), a `remote` element (the fully qualified name of the bean's remote interface), and an optional `ejb-link` element (the name of another bean to which the current bean is linked).

ejb-local-ref

The `ejb-local-ref` element declares a reference to the local home of an enterprise bean. It has the same attributes and is used in the same way as the `ejb-ref` element, with the exception that `local-home` is used in place of `home`.

A SAMPLE WEB
APPLICATION: AN
ONLINE BOAT SHOP

Topics in This Chapter

- Defining and using a larger Web application
- The interaction among components in a Web application
- Using sessions for per-user data
- Using the servlet context for multiuser data
- Managing information that is accessed by multiple servlets and JSP pages
- Eliminating dependencies on the Web application name

Chapter 6

Many people find it helpful to see a variety of individual capabilities brought together in a single example. This chapter walks you through a small application (an online boat shop) that contains many of the different components discussed up to this point in the book. In particular, it illustrates:

- Web application definition, structure, and use
- The *web.xml* file
- The use of relative URLs by servlets and JSP pages at various locations within the Web application
- Custom tags that are used by JSP pages in various directories
- Shared beans
- Session tracking
- The use of the `ServletContext` to share data among multiple pages
- The MVC architecture applied within a Web application
- The elimination of any dependency on the Web application name

6.1   General Configuration Files

Registering a Web application (designating the location of the top-level directory and specifying a URL prefix) is a completely server-specific process. For information on the registration process, see Section 4.1 (Registering Web Applications). Here, I'll just show the settings necessary for Tomcat.

Listing 6.1 presents the relevant part of the Tomcat *server.xml* file. Recall that, if you use the default Web application settings, it is only necessary to edit *server.xml* in Tomcat 3. In Tomcat 4, just drop the *boats* directory into *install_dir/webapps*.

Listing 6.1   *install_dir/conf/server.xml* for Tomcat (partial)

```
<?xml version="1.0" encoding="ISO-8859-1"?>
<Server>
  ...
  <Context path="/boats" docBase="boats" />
</Server>
```

Listing 6.2 shows the complete *web.xml* file. Recall from Section 5.2 (The Order of Elements within the Deployment Descriptor) that it is important to arrange the *web.xml* elements within web-app in the proper order. Also, because the boats application does not use filters, life-cycle event handlers, or other new features, it uses the servlet 2.2 DTD to maximize portability.

This version of *web.xml* specifies the following behaviors:

- The ShowItem servlet can be accessed with the URL *http://host/boats/DisplayItem* instead of the default URL of *http://host/boats/servlet/moreservlets.ShowItem*.

- Similarly, the ShowPurchases servlet can be accessed with the URL *http://host/boats/DisplayPurchases* instead of *http://host/boats/servlet/moreservlets.ShowPurchases*.

- The file *index.jsp* (if it exists) should be used as the default filename for URLs that name a directory but not a file. If *index.jsp* is not found, *index.html* should be used. If neither is found, the result is server specific.

For more information on using the *web.xml* file, see Chapter 5 (Controlling Web Application Behavior with web.xml).

Listing 6.2   *boats/WEB-INF/web.xml*

```xml
<?xml version="1.0" encoding="ISO-8859-1"?>
<!DOCTYPE web-app PUBLIC
    "-//Sun Microsystems, Inc.//DTD Web Application 2.2//EN"
    "http://java.sun.com/j2ee/dtds/web-app_2_2.dtd">

<web-app>
  <!-- Register names for the ShowItem and ShowPurchases
       servlets. These names will be used with servlet-mapping
       to set custom URLs.
  -->
  <servlet>
    <servlet-name>ShowItem</servlet-name>
    <servlet-class>moreservlets.ShowItem</servlet-class>
  </servlet>
  <servlet>
    <servlet-name>ShowPurchases</servlet-name>
    <servlet-class>moreservlets.ShowPurchases</servlet-class>
  </servlet>

  <!-- Set the URL http://host/webAppName/DisplayPurchases
       to invoke the servlet that would otherwise be
       available with the URL
       http://host/webAppName/servlet/moreservlets.ShowPurchases
  -->
  <servlet-mapping>
    <servlet-name>ShowPurchases</servlet-name>
    <url-pattern>/DisplayPurchases</url-pattern>
  </servlet-mapping>

  <!-- Set the URL http://host/webAppName/DisplayItem
       to invoke the servlet that would otherwise be
       available with the URL
       http://host/webAppName/servlet/moreservlets.ShowItem
  -->
  <servlet-mapping>
    <servlet-name>ShowItem</servlet-name>
    <url-pattern>/DisplayItem</url-pattern>
  </servlet-mapping>
```

Listing 6.2	*boats/WEB-INF/web.xml (continued)*

```
<!-- If URL gives a directory but no filename, try index.jsp
     first and index.html second. If neither is found,
     the result is server specific (e.g., a directory
     listing).
-->

<welcome-file-list>
  <welcome-file>index.jsp</welcome-file>
  <welcome-file>index.html</welcome-file>
</welcome-file-list>
</web-app>
```

6.2 The Top-Level Page

Listing 6.3 shows *index.jsp*, the top-level page for the boat store. The result is shown in Figure 6–1. There are a couple of things to note about this page.

First, since the style sheet *app-styles.css* is also in the top-level *boats* directory, the LINK element in the HEAD of the page can simply use the style sheet filename for the HREF attribute. See the source code archive at *http://www.moreservlets.com* if you want the source for *app-styles.css*. Similarly, the hypertext links to the yachts, tankers, and carriers JSP pages require only a simple filename within the HREF attribute. One of the goals of a Web application is that it require no modifications when it is moved from server to server or when the URL prefix is changed. Section 4.5 (Handling Relative URLs in Web Applications) gives details on handling relative URLs so that they don't need modifications when the URL prefix changes, but the approach is trivial for URLs that refer to files in the same directory—just use the filename.

Second, since the yacht image is in the *boats/images/* directory, the IMG element uses a URL of *images/yacht.jpg*.

Third, the taglib element uses a uri of */WEB-INF/tlds/count-taglib.tld*. Although this URL begins with a slash, it refers to the */tlds* subdirectory of the *WEB-INF* directory within the *boats* directory, not to the *tlds* directory of the server's top-level *WEB-INF* directory. The reason for this behavior is that the URL is resolved by the server, not sent to the client, and the server resolves this type of URL within the Web application. See Listings 6.4 through 6.6 for the tag library definition and the tag library descriptor file.

Finally, as Listings 6.4 and 6.5 show, the count tag uses the servlet context to store the access count. As illustrated in Section 4.6 (Sharing Data Among Web Applications), each Web application has its own servlet context. Thus, servlets and JSP pages in other Web apps do not interfere with the access count, even if they use the same tag library.

Listings 6.4 and 6.5 give the source code for the custom tag used to keep the access count for this page and the other pages on the boats site. Listing 6.6 shows the tag library descriptor file that associates the CounterTag code with the base tag name of count.

Listing 6.3 *boats/index.jsp*

```
<!DOCTYPE HTML PUBLIC "-//W3C//DTD HTML 4.0 Transitional//EN">
<HTML>
<HEAD>
<TITLE>Boats</TITLE>
<LINK REL=STYLESHEET
      HREF="app-styles.css"
      TYPE="text/css">
</HEAD>

<BODY>
<TABLE BORDER=5 ALIGN="CENTER">
  <TR><TH CLASS="TITLE">Boats!</TABLE>
<P>
Looking for a hole in the water into which to pour your money?
You've come to the right place. We offer a wide selection of
reasonably priced boats for everyday use.

<IMG SRC="images/yacht.jpg" WIDTH=240 HEIGHT=367
     ALIGN="RIGHT" ALT="Base-model yacht">
<H2>Yachts</H2>
Starting at a mere 72 million, these entry-level models are
perfect for the cost-conscious buyer.
Click <A HREF="yachts.jsp">here</A> for details.

<H2>Oil Tankers</H2>
Looking for something a bit bigger and sturdier? These
roomy models come complete with large swimming pools.
Click <A HREF="tankers.jsp">here</A> for details.
```

Listing 6.3	*boats/index.jsp (continued)*

```
<H2>Aircraft Carriers</H2>
Concerned about security? These high-tech models come
equipped with the latest anti-theft devices.
Click <A HREF="carriers.jsp">here</A> for details.
<P>

<%@ taglib uri="/WEB-INF/tlds/count-taglib.tld" prefix="boats" %>
<boats:count />

</BODY>
</HTML>
```

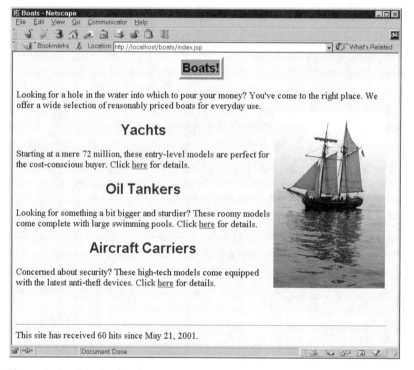

Figure 6–1   Result of *index.jsp*.

Listing 6.4   *boats/WEB-INF/classes/moreservlets/CounterTag.java*[*]

```
package moreservlets;

import javax.servlet.*;
import javax.servlet.jsp.*;
import javax.servlet.jsp.tagext.*;
import java.io.*;
import java.text.*;

/** Tag that outputs a Web-app-specific hit count.
 *  For boats example.
 *  <P>
 *  The actual name of the tag is not defined here;
 *  that is given by the Tag Library Descriptor (TLD)
 *  file that is referenced by the taglib directive
 *  in the JSP file.
 */

public class CounterTag extends TagSupport {
  public int doStartTag() {
    try {
      ServletContext application =
        pageContext.getServletContext();
      Count count = (Count)application.getAttribute("count");
      if (count == null) {
        count = new Count();
        application.setAttribute("count", count);
      }
      DateFormat formatter =
        DateFormat.getDateInstance(DateFormat.MEDIUM);
      JspWriter out = pageContext.getOut();
      out.println("<BR CLEAR=\"ALL\"><BR><HR>");
      out.println("This site has received " +
                  count.getCount() + " hits since " +
                  formatter.format(count.getStartDate()) +
                  ".");
      count.incrementCount();
    } catch(IOException ioe) {
      System.out.println("Error in CounterTag: " + ioe);
    }
    return(SKIP_BODY);
  }
}
```

---

[*] Technically, only the *.class* file needs to go in this directory. The only requirement for the source code is that it go in a directory matching the package name (`moreservlets`).

Listing 6.5	*boats/WEB-INF/classes/moreservlets/Count.java*[*]

```java
package moreservlets;

import java.util.Date;

/** Simple bean used by CounterTag. For boats example. */

public class Count {
  private int count = 1;
  private Date startDate = new Date();

  public int getCount() {
    return(count);
  }

  public void incrementCount() {
    count++;
  }

  public Date getStartDate() {
    return(startDate);
  }
}
```

[*] Technically, only the *.class* file needs to go in this directory.

Listing 6.6	*boats/WEB-INF/tlds/count-taglib.tld*

```xml
<?xml version="1.0" encoding="ISO-8859-1" ?>
<!DOCTYPE taglib
 PUBLIC "-//Sun Microsystems, Inc.//DTD JSP Tag Library 1.1//EN"
 "http://java.sun.com/j2ee/dtds/web-jsptaglibrary_1_1.dtd">

<taglib>
  <tlibversion>1.0</tlibversion>
  <jspversion>1.1</jspversion>
  <shortname>Counts</shortname>
  <info>
    A tag library for counters. From More Servlets and
    JavaServer Pages, http://www.moreservlets.com.
  </info>
  <tag>
    <name>count</name>
    <tagclass>moreservlets.CounterTag</tagclass>
    <bodycontent>empty</bodycontent>
    <info>Hit count</info>
  </tag>
</taglib>
```

6.3   The Second-Level Pages

The top-level page introduces the site and gives links to each of the three second-level pages that describe specific varieties of boats: yachts (Listing 6.7, Figure 6–2), oil tankers (Listing 6.8, Figure 6–3), and aircraft carriers (Listing 6.9, Figure 6–4). Note that simple relative URLs are used for the style sheet and for the servlet with which the form communicates when the user asks for details. Note also that the custom tag maintains the count from the top-level page. That's because the servlet context is shared by all pages in the Web app.

Once the user chooses a particular model and asks for more information on it, the item display servlet is invoked. Since the *web.xml* file (Listing 6.2) registers this servlet with the URL suffix *DisplayItem*, a simple relative URL can be used for the ACTION attribute of the FORM element. As described in Section 4.5 (Handling Relative URLs in Web Applications), this capability is important because it permits the servlet to use simple relative URLs either directly or by means of JSP pages to which it forwards the request. That means that the Web application name can be changed without necessitating changes to these JSP pages. See the following subsection for details on the item display servlet.

Listing 6.7   *boats/yachts.jsp*

```
<!DOCTYPE HTML PUBLIC "-//W3C//DTD HTML 4.0 Transitional//EN">
<HTML>
<HEAD>
<TITLE>Yachts</TITLE>
<LINK REL=STYLESHEET
      HREF="app-styles.css"
      TYPE="text/css">
</HEAD>

<BODY>
<TABLE BORDER=5 ALIGN="CENTER">
  <TR><TH CLASS="TITLE">Yachts</TABLE>
<P>
Luxurious models for the <S>wasteful</S>
wealthy buyer.

<H2>Available Models</H2>
Choose a model to see a picture along with price and
availability information.
```

Listing 6.7   *boats/yachts.jsp (continued)*

```
<FORM ACTION="DisplayItem">
<INPUT TYPE="RADIO" NAME="itemNum" VALUE="BM1">
Base Model -- Includes 4-car garage<BR>
<INPUT TYPE="RADIO" NAME="itemNum" VALUE="MR1">
Mid Range -- Has 15 bedrooms and a helipad<BR>
<INPUT TYPE="RADIO" NAME="itemNum" VALUE="HE1">
High End -- Free tropical island nation included
<P>
<CENTER>
<INPUT TYPE="SUBMIT" VALUE="Get Details">
</CENTER>
</FORM>

<%-- Note the lack of "boats" at the front of URI below --%>
<%@ taglib uri="/WEB-INF/tlds/count-taglib.tld" prefix="boats" %>
<boats:count />
</BODY>
</HTML>
```

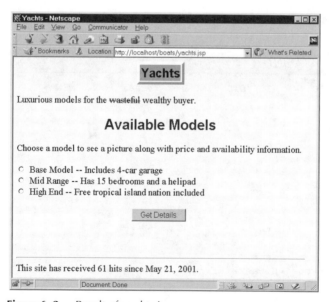

Figure 6–2   Result of *yachts.jsp*.

Listing 6.8 *boats/tankers.jsp*

```
<!DOCTYPE HTML PUBLIC "-//W3C//DTD HTML 4.0 Transitional//EN">
<HTML>
<HEAD>
<TITLE>Oil Tankers</TITLE>
<LINK REL=STYLESHEET
      HREF="app-styles.css"
      TYPE="text/css">
</HEAD>

<BODY>
<TABLE BORDER=5 ALIGN="CENTER">
  <TR><TH CLASS="TITLE">Oil Tankers</TABLE>
<P>
Stable and roomy models for the <S>uninformed</S>
innovative buyer.

<H2>Available Models</H2>
Choose a model to see a picture along with price and
availability information.

<FORM ACTION="DisplayItem">
<INPUT TYPE="RADIO" NAME="itemNum" VALUE="Valdez">
Valdez -- Slightly damaged model available at discount<BR>
<INPUT TYPE="RADIO" NAME="itemNum" VALUE="BigBertha">
Big Bertha -- Includes 10 million gallon swimming pool<BR>
<INPUT TYPE="RADIO" NAME="itemNum" VALUE="EcoDisaster">
ED I -- For those who don't mind political incorrectness
<P>
<CENTER>
<INPUT TYPE="SUBMIT" VALUE="Get Details">
</CENTER>
</FORM>

<%-- Note the lack of "boats" at the front of URI below --%>
<%@ taglib uri="/WEB-INF/tlds/count-taglib.tld" prefix="boats" %>
<boats:count />
</BODY>
</HTML>
```

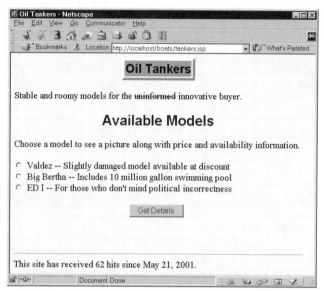

Figure 6–3   Result of *tankers.jsp*.

Listing 6.9   *boats/carriers.jsp*

```
<!DOCTYPE HTML PUBLIC "-//W3C//DTD HTML 4.0 Transitional//EN">
<HTML>
<HEAD>
<TITLE>Aircraft Carriers</TITLE>
<LINK REL=STYLESHEET
      HREF="app-styles.css"
      TYPE="text/css">
</HEAD>

<BODY>
<TABLE BORDER=5 ALIGN="CENTER">
  <TR><TH CLASS="TITLE">Aircraft Carriers</TABLE>
<P>
High-security models for the <S>paranoid</S> careful buyer.

<H2>Available Models</H2>
Choose a model to see a picture along with price and
availability information.
```

| Listing 6.9 | *boats/carriers.jsp (continued)* |

```
<FORM ACTION="DisplayItem">
<INPUT TYPE="RADIO" NAME="itemNum" VALUE="SafeT-1A">
SafeT-1A -- Our Most Popular Model<BR>
<INPUT TYPE="RADIO" NAME="itemNum" VALUE="SafeT-1B">
SafeT-1B -- 1000-man crew included<BR>
<INPUT TYPE="RADIO" NAME="itemNum" VALUE="Lubber-1">
Land Lubber I -- Land-based replica; no water to worry about!
<P>
<CENTER>
<INPUT TYPE="SUBMIT" VALUE="Get Details">
</CENTER>
</FORM>

<%-- Note the lack of "boats" at the front of URI below --%>
<%@ taglib uri="/WEB-INF/tlds/count-taglib.tld" prefix="boats" %>
<boats:count />
</BODY>
</HTML>
```

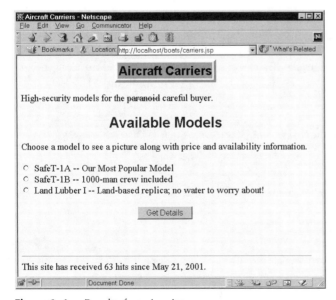

Figure 6–4   Result of *carriers.jsp.*

6.4   The Item Display Servlet

Since prices, descriptions, and pictures of sale items can change, you don't want to create item description pages by hand. Instead, pages of this sort should be automatically generated. In real life, the data source would probably be a database that is accessed with JDBC (see Chapter 18 of *Core Servlets and JavaServer Pages*, available in PDF at *http://www.moreservlets.com*). In this case, a simple data file is used so that the example is short and so that you can run the it without a database.

The item display servlet uses the MVC architecture (see Section 3.8) to display information. First, the servlet (Listing 6.10) reads the `itemNum` request parameter. If the item number is found, the servlet uses the number as a key into the table of ships (Listing 6.13, a subclass of the more general table shown in Listing 6.14) and creates a `SimpleItem` object (Listing 6.15) from the result. The servlet then places the `SimpleItem` in the request object and forwards the request to the *ShowItem.jsp* page (Listing 6.11, Figure 6–5). The *ShowItem.jsp* page uses `jsp:useBean` (Section 3.6) to access the `SimpleItem` object, then uses that object to look up the item's description, its cost, and the location of an image file that illustrates it. If, however, the item number is missing, the `ShowItem` servlet sends the request to *MissingItem.jsp* (Listing 6.12, Figure 6–6).

Note the importance of using the *web.xml* file to give the servlet a URL at the top level of the Web app (e.g., *http://host/boats/DisplayItem*), rather than using the default URL (e.g., *http://host/boats/servlet/moreservlets.ShowItem*). Because of this simplification, the JSP page need not call `getContextPath` before using relative URLs. See Section 4.5 (Handling Relative URLs in Web Applications) for details.

Listing 6.10	*boats/WEB-INF/classes/moreservlets/ShowItem.java*[*]

```
package moreservlets;

import java.io.*;
import javax.servlet.*;
import javax.servlet.http.*;

/** Servlet that looks up information on an item that is for
 *  sale. Uses the MVC architecture, with either
 *  MissingItem.jsp or ShowItem.jsp doing the presentation.
 *  Used in the boats Web app.
 */

public class ShowItem extends HttpServlet {
  public void doGet(HttpServletRequest request,
                    HttpServletResponse response)
       throws ServletException, IOException {
```

Listing 6.10 boats/WEB-INF/classes/moreservlets/ShowItem.java[*]
(continued)

```java
    String itemNum = request.getParameter("itemNum");
    String destination;
    if (itemNum == null) {
      destination = "/MissingItem.jsp";
    } else {
      destination = "/ShowItem.jsp";
      ItemTable shipTable = ShipTable.getShipTable();
      SimpleItem item = shipTable.getItem(itemNum);
      request.setAttribute("item", item);
    }
    RequestDispatcher dispatcher =
      getServletContext().getRequestDispatcher(destination);
    dispatcher.forward(request, response);
  }
}
```

[*] Technically, only the *.class* file needs to go in this directory.

Listing 6.11 boats/ShowItem.jsp

```jsp
<!DOCTYPE HTML PUBLIC "-//W3C//DTD HTML 4.0 Transitional//EN">
<HTML>
<HEAD>
<jsp:useBean id="item"
             class="moreservlets.SimpleItem"
             scope="request" />
<TITLE><jsp:getProperty name="item" property="itemNum" /></TITLE>
<LINK REL=STYLESHEET
      HREF="app-styles.css"
      TYPE="text/css">
</HEAD>

<BODY>
<TABLE BORDER=5 ALIGN="CENTER">
  <TR><TH CLASS="TITLE">
  <jsp:getProperty name="item" property="itemNum" /></TABLE>
<P>
<IMG SRC="<jsp:getProperty name='item' property='imageURL' />"
     ALIGN="RIGHT">

<H3>Item Number</H2>
<jsp:getProperty name="item" property="itemNum" />

<H3>Description</H2>
<jsp:getProperty name="item" property="description" />
```

Listing 6.11	*boats/ShowItem.jsp (continued)*

```
<H3>Cost</H2>
<jsp:getProperty name="item" property="costString" />.
A real bargain!

<H3>Ordering</H2>
<FORM ACTION="DisplayPurchases">
  <INPUT TYPE="HIDDEN" NAME="itemNum"
         VALUE="<jsp:getProperty name='item'
                                  property='itemNum' />">
  <INPUT TYPE="SUBMIT" VALUE="Submit Order">
</FORM>

<%-- Note the lack of "boats" at the front of URI below --%>
<%@ taglib uri="/WEB-INF/tlds/count-taglib.tld" prefix="boats" %>
<boats:count />
</BODY>
</HTML>
```

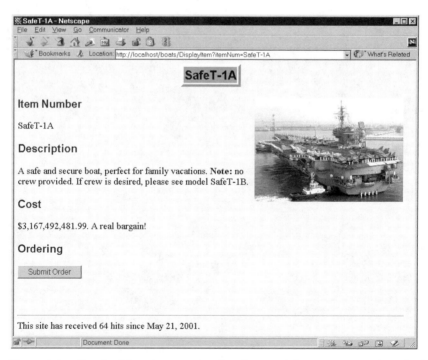

Figure 6–5   Result of the `ShowItem` servlet when model `SafeT-1A` is selected. The servlet is invoked with the registered name (`DisplayItem`) and forwards the request to *ShowItem.jsp*.

Listing 6.12 *boats/MissingItem.jsp*

```
<!DOCTYPE HTML PUBLIC "-//W3C//DTD HTML 4.0 Transitional//EN">
<HTML>
<HEAD>
<TITLE>Missing Item Number</TITLE>
<LINK REL=STYLESHEET
      HREF="app-styles.css"
      TYPE="text/css">
</HEAD>

<BODY>
<TABLE BORDER=5 ALIGN="CENTER">
  <TR><TH CLASS="TITLE">Missing Item Number</TABLE>
<P>

<H2>Error</H2>
<SPAN CLASS="ERROR">You must supply an item number!</SPAN>

<%-- Note the lack of "boats" at the front of URI below --%>
<%@ taglib uri="/WEB-INF/tlds/count-taglib.tld" prefix="boats" %>
<boats:count />
</BODY>
</HTML>
```

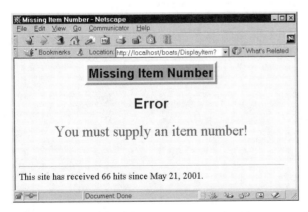

Figure 6–6 Result of the ShowItem servlet when no model number is selected. The servlet is invoked with the registered name (DisplayItem) and forwards the request to *MissingItem.jsp*.

Listing 6.13   *boats/WEB-INF/classes/moreservlets/ShipTable.java*[*]

```java
package moreservlets;

/** A small collection of ships. Used in the boats Web app. */

public class ShipTable {
  private static SimpleItem[] ships =
  { // Yachts
    new SimpleItem
      ("BM1",
        "Base model yacht. Features sauna, two kitchens, " +
          "and four-car garage. <B>Perfect entry-level " +
          "yacht for the first-time buyer</B>.",
        "images/yacht.jpg",
        72678922.99),
    new SimpleItem
      ("MR1",
        "Mid-range yacht. Features helipad, bowling alley, " +
          "and 15 bedrooms. <B>Trade up from a BM1 " +
          "today!</B>.",
        "images/yacht.jpg",
        145357845.98),
    new SimpleItem
      ("HE1",
        "High-end yacht. Features onboard 18-hole golf " +
          "course, onboard polo grounds, and ski jump. " +
          "<B>Bonus: for a limited time only, a mid-sized " +
          "tropical island country will be included at " +
          "no extra cost.</B>",
        "images/yacht.jpg",
        7267892299.00),
    // Oil Tankers
    new SimpleItem
      ("Valdez",
        "Slightly damaged former Alaskan touring boat. " +
          "<B>Special price won't last long!</B>",
        "images/tanker.jpg",
        9.95),
    new SimpleItem
      ("BigBertha",
        "Tired of cramped quarters on your boat? " +
          "This roomy model has plenty of space to stretch " +
          "your legs. <B>10 million gallon onboard " +
          "swimming pool included!</B>",
        "images/tanker.jpg",
        20000000.00),
```

```
      new SimpleItem
        ("EcoDisaster",
         "OK, ok, so this model is not exactly politically " +
           "correct. <B>But you're not one to pass up " +
           "a bargain just because of a few " +
           "<S>Greenpeace</S> pesky demonstrators, " +
           "are you?</B>.",
         "images/tanker.jpg",
         100000000),
      // Aircraft Carriers
      new SimpleItem
        ("SafeT-1A",
         "A safe and secure boat, perfect for family " +
           "vacations. <B>Note:</B> no crew provided. If crew " +
           "is desired, please see model SafeT-1B.",
         "images/carrier.jpg",
         3167492481.99),
       new SimpleItem
        ("SafeT-1B",
         "Just like the 1A model, but we provide the crew. " +
           "<B>Note:</B> You must pay the one million dollar " +
           "annual salary for the crew.",
         "images/carrier.jpg",
         3267492481.99),
      new SimpleItem
        ("Lubber-1",
         "All the comfort of the other models, but without " +
           "the danger. Realistic simulation provides " +
           "continuous water sounds. <B>Note:</B> " +
           "currently located in Siberia. Shipping and " +
           "handling not included.",
         "images/carrier.jpg",
         152.99)
  };

  private static ItemTable shipTable =
    new ItemTable(ships);

  public static ItemTable getShipTable() {
    return(shipTable);
  }
}
```

[*] Technically, only the *.class* file needs to go in this directory.

Listing 6.14 *boats/WEB-INF/classes/moreservlets/ItemTable.java*[*]

```java
package moreservlets;

import java.util.HashMap;

/** Small class that puts an array of items into a
 *  hash table, making the item number the key.
 *  Used in the boats Web app example.
 */

public class ItemTable {
  private HashMap itemMap = new HashMap();

  public ItemTable(SimpleItem[] items) {
    if (items != null) {
      SimpleItem item;
      for(int i=0; i<items.length; i++) {
        item = items[i];
        itemMap.put(item.getItemNum(), item);
      }
    }
  }

  public SimpleItem getItem(String itemNum) {
    return((SimpleItem)itemMap.get(itemNum));
  }
}
```

* Technically, only the *.class* file needs to go in this directory.

Listing 6.15 *boats/WEB-INF/classes/moreservlets/SimpleItem.java*[*]

```java
package moreservlets;

import java.text.*;

/** An item that is for sale. Used in the boats Web app. */

public class SimpleItem {
  private String itemNum = "Missing item number";
  private String description = "Missing description";
  private String imageURL = "Missing image URL";
  private double cost;
  private NumberFormat formatter =
    NumberFormat.getCurrencyInstance();
```

Listing 6.15	*boats/WEB-INF/classes/moreservlets/SimpleItem.java* [*] *(continued)*

```java
public SimpleItem(String itemNum,
                  String description,
                  String imageURL,
                  double cost) {
  setItemNum(itemNum);
  setDescription(description);
  setImageURL(imageURL);
  setCost(cost);
}

public SimpleItem() {}

public String getItemNum() {
  return(itemNum);
}

private void setItemNum(String  itemNum) {
  this.itemNum = itemNum;
}

public String getDescription() {
  return(description);
}

private void setDescription(String  description) {
  this.description = description;
}

public String getImageURL() {
  return(imageURL);
}

private void setImageURL(String   imageURL) {
  this.imageURL = imageURL;
}

public double getCost() {
  return(cost);
}

private void setCost(double cost) {
  this.cost = cost;
}

public String getCostString() {
  return(formatter.format(getCost()));
}
}
```

[*] Technically, only the *.class* file needs to go in this directory.

6.5   The Purchase Display Page

Section 9.4 of *Core Servlets and JavaServer Pages* gives detailed code for creating and using a shopping cart. (Remember that *Core Servlets and JavaServer Pages* is available in its entirety in PDF at *http://www.moreservlets.com.*) Here, I use a much more simplified "cart" to illustrate how session tracking fits in with Web applications. When a user presses the Submit Order button from one of the item display pages of the previous subsection, the item number is sent to the ShowPurchases servlet of Listing 6.16 (by means of the registered name of DisplayPurchases). This servlet looks up the item associated with the item number, puts the item into an ItemList (Listing 6.17), and forwards the request to the *sucker.jsp* page (Listing 6.18) to display all the items being purchased by that client in this session. See Figure 6–7 for a typical result.

Listing 6.16   *boats/WEB-INF/classes/moreservlets/ShowPurchases.java*[*]

```
package moreservlets;

import java.io.*;
import javax.servlet.*;
import javax.servlet.http.*;

/** A simple servlet that shows a table of purchases. */

public class ShowPurchases extends HttpServlet {
  public void doGet(HttpServletRequest request,
                    HttpServletResponse response)
      throws ServletException, IOException {
    String itemNum = request.getParameter("itemNum");
    ItemTable shipTable = ShipTable.getShipTable();
    SimpleItem item = shipTable.getItem(itemNum);
    HttpSession session = request.getSession(true);
    ItemList previousItems =
      (ItemList)session.getAttribute("items");
    if (previousItems == null) {
      previousItems = new ItemList();
      session.setAttribute("items", previousItems);
    }
    previousItems.setNewItem(item);
    RequestDispatcher dispatcher =
      getServletContext().getRequestDispatcher("/sucker.jsp");
    dispatcher.forward(request, response);
  }
}
```

[*] Technically, only the *.class* file needs to go in this directory.

Note that the `ItemList` class (Listing 6.17) uses an `ArrayList`, not a `Vector`. Version 2.3 of the servlet API mandates the use of the Java 2 platform, so this usage does not limit portability.

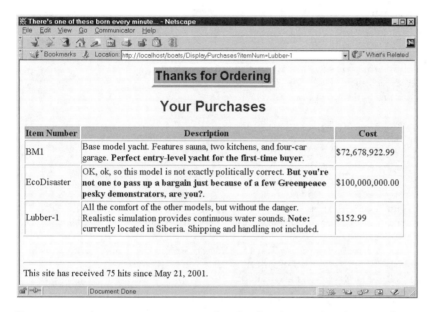

Figure 6–7   The `ShowPurchases` servlet after the client makes three small acquisitions. The servlet is invoked with the registered name (`DisplayPurchases`) and uses the *sucker.jsp* page to present the results.

Listing 6.17   *boats/WEB-INF/classes/moreservlets/ItemList.java*[*]

```
package moreservlets;

import java.util.*;

/** Very simple pseudo shopping cart. Maintains a list
 *  of items and can format them in an HTML table.
 *  Used in the boats Web app example to show that
 *  each Web app maintains its own set of sessions.
 */

public class ItemList {
  private ArrayList items = new ArrayList();
```

Listing 6.17	*boats/WEB-INF/classes/moreservlets/ItemList.java** *(continued)*

```java
public synchronized void setNewItem(SimpleItem newItem) {
  if (newItem != null) {
    items.add(newItem);
  }
}

public synchronized String getItemTable() {
  if (items.size() == 0) {
    return("<H3>No items...</H3>");
  }
  String tableString =
    "<TABLE BORDER=1>\n" +
    "  <TR CLASS=\"COLORED\">\n" +
    "      <TH>Item Number\n" +
    "      <TH>Description\n" +
    "      <TH>Cost\n";
  for(int i=0; i<items.size(); i++) {
    SimpleItem item = (SimpleItem)items.get(i);
    tableString +=
      "  <TR><TD>" + item.getItemNum() + "\n" +
      "      <TD>" + item.getDescription() + "\n" +
      "      <TD>" + item.getCostString() + "\n";
  }
  tableString += "</TABLE>";
  return(tableString);
}

public synchronized String toString() {
  return("[Item List: " + items.size() + " entries.]");
}
}
```

---

* Technically, only the *.class* file needs to go in this directory.

Listing 6.18 *boats/sucker.jsp*

```
<!DOCTYPE HTML PUBLIC "-//W3C//DTD HTML 4.0 Transitional//EN">
<HTML>
<HEAD>
<TITLE>There's one of these born every minute...</TITLE>
<LINK REL=STYLESHEET
      HREF="app-styles.css"
      TYPE="text/css">
</HEAD>

<BODY>
<TABLE BORDER=5 ALIGN="CENTER">
  <TR><TH CLASS="TITLE">Thanks for Ordering</TABLE>

<H2>Your Purchases</H2>
<jsp:useBean id="items"
             class="moreservlets.ItemList"
             scope="session" />
<jsp:getProperty name="items" property="itemTable" />

<%-- Note the lack of "boats" at the front of URI below --%>
<%@ taglib uri="/WEB-INF/tlds/count-taglib.tld" prefix="boats" %>
<boats:count />
</BODY>
</HTML>
```

WEB
APPLICATION
SECURITY

Part III

DECLARATIVE
SECURITY

Topics in This Chapter

- Understanding the major aspects of Web application security
- Authenticating users with HTML forms
- Using BASIC HTTP authentication
- Defining passwords in Tomcat, JRun, and ServletExec
- Designating protected resources with the `security-constraint` element
- Using `login-config` to specify the authentication method
- Mandating the use of SSL
- Configuring Tomcat to use SSL

Chapter 7

There are two major aspects to securing Web applications:

1. **Preventing unauthorized users from accessing sensitive data.**
   This process involves *access restriction* (identifying which resources
   need protection and who should have access to them) and *authentication* (identifying users to determine if they are one of the authorized
   ones). Simple authentication involves the user entering a username
   and password in an HTML form or a dialog box; stronger authentication involves the use of X509 certificates sent by the client to the
   server. This aspect applies to virtually all secure applications. Even
   intranets at locations with physical access controls usually require
   some sort of user authentication.

2. **Preventing attackers from stealing network data while it is in
   transit.** This process involves the use of *Secure Sockets Layer* (SSL)
   to encrypt the traffic between the browser and the server. This capability is generally reserved for particularly sensitive applications or
   particularly sensitive pages within a larger application. After all, unless
   the attackers are on your local subnet, it is exceedingly difficult for
   them to gain access to your network traffic.

These two security aspects are mostly independent. The approaches to access
restriction are the same regardless of whether or not you use SSL. With the exception of client certificates (which apply only to SSL), the approaches to authentication
are also identical whether or not you use SSL.

Within the Web application framework, there are two general approaches to this type of security:

1. **Declarative security.** With declarative security, the topic of this chapter, none of the individual servlets or JSP pages need any security-aware code. Instead, both of the major security aspects are handled by the server.

    To prevent unauthorized access, you use the Web application deployment descriptor (*web.xml*) to declare that certain URLs need protection. You also designate the authentication method that the server should use to identify users. At request time, the server automatically prompts users for usernames and passwords when they try to access restricted resources, automatically checks the results against a predefined set of usernames and passwords, and automatically keeps track of which users have previously been authenticated. This process is completely transparent to the servlets and JSP pages.

    To safeguard network data, you use the deployment descriptor to stipulate that certain URLs should only be accessible with SSL. If users try to use a regular HTTP connection to access one of these URLs, the server automatically redirects them to the HTTPS (SSL) equivalent.

2. **Programmatic security.** With programmatic security, the topic of the next chapter, protected servlets and JSP pages at least partially manage their own security.

    To prevent unauthorized access, *each* servlet or JSP page must either authenticate the user or verify that the user has been authenticated previously.

    To safeguard network data, each servlet or JSP page has to check the network protocol used to access it. If users try to use a regular HTTP connection to access one of these URLs, the servlet or JSP page must manually redirect them to the HTTPS (SSL) equivalent.

7.1   Form-Based Authentication

The most common type of declarative security uses regular HTML forms. The developer uses the deployment descriptor to identify the protected resources and to designate a page that has a form to collect usernames and passwords. A user who attempts to access protected resources is redirected to the page containing the form. When the form is submitted, the server checks the username and password against a list of usernames, passwords and roles. If the login is successful and the user belongs to a role that is permitted access to the page, the user is granted access to the page originally requested. If the login is unsuccessful, the user is sent to a designated error page. Behind the scenes, the system uses some variation of session tracking to remember which users have already been validated.

The whole process is automatic: redirection to the login page, checking of user names and passwords, redirection back to the original resource, and tracking of already authenticated users are all performed by the container (server) in a manner that is completely transparent to the individual resources. However, there is one major caveat: the servlet specification explicitly says that form-based authentication is not guaranteed to work when the server is set to perform session tracking based on URL rewriting instead of cookies (the default session tracking mechanism).

Core Warning

Depending on your server, form-based authentication might fail when you use URL rewriting as the basis of session tracking.

This type of access restriction and authentication is completely independent of the protection of the network traffic. You can stipulate that SSL be used for all, some, or none of your application; but doing so does not change the way you restrict access or authenticate users. Nor does the use of SSL require your individual servlets or JSP pages to participate in the security process; redirection to the URL that uses SSL and encryption/decryption of the network traffic are all performed by the server in a manner that is transparent to the servlets and JSP pages.

Seven basic steps are required to set up your system to use this type of form-based security. I'll summarize the steps here, then give details on each step in the following subsections. All the steps except for the first are standardized and portable across all servers that support version 2.2 or later of the servlet API. Section 7.2 illustrates the concepts with a small application.

1. **Set up usernames, passwords, and roles.** In this step, you designate a list of users and associate each with a password and one or more abstract roles (e.g., normal user or administrator). This is a completely server-specific process. In general, you'll have to read your server's documentation, but I'll summarize the process for Tomcat, JRun, and ServletExec.

2. **Tell the server that you are using form-based authentication. Designate the locations of the login and login-failure page.** This process uses the *web.xml* `login-config` element with an `auth-method` subelement of `FORM` and a `form-login-config` subelement that gives the locations of the two pages.

3. **Create a login page.** This page must have a form with an `ACTION` of `j_security_check`, a `METHOD` of `POST`, a textfield named `j_username`, and a password field named `j_password`.

4. **Create a page to report failed login attempts.** This page can simply say something like "username and password not found" and perhaps give a link back to the login page.

5. **Specify which URLs should be password protected.** For this step, you use the `security-constraint` element of *web.xml*. This element, in turn, uses `web-resource-collection` and `auth-constraint` subelements. The first of these (`web-resource-collection`) designates the URL patterns to which access should be restricted, and the second (`auth-constraint`) specifies the abstract roles that should have access to the resources at the given URLs.

6. **Specify which URLs should be available only with SSL.** If your server supports SSL, you can stipulate that certain resources are available *only* through encrypted HTTPS (SSL) connections. You use the `user-data-constraint` subelement of `security-constraint` for this purpose.

7. **Turn off the invoker servlet.** If your application restricts access to servlets, the access restrictions are placed on the custom URLs that you associate with the servlets. But, most servers have a default servlet URL: *http://host/webAppPrefix/servlet/ServletName*. To prevent users from bypassing the security settings, disable default servlet URLs of this form. To disable these URLs, use the `servlet-mapping` element with a `url-pattern` subelement that designates a pattern of `/servlet/*`.

Details follow.

Setting Up Usernames, Passwords, and Roles

When a user attempts to access a protected resource in an application that is using form-based authentication, the system uses an HTML form to ask for a username and password, verifies that the password matches the user, determines what abstract roles (regular user, administrator, executive, etc.) that user belongs to, and sees whether any of those roles has permission to access the resource. If so, the server redirects the user to the originally requested page. If not, the server redirects the user to an error page.

The good news regarding this process is that the server (container) does a lot of the work for you. The bad news is that the task of associating users with passwords and logical roles is server specific. So, although you would not have to change the *web.xml* file or any of the actual servlet and JSP code to move a secure Web application from system to system, you would still have to make custom changes on each system to set up the users and passwords.

In general, you will have to read your server's documentation to determine how to assign passwords and role membership to users. However, I'll summarize the process for Tomcat, JRun, and ServletExec.

Setting Passwords with Tomcat

Tomcat permits advanced developers to configure custom username and password management schemes (e.g., by accessing a database, looking in the Unix */etc/passwd* file, checking the Windows NT/2000 User Account settings, or making a Kerberos call). For details, see *http://jakarta.apache.org/tomcat/tomcat-4.0-doc/realm-howto.html*. However, this configuration is a lot of work, so Tomcat also provides a default mechanism. With this mechanism, Tomcat stores usernames, passwords, and roles in *install_dir/conf/tomcat-users.xml*. This file should contain an XML header followed by a `tomcat-users` element containing any number of `user` elements. Each user element should have three attributes: `name` (the username), `password` (the plain text password), and `roles` (a comma-separated list of logical role names). Listing 7.1 presents a simple example that defines four users (`valjean`, `bishop`, `javert`, `thenardier`), each of whom belongs to two logical roles.

Listing 7.1   *install_dir/conf/tomcat-users.xml* (Sample)

```
<?xml version="1.0" encoding="ISO-8859-1"?>
<tomcat-users>
  <user name="valjean" password="forgiven"
        roles="lowStatus,nobleSpirited" />
  <user name="bishop" password="mercy"
        roles="lowStatus,nobleSpirited" />
  <user name="javert" password="strict"
        roles="highStatus,meanSpirited" />
  <user name="thenardier" password="grab"
        roles="lowStatus,meanSpirited" />
</tomcat-users>
```

Note that the default Tomcat strategy of storing unencrypted passwords is a poor one. First, an intruder that gains access to the server's file system can obtain all the passwords. Second, even system administrators who are authorized to access server resources should not be able to obtain user's passwords. In fact, since many users reuse passwords on multiple systems, passwords should *never* be stored in clear text. Instead, they should be encrypted with an algorithm that cannot easily be reversed. Then, when a user supplies a password, it is encrypted and the encrypted version is compared with the stored encrypted password. Nevertheless, the default Tomcat approach makes it easy to set up and test secure Web applications. Just keep in mind that for real applications you'll want to replace the simple file-based password scheme with something more robust (e.g., a database or a system call to Kerberos or the Windows NT/2000 User Account system).

Setting Passwords with JRun

JRun, like Tomcat, permits developers to customize the username and password management scheme. For details, see Chapter 39 (Web Application Authentication) of *http://www.allaire.com/documents/jr31/devapp.pdf*. Also like Tomcat, JRun provides a file-based default mechanism. Unlike Tomcat, however, JRun encrypts the passwords before storing them in the file. This approach makes the default JRun strategy usable even in real-world applications.

With the default mechanism, JRun stores usernames, encrypted passwords, and roles in *install_dir/lib/users.properties*. This file contains entries of three types: `user.`*username* entries that associate a password with a user; `group.`*groupname* entries that group users together; and `role.`*rolename* entries that place users and/ or groups into logical roles. Encrypted passwords can be obtained from an existing Unix-based password or *.htaccess* file or by using the `PropertyFileAuthentica-tion` class supplied with JRun. To use this class, temporarily set your `CLASSPATH` (not the server's `CLASSPATH`) to include *install_dir/lib/jrun.jar* and *install_dir/lib/ ext/servlet.jar*, change directory to *install_dir/lib*, and add a user at a time with the `-add` flag, as below. For real applications you would probably set up the server to automate this process.

```
java allaire.jrun.security.PropertyFileAuthentication valjean grace
```

After adding the users, edit the file to assign the roles. Listing 7.2 shows an example that sets up the same users, passwords, and roles as in the previous Tomcat example (Listing 7.1).

Listing 7.2	*install_dir/lib/users.properties* (Sample)

```
user.valjean=vaPoR2yIzbfdI
user.bishop=bic5wknlJ8QFE
user.javert=jaLULvqM82wfk
user.thenardier=thvwKJbcM0s7o

role.lowStatus=valjean,thenardier
role.highStatus=bishop,javert
role.nobleSpirited=valjean,bishop
role.meanSpirited=javert,thenardier
```

Setting Passwords with ServletExec

The process of setting up usernames, passwords, and roles is particularly simple with ServletExec. Simply open the administrator home page and select Users within the Web Applications heading (Figure 7–1). From there, you can interactively enter usernames, passwords, and roles (Figure 7–2). Voila!

With the free desktop debugger version, ServletExec stores the usernames and passwords in plain text in *install_dir/ServletExec Data/users.properties*. The passwords are encrypted in the deployment version.

Figure 7–1   ServletExec user editing interface.

Figure 7–2 Adding a user, password, and role in ServletExec.

Telling the Server You Are Using Form-Based Authentication; Designating Locations of Login and Login-Failure Pages

You use the `login-config` element in the deployment descriptor (*web.xml*) to control the authentication method. Recall from Chapters 4 and 5 that this file goes in the *WEB-INF* directory of your Web application. Although a few servers support nonstandard *web.xml* files (e.g., Tomcat has one in *install_dir/conf* that provides defaults for multiple Web applications), those files are entirely server specific. I am addressing only the standard version that goes in the Web application's *WEB-INF* directory.

To use form-based authentication, supply a value of `FORM` for the `auth-method` subelement and use the `form-login-config` subelement to give the locations of the login (`form-login-page`) and login-failure (`form-error-page`) pages. In the next sections I'll explain exactly what these two files should contain. But for now, note that nothing mandates that they use dynamic content. Thus, these pages can consist of either JSP or ordinary HTML.

For example, Listing 7.3 shows part of a *web.xml* file that stipulates that the container use form-based authentication. Unauthenticated users who attempt to access protected resources will be redirected to *http://host/webAppPrefix/login.jsp*. If they log in successfully, they will be returned to whatever resource they first attempted to access. If their login attempt fails, they will be redirected to *http://host/webAppPrefix/login-error.html*.

Listing 7.3 *web.xml* (Excerpt designating form-based authentication)

```
<?xml version="1.0" encoding="ISO-8859-1"?>
<!DOCTYPE web-app PUBLIC
    "-//Sun Microsystems, Inc.//DTD Web Application 2.2//EN"
    "http://java.sun.com/j2ee/dtds/web-app_2_2.dtd">

<web-app>
  <!-- ... -->
  <security-constraint>...</security-constraint>
  <login-config>
    <auth-method>FORM</auth-method>
    <form-login-config>
      <form-login-page>/login.jsp</form-login-page>
      <form-error-page>/login-error.html</form-error-page>
    </form-login-config>
  </login-config>
  <!-- ... -->
</web-app>
```

Creating the Login Page

OK, so the `login-config` element tells the server to use form-based authentication and to redirect unauthenticated users to a designated page. Fine. But what should you put *in* that page? The answer is surprisingly simple: all the login page requires is a form with an ACTION of j_security_check, a textfield named j_username, and a password field named j_password. And, since using GET defeats the whole point of password fields (protecting the password from prying eyes looking over the user's shoulder), *all* forms that have password fields should use a METHOD of POST. Note that j_security_check is a "magic" name; you don't preface it with a slash even if your login page is in a subdirectory of the main Web application directory. Listing 7.4 gives an example.

Listing 7.4   *login.jsp*

```
<!DOCTYPE HTML PUBLIC "-//W3C//DTD HTML 4.0 Transitional//EN">
<HTML><HEAD><TITLE>...</TITLE></HEAD>
<BODY>
...
<FORM ACTION="j_security_check" METHOD="POST">
<TABLE>
<TR><TD>User name: <INPUT TYPE="TEXT" NAME="j_username">
<TR><TD>Password: <INPUT TYPE="PASSWORD" NAME="j_password">
<TR><TH><INPUT TYPE="SUBMIT" VALUE="Log In">
</TABLE>
</FORM>
...
</BODY></HTML>
```

OK, that was the page for logging *in*. What about a page for logging *out*? The session should time out eventually, but what if users want to log out immediately without closing the browser? Well, the servlet specification says that invalidating the HttpSession should log out users and cause them to be reauthenticated the next time they try to access a protected resource. So, in principle you should be able to create a logout page by making servlet or JSP page that looks up the session and calls invalidate on it. In practice, however, not all servers support this process. Fortunately, changing users is simple: you just visit the login page a second time. This is in contrast to BASIC authentication (Section 7.3), where neither logging out nor changing your username is supported without the user quitting and restarting the browser.

Creating the Page to Report Failed Login Attempts

The main login page must contain a form with a special-purpose ACTION (j_security_check), a textfield with a special name (j_username), and a password field with yet another reserved name (j_password). So, what is required to be in the login-failure page? Nothing! This page is arbitrary; it can contain a link to an unrestricted section of the Web application, a link to the login page, or a simple "login failed" message.

Specifying URLs That Should Be Password Protected

The login-config element tells the server which authentication method to use. Good, but how do you designate the specific URLs to which access should be

restricted? Designating restricted URLs and describing the protection they should
have is the purpose of the `security-constraint` element.

The `security-constraint` element should come immediately before
`login-config` in *web.xml* and contains four possible subelements: `display-name`
(an optional element giving a name for IDEs to use), `web-resource-collection`
(a required element that specifies the URLs that should be protected), `auth-
constraint` (an optional element that designates the abstract roles that should have
access to the URLs), and `user-data-constraint` (an optional element that specifies whether SSL is required). Note that multiple `web-resource-collection`
entries are permitted within `security-constraint`.

For a quick example of the use of `security-constraint`, Listing 7.5 instructs
the server to require passwords for all URLs of the form *http://host/webAppPrefix/
sensitive/blah*. Users who supply passwords and belong to the `administrator` or
`executive` logical roles should be granted access; all others should be denied access.
The rest of this subsection provides details on the `web-resource-collection`,
`auth-constraint`, and `display-name` elements. The role of `user-data-
constraint` is explained in the next subsection (Specifying URLs That Should Be
Available Only with SSL).

Listing 7.5   *web.xml* (Excerpt specifying protected URLs)

```
<?xml version="1.0" encoding="ISO-8859-1"?>
<!DOCTYPE web-app PUBLIC
    "-//Sun Microsystems, Inc.//DTD Web Application 2.2//EN"
    "http://java.sun.com/j2ee/dtds/web-app_2_2.dtd">

<web-app>
  <!-- ... -->
  <security-constraint>
    <web-resource-collection>
      <web-resource-name>Sensitive</web-resource-name>
      <url-pattern>/sensitive/*</url-pattern>
    </web-resource-collection>
    <auth-constraint>
      <role-name>administrator</role-name>
      <role-name>executive</role-name>
    </auth-constraint>
  </security-constraint>
  <login-config>...</login-config>
  <!-- ... -->
</web-app>
```

display-name

This rarely used optional subelement of `security-constraint` gives a name to the security constraint entry. This name might be used by an IDE or other graphical tool.

web-resource-collection

This subelement of `security-constraint` identifies the resources that should be protected. Each `security-constraint` element must contain one or more `web-resource-collection` entries; all other `security-constraint` subelements are optional. The `web-resource-collection` element consists of a `web-resource-name` element that gives an arbitrary identifying name, a `url-pattern` element that identifies the URLs that should be protected, an optional `http-method` element that designates the HTTP commands to which the protection applies (`GET`, `POST`, etc.; the default is all methods), and an optional `description` element providing documentation. For example, the following `web-resource-collection` entries (within a `security-constraint` element) specify that password protection should be applied to all documents in the *proprietary* directory (and subdirectories thereof) and to the *delete-account.jsp* page in the *admin* directory.

```
<security-constraint>
  <web-resource-collection>
    <web-resource-name>Proprietary</web-resource-name>
    <url-pattern>/proprietary/*</url-pattern>
  </web-resource-collection>
  <web-resource-collection>
    <web-resource-name>Account Deletion</web-resource-name>
    <url-pattern>/admin/delete-account.jsp</url-pattern>
  </web-resource-collection>
  <!-- ... -->
</security-constraint>
```

It is important to note that the `url-pattern` applies only to clients that access the resources directly. In particular, it does *not* apply to pages that are accessed through the MVC architecture with a `RequestDispatcher` (Section 3.8) or by the similar means of `jsp:forward` or `jsp:include` (Section 3.5). This asymmetry is good if used properly. For example, with the MVC architecture a servlet looks up data, places it in beans, and forwards the request to a JSP page that extracts the data from the beans and displays it. You want to ensure that the JSP page is never accessed directly but instead is accessed only through the servlet that sets up the beans the page will use. The `url-pattern` and `auth-constraint` (see next subsection) elements can provide this guarantee by declaring that *no* user is permitted direct access to the JSP page. But, this asymmetric behavior can catch developers off guard and allow them to accidentally provide unrestricted access to resources that should be protected.

Core Warning

These protections apply only to direct client access. The security model does not apply to pages accessed by means of a RequestDispatcher, jsp:forward, or jsp:include.

auth-constraint

Whereas the web-resource-collection element designates the URLs that should be protected, the auth-constraint element designates the users that should have access to protected resources. It should contain one or more role-name elements identifying the class of users that have access and, optionally, a description element describing the role. For instance, the following part of the security-constraint element in *web.xml* states that only users who are designated as either Administrators or Big Kahunas (or both) should have access to the designated resource.

```
<security-constraint>
  <web-resource-collection>...</web-resource-collection>
  <auth-constraint>
    <role-name>administrator</role-name>
    <role-name>kahuna</role-name>
  </auth-constraint>
</security-constraint>
```

If you want all authenticated users to have access to a resource, use * as the role-name. Technically, the auth-constraint element is optional. Omitting it means that *no* roles have access. Although at first glance it appears pointless to deny access to all users, remember that these security restrictions apply only to direct client access. So, for example, suppose you had a JSP snippet that is intended to be inserted into another file with jsp:include (Section 3.5). Or, suppose you have a JSP page that is the forwarding destination of a servlet that is using a RequestDispatcher as part of the MVC architecture (Section 3.8). In both cases, users should be prohibited from directly accessing the JSP page. A security-constraint element with no auth-constraint would enforce this restriction nicely.

Specifying URLs That Should Be Available Only with SSL

Suppose your servlet or JSP page collects credit card numbers. User authentication keeps out unauthorized users but does nothing to protect the network traffic. So, for instance, an attacker that runs a packet sniffer on the end user's local area network could see that user's credit card number. This scenario is exactly what SSL protects against—it encrypts the traffic between the browser and the server.

Use of SSL does not change the basic way that form-based authentication works. Regardless of whether you are using SSL, you use the `login-config` element to indicate that you are using form-based authentication and to identify the login and login-failure pages. With or without SSL, you designate the protected resources with the `url-pattern` subelement of `web-resource-collection`. None of your servlets or JSP pages need to be modified or moved to different locations when you enable or disable SSL. That's the beauty of declarative security.

The `user-data-constraint` subelement of `security-constraint` can mandate that certain resources be accessed only with SSL. So, for example, attempts to access *https://host/webAppPrefix/specialURL* are handled normally, whereas attempts to access *http://host/webAppPrefix/specialURL* are redirected to the *https* URL. This behavior does not mean that you cannot supply an explicit *https* URL for a hypertext link or the `ACTION` of a form; it just means that you aren't *required* to. You can stick with the simpler and more easily maintained relative URLs and still be assured that certain URLs will only be accessed with SSL.

The `user-data-constraint` element, if used, must contain a `transport-guarantee` subelement (with legal values NONE, INTEGRAL, or CONFIDENTIAL) and can optionally contain a `description` element. A value of NONE for `transport-guarantee` puts no restrictions on the communication protocol used. Since NONE is the default, there is little point in using `user-data-constraint` or `transport-guarantee` if you specify NONE. A value of INTEGRAL means that the communication must be of a variety that prevents data from being changed in transit without detection. A value of CONFIDENTIAL means that the data must be transmitted in a way that prevents anyone who intercepts it from reading it. Although in principle (and perhaps in future HTTP versions) there may be a distinction between INTEGRAL and CONFIDENTIAL, in current practice they both simply mandate the use of SSL.

For example, the following instructs the server to permit only *https* connections to the associated resource:

```
<security-constraint>
  <!-- ... -->
  <user-data-constraint>
    <transport-guarantee>CONFIDENTIAL</transport-guarantee>
  </user-data-constraint>
</security-constraint>
```

In addition to simply requiring SSL, the servlet API provides a way to stipulate that users must authenticate themselves with client certificates. You supply a value of `CLIENT-CERT` for the `auth-method` subelement of `login-config` (see "Specifying URLs That Should Be Password Protected" earlier in this section). However, only servers that have full J2EE support are required to support this capability.

Now, although the method of prohibiting non-SSL access is standardized, servers that are compliant with the servlet 2.3 and JSP 1.2 specifications are *not* required to support SSL. So, Web applications that use a `transport-guarantee` of `CONFIDENTIAL` (or, equivalently, `INTEGRAL`) are not necessarily portable. For example, JRun and ServletExec are usually used as plugins in Web servers like iPlanet/Netscape or IIS. In this scenario, the network traffic between the client and the Web server is encrypted with SSL, but the local traffic from the Web server to the servlet/JSP container is not encrypted. Consequently, a `CONFIDENTIAL transport-guarantee` will fail. Tomcat, however, can be set up to use SSL directly. Details on this process are given in Section 7.5. Some server plugins maintain SSL even on the local connection between the main Web server and the servlet/JSP engine; for example, the BEA WebLogic plugin for IIS, Apache, and Netscape Enterprise Server does so. Furthermore, integrated application servers like the standalone version of WebLogic have no "separate" servlet and JSP engine, so SSL works exactly as described here. Nevertheless, it is important to realize that these features, although useful, are not mandated by the servlet and JSP specifications.

Core Warning

Web applications that rely on SSL are not necessarily portable.

Turning Off the Invoker Servlet

When you restrict access to certain resources, you do so by specifying the URL patterns to which the restrictions apply. This pattern, in turn, matches a pattern that you set with the `servlet-mapping` *web.xml* element (see Section 5.3, "Assigning Names and Custom URLs"). However, most servers use an "invoker servlet" that provides a default URL for servlets: *http://host/webAppPrefix/servlet/ServletName*. You need to make sure that users don't access protected servlets with this URL, thus bypassing the access restrictions that were set by the `url-pattern` subelement of `web-resource-collection`.

For example, suppose that you use `security-constraint`, `web-resource-collection`, and `url-pattern` to say that the URL */admin/DeclareChapter11* should be protected. You also use the `auth-constraint` and `role-name` elements to say that only users in the `director` role can access this URL. Next, you use the `servlet` and `servlet-mapping` elements to say that the servlet *BankruptcyServlet.class* in the `disaster` package should correspond to */admin/DeclareChapter11*. Now, the security restrictions are in force when clients use the URL *http://host/webAppPrefix/admin/DeclareChapter11*. No restrictions apply to *http://host/webAppPrefix/servlet/disaster.BankruptcyServlet*. Oops.

Section 5.4 (Disabling the Invoker Servlet) discusses server-specific approaches to turning off the invoker. The most portable approach, however, is to simply remap the */servlet* pattern in your Web application so that all requests that include the pattern are sent to the same servlet. To remap the pattern, you first create a simple servlet that prints an error message or redirects users to the top-level page. Then, you use the `servlet` and `servlet-mapping` elements (Section 5.3) to send requests that include the */servlet* pattern to that servlet. Listing 7.6 gives a brief example.

Listing 7.6	*web.xml* (Excerpt redirecting requests from default servlet URLs to an error-message servlet)

```
<?xml version="1.0" encoding="ISO-8859-1"?>
<!DOCTYPE web-app PUBLIC
    "-//Sun Microsystems, Inc.//DTD Web Application 2.2//EN"
    "http://java.sun.com/j2ee/dtds/web-app_2_2.dtd">

<web-app>
  <!-- ... -->
  <servlet>
    <servlet-name>Error</servlet-name>
    <servlet-class>somePackage.ErrorServlet</servlet-class>
  </servlet>
  <!-- ... -->
  <servlet-mapping>
    <servlet-name>Error</servlet-name>
    <url-pattern>/servlet/*</url-pattern>
  </servlet-mapping>
  <!-- ... -->
</web-app>
```

7.2 Example: Form-Based Authentication

In this section I'll work through a small Web site for a fictional company called hot-dot-com.com. I'll start by showing the home page, then list the *web.xml* file, summarize the various protection mechanisms, show the password file, present the login and login-failure pages, and give the code for each of the protected resources.

The Home Page

Listing 7.7 shows the top-level home page for the Web application. The application is registered with a URL prefix of */hotdotcom* so the home page can be accessed with the URL *http://host/hotdotcom/index.jsp* as shown in Figure 7–3. If you've forgotten how to assign URL prefixes to Web applications, review Section 4.1 (Registering Web Applications).

Now, the main home page has no security protections and consequently does not absolutely require an entry in *web.xml*. However, many users expect URLs that list a directory but no file to invoke the default file from that directory. So, I put a welcome-file-list entry in *web.xml* (see Listing 7.8 in the next section) to ensure that *http://host/hotdotcom/* would invoke *index.jsp*.

Listing 7.7 *index.jsp* (Top-level home page)

```
<!DOCTYPE HTML PUBLIC "-//W3C//DTD HTML 4.0 Transitional//EN">
<HTML>
<HEAD>
<TITLE>hot-dot-com.com!</TITLE>
<LINK REL=STYLESHEET
      HREF="company-styles.css"
      TYPE="text/css">
</HEAD>
<BODY>
<TABLE BORDER=5 ALIGN="CENTER">
  <TR><TH CLASS="TITLE">hot-dot-com.com!</TABLE>
<P>
<H3>Welcome to the ultimate dot-com company!</H3>
Please select one of the following:
<UL>
  <LI><A HREF="investing/">Investing</A>.
      Guaranteed growth for your hard-earned dollars!
  <LI><A HREF="business/">Business Model</A>.
      New economy strategy!
  <LI><A HREF="history/">History</A>.
      Fascinating company history.
</UL>
</BODY>
</HTML>
```

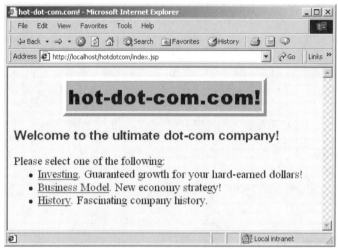

Figure 7–3   Home page for hot-dot-com.com.

The Deployment Descriptor

Listing 7.8 shows the complete deployment descriptor used with the `hotdotcom` Web application. Recall that the order of the subelements within the `web-app` element of *web.xml* is not arbitrary—you must use the standard ordering. For details, see Section 5.2 (The Order of Elements within the Deployment Descriptor).

The `hotdotcom` deployment descriptor specifies several things:

- URLs that give a directory but no filename result in the server first trying to use *index.jsp* and next trying *index.html*. If neither file is available, the result is server specific (e.g., a directory listing).
- URLs that use the default servlet mapping (i.e., *http://host/hotdotcom/servlet/ServletName*) are redirected to the main home page.
- Requests to *http://host/hotdotcom/ssl/buy-stock.jsp* are redirected to *https://host/hotdotcom/ssl/buy-stock.jsp*. Requests directly to *https://host/hotdotcom/ssl/buy-stock.jsp* require no redirection. Similarly, requests to *http://host/hotdotcom/ssl/FinalizePurchase* are redirected to *https://host/hotdotcom/ssl/FinalizePurchase*. See Section 7.5 for information on setting up Tomcat to use SSL.
- URLs in the *investing* directory can be accessed only by users in the `registered-user` or `administrator` roles.
- The *delete-account.jsp* page in the *admin* directory can be accessed only by users in the `administrator` role.

- Requests for restricted resources by unauthenticated users are
  redirected to the *login.jsp* page in the *admin* directory. Users who are
  authenticated successfully get sent to the page they tried to access
  originally. Users who fail authentication are sent to the *login-error.jsp*
  page in the *admin* directory.

Listing 7.8 *WEB-INF/web.xml*
(Complete version for *hot-dot-com.com*)

```xml
<?xml version="1.0" encoding="ISO-8859-1"?>
<!DOCTYPE web-app PUBLIC
    "-//Sun Microsystems, Inc.//DTD Web Application 2.2//EN"
    "http://java.sun.com/j2ee/dtds/web-app_2_2.dtd">

<web-app>
  <!-- Give name to FinalizePurchaseServlet. This servlet
       will later be mapped to the URL /ssl/FinalizePurchase
       (by means of servlet-mapping and url-pattern).
       Then, that URL will be designated as one requiring
       SSL (by means of security-constraint and
       transport-guarantee). -->
  <servlet>
    <servlet-name>
      FinalizePurchaseServlet
    </servlet-name>
    <servlet-class>
      hotdotcom.FinalizePurchaseServlet
    </servlet-class>
  </servlet>

  <!-- A servlet that redirects users to the home page. -->
  <servlet>
    <servlet-name>Redirector</servlet-name>
    <servlet-class>hotdotcom.RedirectorServlet</servlet-class>
  </servlet>

  <!-- Associate previously named servlet with custom URL. -->
  <servlet-mapping>
    <servlet-name>
      FinalizePurchaseServlet
    </servlet-name>
    <url-pattern>
      /ssl/FinalizePurchase
    </url-pattern>
  </servlet-mapping>
```

```xml
<!-- Turn off invoker. Send requests to index.jsp. -->
<servlet-mapping>
  <servlet-name>Redirector</servlet-name>
  <url-pattern>/servlet/*</url-pattern>
</servlet-mapping>

<!-- If URL gives a directory but no filename, try index.jsp
     first and index.html second. If neither is found,
     the result is server-specific (e.g., a directory
     listing). -->
<welcome-file-list>
  <welcome-file>index.jsp</welcome-file>
  <welcome-file>index.html</welcome-file>
</welcome-file-list>

<!-- Protect everything within the "investing" directory. -->
<security-constraint>
  <web-resource-collection>
    <web-resource-name>Investing</web-resource-name>
    <url-pattern>/investing/*</url-pattern>
  </web-resource-collection>
  <auth-constraint>
    <role-name>registered-user</role-name>
    <role-name>administrator</role-name>
  </auth-constraint>
</security-constraint>

<!-- URLs of the form http://host/webAppPrefix/ssl/blah
     require SSL and are thus redirected to
     https://host/webAppPrefix/ssl/blah. -->
<security-constraint>
  <web-resource-collection>
    <web-resource-name>Purchase</web-resource-name>
    <url-pattern>/ssl/*</url-pattern>
  </web-resource-collection>
  <auth-constraint>
    <role-name>registered-user</role-name>
  </auth-constraint>
  <user-data-constraint>
    <transport-guarantee>CONFIDENTIAL</transport-guarantee>
  </user-data-constraint>
</security-constraint>
```

Listing 7.8	*WEB-INF/web.xml* (Complete version for *hot-dot-com.com*) *(continued)*

```
<!-- Only users in the administrator role can access
     the delete-account.jsp page within the admin
     directory. -->
<security-constraint>
  <web-resource-collection>
    <web-resource-name>Account Deletion</web-resource-name>
    <url-pattern>/admin/delete-account.jsp</url-pattern>
  </web-resource-collection>
  <auth-constraint>
    <role-name>administrator</role-name>
  </auth-constraint>
</security-constraint>

<!-- Tell the server to use form-based authentication. -->
<login-config>
  <auth-method>FORM</auth-method>
  <form-login-config>
    <form-login-page>/admin/login.jsp</form-login-page>
    <form-error-page>/admin/login-error.jsp</form-error-page>
  </form-login-config>
</login-config>
</web-app>
```

The Password File

With form-based authentication, the server (container) performs a lot of the work for you. That's good. However, shifting so much work to the server means that there is a server-specific component: the assignment of passwords and roles to individual users (see Section 7.1).

Listing 7.9 shows the password file used by Tomcat for this Web application. It defines four users: john (in the registered-user role), jane (also in the registered-user role), juan (in the administrator role), and juana (in the registered-user and administrator roles).

Listing 7.9 *install_dir/conf/tomcat-users.xml* (First four users)

```
<?xml version="1.0" encoding="ISO-8859-1"?>
<tomcat-users>
  <user name="john" password="nhoj"
        roles="registered-user" />
  <user name="jane" password="enaj"
        roles="registered-user" />
  <user name="juan" password="nauj"
        roles="administrator" />
  <user name="juana" password="anauj"
        roles="administrator,registered-user" />
</tomcat-users>
```

The Login and Login-Failure Pages

This Web application uses form-based authentication. Attempts by not-yet-authenticated users to access any password-protected resource will be sent to the *login.jsp* page in the *admin* directory. This page, shown in Listing 7.10, collects the username in a field named j_username and the password in a field named j_password. The results are sent by POST to a resource called j_security_check. Successful login attempts are redirected to the page that was originally requested. Failed attempts are redirected to the *login-error.jsp* page in the *admin* directory (Listing 7.11).

Listing 7.10 *admin/login.jsp*

```
<!DOCTYPE HTML PUBLIC "-//W3C//DTD HTML 4.0 Transitional//EN">
<HTML>
<HEAD>
<TITLE>Log In</TITLE>
<LINK REL=STYLESHEET
      HREF="../company-styles.css"
      TYPE="text/css">
</HEAD>

<BODY>
<TABLE BORDER=5 ALIGN="CENTER">
  <TR><TH CLASS="TITLE">Log In</TABLE>
<P>
<H3>Sorry, you must log in before accessing this resource.</H3>
<FORM ACTION="j_security_check" METHOD="POST">
```

Listing 7.10 *admin/login.jsp (continued)*

```
<TABLE>
<TR><TD>User name: <INPUT TYPE="TEXT" NAME="j_username">
<TR><TD>Password: <INPUT TYPE="PASSWORD" NAME="j_password">
<TR><TH><INPUT TYPE="SUBMIT" VALUE="Log In">
</TABLE>
</FORM>

</BODY>
</HTML>
```

Listing 7.11 *admin/login-error.jsp*

```
<!DOCTYPE HTML PUBLIC "-//W3C//DTD HTML 4.0 Transitional//EN">
<HTML>
<HEAD>
<TITLE>Begone!</TITLE>
<LINK REL=STYLESHEET
      HREF="../company-styles.css"
      TYPE="text/css">
</HEAD>

<BODY>
<TABLE BORDER=5 ALIGN="CENTER">
  <TR><TH CLASS="TITLE">Begone!</TABLE>

<H3>Begone, ye unauthorized peon.</H3>

</BODY>
</HTML>
```

The investing Directory

The *web.xml* file for the hotdotcom Web application (Listing 7.8) specifies that all URLs that begin with *http://host/hotdotcom/investing/* should be password protected, accessible only to users in the registered-user role. So, the first attempt by any user to access the home page of the *investing* directory (Listing 7.12) results in the login form shown earlier in Listing 7.10. Figure 7–4 shows the initial result, Figure 7–5 shows the result of an unsuccessful login attempt, and Figure 7–6 shows the investing home page—the result of a successful login.

Once authenticated, a user can browse other pages and return to a protected page without reauthentication. The system uses some variation of session tracking to remember which users have previously been authenticated.

Listing 7.12   *investing/index.html*

```
<!DOCTYPE HTML PUBLIC "-//W3C//DTD HTML 4.0 Transitional//EN">
<HTML>
<HEAD>
<TITLE>Investing</TITLE>
<LINK REL=STYLESHEET
      HREF="../company-styles.css"
      TYPE="text/css">
</HEAD>
<BODY>
<TABLE BORDER=5 ALIGN="CENTER">
  <TR><TH CLASS="TITLE">Investing</TABLE>
<H3><I>hot-dot-com.com</I> welcomes the discriminating investor!
</H3>
Please choose one of the following:
<UL>
  <LI><A HREF="../ssl/buy-stock.jsp">Buy stock</A>.
      Astronomic growth rates!
  <LI><A HREF="account-status.jsp">Check account status</A>.
      See how much you've already earned!
</UL>
</BODY>
</HTML>
```

Figure 7–4   Users who are not yet authenticated get redirected to the login page when they attempt to access the investing page.

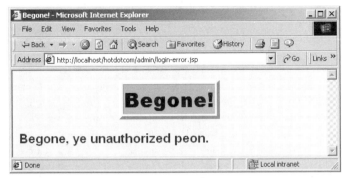

Figure 7–5   Failed login attempts result in the *login-error.jsp* page. Internet Explorer users have to turn off "friendly" HTTP error messages (under Tools, Internet Options, Advanced) to see the real error page instead of a default error page.

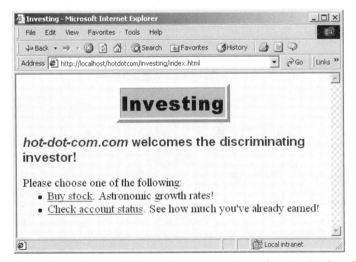

Figure 7–6   Successful login attempts result in redirection back to the originally requested page.

The ssl Directory

The stock purchase page (Listings 7.13 and 7.14) submits data to the purchase finalization servlet (Listing 7.15) which, in turn, dispatches to the confirmation page (Listing 7.16).

Note that the purchase finalization servlet is not really in the *ssl* directory; it is in *WEB-INF/classes/hotdotcom*. However, the deployment descriptor (Listing 7.8) uses `servlet-mapping` to assign a URL that makes the servlet appear (to the client) to be in the *ssl* directory. This mapping serves two purposes.

First, it lets the HTML form of Listing 7.13 use a simple relative URL to refer to the servlet. This is convenient because absolute URLs require modification every time your hostname or URL prefix changes. However, if you use this approach, it is important that *both* the original form and the servlet it talks to are accessed with SSL. If the original form used a relative URL for the `ACTION` and was accessed with a normal HTTP connection, the browser would first submit the data by HTTP and then get redirected to HTTPS. Too late: an attacker with access to the network traffic could have obtained the data from the initial HTTP request. On the other hand, if the `ACTION` of a form is an absolute URL that uses *https*, it is not necessary for the original form to be accessed with SSL.

Second, using `servlet-mapping` in this way guarantees that SSL will be used to access the servlet, even if the user tries to bypass the HTML form and access the servlet URL directly. This guarantee is in effect because the `transport-guarantee` element (with a value of `CONFIDENTIAL`) applies to the pattern `/ssl/*`. Figures 7–7 through 7–9 show the results.

Listing 7.13 *ssl/buy-stock.jsp*

```
<!DOCTYPE HTML PUBLIC "-//W3C//DTD HTML 4.0 Transitional//EN">
<HTML>
<HEAD>
<TITLE>Purchase</TITLE>
<LINK REL=STYLESHEET
      HREF="../company-styles.css"
      TYPE="text/css">
</HEAD>
<BODY>
<TABLE BORDER=5 ALIGN="CENTER">
  <TR><TH CLASS="TITLE">Purchase</TABLE>
<P>
<H3><I>hot-dot-com.com</I> congratulates you on a wise
investment!</H3>
<jsp:useBean id="stock" class="hotdotcom.StockInfo" />
```

Listing 7.13 *ssl/buy-stock.jsp (continued)*

```
<UL>
  <LI>Current stock value:
      <jsp:getProperty name="stock" property="currentValue" />
  <LI>Predicted value in one year:
      <jsp:getProperty name="stock" property="futureValue" />
</UL>
<FORM ACTION="FinalizePurchase" METHOD="POST">
  <DL>
    <DT>Number of shares:
    <DD><INPUT TYPE="RADIO" NAME="numShares" VALUE="1000">
        1000
    <DD><INPUT TYPE="RADIO" NAME="numShares" VALUE="10000">
        10000
    <DD><INPUT TYPE="RADIO" NAME="numShares" VALUE="100000"
              CHECKED>
        100000
  </DL>
  Full name: <INPUT TYPE="TEXT" NAME="fullName"><BR>
  Credit card number: <INPUT TYPE="TEXT" NAME="cardNum"><P>
  <CENTER><INPUT TYPE="SUBMIT" VALUE="Confirm Purchase"></CENTER>
</FORM>
</BODY>
</HTML>
```

Listing 7.14 *WEB-INF/classes/hotdotcom/StockInfo.java*
(Bean used by *buy-stock.jsp*)

```
package hotdotcom;

public class StockInfo {
  public String getCurrentValue() {
    return("$2.00");
  }

  public String getFutureValue() {
    return("$200.00");
  }
}
```

Listing 7.15   *WEB-INF/classes/hotdotcom/FinalizePurchaseServlet.java*

```java
package hotdotcom;

import java.io.*;
import javax.servlet.*;
import javax.servlet.http.*;

/** Servlet that reads credit card information,
 *  performs a stock purchase, and displays confirmation page.
 */

public class FinalizePurchaseServlet extends HttpServlet {

  /** Use doPost for non-SSL access to prevent
   *  credit card number from showing up in URL.
   */

  public void doPost(HttpServletRequest request,
                     HttpServletResponse response)
    throws ServletException, IOException {
    String fullName = request.getParameter("fullName");
    String cardNum = request.getParameter("cardNum");
    confirmPurchase(fullName, cardNum);
    String destination = "/investing/sucker.jsp";
    RequestDispatcher dispatcher =
      getServletContext().getRequestDispatcher(destination);
    dispatcher.forward(request, response);
  }

  /** doGet calls doPost. Servlets that are
   *  redirected to through SSL must have doGet.
   */

  public void doGet(HttpServletRequest request,
                    HttpServletResponse response)
    throws ServletException, IOException {
    doPost(request, response);
  }

  private void confirmPurchase(String fullName,
                               String cardNum) {
    // Details removed to protect the guilty.
  }
}
```

Listing 7.16 *investing/sucker.jsp*
(Dispatched to from *FinalizePurchaseServlet.java*)

```
<!DOCTYPE HTML PUBLIC "-//W3C//DTD HTML 4.0 Transitional//EN">
<HTML>
<HEAD>
<TITLE>Thanks!</TITLE>
<LINK REL=STYLESHEET
      HREF="../company-styles.css"
      TYPE="text/css">
</HEAD>
<BODY>
<TABLE BORDER=5 ALIGN="CENTER">
  <TR><TH CLASS="TITLE">Thanks!</TABLE>
<H3><I>hot-dot-com.com</I> thanks you for your purchase.</H3>
You'll be thanking yourself soon!
</BODY>
</HTML>
```

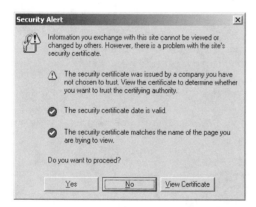

Figure 7–7 Warning when user first accesses `FinalizePurchaseServlet` when Tomcat is using a self-signed certificate. Self-signed certificates result in warnings and are for test purposes only. See Section 7.5 for details on creating them for use with Tomcat and for information on suppressing warnings for future requests.

Figure 7–8 The stock purchase page must be accessed with SSL. Since the form's ACTION uses a simple relative URL, the initial form submission uses the same protocol as the request for the form itself. If you were concerned about overloading your SSL server (HTTPS connections are much slower than HTTP connections), you could access the form with a non-SSL connection and then supply an absolute URL specifying *https* for the form's ACTION. This approach, although slightly more efficient, is significantly harder to maintain.

Figure 7–9 To protect the credit card number in transit, you must use SSL to access the FinalizePurchase servlet. Although FinalizePurchaseServlet dispatches to *sucker.js*p, no *web.xml* entry is needed for that JSP page. Access restrictions apply to the client's URL, not to the behind-the-scenes file locations.

Listing 7.17   *investing/account-status.jsp*

```
<!DOCTYPE HTML PUBLIC "-//W3C//DTD HTML 4.0 Transitional//EN">
<HTML>
<HEAD>
<TITLE>Account Status</TITLE>
<LINK REL=STYLESHEET
      HREF="../company-styles.css"
      TYPE="text/css">
</HEAD>
<BODY>
<TABLE BORDER=5 ALIGN="CENTER">
  <TR><TH CLASS="TITLE">Account Status</TABLE>
<P>
<H3>Your stock is basically worthless now.</H3>
But, hey, that makes this a buying opportunity.
Why don't you <A HREF="../ssl/buy-stock.jsp">buy
some more</A>?
</BODY>
</HTML>
```

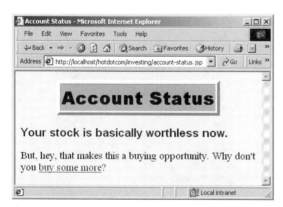

Figure 7–10   Selecting the Account Status link on the investing home page does not result in reauthentication, even if the user has accessed other pages since being authenticated. The system uses a variation of session tracking to remember which users have already been authenticated.

The admin Directory

URLs in the *admin* directory are not uniformly protected as are URLs in the *investing* directory. I already discussed the login and login-failure pages (Listings 7.10 and 7.11, Figures 7–4 and 7–5). This just leaves the Delete Account page (Listing 7.18). This page has been designated as accessible only to users in the `administrator` role. So, when users that are only in the `registered-user` role attempt to access the page, they are denied permission (see Figure 7–11). Note that the permission-denied page of Figure 7–11 is generated automatically by the server and applies to authenticated users whose roles do not match any of the required ones—it is not the same as the login error page that applies to users who cannot be authenticated.

A user in the `administrator` role can access the page without difficulty (Figure 7–12).

Listing 7.18 *admin/delete-account.jsp*

```
<!DOCTYPE HTML PUBLIC "-//W3C//DTD HTML 4.0 Transitional//EN">
<HTML>
<HEAD>
<TITLE>Delete Account</TITLE>
<LINK REL=STYLESHEET
      HREF="../company-styles.css"
      TYPE="text/css">
</HEAD>

<BODY>
<TABLE BORDER=5 ALIGN="CENTER">
  <TR><TH CLASS="TITLE">Delete Account</TABLE>
<P>

<FORM ACTION="confirm-deletion.jsp">
  Username: <INPUT TYPE="TEXT" NAME="userName"><BR>
  <CENTER><INPUT TYPE="SUBMIT" VALUE="Confirm Deletion"></CENTER>
</FORM>

</BODY>
</HTML>
```

Figure 7–11   When John and Jane attempt to access the Delete Account page, they are denied (even though they are authenticated). That's because they belong to the `registered-user` role and the *web.xml* file stipulates that only users in the `administrator` role should be able to access this page.

Figure 7–12   Once authenticated, Juan or Juana (in the `administrator` role) can access the Delete Account page.

The Redirector Servlet

Web applications that have protected servlets should always disable the invoker servlet so that users cannot bypass security by using *http://host/webAppPrefix/servlet/ServletName* when the access restrictions are assigned to a custom servlet URL. In the `hotdotcom` application, I used the `servlet` and `servlet-mapping` elements to register the `RedirectorServlet` with requests to *http://host/hotdotcom/servlet/ anything*. This servlet, shown in Listing 7.19, simply redirects all such requests to the application's home page.

| Listing 7.19 | *WEB-INF/classes/hotdotcom/RedirectorServlet.java* |

```
package hotdotcom;

import java.io.*;
import javax.servlet.*;
import javax.servlet.http.*;

/** Servlet that simply redirects users to the
 *  Web application home page. Registered with the
 *  default servlet URL to prevent access to servlets
 *  through URLs that have no security settings.
 */

public class RedirectorServlet extends HttpServlet {
  public void doGet(HttpServletRequest request,
                    HttpServletResponse response)
     throws ServletException, IOException {
    response.sendRedirect(request.getContextPath());
  }

  public void doPost(HttpServletRequest request,
                     HttpServletResponse response)
     throws ServletException, IOException {
    doGet(request, response);
  }
}
```

Unprotected Pages

The fact that *some* pages in a Web application have access restrictions does not imply that *all* pages in the application need such restrictions. Resources that have no access restrictions need no special handling regarding security. There are two points to keep in mind, however.

First, if you use default pages such as *index.jsp* or *index.html*, you should have an explicit `welcome-file-list` entry in *web.xml*. Without a `welcome-file-list` entry, servers are not required to use those files as the default file when a user supplies a URL that gives only a directory. See Section 5.7 (Specifying Welcome Pages) for details on the `welcome-file-list` element.

Second, you should use relative URLs to refer to images or style sheets so that your pages don't need modification if the Web application's URL prefix changes. For more information, see Section 4.5 (Handling Relative URLs in Web Applications).

Listings 7.20 and 7.21 (Figures 7–13 and 7–14) give two examples.

Listing 7.20 *business/index.html*

```
<!DOCTYPE HTML PUBLIC "-//W3C//DTD HTML 4.0 Transitional//EN">
<HTML>
<HEAD>
<TITLE>Business Model</TITLE>
<LINK REL=STYLESHEET
      HREF="../company-styles.css"
      TYPE="text/css">
</HEAD>
<BODY>
<TABLE BORDER=5 ALIGN="CENTER">
  <TR><TH CLASS="TITLE">Business Model</TABLE>
<P>
<H3>Who needs a business model?</H3>
Hey, this is the new economy. We don't need a real business
model, do we?
<P>
OK, ok, if you insist:
<OL>
  <LI>Start a dot-com.
  <LI>Have an IPO.
  <LI>Get a bunch of suckers to work for peanuts
      plus stock options.
  <LI>Retire.
</OL>
Isn't that what many other dot-coms did?
</BODY>
</HTML>
```

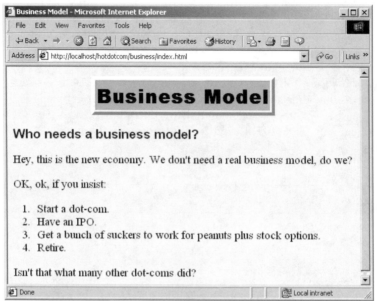

Figure 7–13   The hotdotcom business model.

Listing 7.21   *history/index.html*

```
<!DOCTYPE HTML PUBLIC "-//W3C//DTD HTML 4.0 Transitional//EN">
<HTML>
<HEAD>
<TITLE>History</TITLE>
<LINK REL=STYLESHEET
     HREF="../company-styles.css"
     TYPE="text/css">
</HEAD>
<BODY>
<TABLE BORDER=5 ALIGN="CENTER">
  <TR><TH CLASS="TITLE">History</TABLE>
<P>
<H3>None yet...</H3>
</BODY>
</HTML>
```

Figure 7–14   The distinguished `hotdotcom` heritage.

7.3   BASIC Authentication

The most common type of container-managed security is built on form-based authentication, discussed in Section 7.1. There, the server automatically redirects unauthenticated users to an HTML form, checks their username and password, determines which logical roles they are in, and sees whether any of those roles is permitted to access the resource in question. Then, it uses a variation of session tracking to remember the users that have already been authenticated.

This approach has the advantage that the login form can have the same look and feel as the rest of the Web site. However, it has a few disadvantages. For example, if the client's browser does not support cookies, session tracking would have to be performed with URL rewriting. Or, the server might be configured to always use URL rewriting. The servlet specification explicitly states that form-based authentication is not guaranteed to work in such a case.

So, another approach is to use the standard HTTP BASIC security. With BASIC security, the browser uses a dialog box instead of an HTML form to collect the username and password. Then, the `Authorization` request header is used to remember which users have already been authenticated. As with form-based security, you must use SSL if you are concerned with protecting the network traffic. However, doing so neither changes the way BASIC authentication is set up nor necessitates changes in the individual servlets or JSP pages.

There is also DIGEST security and security based on client certificates. However, few browsers or servers support DIGEST, and only fully J2EE-compliant servers are required to support client certificates. For more information on client certificates, see Section 8.5 (Using Programmatic Security with SSL).

Compared to form-based authentication, the two main disadvantages of BASIC authentication are that the input dialog looks glaringly different than the rest of your application and that it is very difficult to log in as a different user once you are authenticated. In fact, once authenticated, you have to quit the browser and restart if you want to log in as a different user! Now, in principle it is possible to write a "relogin" servlet that sends a 401 (Unauthorized) status code and a WWW-Authenticate header containing the appropriate realm. But, that is hardly "declarative" security!

Use of BASIC security involves five steps, as shown below. Each of the steps except for the second is identical to the corresponding step used in form-based authentication.

1. **Set up usernames, passwords, and roles.** In this step, you designate a list of users and associate each with a password and one or more abstract roles (e.g., normal user, administrator, etc.). This is a completely server-specific process.

2. **Tell the server that you are using BASIC authentication. Designate the realm name.** This process uses the *web.xml* login-config element with an auth-method subelement of BASIC and a realm-name subelement that specifies the realm (which is generally used as part of the title of the dialog box that the browser opens).

3. **Specify which URLs should be password protected.** For this step, you use the security-constraint element of *web.xml*. This element, in turn, uses web-resource-collection and auth-constraint subelements. The first of these designates the URL patterns to which access should be restricted, and the second specifies the abstract roles that should have access to the resources at the given URLs.

4. **Specify which URLs should be available only with SSL.** If your server supports SSL, you can stipulate that certain resources are available *only* through encrypted *https* (SSL) connections. You use the user-data-constraint subelement of security-constraint for this purpose.

5. **Turn off the invoker servlet.** If your application restricts access to servlets, the access restrictions are placed only on the custom URL that you associate with the servlet. To prevent users from bypassing the security settings, disable default servlet URLs of the form *http://host/webAppPrefix/servlet/ServletName*. To disable these URLs, use the servlet-mapping element with a url-pattern subelement that designates a pattern of /servlet/*.

Details on these steps are given in the following sections.

Setting Up Usernames, Passwords, and Roles

This step is exactly the same when BASIC authentication is used as when form-based authentication is used. See Section 7.1 for details. For a quick summary, recall that this process is completely server specific. Tomcat uses *install_dir/conf/tomcat-users.xml* to store this information, JRun uses *install_dir/lib/users.properties*, and ServletExec has an interactive user interface to enable you to specify the information.

Telling the Server You Are Using BASIC Authentication; Designating Realm

You use the `login-config` element in the deployment descriptor to control the authentication method. To use BASIC authentication, supply a value of `BASIC` for the `auth-method` subelement and use the `realm-name` subelement to designate the realm that will be used by the browser in the popup dialog box and in the `Authorization` request header. Listing 7.22 gives an example.

Listing 7.22   *web.xml* (Excerpt designating BASIC authentication)

```xml
<?xml version="1.0" encoding="ISO-8859-1"?>
<!DOCTYPE web-app PUBLIC
    "-//Sun Microsystems, Inc.//DTD Web Application 2.2//EN"
    "http://java.sun.com/j2ee/dtds/web-app_2_2.dtd">

<web-app>
  <!-- ... -->
  <security-constraint>...</security-constraint>
  <login-config>
    <auth-method>BASIC</auth-method>
    <realm-name>Some Name</realm-name>
  </login-config>
  <!-- ... -->
</web-app>
```

Specifying URLs That Should Be Password Protected

You designate password-protected resources in the same manner with BASIC authentication as you do with form-based authentication. See Section 7.1 for details. For a quick summary, you use the `security-constraint` element to specify restricted URLs and the roles that should have access to them. The `security-constraint` element should come immediately before `login-config` in *web.xml* and contains four possible subelements: `display-name` (an optional element giving a name for IDEs to use), `web-resource-collection` (a required element that specifies the URLs that should be protected), `auth-constraint` (an optional element that designates the abstract roles that should have access to the URLs), and `user-data-constraint` (an optional element that specifies whether SSL is required). Multiple `web-resource-collection` entries are permitted within `security-constraint`.

Specifying URLs That Should Be Available Only with SSL

You designate SSL-only resources in the same manner with BASIC authentication as you do with form-based authentication. See Section 7.1 for details. To summarize: use the `user-data-constraint` subelement of `security-constraint` with a `transport-guarantee` subelement specifying `INTEGRAL` or `CONFIDENTIAL`.

In addition to simply requiring SSL, the servlet API provides a way for stipulating that users must authenticate themselves with client certificates. You supply a value of `CLIENT-CERT` for the `auth-method` subelement of `login-config` (see "Specifying URLs That Should Be Password Protected" in Section 7.1). However, only application servers that have full J2EE support are required to support this capability.

7.4 Example: BASIC Authentication

In Section 7.2, I showed the external Web site for a fictional company named hot-dot-com.com. In this section, I'll show their intranet. Since applications that use form-based authentication vary only slightly from those that use BASIC authentication, I'll just concentrate on the differences here. I'll start by showing the home page, then list the *web.xml* file, summarize the various protection mechanisms, show the password file, and give the code for each of the protected resources.

The Home Page

Listing 7.23 shows the top-level home page for the Web application. The application is registered with a URL prefix of */hotdotcom-internal* so the home page can be accessed with the URL *http://host/hotdotcom-internal/index.jsp* as shown in Figure 7–15. If you've forgotten how to assign URL prefixes to Web applications, review Section 4.1 (Registering Web Applications).

Now, the main home page has no security protections and consequently does not absolutely require an entry in *web.xml*. However, many users expect URLs that list a directory but no file to invoke the default file from that directory. So, I put a welcome-file-list entry in *web.xml* (see Listing 7.24 in the next section) to ensure that *http://host/hotdotcom-internal/* invokes *index.jsp*.

Listing 7.23 *index.jsp* (Top-level home page)

```
<!DOCTYPE HTML PUBLIC "-//W3C//DTD HTML 4.0 Transitional//EN">
<HTML>
<HEAD>
<TITLE>hot-dot-com.com!</TITLE>
<LINK REL=STYLESHEET
      HREF="company-styles.css"
      TYPE="text/css">
</HEAD>
<BODY>
<TABLE BORDER=5 ALIGN="CENTER">
  <TR><TH CLASS="TITLE">hot-dot-com.com!</TABLE>
<P>
<H3>Welcome to the hot-dot-com intranet</H3>
Please select one of the following:
<UL>
  <LI><A HREF="financial-plan.html">Financial Plan</A>.
      Available to all employees.
  <LI><A HREF="business-plan.html">Business Plan</A>.
      Available only to corporate executives.
  <LI><A HREF="employee-pay.jsp">Employee Compensation Plans</A>.
      Available to all employees.
</UL>
</BODY>
</HTML>
```

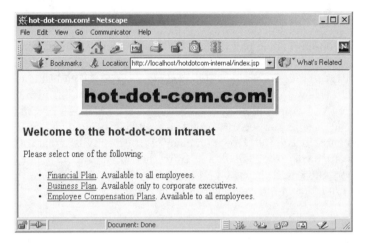

Figure 7–15   Home page for the hot-dot-com.com intranet.

The Deployment Descriptor

Listing 7.24 shows the complete deployment descriptor used with the `hotdot-com-internal` Web application. Again, remember that the order of the sub-elements within the `web-app` element of *web.xml* is not arbitrary—you must use the standard ordering. For details, see Section 5.2 (The Order of Elements within the Deployment Descriptor).

The deployment descriptor specifies several things:

- URLs that give a directory but no filename result in the server first trying to use *index.jsp* and next trying *index.html*. If neither file is available, the result is server specific (e.g., a directory listing).

- URLs that use the default servlet mapping (i.e., *http://host/hotdotcom/servlet/ServletName*) are redirected to the main home page.

- The *financial-plan.html* page can be accessed only by company employees or executives.

- The *business-plan.html* page can be accessed only by company executives.

Listing 7.24	*WEB-INF/web.xml* (Complete version for *hot-dot-com.com* intranet)

```xml
<?xml version="1.0" encoding="ISO-8859-1"?>
<!DOCTYPE web-app PUBLIC
    "-//Sun Microsystems, Inc.//DTD Web Application 2.2//EN"
    "http://java.sun.com/j2ee/dtds/web-app_2_2.dtd">

<web-app>
  <!-- A servlet that redirects users to the home page. -->
  <servlet>
    <servlet-name>Redirector</servlet-name>
    <servlet-class>hotdotcom.RedirectorServlet</servlet-class>
  </servlet>

  <!-- Turn off invoker. Send requests to index.jsp. -->
  <servlet-mapping>
    <servlet-name>Redirector</servlet-name>
    <url-pattern>/servlet/*</url-pattern>
  </servlet-mapping>

  <!-- If URL gives a directory but no filename, try index.jsp
       first and index.html second. If neither is found,
       the result is server specific (e.g., a directory
       listing). -->
  <welcome-file-list>
    <welcome-file>index.jsp</welcome-file>
    <welcome-file>index.html</welcome-file>
  </welcome-file-list>

  <!-- Protect financial plan. Employees or executives. -->
  <security-constraint>
    <web-resource-collection>
      <web-resource-name>Financial Plan</web-resource-name>
      <url-pattern>/financial-plan.html</url-pattern>
    </web-resource-collection>
    <auth-constraint>
      <role-name>employee</role-name>
      <role-name>executive</role-name>
    </auth-constraint>
  </security-constraint>
```

Listing 7.24	*WEB-INF/web.xml* (Complete version for *hot-dot-com.com* intranet) *(continued)*

```
<!-- Protect business plan. Executives only. -->
<security-constraint>
  <web-resource-collection>
    <web-resource-name>Business Plan</web-resource-name>
    <url-pattern>/business-plan.html</url-pattern>
  </web-resource-collection>
  <auth-constraint>
    <role-name>executive</role-name>
  </auth-constraint>
</security-constraint>

<!-- Tell the server to use BASIC authentication. -->
<login-config>
  <auth-method>BASIC</auth-method>
  <realm-name>Intranet</realm-name>
</login-config>
</web-app>
```

The Password File

Password files are not specific to Web applications; they are general to the server. Listing 7.25 shows the password file used by Tomcat for this Web application. It defines three new users: `gates` and `ellison` in the `employee` role and `mcnealy` in the `executive` role.

Listing 7.25	*install_dir/conf/tomcat-users.xml* (Three new users)

```
<?xml version="1.0" encoding="ISO-8859-1"?>
<tomcat-users>
  <user name="john" password="nhoj"
        roles="registered-user" />
  <user name="jane" password="enaj"
        roles="registered-user" />
  <user name="juan" password="nauj"
        roles="administrator" />
  <user name="juana" password="anauj"
        roles="administrator,registered-user" />
  <user name="gates" password="llib"
        roles="employee" />
  <user name="ellison" password="yrral"
        roles="employee" />
  <user name="mcnealy" password="ttocs"
        roles="executive" />
</tomcat-users>
```

The Financial Plan

Listing 7.26 shows the first of the protected pages at the `hotdotcom-internal` site. Figure 7–16 shows the dialog box presented by Netscape to unauthenticated users who attempt to access the page. Figures 7–17 and 7–18 show unsuccessful and successful login attempts, respectively.

Listing 7.26	*financial-plan.html*

```
<!DOCTYPE HTML PUBLIC "-//W3C//DTD HTML 4.0 Transitional//EN">
<HTML>
<HEAD>
<TITLE>Financial Plan</TITLE>
<LINK REL=STYLESHEET
      HREF="company-styles.css"
      TYPE="text/css">
</HEAD>
<BODY>
<TABLE BORDER=5 ALIGN="CENTER">
  <TR><TH CLASS="TITLE">Financial Plan</TABLE>
<P>
<H3>Steps:</H3>
<OL>
  <LI>Make lots of money.
  <LI>Increase value of stock options.
  <LI>Make more money.
  <LI>Increase stock option value further.
</OL>
</BODY>
</HTML>
```

Figure 7–16 Unauthenticated users who attempt to access protected resources are presented with a dialog box.

Figure 7–17   A failed login attempt.

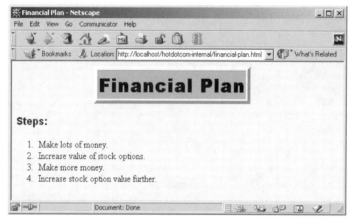

Figure 7–18   A successful login attempt.

The Business Plan

The financial plan of the previous section is available to all employees and executives. The business plan (Listing 7.27), in contrast, is available only to executives. Thus, it is possible for an authenticated user to be denied access to it. Figure 7–19 shows this result. OK, so you have access to more than one username/password combination. You were authenticated as a user with restricted privileges. You now want to log in as a user with additional privileges. How do you do so? Unfortunately, the answer is: quit the browser and restart. Boo. That's one of the downsides of BASIC authentication.

Figure 7–20 shows the result after the browser is restarted and the client logs in as a user in the `executive` role (`mcnealy` in this case).

Listing 7.27	*business-plan.html*

```
<!DOCTYPE HTML PUBLIC "-//W3C//DTD HTML 4.0 Transitional//EN">
<HTML>
<HEAD>
<TITLE>Business Plan</TITLE>
<LINK REL=STYLESHEET
      HREF="company-styles.css"
      TYPE="text/css">
</HEAD>
<BODY>
<TABLE BORDER=5 ALIGN="CENTER">
  <TR><TH CLASS="TITLE">Business Plan</TABLE>
<P>
<H3>Steps:</H3>
<OL>
  <LI>Inflate name recognition by buying meaningless ads
      on high-profile TV shows.
  <LI>Decrease employee pay by promising stock options instead.
  <LI>Increase executive pay with lots of perks and bonuses.
  <LI>Get bought out before anyone notices we have no
      business plan.
</OL>
</BODY>
</HTML>
```

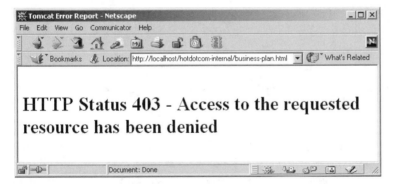

Figure 7–19 Attempt to access the business plan by an authenticated user who is not in the `executive` role. This result is different from that of failed authentication, which is shown in Figure 7–17.

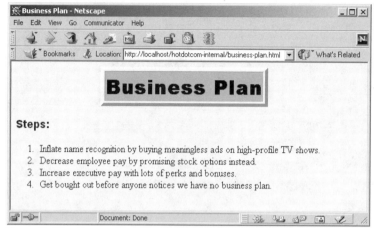

Figure 7–20 Attempt to access the business plan by an authenticated user who is in the `executive` role.

The Redirector Servlet

As it currently stands, the `hotdotcom-internal` application has no protected servlets. So, it is not absolutely necessary to disable the invoker servlet and redirect requests that are sent to *http://host/hotdotcom-internal/servlet/something*. However, it is a good idea to plan ahead and disable the invoker servlet as a matter of course in *all* Web applications that have restricted resources.

This application uses the same redirector servlet (Listing 7.19) and `url-pattern` entry in *web.xml* (Listing 7.24) as does the external `hotdotcom` application.

7.5 Configuring Tomcat to Use SSL

Servlet and JSP containers are not required to support SSL, even in fully J2EE-compliant application servers or with version 2.3 of the servlet specification. Of the three servers that are free for development use and are most commonly discussed throughout the book (Tomcat, JRun, and ServletExec), only Tomcat can directly support SSL. With JRun and ServletExec, traffic between the client and the Web server can be encrypted with SSL, but local communication between the Web server and the JRun or ServletExec plugin does not use SSL. So, Web applications that rely on SSL are not necessarily portable.

Nevertheless, SSL is extremely useful, and many applications make use of it. For example, many application servers are self-contained; they do not have a servlet/JSP plugin that is separate from the main Web server. In addition, some server plugins use SSL even for the communication between the Web server and the plugin. The BEA WebLogic plugin and IBM WebSphere support this very useful capability, for example.

Even with Tomcat, the default configuration lacks SSL support; you have to install some extra packages to add this support. This section summarizes the steps necessary to do so. For more details, see *http://jakarta.apache.org/tomcat/tomcat-4.0-doc/ssl-howto.html*.

1. **Download the Java Secure Socket Extension (JSSE).** Obtain it from *http://java.sun.com/products/jsse/index-102.html*. Note that this step is unnecessary if you are using JDK 1.4 or later; JSSE is integrated into the JDK in such case.

2. **Put the JSSE JAR files in Tomcat's `CLASSPATH`.** JSSE consists of three JAR files: *jcert.jar, jnet.jar,* and *jsse.jar*. The server needs access to all of them. The easiest way to accomplish this step is to put the JAR files into *jdk_install_dir/jre/lib/ext*, thereby making JSSE an installed extension. Note that the Tomcat documentation describes another approach: setting the `JSSE_HOME` environment variable. As of Tomcat 4.0, this approach fails because of a bug in the way Tomcat processes the variable (Tomcat erroneously looks for *jsse.jar* in *JSSE_HOME* instead of *JSSE_HOME/lib*).

3. **Create a self-signed public key certificate.** SSL-based servers use X509 certificates to validate to clients that they are who they claim to be. This prevents attackers from hacking DNS servers to redirect SSL requests to their site. For real-world use, the certificate needs to be signed by a trusted authority like Verisign. For testing purposes, however, a self-signed certificate is sufficient. To generate one that will be valid for two years (730 days), execute the following:

```
keytool -genkey -alias tomcat -keyalg RSA -validity 730
```

   The system will prompt you for a variety of information starting with your first and last name. For a server certificate, this should be the server's name, not your name! For example, with a server that will be accessed from multiple machines, respond with the hostname (*www.yourcompany.com*) or the IP address (*207.46.230.220*) when asked "What is your first and last name?" For a development server that will run on your desktop, use *localhost*. Remember that, for deployment purposes, self-signed certificates are not sufficient. You would need to get your certificate signed by a trusted Certificate Authority. You can use certificates from `keytool` for this purpose also; it just requires a lot more work. For testing purposes, however, self-signed certificates are just as good as trusted ones.

Core Approach

Supply the server's hostname or IP address when asked for your first and last name. Use localhost *for a desktop development server.*

The system will also prompt you for your organization, your location, a keystore password, and a key password. Be sure to use the same value for both passwords. The system will then create a file called *.keystore* in your home directory (e.g., */home/username* on Unix or *C:\Documents and Settings\username* on Windows 2000). You can also use the -keystore argument to change where this file is created.

For more details on keytool (including information on creating trusted certificates that are signed by a standard Certificate Authority), see *http://java.sun.com/j2se/1.3/docs/tooldocs/win32/keytool.html*.

4. **Copy the keystore file to the Tomcat installation directory.** Copy the *.keystore* file just created from your home directory to *tomcat_install_dir*.

5. **Uncomment and edit the SSL connector entry in** *tomcat_install_dir/conf/server.xml*. Look for a commented-out Connector element that encloses a Factory element referring to the SSLServerSocketFactory class. Remove the enclosing comment tags (<!--...-->). Change the port from 8443 to the default SSL value of 443. Add a keystoreFile attribute to Factory designating the name of the keystore file. Add a keystorePass attribute to Factory designating the password. Here is an example (class names shortened and line breaks added for readability).

```
<Connector className="...http.HttpConnector"
        port="443" minProcessors="5"
        maxProcessors="75" enableLookups="true"
        acceptCount="10" debug="0"
        scheme="https" secure="true">
  <Factory className="...net.SSLServerSocketFactory"
        clientAuth="false" protocol="TLS"
        keystoreFile=".keystore"
        keystorePass="your-password"/>
</Connector>
```

6. **Change the main connector entry in** *tomcat_install_dir/conf/*
   server.xml **to use port 443 for SSL redirects.** Use the `redirect-`
   `Port` attribute to specify this. Here is an example.

```
<Connector className="...http.HttpConnector"
           port="80" minProcessors="5" maxProcessors="75"
           enableLookups="true" redirectPort="443"
           acceptCount="10" debug="0"
           connectionTimeout="60000"/>
```

7. **Restart the server.**
8. **Access https://localhost/.** (Note that this URL starts with *https*, not
   http.) With Netscape, you should see initial warnings like those of Figures 7–21 through 7–25. Once you have accepted the certificate, you
   should see the Tomcat home page (Figure 7–26). With Internet
   Explorer, you will see an initial warning like that of Figure 7–27. For
   future requests, you can suppress the warnings by viewing and importing the certificate (Figures 7–28 and 7–29).

Figure 7–21 First new-certificate window supplied by Netscape.

Figure 7–22   Second new-certificate window supplied by Netscape. Self-signed certificates are for testing purposes only.

Figure 7–23   Third new-certificate window supplied by Netscape. By choosing to accept the certificate permanently you suppress future warnings.

Figure 7–24 Fourth new-certificate window supplied by Netscape.

Figure 7–25 Fifth new-certificate window supplied by Netscape.

Figure 7–26 A successful attempt to access the Tomcat home page using SSL.

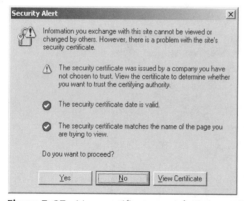

Figure 7–27 New-certificate page for Internet Explorer. View and import the certificate to suppress future warnings. Again, self-signed certificates would not be trusted in real-world applications; they are for testing purposes only.

Figure 7–28 Result of choosing View Certificate in Internet Explorer's new-certificate page.

Figure 7–29 Importing self-signed certificates in Internet Explorer lets you suppress warnings that the certificate comes from a company that you have not chosen to trust.

PROGRAMMATIC SECURITY

Topics in This Chapter

- Combining container-managed and programmatic security
- Using the `isUserInRole` method
- Using the `getRemoteUser` method
- Using the `getUserPrincipal` method
- Programmatically controlling all aspects of security
- Using SSL with programmatic security

Chapter 8

Chapter 7 introduced two fundamental aspects of Web application security:

1. **Preventing unauthorized users from accessing sensitive data.**
   This process involves *access restriction* (identifying which resources
   need protection and who should have access to them) and *authentication* (identifying the user to determine if they are one of the authorized ones). This aspect applies to virtually all secure applications;
   even intranets at locations with physical access controls usually require
   some sort of user authentication.
2. **Preventing attackers from stealing network data while it is in
   transit.** This process involves the use of Secure Sockets Layer (SSL)
   to encrypt the traffic between the browser and the server. This capability is generally reserved for particularly sensitive applications or
   particularly sensitive pages within a larger application.

There are two general strategies for implementing these security aspects: *declarative security* and *programmatic security.*

With declarative security, the topic of the previous chapter, none of the individual servlets or JSP pages need any security-aware code. Instead, both of the major
security aspects are handled by the server. To prevent unauthorized access, you use
the Web application deployment descriptor (*web.xml*) to declare that certain URLs
need protection. You also designate the authentication method that the server
should use to identify users. At request time, the server automatically prompts users
for usernames and passwords when they try to access restricted resources, automat-

ically checks the results against a predefined set of usernames and passwords, and automatically keeps track of which users have previously been authenticated. This process is completely transparent to the servlets and JSP pages. To safeguard network data, you use the deployment descriptor to stipulate that certain URLs should only be accessible with SSL. If users try to use a regular HTTP connection to access one of these URLs, the server automatically redirects them to the HTTPS (SSL) equivalent.

Declarative security is all well and good. In fact, it is by far the most common approach to Web application security. But, what if you want your servlets to be completely independent of any server-specific settings such as password files? Or, what if you want to let users in various roles access a particular resource but customize the data depending on the role that they are in? Or, what if you want to authenticate users other than by requiring an exact match from a fixed set of usernames and passwords? That's where programmatic security comes in.

With programmatic security, the topic of this chapter, protected servlets and JSP pages at least partially manage their own security. To prevent unauthorized access, each servlet or JSP page must either authenticate the user or verify that the user has been authenticated previously. Even after the servlet or JSP page grants access to a user, it can still customize the results for different individual users or categories of users. To safeguard network data, each servlet or JSP page has to check the network protocol used to access it. If users try to use a regular HTTP connection to access one of these URLs, the servlet or JSP page must manually redirect them to the HTTPS (SSL) equivalent.

8.1   Combining Container-Managed and Programmatic Security

Declarative security is very convenient: you set up usernames, passwords, access mechanisms (HTML forms vs. BASIC authentication) and transport-layer requirements (SSL vs. normal HTTP), all without putting any security-related code in any of the individual servlets or JSP pages. However, declarative security provides only two levels of access for each resource: allowed and denied. Declarative security provides no options to permit resources to customize their output depending on the username or role of the client that accesses them.

It would be nice to provide this customization without giving up the convenience of container-managed security for the usernames, passwords, and roles as would be required if a servlet or JSP page completely managed its own security (as in Section 8.3). To support this type of hybrid security, the servlet specification provides three methods in `HttpServletRequest`:

- **isUserInRole.** This method determines if the currently authenticated user belongs to a specified role. For example, given the usernames, passwords, and roles of Listings 7.1 and 7.2 (Section 7.1), if the client has successfully logged in as user `valjean`, the following two expressions would return `true`.

  ```
  request.isUserInRole("lowStatus")
  request.isUserInRole("nobleSpirited")
  ```

  Tests for all other roles would return `false`. If no user is currently authenticated (e.g., if authorization failed or if `isUserInRole` is called from an unrestricted page and the user has not yet accessed a restricted page), `isUserInRole` returns `false`. In addition to the standard security roles given in the password file, you can use the `security-role-ref` element to define aliases for the standard roles. See the next subsection for details.
- **getRemoteUser.** This method returns the name of the current user. For example, if the client has successfully logged in as user `valjean`, `request.getRemoteUser()` would return `"valjean"`. If no user is currently authenticated (e.g., if authorization failed or if `isUserInRole` is called from an unrestricted page and the user has not yet accessed a restricted page), `getRemoteUser` returns `null`.
- **getUserPrincipal.** This method returns the current username wrapped inside a `java.security.Principal` object. The `Principal` object contains little information beyond the username (available with the `getName` method). So, the main reason for using `getUserPrincipal` in lieu of `getRemoteUser` is to be compatible with preexisting security code (the `Principal` class is not specific to the servlet and JSP API and has been part of the Java platform since version 1.1). If no user is currently authenticated, `getUserPrincipal` returns `null`.

It is important to note that this type of programmatic security does not negate the benefits of container-managed security. With this approach, you can still set up usernames, passwords, and roles by using your server's mechanisms. You still use the `login-config` element to tell the server whether you are using form-based or BASIC authentication. If you choose form-based authentication, you still use an HTML form with an `ACTION` of `j_security_check`, a textfield named `j_username`, and a password field named `j_password`. Unauthenticated users are still automatically sent to the page containing this form, and the server still automatically keeps track of which users have been authenticated. You still use the `security-constraint` element to designate the URLs to which the access restrictions apply. You still use the `user-data-constraint` element to specify that certain URLs require SSL. For details on all of these topics, see Section 7.1.

Security Role References

The security-role-ref subelement of servlet lets you define servlet-specific synonyms for existing role names. This element should contain three possible subelements: description (optional descriptive text), role-name (the new synonym), and role-link (the existing security role).

For instance, suppose that you are creating an online bookstore and your server's password file stipulates that user marty is in role author. However, you want to reuse a servlet of type BookInfo (in the catalog package) that was created elsewhere. The problem is that this servlet calls the role writer, not author. Rather than modifying the password file, you can use security-role-ref to provide writer as an alias for author.

Suppose further that you have a servlet of class EmployeeData (in the hr package) that provides one type of information to a goodguy and another type to a meanie. You want to use this servlet with the password file defined in Listings 7.1 and 7.2 (Section 7.1) that assign users to the nobleSpirited and meanSpirited roles. To accomplish this task, you can use security-role-ref to say that isUserInRole("goodguy") should return true for the same users that isUserInRole("nobleSpirited") already would. Similarly, you can use security-role-ref to say that isUserInRole("meanie") should return true for the same users that isUserInRole("meanSpirited") would.

Listing 8.1 shows a deployment descriptor that accomplishes both of these tasks.

Listing 8.1   *web.xml* (Excerpt illustrating security role aliases)

```xml
<?xml version="1.0" encoding="ISO-8859-1"?>
<!DOCTYPE web-app PUBLIC
    "-//Sun Microsystems, Inc.//DTD Web Application 2.2//EN"
    "http://java.sun.com/j2ee/dtds/web-app_2_2.dtd">

<web-app>
  <!-- ... -->
  <servlet>
    <servlet-name>BookInformation</servlet-name>
    <servlet-class>catalog.BookInfo</servlet-class>
    <security-role-ref>
      <role-name>writer</role-name> <!-- New alias. -->
      <role-link>author</role-link> <!-- Preexisting role. -->
    </security-role-ref>
  </servlet>
```

| Listing 8.1 | *web.xml* (Excerpt illustrating security role aliases) *(continued)* |

```
<servlet>
  <servlet-name>EmployeeInformation</servlet-name>
  <servlet-class>hr.EmployeeData</servlet-class>
  <security-role-ref>
    <role-name>goodguy</role-name>          <!-- New. -->
    <role-link>nobleSpirited</role-link> <!-- Preexisting. -->
  </security-role-ref>
  <security-role-ref>
    <role-name>meanie</role-name>           <!-- New. -->
    <role-link>meanSpirited</role-link> <!-- Preexisting. -->
  </security-role-ref>
</servlet>
<!-- ... -->
<security-constraint>...</security-constraint>
<login-config>...</login-config>
<!-- ... -->
</web-app>
```

8.2 Example: Combining Container-Managed and Programmatic Security

Listing 8.2 presents a JSP page that augments the internal Web site for hot-dot-com.com that is introduced in Section 7.4. The page shows plans for employee pay. Because of entries in *web.xml* (Listing 8.3), the page can be accessed only by users in the employee or executive roles. Although both groups can access the page, they see substantially different results. In particular, the planned pay scales for executives is hidden from the normal employees.

Figure 8–1 shows the page when it is accessed by user gates or ellison (both in the employee role; see Listing 7.25). Figure 8–2 shows the page when it is accessed by user mcnealy (in the executive role). Remember that BASIC security provides no simple mechanism for changing your username once you are validated (see Section 7.3). So, for example, switching from user gates to user mcnealy requires you to quit and restart your browser.

Listing 8.2 *employee-pay.jsp*

```
<!DOCTYPE HTML PUBLIC "-//W3C//DTD HTML 4.0 Transitional//EN">
<HTML>
<HEAD>
<TITLE>Compensation Plans</TITLE>
<LINK REL=STYLESHEET
      HREF="company-styles.css"
      TYPE="text/css">
</HEAD>
<BODY>
<TABLE BORDER=5 ALIGN="CENTER">
  <TR><TH CLASS="TITLE">Compensation Plans</TABLE>
<P>
Due to temporary financial difficulties, we are scaling
back our very generous plans for salary increases. Don't
worry, though: your valuable stock options more than
compensate for any small drops in direct salary.

<H3>Regular Employees</H3>
Pay for median-level employee (Master's degree, eight year's
experience):
<UL>
  <LI><B>2002:</B> $50,000.
  <LI><B>2003:</B> $30,000.
  <LI><B>2004:</B> $25,000.
  <LI><B>2005:</B> $20,000.
</UL>

<% if (request.isUserInRole("executive")) { %>
<H3>Executives</H3>
Median pay for corporate executives:
<UL>
  <LI><B>2002:</B> $500,000.
  <LI><B>2003:</B> $600,000.
  <LI><B>2004:</B> $700,000.
  <LI><B>2005:</B> $800,000.
</UL>
<% } %>
</BODY>
</HTML>
```

Listing 8.3	*web.xml* (For augmented hotdotcom intranet)

```xml
<?xml version="1.0" encoding="ISO-8859-1"?>
<!DOCTYPE web-app PUBLIC
    "-//Sun Microsystems, Inc.//DTD Web Application 2.2//EN"
    "http://java.sun.com/j2ee/dtds/web-app_2_2.dtd">

<web-app>
  <!-- A servlet that redirects users to the home page. -->
  <servlet>
    <servlet-name>Redirector</servlet-name>
    <servlet-class>hotdotcom.RedirectorServlet</servlet-class>
  </servlet>

  <!-- Turn off invoker. Send requests to index.jsp. -->
  <servlet-mapping>
    <servlet-name>Redirector</servlet-name>
    <url-pattern>/servlet/*</url-pattern>
  </servlet-mapping>

  <!-- If URL gives a directory but no filename, try index.jsp
       first and index.html second. If neither is found,
       the result is server specific (e.g., a directory
       listing). -->
  <welcome-file-list>
    <welcome-file>index.jsp</welcome-file>
    <welcome-file>index.html</welcome-file>
  </welcome-file-list>

  <!-- Protect financial plan. Employees or executives. -->
  <security-constraint>
    <web-resource-collection>
      <web-resource-name>Financial Plan</web-resource-name>
      <url-pattern>/financial-plan.html</url-pattern>
    </web-resource-collection>
    <auth-constraint>
      <role-name>employee</role-name>
      <role-name>executive</role-name>
    </auth-constraint>
  </security-constraint>
```

| Listing 8.3 | *web.xml* (For augmented hotdotcom intranet) *(continued)* |

```
<!-- Protect business plan. Executives only. -->
<security-constraint>
  <web-resource-collection>
    <web-resource-name>Business Plan</web-resource-name>
    <url-pattern>/business-plan.html</url-pattern>
  </web-resource-collection>
  <auth-constraint>
    <role-name>executive</role-name>
  </auth-constraint>
</security-constraint>

<!-- Protect compensation plan. Employees or executives. -->
<security-constraint>
  <web-resource-collection>
    <web-resource-name>Compensation Plan</web-resource-name>
    <url-pattern>/employee-pay.jsp</url-pattern>
  </web-resource-collection>
  <auth-constraint>
    <role-name>employee</role-name>
    <role-name>executive</role-name>
  </auth-constraint>
</security-constraint>

<!-- Tell the server to use BASIC authentication. -->
<login-config>
  <auth-method>BASIC</auth-method>
  <realm-name>Intranet</realm-name>
</login-config>
</web-app>
```

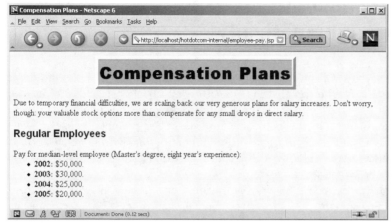

Figure 8–1   The *employee-pay.jsp* page when accessed by a user who is in the `employee` role.

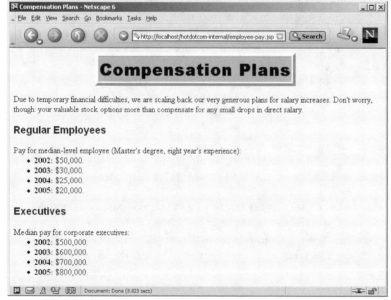

Figure 8–2   The *employee-pay.jsp* page when accessed by a user who is in the `executive` role.

8.3   Handling All Security Programmatically

Declarative security (Chapter 7) offers a number of advantages to the developer. Chief among them is the fact that individual servlets and JSP pages need no security-conscious code: the container (server) handles authentication in a manner that is completely transparent to the individual resources. For example, you can switch from form-based authentication to BASIC authentication or from regular HTTP connections to encrypted HTTPS connections, all without any changes to the individual servlets or JSP pages.

Even when you want a bit more control than just "access allowed" or "access denied," it is convenient to let the server maintain and process the usernames and passwords, as discussed in Section 8.1.

However, the convenience of container-managed security comes at a price: it requires a server-specific component. The method for setting up usernames, passwords, and user roles is not standardized and thus is not portable across different servers. In most situations, this disadvantage is outweighed by the faster and simpler servlet and JSP development process that results from leaving some or all of the authorization tasks to the server. In some cases, however, you might want a servlet or JSP page to be entirely self-contained with no dependencies on server-specific settings or even *web.xml* entries. Although this approach requires a lot more work, it means that the servlet or JSP page can be ported from server to server with much less effort than with container-managed security. Furthermore, it lets the servlet or JSP page use username and password schemes other than an exact match to a pre-configured list.

HTTP supports two varieties of authentication: BASIC and DIGEST. Few browsers support DIGEST, so I'll concentrate on BASIC here.

Here is a summary of the steps involved for BASIC authorization.

1. **Check whether there is an `Authorization` request header.**
   If there is no such header, go to Step 5.
2. **Get the encoded username/password string.** If there is an `Authorization` header, it should have the following form:

   `Authorization: Basic encodedData`

   Skip over the word `Basic`—the remaining part is the username and password represented in base64 encoding.
3. **Reverse the base64 encoding of the username/password string.**
   Use the `decodeBuffer` method of the `BASE64Decoder` class. This method call results in a string of the form `username:password`. The `BASE64Decoder` class is bundled with the JDK; in JDK 1.3 it can be found in the `sun.misc` package in *jdk_install_dir/jre/lib/rt.jar*.

4. **Check the username and password.** The most common approach is to use a database or a file to obtain the real usernames and passwords. For simple cases, it is also possible to place the password information directly in the servlet. In such a case, remember that access to the servlet source code or class file provides access to the passwords. If the incoming username and password match one of the reference username/password pairs, return the page. If not, go to Step 5. With this approach you can provide your own definition of "match." With container-managed security, you cannot.

5. **When authentication fails, send the appropriate response to the client.** Return a 401 (Unauthorized) response code and a header of the following form:

```
WWW-Authenticate: BASIC realm="some-name"
```

This response instructs the browser to pop up a dialog box telling the user to enter a name and password for some-name, then to reconnect with that username and password embedded in a single base64 string inside the Authorization header.

If you care about the details, base64 encoding is explained in RFC 1521. To retrieve RFCs, start at *http://www.rfc-editor.org/* to get a current list of the RFC archive sites. However, there are probably only two things you need to know about base64 encoding.

First, it is not intended to provide security, since the encoding can be easily reversed. So, base64 encoding does not obviate the need for SSL (see Section 7.5) to thwart attackers who might be able to snoop on your network connection (no easy task unless they are on your local subnet). SSL, or Secure Sockets Layer, is a variation of HTTP where the entire stream is encrypted. It is supported by many commercial servers and is generally invoked by use of *https* in the URL instead of *http*. Servlets can run on SSL servers just as easily as on standard servers, and the encryption and decryption are handled transparently before the servlets are invoked. See Sections 7.1 and 8.6 for examples.

The second point you should know about base64 encoding is that Sun provides the sun.misc.BASE64Decoder class, distributed with JDK 1.1 and later, to decode strings that were encoded with base64. In JDK 1.3 it can be found in the sun.misc package in *jdk_install_dir/jre/lib/rt.jar*. Just be aware that classes in the sun package hierarchy are not part of the official language specification and thus are not guaranteed to appear in all implementations. So, if you use this decoder class, make sure that you explicitly include the class file when you distribute your application. One possible approach is to make the class available to all Web applications on your server and then to explicitly record the fact that your applications depend on it. For details on this process, see Section 4.4 (Recording Dependencies on Server Libraries).

8.4 Example: Handling All Security Programmatically

Listing 8.4 shows a servlet that generates hot stock recommendations. If it were made freely available on the Web, it would put half the financial advisors out of business. So, it needs to be password protected, available only to people who have paid the very reasonable $2000 access fee.

Furthermore, the servlet needs to be as portable as possible because ISPs keep shutting it down (they claim fraud, but no doubt they are really being pressured by the financial services companies that the servlet outperforms). So, it uses complete programmatic security and is entirely self-contained: absolutely no changes or server-specific customizations are required to move the servlet from system to system.

Finally, requiring an exact match against a static list of usernames and passwords (as is required in container-managed security) is too limiting for this application. So, the servlet uses a custom algorithm (see the `areEqualReversed` method) for determining if an incoming username and password are legal.

Figure 8–3 shows what happens when the user first tries to access the servlet. Figure 8–4 shows the result of a failed authorization attempt; Figure 8–5 shows what happens if the user gives up at that point. Figure 8–6 shows the result of successful authorization.

Listing 8.4 *StockTip.java*

```java
package stocks;

import java.io.*;
import javax.servlet.*;
import javax.servlet.http.*;
import sun.misc.BASE64Decoder;

/** Servlet that gives very hot stock tips. So hot that
 *  only authorized users (presumably ones who have paid
 *  the steep financial advisory fee) can access the servlet.
 */

public class StockTip extends HttpServlet {

  /** Denies access to all users except those who know
   *  the secret username/password combination.
   */
```

| Listing 8.4 | *StockTip.java (continued)* |

```java
public void doGet(HttpServletRequest request,
                  HttpServletResponse response)
    throws ServletException, IOException {
  String authorization = request.getHeader("Authorization");
  if (authorization == null) {
    askForPassword(response);
  } else {
    // Authorization headers looks like "Basic blahblah",
    // where blahblah is the base64 encoded username and
    // password. We want the part after "Basic ".
    String userInfo = authorization.substring(6).trim();
    BASE64Decoder decoder = new BASE64Decoder();
    String nameAndPassword =
      new String(decoder.decodeBuffer(userInfo));
    // Decoded part looks like "username:password".
    int index = nameAndPassword.indexOf(":");
    String user = nameAndPassword.substring(0, index);
    String password = nameAndPassword.substring(index+1);
    // High security: username must be reverse of password.
    if (areEqualReversed(user, password)) {
      showStock(request, response);
    } else {
      askForPassword(response);
    }
  }
}

// Show a Web page giving the symbol of the next hot stock.

private void showStock(HttpServletRequest request,
                       HttpServletResponse response)
    throws ServletException, IOException {
      response.setContentType("text/html");
  PrintWriter out = response.getWriter();
  String docType =
    "<!DOCTYPE HTML PUBLIC \"-//W3C//DTD HTML 4.0 " +
    "Transitional//EN\">\n";
  out.println(docType +
              "<HTML>\n" +
              "<HEAD><TITLE>Hot Stock Tip!</TITLE></HEAD>\n" +
              "<BODY BGCOLOR=\"#FDF5E6\">\n" +
              "<H1>Today's Hot Stock:");
```

Listing 8.4 *StockTip.java (continued)*

```java
      for(int i=0; i<3; i++) {
        out.print(randomLetter());
      }
      out.println("</H1>\n" +
                  "</BODY></HTML>");
  }

  // If no Authorization header was supplied in the request.

  private void askForPassword(HttpServletResponse response) {
    response.setStatus(response.SC_UNAUTHORIZED); // I.e., 401
    response.setHeader("WWW-Authenticate",
                       "BASIC realm=\"Insider-Trading\"");
  }

  // Returns true if s1 is the reverse of s2.
  // Empty strings don't count.

  private boolean areEqualReversed(String s1, String s2) {
    s2 = (new StringBuffer(s2)).reverse().toString();
    return((s1.length() > 0) && s1.equals(s2));
  }

  private final String ALPHABET = "ABCDEFGHIJKLMNOPQRSTUVWXYZ";

  // Returns a random number from 0 to n-1 inclusive.

  private int randomInt(int n) {
    return((int)(Math.random() * n));
  }

  // A random letter from the alphabet.

  private char randomLetter() {
    return(ALPHABET.charAt(randomInt(ALPHABET.length())));
  }
}
```

Figure 8–3 When the browser first receives the 401 (Unauthorized) status code, it opens a dialog box to collect the username and password.

Figure 8–4 When the browser receives the 401 (Unauthorized) status code on later attempts, it indicates that authorization failed. Netscape 6 and Internet Explorer indicate authorization failure by showing the original dialog box with the previously entered username and an empty password field.

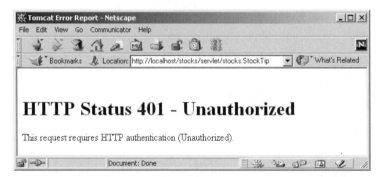

Figure 8–5 Result of cancelled authorization attempt with Tomcat—Tomcat returns an error page along with the 401 (Unauthorized) status code. JRun and ServletExec omit the error page in this case.

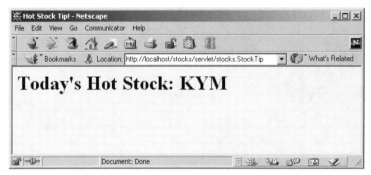

Figure 8–6   Result of successful authorization attempt. Invest now!

8.5   Using Programmatic Security with SSL

SSL can be used with security that is entirely servlet managed, just as it can be with container-managed security (see Section 7.1). As is typical with servlet-managed security, this approach is more portable but requires significantly more effort.

The use of SSL in programmatic security may require one or more of the following capabilities not needed in normal programmatic security.

- Determining if SSL is in use.
- Redirecting non-SSL requests.
- Discovering the number of bits in the key.
- Looking up the encryption algorithm.
- Accessing client X509 certificates.

Details on these capabilities follow.

Determining If SSL Is in Use

The `ServletRequest` interface provides two methods that let you find out if SSL is in use. The `getScheme` method returns `"http"` for regular requests and `"https"` for SSL requests. The `isSecure` method returns `false` for regular requests and `true` for SSL requests.

Redirecting Non-SSL Requests

With container-managed security, you can use the `transport-guarantee` sub-element of `user-data-constraint` to ensure that the server redirects regular (*http*) requests to the SSL (*https*) equivalent. See Section 7.1 for details.

In programmatic security, you might want to explicitly do what the server automatically does with container-managed security. Once you have a URL, redirection is straightforward: use `response.sendRedirect` (Section 2.7).

The difficulty is in generating the URL in the first place. Unfortunately, there is no built-in method that says "give me the complete incoming URL with *http* changed to *https*." So, you have to call `request.getRequestURL` to get the main URL, change *http* to *https* manually, then tack on any form data by using `request.getQueryString`. You pass that result to `response.sendRedirect`.

Even this tedious manual approach runs some portability risks. For example: what if the server is running SSL on a port other than 443 (the default SSL port)? In such a case, the approach outlined here redirects to the wrong port. Unfortunately, there is no general solution to this problem; you simply have to know something about how the server is configured in order to redirect to a nonstandard SSL port. However, since you have to know that the server supports SSL in the first place, this additional burden is not too onerous.

Discovering the Number of Bits in the Key

Suppose that you have a servlet or JSP page that lets authorized users access your company's financial records. You might want to ensure that the most sensitive data is only sent to users that have the strongest (128-bit) level of encryption. Users whose browsers use comparatively weak 40-bit keys should be denied access. To accomplish this task, you need to be able to discover the level of encryption being used.

In version 2.3 of the servlet API, SSL requests automatically result in an attribute named `javax.servlet.request.key_size` being placed in the request object. You can access it by calling `request.getAttribute` with the specified name. The value is an `Integer` that tells you the length of the encryption key. However, since the return type of `getAttribute` is `Object`, you have to perform a typecast to `Integer`. In version 2.2 and earlier, there was no portable way to determine the key size. So, be sure to check if the result is `null` in order to handle non-SSL requests and SSL requests in servers compatible only with version 2.2 of the servlet API. Here is a simple example.

```
String keyAttribute = "javax.servlet.request.key_size";
Integer keySize =
  (Integer)request.getAttribute(keyAttribute);
if (keySize == null) { ... }
```

Looking Up the Encryption Algorithm

In version 2.3 of the servlet API, SSL requests also result in an attribute named `javax.servlet.request.cipher_suite` being placed in the request object. You can access it by calling `request.getAttribute` with the specified name. The value is a `String` that describes the encryption algorithm being used. However, since the return type of `getAttribute` is `Object`, you have to perform a typecast to `String`. Be sure to check if the result is `null` in order to handle non-SSL requests and SSL requests in servers compatible only with version 2.2 of the servlet API. Here is a simple example.

```
String cipherAttribute = "javax.servlet.request.cipher_suite";
String cipherSuite =
  (String)request.getAttribute(cipherAttribute);
if (cipherSuite == null) { ... }
```

Accessing Client X509 Certificates

Rather than using a simple username and password, some browsers permit users to authenticate themselves with X509 certificates. X509 certificates are discussed in RFC 1421. To retrieve RFCs, start at *http://www.rfc-editor.org/* to get a current list of the RFC archive sites.

If the client authenticates himself with an X509 certificate, that certificate is available by means of the `javax.servlet.request.X509Certificate` attribute of the request object. This attribute is available in both version 2.2 and 2.3 of the servlet API. The value is an object of type `java.security.cert.X509Certificate` that contains exhaustive information about the certificate. However, since the return type of `getAttribute` is `Object`, you have to perform a typecast to `X509Certificate`. Be sure to check if the result is `null` in order to handle non-SSL requests and SSL requests that include no certificate. A simple example follows.

```
String certAttribute = "javax.servlet.request.X509Certificate";
X509Certificate certificate =
  (X509Certificate)request.getAttribute(certAttribute);
if (certificate == null) { ... }
```

Once you have an X509 certificate, you can look up the issuer's distinguished name, the serial number, the raw signature value, the public key, and a number of other pieces of information. For details, see *http://java.sun.com/j2se/1.3/docs/api/java/security/cert/X509Certificate.html*.

8.6 Example: Programmatic Security and SSL

Listing 8.5 presents a servlet that redirects non-SSL requests to a URL that is identical to the URL of the original request except that *http* is changed to *https*. When an SSL request is received, the servlet presents a page that displays information on the URL, query data, key size, encryption algorithm, and client certificate. Figures 8–7 and 8–8 show the results.

In a real application, make sure that you redirect users when they access the servlet or JSP page that contains the form that *collects* the data. Once users submit sensitive data to an ordinary non-SSL URL, it is too late to redirect the request: attackers with access to the network traffic could have already obtained the data.

Listing 8.5 *SecurityInfo.java*

```java
package moreservlets;

import java.io.*;
import javax.servlet.*;
import javax.servlet.http.*;
import java.security.cert.*; // For X509Certificate

/** Servlet that prints information on SSL requests. Non-SSL
 *  requests get redirected to SSL.
 */

public class SecurityInfo extends HttpServlet {
  public void doGet(HttpServletRequest request,
                    HttpServletResponse response)
      throws ServletException, IOException {
    // Redirect non-SSL requests to the SSL equivalent.
    if (request.getScheme().equalsIgnoreCase("http")) {
      String origURL = request.getRequestURL().toString();
      String newURL = httpsURL(origURL);
      String formData = request.getQueryString();
      if (formData != null) {
        newURL = newURL + "?" + formData;
      }
      response.sendRedirect(newURL);
    } else {
      String currentURL = request.getRequestURL().toString();
      String formData = request.getQueryString();
```

Listing 8.5   *SecurityInfo.java (continued)*

```java
PrintWriter out = response.getWriter();
String docType =
  "<!DOCTYPE HTML PUBLIC \"-//W3C//DTD HTML 4.0 " +
  "Transitional//EN\">\n";
String title = "Security Info";
out.println
  (docType +
  "<HTML>\n" +
  "<HEAD><TITLE>" + title +
  "</TITLE></HEAD>\n" +
  "<BODY BGCOLOR=\"#FDF5E6\">\n" +
  "<H1>" + title + "</H1>\n" +
  "<UL>\n" +
  "  <LI>URL: " + currentURL + "\n" +
  "  <LI>Data: " + formData);
boolean isSecure = request.isSecure();
if (isSecure) {
  String keyAttribute =
    "javax.servlet.request.key_size";
  // Available only with servlets 2.3
  Integer keySize =
    (Integer)request.getAttribute(keyAttribute);
  String sizeString =
    replaceNull(keySize, "Unknown");
  String cipherAttribute =
    "javax.servlet.request.cipher_suite";
  // Available only with servlets 2.3
  String cipherSuite =
    (String)request.getAttribute(cipherAttribute);
  String cipherString =
    replaceNull(cipherSuite, "Unknown");
  String certAttribute =
    "javax.servlet.request.X509Certificate";
  // Available with servlets 2.2 and 2.3
  X509Certificate certificate =
    (X509Certificate)request.getAttribute(certAttribute);
  String certificateString =
    replaceNull(certificate, "None");
  out.println
    ("  <LI>SSL: true\n" +
    "  <UL>\n" +
    "    <LI>Key Size: " + sizeString + "\n" +
    "    <LI>Cipher Suite: " + cipherString + "\n" +
    "    <LI>Client Certificate: " +
    certificateString + "\n" +
    "  </UL>");
}
```

Listing 8.5	*SecurityInfo.java (continued)*

```java
    out.println
      ("</UL>\n" +
       "</BODY></HTML>");
  }
}

// Given http://blah, return https://blah.

private String httpsURL(String origURL) {
  int index = origURL.indexOf(":");
  StringBuffer newURL = new StringBuffer(origURL);
  newURL.insert(index, 's');
  return(newURL.toString());
}

// If the first argument is null, return the second argument.
// Otherwise, convert first argument to a String and
// return that String.

private String replaceNull(Object obj, String fallback) {
  if (obj == null) {
    return(fallback);
  } else {
    return(obj.toString());
  }
}
}
```

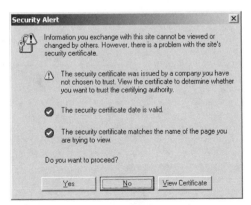

Figure 8–7 New-certificate page for Internet Explorer. View and import the certificate to suppress future warnings. For details on creating self-signed certificates for use with Tomcat, see Section 7.5. Again, self-signed certificates would not be trusted in real-world applications; they are for testing purposes only.

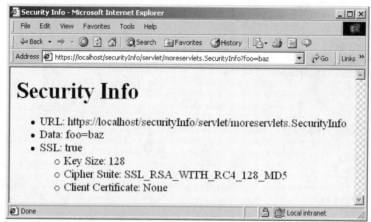

Figure 8–8   Result of the `SecurityInfo` servlet.

MAJOR NEW SERVLET AND JSP CAPABILITIES

Part IV

- Chapter 9
  Servlet and JSP Filters   **434**

- Chapter 10
  The Application Events Framework   **488**

SERVLET AND JSP FILTERS

Topics in This Chapter

- Designing basic filters
- Reading request data
- Accessing the servlet context
- Initializing filters
- Blocking the servlet or JSP response
- Modifying the servlet or JSP response
- Using filters for debugging and logging
- Using filters to monitor site access
- Using filters to replace strings
- Using filters to compress the response

Chapter 9

Perhaps the single most important new capability in version 2.3 of the servlet API is the ability to define filters for servlets and JSP pages. Filters provide a powerful and standard alternative to the nonstandard "servlet chaining" supported by some early servers.

A filter is a program that runs on the server before the servlet or JSP page with which it is associated. A filter can be attached to one or more servlets or JSP pages and can examine the request information going into these resources. After doing so, it can choose among the following options.

- Invoke the resource (i.e., the servlet or JSP page) in the normal manner.
- Invoke the resource with modified request information.
- Invoke the resource but modify the response before sending it to the client.
- Prevent the resource from being invoked and instead redirect to a different resource, return a particular status code, or generate replacement output.

This capability provides several important benefits.

First, it lets you encapsulate common behavior in a modular and reusable manner. Do you have 30 different servlets or JSP pages that need to compress their content to decrease download time? No problem: make a single compression filter (Section 9.11) and apply it to all 30 resources.

Second, it lets you separate high-level access decisions from presentation code. This is particularly valuable with JSP, where you usually want to keep the page almost entirely focused on presentation, not business logic. For example, do you want to block access from certain sites without modifying the individual pages to which these access restrictions apply? No problem: create an access restriction filter (Section 9.8) and apply it to as many or few pages as you like.

Finally, filters let you apply wholesale changes to many different resources. Do you have a bunch of existing resources that should remain unchanged except that the company name should be changed? No problem: make a string replacement filter (Section 9.10) and apply it wherever appropriate.

Remember, however, that filters work only in servers that are compliant with version 2.3 of the servlet specification. If your Web application needs to support older servers, you cannot use filters.

Core Warning

Filters fail in servers that are compliant only with version 2.2 or earlier versions of the servlet specification.

9.1   Creating Basic Filters

Creating a filter involves five basic steps:

1. **Create a class that implements the `Filter` interface.** Your class will need three methods: `doFilter`, `init`, and `destroy`. The `doFilter` method contains the main filtering code (see Step 2), the `init` method performs setup operations, and the `destroy` method does cleanup.
2. **Put the filtering behavior in the `doFilter` method.** The first argument to the `doFilter` method is a `ServletRequest` object. This object gives your filter full access to the incoming information, including form data, cookies, and HTTP request headers. The second argument is a `ServletResponse`; it is mostly ignored in simple filters. The final argument is a `FilterChain`; it is used to invoke the servlet or JSP page as described in the next step.
3. **Call the `doFilter` method of the `FilterChain` object.** The `doFilter` method of the `Filter` interface takes a `FilterChain` object as one of its arguments. When you call the `doFilter` method

of that object, the next associated filter is invoked. If no other filter is associated with the servlet or JSP page, then the servlet or page itself is invoked.

4. **Register the filter with the appropriate servlets and JSP pages.** Use the `filter` and `filter-mapping` elements in the deployment descriptor (*web.xml*).

5. **Disable the invoker servlet.** Prevent users from bypassing filter settings by using default servlet URLs.

Details follow.

Create a Class That Implements the Filter Interface

All filters must implement `javax.servlet.Filter`. This interface comprises three methods: `doFilter`, `init`, and `destroy`.

public void doFilter(ServletRequest request,
                              ServletResponse response,
                              FilterChain chain)
  throws ServletException, IOException

The `doFilter` method is executed each time a filter is invoked (i.e., once for each request for a servlet or JSP page with which the filter is associated). It is this method that contains the bulk of the filtering logic.

The first argument is the `ServletRequest` associated with the incoming request. For simple filters, most of your filter logic is based on this object. Cast the object to `HttpServletRequest` if you are dealing with HTTP requests and you need access to methods such as `getHeader` or `getCookies` that are unavailable in `ServletRequest`.

The second argument is the `ServletResponse`. You often ignore this argument, but there are two cases when you use it. First, if you want to completely block access to the associated servlet or JSP page, you can call `response.getWriter` and send a response directly to the client. Section 9.7 gives details; Section 9.8 gives an example. Second, if you want to modify the output of the associated servlet or JSP page, you can wrap the response inside an object that collects all output sent to it. Then, after the servlet or JSP page is invoked, the filter can examine the output, modify it if appropriate, and then send it to the client. See Section 9.9 for details.

The final argument to doFilter is a FilterChain object. You call doFilter on this object to invoke the next filter that is associated with the servlet or JSP page. In no other filters are in effect, then the call to doFilter invokes the servlet or JSP page itself.

public void init(FilterConfig config)
   throws ServletException

The init method is executed only when the filter is first initialized. It is not executed each time the filter is invoked. For simple filters you can provide an empty body to this method, but there are two common reasons for using init. First, the FilterConfig object provides access to the servlet context and to the name of the filter that is assigned in the *web.xml* file. So, it is common to use init to store the FilterConfig object in a field so that the doFilter method can access the servlet context or the filter name. This process is described in Section 9.3. Second, the FilterConfig object has a getInit-Parameter method that lets you access filter initialization parameters that are assigned in the deployment descriptor (*web.xml*). Use of initialization parameters is described in Section 9.5.

public void destroy()

This method is called when a server is permanently finished with a given filter object (e.g., when the server is being shut down). Most filters simply provide an empty body for this method, but it can be used for cleanup tasks like closing files or database connection pools that are used by the filter.

Put the Filtering Behavior in the doFilter Method

The doFilter method is the key part of most filters. Each time a filter is invoked, doFilter is executed. With most filters, the steps that doFilter performs are based on the incoming information. So, you will probably make use of the Servlet-Request that is supplied as the first argument to doFilter. This object is frequently typecast to HttpServletRequest to provide access to the more specialized methods of that class.

Call the doFilter Method of the FilterChain Object

The doFilter method of the Filter interface takes a FilterChain object as its third argument. When you call the doFilter method of that object, the next associated filter is invoked. This process normally continues until the last filter in the chain is invoked. When the final filter calls the `doFilter` method of its `FilterChain` object, the servlet or page itself is invoked.

However, any filter in the chain can interrupt the process by omitting the call to the `doFilter` method of its `FilterChain`. In such a case, the servlet of JSP page is never invoked and the filter is responsible for providing output to the client. For details, see Section 9.7 (Blocking the Response).

Register the Filter with the Appropriate Servlets and JSP Pages

Version 2.3 of the deployment descriptor introduced two elements for use with filters: `filter` and `filter-mapping`. The `filter` element registers a filtering object with the system. The `filter-mapping` element specifies the URLs to which the filtering object applies.

The filter Element

The `filter` element goes near the top of deployment descriptor (*web.xml*), before any `filter-mapping`, `servlet`, or `servlet-mapping` elements. (For more information on the use of the deployment descriptor, see Chapters 4 and 5. For details on the required ordering of elements within the deployment descriptor, see Section 5.2.) The `filter` element contains six possible subelements:

- **`icon`**. This is an optional element that declares an image file that an IDE can use.
- **`filter-name`**. This is a required element that assigns a name of your choosing to the filter.
- **`display-name`**. This is an optional element that provides a short name for use by IDEs.
- **`description`**. This is another optional element that gives information for IDEs. It provides textual documentation.
- **`filter-class`**. This is a required element that specifies the fully qualified name of the filter implementation class.
- **`init-param`**. This is an optional element that defines initialization parameters that can be read with the `getInitParameter` method of `FilterConfig`. A single filter element can contain multiple `init-param` elements.

Remember that filters were first introduced in version 2.3 of the servlet specification. So, your *web.xml* file must use version 2.3 of the DTD. Here is a simple example:

```
<?xml version="1.0" encoding="ISO-8859-1"?>
<!DOCTYPE web-app PUBLIC
    "-//Sun Microsystems, Inc.//DTD Web Application 2.3//EN"
    "http://java.sun.com/dtd/web-app_2_3.dtd">

<web-app>
  <filter>
    <filter-name>MyFilter</filter-name>
    <filter-class>myPackage.FilterClass</filter-class>
  </filter>
  <!-- ... -->
  <filter-mapping>...</filter-mapping>
</web-app>
```

The filter-mapping Element

The `filter-mapping` element goes in the *web.xml* file after the `filter` element but before the `servlet` element. It contains three possible subelements:

- **filter-name**. This required element must match the name you gave to the filter when you declared it with the `filter` element.
- **url-pattern**. This element declares a pattern starting with a slash (/) that designates the URLs to which the filter applies. You must supply `url-pattern` or `servlet-name` in all `filter-mapping` elements. You cannot provide multiple `url-pattern` entries with a single `filter-mapping` element, however. If you want the filter to apply to multiple patterns, repeat the entire `filter-mapping` element.
- **servlet-name**. This element gives a name that must match a name given to a servlet or JSP page by means of the `servlet` element. For details on the `servlet` element, see Section 5.3 (Assigning Names and Custom URLs). You cannot provide multiple `servlet-name` elements entries with a single `filter-mapping` element. If you want the filter to apply to multiple servlet names, repeat the entire `filter-mapping` element.

Here is a simple example.

```
<?xml version="1.0" encoding="ISO-8859-1"?>
<!DOCTYPE web-app PUBLIC
    "-//Sun Microsystems, Inc.//DTD Web Application 2.3//EN"
    "http://java.sun.com/dtd/web-app_2_3.dtd">

<web-app>
  <filter>
    <filter-name>MyFilter</filter-name>
    <filter-class>myPackage.FilterClass</filter-class>
```

```
  </filter>
  <!-- ... -->
  <filter-mapping>
    <filter-name>MyFilter</filter-name>
    <url-pattern>/someDirectory/SomePage.jsp</url-pattern>
  </filter-mapping>
</web-app>
```

Disable the Invoker Servlet

When you apply filters to resources, you do so by specifying the URL pattern or servlet name to which the filters apply. If you supply a servlet name, that name must match a name given in the `servlet` element of *web.xml*. If you use a URL pattern that applies to a servlet, the pattern must match a pattern that you specified with the `servlet-mapping` *web.xml* element (see Section 5.3, "Assigning Names and Custom URLs"). However, most servers use an "invoker servlet" that provides a default URL for servlets: *http://host/webAppPrefix/servlet/ServletName*. You need to make sure that users don't access servlets with this URL, thus bypassing the filter settings.

For example, suppose that you use `filter` and `filter-mapping` to say that the filter named `SomeFilter` applies to the servlet named `SomeServlet`, as below.

```
<filter>
  <filter-name>SomeFilter</filter-name>
  <filter-class>somePackage.SomeFilterClass</filter-class>
</filter>
<!-- ... -->
<filter-mapping>
  <filter-name>SomeFilter</filter-name>
  <servlet-name>SomeServlet</servlet-name>
</filter-mapping>
```

Next, you use `servlet` and `servlet-mapping` to stipulate that the URL *http://host/webAppPrefix/Blah* should invoke `SomeServlet`, as below.

```
<servlet>
  <servlet-name>SomeServlet</servlet-name>
  <servlet-class>somePackage.SomeServletClass</servlet-class>
</servlet>
<!-- ... -->
<servlet-mapping>
  <servlet-name>SomeServlet</servlet-name>
  <url-pattern>/Blah</url-pattern>
</servlet-mapping>
```

Now, the filter is invoked when clients use the URL *http://host/webAppPrefix/ Blah*. No filters apply to *http://host/webAppPrefix/servlet/somePackage.SomeServlet- Class*. Oops.

Section 5.4 (Disabling the Invoker Servlet) discusses server-specific approaches to turning off the invoker. The most portable approach, however, is to simply remap the */servlet* pattern in your Web application so that all requests that include the pattern are sent to the same servlet. To remap the pattern, you first create a simple servlet that prints an error message or redirects users to the top-level page. Then, you use the `servlet` and `servlet-mapping` elements (Section 5.3) to send requests that include the */servlet* pattern to that servlet. Listing 9.1 gives a brief example.

Listing 9.1   *web.xml* (Excerpt that redirects default servlet URLs)

```
<?xml version="1.0" encoding="ISO-8859-1"?>
<!DOCTYPE web-app PUBLIC
    "-//Sun Microsystems, Inc.//DTD Web Application 2.3//EN"
    "http://java.sun.com/dtd/web-app_2_3.dtd">

<web-app>
  <!-- ... -->
  <servlet>
    <servlet-name>Error</servlet-name>
    <servlet-class>somePackage.ErrorServlet</servlet-class>
  </servlet>
  <!-- ... -->
  <servlet-mapping>
    <servlet-name>Error</servlet-name>
    <url-pattern>/servlet/*</url-pattern>
  </servlet-mapping>
  <!-- ... -->
</web-app>
```

9.2   Example: A Reporting Filter

Just to warm up, let's try a simple filter that merely prints a message to standard output whenever the associated servlet or JSP page is invoked. To accomplish this task, the filter has the following capabilities.

1. **A class that implements the `Filter` interface.** This class is called `ReportFilter` and is shown in Listing 9.2. The class provides empty bodies for the `init` and `destroy` methods.

2. **Filtering behavior in the `doFilter` method.** Each time a servlet or JSP page associated with this filter is invoked, the `doFilter` method generates a printout that lists the requesting host and the URL that was invoked. Since the `getRequestURL` method is in `HttpServletRequest`, not `ServletRequest`, I cast the `ServletRequest` object to `HttpServletRequest`.

3. **A call to the `doFilter` method of the `FilterChain`.** After printing the report, the filter calls the `doFilter` method of the `FilterChain` to invoke the servlet or JSP page (or the next filter in the chain if there was one).

4. **Registration with the Web application home page and the servlet that displays the daily special.** First, the `filter` element associates the name `Reporter` with the class `moreservlets.filters.ReportFilter`. Then, the `filter-mapping` element uses a `url-pattern` of `/index.jsp` to associate the filter with the home page. Finally, the `filter-mapping` element uses a `servlet-name` of `TodaysSpecial` to associate the filter with the daily special servlet (the name `TodaysSpecial` is declared in the `servlet` element). See Listing 9.3.

5. **Disablement of the invoker servlet.** First, I created a `RedirectorServlet` (Listing 9.6) that redirects all requests that it receives to the Web application home page. Next, I used the `servlet` and `servlet-mapping` elements (Listing 9.3) to specify that all URLs that begin with *http://host/webAppPrefix/servlet/* should invoke the `RedirectorServlet`.

Given these settings, the filter is invoked each time a client requests the Web application home page (Listing 9.4, Figure 9–1) or the daily special servlet (Listing 9.5, Figure 9–2).

Listing 9.2	*ReportFilter.java*

```
package moreservlets.filters;

import java.io.*;
import javax.servlet.*;
import javax.servlet.http.*;
import java.util.*; // For Date class

/** Simple filter that prints a report on the standard output
 *  each time an associated servlet or JSP page is accessed.
 */
```

Listing 9.2   *ReportFilter.java (continued)*

```java
public class ReportFilter implements Filter {
  public void doFilter(ServletRequest request,
                       ServletResponse response,
                       FilterChain chain)
     throws ServletException, IOException {
    HttpServletRequest req = (HttpServletRequest)request;
    System.out.println(req.getRemoteHost() +
                       " tried to access " +
                       req.getRequestURL() +
                       " on " + new Date() + ".");
    chain.doFilter(request,response);
  }

  public void init(FilterConfig config)
      throws ServletException {
  }

  public void destroy() {}
}
```

Listing 9.3   *web.xml* (Excerpt for reporting filter)

```xml
<?xml version="1.0" encoding="ISO-8859-1"?>
<!DOCTYPE web-app PUBLIC
    "-//Sun Microsystems, Inc.//DTD Web Application 2.3//EN"
    "http://java.sun.com/dtd/web-app_2_3.dtd">

<web-app>
  <!-- Register the name "Reporter" for ReportFilter. -->
  <filter>
    <filter-name>Reporter</filter-name>
    <filter-class>
      moreservlets.filters.ReportFilter
    </filter-class>
  </filter>
  <!-- ... -->

  <!-- Apply the Reporter filter to home page. -->
  <filter-mapping>
    <filter-name>Reporter</filter-name>
    <url-pattern>/index.jsp</url-pattern>
  </filter-mapping>
```

| Listing 9.3 | *web.xml* (Excerpt for reporting filter) *(continued)* |

```
<!-- Also apply the Reporter filter to the servlet named
     "TodaysSpecial".
-->
<filter-mapping>
  <filter-name>Reporter</filter-name>
  <servlet-name>TodaysSpecial</servlet-name>
</filter-mapping>
<!-- ... -->

<!-- Give a name to the Today's Special servlet so that filters
     can be applied to it.
-->
<servlet>
  <servlet-name>TodaysSpecial</servlet-name>
  <servlet-class>
    moreservlets.TodaysSpecialServlet
  </servlet-class>
</servlet>
<!-- ... -->

<!-- Make /TodaysSpecial invoke the servlet
     named TodaysSpecial (i.e., moreservlets.TodaysSpecial).
-->
<servlet-mapping>
  <servlet-name>TodaysSpecial</servlet-name>
  <url-pattern>/TodaysSpecial</url-pattern>
</servlet-mapping>

<!-- Turn off invoker. Send requests to index.jsp. -->
<servlet-mapping>
  <servlet-name>Redirector</servlet-name>
  <url-pattern>/servlet/*</url-pattern>
</servlet-mapping>

  <!-- ... -->
</web-app>
```

Figure 9–1   Home page for filter company. After the page is deployed on an external server and the reporting filter is attached, each client access results in a printout akin to "purchasing.sun.com tried to access http://www.filtersrus.com/filters/index.jsp on Fri Oct 26 13:19:14 EDT 2001."

Figure 9–2   Page advertising a special sale. After the page is deployed on an external server and the reporting filter is attached, each client access results in a printout akin to "admin.microsoft.com tried to access http://www.filtersrus.com/filters/TodaysSpecial on Fri Oct 26 13:21:56 EDT 2001."

Listing 9.4 *index.jsp*

```
<!DOCTYPE HTML PUBLIC "-//W3C//DTD HTML 4.0 Transitional//EN">
<HTML>
<HEAD>
<TITLE>Filters 'R' Us</TITLE>
<LINK REL=STYLESHEET
      HREF="filter-styles.css"
      TYPE="text/css">
</HEAD>
<BODY>
<CENTER>
<TABLE BORDER=5>
  <TR><TH CLASS="TITLE">Filters 'R' Us</TABLE>
<P>
<TABLE>
  <TR>
    <TH><IMG SRC="images/air-filter.jpg" ALT="Air Filter">
    <TH><IMG SRC="images/coffee-filter.gif" ALT="Coffee Filter">
    <TH><IMG SRC="images/pump-filter.jpg" ALT="Pump Filter">
</TABLE>

<H3>We specialize in the following:</H3>
<UL>
  <LI>Air filters
  <LI>Coffee filters
  <LI>Pump filters
  <LI>Camera lens filters
  <LI>Image filters for Adobe Photoshop
  <LI>Web content filters
  <LI>Kalman filters
  <LI>Servlet and JSP filters
</UL>
Check out <A HREF="TodaysSpecial">Today's Special</A>.
</CENTER>
</BODY>
</HTML>
```

Listing 9.5   *TodaysSpecialServlet.java*

```java
package moreservlets;

import java.io.*;
import javax.servlet.*;
import javax.servlet.http.*;

/** Sample servlet used to test the simple filters. */

public class TodaysSpecialServlet extends HttpServlet {
  private String title, picture;

  public void doGet(HttpServletRequest request,
                    HttpServletResponse response)
      throws ServletException, IOException {
    updateSpecials();
    response.setContentType("text/html");
    PrintWriter out = response.getWriter();
    String docType =
      "<!DOCTYPE HTML PUBLIC \"-//W3C//DTD HTML 4.0 " +
      "Transitional//EN\">\n";
    out.println
      (docType +
      "<HTML>\n" +
      "<HEAD><TITLE>Today's Special</TITLE></HEAD>\n" +
      "<BODY BGCOLOR=\"WHITE\">\n" +
      "<CENTER>\n" +
      "<H1>Today's Special: " + title + "s!</H1>\n" +
      "<IMG SRC=\"images/" + picture + "\"\n" +
      "     ALT=\"" + title + "\">\n" +
      "<BR CLEAR=\"ALL\">\n" +
      "Special deal: for only twice the price, you can\n" +
      "<I>buy one, get one free!</I>.\n" +
      "</BODY></HTML>");
  }

  // Rotate among the three available filter images.
```

Listing 9.5   *TodaysSpecialServlet.java (continued)*

```java
  private void updateSpecials() {
    double num = Math.random();
    if (num < 0.333) {
      title = "Air Filter";
      picture = "air-filter.jpg";
    } else if (num < 0.666) {
      title = "Coffee Filter";
      picture = "coffee-filter.gif";
    } else {
      title = "Pump Filter";
      picture = "pump-filter.jpg";
    }
  }
}
```

Listing 9.6   *RedirectorServlet.java*

```java
package moreservlets;

import java.io.*;
import javax.servlet.*;
import javax.servlet.http.*;

/** Servlet that simply redirects users to the
 *  Web application home page. Registered with the
 *  default servlet URL to prevent clients from
 *  using http://host/webAppPrefix/servlet/ServletName
 *  to bypass filters or security settings that
 *  are associated with custom URLs.
 */

public class RedirectorServlet extends HttpServlet {
  public void doGet(HttpServletRequest request,
                    HttpServletResponse response)
      throws ServletException, IOException {
    response.sendRedirect(request.getContextPath());
  }

  public void doPost(HttpServletRequest request,
                     HttpServletResponse response)
      throws ServletException, IOException {
    doGet(request, response);
  }
}
```

9.3 Accessing the Servlet Context from Filters

The ReportFilter of the previous section prints a report on the standard output whenever the designated servlet or JSP page is invoked. A report on the standard output is fine during development—when you run a server on your desktop you typically have a window that displays the standard output. During deployment, however, you are unlikely to have access to this window. So, a natural enhancement is to write the reports into the servlet log file instead of to the standard output.

The servlet API provides two log methods: one that takes a simple String and another that takes a String and a Throwable. These two methods are available from either the GenericServlet or ServletContext classes. Check your server's documentation for the exact location of the log files that these methods use. The problem is that the doFilter method executes *before* the servlet or JSP page with which it is associated. So, you don't have access to the servlet instance and thus can't call the log methods that are inherited from GenericServlet. Furthermore, the API provides no simple way to access the ServletContext from the doFilter method. The only filter-related class that has a method to access the ServletContext is FilterConfig with its getServletContext method. A FilterConfig object is passed to the init method but is not automatically stored in a location that is available to doFilter.

So, you have to store the FilterConfig yourself. Simply create a field of type FilterConfig, then override init to assign its argument to that field. Since you typically use the FilterConfig object only to access the ServletContext and the filter name, you can store the ServletContext and name in fields as well. Here is a simple example:

```
public class SomeFilter implements Filter {
  protected FilterConfig config;
  private ServletContext context;
  private String filterName;

  public void init(FilterConfig config)
      throws ServletException {
    this.config = config; // In case it is needed by subclass.
    context = config.getServletContext();
    filterName = config.getFilterName();
  }

  // doFilter and destroy methods...
}
```

9.4 Example: A Logging Filter

Let's update the `ReportFilter` (Listing 9.2) so that messages go in the log file instead of to the standard output. To accomplish this task, the filter has the following capabilities.

1. **A class that implements the `Filter` interface.** This class is called `LogFilter` and is shown in Listing 9.7. The `init` method of this class stores the `FilterConfig`, `ServletContext`, and filter name in fields of the filter. The class provides an empty body for the `destroy` method.

2. **Filtering behavior in the `doFilter` method.** There are two differences between this behavior and that of the `ReportFilter`: the report is placed in the log file instead of the standard output and the report includes the name of the filter.

3. **A call to the `doFilter` method of the `FilterChain`.** After printing the report, the filter calls the `doFilter` method of the `FilterChain` to invoke the next filter in the chain (or the servlet or JSP page if there are no more filters).

4. **Registration with all URLs.** First, the `filter` element associates the name `LogFilter` with the class `moreservlets.filters.LogFilter`. Next, the `filter-mapping` element uses a `url-pattern` of `/*` to associate the filter with *all* URLs in the Web application. See Listing 9.8.

5. **Disablement of the invoker servlet.** This operation is shown in Section 9.2 and is not repeated here.

After the Web application is deployed on an external server and the logging filter is attached, a client request for the Web application home page results in an entry in the log file like "audits.irs.gov tried to access http://www.filtersrus.com/filters/index.jsp on Fri Oct 26 15:16:15 EDT 2001. (Reported by Logger.)"

Listing 9.7 *LogFilter.java*

```java
package moreservlets.filters;

import java.io.*;
import javax.servlet.*;
import javax.servlet.http.*;
import java.util.*; // For Date class

/** Simple filter that prints a report in the log file
 *  whenever the associated servlets or JSP pages
 *  are accessed.
 */

public class LogFilter implements Filter {
  protected FilterConfig config;
  private ServletContext context;
  private String filterName;

  public void doFilter(ServletRequest request,
                       ServletResponse response,
                       FilterChain chain)
      throws ServletException, IOException {
    HttpServletRequest req = (HttpServletRequest)request;
    context.log(req.getRemoteHost() +
                " tried to access " +
                req.getRequestURL() +
                " on " + new Date() + ". " +
                "(Reported by " + filterName + ".)");
    chain.doFilter(request,response);
  }

  public void init(FilterConfig config)
      throws ServletException {
    this.config = config; // In case it is needed by subclass.
    context = config.getServletContext();
    filterName = config.getFilterName();
  }

  public void destroy() {}
}
```

| Listing 9.8 | *web.xml* (Excerpt for logging filter) |

```xml
<?xml version="1.0" encoding="ISO-8859-1"?>
<!DOCTYPE web-app PUBLIC
    "-//Sun Microsystems, Inc.//DTD Web Application 2.3//EN"
    "http://java.sun.com/dtd/web-app_2_3.dtd">

<web-app>
  <!-- ... -->

  <!-- Register the name "Logger" for LogFilter. -->
  <filter>
    <filter-name>Logger</filter-name>
    <filter-class>
      moreservlets.filters.LogFilter
    </filter-class>
  </filter>
  <!-- ... -->

  <!-- Apply the Logger filter to all servlets and
       JSP pages.
  -->
  <filter-mapping>
    <filter-name>Logger</filter-name>
    <url-pattern>/*</url-pattern>
  </filter-mapping>

  <!-- ... -->
</web-app>
```

9.5   Using Filter Initialization Parameters

With servlets and JSP pages, you can customize the initialization behavior by supply initialization parameters. For details, see Section 5.5 (Initializing and Preloading Servlets and JSP Pages). The reason this capability is useful is that there are three distinct groups that might want to customize the behavior of servlets or JSP pages:

1. **Developers.** They customize the behavior by changing the code of the servlet or JSP page itself.
2. **End users.** They customize the behavior by entering values in HTML forms.
3. **Deployers.** This third group is the one served by initialization parameters. Members of this group are people who take existing Web applications (or individual servlets or JSP pages) and deploy them in a

customized environment. They are not necessarily developers, so it is not realistic to expect them to modify the servlet and JSP code. Besides, you often omit the source code when distributing servlets. So, developers need a standard way to allow deployers to change servlet and JSP behavior.

If these capabilities are useful for servlets and JSP pages, you would expect them to also be useful for the filters that apply to servlets and JSP page. Indeed they are. However, since filters execute before the servlets or JSP pages to which they are attached, it is not normally possible for end users to customize filter behavior. Nevertheless, it is still useful to permit deployers (not just developers) to customize filter behavior by providing initialization parameters. This behavior is accomplished with the following steps.

1. **Define initialization parameters.** Use the `init-param` subelement of `filter` in *web.xml* along with `param-name` and `param-value` subelements, as follows.

```
<filter>
  <filter-name>SomeFilter</filter-name>
  <filter-class>somePackage.SomeFilterClass</filter-class>
  <init-param>
    <param-name>param1</param-name>
    <param-value>value1</param-value>
  </init-param>
  <init-param>
    <param-name>param2</param-name>
    <param-value>value2</param-value>
  </init-param>
</filter>
```

2. **Read the initialization parameters.** Call the `getInitParameter` method of `FilterConfig` from the `init` method of your filter, as follows.

```
public void init(FilterConfig config)
    throws ServletException {
  String val1 = config.getInitParameter("param1");
  String val2 = config.getInitParameter("param2");
  ...
}
```

3. **Parse the initialization parameters.** Like servlet and JSP initialization parameters, each filter initialization value is of type `String`. So, if you want a value of another type, you have to convert it yourself. For example, you would use `Integer.parseInt` to turn the `String` `"7"` into the `int` 7. When parsing, don't forget to check for missing

and malformed data. Missing initialization parameters result in `null` being returned from `getInitParameter`. Even if the parameters exist, you should consider the possibility that the deployer formatted the value improperly. For example, when converting a `String` to an `int`, you should enclose the `Integer.parseInt` call within a `try/ catch` block that catches `NumberFormatException`. This handles `null` and incorrectly formatted values in one fell swoop.

9.6   Example: An Access Time Filter

The `LogFilter` of Section 9.4 prints an entry in the log file every time the associated servlet or JSP page is accessed. Suppose you want to modify it so that it only notes accesses that occur at unusual times. Since "unusual" is situation dependent, the servlet should provide default values for the abnormal time ranges and let deployers override these values by supplying initialization parameters. To implement this functionality, the filter has the following capabilities.

1. **A class that implements the `Filter` interface.** This class is called `LateAccessFilter` and is shown in Listing 9.9. The `init` method of this class reads the `startTime` and `endTime` initialization parameters. It attempts to parse these values as type `int`, using default values if the parameters are `null` or not formatted as integers. It then stores the start and end times, the `FilterConfig`, the `Servlet- Context`, and the filter name in fields of the filter. Finally, `Late- AccessFilter` provides an empty body for the `destroy` method.

2. **Filtering behavior in the `doFilter` method.** This method looks up the current time, sees if it is within the range given by the start and end times, and prints a log entry if so.

3. **A call to the `doFilter` method of the `FilterChain`.** After printing the report, the filter calls the `doFilter` method of the `Filter- Chain` to invoke the next filter in the chain (or the servlet or JSP page if there are no more filters).

4. **Registration with the Web application home page; definition of initialization parameters.** First, the `filter` element associates the name `LateAccessFilter` with the class `moreservlets. filters.LateAccessFilter`. The `filter` element also includes two `init-param` subelements: one that defines the `startTime` parameter and another that defines `endTime`. Since the people that will be accessing the filtersRus home page are programmers, an abnormal range is considered to be between 2:00 a.m. and 10:00 a.m. Finally, the `filter-mapping` element uses a `url-pattern` of

/index.jsp to associate the filter with the Web application home page. See Listing 9.10.

5. **Disablement of the invoker servlet.** This operation is shown in Section 9.2 and is not repeated here.

After the Web application is deployed on an external server and the logging filter is attached, a client request for the Web application home page results in an entry in the log file like "WARNING: hacker6.filtersrus.com accessed http://www.filtersrus.com/filters/index.jsp on Oct 30, 2001 9:22:09 AM."

Listing 9.9 *LateAccessFilter.java*

```
package moreservlets.filters;

import java.io.*;
import javax.servlet.*;
import javax.servlet.http.*;
import java.util.*;
import java.text.*;

/** Filter that keeps track of accesses that occur
 *  at unusual hours.
 */

public class LateAccessFilter implements Filter {
  private FilterConfig config;
  private ServletContext context;
  private int startTime, endTime;
  private DateFormat formatter;

  public void doFilter(ServletRequest request,
                       ServletResponse response,
                       FilterChain chain)
      throws ServletException, IOException {
    HttpServletRequest req = (HttpServletRequest)request;
    GregorianCalendar calendar = new GregorianCalendar();
    int currentTime = calendar.get(calendar.HOUR_OF_DAY);
    if (isUnusualTime(currentTime, startTime, endTime)) {
      context.log("WARNING: " +
                  req.getRemoteHost() +
                  " accessed " +
                  req.getRequestURL() +
                  " on " +
                  formatter.format(calendar.getTime()));
    }
    chain.doFilter(request,response);
  }
```

Listing 9.9   *LateAccessFilter.java (continued)*

```
public void init(FilterConfig config)
    throws ServletException {
  this.config = config;
  context = config.getServletContext();
  formatter =
    DateFormat.getDateTimeInstance(DateFormat.MEDIUM,
                                   DateFormat.MEDIUM);
  try {
    startTime =
      Integer.parseInt(config.getInitParameter("startTime"));
    endTime =
      Integer.parseInt(config.getInitParameter("endTime"));
  } catch(NumberFormatException nfe) { // Malformed or null
    // Default: access at or after 10 p.m. but before 6 a.m.
    // is considered unusual.
    startTime = 22; // 10:00 p.m.
    endTime = 6;    //  6:00 a.m.
  }
}

public void destroy() {}

// Is the current time between the start and end
// times that are marked as abnormal access times?

private boolean isUnusualTime(int currentTime,
                              int startTime,
                              int endTime) {
  // If the start time is less than the end time (i.e.,
  // they are two times on the same day), then the
  // current time is considered unusual if it is
  // between the start and end times.
  if (startTime < endTime) {
    return((currentTime >= startTime) &&
           (currentTime < endTime));
  }
  // If the start time is greater than or equal to the
  // end time (i.e., the start time is on one day and
  // the end time is on the next day), then the current
  // time is considered unusual if it is NOT between
  // the end and start times.
  else {
    return(!isUnusualTime(currentTime, endTime, startTime));
  }
}
}
```

Listing 9.10   *web.xml* (Excerpt for access time filter)

```xml
<?xml version="1.0" encoding="ISO-8859-1"?>
<!DOCTYPE web-app PUBLIC
    "-//Sun Microsystems, Inc.//DTD Web Application 2.3//EN"
    "http://java.sun.com/dtd/web-app_2_3.dtd">

<web-app>
  <!-- ... -->

  <!-- Register the name "LateAccessFilter" for
       moreservlets.filter.LateAccessFilter.
       Supply two initialization parameters:
       startTime and endTime.
  -->
  <filter>
    <filter-name>LateAccessFilter</filter-name>
    <filter-class>
      moreservlets.filters.LateAccessFilter
    </filter-class>
    <init-param>
      <param-name>startTime</param-name>
      <param-value>2</param-value>
    </init-param>
    <init-param>
      <param-name>endTime</param-name>
      <param-value>10</param-value>
    </init-param>
  </filter>
  <!-- ... -->

  <!-- Apply LateAccessFilter to the home page. -->
  <filter-mapping>
    <filter-name>LateAccessFilter</filter-name>
    <url-pattern>/index.jsp</url-pattern>
  </filter-mapping>

  <!-- ... -->
</web-app>
```

9.7 Blocking the Response

Up to now, all the filters discussed have concluded their doFilter methods by calling the doFilter method of the FilterChain object. This approach is the normal one—the call to doFilter invokes the next resource in the chain (another filter or the actual servlet or JSP page).

But what if your filter detects an unusual situation and wants to prevent the original resource from being invoked? How can it block the normal response? The answer is quite simple: just omit the call to the doFilter method of the FilterChain object. Instead, the filter can redirect the user to a different page (e.g., with a call to response.sendRedirect) or generate the response itself (e.g., by calling getWriter on the response and sending output, just as with a regular servlet). Just remember that the first two arguments to the filter's main doFilter method are declared to be of type ServletRequest and ServletResponse. So, if you want to use methods specific to HTTP, cast these arguments to HttpServletRequest and HttpServletResponse, respectively. Here is a brief example:

```
public void doFilter(ServletRequest request,
                     ServletResponse response,
                     FilterChain chain)
    throws ServletException, IOException {
  HttpServletRequest req = (HttpServletRequest)request;
  HttpServletResponse res = (HttpServletResponse)response;
  if (isUnusualCondition(req)) {
    res.sendRedirect("http://www.somesite.com");
  } else {
    chain.doFilter(req,res);
  }
}
```

9.8 Example: A Prohibited-Site Filter

Suppose you have a competitor that you want to ban from your site. For example, this competing company might have a service that accesses your site, removes advertisements and information that identify your organization, and displays them to their customers. Or, they might have links to your site that are in framed pages, thus making it appear that your page is part of their site. You'd like to prevent them from accessing certain pages at your site. However, every time their Web hosting company boots them off, they simply change domain names and register with another ISP. So, you want the ability to easily change the domain names that should be banned.

The solution is to make a filter that uses initialization parameters to obtain a list of banned sites. Requests originating or referred from these sites result in a warning message. Other requests proceed normally. To implement this functionality, the filter has the following capabilities.

1. **A class that implements the `Filter` interface.** This class is called `BannedAccessFilter` and is shown in Listing 9.11. The `init` method of this class first obtains a list of sites from an initialization parameter called `bannedSites`. The filter parses the entries in the resultant `String` with a `StringTokenizer` and stores each individual site name in a `HashMap` that is accessible through an instance variable (i.e., field) of the filter. Finally, `BannedAccessFilter` provides an empty body for the `destroy` method.

2. **Filtering behavior in the `doFilter` method.** This method looks up the requesting and referring hosts by using the `getRemoteHost` method of `ServletRequest` and parsing the `Referer` HTTP request header, respectively.

3. **A conditional call to the `doFilter` method of the `Filter-Chain`.** The filter checks to see if the requesting or referring host is listed in the `HashMap` of banned sites. If so, it calls the `showWarning` method, which sends a custom response to the client. If not, the filter calls `doFilter` on the `FilterChain` object to let the request proceed normally.

4. **Registration with the daily special servlet; definition of initialization parameters.** First, the `filter` element associates the name `BannedAccessFilter` with the class `moreservlets.filters.BannedAccessFilter`. The `filter` element also includes an `init-param` subelement that specifies the prohibited sites (separated by white space). Since the resource that the competing sites abuse is the servlet that shows the daily special, the `filter-mapping` element uses a `servlet-name` of `TodaysSpecial`. The `servlet` element assigns the name `TodaysSpecial` to `moreservlets.TodaysSpecialServlet`. See Listing 9.12.

5. **Disablement of the invoker servlet.** This operation is shown in Section 9.2 and is not repeated here.

Listing 9.13 shows a very simple page that contains little but a link to the daily special servlet. When that page is hosted on a normal site (Figure 9–3), the link results in the expected output (Figure 9–4). But, when the page that contains the link is hosted on a banned site (Figure 9–5), the link results only in a warning page (Figure 9–6)—access to the real servlet is blocked.

Figure 9–3   A page that links to the daily special servlet. This version is hosted on the desktop development server.

Figure 9–4   You can successfully follow the link from the page of Figure 9–3. The `BannedAccessFilter` does not prohibit access from *localhost*.

Figure 9–5   A page that links to the daily special servlet. This version is hosted on *www.moreservlets.com*.

Figure 9–6 You cannot successfully follow the link from the page of Figure 9–5. The `BannedAccessFilter` prohibits access from *www.moreservlets.com* (an unscrupulous competitor to *filtersRus.com*).

Listing 9.11 *BannedAccessFilter.java*

```java
package moreservlets.filters;

import java.io.*;
import javax.servlet.*;
import javax.servlet.http.*;
import java.util.*;
import java.net.*;

/** Filter that refuses access to anyone connecting directly
 *  from or following a link from a banned site.
 */

public class BannedAccessFilter implements Filter {
  private HashSet bannedSiteTable;

  /** Deny access if the request comes from a banned site
   *  or is referred here by a banned site.
   */

  public void doFilter(ServletRequest request,
                       ServletResponse response,
                       FilterChain chain)
      throws ServletException, IOException {
    HttpServletRequest req = (HttpServletRequest)request;
    String requestingHost = req.getRemoteHost();
    String referringHost =
      getReferringHost(req.getHeader("Referer"));
    String bannedSite = null;
    boolean isBanned = false;
```

Listing 9.11 *BannedAccessFilter.java (continued)*

```
  if (bannedSiteTable.contains(requestingHost)) {
    bannedSite = requestingHost;
    isBanned = true;
  } else if (bannedSiteTable.contains(referringHost)) {
    bannedSite = referringHost;
    isBanned = true;
  }
  if (isBanned) {
    showWarning(response, bannedSite);
  } else {
    chain.doFilter(request,response);
  }
}

/** Create a table of banned sites based on initialization
 *  parameters. Remember that version 2.3 of the servlet
 *  API mandates the use of the Java 2 Platform. Thus,
 *  it is safe to use HashSet (which determines whether
 *  a given key exists) rather than the clumsier
 *  Hashtable (which has a value for each key).
 */

public void init(FilterConfig config)
    throws ServletException {
  bannedSiteTable = new HashSet();
  String bannedSites =
    config.getInitParameter("bannedSites");
  // Default token set: white space.
  StringTokenizer tok = new StringTokenizer(bannedSites);
  while(tok.hasMoreTokens()) {
    String bannedSite = tok.nextToken();
    bannedSiteTable.add(bannedSite);
    System.out.println("Banned " + bannedSite);
  }
}

public void destroy() {}

private String getReferringHost(String refererringURLString) {
  try {
    URL referringURL = new URL(refererringURLString);
    return(referringURL.getHost());
  } catch(MalformedURLException mue) { // Malformed or null
    return(null);
  }
}
```

Listing 9.11 *BannedAccessFilter.java (continued)*

```java
      // Replacement response that is returned to users
      // who are from or referred here by a banned site.

      private void showWarning(ServletResponse response,
                               String bannedSite)
          throws ServletException, IOException {
        response.setContentType("text/html");
        PrintWriter out = response.getWriter();
        String docType =
          "<!DOCTYPE HTML PUBLIC \"-//W3C//DTD HTML 4.0 " +
          "Transitional//EN\">\n";
        out.println
          (docType +
          "<HTML>\n" +
          "<HEAD><TITLE>Access Prohibited</TITLE></HEAD>\n" +
          "<BODY BGCOLOR=\"WHITE\">\n" +
          "<H1>Access Prohibited</H1>\n" +
          "Sorry, access from or via " + bannedSite + "\n" +
          "is not allowed.\n" +
          "</BODY></HTML>");
      }
    }
```

Listing 9.12 *web.xml* (Excerpt for prohibited-site filter)

```xml
<?xml version="1.0" encoding="ISO-8859-1"?>
<!DOCTYPE web-app PUBLIC
    "-//Sun Microsystems, Inc.//DTD Web Application 2.3//EN"
    "http://java.sun.com/dtd/web-app_2_3.dtd">

<web-app>
  <!-- ... -->

  <!-- Register the name "BannedAccessFilter" for
       moreservlets.filter.BannedAccessFilter.
       Supply an initialization parameter:
       bannedSites.
  -->
  <filter>
    <filter-name>BannedAccessFilter</filter-name>
    <filter-class>
      moreservlets.filters.BannedAccessFilter
    </filter-class>
```

Listing 9.12 *web.xml* (Excerpt for prohibited-site filter) *(continued)*

```
  <init-param>
    <param-name>bannedSites</param-name>
    <param-value>
      www.competingsite.com
      www.bettersite.com
      www.moreservlets.com
    </param-value>
  </init-param>
</filter>
<!-- ... -->

<!-- Apply BannedAccessFilter to the servlet named
     "TodaysSpecial".
-->
<filter-mapping>
  <filter-name>BannedAccessFilter</filter-name>
  <servlet-name>TodaysSpecial</servlet-name>
</filter-mapping>
<!-- ... -->

<!-- Give a name to the Today's Special servlet so that filters
     can be applied to it.
-->
<servlet>
  <servlet-name>TodaysSpecial</servlet-name>
  <servlet-class>
    moreservlets.TodaysSpecialServlet
  </servlet-class>
</servlet>
<!-- ... -->

<!-- Make /TodaysSpecial invoke the servlet
     named TodaysSpecial (i.e., moreservlets.TodaysSpecial).
-->
<servlet-mapping>
  <servlet-name>TodaysSpecial</servlet-name>
  <url-pattern>/TodaysSpecial</url-pattern>
</servlet-mapping>

<!-- Turn off invoker. Send requests to index.jsp. -->
<servlet-mapping>
  <servlet-name>Redirector</servlet-name>
  <url-pattern>/servlet/*</url-pattern>
</servlet-mapping>

  <!-- ... -->
</web-app>
```

Listing 9.13   *linker.html*

```
<!DOCTYPE HTML PUBLIC "-//W3C//DTD HTML 4.0 Transitional//EN">
<HTML>
<HEAD>
<TITLE>Link to Filter Company</TITLE>
</HEAD>
<BODY>
<H2 ALIGN="CENTER">Link to Filter Company</H2>
Click <A HREF="http://localhost/filters/TodaysSpecial">here</A>
to see the daily special at filtersRus.com.
</BODY>
</HTML>
```

9.9   Modifying the Response

OK, so filters can block access to resources or invoke them normally. But what if filters want to change the response that a resource generates? There don't appear to be any methods that provide access to the response that a resource generates. The second argument to doFilter (the ServletResponse) gives the filter a way to send new output to a client, but it doesn't give the filter access to the output of the servlet or JSP page. How could it? When the doFilter method is first invoked, the servlet or JSP page hasn't even executed yet. Once you call the doFilter method of the FilterChain object, it appears to be too late to modify the response—data has already been sent to the client. Hmm, a quandary.

The solution is to change the response object that is passed to the doFilter method of the FilterChain object. You typically create a version that buffers up all the output that the servlet or JSP page generates. The servlet 2.3 API provides a useful resource for this purpose: the HttpServletResponseWrapper class. Use of this class involves five steps:

1. **Create a response wrapper.** Extend javax.servlet.http. HttpServletResponseWrapper.
2. **Provide a PrintWriter that buffers output.** Override the getWriter method to return a PrintWriter that saves everything sent to it and stores that result in a field that can be accessed later.
3. **Pass that wrapper to doFilter.** This call is legal because HttpServletResponseWrapper implements HttpServletResponse.
4. **Extract and modify the output.** After the call to the doFilter method of the FilterChain, the output of the original resource is available to you through whatever mechanism you provided in Step 2. You can modify or replace it as appropriate for your application.

5. **Send the modified output to the client.** Since the original resource no longer sends output to the client (the output is stored in your response wrapper instead), *you* have to send the output. So, your filter needs to obtain the `PrintWriter` or `OutputStream` from the *original* response object and pass the modified output to that stream.

A Reusable Response Wrapper

Listing 9.14 presents a wrapper that can be used in most applications where you want filters to modify a resource's output. The `CharArrayWrapper` class overrides the `getWriter` method to return a `PrintWriter` that accumulates everything in a big char array. This result is available to the developer through the `toCharArray` (the raw `char[]`) or `toString` (a `String` derived from the `char[]`) method.

Sections 9.10 and 9.11 give two examples of use of this class.

Listing 9.14   *CharArrayWrapper.java*

```
package moreservlets.filters;

import java.io.*;
import javax.servlet.*;
import javax.servlet.http.*;


/** A response wrapper that takes everything the client
 *  would normally output and saves it in one big
 *  character array.
 */

public class CharArrayWrapper
            extends HttpServletResponseWrapper {
  private CharArrayWriter charWriter;

  /** Initializes wrapper.
   *  <P>
   *  First, this constructor calls the parent
   *  constructor. That call is crucial so that the response
   *  is stored and thus setHeader, setStatus, addCookie,
   *  and so forth work normally.
   *  <P>
   *  Second, this constructor creates a CharArrayWriter
   *  that will be used to accumulate the response.
   */
```

Listing 9.14 *CharArrayWrapper.java (continued)*

```java
public CharArrayWrapper(HttpServletResponse response) {
  super(response);
  charWriter = new CharArrayWriter();
}

/** When servlets or JSP pages ask for the Writer,
 *  don't give them the real one. Instead, give them
 *  a version that writes into the character array.
 *  The filter needs to send the contents of the
 *  array to the client (perhaps after modifying it).
 */

public PrintWriter getWriter() {
  return(new PrintWriter(charWriter));
}

/** Get a String representation of the entire buffer.
 *  <P>
 *  Be sure <B>not</B> to call this method multiple times
 *  on the same wrapper. The API for CharArrayWriter
 *  does not guarantee that it "remembers" the previous
 *  value, so the call is likely to make a new String
 *  every time.
 */

public String toString() {
  return(charWriter.toString());
}

/** Get the underlying character array. */

public char[] toCharArray() {
  return(charWriter.toCharArray());
}
}
```

9.10 Example: A Replacement Filter

This section presents one common application of the CharArrayWrapper shown in the previous section: a filter that changes all occurrences of a target string to some replacement string.

A Generic Replacement Filter

Listing 9.15 presents a filter that wraps the response in a `CharArrayWrapper`, passes that wrapper to the `doFilter` method of the `FilterChain` object, extracts a `String` that represents all of the resource's output, replaces all occurrences of a target string with a replacement string, and sends that modified result to the client.

There are two things to note about this filter. First, it is an abstract class. To use it, you must create a subclass that provides implementations of the `getTargetString` and `getReplacementString` methods. The next subsection has an example of this process. Second, it uses a small utility class (Listing 9.16) to do the actual string substitution. If you are fortunate enough to be using JDK 1.4, you can use the new regular expression package instead of the low-level and cumbersome methods in the `String` and `StringTokenizer` classes. For details, see *http://java.sun.com/j2se/1.4/docs/api/java/util/regex/Matcher.html* and *http://java.sun.com/j2se/1.4/docs/api/java/util/regex/Pattern.html*. Just remember that use of this package limits portability; the servlet 2.3 specification mandates the Java 2 Platform but does not specify any particular JDK version within that general umbrella.

Listing 9.15	*ReplaceFilter.java*

```java
package moreservlets.filters;

import java.io.*;
import javax.servlet.*;
import javax.servlet.http.*;
import java.util.*;

/** Filter that replaces all occurrences of a given
 *  string with a replacement. This is an abstract class:
 *  you <I>must</I> override the getTargetString and
 *  getReplacementString methods in a subclass. The
 *  first of these methods specifies the string in
 *  the response that should be replaced. The second
 *  of these specifies the string that should replace
 *  each occurrence of the target string.
 */

public abstract class ReplaceFilter implements Filter {
  private FilterConfig config;

  public void doFilter(ServletRequest request,
                       ServletResponse response,
                       FilterChain chain)
      throws ServletException, IOException {
```

Listing 9.15   *ReplaceFilter.java (continued)*

```
    CharArrayWrapper responseWrapper =
      new CharArrayWrapper((HttpServletResponse)response);
    // Invoke resource, accumulating output in the wrapper.
    chain.doFilter(request,responseWrapper);
    // Turn entire output into one big String.
    String responseString = responseWrapper.toString();
    // In output, replace all occurrences of target string
    // with replacement string.
    responseString =
      FilterUtils.replace(responseString,
                          getTargetString(),
                          getReplacementString());
    // Update the Content-Length header.
    updateHeaders(response, responseString);
    PrintWriter out = response.getWriter();
    out.write(responseString);
  }

  /** Store the FilterConfig object in case subclasses
   *  want it.
   */

  public void init(FilterConfig config)
      throws ServletException {
    this.config = config;
  }

  protected FilterConfig getFilterConfig() {
    return(config);
  }

  public void destroy() {}

  /** The string that needs replacement.
   *  Override this method in your subclass.
   */

  public abstract String getTargetString();

  /** The string that replaces the target.
   *  Override this method in your subclass.
   */

  public abstract String getReplacementString();
```

Listing 9.15   *ReplaceFilter.java (continued)*

```
/** Updates the response headers. This simple version just sets
 *  the Content-Length header, assuming that we are using a
 *  character set that uses 1 byte per character. For other
 *  character sets, override this method to use different logic
 *  or to give up on persistent HTTP connections. In this latter
 *  case, have this method set the Connection header to "close".
 */

public void updateHeaders(ServletResponse response,
                          String responseString) {
  response.setContentLength(responseString.length());
}
}
```

Listing 9.16   *FilterUtils.java*

```
package moreservlets.filters;

/** Small utility to assist with response wrappers that
 *  return strings.
 */

public class FilterUtils {

  /** Change all occurrences of orig in mainString to
   *  replacement.
   */

  public static String replace(String mainString,
                               String orig,
                               String replacement) {
    String result = "";
    int oldIndex = 0;
    int index = 0;
    int origLength = orig.length();
    while((index = mainString.indexOf(orig, oldIndex))
          != -1) {
      result = result +
               mainString.substring(oldIndex, index) +
               replacement;
      oldIndex = index + origLength;
    }
    result = result + mainString.substring(oldIndex);
    return(result);
  }
}
```

A Specific Replacement Filter

Oh no! A competitor bought out filtersRus.com. All the Web pages that refer to the company name are now obsolete. But, the developers hate to change all their Web pages since another takeover could occur anytime (this company is a hot commodity, after all). No problem—Listing 9.17 presents a filter that replaces all occurrences of `filtersRus.com` with `weBefilters.com`. Figure 9–7 shows a page (Listing 9.19) that promotes the filtersRus.com site name. Figure 9–8 shows the page after the filter is applied.

To implement this functionality, the filter has the following capabilities.

1. **A class that implements the `Filter` interface.** This class is called `ReplaceSiteNameFilter` and is shown in Listing 9.17. It extends the generic `ReplaceFilter` of Listing 9.15. The inherited `init` method stores the `FilterConfig` object in a field in case subclasses need access to the servlet context or filter name. The parent class also provides an empty body for the `destroy` method.

2. **A wrapped response object.** The `doFilter` method, inherited from `ReplaceFilter`, wraps the `ServletResponse` object in a `CharArrayWrapper` and passes that wrapper to the `doFilter` method of the `FilterChain` object. After this call completes, all other filters and the final resource have executed and the output is inside the wrapper. So, the original `doFilter` extracts a `String` that represents all of the resource's output and replaces all occurrences of the target string with the replacement string. Finally, `doFilter` sends that modified result to the client by supplying the entire `String` to the `write` method of the `PrintWriter` that is associated with the *original* response.

3. **Registration with the JSP page that promotes filtersRus.com.** First, the `filter` element of *web.xml* (Listing 9.18) associates the name `ReplaceSiteNameFilter` with the class `moreservlets.filters.ReplaceSiteNameFilter`. Next, the `filter-mapping` element uses a `url-pattern` of `/plugSite/page2.jsp` (see Listing 9.19) so that the filter fires each time that JSP page is requested.

4. **Disablement of the invoker servlet.** This operation is shown in Section 9.2 and is not repeated here.

Figure 9–7   A page that promotes the *filtersRus.com* site.

Figure 9–8   The page that promotes the *filtersRus.com* site after its output is modified by the ReplaceSiteNameFilter.

Listing 9.17 *ReplaceSiteNameFilter.java*

```java
package moreservlets.filters;

public class ReplaceSiteNameFilter extends ReplaceFilter {
  public String getTargetString() {
    return("filtersRus.com");
  }

  public String getReplacementString() {
    return("weBefilters.com");
  }
}
```

Listing 9.18 *web.xml* (Excerpt for site name replacement filter)

```xml
<?xml version="1.0" encoding="ISO-8859-1"?>
<!DOCTYPE web-app PUBLIC
    "-//Sun Microsystems, Inc.//DTD Web Application 2.3//EN"
    "http://java.sun.com/dtd/web-app_2_3.dtd">

<web-app>
  <!-- ... -->

  <!-- Register the name "ReplaceSiteNameFilter" for
       moreservlets.filters.ReplaceSiteNameFilter.
  -->
  <filter>
    <filter-name>ReplaceSiteNameFilter</filter-name>
    <filter-class>
      moreservlets.filters.ReplaceSiteNameFilter
    </filter-class>
  </filter>
  <!-- ... -->


  <!-- Apply ReplaceSiteNameFilter to page2.jsp page
       in the plugSite directory
  -->
  <filter-mapping>
    <filter-name>ReplaceSiteNameFilter</filter-name>
    <url-pattern>/plugSite/page2.jsp</url-pattern>
  </filter-mapping>

  <!-- ... -->
</web-app>
```

Listing 9.19 *page1.jsp* (Identical to *page2.jsp*)

```
<!DOCTYPE HTML PUBLIC "-//W3C//DTD HTML 4.0 Transitional//EN">
<HTML>
<HEAD>
<TITLE>filtersRus.com</TITLE>
<LINK REL=STYLESHEET
      HREF="../filter-styles.css"
      TYPE="text/css">
</HEAD>
<BODY>
<CENTER>
<TABLE BORDER=5>
  <TR><TH CLASS="TITLE">filtersRus.com</TABLE>
<P>
<TABLE>
  <TR>
    <TH><IMG SRC="../images/air-filter.jpg"
            ALT="Air Filter">
    <TH><IMG SRC="../images/coffee-filter.gif"
            ALT="Coffee Filter">
    <TH><IMG SRC="../images/pump-filter.jpg"
            ALT="Pump Filter">
</TABLE>

<H3>filtersRus.com specializes in the following:</H3>
<UL>
  <LI>Air filters
  <LI>Coffee filters
  <LI>Pump filters
  <LI>Camera lens filters
  <LI>Image filters for Adobe Photoshop
  <LI>Web content filters
  <LI>Kalman filters
  <LI>Servlet and JSP filters
</UL>
Check out <A HREF="../TodaysSpecial">Today's Special</A>.
</CENTER>
</BODY>
</HTML>
```

9.11 Example: A Compression Filter

Several recent browsers can handle gzipped content, automatically uncompressing documents that have gzip as the value of the Content-Encoding response header and then treating the result as though it were the original document. Sending such compressed content can be a real time saver because the time required to compress the document on the server and then uncompress it on the client is typically dwarfed by the savings in download time, especially when dialup connections are used. For example, Listing 9.21 shows a servlet that has very long, repetitive, plain text output: a ripe candidate for compression. If gzip could be applied, it could compress the output by a factor of over 300!

However, although most browsers support this type of encoding, a fair number do not. Sending compressed content to browsers that don't support gzip encoding results in a totally garbled result. Browsers that support content encoding include most versions of Netscape for Unix, most versions of Internet Explorer for Windows, and Netscape 4.7 and later for Windows. So, this compression cannot be done blindly—it is only valid for clients that use the Accept-Encoding request header to specify that they support gzip.

A compression filter can use the CharArrayWrapper of Section 9.9 to compress content when the browser supports such a capability. Accomplishing this task requires the following:

1. **A class that implements the Filter interface.** This class is called CompressionFilter and is shown in Listing 9.20. The init method stores the FilterConfig object in a field in case subclasses need access to the servlet context or filter name. The body of the destroy method is left empty.

2. **A wrapped response object.** The doFilter method wraps the ServletResponse object in a CharArrayWrapper and passes that wrapper to the doFilter method of the FilterChain object. After this call completes, all other filters and the final resource have executed and the output is inside the wrapper. So, the original doFilter extracts a character array that represents all of the resource's output. If the client indicates that it supports compression (i.e., has gzip as one of the values of its Accept-Encoding header), the filter attaches a GZIPOutputStream to a ByteArrayOutputStream, copies the character array into that stream, and sets the Content-Encoding response header to gzip. If the client does not support gzip, the unmodified character array is copied to the ByteArrayOutput-

Stream. Finally, doFilter sends that result to the client by writing the entire byte array (possibly compressed) to the OutputStream that is associated with the *original* response.

3. **Registration with long servlet.** First, the filter element of *web.xml* (Listing 9.22) associates the name CompressionFilter with the class moreservlets.filters.CompressionFilter. Next, the filter-mapping element uses a servlet-name of LongServlet so that the filter fires each time that long servlet (Listing 9.21) is requested. The servlet and servlet-mapping elements assign the name LongServlet to the servlet and specify the URL that corresponds to the servlet.

4. **Disablement of the invoker servlet.** This operation is shown in Section 9.2 and is not repeated here.

When the filter is attached, the body of the servlet is reduced three *hundred* times and the time to access the servlet on a 28.8K modem is reduced by more than a factor of *ten* (more than 50 seconds uncompressed; less than 5 seconds compressed). A huge savings! However, two small warnings are in order here.

First, there is a saying in the software industry that there are three kinds of lies: lies, darn lies, and benchmarks. The point of this maxim is that people always rig benchmarks to show their point in the most favorable light possible. I did the same thing by using a servlet with long simple output and using a slow modem connection. So, I'm not promising that you will always get a tenfold performance gain. But, it is a simple matter to attach or detach the compression filter. That's the beauty of filters. Try it yourself and see how much it buys you in typical usage conditions.

Second, although the specification does not officially mandate that you set response headers before calling the doFilter method of the FilterChain, some servers (e.g., ServletExec 4.1) require you to do so. This is to prevent you from attempting to set a response header after a resource has sent content to the client. So, for portability, be sure to set response headers before calling chain.doFilter.

Core Warning

If your filter sets response headers, be sure it does so before calling the doFilter method of the FilterChain object.

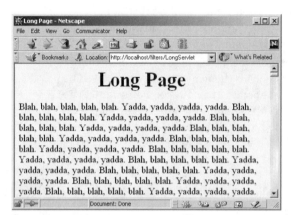

Figure 9–9 The `LongServlet`. The content is more than three hundred times smaller when gzip is used, resulting in more than a tenfold speedup when the servlet is accessed with a 28.8K modem.

Listing 9.20 *CompressionFilter.java*

```java
package moreservlets.filters;

import java.io.*;
import javax.servlet.*;
import javax.servlet.http.*;
import java.util.zip.*;

/** Filter that compresses output with gzip
 *  (assuming that browser supports gzip).
 */

public class CompressionFilter implements Filter {
  private FilterConfig config;

  /** If browser does not support gzip, invoke resource
   *  normally. If browser <I>does</I> support gzip,
   *  set the Content-Encoding response header and
   *  invoke resource with a wrapped response that
   *  collects all the output. Extract the output
   *  and write it into a gzipped byte array. Finally,
   *  write that array to the client's output stream.
   */
```

Listing 9.20   *CompressionFilter.java (continued)*

```java
public void doFilter(ServletRequest request,
                     ServletResponse response,
                     FilterChain chain)
    throws ServletException, IOException {
  HttpServletRequest req = (HttpServletRequest)request;
  HttpServletResponse res = (HttpServletResponse)response;
  if (!isGzipSupported(req)) {
    // Invoke resource normally.
    chain.doFilter(req,res);
  } else {
    // Tell browser we are sending it gzipped data.
    res.setHeader("Content-Encoding", "gzip");

    // Invoke resource, accumulating output in the wrapper.
    CharArrayWrapper responseWrapper =
      new CharArrayWrapper(res);
    chain.doFilter(req,responseWrapper);

    // Get character array representing output.
    char[] responseChars = responseWrapper.toCharArray();

    // Make a writer that compresses data and puts
    // it into a byte array.
    ByteArrayOutputStream byteStream =
      new ByteArrayOutputStream();
    GZIPOutputStream zipOut =
      new GZIPOutputStream(byteStream);
    OutputStreamWriter tempOut =
      new OutputStreamWriter(zipOut);

    // Compress original output and put it into byte array.
    tempOut.write(responseChars);

    // Gzip streams must be explicitly closed.
    tempOut.close();

    // Update the Content-Length header.
    res.setContentLength(byteStream.size());

    // Send compressed result to client.
    OutputStream realOut = res.getOutputStream();
    byteStream.writeTo(realOut);
  }
}
```

Listing 9.20 *CompressionFilter.java (continued)*

```java
/** Store the FilterConfig object in case subclasses
 *  want it.
 */

public void init(FilterConfig config)
    throws ServletException {
  this.config = config;
}

protected FilterConfig getFilterConfig() {
  return(config);
}

public void destroy() {}

private boolean isGzipSupported(HttpServletRequest req) {
  String browserEncodings =
    req.getHeader("Accept-Encoding");
  return((browserEncodings != null) &&
         (browserEncodings.indexOf("gzip") != -1));
}
}
```

Listing 9.21 *LongServlet.java*

```java
package moreservlets;

import java.io.*;
import javax.servlet.*;
import javax.servlet.http.*;

/** Servlet with <B>long</B> output. Used to test
 *  the effect of the compression filter of Chapter 9.
 */

public class LongServlet extends HttpServlet {
  public void doGet(HttpServletRequest request,
                    HttpServletResponse response)
      throws ServletException, IOException {
    response.setContentType("text/html");
    PrintWriter out = response.getWriter();
```

Listing 9.21 *LongServlet.java (continued)*

```
    String docType =
      "<!DOCTYPE HTML PUBLIC \"-//W3C//DTD HTML 4.0 " +
      "Transitional//EN\">\n";
    String title = "Long Page";
    out.println
      (docType +
       "<HTML>\n" +
       "<HEAD><TITLE>" + title + "</TITLE></HEAD>\n" +
       "<BODY BGCOLOR=\"#FDF5E6\">\n" +
       "<H1 ALIGN=\"CENTER\">" + title + "</H1>\n");
    String line = "Blah, blah, blah, blah, blah. " +
                  "Yadda, yadda, yadda, yadda.";
    for(int i=0; i<10000; i++) {
      out.println(line);
    }
    out.println("</BODY></HTML>");
  }
}
```

Listing 9.22 *web.xml* (Excerpt for compression filter)

```
<?xml version="1.0" encoding="ISO-8859-1"?>
<!DOCTYPE web-app PUBLIC
    "-//Sun Microsystems, Inc.//DTD Web Application 2.3//EN"
    "http://java.sun.com/dtd/web-app_2_3.dtd">

<web-app>
  <!-- ... -->

  <!-- Register the name "CompressionFilter" for
       moreservlets.filters.CompressionFilter.
  -->
  <filter>
    <filter-name>CompressionFilter</filter-name>
    <filter-class>
      moreservlets.filters.CompressionFilter
    </filter-class>
  </filter>
  <!-- ... -->
```

Listing 9.22 | *web.xml* (Excerpt for compression filter) *(continued)*

```
<!-- Apply CompressionFilter to the servlet named
     "LongServlet".
-->
<filter-mapping>
  <filter-name>CompressionFilter</filter-name>
  <servlet-name>LongServlet</servlet-name>
</filter-mapping>
<!-- ... -->

<!-- Give a name to the servlet that generates long
     (but very exciting!) output.
-->
<servlet>
  <servlet-name>LongServlet</servlet-name>
  <servlet-class>moreservlets.LongServlet</servlet-class>
</servlet>
<!-- ... -->

<!-- Make /LongServlet invoke the servlet
     named LongServlet (i.e., moreservlets.LongServlet).
-->
<servlet-mapping>
  <servlet-name>LongServlet</servlet-name>
  <url-pattern>/LongServlet</url-pattern>
</servlet-mapping>

<!-- Turn off invoker. Send requests to index.jsp. -->
<servlet-mapping>
  <servlet-name>Redirector</servlet-name>
  <url-pattern>/servlet/*</url-pattern>
</servlet-mapping>

<!-- ... -->
</web-app>
```

9.12 The Complete Filter Deployment Descriptor

The previous sections showed various excerpts of the *web.xml* file for filtersRus.com. This section shows the file in its entirety.

> **Listing 9.23** *web.xml* (Complete version for filter examples)

```
<?xml version="1.0" encoding="ISO-8859-1"?>
<!DOCTYPE web-app PUBLIC
    "-//Sun Microsystems, Inc.//DTD Web Application 2.3//EN"
    "http://java.sun.com/dtd/web-app_2_3.dtd">

<web-app>
  <!-- Order matters in web.xml! For the elements
       used in this example, this order is required:
           filter
           filter-mapping
           servlet
           servlet-mapping
           welcome-file-list
  -->

  <!-- Register the name "Reporter" for ReportFilter. -->
  <filter>
    <filter-name>Reporter</filter-name>
    <filter-class>
      moreservlets.filters.ReportFilter
    </filter-class>
  </filter>

  <!-- Register the name "Logger" for LogFilter. -->
  <filter>
    <filter-name>Logger</filter-name>
    <filter-class>
      moreservlets.filters.LogFilter
    </filter-class>
  </filter>

  <!-- Register the name "LateAccessFilter" for
       moreservlets.filter.LateAccessFilter.
       Supply two initialization parameters:
       startTime and endTime.
  -->
  <filter>
    <filter-name>LateAccessFilter</filter-name>
    <filter-class>
      moreservlets.filters.LateAccessFilter
    </filter-class>
    <init-param>
      <param-name>startTime</param-name>
      <param-value>2</param-value>
    </init-param>
```

| Listing 9.23 | *web.xml* (Complete version for filter examples) *(continued)* |

```
<init-param>
  <param-name>endTime</param-name>
  <param-value>10</param-value>
</init-param>
</filter>

<!-- Register the name "BannedAccessFilter" for
     moreservlets.filter.BannedAccessFilter.
     Supply an initialization parameter:
     bannedSites.
-->
<filter>
  <filter-name>BannedAccessFilter</filter-name>
  <filter-class>
    moreservlets.filters.BannedAccessFilter
  </filter-class>
  <init-param>
    <param-name>bannedSites</param-name>
    <param-value>
      www.competingsite.com
      www.bettersite.com
      www.moreservlets.com
    </param-value>
  </init-param>
</filter>

<!-- Register the name "ReplaceSiteNameFilter" for
     moreservlets.filters.ReplaceSiteNameFilter.
-->
<filter>
  <filter-name>ReplaceSiteNameFilter</filter-name>
  <filter-class>
    moreservlets.filters.ReplaceSiteNameFilter
  </filter-class>
</filter>

<!-- Register the name "CompressionFilter" for
     moreservlets.filters.CompressionFilter.
-->
<filter>
  <filter-name>CompressionFilter</filter-name>
  <filter-class>
    moreservlets.filters.CompressionFilter
  </filter-class>
</filter>
```

```xml
<!-- Apply the Reporter filter to the servlet named
     "TodaysSpecial".
-->
<filter-mapping>
  <filter-name>Reporter</filter-name>
  <servlet-name>TodaysSpecial</servlet-name>
</filter-mapping>

<!-- Also apply the Reporter filter to home page. -->
<filter-mapping>
  <filter-name>Reporter</filter-name>
  <url-pattern>/index.jsp</url-pattern>
</filter-mapping>

<!-- Apply the Logger filter to all servlets and
     JSP pages.
-->
<filter-mapping>
  <filter-name>Logger</filter-name>
  <url-pattern>/*</url-pattern>
</filter-mapping>

<!-- Apply LateAccessFilter to the home page. -->
<filter-mapping>
  <filter-name>LateAccessFilter</filter-name>
  <url-pattern>/index.jsp</url-pattern>
</filter-mapping>

<!-- Apply BannedAccessFilter to the servlet named
     "TodaysSpecial".
-->
<filter-mapping>
  <filter-name>BannedAccessFilter</filter-name>
  <servlet-name>TodaysSpecial</servlet-name>
</filter-mapping>

<!-- Apply ReplaceSiteNameFilter to page2.jsp page
     in the plugSite directory
-->
<filter-mapping>
  <filter-name>ReplaceSiteNameFilter</filter-name>
  <url-pattern>/plugSite/page2.jsp</url-pattern>
</filter-mapping>
```

Listing 9.23	*web.xml* (Complete version for filter examples) *(continued)*

```
<!-- Apply CompressionFilter to the servlet named
     "LongServlet".
-->
<filter-mapping>
  <filter-name>CompressionFilter</filter-name>
  <servlet-name>LongServlet</servlet-name>
</filter-mapping>

<!-- Give a name to the Today's Special servlet so that filters
     can be applied to it.
-->
<servlet>
  <servlet-name>TodaysSpecial</servlet-name>
  <servlet-class>
    moreservlets.TodaysSpecialServlet
  </servlet-class>
</servlet>

<!-- Give a name to the servlet that redirects users
     to the home page.
-->
<servlet>
  <servlet-name>Redirector</servlet-name>
  <servlet-class>moreservlets.RedirectorServlet</servlet-class>
</servlet>

<!-- Give a name to the servlet that generates long
     (but very exciting!) output.
-->
<servlet>
  <servlet-name>LongServlet</servlet-name>
  <servlet-class>moreservlets.LongServlet</servlet-class>
</servlet>

<!-- Make /TodaysSpecial invoke the servlet
     named TodaysSpecial (i.e., moreservlets.TodaysSpecial).
-->
<servlet-mapping>
  <servlet-name>TodaysSpecial</servlet-name>
  <url-pattern>/TodaysSpecial</url-pattern>
</servlet-mapping>
```

Listing 9.23	*web.xml* (Complete version for filter examples) *(continued)*

```
<!-- Make /LongServlet invoke the servlet
     named LongServlet (i.e., moreservlets.LongServlet).
-->
<servlet-mapping>
  <servlet-name>LongServlet</servlet-name>
  <url-pattern>/LongServlet</url-pattern>
</servlet-mapping>

<!-- Turn off invoker. Send requests to index.jsp. -->
<servlet-mapping>
  <servlet-name>Redirector</servlet-name>
  <url-pattern>/servlet/*</url-pattern>
</servlet-mapping>

<!-- If URL gives a directory but no filename, try index.jsp
     first and index.html second. If neither is found,
     the result is server specific (e.g., a directory
     listing).  Order of elements in web.xml matters.
     welcome-file-list needs to come after servlet but
     before error-page.
-->
<welcome-file-list>
  <welcome-file>index.jsp</welcome-file>
  <welcome-file>index.html</welcome-file>
</welcome-file-list>

</web-app>
```

THE APPLICATION
EVENTS FRAMEWORK

Topics in This Chapter

- Understanding the general event-handling strategy
- Monitoring servlet context initialization and shutdown
- Setting application-wide values
- Detecting changes in attributes of the servlet context
- Recognizing creation and destruction of HTTP sessions
- Analyzing overall session usage
- Watching for changes in session attributes
- Tracking purchases at an e-commerce site
- Using multiple cooperating listeners
- Packaging listeners in JSP tag libraries

Chapter 10

Developers have many tools at their disposal for handling the life cycle of individual servlets or JSP pages. The servlet `init` method (Section 2.3) fires when a servlet is first instantiated. JSP pages use the nearly identical `jspInit` method (Section 3.3). Both methods can use initialization parameters that are specified with the `init-param` subelement of the *web.xml* `servlet` element (Section 5.5). Requests are handled with `service` and `_jspService`, and destruction is handled with `destroy` and `jspDestroy`.

This is all fine for *individual* resources. But what if you want to respond to major events in the life cycle of the Web application itself? What if you want to create application-wide connection pools, locate resources, or set up shared network connections? For example, suppose you want to record the email address of the support group at your company, an address that will be used by many different servlets and JSP pages. Sure, you can use the following to store the information:

```
context.setAttribute("supportAddress", "balmer@microsoft.com");
```

Better yet, you could use the *web.xml* `context-param` element (Section 5.5) to designate the address, then read it with the `getInitParameter` method of `ServletContext`. Fine. But which servlet or JSP page should perform this task? Or you could read the address from a database. Fine. But which servlet or JSP page should establish the database connection? There is no good answer to this question; you don't know which resources will be accessed first, so the code that performs these tasks would have to be repeated many different places. You want more global control than any one servlet or JSP page can provide. That's where application life-cycle event listeners come in.

There are four kinds of event listeners that respond to Web application life-cycle events.

- **Servlet context listeners.** These listeners are notified when the servlet context (i.e., the Web application) is initialized and destroyed.
- **Servlet context attribute listeners.** These listeners are notified when attributes are added to, removed from, or replaced in the servlet context.
- **Session listeners.** These listeners are notified when session objects are created, invalidated, or timed out.
- **Session attribute listeners.** These listeners are notified when attributes are added to, removed from, or replaced in any session.

Using these listeners involves six basic steps. I'll give a general outline here, then provide listener-specific details in the following sections.

1. **Implement the appropriate interface.** Use `ServletContext-Listener`, `ServletContextAttributeListener`, `Http-SessionListener`, or `HttpSessionAttributeListener`. The first two interfaces are in the `javax.servlet` package; the second two are in `javax.servlet.http`.

2. **Override the methods needed to respond to the events of interest.** Provide empty bodies for the other methods in the interface. For example, the `ServletContextListener` interface defines two methods: `contextInitialized` (the Web application was just loaded and the servlet context was initialized) and `contextDestroyed` (the Web application is being shut down and the servlet context is about to be destroyed). If you wanted to define an application-wide servlet context entry, you could provide a real implementation for `contextInitialized` and an empty body for `contextDestroyed`.

3. **Obtain access to the important Web application objects.** There are six important objects that you are likely to use in your event-handling methods: the servlet context, the name of the servlet context attribute that changed, the value of the servlet context attribute that changed, the session object, the name of the session attribute that changed, and the value of the session attribute that changed.

4. **Use these objects.** This process is application specific, but there are some common themes. For example, with the servlet context, you are most likely to read initialization parameters (`getInitParameter`), store data for later access (`setAttribute`), and read previously stored data (`getAttribute`).

5. **Declare the listener.** You do this with the `listener` and `listener-class` elements of the general Web application deployment descriptor (*web.xml*) or of a tag library descriptor file.

6. **Provide any needed initialization parameters.** Servlet context listeners commonly read context initialization parameters to use as the basis of data that is made available to all servlets and JSP pages. You use the `context-param` *web.xml* element to provide the names and values of these initialization parameters.

If servlet and JSP filters are the most important new feature in version 2.3 of the servlet specification, then application life-cycle events are the second most important new capability. Remember, however, that these event listeners work only in servers that are compliant with version 2.3 of the servlet specification. If your Web application needs to support older servers, you cannot use life-cycle listeners.

Core Warning

Application life-cycle listeners fail in servers that are compliant only with version 2.2 or earlier versions of the servlet specification.

10.1 Monitoring Creation and Destruction of the Servlet Context

The `ServletContextListener` class responds to the initialization and destruction of the servlet context. These events correspond to the creation and shutdown of the Web application itself. The `ServletContextListener` is most commonly used to set up application-wide resources like database connection pools and to read the initial values of application-wide data that will be used by multiple servlets and JSP pages. Using the listener involves the following six steps.

1. **Implement the `ServletContextListener` interface.** This interface is in the `javax.servlet` package.

2. **Override `contextInitialized` and `contextDestroyed`.** The first of these (`contextInitialized`) is triggered when the Web application is first loaded and the servlet context is created. The two most common tasks performed by this method are creating application-wide data (often by reading context initialization parameters) and storing that data in an easily accessible location (often in attributes of the servlet context). The second method (`contextDestroyed`) is

triggered when the Web application is being shut down and the servlet context is about to be destroyed. The most common task performed by this method is the releasing of resources. For example, `context-Destroyed` can be used to close database connections associated with a now-obsolete connection pool. However, since the servlet context will be destroyed (and garbage collected if the server itself continues to execute), there is no need to use `contextDestroyed` to remove normal objects from servlet context attributes.

3. **Obtain a reference to the servlet context.** The `context-Initialized` and `contextDestroyed` methods each take a `ServletContextEvent` as an argument. The `ServletContext-Event` class has a `getServletContext` method that returns the servlet context.

4. **Use the servlet context.** You read initialization parameters with `getInitParameter`, store data with `setAttribute`, and make log file entries with `log`.

5. **Declare the listener.** Use the `listener` and `listener-class` elements to simply list the fully qualified name of the listener class, as below.

```
<listener>
  <listener-class>somePackage.SomeListener</listener-class>
</listener>
```

For now, assume that this declaration goes in the *web.xml* file (immediately before the `servlet` element). However, in Section 10.5 you'll see that if you package listeners with tag libraries, you can use the identical declaration within the TLD (tag library descriptor) file of the tag library.

6. **Provide any needed initialization parameters.** Once you have a reference to the servlet context (see Step 3), you can use the `get-InitParameter` method to read context initialization parameters as the basis of data that will be made available to all servlets and JSP pages. You use the `context-param` *web.xml* element to provide the names and values of these initialization parameters, as follows.

```
<context-param>
  <param-name>name</param-name>
  <param-value>value</param-value>
</context-param>
```

10.2 Example: Initializing Commonly Used Data

Suppose that you are developing a Web site for a dot-com company that is a hot commodity. So hot, in fact, that it is constantly being bought out by larger companies. As a result, the company name keeps changing. Rather than changing zillions of separate servlets and JSP pages each time you change the company name, you could read the company name when the Web application is loaded, store the value in the servlet context, and design all your servlets and JSP pages to read the name from this location. To prevent confusion among customers, the site can also prominently display the former company name, initializing and using it in a manner similar to the current company name.

The following steps summarize a listener that accomplishes this task.

1. **Implement the `ServletContextListener` interface.** Listing 10.1 shows a class (`InitialCompanyNameListener`) that implements this interface.

2. **Override `contextInitialized` and `contextDestroyed`.** The `InitialCompanyNameListener` class uses `context-Initialized` to read the current and former company names and store them in the servlet context. Since the `contextDestroyed` method is not needed, an empty body is supplied.

3. **Obtain a reference to the servlet context.** The `context-Initialized` method calls `getServletContext` on the `ServletContextEvent` argument and stores the result in the `context` local variable.

4. **Use the servlet context.** The listener needs to read the `company-Name` and `formerCompanyName` initialization parameters and store them in a globally accessible location. So, it calls `getInit-Parameter` on the `context` variable, checks for missing values, and uses `setAttribute` to store the result in the servlet context.

5. **Declare the listener.** The listener is declared in the deployment descriptor with the `listener` and `listener-class` elements, as below.

```
<listener>
  <listener-class>
    moreservlets.listeners.InitialCompanyNameListener
  </listener-class>
</listener>
```

The *web.xml* file is shown in Listing 10.2.

6. **Provide any needed initialization parameters.** The company-Name and formerCompanyName init parameters are defined in *web.xml* (Listing 10.2) as follows.

```
<context-param>
  <param-name>companyName</param-name>
  <param-value>not-dot-com.com</param-value>
</context-param>
<context-param>
  <param-name>formerCompanyName</param-name>
  <param-value>hot-dot-com.com</param-value>
</context-param>
```

Listings 10.3 and 10.4 present two JSP pages that use the predefined application variable (i.e., the servlet context) to access the companyName and former-CompanyName attributes. Figures 10–1 and 10–2 show the results. See Section 3.3 for a full list of the predefined JSP variables (request, response, application, etc.).

Listing 10.1	*InitialCompanyNameListener.java*

```
package moreservlets.listeners;

import java.io.*;
import javax.servlet.*;
import javax.servlet.http.*;

/** Listener that looks up the name of the company when
 *  the Web application is first loaded. Stores this
 *  name in the companyName servlet context attribute.
 *  Various servlets and JSP pages will extract it
 *  from that location.
 *  <P>
 *  Also looks up and stores the former company name and
 *  stores it in the formerCompanyName attribute.
 */

public class InitialCompanyNameListener
    implements ServletContextListener {
  private static final String DEFAULT_NAME =
    "MISSING-COMPANY-NAME";
```

Listing 10.1   *InitialCompanyNameListener.java (continued)*

```java
/** Looks up the companyName and formerCompanyName
 *  init parameters and puts them into the servlet context.
 */

public void contextInitialized(ServletContextEvent event) {
    ServletContext context = event.getServletContext();
    setInitialAttribute(context,
                        "companyName",
                        DEFAULT_NAME);
    setInitialAttribute(context,
                        "formerCompanyName",
                        "");
}

public void contextDestroyed(ServletContextEvent event) {}

// Looks for a servlet context init parameter with a given name.
// If it finds it, it puts the value into a servlet context
// attribute with the same name. If the init parameter is missing,
// it puts a default value into the servlet context attribute.

private void setInitialAttribute(ServletContext context,
                                 String initParamName,
                                 String defaultValue) {
    String initialValue =
        context.getInitParameter(initParamName);
    if (initialValue != null) {
        context.setAttribute(initParamName, initialValue);
    } else {
        context.setAttribute(initParamName, defaultValue);
    }
}

/** Static method that returns the servlet context
 *  attribute named "companyName" if it is available.
 *  Returns a default value if the attribute is unavailable.
 */

public static String getCompanyName(ServletContext context) {
    String name =
        (String)context.getAttribute("companyName");
    if (name == null) {
        name = DEFAULT_NAME;
    }
    return(name);
}
```

Listing 10.1 *InitialCompanyNameListener.java (continued)*

```java
/** Static method that returns the servlet context
 *  attribute named "formerCompanyName" if it is available.
 *  Returns an empty string if the attribute is
 *  unavailable.
 */

public static String getFormerCompanyName
                                (ServletContext context) {
  String name =
    (String)context.getAttribute("formerCompanyName");
  if (name == null) {
    name = "";
  }
  return(name);
}
}
```

Listing 10.2 *web.xml* (Excerpt for initial company name listener)

```xml
<?xml version="1.0" encoding="ISO-8859-1"?>
<!DOCTYPE web-app PUBLIC
    "-//Sun Microsystems, Inc.//DTD Web Application 2.3//EN"
    "http://java.sun.com/dtd/web-app_2_3.dtd">

<web-app>

  <!-- Since the company name changes so frequently,
       supply it as a servlet context parameter instead
       of embedding it into lots of different servlets and
       JSP pages. The InitialCompanyNameListener will
       read this value and store it in the servlet context. -->
  <context-param>
    <param-name>companyName</param-name>
    <param-value>not-dot-com.com</param-value>
  </context-param>

  <!-- Also store the previous company name. -->
  <context-param>
    <param-name>formerCompanyName</param-name>
    <param-value>hot-dot-com.com</param-value>
  </context-param>
  <!-- ... -->
```

Listing 10.2 *web.xml* (Excerpt for initial company name listener) *(continued)*

```
<!-- Register the listener that sets up the
     initial company name. -->
<listener>
  <listener-class>
    moreservlets.listeners.InitialCompanyNameListener
  </listener-class>
</listener>
<!-- ... -->

<!-- If URL gives a directory but no filename, try index.jsp
     first and index.html second. If neither is found,
     the result is server specific (e.g., a directory
     listing).  Order of elements in web.xml matters.
     welcome-file-list needs to come after servlet but
     before error-page.
-->
<welcome-file-list>
  <welcome-file>index.jsp</welcome-file>
  <welcome-file>index.html</welcome-file>
</welcome-file-list>

<!-- ... -->
</web-app>
```

Listing 10.3 *index.jsp*

```
<!DOCTYPE HTML PUBLIC "-//W3C//DTD HTML 4.0 Transitional//EN">
<HTML>
<HEAD>
<%@ page import="moreservlets.listeners.*" %>
<%
String companyName =
  InitialCompanyNameListener.getCompanyName(application);
String formerCompanyName =
  InitialCompanyNameListener.getFormerCompanyName(application);
String formerCompanyDescription = "";
if (!formerCompanyName.equals("")) {
  formerCompanyDescription =
    "(formerly " + formerCompanyName + ")";
}
%>
```

Listing 10.3 *index.jsp (continued)*

```
<TITLE><%= companyName %></TITLE>
<LINK REL=STYLESHEET
      HREF="events-styles.css"
      TYPE="text/css">
</HEAD>

<BODY>
<TABLE BORDER=5 ALIGN="CENTER">
  <TR><TH CLASS="TITLE">
      <%= companyName %><BR>
      <%= formerCompanyDescription %>
</TABLE>
<P>
Welcome to the home page of <B><%= companyName %></B>
<%= formerCompanyDescription %>
<P>
<B><%= companyName %></B> is a high-flying, fast-growing,
big-potential company. A perfect choice for your
retirement portfolio!
<P>
Click <A HREF="company-info.jsp">here</A> for more information.
</BODY>
</HTML>
```

Listing 10.4 *company-info.jsp*

```
<!DOCTYPE HTML PUBLIC "-//W3C//DTD HTML 4.0 Transitional//EN">
<HTML>
<HEAD>
<%@ page import="moreservlets.listeners.*" %>
<%
String companyName =
  InitialCompanyNameListener.getCompanyName(application);
String formerCompanyName =
  InitialCompanyNameListener.getFormerCompanyName(application);
String formerCompanyDescription = "";
if (!formerCompanyName.equals("")) {
  formerCompanyDescription =
    "(formerly " + formerCompanyName + ")";
}
%>
```

Listing 10.4 *company-info.jsp (continued)*

```
<TITLE><%= companyName %></TITLE>
<LINK REL=STYLESHEET
      HREF="events-styles.css"
      TYPE="text/css">
</HEAD>

<BODY>
<TABLE BORDER=5 ALIGN="CENTER">
  <TR><TH CLASS="TITLE">
      <%= companyName %><BR>
      <%= formerCompanyDescription %>
</TABLE>
<P>
Learn more about <B><%= companyName %></B>
<%= formerCompanyDescription %>
<UL>
  <LI><A HREF="products.jsp"><%= companyName %> products</A>
  <LI><A HREF="services.jsp"><%= companyName %> services</A>
  <LI><A HREF="history.jsp"><%= companyName %> history</A>
  <LI><A HREF="invest.jsp">investing in <%= companyName %></A>
  <LI><A HREF="contact.jsp">contacting <%= companyName %></A>
</UL>

</BODY>
</HTML>
```

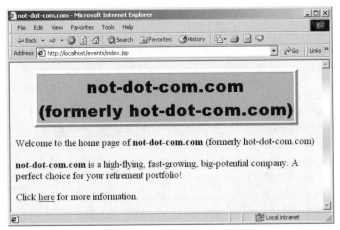

Figure 10–1 Home page for the company with the frequently changing name.

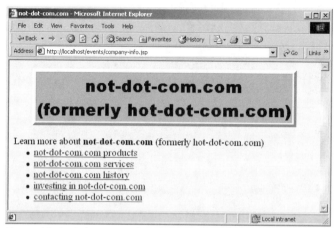

Figure 10–2   Informational page for the company with the frequently changing name.

10.3 Detecting Changes in Servlet Context Attributes

OK, when the Web application is loaded, you can set up *initial* values of resources and store references to them in the servlet context. But what if you want to be notified whenever these resources *change*? For example, what if the value of resource B depends on the value of resource A? If resource A changes, you need to automatically update the value of resource B. Handling this situation is the job of servlet context attribute listeners. Using them involves the following steps.

1. **Implement the `ServletContextAttributeListener` interface.** This interface is in the `javax.servlet` package.
2. **Override `attributeAdded`, `attributeReplaced`, and `attributeRemoved`.** The `attributeAdded` method is triggered when a new attribute is added to the servlet context. When a new value is assigned to an existing servlet context attribute, `attributeAdded` is triggered with the new value and `attributeReplaced` is triggered with the old value (i.e., the value being replaced). The `attributeRemoved` method is triggered when a servlet context attribute is removed altogether.
3. **Obtain references to the attribute name, attribute value, and servlet context.** Each of the three `ServletContextAttributeListener` methods takes a `ServletContextAttributeEvent` as an argument. The `ServletContextAttributeEvent` class has

three useful methods: `getName` (the name of the attribute that was changed), `getValue` (the value of the changed attribute—the new value for `attributeAdded` and the previous value for `attribute-Replaced` and `attributeRemoved`), and `getServletContext` (the servlet context).

4. **Use the objects.** You normally compare the attribute name to a stored name to see if it is the one you are monitoring. The attribute value is used in an application-specific manner. The servlet context is usually used to read previously stored attributes (`getAttribute`), store new or changed attributes (`setAttribute`), and make entries in the log file (`log`).

5. **Declare the listener.** Use the `listener` and `listener-class` elements to simply list the fully qualified name of the listener class, as below.

```
<listener>
  <listener-class>somePackage.SomeListener</listener-class>
</listener>
```

For now, assume that this declaration goes in the *web.xml* file immediately before any `servlet` elements. However, in Section 10.5 you'll see that if you package listeners with tag libraries, you can use the identical declaration within the TLD (tag library descriptor) file of the tag library.

The following section gives an example.

10.4 Example: Monitoring Changes to Commonly Used Data

Section 10.2 shows how to read the current and former company names when the Web application is loaded and how to make use of those values in JSP pages. But what if you want to change the company name during the execution of the Web application? It is reasonable to expect a routine that makes this change to modify the `companyName` servlet context attribute. After all, in this context, that's what it means to change the company name. It is not reasonable, however, to expect that routine to modify (or even know about) the `formerCompanyName` attribute. But, if the company name changes, the former company name must change as well. Enter servlet context attribute listeners!

The following steps summarize a listener that automatically updates the former company name whenever the current company name changes.

1. **Implement the `ServletContextAttributeListener` interface.** Listing 10.5 shows a class (`ChangedCompanyNameListener`) that implements this interface.
2. **Override `attributeAdded`, `attributeReplaced`, and `attributeRemoved`.** The `attributeReplaced` method is used to detect modification to context attributes. Empty bodies are supplied for the `attributeAdded` and `attributeRemoved` methods.
3. **Obtain references to the attribute name, attribute value, and servlet context.** The `attributeReplaced` method calls `getName` and `getValue` on its `ServletContextAttributeEvent` argument to obtain the name and value of the modified attribute. The method also calls `getServletContext` on its argument to get a reference to the servlet context.
4. **Use the objects.** The attribute name is compared to `"company-Name"`. If the name matches, the attribute value is used as the new value of the `formerCompanyName` servlet context attribute.
5. **Declare the listener.** The listener is declared in the deployment descriptor with the `listener` and `listener-class` elements, as below.

```
<listener>
  <listener-class>
    moreservlets.listeners.ChangedCompanyNameListener
  </listener-class>
</listener>
```

The *web.xml* file is shown in Listing 10.6.

Listing 10.7 presents a JSP page containing a form that displays the current company name, lets users enter a new name, and submits the new name to the `Change-CompanyName` servlet (Listing 10.8). Since changing the company name is a privileged operation, access to the form and the servlet should be restricted.

So, the form is placed in the *admin* directory and the `servlet` and `servlet-mapping` elements are used to assign the servlet a URL that also starts with */admin*. See Section 5.3 (Assigning Names and Custom URLs) for details on `servlet` and `servlet-mapping`; see the deployment descriptor in Listing 10.6 for the usage in this example.

Next, the `security-constraint` element is used to stipulate that only authenticated users in the `ceo` role can access the *admin* directory. Then, the `login-config` element is used to specify that form-based authentication be used, with *login.jsp* (Listing 10.9) collecting usernames and passwords and *login-error.jsp* (Listing 10.10) displaying messages to users who failed authentication. Listing 10.11 shows a Tomcat-specific password file used to designate a user who is in the ceo role. See Section 7.1 (Form-Based Authentication) for details on these types of security settings; see the deployment descriptor in Listing 10.6 for the usage in this example.

Figures 10–3 through 10–8 show the results of logging in, changing the company name, and revisiting the pages that display the current and former company names.

Listing 10.5	*ChangedCompanyNameListener.java*

```java
package moreservlets.listeners;

import java.io.*;
import javax.servlet.*;
import javax.servlet.http.*;

/** Listener that monitors changes in the company
 *  name (which is stored in the companyName attribute
 *  of the servlet context).
 */

public class ChangedCompanyNameListener
    implements ServletContextAttributeListener {

  /** When the companyName attribute changes, put
   *  the previous value into the formerCompanyName
   *  attribute.
   */

  public void attributeReplaced
                  (ServletContextAttributeEvent event) {
    if (event.getName().equals("companyName")) {
      String oldName = (String)event.getValue();
      ServletContext context = event.getServletContext();
      context.setAttribute("formerCompanyName", oldName);
    }
  }

  public void attributeAdded
                  (ServletContextAttributeEvent event) {}

  public void attributeRemoved
                  (ServletContextAttributeEvent event) {}
}
```

Listing 10.6 *web.xml* (Excerpt for changed company name listener)

```xml
<?xml version="1.0" encoding="ISO-8859-1"?>
<!DOCTYPE web-app PUBLIC
    "-//Sun Microsystems, Inc.//DTD Web Application 2.3//EN"
    "http://java.sun.com/dtd/web-app_2_3.dtd">

<web-app>
  <!-- ... -->

  <!-- Register the listener that monitors changes to
       the company name.
  -->
  <listener>
    <listener-class>
      moreservlets.listeners.ChangedCompanyNameListener
    </listener-class>
  </listener>
  <!-- ... -->

  <!-- Assign the name ChangeCompanyName to
       moreservlets.ChangeCompanyName. -->
  <servlet>
    <servlet-name>ChangeCompanyName</servlet-name>
    <servlet-class>moreservlets.ChangeCompanyName</servlet-class>
  </servlet>

  <!-- Give a name to the servlet that redirects users
       to the home page.
  -->
  <servlet>
    <servlet-name>Redirector</servlet-name>
    <servlet-class>moreservlets.RedirectorServlet</servlet-class>
  </servlet>

  <!-- Assign the URL /admin/ChangeCompanyName to the
       servlet that is named ChangeCompanyName.
  -->
  <servlet-mapping>
    <servlet-name>ChangeCompanyName</servlet-name>
    <url-pattern>/admin/ChangeCompanyName</url-pattern>
  </servlet-mapping>
```

Listing 10.6   *web.xml* (Excerpt for changed company name listener) *(continued)*

```
<!-- Turn off invoker. Send requests to index.jsp. -->
<servlet-mapping>
  <servlet-name>Redirector</servlet-name>
  <url-pattern>/servlet/*</url-pattern>
</servlet-mapping>
<!-- ... -->

<!-- Protect everything within the "admin" directory.
     Direct client access to this directory requires
     authentication.
-->
<security-constraint>
  <web-resource-collection>
    <web-resource-name>Admin</web-resource-name>
    <url-pattern>/admin/*</url-pattern>
  </web-resource-collection>
  <auth-constraint>
    <role-name>ceo</role-name>
  </auth-constraint>
</security-constraint>

<!-- Tell the server to use form-based authentication. -->
<login-config>
  <auth-method>FORM</auth-method>
  <form-login-config>
    <form-login-page>/admin/login.jsp</form-login-page>
    <form-error-page>/admin/login-error.jsp</form-error-page>
  </form-login-config>
</login-config>
</web-app>
```

Listing 10.7   *change-company-name.jsp*

```
<!DOCTYPE HTML PUBLIC "-//W3C//DTD HTML 4.0 Transitional//EN">
<HTML>
<HEAD>
<%@ page import="moreservlets.listeners.*" %>
<%
String companyName =
  InitialCompanyNameListener.getCompanyName(application);
%>
<TITLE>Changing Company Name</TITLE>
<LINK REL=STYLESHEET
      HREF="../events-styles.css"
      TYPE="text/css">
</HEAD>

<BODY>
<TABLE BORDER=5 ALIGN="CENTER">
  <TR><TH CLASS="TITLE">Changing Company Name
</TABLE>
<P>

<FORM ACTION="ChangeCompanyName">
New name:
<INPUT TYPE="TEXT" NAME="newName" VALUE="<%= companyName %>">
<P>
<CENTER><INPUT TYPE="SUBMIT" VALUE="Submit Change"></CENTER>
</FORM>

</BODY>
</HTML>
```

Listing 10.8 *ChangeCompanyName.java*

```java
package moreservlets;

import java.io.*;
import javax.servlet.*;
import javax.servlet.http.*;

/** Servlet that changes the company name. The web.xml
 *  file specifies that only authenticated users in the
 *  ceo role can access the servlet. A servlet context
 *  attribute listener updates the former company name
 *  when this servlet (or any other program) changes
 *  the current company name.
 */

public class ChangeCompanyName extends HttpServlet {
  public void doGet(HttpServletRequest request,
                    HttpServletResponse response)
      throws ServletException, IOException {
    boolean isNameChanged = false;
    String newName = request.getParameter("newName");
    if ((newName != null) && (!newName.equals(""))) {
      isNameChanged = true;
      getServletContext().setAttribute("companyName",
                                       newName);
    }
    response.setContentType("text/html");
    PrintWriter out = response.getWriter();
    String docType =
      "<!DOCTYPE HTML PUBLIC \"-//W3C//DTD HTML 4.0 " +
      "Transitional//EN\">\n";
    String title = "Company Name";
    out.println
      (docType +
      "<HTML>\n" +
      "<HEAD><TITLE>" + title + "</TITLE></HEAD>\n" +
      "<BODY BGCOLOR=\"#FDF5E6\">\n" +
      "<H2 ALIGN=\"CENTER\">" + title + "</H2>");
    if (isNameChanged) {
      out.println("Company name changed to " + newName + ".");
    } else {
      out.println("Company name not changed.");
    }
    out.println("</BODY></HTML>");
  }
}
```

Listing 10.9 *login.jsp*

```
<!DOCTYPE HTML PUBLIC "-//W3C//DTD HTML 4.0 Transitional//EN">
<HTML>
<HEAD>
<TITLE>Log In</TITLE>
<LINK REL=STYLESHEET
      HREF="../events-styles.css"
      TYPE="text/css">
</HEAD>

<BODY>
<TABLE BORDER=5 ALIGN="CENTER">
  <TR><TH CLASS="TITLE">Log In</TABLE>
<P>
<H3>Sorry, you must log in before accessing this resource.</H3>
<FORM ACTION="j_security_check" METHOD="POST">
<TABLE>
<TR><TD>User name: <INPUT TYPE="TEXT" NAME="j_username">
<TR><TD>Password: <INPUT TYPE="PASSWORD" NAME="j_password">
<TR><TH><INPUT TYPE="SUBMIT" VALUE="Log In">
</TABLE>
</FORM>

</BODY>
</HTML>
```

Listing 10.10 *login-error.jsp*

```
<!DOCTYPE HTML PUBLIC "-//W3C//DTD HTML 4.0 Transitional//EN">
<HTML>
<HEAD>
<TITLE>Begone!</TITLE>
<LINK REL=STYLESHEET
      HREF="../events-styles.css"
      TYPE="text/css">
</HEAD>

<BODY>
<TABLE BORDER=5 ALIGN="CENTER">
  <TR><TH CLASS="TITLE">Begone!</TABLE>

<H3>Begone, ye unauthorized peon.</H3>

</BODY>
</HTML>
```

Listing 10.11	*tomcat-users.xml* (Excerpt for events examples)

```
<?xml version="1.0" encoding="ISO-8859-1"?>
<tomcat-users>
  <!-- ... -->
  <user name="gerstner" password="lou"
        roles="ceo" />
</tomcat-users>
```

Figure 10–3 Only users who are in the ceo role can access the form that changes the company name.

Figure 10–4 A failed login attempt.

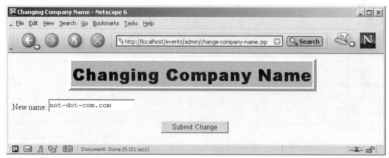

Figure 10–5 The form to change the company name when the page is accessed by an authenticated user who is in the ceo role.

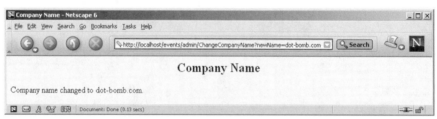

Figure 10–6 The name change confirmation page.

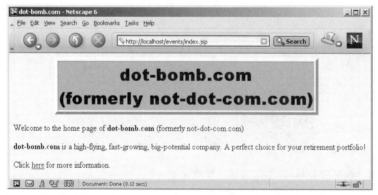

Figure 10–7 When the company name changes, the company home page (Listing 10.3) is automatically updated.

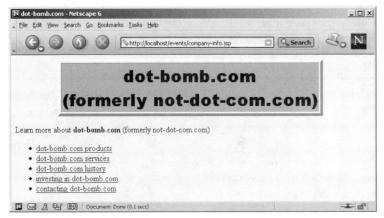

Figure 10–8 When the company name changes, the company information page (Listing 10.4) is also updated automatically.

10.5 Packaging Listeners with Tag Libraries

JSP tag libraries (Section 3.7, Chapter 11) provide a great way of encapsulating content that will be accessed by multiple JSP pages. But what if that content depends on life-cycle event listeners? If the `listener` and `listener-class` elements of *web.xml* were the only option for declaring listeners, tag library maintenance would be much more difficult. Normally, the user of a tag library can deploy it by simply dropping a JAR file in *WEB-INF/lib* and putting a TLD file in *WEB-INF*. Users of the tag libraries need no knowledge of the individual classes within the library, only of the tags that the library defines. But if the tag libraries used listeners, users of the libraries would need to discover the name of the listener classes and make *web.xml* entries for each one. This would be significantly more work.

Fortunately, the JSP 1.2 specification lets you put the listener declarations in the tag library descriptor file instead of in the deployment descriptor. But, wait! Event listeners need to run when the Web application is first loaded, not just the first time a JSP page that uses a custom library is accessed. How does the system handle this? The answer is that, when the Web application is loaded, the system automatically searches *WEB-INF* and its subdirectories for files with *.tld* extensions and uses all listener declarations that it finds. This means that your TLD files *must* be in the *WEB-INF* directory or a subdirectory thereof. In fact, although few servers enforce the restriction, the JSP 1.2 specification requires all TLD files to be in *WEB-INF* anyhow. Besides, putting the TLD files in *WEB-INF* is a good strategy to prevent users from retrieving them. So, you should make *WEB-INF* the standard TLD file location, regardless of whether your libraries use event handlers.

Core Approach

Always put your TLD files in the WEB-INF *directory or a subdirectory thereof.*

Unfortunately, there is a problem with this approach: Tomcat 4.0 improperly ignores TLD files at Web application startup time unless there is also a `taglib` entry in *web.xml* of the following form:

```
<taglib>
  <taglib-uri>/someName.tld</taglib-uri>
  <taglib-location>/WEB-INF/realName.tld</taglib-location>
</taglib>
```

As discussed in Section 5.13 (Locating Tag Library Descriptors), this entry is a good idea when the name of your tag library changes frequently. However, the JSP 1.2 specification does not require its use, and servers such as ServletExec 4.1 properly handle listener declarations in TLD files when there is no such entry. Nevertheless, Tomcat 4.0 requires it.

Core Warning

Tomcat 4.0 only reads listener declarations from TLD files that have `taglib` *entries in* web.xml.

Since listener declarations are a new capability in version 1.2 of the JSP specification, you must use the JSP 1.2 format of the tag library descriptor file. This format differs in two ways from the JSP 1.1 format.

First, the `DOCTYPE` declaration must use the JSP 1.2 Document Type Definition (DTD), not the 1.1 one. Here is the JSP 1.2 version:

```
<!DOCTYPE taglib
 PUBLIC "-//Sun Microsystems, Inc.//DTD JSP Tag Library 1.2//EN"
 "http://java.sun.com/dtd/web-jsptaglibrary_1_2.dtd">
```

Here is the JSP 1.1 version:

```
<!DOCTYPE taglib
 PUBLIC "-//Sun Microsystems, Inc.//DTD JSP Tag Library 1.1//EN"
 "http://java.sun.com/j2ee/dtds/web-jsptaglibrary_1_1.dtd">
```

Second, a number of elements within the TLD file have changed their names slightly. In particular, hyphens were added to the `tlibversion`, `jspversion`, `shortname`, `tagclass`, and `bodycontent` elements. Also, the `info` element was renamed to `description`. These changes are summarized in Table 10.1.

Table 10.1   Changes in tag library element names. You must use the new element names if you use the 1.2 DTD (which is required if you use new capabilities such as listeners).

JSP 1.2 Name	*JSP 1.1 Name*
tlib-version	tlibversion
jsp-version	jspversion
short-name	shortname
description	info
tag-class	tagclass
body-content	bodycontent

Given the changes to the DOCTYPE declaration and the element names, Listing 10.12 shows the template for a TLD file in JSP 1.2. For comparison, Listing 10.13 shows the JSP 1.1 template.

Listing 10.12   JSP 1.2 Tag Library Descriptor (Template)

```
<?xml version="1.0" encoding="ISO-8859-1" ?>
<!DOCTYPE taglib
 PUBLIC "-//Sun Microsystems, Inc.//DTD JSP Tag Library 1.2//EN"
 "http://java.sun.com/dtd/web-jsptaglibrary_1_2.dtd">

<taglib>
  <tlib-version>1.0</tlib-version>
  <jsp-version>1.2</jsp-version>
  <short-name>some-name</short-name>
  <description>
    Tag library documentation.
  </description>
```

Listing 10.12   JSP 1.2 Tag Library Descriptor (Template) *(continued)*

```
<taglib>
  <!-- listener elements, if any, each of the following form:
    <listener>
      <listener-class>somePackage.SomeListener</listener-class>
    </listener>
  -->

  <tag>
    <name>tagName</name>
    <tag-class>somePackage.SomeTag</tag-class>
    <body-content>...</body-content>
    <description>Tag documentation.</description>
  </tag>

  <!-- Other tag elements, if any. -->
</taglib>
```

Listing 10.13   JSP 1.1 Tag Library Descriptor (Template)

```
<?xml version="1.0" encoding="ISO-8859-1" ?>
<!DOCTYPE taglib
 PUBLIC "-//Sun Microsystems, Inc.//DTD JSP Tag Library 1.1//EN"
 "http://java.sun.com/j2ee/dtds/web-jsptaglibrary_1_1.dtd">

<taglib>
  <tlibversion>1.0</tlibversion>
  <jspversion>1.1</jspversion>
  <shortname>some-name</shortname>
  <info>
    Tag library documentation.
  </info>

  <taglib>
    <tag>
      <name>tagName</name>
      <tagclass>somePackage.SomeTag</tagclass>
      <bodycontent>...</bodycontent>
      <info>Tag documentation.</info>
    </tag>

    <!-- Other tag elements, if any. -->
  </taglib>
```

10.6 Example: Packaging the Company Name Listeners

The listeners shown in Sections 10.2 and 10.4 are very effective in keeping track of the current and former company names. However, the pages that display the names (*index.jsp*, Listing 10.3 and *company-info.jsp*, Listing 10.4) are a bit difficult to read and maintain. This difficulty is due to the need for checking if the former company name is missing before trying to display it, a test that results in quite a bit of explicit Java code in the JSP page. A perfect job for a simple custom tag!

Listings 10.14 and 10.15 show custom tags that print out the current and former company names, respectively. The first tag simply prints the current company name. The second tag uses a `fullDescription` attribute to decide whether to simply print the former company name (e.g., `some-company.com`) or the company name inside parentheses (e.g., `(formerly some-company.com)`). Listing 10.16 shows the TLD file for this library: the `listener` elements of Sections 10.2 and 10.4 are moved out of the *web.xml* file and into the TLD file, which is then placed in the *WEB-INF* directory. Listing 10.17 shows the *web.xml* file: the previous `listener` elements are removed, and a `taglib` entry is added that makes it easier to update the name of the TLD file and lets the listeners be detected at Web application startup time by Tomcat 4.0.

Finally, Listings 10.18 and 10.19 show the company home page (see Listing 10.3) and company information page (see Listing 10.4) reworked with the new custom tags. Note that for the `uri` attribute of the `taglib` directive, these pages use `"/company-name-taglib.tld"` (the alias defined with the *web.xml* `taglib` element), not `"/WEB-INF/company-name-taglib.tld"` (the real location). Figures 10–9 and 10–10 show the results—identical to those shown earlier in Figures 10–1 and 10–2.

Listing 10.14   *CompanyNameTag.java*

```
package moreservlets.tags;

import javax.servlet.*;
import javax.servlet.jsp.*;
import javax.servlet.jsp.tagext.*;
import java.io.*;
import moreservlets.listeners.*;
```

Listing 10.14 *CompanyNameTag.java (continued)*

```java
/** The InitialCompanyNameListener class has static
 *  methods that permit access to the current and former
 *  company names. But, using these methods in JSP requires
 *  explicit Java code, and creating beans that provided
 *  the information would have yielded a cumbersome result.
 *  So, we simply move the code into a custom tag.
 */

public class CompanyNameTag extends TagSupport {
  public int doStartTag() {
    try {
      ServletContext context = pageContext.getServletContext();
      String companyName =
        InitialCompanyNameListener.getCompanyName(context);
      JspWriter out = pageContext.getOut();
      out.print(companyName);
    } catch(IOException ioe) {
      System.out.println("Error printing company name.");
    }
    return(SKIP_BODY);
  }
}
```

Listing 10.15 *FormerCompanyNameTag.java*

```java
package moreservlets.tags;

import javax.servlet.*;
import javax.servlet.jsp.*;
import javax.servlet.jsp.tagext.*;
import java.io.*;
import moreservlets.listeners.*;

/** The InitialCompanyNameListener class has static
 *  methods that permit access to the current and former
 *  company names. But, using these methods in JSP requires
 *  explicit Java code, and creating beans that provided
 *  the information would have yielded a cumbersome result.
 *  So, we simply move the code into a custom tag.
 */
```

Listing 10.15 *FormerCompanyNameTag.java (continued)*

```java
public class FormerCompanyNameTag extends TagSupport {
  private boolean useFullDescription = false;

  public int doStartTag() {
    try {
      ServletContext context = pageContext.getServletContext();
      String formerCompanyName =
       InitialCompanyNameListener.getFormerCompanyName(context);
      JspWriter out = pageContext.getOut();
      if (useFullDescription) {
        String formerCompanyDescription = "";
        if (!formerCompanyName.equals("")) {
          formerCompanyDescription =
            "(formerly " + formerCompanyName + ")";
        }
        out.print(formerCompanyDescription);
      } else {
        out.print(formerCompanyName);
      }
    } catch(IOException ioe) {
      System.out.println("Error printing former company name.");
    }
    return(SKIP_BODY);
  }

  /** If the user supplies a fullDescription attribute
   *  with the value "true" (upper, lower, or mixed case),
   *  set the useFullDescription instance variable to true.
   *  Otherwise, leave it false.
   */

  public void setFullDescription(String flag) {
    if (flag.equalsIgnoreCase("true")) {
      useFullDescription = true;
    }
  }

  /** Servers are permitted to reuse tag instances
   *  once a request is finished. So, this resets
   *  the useFullDescription field. This method
   *  is automatically called after the system is
   *  finished using the tag.
   */

  public void release() {
    useFullDescription = false;
  }
}
```

Listing 10.16   *company-name-taglib.tld*

```xml
<?xml version="1.0" encoding="ISO-8859-1" ?>
<!DOCTYPE taglib
 PUBLIC "-//Sun Microsystems, Inc.//DTD JSP Tag Library 1.2//EN"
 "http://java.sun.com/dtd/web-jsptaglibrary_1_2.dtd">

<!-- a tag library descriptor -->

<taglib>
  <tlib-version>1.0</tlib-version>
  <jsp-version>1.2</jsp-version>
  <short-name>company-name-tags</short-name>
  <description>
    A tag library to print out the ever-changing current
    and former company names (which are monitored by event
    listeners).
  </description>

  <!-- Register the listener that sets up the
       initial company name. -->
  <listener>
    <listener-class>
      moreservlets.listeners.InitialCompanyNameListener
    </listener-class>
  </listener>

  <!-- Register the listener that monitors changes to
       the company name.
  -->
  <listener>
    <listener-class>
      moreservlets.listeners.ChangedCompanyNameListener
    </listener-class>
  </listener>

  <!-- Define a tag that prints out the current name. -->
  <tag>
    <name>companyName</name>
    <tag-class>moreservlets.tags.CompanyNameTag</tag-class>
    <body-content>empty</body-content>
    <description>The current company name</description>
  </tag>
```

Listing 10.16 *company-name-taglib.tld (continued)*

```
<!-- Define a tag that prints out the previous name. -->
<tag>
  <name>formerCompanyName</name>
  <tag-class>moreservlets.tags.FormerCompanyNameTag</tag-class>
  <body-content>empty</body-content>
  <description>The previous company name</description>
  <attribute>
    <name>fullDescription</name>
    <required>false</required>
  </attribute>
</tag>
</taglib>
```

Listing 10.17 *web.xml* (Excerpt for custom tags)

```
<?xml version="1.0" encoding="ISO-8859-1"?>
<!DOCTYPE web-app PUBLIC
    "-//Sun Microsystems, Inc.//DTD Web Application 2.3//EN"
    "http://java.sun.com/dtd/web-app_2_3.dtd">

<web-app>
  <!-- ... -->

  <!-- Removed declarations for initial and changed company
       name listeners. They are now in TLD file. -->
  <!-- ... -->

  <!-- Register the company-name tag library. -->
  <taglib>
    <taglib-uri>
      /company-name-taglib.tld
    </taglib-uri>
    <taglib-location>
      /WEB-INF/company-name-taglib.tld
    </taglib-location>
  </taglib>

  <!-- ... -->
</web-app>
```

Listing 10.18 *index2.jsp*

```
<!DOCTYPE HTML PUBLIC "-//W3C//DTD HTML 4.0 Transitional//EN">
<HTML>
<HEAD>
<%@ taglib uri="/company-name-taglib.tld" prefix="msajsp" %>
<TITLE><msajsp:companyName/></TITLE>
<LINK REL=STYLESHEET
      HREF="events-styles.css"
      TYPE="text/css">
</HEAD>

<BODY>
<TABLE BORDER=5 ALIGN="CENTER">
  <TR><TH CLASS="TITLE">
      <msajsp:companyName/><BR>
      <msajsp:formerCompanyName fullDescription="true"/>
</TABLE>
<P>
Welcome to the home page of <B><msajsp:companyName/></B>
<msajsp:formerCompanyName fullDescription="true"/>
<P>
<B><msajsp:companyName/></B> is a high-flying, fast-growing,
big-potential company. A perfect choice for your
retirement portfolio!
<P>
Click <A HREF="company-info2.jsp">here</A> for more information.
</BODY>
</HTML>
```

Listing 10.19 *company-info2.jsp*

```
<!DOCTYPE HTML PUBLIC "-//W3C//DTD HTML 4.0 Transitional//EN">
<HTML>
<HEAD>
<%@ taglib uri="/company-name-taglib.tld" prefix="msajsp" %>
<TITLE><msajsp:companyName/></TITLE>
<LINK REL=STYLESHEET
      HREF="events-styles.css"
      TYPE="text/css">
</HEAD>
```

Listing 10.19 *company-info2.jsp (continued)*

```
<BODY>
<TABLE BORDER=5 ALIGN="CENTER">
  <TR><TH CLASS="TITLE">
      <msajsp:companyName/><BR>
      <msajsp:formerCompanyName fullDescription="true"/>
</TABLE>
<P>
Learn more about <B><msajsp:companyName/></B>
<msajsp:formerCompanyName fullDescription="true"/>
<UL>
  <LI><A HREF="products.jsp"><msajsp:companyName/> products</A>
  <LI><A HREF="services.jsp"><msajsp:companyName/> services</A>
  <LI><A HREF="history.jsp"><msajsp:companyName/> history</A>
  <LI><A HREF="invest.jsp">investing in <msajsp:companyName/></A>
  <LI><A HREF="contact.jsp">contacting <msajsp:companyName/></A>
</UL>

</BODY>
</HTML>
```

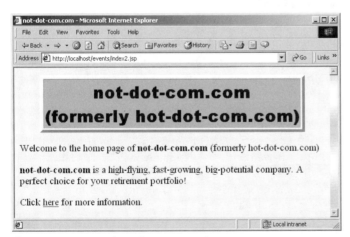

Figure 10–9 Reworking the company home page to use custom tags results in an identical appearance (compare Figure 10–1) but yields JSP code that is significantly easier to read and maintain.

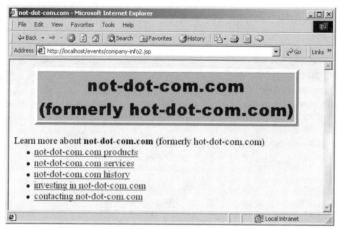

Figure 10–10 Reworking the company information page to use custom tags results in an identical appearance (compare Figure 10–2) but yields JSP code that is significantly easier to read and maintain.

10.7 Recognizing Session Creation and Destruction

Classes that implement the `ServletContextListener` and `ServletContext-AttributeListener` interfaces respond to changes in the servlet context, which is shared by all servlets and JSP pages in the Web application. But, with session tracking (Section 2.10), data is stored in per-user `HttpSession` objects, not in the servlet context. What if you want to monitor changes to this user-specific data? That's the job of the `HttpSessionListener` and `HttpSessionAttributeListener` interfaces. This section discusses `HttpSessionListener`, the listener that is notified when a session is created or destroyed (either deliberately with `invalidate` or by timing out). Section 10.9 discusses `HttpSessionAttributeListener`, the listener that is notified when session attributes are added, replaced, or removed.

Using `HttpSessionListener` involves the following steps.

1. **Implement the `HttpSessionListener` interface.** This interface is in the `javax.servlet.http` package.
2. **Override `sessionCreated` and `sessionDestroyed`.** The first of these (`sessionCreated`) is triggered when a new session is created. The second method (`sessionDestroyed`) is triggered when a a session is destroyed. This destruction could be due to an explicit call to the `invalidate` method or because the elapsed time since the last client access exceeds the session timeout.

3. **Obtain a reference to the session and possibly to the servlet context.** Each of the two `HttpSessionListener` methods takes an `HttpSessionEvent` as an argument. The `HttpSessionEvent` class has a `getSession` method that provides access to the session object. You almost always want this reference; you occasionally also want a reference to the servlet context. If so, first obtain the session object and then call `getServletContext` on it.

4. **Use the objects.** Surprisingly, one of the only methods you usually call on the session object is the `setAttribute` method. You do this in `sessionCreated` if you want to guarantee that all sessions have a certain attribute. Wait! What about `getAttribute`? Nope; you don't use it. In `sessionCreated`, there is nothing in the session yet, so `getAttribute` is pointless. In addition, all attributes are removed *before* `sessionDestroyed` is called, so calling `getAttribute` is also pointless there. If you want to clean up attributes that are left in sessions that time out, you use the `attributeRemoved` method of `HttpSessionAttributeListener` (Section 10.9). Consequently, `sessionDestroyed` is mostly reserved for listeners that are simply keeping track of the number of sessions in use.

5. **Declare the listener.** In the *web.xml* or TLD file, use the `listener` and `listener-class` elements to simply list the fully qualified name of the listener class, as below.

```
<listener>
  <listener-class>somePackage.SomeListener</listener-class>
</listener>
```

10.8 Example: A Listener That Counts Sessions

Session tracking can significantly increase the server's memory load. For example, if a site that uses session tracking has 1,000 unique visitors per hour and the server uses a two-hour session timeout, the system will have approximately 2,000 sessions in memory at any one time. Reducing the timeout to one hour would cut the session memory requirements in half but would risk having active sessions prematurely time out. You need to track typical usage before you can decide on the appropriate solution.

So, you need a listener that will keep track of how many sessions are created, how many are destroyed, and how many are in memory at any one time. Assuming that you have no explicit calls to `invalidate`, the session destructions correspond to expired timeouts.

The following steps summarize a listener that accomplishes this task.

1. **Implement the `HttpSessionListener` interface.** Listing 10.20 shows a class (`SessionCounter`) that implements this interface.
2. **Override `sessionCreated` and `sessionDestroyed`.** The first of these (`sessionCreated`) increments two counters: `totalSession-Count` and `currentSessionCount`. If the current count is greater than the previous maximum count, the method also increments the `maxSessionCount` variable. The second method (`session-Destroyed`) decrements the `currentSessionCount` variable.
3. **Obtain and use the servlet context.** In this application, no specific use is made of the session object. The only thing that matters is the fact that a session was created or destroyed, not any details about the session itself. But, the session counts have to be placed in a location that is easily accessible to servlets and JSP pages that will display the counts. So, the first time `sessionCreated` is called, it obtains the session object, calls `getServletContext` on it, and then calls `set-Attribute` to store the listener object in the servlet context.
4. **Declare the listener.** Listing 10.21 shows the *web.xml* file. It declares the listener with the `listener` and `listener-class` elements, as below.

```
<listener>
  <listener-class>
    moreservlets.listeners.SessionCounter
  </listener-class>
</listener>
```

Listing 10.22 shows a JSP page that displays the session counts. Figure 10–11 shows a typical result.

In order to test session creation and timeout, I made three temporary changes.

First, I disabled cookies in my browser. Since my servers are set to use cookies for session tracking, this had the result of making each request be a new session. See the following subsection for information on disabling cookies in Netscape and Internet Explorer.

Second, I created an HTML page (Listing 10.23, Figure 10–12) that used frames with four rows and four columns to request the same JSP page (Listing 10.24) 16 times. In an environment that has cookies disabled, a request for the framed page results in 16 new sessions being created on the server (recall that JSP pages perform session tracking automatically unless the `session` attribute of the `page` directive is set to `false`—see Section 3.4).

Third, I chose an extremely low session timeout: two minutes. This saved me from waiting for hours to test the session-counting listener. Changing the default session timeout is discussed in Section 5.10, but it simply amounts to creating a `session-config` entry in *web.xml*, as follows:

```
<session-config>
  <session-timeout>2</session-timeout>
</session-config>
```

Listing 10.20	*SessionCounter.java*

```java
package moreservlets.listeners;

import java.io.*;
import javax.servlet.*;
import javax.servlet.http.*;

/** Listener that keeps track of the number of sessions
 *  that the Web application is currently using and has
 *  ever used in its life cycle.
 */

public class SessionCounter implements HttpSessionListener {
  private int totalSessionCount = 0;
  private int currentSessionCount = 0;
  private int maxSessionCount = 0;
  private ServletContext context = null;

  public void sessionCreated(HttpSessionEvent event) {
    totalSessionCount++;
    currentSessionCount++;
    if (currentSessionCount > maxSessionCount) {
      maxSessionCount = currentSessionCount;
    }
    if (context == null) {
      storeInServletContext(event);
    }
  }

  public void sessionDestroyed(HttpSessionEvent event) {
    currentSessionCount--;
  }

  /** The total number of sessions created. */

  public int getTotalSessionCount() {
    return(totalSessionCount);
  }

  /** The number of sessions currently in memory. */

  public int getCurrentSessionCount() {
    return(currentSessionCount);
  }
```

Listing 10.20 *SessionCounter.java (continued)*

```java
/** The largest number of sessions ever in memory
 *  at any one time.
 */

public int getMaxSessionCount() {
  return(maxSessionCount);
}

// Register self in the servlet context so that
// servlets and JSP pages can access the session counts.

private void storeInServletContext(HttpSessionEvent event) {
  HttpSession session = event.getSession();
  context = session.getServletContext();
  context.setAttribute("sessionCounter", this);
}
}
```

Listing 10.21 *web.xml* (Excerpt for session counting listener)

```xml
<?xml version="1.0" encoding="ISO-8859-1"?>
<!DOCTYPE web-app PUBLIC
    "-//Sun Microsystems, Inc.//DTD Web Application 2.3//EN"
    "http://java.sun.com/dtd/web-app_2_3.dtd">

<web-app>
  <!-- ... -->

  <!-- Register the session counting event listener. -->
  <listener>
    <listener-class>
      moreservlets.listeners.SessionCounter
    </listener-class>
  </listener>
  <!-- ... -->

  <!-- Set the default session timeout to two minutes. -->
  <session-config>
    <session-timeout>2</session-timeout>
  </session-config>

  <!-- ... -->
</web-app>
```

Listing 10.22 *session-counts.jsp*

```
<!DOCTYPE HTML PUBLIC "-//W3C//DTD HTML 4.0 Transitional//EN">
<HTML>
<HEAD>
<TITLE>Session Info</TITLE>
<LINK REL=STYLESHEET
      HREF="events-styles.css"
      TYPE="text/css">
</HEAD>

<BODY>
<TABLE BORDER=5 ALIGN="CENTER">
  <TR><TH CLASS="TITLE">Session Info</TABLE>
<P>

<jsp:useBean class="moreservlets.listeners.SessionCounter"
             id="sessionCounter" scope="application" />
<UL>
<LI>Total number of sessions in the life of this
    Web application:
    <jsp:getProperty name="sessionCounter"
                     property="totalSessionCount" />.
<LI>Number of sessions currently in memory:
    <jsp:getProperty name="sessionCounter"
                     property="currentSessionCount" />.
<LI>Maximum number of sessions that have ever been in
    memory at any one time:
    <jsp:getProperty name="sessionCounter"
                     property="maxSessionCount" />.
</UL>

</BODY>
</HTML>
```

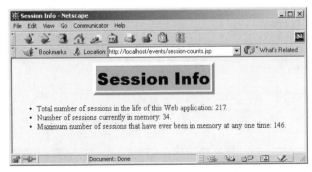

Figure 10–11 The SessionCounter listener keeps track of the sessions used in the Web application.

Listing 10.23 *make-sessions.html*

```
<!DOCTYPE HTML PUBLIC "-//W3C//DTD HTML 4.0 Frameset//EN">
<HTML>
<HEAD>
  <TITLE>Session Testing...</TITLE>
</HEAD>

<FRAMESET ROWS="*,*,*,*" COLS="*,*,*,*">
  <FRAME SRC="test.jsp">
  <FRAME SRC="test.jsp">
  <FRAME SRC="test.jsp">
  <FRAME SRC="test.jsp">
  <FRAME SRC="test.jsp">
  <FRAME SRC="test.jsp">
  <FRAME SRC="test.jsp">
  <FRAME SRC="test.jsp">
  <FRAME SRC="test.jsp">
  <FRAME SRC="test.jsp">
  <FRAME SRC="test.jsp">
  <FRAME SRC="test.jsp">
  <FRAME SRC="test.jsp">
  <FRAME SRC="test.jsp">
  <FRAME SRC="test.jsp">
  <FRAME SRC="test.jsp">
  <NOFRAMES><BODY>
    This example requires a frame-capable browser.
  </BODY></NOFRAMES>
</FRAMESET>
</HTML>
```

Listing 10.24 *test.jsp*

```
<!DOCTYPE HTML PUBLIC "-//W3C//DTD HTML 4.0 Transitional//EN">
<!-- The purpose of this page is to force the system
     to create a session. -->
<HTML>
<HEAD><TITLE>Test</TITLE></HEAD>

<%@ page import="moreservlets.*" %>
<BODY BGCOLOR="<%= ColorUtils.randomColor() %>">

</BODY></HTML>
```

Listing 10.25 *ColorUtils.java*

```java
package moreservlets;

/** Small utility to generate random HTML color names. */

public class ColorUtils {
  // The official HTML color names.
  private static String[] htmlColorNames =
    { "AQUA", "BLACK", "BLUE", "FUCHSIA", "GRAY", "GREEN",
      "LIME", "MAROON", "NAVY", "OLIVE", "PURPLE", "RED",
      "SILVER", "TEAL", "WHITE", "YELLOW" };

  public static String randomColor() {
    int index = randomInt(htmlColorNames.length);
    return(htmlColorNames[index]);
  }

  // Returns a random number from 0 to n-1 inclusive.

  private static int randomInt(int n) {
    return((int)(Math.random() * n));
  }
}
```

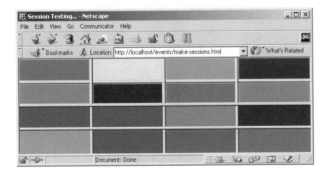

Figure 10–12 Session management was tested with a frame-based page that was invoked after cookies were disabled. So, each request resulted in 16 different sessions.

Disabling Cookies

Figures 10–13 through 10–15 summarize the approach to disabling cookies in Netscape 4, Netscape 6, and Internet Explorer 5. As discussed in the previous sub-section, temporarily disabling cookies is useful for testing session usage.

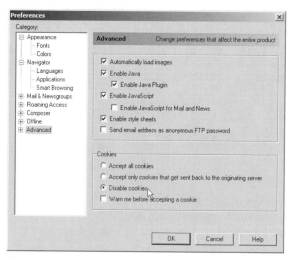

Figure 10–13 To disable cookies in Netscape 4, choose the Edit menu, then Preferences, then Advanced. Select "Disable cookies." Reset the browser after you are done testing; my preferred setting is "Accept only cookies that get sent back to the originating server."

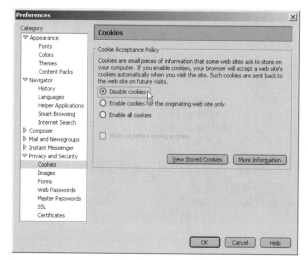

Figure 10–14 To disable cookies in Netscape 6, choose the Edit menu, then Preferences, then Privacy and Security, then Cookies. Select "Disable cookies." Reset the browser after you are done testing; my preferred setting is "Enable cookies for the originating web site only."

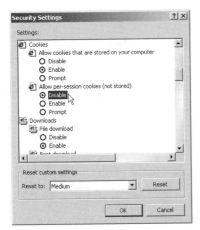

Figure 10–15 To disable cookies in Internet Explorer 5, choose the Tools menu, then Internet Options, then Security, then Custom Level. Since the goal here is to generate multiple sessions, you only need to disable per-session cookies. When done testing, reset the browser by changing the setting back to Enable.

10.9 Watching for Changes in Session Attributes

OK, so `HttpSessionListener` lets you detect when a session is created or destroyed. But, since session attributes are removed before session destruction, this listener does not let you clean up attributes that are in destroyed sessions. That's the job of the `HttpSessionAttributeListener` interface. Use of this interface involves the following steps.

1. **Implement the `HttpSessionAttributeListener` interface.**
   This interface is in the `javax.servlet.http` package.

2. **Override `attributeAdded`, `attributeReplaced`, and `attributeRemoved`.** The `attributeAdded` method is triggered when a new attribute is added to a session. When a new value is assigned to an existing session attribute, `attributeAdded` is triggered with the new value and `attributeReplaced` is triggered with the old value (i.e., the value being replaced). The `attribute-Removed` method is triggered when a session attribute is removed altogether. This removal can be due to an explicit programmer call to `removeAttribute`, but is more commonly due to the system remov-

ing all attributes of sessions that are about to be deleted because their timeout expired.

3. **Obtain references to the attribute name, attribute value, session, and servlet context.** Each of the three `HttpSession-AttributeListener` methods takes an `HttpSessionBinding-Event` as an argument. The `HttpSessionBindingEvent` class has three useful methods: `getName` (the name of the attribute that was changed), `getValue` (the value of the changed attribute—the new value for `attributeAdded` and the previous value for `attribute-Replaced` and `attributeRemoved`), and `getSession` (the `HttpSession` object). If you also want access to the servlet context, first obtain the session and then call `getServletContext` on it.

4. **Use the objects.** The attribute name is usually compared to a stored name to see if it is the one you are monitoring. The attribute value is used in an application-specific manner. The session is usually used to read previously stored attributes (`getAttribute`) or to store new or changed attributes (`setAttribute`).

5. **Declare the listener.** In the *web.xml* or TLD file, use the `listener` and `listener-class` elements to simply list the fully qualified name of the listener class, as below.

```
<listener>
  <listener-class>somePackage.SomeListener</listener-class>
</listener>
```

10.10 Example: Monitoring Yacht Orders

You're "promoted" to sales manager. (OK, ok, so that is too horrible a fate to contemplate. All right then, you are asked to help the sales manager.) You want to track buying patterns for a specific item (a yacht, in this case). Of course, you could try to find all servlets and JSP pages that process orders and change each one to record yacht purchases. That's an awful lot of work for what sounds like a simple request, though. Pretty hard to maintain, anyhow.

A much better option is to create a session attribute listener that monitors the attributes corresponding to order reservations or purchases and that records the information in the log file for later perusal by the sales manager.

The following steps summarize a listener that accomplishes this task.

1. **Implement the `HttpSessionAttributeListener` interface.** Listing 10.26 shows a class (`YachtWatcher`) that implements this interface.

2. **Override `attributeAdded`, `attributeReplaced`, and `attributeRemoved`.** The first of these (`attributeAdded`) is used to log the fact that a yacht was reserved (tentative) or purchased (permanent). The other two methods are used to print retractions of order reservations (but not purchases—all sales are final).

3. **Obtain references to the attribute name, attribute value, session, and servlet context.** Each of the three methods calls `getName` and `getValue` on its `HttpSessionBindingEvent` argument to obtain the name and value of the modified attribute. The methods also call `getServletContext` on the session object (obtained with `getSession`) to get a reference to the servlet context.

4. **Use the objects.** The attribute name is compared to `"orderedItem"` (attribute addition, replacement, and removal) and `"purchasedItem"` (attribute addition only). If the name matches, then the attribute value is compared to `"yacht"`. If that comparison also succeeds, then the `log` method of the servlet context is called.

5. **Declare the listener.** Listing 10.27 shows the *web.xml* file. It declares the listener with the `listener` and `listener-class` elements, as below.

```
<listener>
  <listener-class>
    moreservlets.listeners.YachtWatcher
  </listener-class>
</listener>
```

Listings 10.28 and 10.29 show a servlet that handles orders and an HTML form that sends it data, respectively. Figures 10–16 through 10–19 show the results. Listing 10.30 shows a portion of the resultant log file.

Listing 10.26 *YachtWatcher.java*

```java
package moreservlets.listeners;

import java.io.*;
import javax.servlet.*;
import javax.servlet.http.*;

/** Listener that keeps track of yacht purchases by monitoring
 *  the orderedItem and purchasedItem session attributes.
 */

public class YachtWatcher
    implements HttpSessionAttributeListener {
```

Listing 10.26 *YachtWatcher.java (continued)*

```java
private String orderAttributeName = "orderedItem";
private String purchaseAttributeName = "purchasedItem";
private String itemName = "yacht";

/** Checks for initial ordering and final purchase of
 *  yacht. Records "Customer ordered a yacht" if the
 *  orderedItem attribute matches "yacht".
 *  Records "Customer finalized purchase of a yacht" if the
 *  purchasedItem attribute matches "yacht".
 */

public void attributeAdded(HttpSessionBindingEvent event) {
  checkAttribute(event, orderAttributeName, itemName,
                 " ordered a ");
  checkAttribute(event, purchaseAttributeName, itemName,
                 " finalized purchase of a ");
}

/** Checks for order cancellation: was an order for "yacht"
 *  cancelled?  Records "Customer cancelled an order for
 *  a yacht" if the orderedItem attribute matches "yacht".
 */

public void attributeRemoved(HttpSessionBindingEvent event) {
  checkAttribute(event, orderAttributeName, itemName,
                 " cancelled an order for a ");
}

/** Checks for item replacement: was "yacht" replaced
 *  by some other item? Records "Customer changed to a new
 *  item instead of a yacht" if the orderedItem attribute
 *  matches "yacht".
 */

public void attributeReplaced(HttpSessionBindingEvent event) {
  checkAttribute(event, orderAttributeName, itemName,
                 " changed to a new item instead of a ");
}

private void checkAttribute(HttpSessionBindingEvent event,
                            String orderAttributeName,
                            String keyItemName,
                            String message) {
  String currentAttributeName = event.getName();
  String currentItemName = (String)event.getValue();
  if (currentAttributeName.equals(orderAttributeName) &&
      currentItemName.equals(keyItemName)) {
```

Listing 10.26   *YachtWatcher.java (continued)*

```
        ServletContext context =
          event.getSession().getServletContext();
        context.log("Customer" + message + keyItemName + ".");
      }
    }
  }
```

Listing 10.27   *web.xml* (Excerpt for yacht-watching listener)

```xml
<?xml version="1.0" encoding="ISO-8859-1"?>
<!DOCTYPE web-app PUBLIC
    "-//Sun Microsystems, Inc.//DTD Web Application 2.3//EN"
    "http://java.sun.com/dtd/web-app_2_3.dtd">

<web-app>
  <!-- ... -->

  <!-- Register the yacht-watching event listener. -->
  <listener>
    <listener-class>
      moreservlets.listeners.YachtWatcher
    </listener-class>
  </listener>
  <!-- ... -->

<!-- Assign the name OrderHandlingServlet to
     moreservlets.OrderHandlingServlet. -->
  <servlet>
    <servlet-name>OrderHandlingServlet</servlet-name>
    <servlet-class>
      moreservlets.OrderHandlingServlet
    </servlet-class>
  </servlet>
  <!-- ... -->

  <!-- Assign the URL /HandleOrders to the
       servlet that is named OrderHandlingServlet.
  -->
  <servlet-mapping>
    <servlet-name>OrderHandlingServlet</servlet-name>
    <url-pattern>/HandleOrders</url-pattern>
  </servlet-mapping>

  <!-- ... -->
</web-app>
```

Listing 10.28 *OrderHandlingServlet.java*

```java
package moreservlets;

import java.io.*;
import javax.servlet.*;
import javax.servlet.http.*;

/** Servlet that handles submissions from the order form. If the
 *  user selects the "Reserve Order" button, the selected item
 *  is put into the orderedItem attribute. If the user selects
 *  the "Cancel Order" button, the orderedItem attribute is
 *  deleted. If the user selects the "Purchase Item" button,
 *  the selected item is put into the purchasedItem attribute.
 */

public class OrderHandlingServlet extends HttpServlet {
  private String title, picture;

  public void doGet(HttpServletRequest request,
                    HttpServletResponse response)
      throws ServletException, IOException {
    HttpSession session = request.getSession(true);
    String itemName = request.getParameter("itemName");
    if ((itemName == null) || (itemName.equals(""))) {
      itemName = "<B>MISSING ITEM</B>";
    }
    String message;
    if (request.getParameter("order") != null) {
      session.setAttribute("orderedItem", itemName);
      message = "Thanks for ordering " + itemName + ".";
    } else if (request.getParameter("cancel") != null) {
      session.removeAttribute("orderedItem");
      message = "Thanks for nothing.";
    } else {
      session.setAttribute("purchasedItem", itemName);
      message = "Thanks for purchasing " + itemName + ".";
    }
    response.setContentType("text/html");
    PrintWriter out = response.getWriter();
    String docType =
      "<!DOCTYPE HTML PUBLIC \"-//W3C//DTD HTML 4.0 " +
      "Transitional//EN\">\n";
    out.println
      (docType +
       "<HTML>\n" +
       "<HEAD><TITLE>" + message + "</TITLE></HEAD>\n" +
       "<BODY BGCOLOR=\"#FDF5E6\">\n" +
       "<H2 ALIGN=\"CENTER\">" + message + "</H2>\n" +
       "</BODY></HTML>");
  }
}
```

Listing 10.29 *orders.html*

```html
<!DOCTYPE HTML PUBLIC "-//W3C//DTD HTML 4.0 Transitional//EN">
<HTML>
<HEAD>
<TITLE>Orders</TITLE>
<LINK REL=STYLESHEET
      HREF="events-styles.css"
      TYPE="text/css">
</HEAD>

<BODY>
<TABLE BORDER=5 ALIGN="CENTER">
  <TR><TH CLASS="TITLE">Orders
</TABLE>
<P>
Choose a valuable item below.
<P>
Select "Reserve Order" to hold the order for 30 days. Due to
unprecedented demand, you can only reserve a single item:
selecting another item will replace the previous choice.
<P>
Select "Purchase Item" to finalize your purchase. After
finalizing a purchase, you can reserve a new item.
<FORM ACTION="HandleOrders">
<DL>
  <DT><B>Item:</B>
  <DD><INPUT TYPE="RADIO" NAME="itemName" VALUE="yacht">Yacht
  <DD><INPUT TYPE="RADIO" NAME="itemName" VALUE="chalet">Chalet
  <DD><INPUT TYPE="RADIO" NAME="itemName" VALUE="car">Lamborghini
  <DD><INPUT TYPE="RADIO" NAME="itemName" VALUE="msajsp" CHECKED>
      <I>More Servlets and JavaServer Pages</I>
  <DD><INPUT TYPE="RADIO" NAME="itemName" VALUE="csajsp">
      <I>Core Servlets and JavaServer Pages</I>
</DL>
<CENTER>
<INPUT TYPE="SUBMIT" NAME="order" VALUE="Reserve Order">
<INPUT TYPE="SUBMIT" NAME="cancel" VALUE="Cancel Order">
<INPUT TYPE="SUBMIT" NAME="purchase" VALUE="Purchase Item">
</CENTER>
</FORM>

</BODY>
</HTML>
```

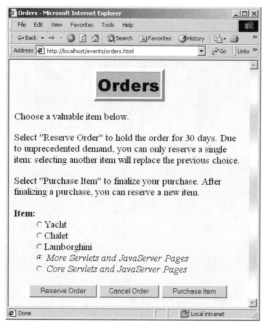

Figure 10–16 The order form that sends data to the order handling servlet (Listing 10.28). That servlet adds, replaces, and removes values in the `orderedItem` and `purchasedItem` session attributes, which in turn triggers the yacht-watching listener (Listing 10.26).

Figure 10–17 Result of reserving an order for a yacht. The yacht-watching listener makes an entry in the log file (Listing 10.30) saying that a customer ordered a yacht.

Figure 10–18 Result of cancelling an order. If the user had previously reserved an order for a yacht, the yacht-watching listener makes an entry in the log file (Listing 10.30) saying that a customer replaced a yacht order with something else.

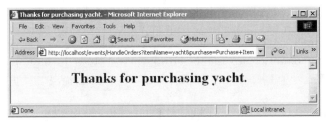

Figure 10–19 Result of purchasing a yacht. The yacht-watching listener makes an entry in the log file (Listing 10.30) saying that a customer purchased a yacht.

Listing 10.30	Sample Log File Entries

```
2001-11-07 11:50:59 Customer ordered a yacht.
2001-11-07 11:51:06 Customer changed to a new item instead of a
yacht.
2001-11-07 11:52:37 Customer cancelled an order for a yacht.
2001-11-07 11:53:05 Customer finalized purchase of a yacht.
2001-11-07 11:53:35 Customer ordered a yacht.
2001-11-07 11:53:50 Customer cancelled an order for a yacht.
2001-11-07 11:54:20 Customer changed to a new item instead of a
yacht.
2001-11-07 11:54:27 Customer changed to a new item instead of a
yacht.
2001-11-07 11:54:42 Customer cancelled an order for a yacht.
2001-11-07 11:54:44 Customer ordered a yacht.
2001-11-07 11:54:47 Customer changed to a new item instead of a
yacht.
```

10.11 Using Multiple Cooperating Listeners

Now, the listeners discussed in this chapter are all well and good. There are plenty of applications where one of them is useful. However, there are also plenty of applications where no *single* listener can, in isolation, accomplish the necessary tasks. *Multiple* listeners need to work together.

For example, suppose that your yacht-watching listener was so successful that you are asked to expand it. Rather than tracking buying patterns of a fixed item such as a yacht, you should track orders for the current daily special to let management discover if their specials are effective. Accomplishing this task requires *three* listeners to cooperate: a `ServletContextListener` to set up application-wide information about the session attributes that store daily specials, a `ServletContext-AttributeListener` to monitor changes to the attributes that store the information, and an `HttpSessionAttributeListener` to keep a running count of orders for the daily special.

The three listeners are described in more detail in the following subsections.

Tracking Orders for the Daily Special

As the first step in creating an order-tracking system, you need a servlet context listener to read initialization parameters that specify which session attributes correspond to orders and which items are the current daily specials. These values should be stored in the servlet context so other resources can determine what the daily specials are. Listing 10.31 shows this listener.

Second, you need a session attribute listener to keep a running count of orders for the daily special. The count will be incremented every time a designated attribute name is added with any of the daily specials as its value. The count will be decremented every time a designated attribute is replaced or removed and the previous value is one of the daily specials. Listing 10.32 shows this listener.

Listing 10.33 shows the deployment descriptor that registers the two listeners and sets up the servlet context initialization parameters that designate the names of order-related session attributes and the names of the daily specials.

Listing 10.34 shows a JSP page that prints the current order count. Figures 10–20 through 10–22 show some typical results.

Listing 10.31 *DailySpecialRegistrar.java*

```java
package moreservlets.listeners;

import java.io.*;
import javax.servlet.*;
import javax.servlet.http.*;
import java.util.*;

/** Listener that records how to detect orders
 *  of the daily special. It reads a list of attribute
 *  names from an init parameter: these correspond to
 *  session attributes that are used to record orders.
 *  It also reads a list of item names: these correspond
 *  to the names of the daily specials. Other listeners
 *  will watch to see if any daily special names appear
 *  as values of attributes that are hereby designated
 *  to refer to orders.
 */

public class DailySpecialRegistrar
    implements ServletContextListener {

  /** When the Web application is loaded, record the
   *  attribute names that correspond to orders and
   *  the attribute values that are the daily specials.
   *  Also set to zero the count of daily specials that have
   *  been ordered.
   */

  public void contextInitialized(ServletContextEvent event) {
    ServletContext context = event.getServletContext();
    addContextEntry(context, "order-attribute-names");
    addContextEntry(context, "daily-special-item-names");
    context.setAttribute("dailySpecialCount", new Integer(0));
  }

  public void contextDestroyed(ServletContextEvent event) {}

  /** Read the designated context initialization parameter,
   *  put the values into an ArrayList, and store the
   *  list in the ServletContext with an attribute name
   *  that is identical to the initialization parameter name.
   */
```

Listing 10.31   *DailySpecialRegistrar.java (continued)*

```java
  private void addContextEntry(ServletContext context,
                               String initParamName) {
    ArrayList paramValues = new ArrayList();
    String attributeNames =
      context.getInitParameter(initParamName);
    if (attributeNames != null) {
      StringTokenizer tok = new StringTokenizer(attributeNames);
      String value;
      while(tok.hasMoreTokens()) {
        value = tok.nextToken();
        paramValues.add(value);
      }
      context.setAttribute(initParamName, paramValues);
    }
  }

  /** Returns a string containing the daily special
   *  names. For insertion inside an HTML text area.
   */

  public static String dailySpecials(ServletContext context) {
    String attributeName = "daily-special-item-names";
    ArrayList itemNames =
      (ArrayList)context.getAttribute(attributeName);
    String itemString = "";
    for(int i=0; i<itemNames.size(); i++) {
      itemString = itemString + (String)itemNames.get(i) + "\n";
    }
    return(itemString);
  }

  /** Returns a UL list containing the daily special
   *  names. For insertion within the body of a JSP page.
   */

  public static String specialsList(ServletContext context) {
    String attributeName = "daily-special-item-names";
    ArrayList itemNames =
      (ArrayList)context.getAttribute(attributeName);
    String itemString = "<UL>\n";
    for(int i=0; i<itemNames.size(); i++) {
      itemString = itemString + "<LI>" +
                   (String)itemNames.get(i) + "\n";
    }
    itemString = itemString + "</UL>";
    return(itemString);
  }
}
```

Listing 10.32   *DailySpecialWatcher.java*

```java
package moreservlets.listeners;

import java.io.*;
import javax.servlet.*;
import javax.servlet.http.*;
import java.util.*;

/** Listener that keeps track of orders of the
 *  current daily special.
 */

public class DailySpecialWatcher
    implements HttpSessionAttributeListener {
  private static int dailySpecialCount = 0;

  /** If the name of the session attribute that was added
   *  matches one of the stored order-attribute-names AND
   *  the value of the attribute matches one of the
   *  stored daily-special-item-names, then increment
   *  the count of daily specials ordered.
   */

  public void attributeAdded(HttpSessionBindingEvent event) {
    checkForSpecials(event, 1);
  }

  /** If the name of the session attribute that was removed
   *  matches one of the stored order-attribute-names AND
   *  the value of the attribute matches one of the
   *  stored daily-special-item-names, then decrement
   *  the count of daily specials ordered.
   */

  public void attributeRemoved(HttpSessionBindingEvent event) {
    checkForSpecials(event, -1);
  }

  /** If the name of the session attribute that was replaced
   *  matches one of the stored order-attribute-names AND
   *  the value of the attribute matches one of the
   *  stored daily-special-item-names, then increment
   *  the count of daily specials ordered. Note that the
   *  value here is the old value (the one being replaced);
   *  the attributeAdded method will handle the new value
   *  (the replacement).
   */
```

Listing 10.32 *DailySpecialWatcher.java (continued)*

```java
public void attributeReplaced(HttpSessionBindingEvent event) {
  checkForSpecials(event, -1);
}

// Check whether the attribute that was just added or removed
// matches one of the stored order-attribute-names AND
// the value of the attribute matches one of the
// stored daily-special-item-names. If so, add the delta
// (+1 or -1) to the count of daily specials ordered.

private void checkForSpecials(HttpSessionBindingEvent event,
                              int delta) {
  ServletContext context =
    event.getSession().getServletContext();
  ArrayList attributeNames =
    getList(context, "order-attribute-names");
  ArrayList itemNames =
    getList(context, "daily-special-item-names");
  synchronized(attributeNames) {
    for(int i=0; i<attributeNames.size(); i++) {
      String attributeName = (String)attributeNames.get(i);
      for(int j=0; j<itemNames.size(); j++) {
        String itemName = (String)itemNames.get(j);
        if (attributeName.equals(event.getName()) &&
            itemName.equals((String)event.getValue())) {
          dailySpecialCount = dailySpecialCount + delta;
        }
      }
    }
  }
  context.setAttribute("dailySpecialCount",
                       new Integer(dailySpecialCount));
}

// Get either the order-attribute-names or
// daily-special-item-names list.

private ArrayList getList(ServletContext context,
                          String attributeName) {
  ArrayList list =
    (ArrayList)context.getAttribute(attributeName);
  return(list);
}
```

Listing 10.32   *DailySpecialWatcher.java (continued)*

```
/** Reset the count of daily specials that have
 *  been ordered. This operation is normally performed
 *  only when the daily special changes.
 */

public static void resetDailySpecialCount() {
  dailySpecialCount = 0;
}
}
```

Listing 10.33   *web.xml* (Excerpt for tracking daily special orders)

```xml
<?xml version="1.0" encoding="ISO-8859-1"?>
<!DOCTYPE web-app PUBLIC
    "-//Sun Microsystems, Inc.//DTD Web Application 2.3//EN"
    "http://java.sun.com/dtd/web-app_2_3.dtd">

<web-app>
  <!-- ... -->

  <!-- Register the listener that sets up the entries
       that will be used to monitor orders for the daily
       special. -->
  <listener>
    <listener-class>
      moreservlets.listeners.DailySpecialRegistrar
    </listener-class>
  </listener>

  <!-- Register the listener that counts orders for the daily
       special. -->
  <listener>
    <listener-class>
      moreservlets.listeners.DailySpecialWatcher
    </listener-class>
  </listener>

  <!-- ... -->
</web-app>
```

Listing 10.34 *track-daily-specials.jsp*

```
<!DOCTYPE HTML PUBLIC "-//W3C//DTD HTML 4.0 Transitional//EN">
<HTML>
<HEAD>
<TITLE>Tracking Daily Special Orders</TITLE>
<LINK REL=STYLESHEET
      HREF="events-styles.css"
      TYPE="text/css">
</HEAD>
<BODY>
<CENTER>
<TABLE BORDER=5>
  <TR><TH CLASS="TITLE">Tracking Daily Special Orders
</TABLE>

<H2>Current Specials:</H2>
<%@ page import="moreservlets.listeners.*" %>
<%= DailySpecialRegistrar.specialsList(application) %>

<H2>Number of Orders:
<%= application.getAttribute("dailySpecialCount") %>
</H2>

</CENTER>
</BODY>
</HTML>
```

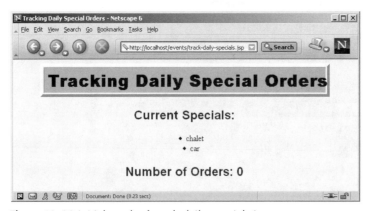

Figure 10–20 Initial result of *track-daily-specials.jsp*.

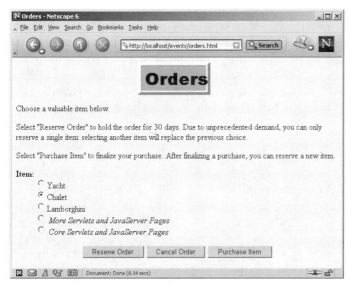

Figure 10–21 Ordering the daily special.

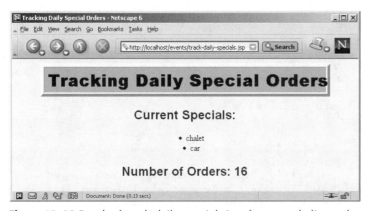

Figure 10–22 Result of *track-daily-specials.jsp* after several clients placed orders.

Resetting the Daily Special Order Count

The two listeners shown in the previous subsection are sufficient if you restart the server every time you change the daily specials.

However, if you change the daily specials while the server is running, you need a servlet context attribute listener to detect changes in the attribute that stores the names of the daily specials. In particular, when the daily specials change, you need to reset the running count of orders for the specials. Listing 10.35 shows this listener.

Listing 10.36 shows a JSP page that displays the current daily specials in a text area. It lets the user change the values and send them to a servlet (Listing 10.37) that records the changes in the servlet context. The JSP page is in the *admin* directory and the servlet is assigned a URL beginning with */admin* (see the *web.xml* file in Listing 10.38), so the security restrictions discussed in Section 10.4 apply.

When an authorized user changes the names of the daily specials, the order count is reset. Figures 10–23 through 10–27 show some representative results.

Listing 10.35 *ChangedDailySpecialListener.java*

```java
package moreservlets.listeners;

import java.io.*;
import javax.servlet.*;
import javax.servlet.http.*;

/** Listener that monitors changes to the names
 *  of the daily specials (which are stored in
 *  the daily-special-item-names attribute of
 *  the servlet context). If the names change, the
 *  listener resets the running count of the number
 *  of daily specials being ordered.
 */

public class ChangedDailySpecialListener
    implements ServletContextAttributeListener {

  /** When the daily specials change, reset the
   *  order counts.
   */

  public void attributeReplaced
                (ServletContextAttributeEvent event) {
    if (event.getName().equals("daily-special-item-names")) {
      ServletContext context = event.getServletContext();
      context.setAttribute("dailySpecialCount",
                    new Integer(0));
      DailySpecialWatcher.resetDailySpecialCount();
    }
  }

  public void attributeAdded
                (ServletContextAttributeEvent event) {}

  public void attributeRemoved
                (ServletContextAttributeEvent event) {}
}
```

Listing 10.36   *change-daily-specials.jsp*

```
<!DOCTYPE HTML PUBLIC "-//W3C//DTD HTML 4.0 Transitional//EN">
<HTML>
<HEAD>
<TITLE>Changing Daily Specials</TITLE>
<LINK REL=STYLESHEET
      HREF="../events-styles.css"
      TYPE="text/css">
</HEAD>

<BODY>
<CENTER>
<TABLE BORDER=5>
  <TR><TH CLASS="TITLE">Changing Daily Specials
</TABLE>
<P>
<FORM ACTION="ChangeDailySpecial">
New specials:<BR>
<%@ page import="moreservlets.listeners.*" %>
<TEXTAREA NAME="newSpecials" ROWS=4 COLS=30>
<%= DailySpecialRegistrar.dailySpecials(application) %>
</TEXTAREA>
<P>
<INPUT TYPE="SUBMIT" VALUE="Submit Change">
</FORM>
</CENTER>
</BODY>
</HTML>
```

Listing 10.37   *ChangeDailySpecial.java*

```
package moreservlets;

import java.io.*;
import javax.servlet.*;
import javax.servlet.http.*;
import java.util.*;

/** Servlet that changes the daily specials. The web.xml
 *  file specifies that only authenticated users in the
 *  ceo role can access the servlet. A servlet context
 *  attribute listener resets the count of daily special
 *  orders when this servlet (or any other program) changes
 *  the daily specials.
 */
```

Listing 10.37 *ChangeDailySpecial.java (continued)*

```java
public class ChangeDailySpecial extends HttpServlet {
  public void doGet(HttpServletRequest request,
                    HttpServletResponse response)
      throws ServletException, IOException {
    String dailySpecialNames =
      request.getParameter("newSpecials");
    if ((dailySpecialNames == null) ||
        (dailySpecialNames.equals(""))) {
      dailySpecialNames = "MISSING-VALUE";
    }
    ArrayList specials = new ArrayList();
    StringTokenizer tok =
      new StringTokenizer(dailySpecialNames);
    while(tok.hasMoreTokens()) {
      specials.add(tok.nextToken());
    }
    ServletContext context = getServletContext();
    context.setAttribute("daily-special-item-names",
                         specials);
    response.setContentType("text/html");
    PrintWriter out = response.getWriter();
    String docType =
      "<!DOCTYPE HTML PUBLIC \"-//W3C//DTD HTML 4.0 " +
      "Transitional//EN\">\n";
    String title = "New Daily Specials";
    out.println
      (docType +
       "<HTML>\n" +
       "<HEAD><TITLE>" + title + "</TITLE></HEAD>\n" +
       "<BODY BGCOLOR=\"#FDF5E6\">\n" +
       "<H2 ALIGN=\"CENTER\">" + title + "</H2>\n" +
       "<UL>");
    String special;
    for(int i=0; i<specials.size(); i++) {
      special = (String)specials.get(i);
      out.println("<LI>" + special);
    }
    out.println("</UL>\n" +
                "</BODY></HTML>");
  }
}
```

Listing 10.38 *web.xml* (Excerpt for resetting order counts)

```
<?xml version="1.0" encoding="ISO-8859-1"?>
<!DOCTYPE web-app PUBLIC
    "-//Sun Microsystems, Inc.//DTD Web Application 2.3//EN"
    "http://java.sun.com/dtd/web-app_2_3.dtd">

<web-app>
  <!-- ... -->

  <!-- Register the listener that resets the order counts
       when the names of the daily specials change. -->
  <listener>
    <listener-class>
      moreservlets.listeners.ChangedDailySpecialListener
    </listener-class>
  </listener>
  <!-- ... -->

  <!-- Assign the name ChangeDailySpecial to
       moreservlets.ChangeDailySpecial. -->
  <servlet>
    <servlet-name>ChangeDailySpecial</servlet-name>
    <servlet-class>
      moreservlets.ChangeDailySpecial
    </servlet-class>
  </servlet>
  <!-- ... -->

  <!-- Assign the URL /admin/ChangeDailySpecial to the
       servlet that is named ChangeDailySpecial.
  -->
  <servlet-mapping>
    <servlet-name>ChangeDailySpecial</servlet-name>
    <url-pattern>/admin/ChangeDailySpecial</url-pattern>
  </servlet-mapping>

  <!-- ... -->
</web-app>
```

Figure 10–23 Requests by unauthenticated users for *change-daily-specials.jsp* get sent to the login page (Listing 10.9).

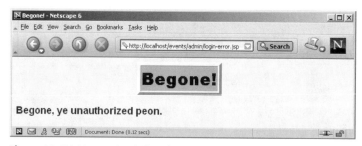

Figure 10–24 Users who fail authentication are shown the login-failure page (Listing 10.10).

Figure 10–25 Users who pass authentication and are in the designated role (ceo) are shown the form for changing the daily specials (Listing 10.36). The current daily specials are displayed as the initial value of the text area.

Figure 10–26 Result of submitting the form for changing daily specials after `yacht` and `chalet` are entered in the text area.

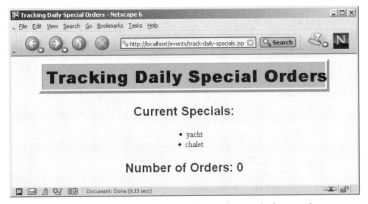

Figure 10–27 When the daily specials are changed, the servlet context attribute listener (Listing 10.35) resets the order count.

10.12 The Complete Events Deployment Descriptor

The previous sections showed various excerpts of the *web.xml* file for the application events examples. This section shows the file in its entirety.

Listing 10.39 *web.xml* (Complete version for events examples)

```xml
<?xml version="1.0" encoding="ISO-8859-1"?>
<!DOCTYPE web-app PUBLIC
    "-//Sun Microsystems, Inc.//DTD Web Application 2.3//EN"
    "http://java.sun.com/dtd/web-app_2_3.dtd">

<web-app>
  <!-- Order matters in web.xml! For the elements
       used in this example, this order is required:
          context-param
          listener
          servlet
          servlet-mapping
          session-config
          welcome-file-list
          taglib
          security-constraint
          login-config
  -->

  <!-- Since the company name changes so frequently,
       supply it as a servlet context parameter instead
       of embedding it into lots of different servlets and
       JSP pages. The InitialCompanyNameListener will
       read this value and store it in the servlet context. -->
  <context-param>
    <param-name>companyName</param-name>
    <param-value>not-dot-com.com</param-value>
  </context-param>

  <!-- Also store the previous company name. -->
  <context-param>
    <param-name>formerCompanyName</param-name>
    <param-value>hot-dot-com.com</param-value>
  </context-param>

  <!-- Declare the names of the session attributes that
       are used to store items that customers are
       purchasing. The daily special listener will
       track changes to the values of these attributes. -->
  <context-param>
    <param-name>order-attribute-names</param-name>
    <param-value>
      orderedItem
      purchasedItem
    </param-value>
  </context-param>
```

Listing 10.39   *web.xml* (Complete version for events examples) *(continued)*

```
<!-- The item names of the current daily specials. -->
<context-param>
  <param-name>daily-special-item-names</param-name>
  <param-value>
    chalet
    car
  </param-value>
</context-param>

<!-- Register the listener that sets up the
     initial company name. -->
<!-- Listener declaration moved to tag library...
  <listener>
    <listener-class>
      moreservlets.listeners.InitialCompanyNameListener
    </listener-class>
  </listener>
-->

<!-- Register the listener that monitors changes to
     the company name.
  -->
<!-- Listener declaration moved to tag library...
  <listener>
    <listener-class>
      moreservlets.listeners.ChangedCompanyNameListener
    </listener-class>
  </listener>
-->

<!-- Register the session counting event listener. -->
<listener>
  <listener-class>
    moreservlets.listeners.SessionCounter
  </listener-class>
</listener>

<!-- Register the yacht-watching event listener. -->
<listener>
  <listener-class>
    moreservlets.listeners.YachtWatcher
  </listener-class>
</listener>
```

Listing 10.39   *web.xml* (Complete version for events examples) *(continued)*

```
<!-- Register the listener that sets up the entries
     that will be used to monitor orders for the daily
     special. -->
<listener>
  <listener-class>
    moreservlets.listeners.DailySpecialRegistrar
  </listener-class>
</listener>

<!-- Register the listener that counts orders for the daily
     special. -->
<listener>
  <listener-class>
    moreservlets.listeners.DailySpecialWatcher
  </listener-class>
</listener>

<!-- Register the listener that resets the order counts
     when the names of the daily specials change. -->
<listener>
  <listener-class>
    moreservlets.listeners.ChangedDailySpecialListener
  </listener-class>
</listener>

<!-- Assign the name ChangeCompanyName to
     moreservlets.ChangeCompanyName. -->
<servlet>
  <servlet-name>ChangeCompanyName</servlet-name>
  <servlet-class>moreservlets.ChangeCompanyName</servlet-class>
</servlet>

<!-- Assign the name OrderHandlingServlet to
     moreservlets.OrderHandlingServlet. -->
<servlet>
  <servlet-name>OrderHandlingServlet</servlet-name>
  <servlet-class>
    moreservlets.OrderHandlingServlet
  </servlet-class>
</servlet>
```

Listing 10.39 *web.xml* (Complete version for events examples) *(continued)*

```
<!-- Assign the name ChangeDailySpecial to
     moreservlets.ChangeDailySpecial. -->
<servlet>
  <servlet-name>ChangeDailySpecial</servlet-name>
  <servlet-class>
    moreservlets.ChangeDailySpecial
  </servlet-class>
</servlet>

<!-- Give a name to the servlet that redirects users
     to the home page.
-->
<servlet>
  <servlet-name>Redirector</servlet-name>
  <servlet-class>moreservlets.RedirectorServlet</servlet-class>
</servlet>

<!-- Assign the URL /admin/ChangeCompanyName to the
     servlet that is named ChangeCompanyName.
-->
<servlet-mapping>
  <servlet-name>ChangeCompanyName</servlet-name>
  <url-pattern>/admin/ChangeCompanyName</url-pattern>
</servlet-mapping>

<!-- Assign the URL /HandleOrders to the
     servlet that is named OrderHandlingServlet.
-->
<servlet-mapping>
  <servlet-name>OrderHandlingServlet</servlet-name>
  <url-pattern>/HandleOrders</url-pattern>
</servlet-mapping>

<!-- Assign the URL /admin/ChangeDailySpecial to the
     servlet that is named ChangeDailySpecial.
-->
<servlet-mapping>
  <servlet-name>ChangeDailySpecial</servlet-name>
  <url-pattern>/admin/ChangeDailySpecial</url-pattern>
</servlet-mapping>
```

Listing 10.39 *web.xml* (Complete version for events examples) *(continued)*

```
<!-- Turn off invoker. Send requests to index.jsp. -->
<servlet-mapping>
  <servlet-name>Redirector</servlet-name>
  <url-pattern>/servlet/*</url-pattern>
</servlet-mapping>

<!-- Set the default session timeout to two minutes. -->
<session-config>
  <session-timeout>2</session-timeout>
</session-config>

<!-- If URL gives a directory but no filename, try index.jsp
     first and index.html second. If neither is found,
     the result is server specific (e.g., a directory
     listing). Order of elements in web.xml matters.
     welcome-file-list needs to come after servlet but
     before error-page.
-->
<welcome-file-list>
  <welcome-file>index.jsp</welcome-file>
  <welcome-file>index.html</welcome-file>
</welcome-file-list>

<!-- Register the company-name tag library. -->
<taglib>
  <taglib-uri>
    /company-name-taglib.tld
  </taglib-uri>
  <taglib-location>
    /WEB-INF/company-name-taglib.tld
  </taglib-location>
</taglib>

<!-- Protect everything within the "admin" directory.
     Direct client access to this directory requires
     authentication.
-->
<security-constraint>
  <web-resource-collection>
    <web-resource-name>Admin</web-resource-name>
    <url-pattern>/admin/*</url-pattern>
  </web-resource-collection>
  <auth-constraint>
    <role-name>ceo</role-name>
  </auth-constraint>
</security-constraint>
```

Listing 10.39	*web.xml* (Complete version for events examples) *(continued)*

```
<!-- Tell the server to use form-based authentication. -->
<login-config>
  <auth-method>FORM</auth-method>
  <form-login-config>
    <form-login-page>/admin/login.jsp</form-login-page>
    <form-error-page>/admin/login-error.jsp</form-error-page>
  </form-login-config>
</login-config>
</web-app>
```

NEW TAG
LIBRARY
CAPABILITIES

Part V

NEW TAG LIBRARY
FEATURES IN JSP 1.2

Topics in This Chapter

- Converting TLD files to the new format

- Bundling life-cycle event listeners with tag libraries

- Checking custom tag syntax with `TagLibraryValidator`

- Using the Simple API for XML (SAX) in validators

- Handling errors with the `TryCatchFinally` interface

- Changing names of method return values

- Looping without creating `BodyContent`

- Declaring scripting variables in the TLD file

Chapter 11

Section 3.7 (Defining Custom JSP Tag Libraries) describes the creation and use of tag libraries in JSP 1.1. You do not need to modify JSP 1.1 tag libraries to make them work in JSP 1.2; they are totally compatible. However, JSP 1.2 has a number of new capabilities that are unavailable in JSP 1.1. Tag libraries that use these new capabilities must use a slightly different format for the TLD file. This chapter first describes that new format and then explains the use of each of the new capabilities. The following list gives a brief summary; details are provided in the following sections.

- **New TLD format.** The `DOCTYPE` definition has changed, some existing elements have been renamed (mostly by the addition of dashes), and several new elements have been introduced.

- **Ability to bundle listeners with tag libraries.** The servlet 2.3 specification introduced application life-cycle listeners. The JSP 1.2 specification added the ability to bundle these listeners with tag libraries.

- **`TagLibraryValidator` for translation-time syntax checking.** JSP 1.2 permits you to create a class that, at page translation time, can read an entire JSP file (represented in XML) and check that the custom tags are used properly.

- **`TryCatchFinally` interface.** JSP 1.2 introduced a new interface with two methods: `doCatch` and `doFinally`. These methods help tags handle uncaught exceptions that occur in any of the tag life-cycle methods or during the processing of the tag body.

- **New return values.** In JSP 1.1, EVAL_BODY_TAG was used in two distinct situations. In JSP 1.2, the constant is replaced with EVAL_BODY_BUFFERED and EVAL_BODY_AGAIN to better differentiate the two cases.
- **Looping without creating BodyContent.** In JSP 1.1, iteration-related tags extended BodyTagSupport and returned EVAL_BODY_TAG from doAfterBody to indicate that the tag body should be reevaluated and made available in a BodyContent object. In JSP 1.2, you can extend TagSupport and return EVAL_BODY_AGAIN to indicate that the body should be reevaluated and sent to the client with no intervening BodyContent. This yields an implementation that is easier to read and more efficient.
- **The variable element for introducing scripting variables.** Instead of declaring variables only in the TagExtraInfo class, JSP 1.2 lets you declare them in the TLD file.

11.1 Using the New Tag Library Descriptor Format

Tag libraries that make use of any new JSP 1.2 capabilities must use a new format for their tag library descriptor (TLD) files. However, libraries that are compatible with JSP 1.1 are allowed to use the JSP 1.1 TLD format.

TLD files in JSP 1.2 differ in the following ways from JSP 1.1 TLD files:

- The DOCTYPE declaration has changed.
- Several elements have been renamed.
- New elements have been added.

Each of these changes is described in one of the following subsections. The final subsection gives a side-by-side comparison of the JSP 1.2 and 1.1 TLD file formats.

New DOCTYPE Declaration

Tag library descriptor files start with an XML header, then have a DOCTYPE declaration and a taglib element. The XML header is unchanged from JSP 1.1 to 1.2, but for the DOCTYPE declaration, you now use:

```
<!DOCTYPE taglib
 PUBLIC "-//Sun Microsystems, Inc.//DTD JSP Tag Library 1.2//EN"
 "http://java.sun.com/dtd/web-jsptaglibrary_1_2.dtd">
```

In JSP 1.1 you used:

```
<!DOCTYPE taglib
 PUBLIC "-//Sun Microsystems, Inc.//DTD JSP Tag Library 1.1//EN"
 "http://java.sun.com/j2ee/dtds/web-jsptaglibrary_1_1.dtd">
```

Listing 11.1 briefly outlines the resultant file.

Listing 11.1   JSP 1.2 TLD File (Excerpt 1)

```
<?xml version="1.0" encoding="ISO-8859-1" ?>
<!DOCTYPE taglib
 PUBLIC "-//Sun Microsystems, Inc.//DTD JSP Tag Library 1.2//EN"
 "http://java.sun.com/dtd/web-jsptaglibrary_1_2.dtd">

<taglib>
  <!-- ... -->
</taglib>
```

Renamed Elements

Within the `taglib` element in JSP 1.2, dashes were added to the `tlibversion`, `jspversion`, and `shortname` elements, yielding `tlib-version`, `jsp-version`, and `short-name`, respectively. The `tlib-version` element indicates the version number of the tag library (an arbitrary number), `jsp-version` indicates the JSP version needed (1.2), and `short-name` defines a name that IDEs can use to refer to the library (no spaces are allowed because IDEs might use `short-name` as the default tag prefix). The JSP 1.1 `info` element (used for documentation) was renamed to `description`.

Within the `tag` element, dashes were added to `tagclass`, `teiclass`, and `bodycontent` elements, yielding `tag-class`, `tei-class`, and `body-content`, respectively. The `tag-class` element gives the fully qualified name of the tag implementation class, `tei-class` defines a `TagExtraInfo` class for validation (this is optional; see Section 11.3 for a new and better alternative), and body-content provides IDEs a hint as to whether the tag is empty (i.e., uses no separate end tag) or uses a tag body between its start and end tags. The JSP 1.1 `info` element (used for documentation) was renamed to `description`.

Listing 11.2 gives a brief outline of a typical TLD file. Remember that the order of elements within XML files is not arbitrary. You must use the elements in the order shown here.

Listing 11.2   JSP 1.2 TLD File (Excerpt 2)

```
<?xml version="1.0" encoding="ISO-8859-1" ?>
<!DOCTYPE taglib
  PUBLIC "-//Sun Microsystems, Inc.//DTD JSP Tag Library 1.2//EN"
  "http://java.sun.com/dtd/web-jsptaglibrary_1_2.dtd">

<taglib>
  <tlib-version>some-number</tlib-version>
  <jsp-version>1.2</jsp-version>
  <short-name>some-name</short-name>
  <description>Tag library documentation.</description>

  <tag>
    <name>tag-name</name>
    <tag-class>somePackage.SomeTag</tag-class>
    <body-content>empty, JSP, or tagdependent</body-content>
    <description>Tag documentation.</description>
  </tag>

  <!-- Other tag elements, if any. -->
</taglib>
```

New Elements

Within the `taglib` element, five new elements were added: `display-name`, `small-icon`, `large-icon`, `validator`, and `listener`. All are optional.

The first three of these supply information for IDEs and other authoring tools. If used, they must appear in the order listed here and must be placed immediately before the `description` element within `taglib`. The `display-name` element gives a short name that the IDEs can present to the author; it differs from `short-name` in that it can contain white space (`short-name` cannot) and is used only for identification, not as a preferred prefix in a `taglib` directive (as `short-name` could be). The `small-icon` element gives the location of a 16 × 16 GIF or JPEG image that can be used by the IDE. The `large-icon` element gives the location of a 32 × 32 image, also in GIF or JPEG format.

The `validator` element declares a `TagLibraryValidator` class to be used for page translation-time syntax checking. Its use is discussed in Section 11.3. This element, if used, must appear in the `taglib` element after `description` but before `listener` (if used) and `tag`.

The `listener` element declares an application life-cycle event listener that will be loaded when the Web application is loaded (not when the tag library is first used!). Use of the `listener` element is discussed in Section 11.2; use of life-cycle listeners in general is described in Chapter 10. The `listener` element, if used, must be the last element before `tag`.

There were also five new elements that can appear within the `tag` element: `display-name`, `small-icon`, `large-icon`, `variable`, and `example`. All are optional. The first three (`display-name`, `small-icon`, and `large-icon`) are used for IDE documentation in the same way as just described for the `taglib` element. The elements, if used, must appear after `body-content` but before `description`. The `variable` element is used to introduce scripting variables. It must appear after `description` but before `attribute`; its use is described in Section 11.8. Finally, the `example` element gives a simple textual example of the use of the tag. If used, the `example` element must be the last subelement within `tag`.

Summary

Table 11.1 summarizes the first-, second-, and third-level elements in tag library descriptor files, listed in the order in which they must be used. Items in bold indicate changes from JSP 1.1. Elements marked with an asterisk are optional.

Table 11.1   Tag library descriptor format.

JSP 1.2	*JSP 1.1*
`<?xml version="1.0"` `        encoding="ISO-8859-1" ?>`	`<?xml version="1.0"` `        encoding="ISO-8859-1" ?>`
JSP 1.2 DOCTYPE declaration	JSP 1.1 DOCTYPE declaration
`taglib`	`taglib`
`tlib-version`	`tlibversion`
`jsp-version`	`jspversion`
`short-name`	`shortname`
`uri`°	`uri`°
`display-name`°	
`small-icon`°	
`large-icon`°	
`description`°	`info`°
`validator`° **`validator-class`** **`init-param`**° **`description`**°	

Table 11.1 Tag library descriptor format. *(continued)*

JSP 1.2   *JSP 1.1*

```
listener°
  listener-class

tag                                               tag
  name                                              name
  tag-class                                         tagclass
  tei-class°                                        teiclass°
  body-content°                                     bodycontent°
  display-name°
  small-icon°
  large-icon°
  description°                                      info°
  variable°
  attribute°                                        attribute°
  example°
```

11.2 Bundling Listeners with Tag Libraries

Application life-cycle event listeners are described in Chapter 10. They provide a powerful new capability that lets you respond to the creation and deletion of the servlet context and `HttpSession` objects and lets you monitor changes in servlet context and session attributes. In most cases, listeners are declared with the `listener` element of the deployment descriptor (*web.xml*).

However, suppose that the behavior of a tag library depends upon an event listener. In such a case, you would want to be certain that the listeners were available in all Web applications that used the tag library.

If the `listener` and `listener-class` elements of *web.xml* were the only option for declaring listeners, tag library maintenance would be difficult. Normally, the user of a tag library deploys it by simply dropping a JAR file in *WEB-INF/lib* and putting a TLD file in *WEB-INF*. Users of the tag libraries need no knowledge of the individual classes within the library, only of the tags that the library defines. But if the tag libraries used listeners, users of the libraries would need to discover the name of the listener classes and make *web.xml* entries for each one. This would be less flexible and harder to maintain.

Fortunately, the JSP 1.2 specification lets you put the listener declarations in the tag library descriptor file instead of in the deployment descriptor. "Hold on!" you say, "Event listeners need to run when the Web application is first loaded, not just the first time a JSP page that uses a custom library is accessed. I thought TLD files were only loaded the first time a user requests a page that refers to it. How can this work?" Good question. JSP 1.2 introduced a new TLD search mechanism to handle this situation. When a Web application is loaded, the system automatically searches *WEB-INF* and its subdirectories for files with *.tld* extensions and uses all `listener` declarations that it finds in them. This means that your TLD files *must* be in the *WEB-INF* directory or a subdirectory thereof. In fact, although few servers enforce the restriction, the JSP 1.2 specification requires all TLD files to be in *WEB-INF* anyhow. Besides, putting the TLD files in *WEB-INF* is a good strategy to prevent users from retrieving them. So, you should make *WEB-INF* the standard TLD file location, regardless of whether your libraries use event handlers.

Core Approach

Always put your TLD files in the WEB-INF *directory or a subdirectory thereof.*

Unfortunately, there is a problem with this approach: Tomcat 4.0 ignores TLD files at Web application startup time unless there is a `taglib` entry in *web.xml* of the following form:

```
<taglib>
  <taglib-uri>/someName.tld</taglib-uri>
  <taglib-location>/WEB-INF/realName.tld</taglib-location>
</taglib>
```

As discussed in Section 5.13 (Locating Tag Library Descriptors), this entry is a good idea when the name of your tag library changes frequently. However, the JSP 1.2 specification does not require its use, and servers such as ServletExec 4.1 properly handle listener declarations in TLD files when there is no such entry. Nevertheless, Tomcat 4.0 requires it.

Core Warning

Tomcat 4.0 reads listener declarations only from TLD files that have `taglib` *entries in* web.xml.

Tracking Active Sessions

At busy sites, a significant portion of the server's memory can be spent storing `HttpSession` objects. You might like to track session usage so that you can decide if you should lower the session timeout, increase the server's memory allotment, or even use a database instead of the servlet session API.

Listing 11.3 shows a session listener that keeps a running count of the number of sessions in memory. The count is incremented each time a session is created; it is decremented whenever a session is destroyed (regardless of whether the session destruction is from an explicit call to `invalidate` or from timing out).

Listing 11.4 gives a custom tag that simply prints the count of active sessions. Listing 11.5 presents a related tag that prints a large, red warning if the number of sessions in memory exceeds a predefined maximum. Nothing is printed if the number of active sessions is within bounds.

Since it doesn't make sense to use these tags unless the listener is in effect, the TLD file that declares the tags (Listing 11.6) also declares the listener. Finally, an alias for the TLD file is created with the `taglib` element of the *web.xml* deployment descriptor (Listing 11.7) to ensure that Tomcat will read the TLD file when the Web application is loaded and to allow developers to change the name of the TLD file without modifying the JSP pages that use it.

Listing 11.8 shows a JSP page that uses both of the custom tags. Figures 11–1 and 11–2 show the results when the number of sessions is below and above the predefined limit, respectively.

Listing 11.3 *ActiveSessionCounter.java*

```
package moreservlets.listeners;

import java.io.*;
import javax.servlet.*;
import javax.servlet.http.*;
import java.util.*;

/** Listener that keeps track of the number of sessions
 *  that the Web application is currently using.
 */

public class ActiveSessionCounter
                          implements HttpSessionListener {
  private static int sessionCount = 0;
  private static int sessionLimit = 1000;
  private ServletContext context = null;

  /** Each time a session is created, increment the
   *  running count. If the count exceeds the limit,
   *  print a warning in the log file.
   */
```

Listing 11.3   *ActiveSessionCounter.java (continued)*

```java
public void sessionCreated(HttpSessionEvent event) {
  sessionCount++;
  if (context == null) {
    recordServletContext(event);
  }
  String warning = getSessionCountWarning();
  if (warning != null) {
    context.log(warning);
  }
}

/** Each time a session is destroyed, decrement the
 *  running count. A session can be destroyed when a
 *  servlet makes an explicit call to invalidate, but it
 *  is more commonly destroyed by the system when the time
 *  since the last client access exceeds a limit.
 */

public void sessionDestroyed(HttpSessionEvent event) {
  sessionCount--;
}

/** The number of sessions currently in memory. */

public static int getSessionCount() {
  return(sessionCount);
}

/** The limit on the session count. If the number of
 *  sessions in memory exceeds this value, a warning
 *  should be issued.
 */

public static int getSessionLimit() {
  return(sessionLimit);
}

/** If the number of active sessions is over the limit,
 *  this returns a warning string. Otherwise, it returns
 *  null.
 */
```

Listing 11.3   *ActiveSessionCounter.java (continued)*

```java
public static String getSessionCountWarning() {
  String warning = null;
  if (sessionCount > sessionLimit) {
    warning = "WARNING: the number of sessions in memory " +
              "(" + sessionCount + ") exceeds the limit " +
              "(" + sessionLimit + "). Date/time: " +
              new Date();
  }
  return(warning);
}

private void recordServletContext(HttpSessionEvent event) {
  HttpSession session = event.getSession();
  context = session.getServletContext();
}
```

Listing 11.4   *SessionCountTag.java*

```java
package moreservlets.tags;

import javax.servlet.*;
import javax.servlet.jsp.*;
import javax.servlet.jsp.tagext.*;
import java.io.*;
import moreservlets.listeners.*;

/** Prints out the number of active sessions. */

public class SessionCountTag extends TagSupport {
  public int doStartTag() {
    try {
      JspWriter out = pageContext.getOut();
      out.print(ActiveSessionCounter.getSessionCount());
    } catch(IOException ioe) {
      System.out.println("Error printing session count.");
    }
    return(SKIP_BODY);
  }
}
```

Listing 11.5 *SessionCountWarningTag.java*

```
package moreservlets.tags;

import javax.servlet.*;
import javax.servlet.jsp.*;
import javax.servlet.jsp.tagext.*;
import java.io.*;
import moreservlets.listeners.*;

/** If the number of active sessions is above the limit,
 *  this prints a warning. Otherwise, it does nothing.
 */

public class SessionCountWarningTag extends TagSupport {
  public int doStartTag() {
    try {
      String warning =
        ActiveSessionCounter.getSessionCountWarning();
      if (warning != null) {
        JspWriter out = pageContext.getOut();
        out.println("<H1><FONT COLOR=\"RED\">");
        out.println(warning);
        out.println("</FONT></H1>");
      }
    } catch(IOException ioe) {
      System.out.println("Error printing session warning.");
    }
    return(SKIP_BODY);
  }
}
```

Listing 11.6 *session-count-taglib-0.9-beta.tld*

```
<?xml version="1.0" encoding="ISO-8859-1" ?>
<!DOCTYPE taglib
 PUBLIC "-//Sun Microsystems, Inc.//DTD JSP Tag Library 1.2//EN"
 "http://java.sun.com/dtd/web-jsptaglibrary_1_2.dtd">

<taglib>
  <tlib-version>0.9</tlib-version>
  <jsp-version>1.2</jsp-version>
  <short-name>company-name-tags</short-name>
```

Listing 11.6 *session-count-taglib-0.9-beta.tld (continued)*

```
<description>
  A tag library that lets you print out the number of
  sessions currently in memory and/or a warning about
  the session count exceeding the limit.

  The tlib-version number and the TLD filename are intended
  to suggest that this tag library is in development. In
  such a situation, you want to use the web.xml taglib
  element to define an alias for the TLD filename. You
  would want to do so even if you weren't trying
  to accommodate Tomcat 4.0, which only reads listener
  declarations from TLD files that are declared that way.
</description>

<!-- Register the listener that records the counts. -->
<listener>
  <listener-class>
    moreservlets.listeners.ActiveSessionCounter
  </listener-class>
</listener>

<!-- Define a tag that prints out the session count. -->
<tag>
  <name>sessionCount</name>
  <tag-class>
    moreservlets.tags.SessionCountTag
  </tag-class>
  <body-content>empty</body-content>
  <description>The number of active sessions.</description>
</tag>

<!-- Define a tag that prints out an optional
     session-count warning. -->
<tag>
  <name>sessionCountWarning</name>
  <tag-class>
    moreservlets.tags.SessionCountWarningTag
  </tag-class>
  <body-content>empty</body-content>
  <description>
    If the number of sessions exceeds the limit,
    this prints a warning. Otherwise, it does nothing.
  </description>
</tag>
</taglib>
```

Listing 11.7	*web.xml* (For session-counting tags)

```xml
<?xml version="1.0" encoding="ISO-8859-1"?>
<!DOCTYPE web-app PUBLIC
    "-//Sun Microsystems, Inc.//DTD Web Application 2.3//EN"
    "http://java.sun.com/dtd/web-app_2_3.dtd">

<web-app>
  <!-- If URL gives a directory but no filename, try index.jsp
       first and index.html second. If neither is found,
       the result is server specific (e.g., a directory
       listing).  Order of elements in web.xml matters.
       welcome-file-list needs to come after servlet but
       before error-page.
  -->
  <welcome-file-list>
    <welcome-file>index.jsp</welcome-file>
    <welcome-file>index.html</welcome-file>
  </welcome-file-list>

  <!-- Register the company-name tag library. Declare an alias
       for the TLD filename since the tag library is under
       development and thus the TLD filename might change.
       You don't want to change all the JSP files each time
       the TLD file changes. Besides, Tomcat 4.0 won't pick
       up listener declarations from TLD files unless they
       are declared this way.
  -->
  <taglib>
    <taglib-uri>
      /session-count-taglib.tld
    </taglib-uri>
    <taglib-location>
      /WEB-INF/session-count-taglib-0.9-beta.tld
    </taglib-location>
  </taglib>
</web-app>
```

Listing 11.8   *index.jsp*

```
<!DOCTYPE HTML PUBLIC "-//W3C//DTD HTML 4.0 Transitional//EN">
<HTML>
<HEAD>
<TITLE>VIP</TITLE>
<LINK REL=STYLESHEET
      HREF="styles.css"
      TYPE="text/css">
</HEAD>

<BODY>
<TABLE BORDER=5 ALIGN="CENTER">
  <TR><TH CLASS="TITLE">
      Very Important Page
</TABLE>
<P>
Blah, blah, blah.
<P>
Yadda, yadda, yadda.
<HR>
<!-- Note that the uri refers to the location defined by
     the taglib element of web.xml, not to the real
     location of the TLD file. -->
<%@ taglib uri="/session-count-taglib.tld" prefix="counts" %>
Number of sessions in memory:  <counts:sessionCount/>
<counts:sessionCountWarning/>
</BODY>
</HTML>
```

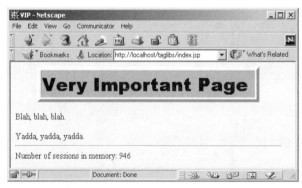

Figure 11–1   When the number of sessions in memory is less than the limit, the sessionCountWarning tag does not generate any output.

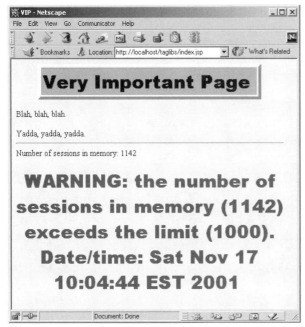

Figure 11–2 When the number of sessions in memory exceeds the limit, the `sessionCountWarning` tag generates a warning.

Testing Session Counts

On a development system, it is often difficult to test session usage because few (if any) outside users are accessing the server. So, it is helpful to generate sessions manually. The simplest way to do this is to disable cookies in your browser and access a framed page that loads the same JSP page multiple times. For details on the process, see Section 10.7 (Recognizing Session Creation and Destruction).

To test the session-counting page shown earlier in this section, I used the same JSP page as in Section 10.7—a blank page with a randomized background color (Listing 11.9; uses the utility class of Listing 11.10). Listing 11.11 shows a frame-based page that, each time it is loaded, loads 49 copies of the JSP page. Figure 11–3 shows a typical result.

Listing 11.9 *test.jsp*

```
<!DOCTYPE HTML PUBLIC "-//W3C//DTD HTML 4.0 Transitional//EN">
<!-- The purpose of this page is to force the system
     to create a session. -->
<HTML>
<HEAD><TITLE>Test</TITLE></HEAD>

<%@ page import="moreservlets.*" %>
<BODY BGCOLOR="<%= ColorUtils.randomColor() %>">

</BODY></HTML>
```

Listing11.10 *ColorUtils.java*

```
package moreservlets;

/** Small utility to generate random HTML color names. */

public class ColorUtils {
  // The official HTML color names.
  private static String[] htmlColorNames =
    { "AQUA", "BLACK", "BLUE", "FUCHSIA", "GRAY", "GREEN",
      "LIME", "MAROON", "NAVY", "OLIVE", "PURPLE", "RED",
      "SILVER", "TEAL", "WHITE", "YELLOW" };

  public static String randomColor() {
    int index = randomInt(htmlColorNames.length);
    return(htmlColorNames[index]);
  }

  // Returns a random number from 0 to n-1 inclusive.

  private static int randomInt(int n) {
    return((int)(Math.random() * n));
  }
}
```

Listing11.11 *make-sessions.html*

```
<!DOCTYPE HTML PUBLIC "-//W3C//DTD HTML 4.0 Frameset//EN">
<HTML>
<HEAD>
  <TITLE>Session Testing...</TITLE>
</HEAD>
<!-- Load the same JSP page 49 times. If cookies are
     disabled and the server is using cookies for session
     tracking (the default), loading this HTML page causes
     the system to create 49 new sessions. -->
<FRAMESET ROWS="*,*,*,*,*,*,*" COLS="*,*,*,*,*,*,*">
  <FRAME SRC="test.jsp"><FRAME SRC="test.jsp">
  <FRAME SRC="test.jsp"><FRAME SRC="test.jsp">
  <FRAME SRC="test.jsp"><FRAME SRC="test.jsp">
  <FRAME SRC="test.jsp"><FRAME SRC="test.jsp">
  <FRAME SRC="test.jsp"><FRAME SRC="test.jsp">
  <FRAME SRC="test.jsp"><FRAME SRC="test.jsp">
  <FRAME SRC="test.jsp"><FRAME SRC="test.jsp">
  <FRAME SRC="test.jsp"><FRAME SRC="test.jsp">
  <FRAME SRC="test.jsp"><FRAME SRC="test.jsp">
  <FRAME SRC="test.jsp"><FRAME SRC="test.jsp">
  <FRAME SRC="test.jsp"><FRAME SRC="test.jsp">
  <FRAME SRC="test.jsp"><FRAME SRC="test.jsp">
  <FRAME SRC="test.jsp"><FRAME SRC="test.jsp">
  <FRAME SRC="test.jsp"><FRAME SRC="test.jsp">
  <FRAME SRC="test.jsp"><FRAME SRC="test.jsp">
  <FRAME SRC="test.jsp"><FRAME SRC="test.jsp">
  <FRAME SRC="test.jsp"><FRAME SRC="test.jsp">
  <FRAME SRC="test.jsp"><FRAME SRC="test.jsp">
  <FRAME SRC="test.jsp"><FRAME SRC="test.jsp">
  <FRAME SRC="test.jsp"><FRAME SRC="test.jsp">
  <FRAME SRC="test.jsp"><FRAME SRC="test.jsp">
  <FRAME SRC="test.jsp"><FRAME SRC="test.jsp">
  <FRAME SRC="test.jsp"><FRAME SRC="test.jsp">
  <FRAME SRC="test.jsp"><FRAME SRC="test.jsp">
  <FRAME SRC="test.jsp">
  <NOFRAMES><BODY>
    This example requires a frame-capable browser.
  </BODY></NOFRAMES>
</FRAMESET>
</HTML>
```

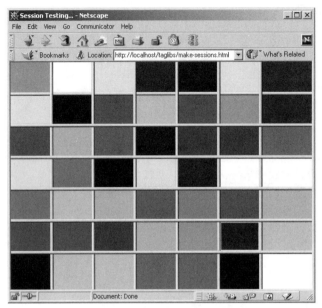

Figure 11–3   The page used to force the system to create new sessions.

11.3 Checking Syntax with TagLibraryValidator

Your tag handlers (i.e., classes that implement the `Tag` interface, usually by extend-ing `TagSupport` or `BodyTagSupport`) can handle some simple usage errors at request time. For instance, if your tag has an attribute that expects an integer, the associated `setXxx` method should convert the incoming `String` to an `int` by put-ting the call to `Integer.parseInt` within a `try/catch` block to handle situations where a malformed value is supplied. In addition to these request time checks, the system will automatically do simple syntax checking at page translation time based on information supplied in the TLD file. For example, if you misspell an attribute or omit one that is listed as required, the system will flag these errors when the JSP page is translated into a servlet.

Both of these approaches are fine for simple cases; neither is sufficient for compli-cated situations. For example, suppose the TLD file lists two attributes as optional, but it doesn't make sense to use one without the other. How do you enforce that both are supplied or both are omitted? In principle, your tag handler could enforce these restrictions, but doing so would make the code significantly more complicated. Besides, errors of this type should be recognized at page translation time; if you can catch them at page translation time, why slow down request time execution by checking for them? Other syntax errors simply cannot be detected by tag handlers. For example, suppose that a certain tag must always contain one of two possible subelements or cannot contain a certain subelement. The nested tags can discover their enclosing tags with `findAncestorWithClass` (see Section 3.7), but how does the enclosing tag enforce which nested tags it contains?

JSP 1.1 provides a `TagExtraInfo` class that lets you perform some of these checks. However, `TagExtraInfo` is difficult to use and limited in capability. So, JSP 1.2 introduced a new class called `TagLibraryValidator` that lets you perform arbitrary page translation-time syntax checks. This class has a `validate` method indirectly giving you an `InputStream` that lets you read the entire JSP page (represented in XML format), so you have full access to all available translation-time information about the page. In most cases you don't read the input directly from the input stream. Instead, you use an XML-based API like SAX, DOM, or JDOM to look at the various XML elements (start tags, end tags, tag attributes, and tag bodies) of the file. In such a situation, the HTML content is represented as the body of a `jsp:text` element and is usually ignored by the validator.

Using a validator consists of the following steps.

1. **Create a subclass of `TagLibraryValidator`.** Note that Tag-LibraryValidator is in the `javax.servlet.jsp.tagext` package.

2. **Override the `validate` method.** This method takes three arguments: two strings giving the `prefix` and `uri` declared in the `taglib` directive of the JSP page using the tag library, and a `PageData` object. Call `getInputStream` on the `PageData` object to obtain a stream that lets you read the XML representation of the JSP page. This stream is typically passed to an XML parser, and your `validate` method deals with the XML elements, not the raw characters. If the syntax checks out properly, return `null` from `validate`. If there are errors, return an array of `ValidationMessage` objects, each of which is built by calling the `ValidationMessage` constructor with the ID of the tag (usually `null` since servers are not required to give IDs to tags) and a `String` describing the problem. Here is a simplified example:

```
public ValidationMessage[] validate(String prefix,
                                     String uri,
                                     PageData page) {
  InputStream stream = page.getInputStream();
  BookOrder[] orders = findBookOrders(stream);
  for(int i=0; i<orders.length; i++) {
    String title = orders[i].getTitle();
    int numOrdered = orders[i].getNumOrdered();
```

```
      if (title.equals("More Servlets and JavaServer Pages") &&
          (numOrdered < 100)) {
        String message = "Too few copies of MSAJSP ordered!";
        ValidationMessage[] errors =
          { new ValidationMessage(null, message) };
        return(errors);
      }
    }
    return(null);
}
```

3. **Optionally override other methods.** You read validator initialization parameters (supplied in the TLD file with the `init-param` subelement of `validator`) with `getInitParameters`. You can set initialization parameters with `setInitParameters`. If you store persistent values in fields of your validator, use `release` to reset the fields—validator instances, like tag instances, can be reused by servers.

4. **Declare the validator in the TLD file.** Use the `validator` element with a `validator-class` subelement and optionally one or more `init-param` subelements and a `description` element. The `validator` element goes after `description` but before `listener` and `tag` in the TLD file. Here is a simplified example:

```
<?xml version="1.0" encoding="ISO-8859-1" ?>
<!DOCTYPE ...>
<taglib>
  <tlib-version>...</tlib-version>
  <jsp-version>1.2</jsp-version>
  <short-name>...</short-name>
  <description>...</description>
  <validator>
    <validator-class>
      somePackage.SomeValidatorClass
    </validator-class>
  </validator>
  <tag>...</tag>
</taglib>
```

5. **Try JSP pages that use the tag library.** First, deploy your Web application. Second, see if you get errors when the JSP pages are translated. If you use `load-on-startup` (see Section 5.5, "Initializing and Preloading Servlets and JSP Pages"), the JSP page is translated into a servlet when the server is loaded. Otherwise, it is translated the first time it is accessed. If the `validate` method returns `null`, no action is taken. If `validate` returns a nonempty array, the server makes the error messages available in some server-specific manner.

Remember, however, that each JSP page is only translated into a servlet once. Unless the JSP page is modified, it doesn't get retranslated *even if the server is restarted*. This means that, during development, you have to be sure to modify your JSP pages whenever you want to test a change in your validator. It is also possible to delete the servlet that resulted from the JSP page, but that servlet is stored in a server-specific location. I usually just add and then delete a space in the JSP page, then redeploy it.

Core Warning

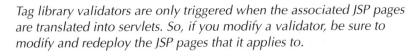

Tag library validators are only triggered when the associated JSP pages are translated into servlets. So, if you modify a validator, be sure to modify and redeploy the JSP pages that it applies to.

Example: Tracing the Tag Structure

To become acquainted with validators, let's make a validator that simply discovers all of the start and end tags, tag attributes, and tag bodies. It will print a summary to standard output and always return `null` to indicate that no syntax errors were found. I'll show a more interesting validator in the next subsection.

Even this simple task would be a lot of work if we had to parse the JSP page ourselves. Fortunately, since the page is represented in XML, we can use an XML parser and one of the standardized APIs like SAX, DOM, or JDOM. I'll use the Apache Xerces parser and the SAX API in this example. I'll also use the Java API for XML Parsing (JAXP) so that I can switch from the Apache parser to another SAX-compliant parser by changing only a single property value. If you aren't familiar with SAX and JAXP, Section 11.4 summarizes their use.

Accomplishing this task involves the following steps.

1. **Creation of a subclass of `TagLibraryValidator`.** Listing 11.12 shows a class called `SAXValidator` that extends `TagLibrary-Validator`.
2. **Overriding of the `validate` method.** I take the third argument to `validate` (the `PageData` object), call `getInputStream`, and pass that to the SAX `InputSource` constructor. I then tell SAX to parse the JSP document using that `InputSource` and a handler called `PrintHandler` (Listing 11.13). This handler simply prints to standard output the start tags (with attributes), the end tags, and the first word of each tag body. Again, see Section 11.4 if you are unfamiliar with the SAX API.

3. **Declaration of the validator in the TLD file.** Listing 11.14 shows an updated version of the TLD file for the session-counting example, with a validator entry added.

4. **Try JSP pages that use the tag library.** Listing 11.15 shows the standard output that results when *index.jsp* (shown earlier in Listing 11.8 and Figures 11–1 and 11–2) is accessed.

Listing11.12 *SAXValidator.java*

```java
import javax.servlet.jsp.tagext.*;
import javax.xml.parsers.*;
import org.xml.sax.*;
import org.xml.sax.helpers.*;

/** A "validator" that really just prints out an outline
 *  of the JSP page (in its XML representation). The
 *  validate method always returns null, so the page is
 *  always considered valid.
 */

public class SAXValidator extends TagLibraryValidator {
  /** Print an outline of the XML representation of
   *  the JSP page.
   */
  public ValidationMessage[] validate(String prefix,
                                      String uri,
                                      PageData page) {
    String jaxpPropertyName =
      "javax.xml.parsers.SAXParserFactory";
    // Pass the parser factory in on the command line with
    // -D to override the use of the Apache parser.
    if (System.getProperty(jaxpPropertyName) == null) {
      String apacheXercesPropertyValue =
        "org.apache.xerces.jaxp.SAXParserFactoryImpl";
      System.setProperty(jaxpPropertyName,
                         apacheXercesPropertyValue);
    }
    DefaultHandler handler = new PrintHandler();
    SAXParserFactory factory = SAXParserFactory.newInstance();
    try {
      SAXParser parser = factory.newSAXParser();
      InputSource source =
        new InputSource(page.getInputStream());
      parser.parse(source, handler);
```

Listing11.12 *SAXValidator.java (continued)*

```
    } catch(Exception e) {
      String errorMessage =
        "SAX parse error: " + e;
      System.err.println(errorMessage);
      e.printStackTrace();
    }
    return(null);
  }
}
```

Listing11.13 *PrintHandler.java*

```
package moreservlets;

import org.xml.sax.*;
import org.xml.sax.helpers.*;
import java.util.StringTokenizer;

/** A SAX handler that prints out the start tags, end tags,
 *  and first word of tag body. Indents two spaces
 *  for each nesting level.
 */

public class PrintHandler extends DefaultHandler {
  private int indentation = 0;

  /** When you see a start tag, print it out and then increase
   *  indentation by two spaces. If the element has
   *  attributes, place them in parens after the element name.
   */

  public void startElement(String namespaceUri,
                           String localName,
                           String qualifiedName,
                           Attributes attributes)
      throws SAXException {
    indent(indentation);
    System.out.print("<" + qualifiedName);
    int numAttributes = attributes.getLength();
    // For <someTag> just print out "<someTag>". But for
    // <someTag att1="Val1" att2="Val2"> (or variations
    // that have extra white space), print out
    // <someTag att1="Val1" att2="Val2">.
```

Listing 11.13 *PrintHandler.java (continued)*

```java
    if (numAttributes > 0) {
      for(int i=0; i<numAttributes; i++) {
        System.out.print(" ");
        System.out.print(attributes.getQName(i) + "=\"" +
                         attributes.getValue(i) + "\"");
      }
    }
    System.out.println(">");
    indentation = indentation + 2;
  }

  /** When you see the end tag, print it out and decrease
   *  indentation level by 2.
   */

  public void endElement(String namespaceUri,
                         String localName,
                         String qualifiedName)
      throws SAXException {
    indentation = indentation - 2;
    indent(indentation);
    System.out.println("</" + qualifiedName + ">");
  }

  /** Print out the first word of each tag body. */

  public void characters(char[] chars,
                         int startIndex,
                         int length) {
    String data = new String(chars, startIndex, length);
    // White space makes up default StringTokenizer delimiters
    StringTokenizer tok = new StringTokenizer(data);
    if (tok.hasMoreTokens()) {
      indent(indentation);
      System.out.print(tok.nextToken());
      if (tok.hasMoreTokens()) {
        System.out.println("...");
      } else {
        System.out.println();
      }
    }
  }

  private void indent(int indentation) {
    for(int i=0; i<indentation; i++) {
      System.out.print(" ");
    }
  }
}
```

Listing 11.14 *session-count-taglib-0.9-beta.tld* (Updated)

```
<?xml version="1.0" encoding="ISO-8859-1" ?>
<!DOCTYPE taglib
 PUBLIC "-//Sun Microsystems, Inc.//DTD JSP Tag Library 1.2//EN"
 "http://java.sun.com/dtd/web-jsptaglibrary_1_2.dtd">

<taglib>
  <tlib-version>0.9</tlib-version>
  <jsp-version>1.2</jsp-version>
  <short-name>company-name-tags</short-name>
  <description>
    A tag library that lets you print out the number of
    sessions currently in memory and/or a warning about
    the session count exceeding the limit.

    The tlib-version number and the TLD filename are intended
    to suggest that this tag library is in development. In
    such a situation, you want to use the web.xml taglib
    element to define an alias for the TLD filename. You
    would want to do so even if you weren't trying
    to accommodate Tomcat 4.0, which only reads listener
    declarations from TLD files that are declared that way.
  </description>

  <!-- Declare a validator to do translation-time checking
       of custom tag syntax. -->
  <validator>
    <validator-class>moreservlets.SAXValidator</validator-class>
  </validator>

  <!-- Register the listener that records the counts. -->
  <listener>
    <listener-class>
      moreservlets.listeners.ActiveSessionCounter
    </listener-class>
  </listener>

  <!-- Define a tag that prints out the session count. -->
  <tag>
    <name>sessionCount</name>
    <tag-class>
      moreservlets.tags.SessionCountTag
    </tag-class>
    <body-content>empty</body-content>
    <description>The number of active sessions.</description>
  </tag>
```

Listing11.14   *session-count-taglib-0.9-beta.tld* (Updated) *(continued)*

```
<!-- Define a tag that prints out an optional
     session-count warning. -->
<tag>
  <name>sessionCountWarning</name>
  <tag-class>
    moreservlets.tags.SessionCountWarningTag
  </tag-class>
  <body-content>empty</body-content>
  <description>
    If the number of sessions exceeds the limit,
    this prints a warning. Otherwise, it does nothing.
  </description>
</tag>
</taglib>
```

Listing11.15   Validator output (for *index.jsp*—Listing 11.8)

```
<jsp:root xmlns:jsp="http://java.sun.com/JSP/Page"
          version="1.2"
          xmlns:counts="/session-count-taglib.tld">
  <jsp:text>
    <!DOCTYPE...
  </jsp:text>
  <jsp:text>
    Number...
  </jsp:text>
  <counts:sessionCount>
  </counts:sessionCount>
  <jsp:text>
  </jsp:text>
  <counts:sessionCountWarning>
  </counts:sessionCountWarning>
  <jsp:text>
    </BODY>...
  </jsp:text>
</jsp:root>
```

Example: Enforcing Tag Nesting Order

The previous subsection showed how to make a simple validator that uses SAX to discover the various tags in the page. Now let's *do* something with those tags. Listings 11.16 and 11.17 show two simple tags: OuterTag and InnerTag. OuterTag should not contain other OuterTag instances, and InnerTag should only appear within OuterTag. Developing a validator to enforce these restrictions involves the following steps.

1. **Creation of a subclass of `TagLibraryValidator`.** Listing 11.18 shows a class called NestingValidator that extends Tag-LibraryValidator.

2. **Overriding of the `validate` method.** I take the third argument to validate (the PageData object), call getInputStream, and pass that to the SAX InputSource constructor. I then tell SAX to parse the JSP document using that InputSource and a handler called NestingHandler (Listing 11.19). The NestingHandler class throws an exception in two situations: if it finds the outer tag when an existing outer tag instance is open and if it finds the inner tag when an existing outer tag instance is not open. The main validator returns null if the handler throws no exceptions. If the handler throws an exception, a 1-element ValidationMessage array is returned that contains a ValidationMessage describing the error.

3. **Declaration of the validator in the TLD file.** Listing 11.20 shows a TLD file that gives tag names to the two tag handlers and declares the validator.

4. **Try JSP pages that use the tag library.** Listings 11.21 and 11.22 show two JSP pages that correctly follow the rules that the outer tag cannot be nested and that the inner tag must appear directly or indirectly within the outer tag. Figures 11–4 and 11–5 show the results— the validator does not affect the output in any way. Listing 11.23 shows a JSP page that incorrectly attempts to use the inner tag when it is not nested within the outer tag. Figures 11–6 and 11–7 show the results in Tomcat 4.0 and ServletExec 4.1, respectively—the normal output is blocked since the JSP page was not successfully translated into a servlet. Listing 11.24 shows a JSP page that incorrectly attempts to nest the outer tag. Figure 11–8 shows the result in Tomcat 4.0.

Listing11.16 *OuterTag.java*

```java
package moreservlets.tags;

import javax.servlet.*;
import javax.servlet.jsp.*;
import javax.servlet.jsp.tagext.*;
import java.io.*;

/** Prints out a simple message. A TagLibraryValidator will
 *  enforce a nesting order for tags associated with this class.
 */

public class OuterTag extends TagSupport {
  public int doStartTag() {
    try {
      JspWriter out = pageContext.getOut();
      out.print("OuterTag");
    } catch(IOException ioe) {
      System.out.println("Error printing OuterTag.");
    }
    return(EVAL_BODY_INCLUDE);
  }
}
```

Listing11.17 *InnerTag.java*

```java
package moreservlets.tags;

import javax.servlet.*;
import javax.servlet.jsp.*;
import javax.servlet.jsp.tagext.*;
import java.io.*;

/** Prints out a simple message. A TagLibraryValidator will
 *  enforce a nesting order for tags associated with this class.
 */

public class InnerTag extends TagSupport {
  public int doStartTag() {
    try {
      JspWriter out = pageContext.getOut();
      out.print("InnerTag");
    } catch(IOException ioe) {
      System.out.println("Error printing InnerTag.");
    }
    return(EVAL_BODY_INCLUDE);
  }
}
```

Listing11.18	*NestingValidator.java*

```java
package moreservlets;

import javax.servlet.jsp.tagext.*;
import javax.xml.parsers.*;
import org.xml.sax.*;
import org.xml.sax.helpers.*;

/** A validator that verifies that tags follow
 *  proper nesting order.
 */

public class NestingValidator extends TagLibraryValidator {

  public ValidationMessage[] validate(String prefix,
                                       String uri,
                                       PageData page) {
    String jaxpPropertyName =
      "javax.xml.parsers.SAXParserFactory";
    // Pass the parser factory in on the command line with
    // -D to override the use of the Apache parser.
    if (System.getProperty(jaxpPropertyName) == null) {
      String apacheXercesPropertyValue =
        "org.apache.xerces.jaxp.SAXParserFactoryImpl";
      System.setProperty(jaxpPropertyName,
                         apacheXercesPropertyValue);
    }
    DefaultHandler handler = new NestingHandler();
    SAXParserFactory factory = SAXParserFactory.newInstance();
    try {
      SAXParser parser = factory.newSAXParser();
      InputSource source =
        new InputSource(page.getInputStream());
      parser.parse(source, handler);
      return(null);
    } catch(Exception e) {
      String errorMessage = e.getMessage();
      // The first argument to the ValidationMessage
      // constructor can be a tag ID. Since tag IDs
      // are not universally supported, use null for
      // portability. The important part is the second
      // argument: the error message.
      ValidationMessage[] messages =
        { new ValidationMessage(null, errorMessage) };
      return(messages);
    }
  }
}
```

Listing11.19 *NestingHandler.java*

```java
package moreservlets;

import org.xml.sax.*;
import org.xml.sax.helpers.*;
import java.util.StringTokenizer;

/** A SAX handler that returns an exception if either of
 *  the following two situations occurs:
 *  <UL>
 *    <LI>The designated outer tag is directly or indirectly
 *        nested within the outer tag (i.e., itself).
 *    <LI>The designated inner tag is <I>not</I> directly
 *        or indirectly nested within the outer tag.
 *  </UL>
 */

public class NestingHandler extends DefaultHandler {
  private String outerTagName = "outerTag";
  private String innerTagName = "innerTag";
  private boolean inOuterTag = false;

  public void startElement(String namespaceUri,
                           String localName,
                           String qualifiedName,
                           Attributes attributes)
      throws SAXException {
    String tagName = mainTagName(qualifiedName);
    if (tagName.equals(outerTagName)) {
      if (inOuterTag) {
        throw new SAXException("\nCannot nest " + outerTagName);
      }
      inOuterTag = true;
    } else if (tagName.equals(innerTagName) && !inOuterTag) {
      throw new SAXException("\n" + innerTagName +
                             " can only appear within " +
                             outerTagName);
    }
  }

  public void endElement(String namespaceUri,
                         String localName,
                         String qualifiedName)
      throws SAXException {
    String tagName = mainTagName(qualifiedName);
    if (tagName.equals(outerTagName)) {
      inOuterTag = false;
    }
  }
```

| Listing11.19 | *NestingHandler.java (continued)* |

```
  private String mainTagName(String qualifiedName) {
    StringTokenizer tok =
      new StringTokenizer(qualifiedName, ":");
    tok.nextToken();
    return(tok.nextToken());
  }
}
```

| Listing11.20 | *nested-tag-taglib.tld* |

```
<?xml version="1.0" encoding="ISO-8859-1" ?>
<!DOCTYPE taglib
 PUBLIC "-//Sun Microsystems, Inc.//DTD JSP Tag Library 1.2//EN"
 "http://java.sun.com/dtd/web-jsptaglibrary_1_2.dtd">

<taglib>
  <tlib-version>1.0</tlib-version>
  <jsp-version>1.2</jsp-version>
  <short-name>nested-tags</short-name>
  <description>
    A tag library that has two tags: outerTag and innerTag.
    A TagLibraryValidator will enforce the following
    nesting rules:
      1) innerTag can only appear inside outerTag. It can
         be nested, however.
      2) outerTag cannot be nested within other outerTag
         instances.
  </description>

  <!-- Declare a validator to do translation-time checking
       of custom tag syntax. -->
  <validator>
    <validator-class>
      moreservlets.NestingValidator
    </validator-class>
  </validator>

  <!-- Define the outerTag tag. -->
  <tag>
    <name>outerTag</name>
    <tag-class>
      moreservlets.tags.OuterTag
    </tag-class>
    <body-content>JSP</body-content>
```

Listing11.20 *nested-tag-taglib.tld (continued)*

```
   <description>
     A simple tag: cannot be nested within other outerTag
     instances.
   </description>
 </tag>

 <!-- Define the innerTag tag. -->
 <tag>
   <name>innerTag</name>
   <tag-class>
     moreservlets.tags.InnerTag
   </tag-class>
   <body-content>JSP</body-content>
   <description>
     A simple tag: can only appear within outerTag.
   </description>
 </tag>
</taglib>
```

Listing11.21 *nesting-test1.jsp* (Proper tag nesting)

```
<!DOCTYPE HTML PUBLIC "-//W3C//DTD HTML 4.0 Transitional//EN">
<HTML>
<HEAD>
<TITLE>Nested Tags: Test 1</TITLE>
<LINK REL=STYLESHEET
      HREF="styles.css"
      TYPE="text/css">
</HEAD>

<BODY>
<TABLE BORDER=5 ALIGN="CENTER">
  <TR><TH CLASS="TITLE">
      Nested Tags: Test 1
</TABLE>

<%@ taglib uri="/WEB-INF/nested-tag-taglib.tld" prefix="test" %>
```

Listing 11.21 *nesting-test1.jsp* (Proper tag nesting) *(continued)*

```
<PRE>
<test:outerTag>
  <test:innerTag/>
  <test:innerTag/>
  <test:innerTag/>
</test:outerTag>
<test:outerTag/>
</PRE>

</BODY>
</HTML>
```

Listing 11.22 *nesting-test2.jsp* (Proper tag nesting)

```
<!DOCTYPE HTML PUBLIC "-//W3C//DTD HTML 4.0 Transitional//EN">
<HTML>
<HEAD>
<TITLE>Nested Tags: Test 2</TITLE>
<LINK REL=STYLESHEET
      HREF="styles.css"
      TYPE="text/css">
</HEAD>

<BODY>
<TABLE BORDER=5 ALIGN="CENTER">
  <TR><TH CLASS="TITLE">
      Nested Tags: Test 2
</TABLE>

<%@ taglib uri="/WEB-INF/nested-tag-taglib.tld" prefix="test" %>

<PRE>
<test:outerTag>
  <test:innerTag>
    <test:innerTag/>
  </test:innerTag>
  <test:innerTag>
    <test:innerTag>
      <test:innerTag/>
    </test:innerTag>
  </test:innerTag>
</test:outerTag>
<test:outerTag/>
</PRE>

</BODY>
</HTML>
```

Listing11.23 *nesting-test3.jsp* (Improper tag nesting)

```
<!DOCTYPE HTML PUBLIC "-//W3C//DTD HTML 4.0 Transitional//EN">
<HTML>
<HEAD>
<TITLE>Nested Tags: Test 3</TITLE>
<LINK REL=STYLESHEET
      HREF="styles.css"
      TYPE="text/css">
</HEAD>

<BODY>
<TABLE BORDER=5 ALIGN="CENTER">
  <TR><TH CLASS="TITLE">
      Nested Tags: Test 3
</TABLE>

<%@ taglib uri="/WEB-INF/nested-tag-taglib.tld" prefix="test" %>

<PRE>
<test:innerTag/>
</PRE>

</BODY>
</HTML>
```

Listing11.24 *nesting-test4.jsp* (Improper tag nesting)

```
<!DOCTYPE HTML PUBLIC "-//W3C//DTD HTML 4.0 Transitional//EN">
<HTML>
<HEAD>
<TITLE>Nested Tags: Test 4</TITLE>
<LINK REL=STYLESHEET
      HREF="styles.css"
      TYPE="text/css">
</HEAD>

<BODY>
<TABLE BORDER=5 ALIGN="CENTER">
  <TR><TH CLASS="TITLE">
      Nested Tags: Test 4
</TABLE>

<%@ taglib uri="/WEB-INF/nested-tag-taglib.tld" prefix="test" %>
```

| Listing11.24 | *nesting-test4.jsp* (Improper tag nesting) *(continued)* |

```
<PRE>
<test:outerTag>
  <test:outerTag/>
</test:outerTag>
</PRE>

</BODY>
</HTML>
```

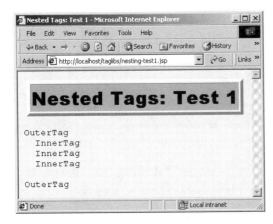

Figure 11–4 Result of *nesting-test1.jsp*. Tags are nested properly, so output is normal.

Figure 11–5 Result of *nesting-test2.jsp*. Tags are nested properly, so output is normal.

Figure 11–6   Result of *nesting-test3.jsp*. Tags are nested improperly, so normal output is prevented—at page translation time, the normal servlet is replaced by one that gives an error message. This output is from Tomcat 4.0.

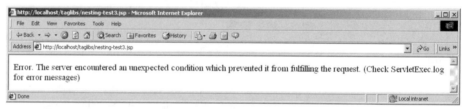

Figure 11–7   The result of *nesting-test3.jsp* when accessed on ServletExec 4.1.

Figure 11–8   Result of *nesting-test4.jsp*. Tags are nested improperly, so normal output is prevented—at page translation time, the normal servlet is replaced by one that gives an error message. This output is from Tomcat 4.0.

11.4 Aside: Parsing XML with SAX 2.0

The `validate` method of `TagLibraryValidator` gives you a `PageData` object from which you can obtain an `InputStream` that is associated with the XML version of the JSP page. You are unlikely to want to read directly from that stream to try to validate proper usage of your custom tags: the input streams and readers in the `java.io` package are too low level to be effective for this usage. Instead, you will probably want to use an XML parser to do the low-level work for you. The validators of Section 11.3 used the SAX 2.0 API, so I'll summarize its use here. More detail on SAX can be found at *http://www.saxproject.org/*. For information on DOM and other XML-related APIs, see *http://www.w3.org/XML/*, one of the many XML and Java texts such as *Java & XML 2nd Edition* (O'Reilly 2001), or the SAX, DOM, and XSLT summary in Chapter 23 of *Core Web Programming 2nd Edition* (Prentice Hall and Sun Microsystems Press 2001).

SAX processing is a lot like writing custom tag handlers: you write methods to handle the start tag, end tag, and tag body. The major difference is that SAX handlers are not associated with specific tags—the same handler fires for all tags. So, with SAX you have to repeatedly check which tag you are working with. Of course, this capability is exactly what makes SAX so useful for checking that different tags are interacting properly.

Installation and Setup

SAX is not a standard part of either Java 2 Standard Edition or the servlet and JSP APIs. So, your first step is to download the appropriate classes and configure them for use in your programs. Here is a summary of what is required.

1. **Download a SAX-compliant parser.** The parser provides the Java classes that follow the SAX 2 API as specified by the WWW Consortium. You can obtain a list of XML parsers in Java at *http://www.xml.com/pub/rg/Java_Parsers*. I use the Apache Xerces-J parser in this book. See *http://xml.apache.org/xerces-j/*. This parser comes with the complete SAX API in Javadoc format.

2. **Download the Java API for XML Processing (JAXP).** This API provides a small layer on top of SAX that lets you plug in different vendor's parsers without making any changes to your basic code. See *http://java.sun.com/xml/*.

3. **Tell your development environment and the server about the SAX classes.** In the case of Apache Xerces, the SAX classes are in *xerces_install_dir/ xerces.jar*. So, for example, to set up your development environment on Windows 98, you would do

```
set CLASSPATH=xerces_install_dir\xerces.jar;%CLASSPATH%
```

To tell the server about the SAX classes, you would either copy the JAR file to the Web application's `lib` directory, unpack the JAR file (using `jar -xvf`) into the server's `classes` directory, or put the JAR file in a shared location (if your server supports such a capability—see Section 4.4, "Recording Dependencies on Server Libraries").

4. **Set your `CLASSPATH` to include the JAXP classes.** These classes are in *jaxp_install_dir/jaxp.jar*. For example, to set up your development environment on Unix/Linux with the C shell, you would do

```
setenv CLASSPATH jaxp_install_dir/jaxp.jar:$CLASSPATH
```

To tell the server about the JAXP classes, see the preceding step.

5. **Bookmark the SAX API.** You can browse the official API at *http://www.saxproject.org/apidoc/index.html*, but the API that comes with Apache Xerces is easier to use because it is on your local system and is integrated with the DOM and JAXP APIs. More information on SAX can be found at *http://www.saxproject.org/*.

Parsing

With SAX processing, there are two high-level tasks: creating a content handler and invoking the parser with the designated content handler. The following list summarizes the detailed steps needed to accomplish these tasks.

1. **Tell the system which parser you want to use.** This can be done in a number of ways: through the `javax.xml.parsers.SAXParser-Factory` system property, through *jre_dir/lib/ jaxp.properties*, through the J2EE Services API and the class specified in *META-INF/services/ javax.xml.parsers.SAXParserFactory*, or with a system-dependent default parser. The system property is the easiest method. For example, the following code permits deployers to specify the parser in the server startup script with the `-D` option to `java`, and uses the Apache Xerces parser otherwise.

```
String jaxpPropertyName =
  "javax.xml.parsers.SAXParserFactory";
if (System.getProperty(jaxpPropertyName) == null) {
  String apacheXercesPropertyValue =
    "org.apache.xerces.jaxp.SAXParserFactoryImpl";
  System.setProperty(jaxpPropertyName,
                     apacheXercesPropertyValue);
}
...
```

2. **Create a parser instance.** First make an instance of a parser factory, then use that to create a parser object.

```
SAXParserFactory factory = SAXParserFactory.newInstance();
SAXParser parser = factory.newSAXParser();
```

Note that you can use the `setNamespaceAware` and `set-Validating` methods on the `SAXParserFactory` to make the parser namespace aware and validating, respectively.

3. **Create a content handler to respond to parsing events.** This handler is typically a subclass of `DefaultHandler`. You override any or all of the following placeholders.

   - **`startDocument, endDocument`**
     Use these methods to respond to the start and end of the document; they take no arguments.

   - **`startElement, endElement`**
     Use these methods to respond to the start and end tags of an element. The `startElement` method takes four arguments: the namespace URI (a `String`; empty if no namespace), the namespace or prefix (a `String`; empty if no namespace), the fully qualified element name (a `String`; i.e., `"prefix:mainName"` if there is a namespace; `"mainName"` otherwise), and an `Attributes` object representing the attributes of the start tag. The `endElement` method takes the same arguments except for the attributes (since end tags are not permitted attributes).

   - **`characters, ignoreableWhitespace`**
     Use these methods to respond to the tag body. They take three arguments: a `char` array, a start index, and an end index. A common approach is to turn the relevant part of the character array into a `String` by passing all three arguments to the `String` constructor. Non-white-space data is always reported to the `characters` method. White space is always reported to the `ignoreable-Whitespace` method when the parser is run in validating mode but can be reported to either method otherwise.

4. **Invoke the parser with the designated content handler.** You invoke the parser by calling the `parse` method, supplying an input stream, URI (represented as a string), or `org.xml.sax.Input-Source` along with the content handler. Note that `InputSource` has a simple constructor that accepts an `InputStream`. Use this constructor to turn the `InputStream` of the `TagLibraryValidator` `validate` method into an `InputSource`.

   ```
   parser.parse(new InputSource(validatorStream), handler);
   ```

   The content handler does the rest.

11.5 Handling Exceptions with the TryCatchFinally Interface

In JSP 1.1, you can trap exceptions that occur in each of your tag handling methods (doStartTag, doEndTag, etc.). But, what happens if an exception occurs during the processing of the body of the tag? What if you want to respond to exceptions in doStartTag, doEndTag, and doAfterBody the same way and don't want to repeat your code?

JSP 1.2 answers these questions by providing a new interface called TryCatchFinally with two methods:

- **doCatch(Throwable t)**
- **doFinally()**

If your tag implements this interface and an exception occurs during *any* of the tag life-cycle methods *or* during the processing of the tag body, the system calls the doCatch method. Regardless of whether an exception occurs, the system calls the doFinally method when done executing the tag. Note, however, that this exception-handling behavior applies only to the tag life-cycle methods and the processing of the tag body. It does *not* apply to the set*Xxx* attribute-setting methods.

Core Warning

The TryCatchFinally interface does not apply to the methods that set the tag attributes.

To illustrate this new exception-handling behavior, Listing 11.25 shows a tag that implements TryCatchFinally. The tag doesn't actually output anything: it just prints a message to standard output when doStartTag, doEndTag, doCatch, and doFinally are called. Listing 11.26 shows the TLD file that declares the tag; no new syntax or entries are needed.

Listing 11.27 shows a JSP page that uses the new tag wrapped around a body that sometimes throws an exception (see Listing 11.28). Figure 11–9 shows the result when none of the tags throws an exception. Listing 11.29 shows the corresponding output—doStartTag, doEndTag, and doFinally are invoked but doCatch is not. Figure 11–10 shows the result when the second invocation of the tag throws an exception—the tag body generates no output but the page processing continues normally. Listing 11.30 shows the corresponding output—doStartTag, doEndTag, and doFinally are invoked each time and doCatch is invoked only in the case when the tag body threw the exception.

Listing 11.25 *CatchTag.java*

```java
package moreservlets.tags;

import javax.servlet.*;
import javax.servlet.jsp.*;
import javax.servlet.jsp.tagext.*;
import java.io.*;

/** Tag that traces the life cycle of tags that
 *  implement the TryCatchFinally interface.
 */

public class CatchTag extends TagSupport
                      implements TryCatchFinally {
  public int doStartTag() {
    System.out.println("CatchTag: start");
    return(EVAL_BODY_INCLUDE);
  }

  public int doEndTag() {
    System.out.println("CatchTag: end");
    return(EVAL_PAGE);
  }

  public void doCatch(Throwable throwable) {
    System.out.println("CatchTag: doCatch: " +
                       throwable.getMessage());
  }

  public void doFinally() {
    System.out.print("CatchTag: doFinally\n");
  }
}
```

Listing 11.26 *catch-tag-taglib.tld*

```xml
<?xml version="1.0" encoding="ISO-8859-1" ?>
<!DOCTYPE taglib
 PUBLIC "-//Sun Microsystems, Inc.//DTD JSP Tag Library 1.2//EN"
 "http://java.sun.com/dtd/web-jsptaglibrary_1_2.dtd">

<taglib>
  <tlib-version>1.0</tlib-version>
  <jsp-version>1.2</jsp-version>
  <short-name>catch-tags</short-name>
  <description>
    A tag library that uses a simple tag to illustrate
    the behavior of the TryCatchFinally interface.

    From More Servlets and JavaServer Pages,
    http://www.moreservlets.com/.
  </description>

  <!-- Define the catchTag tag. -->
  <tag>
    <name>catchTag</name>
    <tag-class>
      moreservlets.tags.CatchTag
    </tag-class>
    <body-content>JSP</body-content>
    <description>
      Implements the TryCatchFinally interface and
      prints simple tag life-cycle information to the
      standard output.
    </description>
  </tag>
</taglib>
```

Listing 11.27 *catchTest.jsp*

```html
<!DOCTYPE HTML PUBLIC "-//W3C//DTD HTML 4.0 Transitional//EN">
<HTML>
<HEAD>
<TITLE>Some Random Numbers</TITLE>
<LINK REL=STYLESHEET
      HREF="styles.css"
      TYPE="text/css">
</HEAD>
```

Listing 11.27 *catchTest.jsp (continued)*

```
<BODY>
<TABLE BORDER=5 ALIGN="CENTER">
  <TR><TH CLASS="TITLE">
     Some Random Numbers
</TABLE>

<%@ taglib uri="/WEB-INF/catch-tag-taglib.tld" prefix="msajsp" %>
<UL>
  <LI><msajsp:catchTag>
     <%= moreservlets.Utils.dangerousMethod() %>
     </msajsp:catchTag>
  <LI><msajsp:catchTag>
     <%= moreservlets.Utils.dangerousMethod() %>
     </msajsp:catchTag>
  <LI><msajsp:catchTag>
     <%= moreservlets.Utils.dangerousMethod() %>
     </msajsp:catchTag>
  <LI><msajsp:catchTag>
     <%= moreservlets.Utils.dangerousMethod() %>
     </msajsp:catchTag>
  <LI><msajsp:catchTag>
     <%= moreservlets.Utils.dangerousMethod() %>
     </msajsp:catchTag>
</UL>
</BODY>
</HTML>
```

Listing 11.28 *Utils.java*

```
package moreservlets;

public class Utils {
  public static String dangerousMethod() throws Exception {
    double num = Math.random();
    if (num < 0.8) {
      return("Random num: " + num);
    } else {
      throw(new Exception("No intelligent life here."));
    }
  }
}
```

Figure 11–9   One possible result of *catchTest.jsp*.

| **Listing11.29** | Output of *catchTest.jsp* corresponding to Figure 11–9 |

```
CatchTag: start
CatchTag: end
CatchTag: doFinally
CatchTag: start
CatchTag: end
CatchTag: doFinally
CatchTag: start
CatchTag: end
CatchTag: doFinally
CatchTag: start
CatchTag: end
CatchTag: doFinally
CatchTag: start
CatchTag: end
CatchTag: doFinally
```

Figure 11–10 Another possible result of *catchTest.jsp*.

Listing11.30 Output of *catchTest.jsp* corresponding to Figure 11–10

```
CatchTag: start
CatchTag: end
CatchTag: doFinally
CatchTag: start
CatchTag: doCatch: No intelligent life here.
CatchTag: doFinally
CatchTag: start
CatchTag: end
CatchTag: doFinally
CatchTag: start
CatchTag: end
CatchTag: doFinally
CatchTag: start
CatchTag: end
CatchTag: doFinally
```

11.6 New Names for Return Values

In JSP 1.1, the EVAL_BODY_TAG constant was used in two totally different situations. First, it was returned from the doStartTag method of TagSupport or BodyTagSupport to indicate that the tag body should be made available in doAfterBody. The default doStartTag method of BodyTagSupport returned this value. Second, it was returned from the doAfterBody method of TagSupport or BodyTagSupport to indicate that the body should be reevaluated.

This dual use of EVAL_BODY_TAG was confusing because it indicated a single evaluation in the first case and multiple evaluations (as in iterative tags) in the second case. To better differentiate the two situations, in JSP 1.2 you return EVAL_BODY_BUFFERED from doStartTag to indicate that the tag body should be made available in doAfterBody. You return EVAL_BODY_AGAIN from doAfter-Body when you want to reevaluate the body.

11.7 Looping Without Generating BodyContent

In JSP 1.1, the only way to make an iterative tag is to return EVAL_BODY_TAG from the doAfterBody method, thus instructing the system to reevaluate the tag body. If the doStartTag returns EVAL_BODY_TAG, the system copies the tag body into a BodyContent object and invokes doAfterBody. The BodyTagSupport class overrides doStartTag to automatically return EVAL_BODY_TAG, so you only need to write doAfterBody when using BodyTagSupport. The problem with this approach is that doAfterBody must manually generate the tag body's output by extracting it from the BodyContent object in which the system wraps the body. This is fine if you actually want to manipulate the body. But, if you merely want to iterate, you must use the somewhat clumsy BodyContent object and the system must repeatedly copy the tag body.

JSP 1.2 provides a solution that is both simpler and more efficient. If a tag implements IterationTag, doStartTag can return EVAL_BODY_INCLUDE to instruct the system to output the tag body without first copying it. Then, if the doAfter-Body method returns EVAL_BODY_AGAIN, the process is repeated. Since the Tag-Support class now implements IterationTag, simple iterative tags in JSP 1.2 need not use BodyTagSupport at all.

The following two subsections present simple examples that contrast the JSP 1.1 and JSP 1.2 approaches.

JSP 1.1 Loop Tag

Listing 11.31 shows a simple iterative tag that uses the JSP 1.1 approach. It extends the BodyTagSupport class, overrides doAfterBody, extracts the tag body from the BodyContent object, and outputs it to the client. The doAfterBody method returns EVAL_BODY_TAG to indicate that looping should continue; it returns SKIP_BODY when done.

Listing 11.32 shows a TLD file that declares the tag; Listing 11.33 shows a JSP page that uses the tag, supplying a request-time form parameter (`repeats`) to dictate how many repetitions should be executed. Figure 11–11 shows the result.

Listing 11.31 *RepeatTag1.java*

```java
package moreservlets.tags;

import javax.servlet.jsp.*;
import javax.servlet.jsp.tagext.*;
import java.io.*;

/** A tag that repeats the body the specified
 *  number of times. JSP 1.1 version.
 */

public class RepeatTag1 extends BodyTagSupport {
  private int reps;

  public void setReps(String repeats) {
    try {
      reps = Integer.parseInt(repeats);
    } catch(NumberFormatException nfe) {
      reps = 1;
    }
  }

  public int doAfterBody() {
    if (reps-- >= 1) {
      BodyContent body = getBodyContent();
      try {
        JspWriter out = body.getEnclosingWriter();
        out.println(body.getString());
        body.clearBody(); // Clear for next evaluation
      } catch(IOException ioe) {
        System.out.println("Error in RepeatTag1: " + ioe);
      }
      return(EVAL_BODY_TAG);
    } else {
      return(SKIP_BODY);
    }
  }
}
```

Listing11.32 *repeat-taglib.tld*

```
<?xml version="1.0" encoding="ISO-8859-1" ?>
<!DOCTYPE taglib
 PUBLIC "-//Sun Microsystems, Inc.//DTD JSP Tag Library 1.2//EN"
 "http://java.sun.com/dtd/web-jsptaglibrary_1_2.dtd">

<taglib>
  <tlib-version>1.0</tlib-version>
  <jsp-version>1.2</jsp-version>
  <short-name>repeat-tags</short-name>
  <description>
    A tag library that has two tags: repeatTag1 and repeatTag2.
    These are JSP 1.1 and JSP 1.2 versions of simple
    looping tags.
  </description>

  <!-- An iterative tag. JSP 1.1 version. -->
  <tag>
    <name>repeat1</name>
    <tag-class>moreservlets.tags.RepeatTag1</tag-class>
    <body-content>JSP</body-content>
    <description>
      Repeats body the specified number of times.
    </description>
    <attribute>
      <name>reps</name>
      <required>true</required>
      <!-- rtexprvalue indicates whether attribute
           can be a JSP expression. -->
      <rtexprvalue>true</rtexprvalue>
    </attribute>
  </tag>

  <!-- An iterative tag. JSP 1.2 version. -->
  <tag>
    <name>repeat2</name>
    <tag-class>moreservlets.tags.RepeatTag2</tag-class>
    <body-content>JSP</body-content>
    <description>
      Repeats body the specified number of times.
    </description>
```

Listing 11.32 *repeat-taglib.tld (continued)*

```
    <attribute>
      <name>reps</name>
      <required>true</required>
      <!-- rtexprvalue indicates whether attribute
           can be a JSP expression. -->
      <rtexprvalue>true</rtexprvalue>
    </attribute>
  </tag>
</taglib>
```

Listing 11.33 *repeat-test1.jsp*

```
<!DOCTYPE HTML PUBLIC "-//W3C//DTD HTML 4.0 Transitional//EN">
<HTML>
<HEAD>
<TITLE>Some Random Numbers</TITLE>
<LINK REL=STYLESHEET
      HREF="styles.css"
      TYPE="text/css">
</HEAD>

<BODY>
<TABLE BORDER=5 ALIGN="CENTER">
  <TR><TH CLASS="TITLE">
      Some Random Numbers
</TABLE>
<P>
<%@ taglib uri="/WEB-INF/repeat-taglib.tld" prefix="msajsp" %>
<UL>
<msajsp:repeat1 reps='<%= request.getParameter("repeats") %>'>
  <LI><%= Math.random() %>
</msajsp:repeat1>
</UL>
</BODY>
</HTML>
```

Figure 11–11 Result of *repeat-test1.jsp* when the user supplies a `repeats` parameter of 25.

JSP 1.2 Loop Tag

Listing 11.34 shows a simple iterative tag that uses the JSP 1.2 approach. It extends the `TagSupport` class, overrides `doStartTag` to return `EVAL_BODY_INCLUDE`, and overrides `doAfterBody` to either return `EVAL_BODY_AGAIN` (keep looping) or `SKIP_BODY` (done). No `BodyContent`: no need for the programmer to extract it, and no need for the system to waste time and memory copying the tag body into it.

Listing 11.35 shows a JSP page that uses the tag, supplying a request-time form parameter (`repeats`) to dictate how many repetitions should be executed. Figure 11–12 shows the result.

Listing 11.34 *RepeatTag2.java*

```java
package moreservlets.tags;

import javax.servlet.jsp.*;
import javax.servlet.jsp.tagext.*;
import java.io.*;

/** A tag that repeats the body the specified
 *  number of times. JSP 1.2 version.
 */

public class RepeatTag2 extends TagSupport {
  private int reps;

  public void setReps(String repeats) {
    try {
      reps = Integer.parseInt(repeats);
    } catch(NumberFormatException nfe) {
      reps = 1;
    }
  }

  public int doStartTag() {
    if (reps >= 1) {
      return(EVAL_BODY_INCLUDE);
    } else {
      return(SKIP_BODY);
    }
  }

  public int doAfterBody() {
    if (reps-- > 1) {
      return(EVAL_BODY_AGAIN);
    } else {
      return(SKIP_BODY);
    }
  }
}
```

Listing11.35 *repeat-test2.jsp*

```
<!DOCTYPE HTML PUBLIC "-//W3C//DTD HTML 4.0 Transitional//EN">
<HTML>
<HEAD>
<TITLE>Some Random Numbers</TITLE>
<LINK REL=STYLESHEET
      HREF="styles.css"
      TYPE="text/css">
</HEAD>

<BODY>
<TABLE BORDER=5 ALIGN="CENTER">
  <TR><TH CLASS="TITLE">
      Some Random Numbers
</TABLE>
<P>
<%@ taglib uri="/WEB-INF/repeat-taglib.tld" prefix="msajsp" %>
<UL>
<msajsp:repeat2 reps='<%= request.getParameter("repeats") %>'>
  <LI><%= Math.random() %>
</msajsp:repeat2>
</UL>
</BODY>
</HTML>
```

11.8 Introducing Scripting Variables in the TLD File

In JSP 1.1, you override the getVariableInfo method of a TagExtraInfo class to declare scripting variables that your tag will introduce. The getVariableInfo method returns an array of VariableInfo objects. The VariableInfo constructor, in turn, takes four arguments:

- The variable name (a String).
- The variable's type (a String representing a fully qualified class name or a class listed in the current page's import statements).
- A boolean indicating whether the variable should be declared (almost always true; this option supports future scripting in other languages).
- An int indicating the variable's scope (NESTED—available between the tag's start and end tags, AT_BEGIN—available anytime after the tag's start tag, or AT_END—available anytime after the tag's end tag).

Figure 11–12 Result of *repeat-test2.jsp* when the user supplies a `repeats` parameter of 25.

Rather than burying this information within the `TagExtraInfo` class, in JSP 1.2 you can declare it directly in the TLD file. To do this, use the `variable` subelement of `tag`. This new element has five possible subelements:

- `name-given`: the variable name.
- `name-from-attribute`: the name of an attribute whose translation-time value will give the variable's name. You must supply either `name-given` or `name-from-attribute`.
- `variable-class`: the variable's type. This element is optional; `java.lang.String` is the default.
- `declare`: whether the variable is declared. This element is optional; `true` is the default.
- `scope`: the variable's scope. This element is optional; `NESTED` is the default.
- `description`: brief documentation on the variable.

The variable element appears within tag after description but before attribute. For example, Listing 11.36 shows a TLD file that declares a simple nested String variable named emailAddress.

Listing11.36 *sample-taglib.tld* (Excerpt)

```
<?xml version="1.0" encoding="ISO-8859-1" ?>
<!DOCTYPE taglib
 PUBLIC "-//Sun Microsystems, Inc.//DTD JSP Tag Library 1.2//EN"
 "http://java.sun.com/dtd/web-jsptaglibrary_1_2.dtd">

<taglib>
  <tlib-version>1.0</tlib-version>
  <jsp-version>1.2</jsp-version>
  <short-name>some-name</short-name>
  <description>Tag library documentation.</description>

  <tag>
    <name>tag-name</name>
    <tag-class>somePackage.SomeTagClass</tag-class>
    <tei-class>somePackage.SomeTEIClass</tei-class>
    <body-content>JSP</body-content>
    <description>Tag documentation.</description>
    <variable>
      <name-given>emailAddress</name-given>
    </variable>
  </tag>
</taglib>
```

THE JSP STANDARD
TAG LIBRARY

Topics in This Chapter

- Downloading and installing the standard JSP tag library
- Reading attributes without using Java syntax
- Accessing bean properties without using Java syntax
- Looping an explicit number of times
- Iterating over various data structures
- Checking iteration status
- Iterating with string-based tokens
- Evaluating expressions conditionally
- Using the expression language to set attributes, return values, and declare scripting variables

Chapter 12

The JSR-052 Expert Group, operating under the Java Community Process, is developing a standard tag library for JSP 1.2 and later. This library, the JSP Standard Tag Library (JSTL), provides standard iteration, conditional-evaluation, and expression-language tags. It also provides simplified access to attributes of the `PageContext`, `HttpServletRequest`, `HttpSession`, and `ServletContext` objects as well as shorthand methods for accessing bean properties. The availability of JSTL is an important addition to JSP technology because it prevents the proliferation of incompatible tag libraries to perform some of the most common JSP tasks.

However, despite more than 18 months of effort by the JSR-052 group, as of the end of 2001 JSTL was still not finalized. So, this chapter describes the 12/2001 version of the library (Early Access release 1.2). There are certain to be at least minor changes to the library before the final release, so this chapter should be viewed as a general guide to the use of JSTL, not a definitive reference. As the chapter progresses, I'll alert you to the parts that are most likely to change and point you to online references that will give the final documentation when it becomes available. For updated information, see *http://www.moreservlets.com*.

Core Warning

The standard tag library was not finalized when this book went to press. The final version is certain to differ in at least minor ways from the version described here.

12.1 Using JSTL: An Overview

The standard tag library consists of two sublibraries. Each of the two sublibraries contains tags for general looping, iterating over the elements in a variety of data structures, evaluating items conditionally, and setting attributes or scripting variables.

The jr and jx Libraries

The first thing to understand about JSTL is that it consists of two nearly identical libraries. The first, the "jr" library, permits request time expressions as the values of its attributes. That is, it specifies `rtexprvalue="true"` in the attribute definitions of the TLD file. The second library, the "jx" library, uses a shorthand expression language to access page attributes and bean properties. In this library, "$" indicates access to an attribute and "." indicates access to a bean property. So, for example, `$customer.name` refers to the result of the `getName` method applied to the object stored in the attribute named `customer`.

In general, the jr library is better when your JSP page directly computes values. The jx library is usually better when you use the MVC architecture (Section 3.8) wherein a servlet computes all the important values, stores them in an attribute, and forwards the request to a JSP page that merely extracts and displays the values. However, many situations fall into a gray area between these two extremes. In such cases, the choice of libraries is mostly a matter of taste.

Core Approach

The jr library is usually better when your JSP pages directly compute values. The jx library is usually better when your JSP pages simply access existing attributes (as is the case when you use the MVC architecture).

For example, JSTL defines an `if` tag that conditionally outputs some result. Suppose that a servlet has stored a value of type `Employee` in a `PageContext` attribute named `employee` and has then forwarded the request to a JSP page. In such a case, the jr library would use the `if` tag as follows to conditionally output the email address.

```
<% Employee employee =
     (Employee)pageContext.getAttribute("employee"); %>
<jr:if test='<%= employee.getName().equals("andreesen") %>'>
  Andreesen's email: <%= employee.getEmailAddress() %>
</jr:if>
```

Don't worry about the details of this code; the `if` tag is discussed in Section 12.6 (Evaluating Items Conditionally). Just note the use of a JSP scriptlet to access the attribute and the use of JSP expressions to access methods of the object stored in the attribute. The jx library would use the following code instead:

```
<jx:if test='$employee.name == "andreesen"'>
  Andreesen's email: <jx:expr value="$employee.emailAddress"/>
</jx:if>
```

Again, don't worry about the details of this code. Just note that $employee is used to access the attribute named `employee`, `.name` is used to access the name bean property (i.e., the result of the `getName` method), and `.emailAddress` is used to access the `emailAddress` bean property (i.e., the result of the `getEmailAddress` method).

Now, I said that the dollar sign provided access to "attributes" from within jx code. Attributes of what? Well, by default the system first looks in the `PageContext` object (i.e., the `pageContext` predefined variable), then the `HttpServletRequest` object (i.e., the `request` predefined variable), then the `HttpSession` object (i.e., the `session` predefined variable), then the `ServletContext` object (i.e., the `application` predefined variable). But, you can also use qualifiers to change where the system looks. Here is a summary:

- **$name**. Look for the attribute in the `PageContext` object, the `HttpServletRequest` object, the `HttpSession` object, the `ServletContext` object. Use the first match found.
- **$page:name**. Look only in the `PageContext` object for the attribute named name.
- **$request:name**. Look only in the `HttpServletRequest` object for the attribute named name.
- **$session:name**. Look only in the `HttpSession` object for the attribute named name.
- **$app:name**. Look only in the `ServletContext` object for the attribute named name.
- **$header:name**. Call `HttpServletRequest.getHeader(name)`.
- **$param:name**. Call `ServletRequest.getParameter(name)`.
- **$paramvalues:name**. Call `ServletRequest.getParameterValues(name)`.

The forEach Iteration Tag

The single most important tag in JSTL is forEach. It provides the ability to loop a specific number of times or to iterate down a data structure. Details are given in Section 12.3 (Looping with the forEach Tag), but here is a quick summary.

- **Looping a specific number of times (jr library).** Use the var, begin, end, and, optionally, step attributes. The iteration count is stored in the PageContext attribute named by var. Access the attribute with a JSP expression. For example:

```
<jr:forEach var="name" begin="x" end="y" step="z">
  Blah, blah <%= pageContext.getAttribute("name") %>
</jr:forEach>
```

- **Looping a specific number of times (jx library).** Use the same basic syntax as with the jr library, but access the attribute with the expr tag. For example:

```
<jx:forEach var="name" begin="x" end="y" step="z">
  Blah, blah <jx:expr value="$name"/>
</jx:forEach>
```

- **Looping down a data structure (jr library).** Use the var and items attributes. The items attribute specifies an array, Collection, Iterator, Enumeration, Map, ResultSet, or comma-separated String. It is also legal to use begin, end, and step so that only some of the items are accessed. Use a JSP expression to define the items and to access the attribute within the loop. For example:

```
<jr:forEach var="name"
            items="<%= expression %>">
  Blah, blah <%= pageContext.getAttribute("name") %>
</jr:forEach>
```

- **Looping down a data structure (jx library).** Use the same basic syntax as with the jr library, but define the items by giving the name of an existing attribute and access the attribute with the expr tag. For example:

```
<jx:forEach var="name"
            items="$existing-attribute-name">
  Blah, blah <jx:expr value="$name"/>
</jx:forEach>
```

The forTokens Iteration Tag

The forTokens tag lets you iterate down a String, using characters of your choice as delimiters between tokens. Details are given in Section 12.5 (Looping with the forTokens Tag), but here is a quick summary.

- **Looping down a String (jr library).** Use the items attribute to specify the String and the delims attribute to specify the delimiters. The var attribute gives the name of the attribute that will store each token. Use a JSP expression to access the attribute from within the loop. For example:

```
<jr:forTokens var="name"
              items="string"
              delims="characters">
  Blah, blah <%= pageContext.getAttribute("name") %>
</jr:forTokens>
```

- **Looping down a String (jx library).** Use the same basic syntax as with the jr library, but access the attribute with the expr tag. For example:

```
<jx:forTokens var="name"
              items="string"
              delims="characters">
  Blah, blah <jx:expr value="$name"/>
</jx:forTokens>
```

Conditional Evaluation Tags

The if and choose tags let you output different content depending on the results of various tests. Details are given in Section 12.6 (Evaluating Items Conditionally), but here is a quick summary.

- **The if tag (jr library).** Use a JSP expression for the test attribute; if the result is true or Boolean.TRUE, the contents of the tag are evaluated. For example:

```
<jr:if test="<% expression %>">
  Blah, blah.
</jr:if>
```

- **The if tag (jx library).** Use the same basic syntax as with the jr library, but specify the test by accessing an existing attribute and comparing it to another value using one of a small set of relational operators. For example:

```
<jx:if test="$attribute.beanProperty == 'value'">
  Blah, blah.
</jx:if>
```

- **The choose tag (jr library).** Use nested when tags; the contents of the first one whose test attribute evaluates to true or Boolean.TRUE is used. If no when tag succeeds and there is an otherwise tag, its contents are used. Use JSP expressions to specify each of the tests. For example:

```
<jr:choose>
  <jr:when test="<% expression1 %>">Blah, blah</jr:when>
  <jr:when test="<% expression2 %>">Blah, blah</jr:when>
  ...
  <jr:when test="<% expressionN %>">Blah, blah</jr:when>
  <jr:otherwise>Blah, blah</jr:otherwise>
</jr:choose>
```

- **The choose tag (jx library).** Use the same basic syntax as with the jr library, but specify the tests as with the jx version of the if tag. For example:

```
<jx:choose>
  <jx:when test="$att.prop1 == 'val1'">Blah, blah</jx:when>
  <jx:when test="$att.prop2 == 'val2'">Blah, blah</jx:when>
  ...
  <jx:when test="$att.propN == 'valN'">Blah, blah</jx:when>
  <jx:otherwise>Blah, blah</jx:otherwise>
</jx:choose>
```

Expression Language Support Tags

The set, expr, and declare tags let you define attributes, evaluate expressions, and declare scripting variables. The first two tags are available only in the jx library; declare is technically available in either library but is primarily used with jx. Details are given in Section 12.7 (Using the Expression Language), but here is a quick summary.

- **The set tag.** This tag defines an attribute. Use var to specify the attribute; use value to specify the value. Recall that in the jx library $attribute.beanProperty means that the system should call the getBeanProperty method of the object referenced by the attribute named attribute. You can also omit the value attribute and put the value between the start and end tags. For example:

```
<jx:set var="name" value="$attribute.beanProperty"/>
```

- **The `expr` tag.** This tag returns a value. Use the `value` attribute to access existing attributes and bean properties with the jx library's shorthand notation. If you use a `default` attribute, its value is used if exceptions are thrown when the system attempts to access the main value. For example:

```
<jx:expr value="$attribute.beanProperty" default="value"/>
```

- **The `declare` tag.** This tag declares a scripting variable that can be accessed by JSP expressions and scriptlets. Use `id` to give the name of the variable; its initial value will be the attribute of the same name. Use `type` to give the fully qualified class name of the variable's type. For example:

```
<jx:declare id="name" type="package.Class"/>
```

12.2 Installing and Configuring JSTL

Before you can use the standard tag library, you must perform the following seven steps.

1. Download the JSTL files.
2. Access the JSTL documentation.
3. Make the JSTL classes available to the server.
4. Put the JSTL TLD files in the *WEB-INF* directory.
5. Create aliases for the TLD file locations.
6. Define the expression language in *web.xml*.
7. Download and install an XML parser.

The following subsections give details on each of these steps.

Downloading the JSTL Files

The home page for JSTL is *http://jakarta.apache.org/taglibs/doc/standard-doc/intro.html*. There should be a prominent link on that page specifying where to obtain the JSTL code. When this book went to press, that link referred to *http://jakarta.apache.org/builds/jakarta-taglibs/releases/standard/*, but that URL is subject to change. In addition, the book's home page at *http://www.moreservlets.com* maintains up-to-date listings of the URLs. The code should come in the form of a zip or tar file and should contain three key pieces of data:

- A JAR file containing the necessary class files. As of release EA 1.2 of JSTL, this file was called *jsptl.jar*. Note that this name is *jsptl.jar*, not *jstl.jar*—they changed the official name from JSPTL to JSTL but have not (yet) updated the filenames.
- The tag library descriptor file for the jr portion of the library. As of release EA 1.2 of JSTL, this file was called *jsptl-jr.tld*.
- The tag library descriptor file for the jx portion of the library. As of release EA 1.2 of JSTL, this file was called *jsptl-jx.tld*.

The file that you download might also contain documentation and examples.

Accessing the JSTL Documentation

When this book went to press, JSTL was not yet standardized. So, it is crucial that you read the latest version of the documentation and check for additions and changes. For the latest version, see *http://jakarta.apache.org/taglibs/doc/standard-doc/index.html* or the book's home page at *http://www.moreservlets.com*.

Making the JSTL Classes Available to the Server

The most portable approach to installing the JSTL classes is to put the appropriate JAR file (e.g., *jsptl.jar*) in the *WEB-INF/lib* directory of each Web application that will use JSTL. The only disadvantage of this approach is that the JAR file has to be copied many times if multiple Web applications use JSTL. This wastes space and can cause maintenance problems if JSTL continues to evolve. So, you might consider using a server-specific mechanism for sharing classes among Web applications, but having each application register its dependence on the classes. For details on this process, see Section 4.4 (Recording Dependencies on Server Libraries).

Putting the JSTL TLD Files in the WEB-INF Directory

Tag library descriptor files must be placed in your Web application's *WEB-INF* directory or in a subdirectory thereof. I normally place the two TLD files in *WEB-INF/jsptl-tlds/*, but no specific subdirectory is required.

Creating Aliases for the TLD File Locations

My convention is to put the JSTL tag library descriptor files in *WEB-INF/jsptl-tlds/jsptl-jr.tld* and *WEB-INF/jsptl-tlds/jsptl-jx.tld*. However, the specification requires no particular location beyond the general requirement that all TLD files go in *WEB-*

INF or a subdirectory of *WEB-INF*. This presents a problem: if the locations of the TLD files are not standardized, how do you ensure that pages that use JSTL are portable? After all, each page that uses JSTL has to specify the location of the TLD file. The solution is to use the `taglib` element of *web.xml* to define standard aliases for the real TLD file locations, then to use the aliases in all the JSP pages that use JSTL. As of the end of 2001, the standard aliases were *http://java.sun.com/jsptl/ea/jr* (for the jr library) and *http://java.sun.com/jsptl/ea/jx* (for the jx library). It is expected that, when the final version of JSTL is released, *jsptl* will change to *jstl* and the *ea* part of the URL will be removed. So, for example, to use the jr library you would put the following element in the *web.xml* file.

```
<taglib>
  <taglib-uri>
    http://java.sun.com/jsptl/ea/jr
  </taglib-uri>
  <taglib-location>
    /WEB-INF/jsptl-tlds/jsptl-jr.tld
  </taglib-location>
</taglib>
```

Then, a JSP page that uses the jr JSTL library would use the following directive.

```
<%@ taglib uri="http://java.sun.com/jsptl/ea/jr" prefix="jr" %>
```

Listing 12.1 shows a representative deployment descriptor.

Listing 12.1 *web.xml* (Excerpt for JSTL TLD aliases)

```
<?xml version="1.0" encoding="ISO-8859-1"?>
<!DOCTYPE web-app PUBLIC
    "-//Sun Microsystems, Inc.//DTD Web Application 2.3//EN"
    "http://java.sun.com/dtd/web-app_2_3.dtd">

<web-app>
  <!-- ... -->

  <!-- Register jr JSTL TLD file. -->
  <taglib>
    <taglib-uri>
      http://java.sun.com/jsptl/ea/jr
    </taglib-uri>
    <taglib-location>
      /WEB-INF/jsptl-tlds/jsptl-jr.tld
    </taglib-location>
  </taglib>
```

Listing 12.1   *web.xml* (Excerpt for JSTL TLD aliases) *(continued)*

```
<!-- Register jx JSTL TLD file. -->
<taglib>
  <taglib-uri>
    http://java.sun.com/jsptl/ea/jx
  </taglib-uri>
  <taglib-location>
    /WEB-INF/jsptl-tlds/jsptl-jx.tld
  </taglib-location>
</taglib>
</web-app>
```

Defining the Expression Language in web.xml

The EA 1.2 version of JSTL supports experimentation with different languages for use in the jx library. The final version is expected to use a superset of SPEL: the Simplest Possible Expression Language. In the meantime, no expression language is predefined; you must use the `javax.servlet.jsptl.ExpressionEvaluatorClass` servlet context parameter to tell the system which expression language you want. To use SPEL, specify a value of `org.apache.taglibs.jsptl.lang.spel.Evaluator`.

Listing 12.2 shows a representative *web.xml* file.

Listing 12.2   *web.xml* (Excerpt for defining expression language)

```
<?xml version="1.0" encoding="ISO-8859-1"?>
<!DOCTYPE web-app PUBLIC
    "-//Sun Microsystems, Inc.//DTD Web Application 2.3//EN"
    "http://java.sun.com/dtd/web-app_2_3.dtd">

<web-app>
  <!-- Use the SPEL for expressions. -->
  <context-param>
    <param-name>
      javax.servlet.jsptl.ExpressionEvaluatorClass
    </param-name>
    <param-value>
      org.apache.taglibs.jsptl.lang.spel.Evaluator
    </param-value>
  </context-param>

  <!-- ... -->
</web-app>
```

Downloading and Installing an XML Parser

JSTL requires an XML parser that supports SAX and DOM. Since neither the servlet 2.3 API nor the JSP 1.2 API requires an XML parser, you might have to install one yourself. Even if your server already includes an XML parser, to guarantee portability you should include the XML parser with the JSTL JAR and TLD files when you distribute your Web application. For details on downloading and installing a parser, see the Installation and Configuration subsection of Section 11.4 (Aside: Parsing XML with SAX 2.0). Note that, for the purposes of JSTL, you need only *install* the parser; you never have to explicitly use it in any of your code.

12.3 Looping with the forEach Tag

Perhaps the single most important tag in JSTL is forEach. It provides the ability to loop with explicit numeric values or to iterate down an array, Collection, Iterator, Enumeration, Map, ResultSet, or comma-separated String. The forEach tag also lets you access an IteratorTagStatus object that provides a variety of information about the loop status.

The forEach tag has six available attributes: var, begin, end, step, items, and status. The following list summarizes their use; the following subsections give details and examples.

- **var.** The iteration variable. When you loop with explicit numeric values, the variable contains the value of the loop index. When you iterate over data structures, the variable contains the individual value from within the data structure.
- **begin.** When you loop with explicit numeric values, this attribute gives the initial value of the loop index. When you loop down a data structure, this attribute gives the index of the first item that should be accessed.
- **end.** When you loop with explicit numeric values, this attribute gives the final value of the loop index. When you loop down a data structure, this attribute gives the index of the last item that should be accessed.
- **step.** This attribute gives the size of the loop index increment.
- **items.** This attribute supplies the value of the data structure to iterate over. It is not used when you loop with explicit numeric values.
- **status.** This attribute gives the name of a variable that will hold an IteratorTagStatus object that provides details on the loop status.

Looping with Explicit Numeric Values

The simplest type of loop is one in which you specify only `var`, `begin`, and `end` attributes. The `var` attribute defines the loop index variable; `begin` and `end` give the initial and final values of the variable.

With the jr library, you access the loop index by retrieving the `PageContext` attribute named by the `var` attribute. For example, the following code outputs a bulleted list containing the numbers 1 through 10.

```
<UL>
<jr:forEach var="i" begin="1" end="10">
  <LI><%= pageContext.getAttribute("i") %>
</jr:forEach>
</UL>
```

With the jx library, you can access attributes by using a dollar sign followed by the attribute name. To simply output an attribute, you use the `expr` tag along with its `value` attribute. So, for example, the following jx code outputs the same bulleted list as the jr code just shown.

```
<UL>
<jx:forEach var="i" begin="1" end="10">
  <LI><jx:expr value="$i"/>
</jx:forEach>
</UL>
```

Listing 12.3 shows a JSP page that uses the jr code; Figure 12–1 shows the result. Listing 12.4 shows a JSP page that uses the jx code; Figure 12–2 shows the result. Listing 12.5 shows the deployment descriptor that both pages require.

Listing 12.3 *simple-loop-jr.jsp*

```
<!DOCTYPE HTML PUBLIC "-//W3C//DTD HTML 4.0 Transitional//EN">
<HTML>
<HEAD>
<TITLE>Simple Loop: "jr" Version</TITLE>
<LINK REL=STYLESHEET
      HREF="../styles.css"
      TYPE="text/css">
</HEAD>
```

| Listing 12.3 | *simple-loop-jr.jsp (continued)* |

```
<BODY>
<TABLE BORDER=5 ALIGN="CENTER">
  <TR><TH CLASS="TITLE">
      Simple Loop: "jr" Version
</TABLE>
<P>
<!-- Note that the uri refers to the location defined by
     the taglib element of web.xml, not to the real
     location of the TLD file. -->
<%@ taglib uri="http://java.sun.com/jsptl/ea/jr" prefix="jr" %>
<UL>
<jr:forEach var="i" begin="1" end="10">
  <LI><%= pageContext.getAttribute("i") %>
</jr:forEach>
</UL>
</BODY>
</HTML>
```

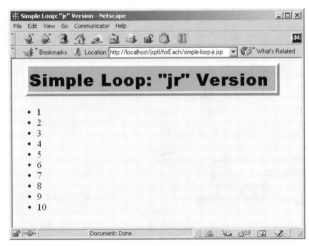

Figure 12–1   Result of *simple-loop-jr.jsp*.

Listing 12.4   *simple-loop-jx.jsp*

```
<!DOCTYPE HTML PUBLIC "-//W3C//DTD HTML 4.0 Transitional//EN">
<HTML>
<HEAD>
<TITLE>Simple Loop: "jx" Version</TITLE>
<LINK REL=STYLESHEET
      HREF="../styles.css"
      TYPE="text/css">
</HEAD>

<BODY>
<TABLE BORDER=5 ALIGN="CENTER">
  <TR><TH CLASS="TITLE">
      Simple Loop: "jx" Version
</TABLE>
<P>
<!-- Note that the uri refers to the location defined by
     the taglib element of web.xml, not to the real
     location of the TLD file. -->
<%@ taglib uri="http://java.sun.com/jsptl/ea/jx" prefix="jx" %>
<UL>
<jx:forEach var="i" begin="1" end="10">
  <LI><jx:expr value="$i"/>
</jx:forEach>
</UL>
</BODY>
</HTML>
```

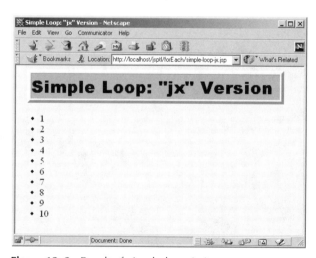

Figure 12–2   Result of *simple-loop-jx.jsp*.

Listing 12.5　*web.xml* (Excerpt for simple-loop examples)

```xml
<?xml version="1.0" encoding="ISO-8859-1"?>
<!DOCTYPE web-app PUBLIC
    "-//Sun Microsystems, Inc.//DTD Web Application 2.3//EN"
    "http://java.sun.com/dtd/web-app_2_3.dtd">

<web-app>
  <!-- Use the SPEL for expressions. -->
  <context-param>
    <param-name>
      javax.servlet.jsptl.ExpressionEvaluatorClass
    </param-name>
    <param-value>
      org.apache.taglibs.jsptl.lang.spel.Evaluator
    </param-value>
  </context-param>

  <!-- If URL gives a directory but no filename, try index.jsp
       first and index.html second. If neither is found, the
       result is server specific (e.g., a directory listing).
       Order of elements in web.xml matters. welcome-file-list
       needs to come after servlet but before error-page.
  -->
  <welcome-file-list>
    <welcome-file>index.jsp</welcome-file>
    <welcome-file>index.html</welcome-file>
  </welcome-file-list>

  <!-- Register jr JSTL TLD file. -->
  <taglib>
    <taglib-uri>
      http://java.sun.com/jsptl/ea/jr
    </taglib-uri>
    <taglib-location>
      /WEB-INF/jsptl-tlds/jsptl-jr.tld
    </taglib-location>
  </taglib>

  <!-- Register jx JSTL TLD file. -->
  <taglib>
    <taglib-uri>
      http://java.sun.com/jsptl/ea/jx
    </taglib-uri>
    <taglib-location>
      /WEB-INF/jsptl-tlds/jsptl-jx.tld
    </taglib-location>
  </taglib>
</web-app>
```

Looping with a Designated Step Size

The forEach tag permits you to use the step attribute to specify how much the loop index will increase each time around the loop. For example, suppose that you want to generate a bulleted list that shows the number of seconds every minute from zero until the session timeout.

With the jr library, this task is straightforward. Simply supply the value of session.getMaxInactiveInterval for the end attribute and 60 for the step attribute, as shown in the following example.

```
<UL>
<jr:forEach var="seconds"
            begin="0"
            end="<%= session.getMaxInactiveInterval() %>"
            step="60">
  <LI><%= pageContext.getAttribute("seconds") %> seconds.
</jr:forEach>
  <LI>Timeout exceeded.
</UL>
```

With the jx library, however, there is a problem. The end attribute does not permit a JSP expression. Furthermore, since session is an implicit object (predefined variable), not an attribute of PageContext, you cannot use the $ notation to access it. (However, the JSR-052 group is considering providing simplified access to the implicit objects in the final version of JSTL.) Now, as we will see in Section 12.7 (Using the Expression Language), the jx library's set tag can be used to assign an attribute based on a JSP expression. However, that approach is not satisfactory since one of the purposes of the jx library is to avoid explicit Java code in the JSP page. So, I create a custom JSP tag that does nothing but store the PageContext object in the pageContext attribute of the PageContext object (i.e., of itself!). After this custom tag is used, the PageContext object can be accessed in the jx library with $pageContext. The various implicit objects can be accessed with $page-Context.request (i.e., by calling getRequest on the PageContext object), $pageContext.response (i.e., by calling getResponse on the PageContext object), $pageContext.session (i.e., by calling getSession on the Page-Context object), etc. So, after this custom tag is used, the following jx code yields the same result as the jr code just shown.

```
<UL>
<jx:forEach var="seconds"
            begin="0"
            end="$pageContext.session.maxInactiveInterval"
            step="60">
  <LI><jx:expr value="$seconds"/> seconds.
</jx:forEach>
  <LI>Timeout exceeded.
</UL>
```

Listing 12.6 shows a JSP page that uses the jr code; Figure 12–3 shows the result. Listing 12.7 shows a JSP page that uses the new custom tag and the jx code; Figure 12–4 shows the result. Listings 12.8 and 12.9 show the custom tag and associated TLD file for a tag that stores the `PageContext` object in the `pageContext` attribute. Listing 12.5 (shown on page 633) presents the deployment descriptor that both pages require.

Listing 12.6 *inactive-interval-loop-jr.jsp*

```
<!DOCTYPE HTML PUBLIC "-//W3C//DTD HTML 4.0 Transitional//EN">
<HTML>
<HEAD>
<TITLE>Session Timeout: "jr" Version</TITLE>
<LINK REL=STYLESHEET
      HREF="../styles.css"
      TYPE="text/css">
</HEAD>

<BODY>
<TABLE BORDER=5 ALIGN="CENTER">
  <TR><TH CLASS="TITLE">
      Session Timeout: "jr" Version
</TABLE>
<P>
<%@ taglib uri="http://java.sun.com/jsptl/ea/jr" prefix="jr" %>
<UL>
<jr:forEach var="seconds"
            begin="0"
            end="<%= session.getMaxInactiveInterval() %>"
            step="60">
  <LI><%= pageContext.getAttribute("seconds") %> seconds.
</jr:forEach>
  <LI>Timeout exceeded.
</UL>
</BODY>
</HTML>
```

Figure 12–3 Result of *inactive-interval-loop-jr.jsp.*

Listing 12.7 *inactive-interval-loop-jx.jsp*

```
<!DOCTYPE HTML PUBLIC "-//W3C//DTD HTML 4.0 Transitional//EN">
<HTML>
<HEAD>
<TITLE>Session Timeout: "jx" Version</TITLE>
<LINK REL=STYLESHEET
      HREF="../styles.css"
      TYPE="text/css">
</HEAD>
<BODY>
<TABLE BORDER=5 ALIGN="CENTER">
  <TR><TH CLASS="TITLE">
      Session Timeout: "jx" Version
</TABLE>
<P>
<%@ taglib uri="/WEB-INF/store-page-context.tld" prefix="init" %>
<init:storePageContext/>
<%@ taglib uri="http://java.sun.com/jsptl/ea/jx" prefix="jx" %>
<UL>
<jx:forEach var="seconds"
            begin="0"
            end="$pageContext.session.maxInactiveInterval"
            step="60">
  <LI><jx:expr value="$seconds"/> seconds.
</jx:forEach>
  <LI>Timeout exceeded.
</UL>
</BODY>
</HTML>
```

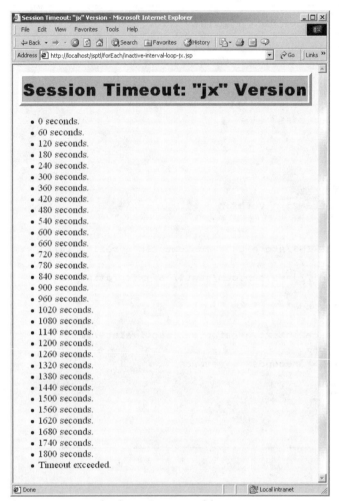

Figure 12–4   Result of *inactive-interval-loop-jx.jsp*.

Listing 12.8 *StorePageContextTag.java*

```java
package moreservlets.tags;

import javax.servlet.*;
import javax.servlet.jsp.*;
import javax.servlet.jsp.tagext.*;
import java.io.*;

/** Stores the PageContext reference in an attribute
 *  of the PageContext. The reason for doing this is to
 *  make it easier for JSTL jx tags to access the request,
 *  response, pageContext, etc.
 */

public class StorePageContextTag extends TagSupport {
  public int doStartTag() {
    pageContext.setAttribute("pageContext", pageContext);
    return(SKIP_BODY);
  }
}
```

Listing 12.9 *store-page-context.tld*

```xml
<?xml version="1.0" encoding="ISO-8859-1" ?>
<!DOCTYPE taglib
 PUBLIC "-//Sun Microsystems, Inc.//DTD JSP Tag Library 1.2//EN"
 "http://java.sun.com/dtd/web-jsptaglibrary_1_2.dtd">

<taglib>
  <tlib-version>1.0</tlib-version>
  <jsp-version>1.2</jsp-version>
  <short-name>store-page-context</short-name>
  <description>
    An extremely simple tag that simply stores a reference
    to the PageContext object in a PageContext attribute.
    This setting is performed because the JSTL jx library
    makes it easy to access attributes but does not make it
    easy to access scripting variables like request, response,
    pageContext, etc.
  </description>
```

> **Listing 12.9** | *store-page-context.tld (continued)*

```
<!-- Define a tag the stores the pageContext attribute. -->
<tag>
  <name>storePageContext</name>
  <tag-class>
    moreservlets.tags.StorePageContextTag
  </tag-class>
  <body-content>empty</body-content>
  <description>Store PageContext in attribute.</description>
</tag>
</taglib>
```

Looping Down Arrays

The previous examples used the begin and end attributes of forEach to specify explicit numeric values for looping. Even more useful is the ability to iterate over a data structure. To do this, you supply an array, Collection, Iterator, Enumeration, Map, ResultSet, or comma-separated String as the value of the items attribute. The var attribute gives the name of the PageContext attribute that will store each individual item from the data structure. It is also legal to use begin, end, and step so that only some of the items are accessed.

For example, the following jr code creates a table of the cookies that were sent by the client on the current request.

```
<TABLE BORDER="1" ALIGN="CENTER">
  <TR><TH CLASS="HEADING">Cookie Name
      <TH CLASS="HEADING">Cookie Value
<jr:forEach var="cookie"
            items="<%= request.getCookies() %>">
  <% Cookie cookie =
       (Cookie)pageContext.getAttribute("cookie"); %>
  <TR><TD><%= cookie.getName() %>
      <TD><%= cookie.getValue() %>
</jr:forEach>
</TABLE>
```

Given the custom tag that stores the PageContext object in the pageContext attribute (see Listings 12.8 and 12.9), the following jx code has the same effect as the jr code just shown. Recall that "$" is used to access attributes and "." is used to access bean properties. So, for example, $pageContext.request.cookies means that the system should retrieve the object stored in the pageContext attribute (i.e., the PageContext object itself), call getRequest on it, then call getCookies on that result.

```
<TABLE BORDER="1" ALIGN="CENTER">
  <TR><TH CLASS="HEADING">Cookie Name
      <TH CLASS="HEADING">Cookie Value
<jx:forEach var="cookie"
            items="$pageContext.request.cookies">
  <TR><TD><jx:expr value="$cookie.name"/>
      <TD><jx:expr value="$cookie.value"/>
</jx:forEach>
</TABLE>
```

Listing 12.10 shows a JSP page that uses the jr code; Figure 12–5 shows the result after a cookie-setting servlet (Listing 12.12) is accessed. Listing 12.11 shows a JSP page that uses the jx code; Figure 12–6 shows the result after the cookie-setting servlet (Listing 12.12) is accessed. Listing 12.13 shows the deployment descriptor needed by the JSP pages and the cookie-setting servlet.

Note that both pages fail if no cookies are sent. We don't yet have the tools to fix this problem; however, in Section 12.7 (Using the Expression Language), you'll see how to use the expr element to supply default values for missing items. Also, in Section 12.6 (Evaluating Items Conditionally) you'll see how to do general conditional evaluation.

Listing 12.10   *cookie-loop-jr.jsp*

```
<!DOCTYPE HTML PUBLIC "-//W3C//DTD HTML 4.0 Transitional//EN">
<HTML>
<HEAD>
<TITLE>Cookies: "jr" Version</TITLE>
<LINK REL=STYLESHEET
      HREF="../styles.css"
      TYPE="text/css">
</HEAD>

<BODY>
<TABLE BORDER=5 ALIGN="CENTER">
  <TR><TH CLASS="TITLE">
      Cookies: "jr" Version
</TABLE>
<P>
<%@ taglib uri="http://java.sun.com/jsptl/ea/jr" prefix="jr" %>
<TABLE BORDER="1" ALIGN="CENTER">
  <TR><TH CLASS="HEADING">Cookie Name
      <TH CLASS="HEADING">Cookie Value
```

Listing 12.10 *cookie-loop-jr.jsp (continued)*

```
<jr:forEach var="cookie"
            items="<%= request.getCookies() %>">
  <% Cookie cookie =
      (Cookie)pageContext.getAttribute("cookie"); %>
  <TR><TD><%= cookie.getName() %>
      <TD><%= cookie.getValue() %>
</jr:forEach>
</TABLE>
</BODY>
</HTML>
```

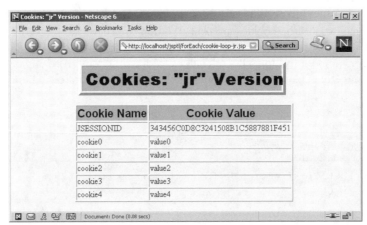

Figure 12–5 Result of *cookie-loop-jr.jsp* after the `DefineCookies` servlet (Listing 12.12) is visited.

Listing 12.11 *cookie-loop-jx.jsp*

```
<!DOCTYPE HTML PUBLIC "-//W3C//DTD HTML 4.0 Transitional//EN">
<HTML>
<HEAD>
<TITLE>Cookies: "jx" Version</TITLE>
<LINK REL=STYLESHEET
      HREF="../styles.css"
      TYPE="text/css">
</HEAD>
```

Listing 12.11 *cookie-loop-jx.jsp (continued)*

```
<BODY>
<TABLE BORDER=5 ALIGN="CENTER">
  <TR><TH CLASS="TITLE">
      Cookies: "jx" Version
</TABLE>
<P>
<%@ taglib uri="/WEB-INF/store-page-context.tld" prefix="init" %>
<init:storePageContext/>
<%@ taglib uri="http://java.sun.com/jsptl/ea/jx" prefix="jx" %>
<TABLE BORDER="1" ALIGN="CENTER">
  <TR><TH CLASS="HEADING">Cookie Name
      <TH CLASS="HEADING">Cookie Value
<jx:forEach var="cookie"
            items="$pageContext.request.cookies">
  <TR><TD><jx:expr value="$cookie.name"/>
      <TD><jx:expr value="$cookie.value"/>
</jx:forEach>
</TABLE>
</BODY>
</HTML>
```

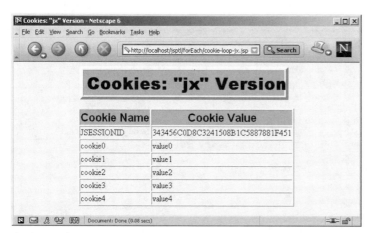

Figure 12–6   Result of *cookie-loop-jx.jsp* after the `DefineCookies` servlet (Listing 12.12) is visited.

Listing 12.12 *DefineCookies.java*

```java
package moreservlets;

import java.io.*;
import javax.servlet.*;
import javax.servlet.http.*;
import java.util.*;

/** Defines a few cookies, then redirects the user
 *  to the cookie-displaying page.
 */

public class DefineCookies extends HttpServlet {
  public void doGet(HttpServletRequest request,
                    HttpServletResponse response)
    throws ServletException, IOException {
    for(int i=0; i<5; i++) {
      Cookie c = new Cookie("cookie" + i, "value" + i);
      response.addCookie(c);
    }
    String cookieDisplayPage =
      request.getContextPath() + "/forEach/cookie-loop-jr.jsp";
    response.sendRedirect(cookieDisplayPage);
  }
}
```

Listing 12.13 *web.xml* (Excerpt for cookie-displaying pages)

```xml
<?xml version="1.0" encoding="ISO-8859-1"?>
<!DOCTYPE web-app PUBLIC
    "-//Sun Microsystems, Inc.//DTD Web Application 2.3//EN"
    "http://java.sun.com/dtd/web-app_2_3.dtd">

<web-app>
  <!-- Use the SPEL for expressions. -->
  <context-param>
    <param-name>
      javax.servlet.jsptl.ExpressionEvaluatorClass
    </param-name>
    <param-value>
      org.apache.taglibs.jsptl.lang.spel.Evaluator
    </param-value>
  </context-param>
```

Listing 12.13 *web.xml* (Excerpt for cookie-displaying pages) *(continued)*

```
<!-- Give a name to the moreservlets.DefineCookies servlet
     so that a custom URL can later be assigned.
-->
<servlet>
  <servlet-name>DefineCookies</servlet-name>
  <servlet-class>moreservlets.DefineCookies</servlet-class>
</servlet>

<!-- Register the URL /forEach/DefineCookies with the
     DefineCookies servlet. This prevents the servlet
     from needing to define a path of "/" for the cookies.
     Instead, the servlet (which sets the cookies) and the
     JSP pages (which display the cookies) have the same
     URL prefix, so no special settings are needed.
-->
<servlet-mapping>
  <servlet-name>DefineCookies</servlet-name>
  <url-pattern>/forEach/DefineCookies</url-pattern>
</servlet-mapping>

<!-- ... -->

<!-- Register jr JSTL TLD file. -->
<taglib>
  <taglib-uri>
    http://java.sun.com/jsptl/ea/jr
  </taglib-uri>
  <taglib-location>
    /WEB-INF/jsptl-tlds/jsptl-jr.tld
  </taglib-location>
</taglib>

<!-- Register jx JSTL TLD file. -->
<taglib>
  <taglib-uri>
    http://java.sun.com/jsptl/ea/jx
  </taglib-uri>
  <taglib-location>
    /WEB-INF/jsptl-tlds/jsptl-jx.tld
  </taglib-location>
</taglib>
</web-app>
```

Looping Down Enumerations

You iterate over a `java.util.Enumeration` object in exactly the same manner as you iterate over an array: you define the iteration variable with the `var` attribute of `forEach` and supply the object with the `items` attribute.

For example, the `getHeaderNames` method of `HttpServletRequest` returns an `Enumeration` of the request headers sent by the client. So, the following jr code will create a table of the names and values of all headers in the request.

```
<TABLE BORDER="1" ALIGN="CENTER">
  <TR><TH CLASS="HEADING">Header Name
      <TH CLASS="HEADING">Header Value
<jr:forEach var="header"
            items="<%= request.getHeaderNames() %>">
  <% String header =
       (String)pageContext.getAttribute("header"); %>
  <TR><TD><%= header %>
      <TD><%= request.getHeader(header) %>
</jr:forEach>
</TABLE>
```

Once again, however, we have a problem performing the same task with the jx library. Given the custom tag that defines the `pageContext` attribute, the `Enumeration` itself can be accessed with `$pageContext.request.headerNames`. However, once you have a header name, how do you get a header value? There is no bean property (i.e., zero-argument `getXxx` method) that gives you a header value, and the jx library provides no way to specify arguments to methods without using Java code. You're stuck: you have to write a special-purpose custom tag or use scripting expressions. Use of the jx library does not always negate the need for explicit Java code.

Even after you resign yourself to using scripting expressions with the jx library, you'd like to minimize their use. A good way to do this is to use the `declare` tag. This element is described in Section 12.7, but the gist of it is that `declare` provides a bridge between jx tags and scripting elements by copying the value of an attribute into a scripting variable. The following jx code uses `declare` to create the same request header table as the previous jr code.

```
<TABLE BORDER="1" ALIGN="CENTER">
  <TR><TH CLASS="HEADING">Header Name
      <TH CLASS="HEADING">Header Value
<jx:forEach var="headerName"
            items="$pageContext.request.headerNames">
  <TR><TD><jx:expr value="$headerName"/>
      <TD><jx:declare id="headerName" type="java.lang.String"/>
         <%= request.getHeader(headerName) %>
</jx:forEach>
</TABLE>
```

Listing 12.14 shows a JSP page that uses the jr code; Figure 12–7 shows the result. Listing 12.15 shows a JSP page that uses the jx code; Figure 12–8 shows the result.

Listing 12.14 *header-loop-jr.jsp*

```
<!DOCTYPE HTML PUBLIC "-//W3C//DTD HTML 4.0 Transitional//EN">
<HTML>
<HEAD>
<TITLE>Headers: "jr" Version</TITLE>
<LINK REL=STYLESHEET
      HREF="../styles.css"
      TYPE="text/css">
</HEAD>

<BODY>
<TABLE BORDER=5 ALIGN="CENTER">
  <TR><TH CLASS="TITLE">
      Headers: "jr" Version
</TABLE>
<P>
<%@ taglib uri="http://java.sun.com/jsptl/ea/jr" prefix="jr" %>
<TABLE BORDER="1" ALIGN="CENTER">
  <TR><TH CLASS="HEADING">Header Name
      <TH CLASS="HEADING">Header Value
<jr:forEach var="header"
            items="<%= request.getHeaderNames() %>">
  <% String header =
       (String)pageContext.getAttribute("header"); %>
  <TR><TD><%= header %>
      <TD><%= request.getHeader(header) %>
</jr:forEach>
</TABLE>
</BODY>
</HTML>
```

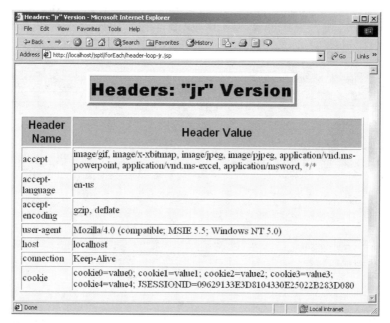

Figure 12–7 Result of *header-loop-jr.jsp*.

Listing 12.15 *header-loop-jx.jsp*

```
<!DOCTYPE HTML PUBLIC "-//W3C//DTD HTML 4.0 Transitional//EN">
<HTML>
<HEAD>
<TITLE>Headers: "jx" Version</TITLE>
<LINK REL=STYLESHEET
      HREF="../styles.css"
      TYPE="text/css">
</HEAD>

<BODY>
<TABLE BORDER=5 ALIGN="CENTER">
  <TR><TH CLASS="TITLE">
      Headers: "jx" Version
</TABLE>
<P>
<%@ taglib uri="/WEB-INF/store-page-context.tld" prefix="init" %>
<init:storePageContext/>
<%@ taglib uri="http://java.sun.com/jsptl/ea/jx" prefix="jx" %>
<TABLE BORDER="1" ALIGN="CENTER">
  <TR><TH CLASS="HEADING">Header Name
      <TH CLASS="HEADING">Header Value
```

Listing 12.15   *header-loop-jx.jsp (continued)*

```
<jx:forEach var="headerName"
            items="$pageContext.request.headerNames">
  <TR><TD><jx:expr value="$headerName"/>
      <TD><jx:declare id="headerName" type="java.lang.String"/>
          <%= request.getHeader(headerName) %>
</jx:forEach>
</TABLE>
</BODY>
</HTML>
```

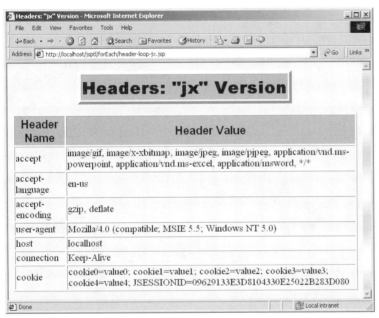

Figure 12–8   Result of *header-loop-jx.jsp.*

Looping Down Entries in a String

In addition to the standard collection data structures (array, Enumeration, Collection, etc.), the standard tag library lets you loop down comma-delimited strings.

For example, the following jr code makes a bulleted list of countries. Note that, since the items attribute can contain objects of various types, you have to use explicit double quotes within the attribute value to designate a String. The easiest way to do this is to use single quotes around the overall value.

```
<UL>
<jr:forEach var="country"
            items='"Australia,Canada,Japan,Philippines,USA"'>
  <LI><%= pageContext.getAttribute("country") %>
</jr:forEach>
</UL>
```

The following jx code yields the same result. Since the `items` attribute cannot accept request time expressions, there is no need to use an extra set of quote marks.

```
<UL>
<jx:forEach var="country"
            items="Australia,Canada,Japan,Philippines,USA">
  <LI><jx:expr value="$country"/>
</jx:forEach>
</UL>
```

Listing 12.16 shows a JSP page that uses the jr code; Figure 12–9 shows the result. Listing 12.17 shows a JSP page that uses the jx code; Figure 12–10 shows the result.

Listing 12.16 *string-loop-jr.jsp*

```
<!DOCTYPE HTML PUBLIC "-//W3C//DTD HTML 4.0 Transitional//EN">
<HTML>
<HEAD>
<TITLE>String: "jr" Version</TITLE>
<LINK REL=STYLESHEET
      HREF="../styles.css"
      TYPE="text/css">
</HEAD>
<BODY>
<TABLE BORDER=5 ALIGN="CENTER">
  <TR><TH CLASS="TITLE">
      Strings: "jr" Version
</TABLE>
<P>
<H3>Marty has given servlet and JSP short courses in:</H3>
<%@ taglib uri="http://java.sun.com/jsptl/ea/jr" prefix="jr" %>
<UL>
<jr:forEach var="country"
            items='"Australia,Canada,Japan,Philippines,USA"'>
  <LI><%= pageContext.getAttribute("country") %>
</jr:forEach>
</UL>
For more details or to schedule a short course at <I>your</I>
company, see <A HREF="http://courses.coreservlets.com">
http://courses.coreservlets.com</A>.
</BODY>
</HTML>
```

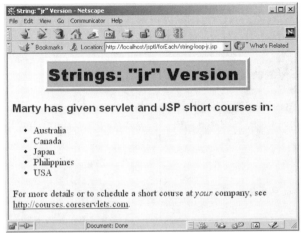

Figure 12–9   Result of *string-loop-jr.jsp*.

Listing 12.17   *string-loop-jx.jsp*

```
<!DOCTYPE HTML PUBLIC "-//W3C//DTD HTML 4.0 Transitional//EN">
<HTML>
<HEAD>
<TITLE>String: "jx" Version</TITLE>
<LINK REL=STYLESHEET
      HREF="../styles.css"
      TYPE="text/css">
</HEAD>
<BODY>
<TABLE BORDER=5 ALIGN="CENTER">
  <TR><TH CLASS="TITLE">
      Strings: "jx" Version
</TABLE>
<P>
<H3>Marty has given servlet and JSP short courses in:</H3>
<%@ taglib uri="http://java.sun.com/jsptl/ea/jx" prefix="jx" %>
<UL>
<jx:forEach var="country"
            items="Australia,Canada,Japan,Philippines,USA">
  <LI><jx:expr value="$country"/>
</jx:forEach>
</UL>
For more details or to schedule a short course at <I>your</I>
company, see <A HREF="http://courses.coreservlets.com">
http://courses.coreservlets.com</A>.
</BODY>
</HTML>
```

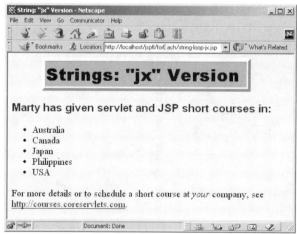

Figure 12–10 Result of *string-loop-jx.jsp*.

Looping Down Multiple Data Types

The `items` attribute of `forEach` can specify an array, `Collection`, `Iterator`, `Enumeration`, `Map`, `ResultSet`, or comma-separated `String`. For all cases except `Map` and `ResultSet`, the value of the iteration variable is obvious: it is the appropriate entry from the data structure.

Since a `Map` consists of both names and values, however, what does the iteration variable return? The answer is that it returns a `Map.Entry` object. The `Map.Entry` interface, in turn, defines `getKey` and `getValue` methods.

The value of the iteration variable when you loop over a `ResultSet` is even more surprising: it is the `ResultSet` itself! The reason that this approach is useful is that the system maintains a cursor that refers to the current row of the `ResultSet`. That cursor is updated each time around the loop.

OK, so I've repeatedly claimed that the real strength of the jx library is when it is used to access attributes that are set in a servlet that forwards the request to the JSP page. Let's test this theory out in a relatively realistic MVC scenario. Listing 12.18 (Figure 12–11) shows an HTML form that collects a variety of data from a user. When the form is submitted, the data is sent to the `ShowData` servlet (Listing 12.19). This servlet creates an array (the values of the `computerLanguages` request parameter), an `Enumeration` (a `StringTokenizer` created from the values of the `spokenLanguages` request parameter), a `Collection` (an `ArrayList` giving predefined favorite foods), a `Map` (a `HashMap` giving predefined usernames and passwords), and a comma-delimited `String` (usernames of people on probation for bad behavior). The servlet stores all of these values in request attributes and then forwards the request to a jr (Listing 12.20) or jx (Listing 12.21) page to display the results (Figures 12–12 and 12–13). Listing 12.22 shows the deployment descriptor.

In this case, the jx version is considerably less complicated than the jr version: no scripting expressions are needed, and the code is significantly more concise.

Listing 12.18 *data-form.html*

```
<!DOCTYPE HTML PUBLIC "-//W3C//DTD HTML 4.0 Transitional//EN">
<HTML>
<HEAD>
<TITLE>Languages</TITLE>
<LINK REL=STYLESHEET
      HREF="../styles.css"
      TYPE="text/css">
</HEAD>

<BODY>
<CENTER>
<TABLE BORDER=5>
  <TR><TH CLASS="TITLE">
      Languages</TABLE>
<P>
<FORM ACTION="ShowData">
<H3>Select the computer languages you know:</H3>
<INPUT TYPE="CHECKBOX" NAME="computerLanguages"
      value="Java">Java<BR>
<INPUT TYPE="CHECKBOX" NAME="computerLanguages"
      value="C++">C++<BR>
<INPUT TYPE="CHECKBOX" NAME="computerLanguages"
      value="Common Lisp">Common Lisp<BR>
<INPUT TYPE="CHECKBOX" NAME="computerLanguages"
      value="Smalltalk">Smalltalk<BR>
<INPUT TYPE="CHECKBOX" NAME="computerLanguages"
      value="Visual Basic">Visual Basic<BR>
<H3>Enter the spoken languages you know:</H3>
<TEXTAREA NAME="spokenLanguages" ROWS=5 COLS=20></TEXTAREA>
<H3>Choose the jr or jx output version:</H3>
<INPUT TYPE="RADIO" NAME="outputVersion" VALUE="jr" CHECKED>jr
    
<INPUT TYPE="RADIO" NAME="outputVersion" VALUE="jx">jx
<P>
<INPUT TYPE="SUBMIT">
</FORM>
</CENTER>
</BODY>
</HTML>
```

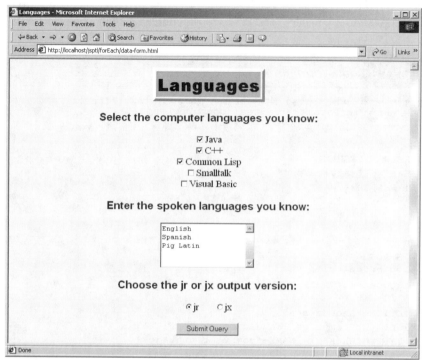

Figure 12–11 Result of *data-form.html*. Data, when submitted, is sent to the ShowData servlet (Listing 12.19). The servlet, in turn, forwards the request to either *show-data-jr.jsp* (Listing 12.20, Figure 12–12) or *show-data-jx.jsp* (Listing 12.21, Figure 12–13).

Listing 12.19   *ShowData.java*

```
package moreservlets;

import java.io.*;
import javax.servlet.*;
import javax.servlet.http.*;
import java.util.*;

/** Servlet that sets up a variety of data structures,
 *  then forwards the request to a JSP page that
 *  uses JSTL to display the values in the
 *  data structures.
 */
```

Listing 12.19 *ShowData.java (continued)*

```java
public class ShowData extends HttpServlet {
  public void doGet(HttpServletRequest request,
                    HttpServletResponse response)
      throws ServletException, IOException {
    String[] computerLanguages =
      request.getParameterValues("computerLanguages");
    if (computerLanguages == null) {
      computerLanguages = new String[0];
    }
    request.setAttribute("computerLanguages",
                         computerLanguages);
    String spokenLanguages =
      request.getParameter("spokenLanguages");
    if (spokenLanguages == null) {
      spokenLanguages = "";
    }
    request.setAttribute("spokenLanguages",
                         new StringTokenizer(spokenLanguages));
    ArrayList favoriteFoods = getFavoriteFoods();
    request.setAttribute("favoriteFoods", favoriteFoods);
    HashMap passwords = getPasswords();
    request.setAttribute("passwords", passwords);
    String bannedUsers = "bill,larry,scott";
    request.setAttribute("bannedUsers", bannedUsers);
    String outputVersion =
      request.getParameter("outputVersion");
    String outputPage = "/forEach/show-data-jx.jsp";
    if ("jr".equals(outputVersion)) {
      outputPage = "/forEach/show-data-jr.jsp";
    }
    gotoPage(outputPage, request, response);
  }

  private void gotoPage(String address,
                        HttpServletRequest request,
                        HttpServletResponse response)
      throws ServletException, IOException {
    RequestDispatcher dispatcher =
      getServletContext().getRequestDispatcher(address);
    dispatcher.forward(request, response);
  }
}
```

Listing 12.19 *ShowData.java (continued)*

```java
  private ArrayList getFavoriteFoods() {
    ArrayList foods = new ArrayList();
    foods.add("Tacos al pastor");
    foods.add("Pan-fried dumplings");
    foods.add("Bulgogi");
    foods.add("Strawberries");
    foods.add("Chocolate");
    return(foods);
  }

  private HashMap getPasswords() {
    HashMap passwords = new HashMap();
    passwords.put("bill", "setag");
    passwords.put("larry", "nosille");
    passwords.put("scott", "ylaencm");
    passwords.put("lou", "rentsreg");
    passwords.put("greg", "hcneod");
    return(passwords);
  }
}
```

Listing 12.20 *show-data-jr.jsp*

```jsp
<!DOCTYPE HTML PUBLIC "-//W3C//DTD HTML 4.0 Transitional//EN">
<HTML>
<HEAD>
<TITLE>Data Display: "jr" Version</TITLE>
<LINK REL=STYLESHEET
      HREF="../styles.css"
      TYPE="text/css">
</HEAD>

<BODY>
<CENTER>
<TABLE BORDER=5>
  <TR><TH CLASS="TITLE">
      Data Display: "jr" Version
</TABLE>
<P>
<%@ taglib uri="http://java.sun.com/jsptl/ea/jr" prefix="jr" %>
```

Listing 12.20 *show-data-jr.jsp (continued)*

```
<TABLE BORDER=1>

<TR>
<TH CLASS="HEADING">Computer<BR>Languages
<TH CLASS="HEADING">Spoken<BR>Languages
<TH CLASS="HEADING">Favorite<BR>Foods
<TH CLASS="HEADING">Passwords
<TH CLASS="HEADING">Banned<BR>Users

<TR>
<TD>
<UL>
<jr:forEach var="lang"
    items='<%= request.getAttribute("computerLanguages") %>'>
  <LI><%= pageContext.getAttribute("lang") %>
</jr:forEach>
</UL>
<CENTER><SMALL>(From Array)</SMALL></CENTER>

<TD>
<UL>
<jr:forEach var="lang"
    items='<%= request.getAttribute("spokenLanguages") %>'>
  <LI><%= pageContext.getAttribute("lang") %>
</jr:forEach>
</UL>
<CENTER><SMALL>(From Enumeration)</SMALL></CENTER>

<TD>
<UL>
<jr:forEach var="food"
    items='<%= request.getAttribute("favoriteFoods") %>'>
  <LI><%= pageContext.getAttribute("food") %>
</jr:forEach>
</UL>
<CENTER><SMALL>(From Collection)</SMALL></CENTER>

<TD>
<TABLE BORDER=1>
  <TR><TH>Username
      <TH>Password
<jr:forEach var="user"
    items='<%= request.getAttribute("passwords") %>'>
  <% java.util.Map.Entry user =
       (java.util.Map.Entry)pageContext.getAttribute("user"); %>
```

Listing 12.20   *show-data-jr.jsp (continued)*

```
  <TR><TD><%= user.getKey() %>
      <TD><%= user.getValue() %>
</jr:forEach>
</TABLE>
<CENTER><SMALL>(From Map)</SMALL></CENTER>

<TD>
<UL>
<jr:forEach var="user"
    items='<%= request.getAttribute("bannedUsers") %>'>
  <LI><%= pageContext.getAttribute("user") %>
</jr:forEach>
</UL>
<CENTER><SMALL>(From String)</SMALL></CENTER>
</TABLE>

</CENTER>
</BODY>
</HTML>
```

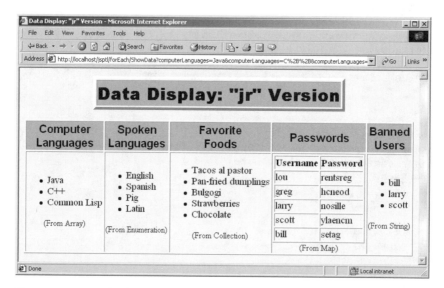

Figure 12–12 Result of the ShowData servlet when it forwards the request to *show-data-jr.jsp.*

Listing 12.21   *show-data-jx.jsp*

```
<!DOCTYPE HTML PUBLIC "-//W3C//DTD HTML 4.0 Transitional//EN">
<HTML>
<HEAD>
<TITLE>Data Display: "jx" Version</TITLE>
<LINK REL=STYLESHEET
      HREF="../styles.css"
      TYPE="text/css">
</HEAD>

<BODY>
<CENTER>
<TABLE BORDER=5>
  <TR><TH CLASS="TITLE">
      Data Display: "jx" Version
</TABLE>
<P>
<%@ taglib uri="http://java.sun.com/jsptl/ea/jx" prefix="jx" %>

<TABLE BORDER=1>

<TR>
<TH CLASS="HEADING">Computer<BR>Languages
<TH CLASS="HEADING">Spoken<BR>Languages
<TH CLASS="HEADING">Favorite<BR>Foods
<TH CLASS="HEADING">Passwords
<TH CLASS="HEADING">Banned<BR>Users

<TR>
<TD>
<UL>
<jx:forEach var="lang" items="$computerLanguages">
  <LI><jx:expr value="$lang"/>
</jx:forEach>
</UL>
<CENTER><SMALL>(From Array)</SMALL></CENTER>

<TD>
<UL>
<jx:forEach var="lang" items="$spokenLanguages">
  <LI><jx:expr value="$lang"/>
</jx:forEach>
</UL>
<CENTER><SMALL>(From Enumeration)</SMALL></CENTER>
```

Listing 12.21 *show-data-jx.jsp (continued)*

```
<TD>
<UL>
<jx:forEach var="food" items="$favoriteFoods">
  <LI><jx:expr value="$food"/>
</jx:forEach>
</UL>
<CENTER><SMALL>(From Collection)</SMALL></CENTER>

<TD>
<TABLE BORDER=1>
  <TR><TH>Username
      <TH>Password
<jx:forEach var="user" items="$passwords">
  <TR><TD><jx:expr value="$user.key"/>
      <TD><jx:expr value="$user.value"/>
</jx:forEach>
</TABLE>
<CENTER><SMALL>(From Map)</SMALL></CENTER>

<TD>
<UL>
<jx:forEach var="user" items="$bannedUsers">
  <LI><jx:expr value="$user"/>
</jx:forEach>
</UL>
<CENTER><SMALL>(From String)</SMALL></CENTER>
</TABLE>

</CENTER>
</BODY>
</HTML>
```

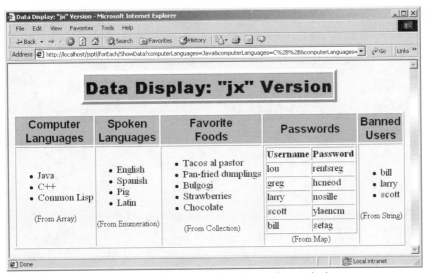

Figure 12–13 Result of the ShowData servlet when it forwards the request to *show-data-jx.jsp.*

Listing 12.22   *web.xml* (Excerpt for the data-displaying pages)

```xml
<?xml version="1.0" encoding="ISO-8859-1"?>
<!DOCTYPE web-app PUBLIC
    "-//Sun Microsystems, Inc.//DTD Web Application 2.3//EN"
    "http://java.sun.com/dtd/web-app_2_3.dtd">

<web-app>
  <!-- Use the SPEL for expressions. -->
  <context-param>
    <param-name>
      javax.servlet.jsptl.ExpressionEvaluatorClass
    </param-name>
    <param-value>
      org.apache.taglibs.jsptl.lang.spel.Evaluator
    </param-value>
  </context-param>

  <!-- ... -->
```

Listing 12.22 *web.xml* (Excerpt for the data-displaying pages) *(continued)*

```xml
<!-- Give a name to the moreservlets.ShowData servlet
     so that a custom URL can later be assigned.
-->
<servlet>
  <servlet-name>ShowData</servlet-name>
  <servlet-class>moreservlets.ShowData</servlet-class>
</servlet>

<!-- ... -->

<!-- Register the URL /forEach/ShowData with the
     ShowData servlet. This lets the HTML form use
     a simple relative URL to invoke the servlet.
-->
<servlet-mapping>
  <servlet-name>ShowData</servlet-name>
  <url-pattern>/forEach/ShowData</url-pattern>
</servlet-mapping>

<!-- ... -->

<!-- Register jr JSTL TLD file. -->
<taglib>
  <taglib-uri>
    http://java.sun.com/jsptl/ea/jr
  </taglib-uri>
  <taglib-location>
    /WEB-INF/jsptl-tlds/jsptl-jr.tld
  </taglib-location>
</taglib>

<!-- Register jx JSTL TLD file. -->
<taglib>
  <taglib-uri>
    http://java.sun.com/jsptl/ea/jx
  </taglib-uri>
  <taglib-location>
    /WEB-INF/jsptl-tlds/jsptl-jx.tld
  </taglib-location>
</taglib>
</web-app>
```

12.4 Accessing the Loop Status

The `forEach` tag defines an optional `status` attribute that specifies the name of an attribute referring to an `IteratorTagStatus` object. This object provides details about the loop status. In particular, the `IteratorTagStatus` object has the following bean properties.

- **current.** The current object, the same as you could obtain from the iteration variable that the `var` attribute specifies. This property corresponds to the `getCurrent` method and is of type `Object`.

- **index.** The actual zero-based index of the current item within its data structure. This property corresponds to the `getIndex` method and is of type `int`.

- **count.** The iteration number. This value starts at 1 and increases by 1 each time around the loop, regardless of the values of the `begin`, `end`, or `step` attributes. This property corresponds to the `getCount` method and is of type `int`.

- **first.** A flag indicating whether the current item is the first in the iteration. Since this is a `boolean` property, it corresponds to the `isFirst` (not `getFirst`!) method.

- **last.** A flag indicating whether the current item is the last in the iteration. Since this is a `boolean` property, it corresponds to the `isLast` (not `getLast`) method.

- **beginSpecified.** A flag indicating whether the `begin` attribute was specified explicitly. Since this is a `boolean` property, it corresponds to the `isBeginSpecified` (not `getBeginSpecified`) method.

- **begin.** The value of the `begin` attribute or –1 if `begin` is not specified. This property corresponds to the `getBegin` method and is of type `int`.

- **endSpecified.** A flag indicating whether the `end` attribute was specified explicitly. Since this is a `boolean` property, it corresponds to the `isEndSpecified` (not `getEndSpecified`) method.

- **end.** The value of the `end` attribute or –1 if `end` is not specified. This property corresponds to the `getBegin` method and is of type `int`.

- **stepSpecified.** A flag indicating whether the `step` attribute was specified explicitly. Since this is a `boolean` property, it corresponds to the `isStepSpecified` (not `getStepSpecified`) method.

- **step.** The value of the `step` attribute or –1 if `step` is not specified. This property corresponds to the `getStep` method and is of type `int`.

Listing 12.23 shows the jr version of a page that loops down a comma-delimited String and displays status information each time around the loop. Figure 12–14 shows the result. Listing 12.24 (Figure 12–15) shows the jx equivalent.

Listing 12.23 *status-loop-jr.jsp*

```
<!DOCTYPE HTML PUBLIC "-//W3C//DTD HTML 4.0 Transitional//EN">
<HTML>
<HEAD>
<TITLE>Loop Status: "jr" Version</TITLE>
<LINK REL=STYLESHEET
      HREF="../styles.css"
      TYPE="text/css">
</HEAD>

<BODY>
<TABLE BORDER=5 ALIGN="CENTER">
  <TR><TH CLASS="TITLE">
     Loop Status: "jr" Version
</TABLE>
<P>
<TABLE BORDER=1>
<TR><TH CLASS="HEADING">Current<BR>Item
    <TH CLASS="HEADING">Index
    <TH CLASS="HEADING">Count
    <TH CLASS="HEADING">First?
    <TH CLASS="HEADING">Last?
    <TH CLASS="HEADING"><CODE>begin</CODE><BR>Specified?
    <TH CLASS="HEADING"><CODE>begin</CODE>
    <TH CLASS="HEADING"><CODE>end</CODE><BR>Specified?
    <TH CLASS="HEADING"><CODE>end</CODE>
    <TH CLASS="HEADING"><CODE>step</CODE><BR>Specified?
    <TH CLASS="HEADING"><CODE>step</CODE>
<%@ taglib uri="http://java.sun.com/jsptl/ea/jr" prefix="jr" %>
<jr:forEach status="status" begin="1" step="2"
   items='"a,b,c,d,e,f,g,h,i,j,k,l,m,n,o,p,q,r,s,t,u,v,w,x,y,z"'>
  <%@ page import="javax.servlet.jsptl.*" %>
  <% IteratorTagStatus status =
       (IteratorTagStatus)pageContext.getAttribute("status"); %>
  <TR><TD><%= status.getCurrent() %>
      <TD><%= status.getIndex() %>
      <TD><%= status.getCount() %>
      <TD><%= status.isFirst() %>
      <TD><%= status.isLast() %>
```

Listing 12.23 *status-loop-jr.jsp (continued)*

```
      <TD><%= status.isBeginSpecified() %>
      <TD><%= status.getBegin() %>
      <TD><%= status.isEndSpecified() %>
      <TD><%= status.getEnd() %>
      <TD><%= status.isStepSpecified() %>
      <TD><%= status.getStep() %>
</jr:forEach>
</TABLE>

</BODY>
</HTML>
```

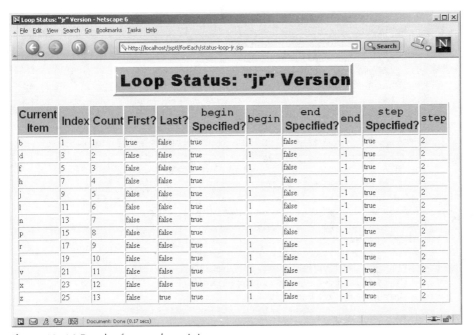

Figure 12–14 Result of *status-loop-jr.jsp*.

Listing 12.24 *status-loop-jx.jsp*

```
<!DOCTYPE HTML PUBLIC "-//W3C//DTD HTML 4.0 Transitional//EN">
<HTML>
<HEAD>
<TITLE>Loop Status: "jx" Version</TITLE>
<LINK REL=STYLESHEET
      HREF="../styles.css"
      TYPE="text/css">
</HEAD>

<BODY>
<TABLE BORDER=5 ALIGN="CENTER">
  <TR><TH CLASS="TITLE">
      Loop Status: "jx" Version
</TABLE>
<P>
<TABLE BORDER=1>
<TR><TH CLASS="HEADING">Current<BR>Item
    <TH CLASS="HEADING">Index
    <TH CLASS="HEADING">Count
    <TH CLASS="HEADING">First?
    <TH CLASS="HEADING">Last?
    <TH CLASS="HEADING"><CODE>begin</CODE><BR>Specified?
    <TH CLASS="HEADING"><CODE>begin</CODE>
    <TH CLASS="HEADING"><CODE>end</CODE><BR>Specified?
    <TH CLASS="HEADING"><CODE>end</CODE>
    <TH CLASS="HEADING"><CODE>step</CODE><BR>Specified?
    <TH CLASS="HEADING"><CODE>step</CODE>
<%@ taglib uri="http://java.sun.com/jsptl/ea/jx" prefix="jx" %>
<jx:forEach status="status" begin="1" step="2"
    items="a,b,c,d,e,f,g,h,i,j,k,l,m,n,o,p,q,r,s,t,u,v,w,x,y,z">
  <TR><TD><jx:expr value="$status.current"/>
      <TD><jx:expr value="$status.index"/>
      <TD><jx:expr value="$status.count"/>
      <TD><jx:expr value="$status.first"/>
      <TD><jx:expr value="$status.last"/>
      <TD><jx:expr value="$status.beginSpecified"/>
      <TD><jx:expr value="$status.begin"/>
      <TD><jx:expr value="$status.endSpecified"/>
      <TD><jx:expr value="$status.end"/>
      <TD><jx:expr value="$status.stepSpecified"/>
      <TD><jx:expr value="$status.step"/>
</jx:forEach>
</TABLE>

</BODY>
</HTML>
```

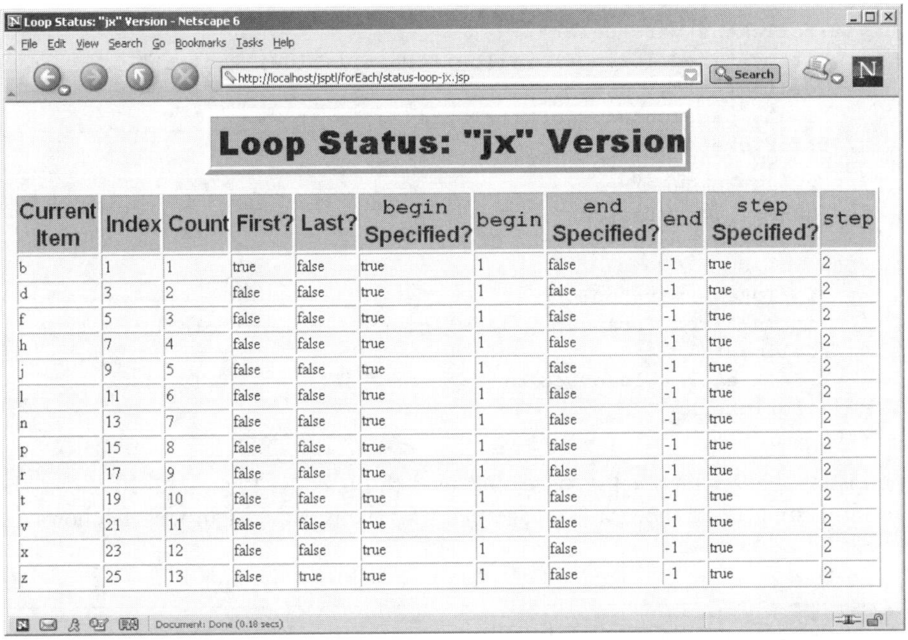

Figure 12–15 Result of *status-loop-jx.jsp*.

12.5 Looping with the forTokens Tag

The `forEach` tag lets you loop down comma-delimited strings. But, what if the tokens are delimited by something other than a comma? Or, what if more than one character can separate the tokens? Enter the `forTokens` tag. In addition to the six attributes available in `forEach` (var, begin, end, step, items, status), for-Tokens has a `delims` attribute. This attribute specifies the delimiters, just as with the second argument to the `StringTokenizer` constructor.

Hmm, `forTokens` sounds an awfully lot like `forEach`. Were the JSTL developers able to leverage the `forEach` code when developing `forTokens`? Yes! And you can too. JSTL provides a class called `IteratorTagSupport` that lets you create custom tags that extend the behavior of the `forEach` tag.

A Simple Token Loop

The following jr code treats parentheses as delimiters and creates a bulleted list of colors.

```
<UL>
<jr:forTokens var="color"
    items="(red (orange) yellow)(green)((blue) violet)"
    delims="()">
  <LI><%= pageContext.getAttribute("color") %>
</jr:forTokens>
</UL>
```

Here is the jx equivalent:

```
<UL>
<jx:forTokens var="color"
    items="(red (orange) yellow)(green)((blue) violet)"
    delims="()">
  <LI><jx:expr value="$color"/>
</jx:forTokens>
</UL>
```

Listing 12.25 shows a JSP page that uses the jr code; Figure 12–16 shows the result. Listing 12.26 shows a JSP page that uses the jx code; Figure 12–17 shows the result.

Listing 12.25 *simple-token-loop-jr.jsp*

```
<!DOCTYPE HTML PUBLIC "-//W3C//DTD HTML 4.0 Transitional//EN">
<HTML>
<HEAD>
<TITLE>Token Loop: "jr" Version</TITLE>
<LINK REL=STYLESHEET
      HREF="../styles.css"
      TYPE="text/css">
</HEAD>

<BODY>
<TABLE BORDER=5 ALIGN="CENTER">
  <TR><TH CLASS="TITLE">
      Token Loop: "jr" Version
</TABLE>
<P>
<%@ taglib uri="http://java.sun.com/jsptl/ea/jr" prefix="jr" %>
<UL>
<jr:forTokens var="color"
    items="(red (orange) yellow)(green)((blue) violet)"
    delims="()">
  <LI><%= pageContext.getAttribute("color") %>
</jr:forTokens>
</UL>
</BODY>
</HTML>
```

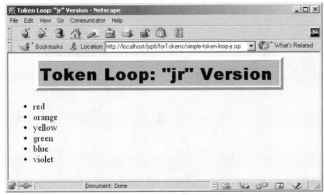

Figure 12–16 Result of *simple-token-loop-jr.jsp*.

Listing 12.26 | *simple-token-loop-jx.jsp*

```
<!DOCTYPE HTML PUBLIC "-//W3C//DTD HTML 4.0 Transitional//EN">
<HTML>
<HEAD>
<TITLE>Token Loop: "jx" Version</TITLE>
<LINK REL=STYLESHEET
      HREF="../styles.css"
      TYPE="text/css">
</HEAD>

<BODY>
<TABLE BORDER=5 ALIGN="CENTER">
  <TR><TH CLASS="TITLE">
      Token Loop: "jx" Version
</TABLE>
<P>
<%@ taglib uri="http://java.sun.com/jsptl/ea/jx" prefix="jx" %>
<UL>
<jx:forTokens var="color"
    items="(red (orange) yellow)(green)((blue) violet)"
    delims="()">
  <LI><jx:expr value="$color"/>
</jx:forTokens>
</UL>
</BODY>
</HTML>
```

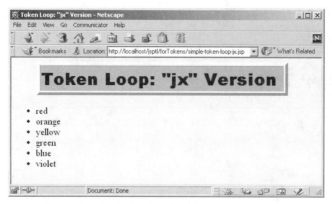

Figure 12–17 Result of *simple-token-loop-jx.jsp*.

Nested Token Loops

One of the nice things about the forTokens tag is that it makes it easy to create nested loops. For example, the following jr code creates two bulleted lists: the first giving colors and the second giving numbers. The two sets of items are separated by parentheses. Within each set, individual items are separated by commas.

```
<jr:forTokens var="entry"
    items="(purple,cyan,black,green)(pi,e,7,6.02 x 10^23)"
    delims="()">
  <UL>
  <jr:forTokens var="subentry"
      items='<%= (String)pageContext.getAttribute("entry") %>'
      delims=",">
    <LI><%= pageContext.getAttribute("subentry") %>
  </jr:forTokens>
  </UL><HR>
</jr:forTokens>
```

Here is the jx equivalent:

```
<jx:forTokens var="entry"
    items="(purple,cyan,black,green)(pi,e,7,6.02 x 10^23)"
    delims="()">
  <UL>
  <jx:forTokens var="subentry" items="$entry" delims=",">
    <LI><jx:expr value="$subentry"/>
  </jx:forTokens>
  </UL><HR>
</jx:forTokens>
```

Listing 12.27 shows a JSP page that uses the jr code; Figure 12–18 shows the result. Listing 12.28 shows a JSP page that uses the jx code; Figure 12–19 shows the result.

Listing 12.27 *nested-token-loop-jr.jsp*

```
<!DOCTYPE HTML PUBLIC "-//W3C//DTD HTML 4.0 Transitional//EN">
<HTML>
<HEAD>
<TITLE>Nested Token Loop: "jr" Version</TITLE>
<LINK REL=STYLESHEET
      HREF="../styles.css"
      TYPE="text/css">
</HEAD>

<BODY>
<TABLE BORDER=5 ALIGN="CENTER">
  <TR><TH CLASS="TITLE">
      Nested Token Loop: "jr" Version
</TABLE>
<H3>Favorite Colors and Numbers:</H3>
<HR>
<%@ taglib uri="http://java.sun.com/jsptl/ea/jr" prefix="jr" %>
<jr:forTokens var="entry"
    items="(purple,cyan,black,green)(pi,e,7,6.02 x 10^23)"
    delims="()">
  <UL>
  <jr:forTokens var="subentry"
      items='<%= (String)pageContext.getAttribute("entry") %>'
      delims=",">
    <LI><%= pageContext.getAttribute("subentry") %>
  </jr:forTokens>
  </UL><HR>
</jr:forTokens>

</BODY>
</HTML>
```

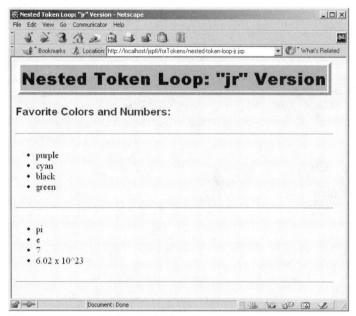

Figure 12–18 Result of *nested-token-loop-jr.jsp*.

Listing 12.28 *nested-token-loop-jx.jsp*

```
<!DOCTYPE HTML PUBLIC "-//W3C//DTD HTML 4.0 Transitional//EN">
<HTML>
<HEAD>
<TITLE>Nested Token Loop: "jx" Version</TITLE>
<LINK REL=STYLESHEET
      HREF="../styles.css"
      TYPE="text/css">
</HEAD>

<BODY>
<TABLE BORDER=5 ALIGN="CENTER">
  <TR><TH CLASS="TITLE">
      Nested Token Loop: "jx" Version
</TABLE>
<H3>Favorite Colors and Numbers:</H3>
```

Listing 12.28 *nested-token-loop-jx.jsp (continued)*

```
<HR>
<%@ taglib uri="http://java.sun.com/jsptl/ea/jx" prefix="jx" %>
<jx:forTokens var="entry"
    items="(purple,cyan,black,green)(pi,e,7,6.02 x 10^23)"
    delims="()">
  <UL>
  <jx:forTokens var="subentry" items="$entry" delims=",">
    <LI><jx:expr value="$subentry"/>
  </jx:forTokens>
  </UL><HR>
</jx:forTokens>

</BODY>
</HTML>
```

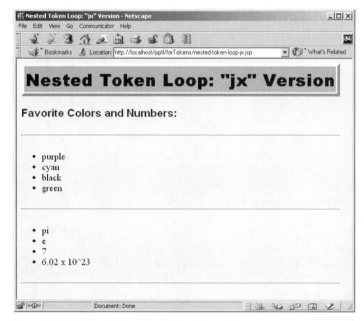

Figure 12–19 Result of *nested-token-loop-jx.jsp.*

12.6 Evaluating Items Conditionally

JSTL provides two main tags for performing conditional evaluation: `if` and `choose`. The `if` tag evaluates its body only when a specified test condition is true. There is no "else" condition—the content is either included or omitted with no alternative content. The following list summarizes the use of `if`; the following subsections give details and examples.

- **The `if` tag in the jr library.** Use a JSP expression for the `test` attribute; if the result is `true` or `Boolean.TRUE`, the contents of the tag are evaluated. For example:

  ```
  <jr:if test="<% expression %>">
    HTML or JSP content.
  </jr:if>
  ```

- **The `if` tag in the jx library.** Use the same basic syntax as with the jr library, but specify the test by accessing an existing attribute and comparing it to another value using one of a small set of relational operators (`==`, `!=`, `<`, `>`, `<=`, or `>=`). For example:

  ```
  <jx:if test="$attribute.beanProperty == 'value'">
    HTML or JSP content.
  </jx:if>
  ```

Whereas the `if` tag provides a single option that is either evaluated or ignored, the `choose` tag lets you specify several different options with nested `when` tags. The content of the first option whose test condition is true is evaluated. You can use the `otherwise` tag to provide default content when no test is true. The following list summarizes the use of `choose`; the following subsections give details and examples.

- **The `choose` tag in the jr library.** Use nested `when` tags; the contents of the first one whose `test` attribute evaluates to `true` or `Boolean.TRUE` is used. If no `when` tag succeeds and there is an `otherwise` tag, its contents are used. Use JSP expressions to specify each of the tests. For example:

  ```
  <jr:choose>
    <jr:when test="<% expression1 %>">Content1</jr:when>
    <jr:when test="<% expression2 %>">Content2</jr:when>
    ...
    <jr:when test="<% expressionN %>">ContentN</jr:when>
    <jr:otherwise>Default Content</jr:otherwise>
  </jr:choose>
  ```

- **The choose tag in the jx library.** Use the same basic syntax as with the jr library, but specify the tests by accessing an existing attribute and comparing it to another value using one of a small set of relational operators (==, !=, <, >, <=, or >=). For example:

```
<jx:choose>
    <jx:when test="$att.prop1 == 'val1'">Content1</jx:when>
    <jx:when test="$att.prop2 == 'val2'">Content2</jx:when>
    ...
    <jx:when test="$att.propN == 'valN'">ContentN</jx:when>
    <jx:otherwise>Default Content</jx:otherwise>
</jx:choose>
```

The if Tag

With the if tag, you simply specify a condition with the test attribute. If it is true (i.e., is the boolean value true or the Boolean value Boolean.TRUE), the content between the start and end tags is evaluated. Otherwise, the tag body is ignored.

For example, the following jr library code prints a bulleted list of the numbers from 1 to 10. If the number is greater than 7, a notation to that effect is placed after the number.

```
<UL>
<jr:forEach var="i" begin="1" end="10">
  <% Integer i = (Integer)pageContext.getAttribute("i"); %>
  <LI><%= i %>
      <jr:if test="<%= i.intValue() > 7 %>">
      (greater than 7)
      </jr:if>
</jr:forEach>
</UL>
```

The jx library follows a similar procedure. The difference is that the test attribute uses existing attributes and one of the following predefined comparisons: ==, !=, <, >, <=, or >=. It is important to realize that these operators do not behave the same as their Java equivalents. In particular, all of the operators support String arguments. For example, the == operator uses the equals method when both arguments are of type String but does not generate an exception when either argument is null. Similarly, >, <, etc., can be applied to strings as well as numbers. If the arguments are both strings, the result is that of the compareTo method of the String class.

Core Warning

The relational operators of the jx library work differently than they do in standard Java code. In particular, all of them can be used to compare String *objects.*

For example, the following jx code generates the same list as the jr code just shown.

```
<UL>
<jx:forEach var="i" begin="1" end="10">
  <LI><jx:expr value="$i"/>
      <jx:if test="$i > 7">
      (greater than 7)
      </jx:if>
</jx:forEach>
</UL>
```

Listing 12.29 shows a JSP page that uses the jr code; Figure 12–20 shows the result. Listing 12.30 shows a JSP page that uses the jx code; Figure 12–21 shows the result.

Listing 12.29 *if-jr.jsp*

```
<!DOCTYPE HTML PUBLIC "-//W3C//DTD HTML 4.0 Transitional//EN">
<HTML>
<HEAD>
<TITLE>If: "jr" Version</TITLE>
<LINK REL=STYLESHEET
      HREF="../styles.css"
      TYPE="text/css">
</HEAD>

<BODY>
<TABLE BORDER=5 ALIGN="CENTER">
  <TR><TH CLASS="TITLE">
      If: "jr" Version
</TABLE>
```

Listing 12.29 *if-jr.jsp (continued)*

```
<P>
<%@ taglib uri="http://java.sun.com/jsptl/ea/jr" prefix="jr" %>
<UL>
<jr:forEach var="i" begin="1" end="10">
  <% Integer i = (Integer)pageContext.getAttribute("i"); %>
  <LI><%= i %>
      <jr:if test="<%= i.intValue() > 7 %>">
      (greater than 7)
      </jr:if>
</jr:forEach>
</UL>
</BODY>
</HTML>
```

Figure 12–20 Result of *if-jr.jsp.*

Listing 12.30 *if-jx.jsp*

```
<!DOCTYPE HTML PUBLIC "-//W3C//DTD HTML 4.0 Transitional//EN">
<HTML>
<HEAD>
<TITLE>If: "jx" Version</TITLE>
<LINK REL=STYLESHEET
      HREF="../styles.css"
      TYPE="text/css">
</HEAD>

<BODY>
<TABLE BORDER=5 ALIGN="CENTER">
  <TR><TH CLASS="TITLE">
      If: "jx" Version
</TABLE>
<P>
<%@ taglib uri="http://java.sun.com/jsptl/ea/jx" prefix="jx" %>
<UL>
<jx:forEach var="i" begin="1" end="10">
  <LI><jx:expr value="$i"/>
      <jx:if test="$i > 7">
      (greater than 7)
      </jx:if>
</jx:forEach>
</UL>
</BODY>
</HTML>
```

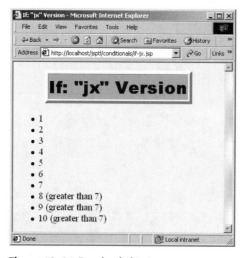

Figure 12–21 Result of *if-jx.jsp*.

The choose, when, and otherwise Tags

With the choose tag, you supply a set of possible results by using nested when tags. Each when tag uses the test attribute in the same manner as with the if tag. The body of the first when tag whose condition is true (i.e., is the boolean value true or the Boolean value Boolean.TRUE) is evaluated. If no when tag is true and there is an otherwise tag, its body is evaluated.

For example, the following jr code generates a bulleted list of numbers. If the number is less than four, it is marked as "small." If the number is greater than or equal to four but less than eight, it is marked as "medium." If the number is greater than eight, it is marked as "large."

```
<UL>
<jr:forEach var="i" begin="1" end="10">
  <% Integer i = (Integer)pageContext.getAttribute("i"); %>
  <LI><%= i %>
      <jr:choose>
        <jr:when test="<%= i.intValue() < 4 %>">
          (small)
        </jr:when>
        <jr:when test="<%= i.intValue() < 8 %>">
          (medium)
        </jr:when>
        <jr:otherwise>
          (large)
        </jr:otherwise>
      </jr:choose>
</jr:forEach>
</UL>
```

Here is the jx equivalent: shorthand tests are used instead of explicit JSP expressions, yielding a more concise and readable result.

```
<UL>
<jx:forEach var="i" begin="1" end="10">
  <LI><jx:expr value="$i"/>
      <jx:choose>
        <jx:when test="$i < 4">
          (small)
        </jx:when>
        <jx:when test="$i < 8">
          (medium)
        </jx:when>
        <jx:otherwise>
          (large)
        </jx:otherwise>
      </jx:choose>
</jx:forEach>
</UL>
```

Listing 12.31 shows a JSP page that uses the jr code; Figure 12–22 shows the result. Listing 12.32 shows a JSP page that uses the jx code; Figure 12–23 shows the result.

Listing 12.31 *choose-jr.jsp*

```
<!DOCTYPE HTML PUBLIC "-//W3C//DTD HTML 4.0 Transitional//EN">
<HTML>
<HEAD>
<TITLE>Choose: "jr" Version</TITLE>
<LINK REL=STYLESHEET
      HREF="../styles.css"
      TYPE="text/css">
</HEAD>

<BODY>
<TABLE BORDER=5 ALIGN="CENTER">
  <TR><TH CLASS="TITLE">
      Choose: "jr" Version
</TABLE>
<P>
<%@ taglib uri="http://java.sun.com/jsptl/ea/jr" prefix="jr" %>
<UL>
<jr:forEach var="i" begin="1" end="10">
   <% Integer i = (Integer)pageContext.getAttribute("i"); %>
   <LI><%= i %>
      <jr:choose>
        <jr:when test="<%= i.intValue() < 4 %>">
          (small)
        </jr:when>
        <jr:when test="<%= i.intValue() < 8 %>">
          (medium)
        </jr:when>
        <jr:otherwise>
          (large)
        </jr:otherwise>
      </jr:choose>
</jr:forEach>
</UL>
</BODY>
</HTML>
```

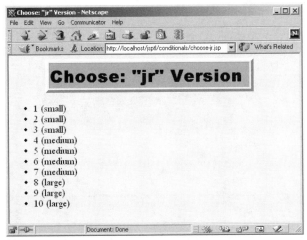

Figure 12–22 Result of *choose-jr.jsp*.

Listing 12.32 *choose-jx.jsp*

```
<!DOCTYPE HTML PUBLIC "-//W3C//DTD HTML 4.0 Transitional//EN">
<HTML>
<HEAD>
<TITLE>Choose: "jx" Version</TITLE>
<LINK REL=STYLESHEET
      HREF="../styles.css"
      TYPE="text/css">
</HEAD>

<BODY>
<TABLE BORDER=5 ALIGN="CENTER">
  <TR><TH CLASS="TITLE">
      Choose: "jx" Version
</TABLE>
<P>
<%@ taglib uri="http://java.sun.com/jsptl/ea/jx" prefix="jx" %>
<UL>
<jx:forEach var="i" begin="1" end="10">
  <LI><jx:expr value="$i"/>
      <jx:choose>
        <jx:when test="$i < 4">
          (small)
        </jx:when>
```

Listing 12.32   *choose-jx.jsp (continued)*

```
        <jx:when test="$i < 8">
           (medium)
        </jx:when>
        <jx:otherwise>
           (large)
        </jx:otherwise>
      </jx:choose>
</jx:forEach>
</UL>
</BODY>
</HTML>
```

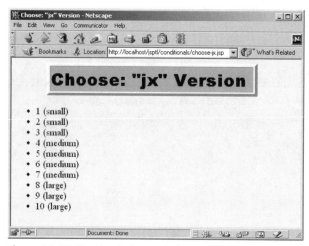

Figure 12–23 Result of *choose-jx.jsp*.

The Use of the set Tag with the choose Tag

In the previous example, the jx version of `choose` yielded more succinct code than did the jr version because the tests were performed on an attribute that was set by the `forEach` tag. When the tests are based on explicit computations, however, the jx code is more complicated.

For example, here is some jr code that prints out the results of ten coin tosses.

```
<UL>
<jr:forEach var="i" begin="1" end="10">
  <% double d = Math.random(); %>
  <LI><jr:choose>
        <jr:when test="<%= d < 0.49 %>">
          Heads.
        </jr:when>
        <jr:when test="<%= d < 0.98 %>">
          Tails.
        </jr:when>
        <jr:otherwise>
          <B>Coin landed on edge!</B>
        </jr:otherwise>
      </jr:choose>
</jr:forEach>
</UL>
```

How would you perform the equivalent tasks in the jx library? The test attribute
of the when tag does not accept a JSP expression. Sure, you could use a scriptlet to
explicitly store the result of the call to Math.random in a PageContext attribute,
but that results in so much scripting code that it negates any advantage that the jx
library might have had. Instead, you can use the set tag to evaluate a JSP expression
and automatically store the result in a PageContext attribute. The set tag is
described in Section 12.7, but the gist is that you can supply a value either with the
value attribute or by enclosing the value between the start and end tags of set. The
result is placed in the PageContext attribute named by the var attribute of set.
Given this behavior of set, the following jx code yields the same result as the previous jr example.

```
<UL>
<jx:forEach var="i" begin="1" end="10">
  <jx:set var="d"><%= Math.random() %></jx:set>
  <LI><jx:choose>
        <jx:when test="$d < '0.49'">
          Heads.
        </jx:when>
        <jx:when test="$d < '0.98'">
          Tails.
        </jx:when>
        <jx:otherwise>
          <B>Coin landed on edge!</B>
        </jx:otherwise>
      </jx:choose>
</jx:forEach>
</UL>
```

Listing 12.33 shows a JSP page that uses the jr code; Figure 12–24 shows the result. Listing 12.34 shows a JSP page that uses the jx code; Figure 12–25 shows the result.

Listing 12.33 *coin-toss-jr.jsp*

```
<!DOCTYPE HTML PUBLIC "-//W3C//DTD HTML 4.0 Transitional//EN">
<HTML>
<HEAD>
<TITLE>Coin Toss: "jr" Version</TITLE>
<LINK REL=STYLESHEET
      HREF="../styles.css"
      TYPE="text/css">
</HEAD>

<BODY>
<TABLE BORDER=5 ALIGN="CENTER">
  <TR><TH CLASS="TITLE">
      Coin Toss: "jr" Version
</TABLE>
<P>
<%@ taglib uri="http://java.sun.com/jsptl/ea/jr" prefix="jr" %>
<UL>
<jr:forEach var="i" begin="1" end="10">
  <% double d = Math.random(); %>
  <LI><jr:choose>
        <jr:when test="<%= d < 0.49 %>">
          Heads.
        </jr:when>
        <jr:when test="<%= d < 0.98 %>">
          Tails.
        </jr:when>
        <jr:otherwise>
          <B>Coin landed on edge!</B>
        </jr:otherwise>
      </jr:choose>
</jr:forEach>
</UL>
</BODY>
</HTML>
```

Figure 12–24 Result of *coin-toss-jr.jsp*.

Listing 12.34	*coin-toss-jx.jsp*

```
<!DOCTYPE HTML PUBLIC "-//W3C//DTD HTML 4.0 Transitional//EN">
<HTML>
<HEAD>
<TITLE>Coin Toss: "jx" Version</TITLE>
<LINK REL=STYLESHEET
      HREF="../styles.css"
      TYPE="text/css">
</HEAD>

<BODY>
<TABLE BORDER=5 ALIGN="CENTER">
  <TR><TH CLASS="TITLE">
      Coin Toss: "jx" Version
</TABLE>
<P>
<%@ taglib uri="http://java.sun.com/jsptl/ea/jx" prefix="jx" %>
<UL>
<jx:forEach var="i" begin="1" end="10">
  <jx:set var="d"><%= Math.random() %></jx:set>
  <LI><jx:choose>
        <jx:when test="$d < '0.49'">
          Heads.
        </jx:when>
        <jx:when test="$d < '0.98'">
          Tails.
        </jx:when>
```

Listing 12.34	*coin-toss-jx.jsp (continued)*

```
      <jx:otherwise>
         <B>Coin landed on edge!</B>
      </jx:otherwise>
    </jx:choose>
</jx:forEach>
</UL>
</BODY>
</HTML>
```

Figure 12–25 Result of *coin-toss-jx.jsp.*

12.7 Using the Expression Language

The set, expr, and declare tags let you use shorthand notation to define attributes, evaluate expressions, and declare scripting variables. The first two tags are available only in the jx library; declare is technically available in either library but is primarily used with jx. Details and examples are provided in the following subsections, but here is a quick summary.

- **set.** This tag defines a PageContext attribute. Use var to specify the name of the attribute; use value to specify its value. When using the value attribute, recall that in the jx library $attribute.bean-Property means that the system should call the getBeanProperty method of the object referenced by the attribute named `attribute`. You can also omit the `value` attribute and put the value between the start and end tags. For example:

```
<jx:set var="name" value="$attribute.beanProperty"/>
```

- **expr.** This tag returns a value. Use the `value` attribute to access existing attributes and bean properties with the jx library's shorthand notation. If you use a `default` attribute, its value is used if exceptions are thrown when the system attempts to access the main value. For example:

```
<jx:expr value="$attribute.beanProperty" default="value"/>
```

- **declare.** This tag provides a bridge between the jx library and scripting code. It declares a scripting variable (i.e., a local variable in `_jspService`) that can be accessed by JSP expressions and scriptlets. Use `id` to give the name of the variable; its initial value will be the attribute of the same name. Use `type` to give the fully qualified class name of the variable's type. For example:

```
<jx:declare id="name" type="package.Class"/>
```

The set Tag

The `set` tag defines a `PageContext` attribute with a name that is specified with the `var` attribute. The `set` tag has two main purposes.

First, `set` can be used to evaluate a JSP expression and store its result in an attribute. This use of `set` applies to situations in which you cannot entirely avoid explicit scripting expressions but you still want to primarily use the jx library. With this usage, the value is placed inside the tag body. For example, in the coin-toss example of the previous section, the following code was used to store the result of `Math.random` in a `PageContext` attribute named d.

```
<jx:set var="d"><%= Math.random() %></jx:set>
```

Second, `set` can be used to store intermediate results. For example, the results of long and complicated expressions can be stored in meaningfully named attributes, thus simplifying the `expr` tags that use the values. With this usage, the value is specified with the `value` attribute. For example, the following code uses `set` to establish the `count`, `index`, and `letter` attributes.

```
<UL>
<jx:forEach status="status" begin="1" step="2"
    items="a,b,c,d,e,f,g,h,i,j,k,l,m,n,o,p,q,r,s,t,u,v,w,x,y,z">
  <jx:set var="count" value="$status.count"/>
  <jx:set var="index" value="$status.index"/>
```

```
    <jx:set var="letter" value="$status.current"/>
    <LI>Item <jx:expr value="$count"/>
        <UL>
          <LI>Index: <jx:expr value="$index"/>
          <LI>Letter: <jx:expr value="$letter"/>
        </UL>
  </jx:forEach>
  </UL>
```

Listing 12.35 shows a JSP page that uses this set code; Figure 12–26 shows the result.

Listing 12.35 *set.jsp*

```
<!DOCTYPE HTML PUBLIC "-//W3C//DTD HTML 4.0 Transitional//EN">
<HTML>
<HEAD>
<TITLE>Setting PageContext Attributes</TITLE>
<LINK REL=STYLESHEET
      HREF="../styles.css"
      TYPE="text/css">
</HEAD>

<BODY>
<TABLE BORDER=5 ALIGN="CENTER">
  <TR><TH CLASS="TITLE">
      Setting PageContext Attributes
</TABLE>
<P>
<%@ taglib uri="http://java.sun.com/jsptl/ea/jx" prefix="jx" %>
<UL>
<jx:forEach status="status" begin="1" step="2"
    items="a,b,c,d,e,f,g,h,i,j,k,l,m,n,o,p,q,r,s,t,u,v,w,x,y,z">
  <jx:set var="count" value="$status.count"/>
  <jx:set var="index" value="$status.index"/>
  <jx:set var="letter" value="$status.current"/>
  <LI>Item <jx:expr value="$count"/>
      <UL>
        <LI>Index: <jx:expr value="$index"/>
        <LI>Letter: <jx:expr value="$letter"/>
      </UL>
</jx:forEach>
</UL>
</BODY>
</HTML>
```

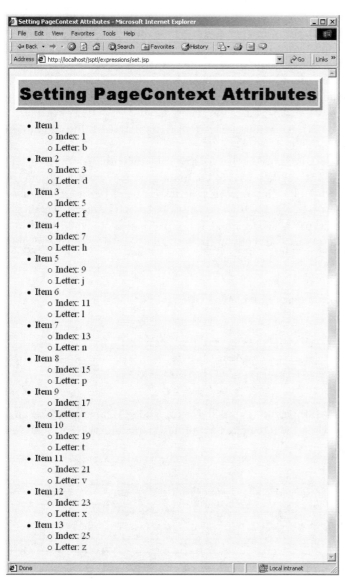

Figure 12–26 Result of *set.jsp*.

The expr Tag

The expr tag normally returns the value specified in its value attribute; I use expr in virtually every jx example in this chapter. However, what happens if value specifies an attribute that does not exist? The result is an error, not simply null. In most cases, this behavior is not a problem: you know the attribute exists because it is specified by an enclosing forEach or forTokens tag, an earlier set tag, or the servlet that forwarded the request to the JSP page. However, suppose that you use the param scoping qualifier to read request parameters with the $param:*paramName* shorthand format? In such a case, you cannot be sure whether the request parameter exists or not: it is supplied by the end user. Similarly, if you use the header scoping qualifier to read a request header, you cannot know in advance whether or not the specified header will exist. In both cases, you get an error, not null, if you try to use the value when it is unavailable.

To handle this problem, the expr tag has a default attribute. Its value is used if an exception occurs when the system tries to compute the value given in the value attribute. For example, the following code uses the alertLevel request parameter to decide what heading to generate. If the alertLevel parameter is not in the request, a default heading is generated. If expr had not been used and $param:alertLevel was used directly in the tests, an error would have resulted when alertLevel was not a request parameter.

```
<jx:set var="level">
  <jx:expr value="$param:alertLevel" default="low"/>
</jx:set>
<jx:choose>
  <jx:when test="$level == 'high'"><H1>Code Red!</H1></jx:when>
  <jx:when test="$level == 'medium'"><H1>Code Blue</H1></jx:when>
  <jx:otherwise><H2>Code White</H2></jx:otherwise>
</jx:choose>
```

Listing 12.36 shows a JSP page that uses this expr code; Figures 12–27 through 12–29 show the results when the alertLevel request parameter is high, medium, and missing, respectively.

Listing 12.36 *expr.jsp*

```
<!DOCTYPE HTML PUBLIC "-//W3C//DTD HTML 4.0 Transitional//EN">
<HTML>
<HEAD>
<TITLE>Expressions with Defaults</TITLE>
<LINK REL=STYLESHEET
      HREF="../styles.css"
      TYPE="text/css">
</HEAD>
```

Listing 12.36 *expr.jsp (continued)*

```
<BODY>
<TABLE BORDER=5 ALIGN="CENTER">
  <TR><TH CLASS="TITLE">
     Expressions with Defaults
</TABLE>
<%@ taglib uri="http://java.sun.com/jsptl/ea/jx" prefix="jx" %>
<jx:set var="level">
  <jx:expr value="$param:alertLevel" default="low"/>
</jx:set>
<jx:choose>
  <jx:when test="$level == 'high'"><H1>Code Red!</H1></jx:when>
  <jx:when test="$level == 'medium'"><H1>Code Blue</H1></jx:when>
  <jx:otherwise><H2>Code White</H2></jx:otherwise>
</jx:choose>
</BODY>
</HTML>
```

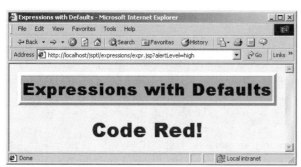

Figure 12–27 Result of *expr.jsp* when invoked with an `alertLevel` request parameter of high.

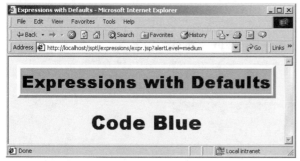

Figure 12–28 Result of *expr.jsp* when invoked with an `alertLevel` request parameter of medium.

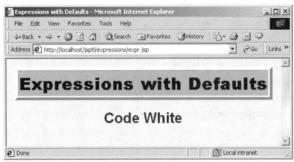

Figure 12–29 Result of *expr.jsp* when invoked with no request parameters.

The declare Tag

The jx library is preferred by developers who want to minimize the amount of explicit scripting code in their JSP pages. In fact, JSTL provides a TagLibraryValidator (see Section 11.3) called ScriptFreeTLV that you can use to verify that certain pages contain no scripting code whatsoever.

However, despite the ability to access attributes and bean properties with shorthand notation, you cannot always avoid the use of scripting elements. When scripting code is necessary, some developers prefer to simply switch to the jr library. Others prefer to stick with jx but keep the scripting code to a minimum. The declare tag is designed for this latter situation. It copies the value of an existing attribute into a scripting variable (i.e., a local variable in the _jspService method) that has the same name. This variable can then be accessed by scripting code.

For example, Listing 12.37 shows a very short JSP page that reads the url request parameter and redirects the user to the specified page. It uses the jx library to take advantage of two capabilities: the param scoping qualifier to simplify access to the request parameter and the default attribute of expr to simplify the situation when the url parameter is missing. However, since the call to sendRedirect requires explicit scripting code, the declare tag copies the value from the url Page-Context attribute into a String variable named url. Figure 12–30 shows the result when the page is accessed without a url request parameter. Figure 12–31 shows the result when url is part of the request data.

Listing 12.37   *declare.jsp*

```
<%@ taglib uri="http://java.sun.com/jsptl/ea/jx" prefix="jx" %>
<jx:set var="url">
  <jx:expr value="$param:url"
           default="http://java.sun.com/products/jsp/"/>
</jx:set>
<jx:declare id="url" type="java.lang.String"/>
<% response.sendRedirect(url); %>
```

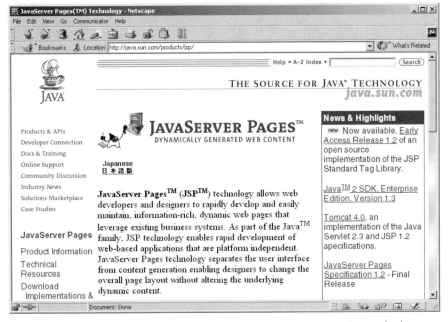

Figure 12–30 Result of *declare.jsp* when no `url` request parameter is supplied (*http://localhost/jsptl/expressions/declare.jsp*).

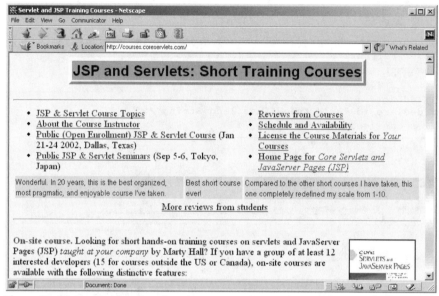

Figure 12–31 Result of *declare.jsp* when a `url` request parameter is supplied (*http://localhost/jsptl/expressions/declare.jsp?**url=http://courses.coreservlets.com***).

SERVER ORGANIZATION AND STRUCTURE

Topics in This Appendix

- Downloading server software
- Accessing servlet and JSP documentation
- Locating servlet JAR files
- Starting and stopping the server
- Storing files for use in the default Web application
- Storing files for use in custom Web applications

Appendix

This appendix summarizes the various files and directories used by Tomcat, JRun, and ServletExec. It also reminds you where to get the server software and documentation.

Download Sites

- **Tomcat.**
  http://jakarta.apache.org/builds/jakarta-tomcat-4.0/release/
- **JRun.**
  http://www.macromedia.com/software/jrun/
- **ServletExec.**
  http://www.newatlanta.com/download.jsp
- **API documentation.**
  http://java.sun.com/products/jsp/download.html

Starting and Stopping the Server

- **Tomcat.**
  In your development directory, make shortcuts to *install_dir/bin/startup.bat* and *install_dir/bin/shutdown.bat*. Double click them to start and stop the server. Use *startup.sh* and *shutdown.sh* on Unix/Linux.

- **JRun.**
  Go to the Start menu, select Programs, select JRun, right-click on the JRun Default Server icon, and select Copy. Then go to your development directory, right-click in the window, and select Paste Shortcut. If desired, repeat the process for the JRun Admin Server and JRun Management Console. Double click the default server icon to start JRun. To stop JRun, click on the icon in the taskbar and select Stop.
- **ServletExec.**
  In your development directory, make shortcut to *install_dir/StartSED.bat*. Double click it to start the server. There is no separate shutdown file; to stop ServletExec, just go to *http://localhost/* and click on the Shutdown link in the General category on the left-hand side. Or, just close the popup window that shows the ServletExec output.

Servlet JAR File Locations

This location needs to be added to the CLASSPATH of your development environment or IDE.

- **Tomcat.**
  install_dir/common/lib/servlet.jar
- **JRun.**
  install_dir/lib/ext/servlet.jar
- **ServletExec.**
  install_dir/ServletExecDebugger.jar

Locations for Files in the Default Web Application

This section summarizes where you place files when you are not using custom Web applications (i.e., when first testing things out). Note that the URLs cited assume that you have changed your server's port to 80 as described in Section 1.3.

Individual Classes that Do Not Use Packages

- **Tomcat.**
  install_dir/webapps/ROOT/WEB-INF/classes
- **JRun.**
  install_dir/servers/default/default-app/WEB-INF/classes

- **ServletExec.**
  install_dir/Servlets
- **Corresponding URL.**
  http://host/servlet/ServletName

Individual Classes That Use Packages

- **Tomcat.**
  install_dir/webapps/ROOT/WEB-INF/classes/packageName
- **JRun.**
  install_dir/servers/default/default-app/WEB-INF/classes/packageName
- **ServletExec Directory.**
  install_dir/Servlets/packageName
- **Corresponding URL.**
  http://host/servlet/packageName.ServletName

Classes That Are Bundled in JAR Files

- **Tomcat.**
  install_dir/webapps/ROOT/WEB-INF/lib
- **JRun.**
  install_dir/servers/default/default-app/WEB-INF/lib
- **ServletExec.**
  install_dir/Servlets
- **Corresponding URLs (Servlets).**
  http://host/servlet/ServletName
  http://host/servlet/packageName.ServletName

HTML and JSP Pages (No Subdirectories)

Images, style sheets, and other Web content go in the same places.

- **Tomcat.**
  install_dir/webapps/ROOT
- **JRun.**
  install_dir/servers/default/default-app
- **ServletExec.**
  install_dir/public_html
- **Corresponding URLs.**
  http://host/SomeFile.html
  http://host/SomeFile.jsp

HTML and JSP Pages (In Subdirectories)

Images, style sheets, and other Web content go in the same places.

- **Tomcat.**
  install_dir/webapps/ROOT/someDirectory
- **JRun.**
  install_dir/servers/default/default-app/someDirectory
- **ServletExec.**
  install_dir/public_html/someDirectory
- **Corresponding URLs.**
  http://host/someDirectory/SomeFile.html
  http://host/someDirectory/SomeFile.jsp

Locations for Files in Custom Web Applications

Autodeploy Directories

These directories are where you drop WAR files or directories containing Web applications. Once you restart the server, you automatically get a custom Web application whose URL prefix matches the main name of the WAR file (minus the *.war* extension) or the directory name. For lots more control over Web application deployment, see Section 4.1 (Registering Web Applications).

- **Tomcat.**
  install_dir/webapps
- **JRun.** (No autodeployment prior to version 4)
  install_dir/servers/default
- **ServletExec.**
  install_dir/webapps/default

Locations for Files Within Web Applications

The following figure summarizes where you place different types of files *within* each of your Web applications. Again, the URLs cited assume that you have customized the server to use port 80 as described in Section 1.3.

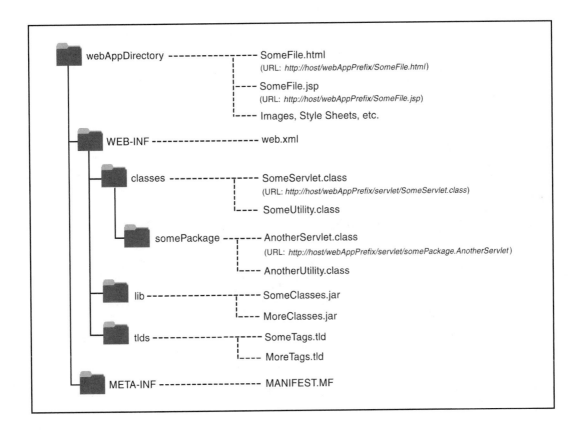

webAppDirectory --------------------------- SomeFile.html
                                             (URL: *http://host/webAppPrefix/SomeFile.html*)

                                       ----- SomeFile.jsp
                                             (URL: *http://host/webAppPrefix/SomeFile.jsp*)

                                       ----- Images, Style Sheets, etc.

WEB-INF ----------------------- web.xml

classes -------------------- SomeServlet.class
                             (URL: *http://host/webAppPrefix/servlet/SomeServlet.class*)

                        ----- SomeUtility.class

somePackage ------- AnotherServlet.class
                    (URL: *http://host/webAppPrefix/servlet/somePackage.AnotherServlet*)

              ----- AnotherUtility.class

lib ------------------ SomeClasses.jar

              ----- MoreClasses.jar

tlds ----------------- SomeTags.tld

              ----- MoreTags.tld

META-INF ------------------- MANIFEST.MF

Index